THE COMPLETE FRENCH CONJUGATION COURSE

DYLANE MOREAU

PREFACE

The Complete French Conjugation Course is a comprehensive book to guide you through French conjugation and its mysteries. It will help you understand how and why a French verb is formed, why it changes a certain way with a specific conjugation and how to remember the conjugation easily. Eventually, you will master all the irregularities that made you scratch your head in the past.

This book is written for French learners of all levels, inspired by French learners. If you are starting French in school, learning by yourself as an adult, or just want to brush up on your French, this is the perfect tool for you. This book is ideal for self-study or as additional practice.

Each chapter looks at a specific conjugation and is divided into grammar notes and exercises for you to stop and practice. The vocabulary used in this book is simple and is inspired by everyday French. The explanations are easy to understand without advanced grammatical jargon, so you can start learning conjugation from the beginning of your French learning journey.

Videos and audios

This book inludes **18 chapters** to master French conjugation, **more than 200 exercises**, **500 verbs**, an annex with the conjugation of **more than 50 verbs** to go back to, as well as **47 video lessons** if you need a "teacher approach."

The video lessons can be found at www.theperfectfrench.com/french-conjugation-course
To access the audios, go to www.theperfectfrench.com/french-conjugation-course-audios

The Complete French Conjugation Course will guide you and help you remember all the how's and why's of French conjugation.

A note from the author

This book was easy to write thanks to all my students. The book is for you and because of you. All of you inspire me every day to push through the traditional teaching methods and find new ways of teaching that will work for you, no matter your first language, no matter your age. Every single question I have ever received about conjugation is translated in this book with a chapter, exercise, and note.

I hope this book will help you acquire an understanding of French conjugation and the most irregular verbs.

To all my past, current, and new students, thank you.

Dylane Moreau

Table of Contents

Introduction 1
Glossary 3

The Present Tense – Le Présent de l'Indicatif 7

When to Use the Present Tense 9
Conjugation of Regular -er Verbs 11
Conjugation of Irregular -er Verbs 17
Conjugation of Regular -ir Verbs 30
Conjugation of Regular -re Verbs 32
Être and Avoir 33
Aller 37
Faire 40
Jouer à – Jouer de – Faire de 43
Prendre 46
Negation 49
Battre and Mettre 53
Venir and Tenir 54
Conjugation of Irregular -ir Verbs 55
Conjugation of Irregular -indre Verbs 58
Conjugation of Verbs with a Stem Including v 59
Conjugation of Verbs with a Stem Including s 60
Conjugation of Verbs Ending in -aître 62
Conjugation of Verbs with a Stem Including y 63
Conjugation of Verbs with a Stem Including qu 63
Devoir, Vouloir and Pouvoir 64
A few Other Verbs 65
Questions 71
Impersonal Verbs 75
COP & DOP 76
COI & IOP 80
Reflexive Verbs 85

The Perfect Tense - Le Passé Composé 101

Building the Passé Composé 103
The Past Participle 104
Passé Composé with Avoir 106
Passé Composé with Être 110
Agreement - Passé Composé with Avoir 113
When to Use the Passé Composé 115
Verbs with Avoir and Être 118
The Passé Composé of Reflexive Verbs 119
Passé Composé and Negation 122
Questions Using the Passé Composé 124

The Imperfect Tense - L'Imparfait 129

Building the Imparfait 131
When to Use the Imparfait 137
Other Important Points about the Imparfait 140

Perfect Tense vs Imperfect - Le Passé Composé vs l'Imparfait - Revision 143

The Recent Past - Le Passé Récent 153

The Future Tense - Le Futur Simple 161

Building the Future Tense 163
When to Use the Future Tense 169

The Near Future - Le Futur Proche 173

Futur Proche and Negation 176

The Present Conditional - Le Conditionnel Présent 179

Building the Conditional 181
When to Use the Conditional 187

The imperative - L'impératif 191

Building the Imperative 193
The Imperative and Negation 195
The Imperative and Object Pronouns 195
The Imperative of Reflexive Verbs 197

Infinitive & Prepositions - Infinitif & Prépositions 201

The Types of Infinitive 203
Verb + Infinitive 204
Verb + à + Infinitive 205
Verb + à + Noun 207
Verb + de + Infinitive 208
Verb + de + Noun 210
Prepositions + Infinitive 212
Faire + Infinitive = Causative 213
Verb + de quoi + Infinitive 215
Être + en train + de + Infinitive 216
Être + sur le point + de + Infinitive 216
Être + Adjective + de + Infinitive 217
Être + Adjective – past participle + à + Infinitive 218
Il est + Adjective + de + Infinitive 219
C'est + Adjective + de + Infinitive 221
C'est + Adjective + à + Infinitive 220
... Seul + à + Infinitive 220
Ordinal Number + Infinitive 221
Il Faut + Infinitive 222
The Past Infinitive 223
The Negative Infinitive 223
Merci de + Infinitive 224

The Subjunctive - Le Subjonctif 227

Building the Subjunctive 229
Building the Subjunctive Past 234
When to Use the Subjunctive 235

The Pluperfect - Le Plus-Que-Parfait 251
Building the Pluperfect 253
When to Use the Pluperfect 254
The Future Perfect - Le Futur Antérieur 259
Building the Future Perfect 261
When to Use The Future Perfect 262
The Conditional Perfect - Le Conditionnel Passé 267
Building the Conditional Perfect 269
When to Use the Conditional Perfect 270
The Present Participle - Le Participe Présent 275
The Gerund - Le Gérondif
Building the Present Participle 277
When to Use the Present Participle 278
When to Use the Gerund 279
Past Participle vs. Gerund 280
The Passive Voice - La Voix Passive 283
The Simple Past - Le Passé Simple 289
Revision 293
The French Tenses and a Table of Verbs 327
Solutions 389

Introduction

Before jumping into the conjugation, here are a few things that you should know to avoid confusion as you navigate through the chapters:

The 3 Groups of Verbs

French verbs belong to 3 different groups:

- Regular verbs ending in **-er** are under the 1st group of verbs.
  Some have spelling changes with some conjugations, but they follow a general pattern most of the time.
  This group represents the majority of French verbs.

- Verbs ending in **-ir** are under the 2nd group of verbs.

- Verbs of the 3rd group are irregular verbs. They are the most used in the French language.

Most verbs in French are built the same way as other verbs. Try to study them together so remembering the conjugation will be easier.

- Some of them include a main verb, such as prendre:
  Prendre = ap**prendre** – com**prendre** – sur**prendre** – re**prendre** – ...

- Others have similar endings:
  T**enir** and V**enir**

Or they have very little in common but follow the same rules of conjugation and irregularities:
Offrir and Couvrir

In the first chapter, verbs are explained and kept by group and similarities, but not as much in the other chapters. If you need to look at what verbs are similarly conjugated, go to the first chapter or the verb annex, where you can see a conjugation model for each verb.

The French Subject Pronouns

Singular	Plural
Je – J' – I	**Nous –** We
Tu – You	**Vous –** You
Il – He	**Ils –** They
Elle – She	**Elles –** They
On – We	

Tu and Vous

Tu and **Vous** both mean you in English.

In French, **tu** is the singular form and is an informal way to address someone. It can be used when talking to friends, family members, colleagues, etc.

Vous, when used for one person, is formal. It is used to address people you don't know or people that you must show respect to, such as a stranger, your boss, the plumber, etc.

Vous in the plural form is used when there is more than one person.

Ils and Elles

In French, the distinction is made between masculine plural and feminine plural.
Ils refers to masculine plural, **elles** refers to feminine plural, which is easy to understand.
However, if you are talking about a mix of men and women, use **ils**. Only use **elles** when the group is women only.

On and Nous

On and **nous** both mean we in French. **Nous** is used more in written French, while **on** is used in spoken French.

The Neutral It

Neutral doesn't exist in French; everything is either masculine or feminine. It translates to *he* or *she*.

Abbreviations used in this book:

adj.	adjective
ex.	example or exercise
s.	singular
f.	feminine (noun or subject)
f.pl	feminine plural noun
inf.	infinitive
m.	masculine (noun or subject)
m.pl.	masculine plural noun
p.	page
pl.	plural
qqch	quelque chose
qqn	quelqu'un
sb	somebody
sth	something

Glossary

Adjective
An adjective is a word that modifies a noun and gives additional information.

Agree
When a past participle changes depending on whether the subject is feminine, masculine, and plural.

Auxiliary verb
Auxiliary verbs in French are **avoir** and **être**. They are used in compound tenses.

Clause
A clause is a group of words, including a verb.

Compound tense
A tense composed by **avoir** or **être** conjugated and followed by the past participle.

Conjugation
A conjugation changes a verb depending on the action that has taken place.

Conjunction
Words that link two words or two sentences together, such as **et**, **mais,** and more.

Direct object
A direct object is a person or a group of words answering the questions qui or quoi. It usually follows the verb.

Direct object pronoun
A direct object pronoun is the direct object under the form of a pronoun.

Elision
An elision happens when a word is used in its shorter version **j'**, **qu'**, etc.

Endings
The endings, **terminaisons** in French, are the part of conjugation added to the stem to form conjugated verbs.

Feminine
Gender of a person, a noun, or an object.

Gender
Whether a noun or an object is feminine or masculine.

Infinitive
A verb without conjugation.

Impersonal verb
A verb that doesn't refer to a person but the weather, for example.

Indirect object
An indirect object is a person of a group of words answering the questions **à qui**, **à quoi**, **de qui**, **de quoi**. It usually follows the verb.

Indirect object pronoun
An indirect object pronoun is the indirect object under the form of a pronoun.

Inversion
Term used for questions when the verb is placed before the object.

Irregular verb
A verb not following the rules of regular conjugation. Ex: **Faire**

Masculine
Gender of a person, a noun, or an object.

Plural
Used to refer to more than one person or object.

Question word
A word used in a question to obtain specific information. Ex: **Quand**.

Reflexive pronoun
A pronoun included in a reflexive verb. In "se laver", the reflexive pronoun is se.

Reflexive verb
A reflexive verb is a verb when the action is being reflected on the subject. Ex: **Se changer**, to get changed.

Regular verb
A verb following the rules of regular conjugation. Ex: **Donner**

Singular
Used to refer to one person or one object.

Stem
The stem is the part of the verb that doesn't change. In donner, the stem is **donn-**

Subject pronoun
A subject pronoun is used instead of a noun, usually placed before a verb. Ex: **Tu**

Tense
A tense is the conjugation of a verb that indicates if you refer to the future, the present or the past.

Verb
A verb is a word used to describe an action or a state. It gives context to the sentence, the conversation.

Past participle
The past participle is used to form compound tenses such as **passé composé**, **plus-que-parfait** and more.

CHAPTER 1

The Present Tense
Le Présent de l'Indicatif

The Present Tense
Le Présent de l'Indicatif

The present tense, called **présent de l'indicatif** in French, is one of the most used tenses. It replaces three English tenses:

The simple present	He eats
The continuous present	He's eating
The emphatic present	He does eat

> In French, the present tense replaces these three conjugations: **Il mange.**

When to Use the Present Tense

AUDIO 2.1

The present tense shares many similarities with the three English conjugations - only a few uses are different. If we look at similar ones, we use the present tense to talk about:

⇨ Things that are happening now, at the moment we are speaking. The sentence sometimes includes an adverb of time such as **aujourd'hui** (today), **maintenant** (now), **en ce moment** (at the moment)...

Je pars maintenant. *I am leaving now.*
Il est au magasin en ce moment. *He is at the store at the moment.*

⇨ Things that happen all the time or some habits that you have:

Je joue au football tous les samedis. *I play football – soccer every Saturday.*
On promène toujours le chien dans ce quartier. *We always walk the dog in this neighborhood.*

⇨ General actions or states:

La maison est à vendre. *The house is for sale.*
J'ai 30 ans. *I am 30 years old.*
Elle cuisine très bien. *She cooks very well.*

⇨ The present tense can also be used to express the future when a word in the sentence refers to a moment in the future:

Son examen est demain matin. *His exam is tomorrow morning.*
J'arrive demain à 2 heures. *I arrive tomorrow at 2 p.m.*
Nous allons en vacances le mois prochain. *We are going on vacation next month.*

The main difference between French and English is that French uses the present tense to talk about things that started in the past but continue in the present. It all comes down to the expression of time.

⇨ With the word **depuis** Since – for

Depuis indicates that the action has been going on for some time. In French, we use the present tense in this case:

J'habite au Canada depuis deux ans. *I have been living in Canada for two years.*
Il est retraité depuis quelques mois. *He has been retired for a few months.*
Il apprend le français depuis novembre. *He has been learning French since November.*

Other ways to tell that the action is ongoing:

Ça fait:
Ça fait deux ans que j'habite au Canada.

Il y a:
Il y a deux ans que j'habite au Canada.

In questions:

Depuis combien de temps + est-ce que + verb:

Depuis combien de temps est-ce que tu as ce plâtre ? *Have long have you had this cast for?*
Je l'ai depuis quelques jours. *I have had it for a few days.*

Depuis quand + est-ce que + verb:

Depuis quand est-ce que vous êtes mariés ? *How long have you been married?*
Nous sommes mariés depuis l'année dernière. *We have been married since last year.*

Conjugation of Regular -er Verbs

Verbs ending in -er are the most common and easiest ones to conjugate, also called verbs of the 1st group. They represent around 80% of French verbs, including a few irregular verbs described in the following pages.

How to conjugate an -er verb?

First, remove the **-er** at the end of the verb, obtaining the stem. Then add the endings to the stem. For -er verbs, these endings are **-e, -es, -e, -ons, -ez,** and **-ent**. That's it!

See the example below with the verb **téléphoner**. After removing -er, the stem is **téléphon-**, the process of adding the endings is described below.

⇨ For the next verbs in this chapter, the conjugation will be simplified by pairing **il - elle - on** and **ils - elles**.

Téléphoner To call AUDIO 3.1

Pr.	Stem + Endings	Conjugated verb	Translation
Je	téléphon - **e**	Je téléphon**e**	I call – I am calling
Tu	téléphon - **es**	Tu téléphon**es**	You call – You are calling
Il	téléphon - **e**	Il téléphon**e**	He calls – He is calling
Elle	téléphon - **e**	Elle téléphon**e**	She calls – She is calling
On	téléphon - **e**	On téléphon**e**	We call – We are calling
Nous	téléphon - **ons**	Nous téléphon**ons**	We call – We are calling
Vous	téléphon - **ez**	Vous téléphon**ez**	You call – You are calling
Ils	téléphon - **ent**	Ils téléphon**ent**	They call – They are calling
Elles	téléphon - **ent**	Elles téléphon**ent**	They call – They are calling

The endings **-e, -es, -ent** have the same pronunciation.

⇨ If the pronunciation is different, there will be a *pronunciation note* at the bottom of the page.

Common regular verbs ending in -er: AUDIO 3.2

Abaisser To lower
Accepter To accept
Accompagner To accompany
Accorder To admit – To grant
Accrocher To hang
Accuser To accuse
Admirer To admire
Adorer To adore
Adresser To address
Aider To help
Aimer To like – To love
Ajouter To add
Amuser To amuse
Apporter To bring
Approcher To approach
Approuver To approve
Armer To arm
Arracher To pull up – out
Arrêter To stop
Arriver To arrive
Assister To attend
Assurer To assure
Attaquer To attack
Attirer To attract
Attraper To catch
Augmenter To increase
Baisser To lower
Bavarder To chat
Blaguer To joke
Blâmer To blame
Blesser To hurt – To offend
Briser To break
Brosser To brush
Brûler To burn
Cacher To hide
Casser To break
Causer To cause
Célébrer To celebrate
Cesser To cease
Chanter To sing
Chasser To hunt
Chercher To look for – To search
Chuchoter To whisper
Coller To stick
Commander To order
Comparer To compare
Compter To count – To intend
Concerner To concern
Conseiller To recommend
Consommer To consume
Continuer To continue
Contrôler To control
Coucher To put to bed
Couper To cut
Coûter To cost
Crier To shout
Cuisiner To cook
Culpabiliser To make one feel guilty
Danser To dance
Déchirer To rip
Décider To decide
Déjeuner To have lunch
Demander To ask
Demeurer To live – To stay
Dépasser To exceed
Dépêcher To hurry
Dépenser To spend
Désirer To desire – To wish
Dessiner To draw
Détester To hate
Détourner To divert
Développer To develop
Deviner To guess
Diminuer To diminish
Dîner To have dinner
Discuter To discuss
Donner To give
Doubler To double
Douter To doubt
Échapper To escape
Échouer To fail
Écouter To listen
Écraser To crush
Éloigner To move away
Embrasser To kiss – To embrace
Empêcher To prevent

*Remember to **download the audio** and to **watch the videos** – see Preface*

Emprunter To borrow
Enregistrer To record – To save
Enseigner To teach
Enterrer To burry
Entraîner To cause
Entrer To enter
Épouser To marry
Étonner To astonish
Étudier To study
Éviter To avoid
Excuser To excuse
Exister To exist
Expliquer To explain
Explorer To explore
Exprimer To express
Féliciter To congratulate
Fermer To close
Fixer To fix
Fonder To found
Fouiller To search
Frapper To knock – To hit
Fumer To smoke
Gagner To win – To earn – To gain
Garder To keep
Gaspiller To waste
Goûter To taste
Gratter To scratch
Grimper To climb
Habiller To dress
Habiter To live
Hésiter To hesitate
Ignorer To ignore
Importer To import
Indiquer To indicate
Informer To inform
Insister To insist
Intéresser To interest
Inventer To invent
Inviter To invite
Jouer To play
Jurer To swear – To vow
Klaxonner To honk
Laisser To leave
Laver To wash
Louer To rent
Manquer To miss
Marcher To walk
Mériter To merit
Mesurer To measure
Monter To climb – To go up
Montrer To show
Moquer To mock
Négocier To negotiate
Nier To deny
Nommer To name – To appoint
Noter To write down
Occuper To occupy
Oublier To forget
Pardonner To forgive
Parler To speak – To talk
Participer To participate
Passer To pass
Pêcher To fish
Peigner To comb
Penser To think
Persuader To persuade
Plaisanter To joke
Planter To plant
Pleurer To cry
Plier To fold
Porter To carry – To wear
Poser To put down
Pousser To push
Préparer To prepare
Présenter To present – To introduce
Prêter To lend
Prier To pray
Proposer To suggest
Prouver To prove
Puer To stink
Quitter To leave
Raconter To tell
Rassurer To reassure
Refuser To refuse
Regarder To look at
Regretter To regret
Remarquer To notice
Remercier To thank
Rencontrer To meet
Rentrer To return

Réparer To repair
Repasser To iron
Reposer To put back
Représenter To represent
Ressembler To look like
Rester To stay
Retourner To return
Retrouver To find
Réveiller To wake up
Rêver To dream
Risquer To risk
Rouler To roll - To drive
Sauter To jump
Sauver To save
Secouer To shake
Séjourner To stay
Sembler To seem
Séparer To separate
Siffler To whistle
Signaler To signal
Signer To sign
Signifier To mean
Skier To ski
Sonner To ring
Souffler To blow
Souhaiter To wish
Supporter To support
Supposer To suppose
Taper To type
Téléphoner To call
Tenter To try
Terminer To end
Tirer To pull
Tomber To fall
Toucher To touch - To affect
Tourner To turn
Tousser To cough
Traiter To treat
Travailler To work
Traverser To cross
Tromper To mislead
Trouver To find
Tuer To kill
User To wear out - To use
Utiliser To use
Varier To vary
Vérifier To verify
Verser To pour
Viser To aim
Visiter To visit
Voler To steal - To fly
Voter To vote

EX. 1.1 *Traduisez le pronom et le verbe au présent.* AUDIO 3.3

1. I cook – ______
2. He studies – ______
3. We look – ______
4. She washes – ______
5. They teach (m) – ______
6. You pour (s) – ______
7. I show – ______
8. We walk – ______
9. They separate (f) – ______
10. I talk – ______
11. He spends – ______
12. They sing (m) – ______
13. We accept – ______
14. It stinks (m) – ______
15. You dream (s) – ______

EX. 1.2 *Conjuguez le verbe entre parenthèses au présent.* AUDIO 3.4

1. Eric ______ la télévision. (regarder)
2. Elle ______ une pomme. (couper)
3. Nous ______ une solution. (trouver)
4. Le docteur ______ le patient. (aider)
5. Elles ______ une chanson. (chanter)
6. Jeff ______ à l'hôtel. (rester)
7. Elle ______ du sel. (ajouter)
8. Le valet ______ la valise. (porter)
9. Il ______ son manteau. (accrocher)
10. Nous ______ le déjeuner. (préparer)
11. Vous ______ un accident. (éviter)

12. Les mariés ______________________________ les invités. (remercier)
13. L'avocat ______________________________ un conseil. (donner)
14. Les enfants ______________________________ le chocolat. (aimer)
15. Elle ______________________________ une tasse. (casser)

EX. 1.3 *Traduisez le pronom et le verbe entre parenthèses.* AUDIO 3.5

1. (We love) ______________________________ les pommes.
2. (She explains) ______________________________ la leçon.
3. (He pushes) ______________________________ la porte.
4. (I type) ______________________________ le numéro.
5. (They listen – f) ______________________________ de la musique.
6. (You steal – s) ______________________________ un biscuit.
7. (He calls) ______________________________ au client.
8. (He shows) ______________________________ ses dessins.
9. (I play) ______________________________ aux cartes.
10. (We cross) ______________________________ la route.
11. (She works) ______________________________ aujourd'hui.
12. (I speak) ______________________________ français.
13. (She signs) ______________________________ le document.
14. (I forget) ______________________________ le mot de passe.
15. (He fishes) ______________________________ un poisson.

EX. 1.4 *Trouvez les erreurs et corrigez-les (si nécessaire).* AUDIO 3.6

1. J'habitent à la campagne. ______________________________
2. On cuisines un poulet. ______________________________
3. Je reste au travail. ______________________________
4. Il amusez le chien. ______________________________
5. Elle couchons les enfants. ______________________________
6. Je chercher mon téléphone. ______________________________
7. Ils négocie le contrat. ______________________________

8. Vous quitte le travail. ____________________

9. Nous invitez des amis. ____________________

10. Tu plante des légumes. ____________________

11. Je termine le film. ____________________

12. Elle rencontrons ses parents. ____________________

13. Nous plie les linges. ____________________

14. Tu vérifies le numéro. ____________________

15. Elle donnez un cadeau. ____________________

Conjugation of Irregular -er Verbs

Irregular verbs ending in **-er** include the following endings in the infinitive form:

- **-cer** and **-ger**
- **-ayer**, **-oyer** and **-uyer**
- **-eler** and **-eter**
- **-eler**, **-ener**, **-eser**, **-eter** and **-ever**
- **-éder**, **-érer**, **-éter**, and **-ébrer**

Verbs ending in -cer and -ger:

The conjugation of verbs ending in **-cer** and **-ger** stays the same as the regular conjugation, except for the conjugation of **nous**, which changes for phonetic reasons.

Lancer To throw AUDIO 4.1

Pr.	Stem + Endings	Conjugated verb
Je	lanc - **e**	Je lance
Tu	lanc - **es**	Tu lances
Il-Elle-On	lanc - **e**	Il-Elle-On lance
Nous	lanç - **ons**	Nous lançons
Vous	lanc - **ez**	Vous lancez
Ils-Elles	lanc - **ent**	Ils-Elles lancent

C turns into **Ç** when the verb is conjugated with **nous.** This change happens for phonetic reasons.

C followed by **e** or **i**, will be pronounced **S.**

Here **C** is followed by **O**, which means that **C** will be pronounced as a hard **C.** By replacing **C** with **Ç**, which is pronounced **S**, the pronunciation of the word stays consistent.

Manger To eat AUDIO 4.2

Pr.	Stem - Endings	Conjugated verb
Je	mang - **e**	Je mange
Tu	mang - **es**	Tu manges
Il-Elle-On	mang - **e**	Il-Elle-On mange
Nous	mang**e** - **ons**	Nous mang**e**ons
Vous	mang - **ez**	Vous mangez
Ils-Elles	mang - **ent**	Ils-Elles mangent

G will also be pronounced as a hard **G** when followed by the letter **O**. But, unlike **C**, **G** doesn't use another letter to keep the pronunciation consistent. By adding an **E** between **G** and **O**, the pronunciation stays as a soft **G**.

Common verbs ending in -cer: AUDIO 4.3

Agacer To annoy
Annoncer To announce
Avancer To advance
Balancer To sway – To swing
Commencer To begin – To start
Dénoncer To denounce
Divorcer To divorce
Effacer To erase – To delete
Forcer To force
Lancer To throw
Menacer To threaten
Placer To put
Prononcer To pronounce
Remplacer To replace
Renoncer To renounce
Sucer To suck
Tracer To draw

Common verbs ending in -ger: AUDIO 4.4

Aménager To furnish
Arranger To arrange
Bouger To move
Changer To change
Charger To charge - To load
Corriger To correct
Décourager To discourage
Dégager To free
Déménager To move
Déranger To disturb
Diriger To direct
Encourager To encourage
Engager To engage – To hire
Envisager To plan
Exiger To demand
Interroger To interrogate – To question
Juger To judge
Loger To lodge
Manger To eat
Mélanger To mix
Nager To swim
Neiger To snow
Obliger To force
Partager To share
Plonger To dive
Protéger To protect
Ranger To tidy
Rédiger To write
Songer To think
Télécharger To download
Venger To avenge
Voyager To travel

EX. 1.5 *Traduisez le pronom et le verbe.* AUDIO 4.5

1. We replace ____________________
2. We judge ____________________
3. We charge ____________________
4. We announce ____________________
5. We share ____________________
6. We annoy ____________________
7. We force ____________________
8. We download ____________________
9. We think ____________________
10. We travel ____________________
11. We throw ____________________
12. We swim ____________________
13. We begin ____________________
14. We put ____________________
15. We move ____________________

Verbs ending in -yer:

Including: **-ayer -oyer -uyer**

Verbs ending in **-yer** can be divided into 2 categories. The first one is verbs ending in **-ayer** and the second is verbs ending in **-oyer** and **-uyer**.

Verbs ending in -**ayer** have two possible conjugations and two different stems, which doesn't happen with **-oyer** and **-uyer**. The first one, in this case, is **essai**- and the second, which has been commonly used recently, is **essay**-. When using **essai**-, you have to change the stem to **essay**- in the **nous** and **vous** forms.

Essayer To try AUDIO 4.6

Pr.	Stem - Endings	Conjugated verb
J'	essai - **e**	J'essaie
Tu	essai - **es**	Tu essaies
Il-Elle-On	essai - **e**	Il-Elle-On essaie
Nous	essay - **ons**	Nous essayons
Vous	essay - **ez**	Vous essayez
Ils-Elles	essai - **ent**	Ils-Elles essaient

> The endings -**aie** - **aies** - **aient** are pronounced as **è.**
> The part of the stem **ay** before **-ons** and **-ez** is pronounced like the infinitive form of the verb.

When using **essay**-, the conjugation and pronunciation are consistent.
Keeping the same spelling and pronunciation as the infinitive verb may be easier. You can choose the one you prefer to use.

Pr.	Stem - Endings	Conjugated verb
J'	essay - **e**	J'essaye
Tu	essay - **es**	Tu essayes
Il-Elle-On	essay - **e**	Il-Elle-On essaye
Nous	essay - **ons**	Nous essayons
Vous	essay - **ez**	Vous essayez
Ils-Elles	essay - **ent**	Ils-Elles essayent

Common verbs ending in **-ayer** following the same rules:

Balayer To sweep
Effrayer To frighten
Égayer To entertain
Essayer To try
Payer To pay

Verbs ending in -oyer and -uyer:

Verbs ending in -**oyer** and -**uyer** don't have 2 different possibilities of conjugation and pronunciation like verbs ending in **-ayer**.

The stem will change from **nettoy**- or **essuy-** to **nettoi**- or **essui-** for all the forms but, changing back to **nettoy- essuy-** for **nous** and **vous**.

Verbs ending in -oyer:

Nettoyer To clean AUDIO 4.7

Pr.	Stem + Endings	Conjugated verb
Je	nettoi - **e**	Je nettoi
Tu	nettoi - **es**	Tu nettoies
Il-Elle-On	nettoi - **e**	Il-Elle-On nettoie
Nous	nettoy - **ons**	Nous nettoyons
Vous	nettoy - **ez**	Vous nettoyez
Ils-Elles	nettoi - **ent**	Ils-Elles nettoient

Common verbs ending in **-oyer:**

Employer To employ – To use
Nettoyer To clean
Tutoyer To use "tu"
Vouvoyer To use "vous"

Verbs ending in -uyer:

Essuyer To wipe AUDIO 4.8

Pr.	Stem + Endings	Conjugated verb
J'	essui - **e**	J'essuie
Tu	essui - **es**	Tu essuies
Il-Elle-On	essui - **e**	Il-Elle-On essuie
Nous	essuy - **ons**	Nous essuyons
Vous	essuy - **ez**	Vous essuyez
Ils-Elles	essui - **ent**	Ils-Elles essuient

Common verbs ending in **-uyer:**

Appuyer To press – To lean
Ennuyer To bore – To annoy
Essuyer To wipe

EX. 1.6 *Conjuguez le verbe au présent en accord avec le pronom.* AUDIO 4.9

1. Je / payer ____________________
2. Nous / nettoyer ____________________
3. Elle / essuyer ____________________
4. Tu / effrayer ____________________
5. Vous / essayer ____________________
6. Ils / employer ____________________
7. On / balayer ____________________
8. Il / appuyer ____________________

Verbs ending in -eler and -eter:

The stem of verbs ending in **-eler** and **-eter** changes for all the forms but not for **nous** and **vous**.
L and **T** will be doubled, and the **E** will be pronounced as **È. E** before a **double L** or a **double T** is pronounced as **È.**

Verbs ending in -eler:

Appeler To call AUDIO 4.10

Pr.	Stem - Endings	Conjugated verb
J'	app**ell** - **e**	J'app**elle**
Tu	app**ell** - **es**	Tu app**elle**s
Il-Elle-On	app**ell** - **e**	Il-Elle-On app**ell**e
Nous	appel - **ons**	Nous appelons
Vous	appel - **ez**	Vous appelez
Ils-Elles	app**ell** - **ent**	Ils-Elles app**ell**ent

Common verbs ending in **-eler** following the same rules:

Appeler To call
Épeler To spell
Rappeler To call back

Verbs ending in -eter:

Jeter To throw AUDIO 4.11

Pr.	Stem - Endings	Conjugated verb
Je	**jett** - **e**	Je **jett**e
Tu	**jett** - **es**	Tu **jett**es
Il-Elle-On	**jett** - **e**	Il-Elle-On **jett**e
Nous	jet - **ons**	Nous jetons
Vous	jet - **ez**	Vous jetez
Ils-Elles	**jett** - **ent**	Ils-Elles **jett**ent

Other **-eter** verbs conjugated the same way contain the verb **jeter**:

Rejeter To reject
Projeter To project

EX. 1.7 *Traduisez le verbe et le pronom.* AUDIO 4.12

1. We call ______________________
2. I reject ______________________
3. She throws ______________________
4. They project ______________________
5. We spell ______________________

Verbs ending in -eler, -ener, -eser, -eter and -ever:

The letter **E** of the last syllable of the stem changes from **E** to **È** in all forms, except in **nous** and **vous** forms.

Verbs ending in -eler:

Geler To freeze AUDIO 4.13

Pr.	Stem - Endings	Conjugated verb
Je	g**è**l - e	Je g**è**le
Tu	g**è**l - **es**	Tu g**è**les
Il-Elle-On	g**è**l - **e**	Il-Elle-On g**è**le
Nous	gel - **ons**	Nous gelons
Vous	gel - **ez**	Vous gelez
Ils-Elles	g**è**l - **ent**	Ils-Elles g**è**lent

Common verbs ending in **-eler**:

Geler To freeze
Peler To peel

Verbs ending in -ener:

Amener To bring AUDIO 4.14

Pr.	Stem - Endings	Conjugated verb
J'	am**è**n - **e**	J'am**è**ne
Tu	am**è**n - **es**	Tu am**è**nes
Il-Elle-On	am**è**n - **e**	Il-Elle-On am**è**ne
Nous	amen - **ons**	Nous amenons
Vous	amen - **ez**	Vous amenez
Ils-Elles	am**è**n - **ent**	Ils-Elles am**è**nent

Common verbs ending in **-ener**:

Amener To bring
Emmener To take
Mener To lead
Promener To walk

Verbs ending in -eser:

Peser To weigh AUDIO 4.15

Pr.	Stem - Endings	Conjugated verb
Je	pès - **e**	Je p**è**se
Tu	pès - **es**	Tu p**è**ses
Il-Elle-On	pès - **e**	Il-Elle-On p**è**se
Nous	pes - **ons**	Nous pesons
Vous	pes - **ez**	Vous pesez
Ils-Elles	pès - **ent**	Ils-Elles p**è**sent

Verbs ending in -eter:

Acheter To buy AUDIO 4.16

Pr.	Stem - Endings	Conjugated verb
J'	achèt - **e**	J'ach**è**te
Tu	achèt - **es**	Tu ach**è**tes
Il-Elle-On	achèt - **e**	Il-Elle-On ach**è**te
Nous	achet - **ons**	Nous achetons
Vous	achet - **ez**	Vous achetez
Ils-Elles	achèt - **ent**	Ils-Elles ach**è**te

Verbs ending in -ever:

Achever To finish AUDIO 4.17

Pr.	Stem - Endings	Conjugated verb
J'	achèv - **e**	J'ach**è**ve
Tu	achèv - **es**	Tu ach**è**ves
Il-Elle-On	achèv - **e**	Il-Elle-On ach**è**ve
Nous	achev - **ons**	Nous achevons
Vous	achev - **ez**	Vous achevez
Ils-Elles	achèv - **ent**	Ils-Elles ach**è**vent

Common verbs ending in **-ever**:

Achever To finish
Élever To raise
Enlever To remove
Lever To get up
Relever To lift up

EX. 1.8 *Conjuguez le verbe au présent avec le pronom correspondant.* AUDIO 4.18

1. Nous achevons => Il ______
2. Tu mènes => Nous ______
3. Elle pèse => Nous ______
4. Vous promenez => Je ______
5. Nous élevons => Ils ______
6. On emmène => Nous ______
7. J'amène => Il ______
8. Il relève => Vous ______
9. Tu achètes => Nous ______
10. Nous enlevons => Ils ______

Verbs ending in -éder, -érer, -éter and -ébrer:

The letter **É** of the last syllable of the stem changes from **É** to **È** in all forms, except in **nous** and **vous** forms. For **nous** and **vous**, it stays **É**.

Verbs ending in -éder:

Céder To yield AUDIO 4.19

Pr.	Stem - Endings	Conjugated verb
Je	cèd - **e**	Je c**è**de
Tu	cèd - **es**	Tu c**è**des
Il-Elle-On	cèd - **e**	Il-Elle-On c**è**de
Nous	céd - **ons**	Nous cédons
Vous	céd - **ez**	Vous cédez
Ils-Elles	cèd - **ent**	Ils-Elles c**è**dent

Common verbs ending in **-éder**:

Céder To yield
Posséder To own - To possess

Verbs ending in -érer:

Espérer To hope AUDIO 4.20

Pr.	Stem - Endings	Conjugated verb
J'	espèr - **e**	J'esp**è**re
Tu	espèr - **es**	Tu esp**è**res
Il-Elle-On	espèr - **e**	Il-Elle-On esp**è**re
Nous	espér - **ons**	Nous espérons
Vous	espér - **ez**	Vous espérez
Ils-Elles	espèr - **ent**	Ils-Elles esp**è**rent

Common verbs ending in **-érer**:

Espérer To hope
Préférer To prefer
Exagérer To exaggerate
Considérer To consider

Verbs ending in -éter:

Répéter To repeat AUDIO 4.21

Pr.	Stem - Endings	Conjugated verb
Je	répèt - **e**	Je rép**è**te
Tu	répèt - **es**	Tu rép**è**tes
Il-Elle-On	répèt - **e**	Il-Elle-On rép**è**te
Nous	répét - **ons**	Nous répétons
Vous	répét - **ez**	Vous répétez
Ils-Elles	répèt - **ent**	Ils-Elles rép**è**tent

Verbs ending in -ébrer:

Célébrer To celebrate AUDIO 4.22

Pr.	Stem - Endings	Conjugated verb
Je	célèbr - **e**	Je cél**è**bre
Tu	célèbr - **es**	Tu cél**è**bres
Il-Elle-On	célèbr - **e**	Il-Elle-On cél**è**bre
Nous	célébr - **ons**	Nous célébrons
Vous	célébr - **ez**	Vous célébrez
Ils-Elles	célèbr - **ent**	Ils-Elles cél**è**brent

EX. 1.9 *Trouvez les erreurs et corrigez-les.* AUDIO 4.23

1. Je préféres ____________________
2. Nous célèbrent ____________________

3. Ils considère ________________

4. Tu répètent ________________

5. On céder ________________

Revision: Verbs ending in -er:

EX. 1.10 *Conjuguez le verbe entre parenthèses au présent.* AUDIO 4.24

1. (Écouter) Il ________________ de la musique.
2. (Tracer) L'architecte ________________ les plans.
3. (Acheter) Le client ________________ du pain.
4. (Séjourner) Nous ________________ à l'hôtel.
5. (Regarder) Elles ________________ la télévision.
6. (Signaler) L'ouvrier ________________ le chantier.
7. (Exagérer) Tu ________________ toujours.
8. (Marcher) Mes parents ________________ deux fois par jour.
9. (Télécharger) Tout le monde ________________illégalement.
10. (Posséder) Sa sœur ________________ une voiture de collection.
11. (Remplacer) Je ________________ une ampoule.
12. (Balayer) Mon mari ________________ la terrasse.
13. (Planter) On ________________ des légumes.
14. (Enlever) J'________________ mon pull.
15. (Manger) Nous ________________ avant de partir.

EX. 1.11 *Trouvez le verbe conjugué et écrivez l'infinitif entre parenthèses. Conjuguez le verbe au présent avec le pronom* ***nous.*** AUDIO 4.25

1. On rentre (________________) Nous ________________
2. On voyage (________________) Nous ________________
3. On considère (________________) Nous ________________
4. On commande (________________) Nous ________________
5. On enlève (________________) Nous ________________

6. On lance (______________________) Nous ______________________
7. On jette (______________________) Nous ______________________
8. On paye (______________________) Nous ______________________
9. On admire (______________________) Nous ______________________
10. On mesure (______________________) Nous ______________________
11. On vote (______________________) Nous ______________________
12. On corrige (______________________) Nous ______________________
13. On chauffe (______________________) Nous ______________________
14. On déménage (______________________) Nous ______________________
15. On tombe (______________________) Nous ______________________

EX. 1.12 *Formez une phrase avec les différentes parties et conjuguez le verbe au présent.*

AUDIO 4.26

1. Le patient / refuser / le traitement

____

2. Je / promener / le chien

____

3. Nous / voyager / toujours / en première classe

____

4. Les enfants / préférer / le chocolat / aux légumes

____

5. Ils / coller / des stickers / dans le livre

____

6. Les jeunes mariés / remercier / les invités

____

7. L'éducateur / diriger / les enfants / vers le terrain de football

____

8. Le garçon / appuyer / sur le bouton

____

9. J' / appeler / mes parents / tous les soirs

____

10. Les voisins / amener / un apéritif

____

11. Les étudiants / travailler / après l'école

____

12. On / regarder / la télé / quand il pleut

____

13. Le comptable / vérifier / les transactions

____

14. La radio / annoncer / une tempête

____

15. J' / essayer / un nouveau pantalon

____

EX. 1.13 *Choisissez le bon verbe entre parenthèses et conjuguez-le au présent.* AUDIO 4.27

1. (Laver / Casser) Le lave-vaisselle ____________________ les assiettes.
2. (Achever / Adorer) Il ____________________ se rouler dans l'herbe.
3. (Répéter / Téléphoner) La réceptionniste ____________________ le numéro.
4. (Corriger / Effacer) Le professeur ____________________ les devoirs.
5. (Aimer / Dépêcher) J'____________________ le jus d'orange.
6. (Cacher / Siffler) Le chien ____________________ un os.
7. (Effacer / Embrasser) La maman ____________________ son enfant.
8. (Siffler / Pêcher) L'homme ____________________ en marchant.
9. (Changer / Nettoyer) Elles ____________________ leur chambre.
10. (Partager / Enlever) Les enfants ____________________ leurs goûters.

Conjugation of Regular -ir Verbs

Verbs ending in **-ir** are part of the second most common group, also called verbs of the 2nd group. There are around 400 verbs in this group, including a few irregular verbs described in the next pages.

How to conjugate an -ir verb?

Just like verbs ending in -er, you obtain the stem after removing the **-ir** from the verb. Then add the endings to the stem. For **-ir** verbs, the endings are **-is, -is, -it, -issons, -issez** and **-issent.**

Finir To finish AUDIO 5.1

Pr.	Stem - Endings	Conjugated verb
Je	fin - **is**	Je finis
Tu	fin - **is**	Tu finis
Il-Elle-On	fin - **it**	Il-Elle-On finit
Nous	fin - **issons**	Nous finissons
Vous	fin - **issez**	Vous finissez
Ils-Elles	fin - **issent**	Ils-Elles finissent

Note that **not** all verbs ending in -ir belong to the 2nd group of verbs and conjugate this way. Many other verbs such as «ouvrir, dormir, partir» and more are in the 3rd group of verbs. We will see them in the next chapter.

Common verbs ending in -ir: AUDIO 5.2

Affaiblir To weaken
Agir To act
Bâtir To build
Blanchir To whiten
Choisir To choose
Démolir To demolish
Désobéir To disobey
Finir To finish
Fournir To provide
Grandir To grow up
Grossir To gain weight
Guérir To heal
Jaunir To turn yellow
Jouir To enjoy
Maigrir To lose weight
Nourrir To feed
Obéir To obey
Ralentir To slow down
Réfléchir To think/To reflect
Remplir To fill up
Réunir To gather
Réussir To succeed
Rougir To blush
Saisir To seize
Salir To soil
Subir To undergo
Trahir To betray
Unir To join
Vieillir To age

EX. 1.14 *Conjuguez le verbe entre parenthèses au présent.* AUDIO 5.3

1. (Choisir) Mon père ________________ ce qu'il veut manger.
2. (Réunir) Elle ________________ les papiers.
3. (Finir) Les enfants ________________ leurs goûters.
4. (Nourrir) La maman ________________ son enfant.
5. (Vieillir) Elles ________________ vite.
6. (Ralentir) La voiture ________________ avant de tourner.
7. (Jaunir) Les habits blancs ________________ facilement.
8. (Finir) Je ________________ de préparer ma valise.
9. (Agir) Il ________________ comme un enfant.
10. (Maigrir) Je ne ________________ pas beaucoup.
11. (Réussir) Mon frère ________________ tous ses examens.
12. (Grandir) Tu ________________ tellement vite.
13. (Bâtir) Le couple ________________ une nouvelle maison.
14. (Démolir) Le constructeur ________________ le bâtiment.
15. (Affaiblir) La maladie ________________ les patients.

EX. 1.15 *Trouvez le verbe conjugué et écrivez l'infinitif entre parenthèses. Conjuguez le verbe au présent avec le pronom **vous**.* AUDIO 5.4

1. Tu saisis (________________) Vous ________________
2. Tu trahis (________________) Vous ________________
3. Tu fournis (________________) Vous ________________
4. Tu subis (________________) Vous ________________
5. Tu réfléchis (________________) Vous ________________
6. Tu grossis (________________) Vous ________________
7. Tu salis (________________) Vous ________________
8. Tu unis (________________) Vous ________________
9. Tu remplis (________________) Vous ________________
10. Tu désobéis (________________) Vous ________________

Conjugation of -re Verbs

Verbs in the 3rd group are mostly irregular. However, some of them follow the same pattern. The main type being the verbs ending in **-re.** Keep in mind that this type includes less than 20 verbs.

How to conjugate an -re verb?

Just like verbs ending in -er and -ir, remove the **-re** from the verb, leaving you with the stem ending in **d-**. Then add the endings to the stem. For **-re** verbs, the endings are **-s -s** *-nothing* **-ons -ez -ent.**

Remember that for **il**, **elle** and **on**, there is no ending in this conjugation.

Entendre To hear AUDIO 6.1

Pr.	Stem - Endings	Conjugated verb
J'	entend – **s**	J'entends
Tu	entend – **s**	Tu entends
Il-Elle-On	entend –	Il-Elle-On entend
Nous	entend – **ons**	Nous entendons
Vous	entend – **ez**	Vous entendez
Ils-Elles	entend – **ent**	Ils-Elles entendent

Common verbs ending in -re: AUDIO 6.2

Attendre To wait
Confondre To confuse
Correspondre To correspond
Défendre To defend
Dépendre To depend
Descendre To go down – To descend
Entendre To hear
Étendre To stretch
Fondre To melt

Pendre To hang
Perdre To lose
Rendre To give back
Répondre To answer
Tendre To tend
Tondre To mow
Tordre To twist
Vendre To sell

EX. 1.16 *Trouvez les erreurs et corrigez-les.* AUDIO 6.3

1. Nous correspondez par email. ____________________
2. Tu répons au téléphone. ____________________
3. Le voisin tondt la pelouse. ____________________
4. Le magasin vens des cartes. ____________________
5. Ils attende le train. ____________________

6. Je descendu les escaliers. ______________________________

7. Le beurre fond dans la poêle. ______________________________

8. Je perd toujours mes clés. ______________________________

9. Il rendent les clés au propriétaire. ______________________________

10. Elle confonds le rouge et le bleu. ______________________________

Être and Avoir

Être and **avoir** are both verbs and auxiliary. They are used to describe yourself, what you have, etc. But they are more than that! They are both used in the conjugation of compound tenses such as the *passé composé.*

Être is also used as an impersonal verb.

They are 2 of the most used verbs in French and are both irregular. To master the French language, you should know them by heart.

Être To be AUDIO 7-8.1

Je **suis**	Nous **sommes**
Tu **es**	Vous **êtes**
Il-Elle-On **est**	Ils-Elles **sont**

Avoir To have AUDIO 7-8.2

J'**ai**	Nous **avons**
Tu **as**	Vous **avez**
Il-Elle-On **a**	Ils-Elles **ont**

EX. 1.17 *Traduisez les pronoms et les verbes* ***être*** *et* ***avoir.*** AUDIO 7-8.3

1. I am ______________________________
2. You have ______________________________
3. They have (f) ______________________________
4. You are (form) ______________________________
5. He is ______________________________

Expressions and idioms with être: AUDIO 7-8.4

Être + nationality To be + nationality
Être de To be from

Être à (qqn) To belong to sb
Être à l'heure To be on time
Être au courant To be informed

Être d'accord To agree
Être de bonne humeur To be in a good mood
Être de mauvaise humeur To be in a bad mood
Être de retour To be back

Être en avance To be early
Être en retard To be late
Être en colère To be angry
Être en vie To be alive
Être en train de (+ inf) To be in the process of (doing)
Être en forme To be in shape
Être en bonne santé To be healthy
Être en panne To be out of order

Être sur le point de (+ inf) To be about to (do)

Être bien dans sa peau To feel comfortable with oneself – To be confident
Être bouche bée – Être sans voix To be speechless
Être dans la lune – Être dans les nuages To daydream
Être dans le doute To doubt – To be doubtful
Être sur son trente et un To be dressed to the nines

EX. 1.18 *Conjuguez le verbe **être**.* AUDIO 7-8.5

1. La machine ______________________ en panne.
2. Le client ______________________ en avance.
3. Le chat ______________________ de mauvaise humeur.
4. Je ______________________ de Londres.
5. Il ______________________ de retour.
6. Ce sac ______________________ à cette dame.
7. Est-ce que tu ______________________ d'accord ?
8. Les élèves ______________________ dans la lune.
9. Mon oncle n' ______________________ jamais en colère.
10. J'espère qu'il ______________________ en bonne santé.

*Remember to **download the audio** and to **watch the videos** – see Preface*

Expressions and idioms with avoir:

Expressions with **avoir** are even more important than the ones with être. This is where it gets confusing for a lot of French learners. In English, the most common expressions are used with the verb To be (être). The same expressions are used with the verb Avoir (to have) in French.

AUDIO 7-8.6

Avoir ______ ans To be ______ years old
Avoir faim To be hungry
Avoir soif To be thirsty
Avoir chaud To be hot
Avoir froid To be cold
Avoir sommeil To be sleepy
Avoir peur (de) To be afraid (of)
Avoir raison To be right
Avoir tort To be wrong
Avoir mal To be in pain
Avoir de la chance To be lucky
Avoir l'habitude de To be in the habit of
Avoir honte de To be ashamed of

Il y a There is – There are
Avoir besoin de To need
Avoir envie de To want
En avoir marre de To be fed up with
Avoir l'air To seem
Avoir hâte de + inf. Can't wait to + inf.
Avoir du mal à To have a hard time to

Avoir des étoiles plein les yeux To be amazed – To be in love
Avoir deux mains gauches To be clumsy
Avoir les yeux plus gros que le ventre To have eyes bigger than one's stomach – To be greedy
Avoir du bol To be lucky
Avoir la pêche – Avoir la banane To be happy
Avoir le cafard To be depressed
Avoir un petit creux To be a little bit hungry
Avoir une faim de loup To be very hungry

Avoir mal à + body part To have a(n) ______ ache
Avoir mal à la tête To have a headache
Avoir mal à la gorge To have a sore throat
Avoir mal au ventre To have a stomachache
Avoir mal au dos To have back pain

Avoir mal aux dents To have a toothache

EX. 1.19 *Conjuguez le verbe au présent et mettez la phrase dans le bon ordre.* AUDIO 7-8.7

1. Avoir mal / tu / au pied

 ____

2. Avoir besoin de / il / un nouveau manteau

 ____

3. Avoir hâte de / nous / partir / en vacances

 ____

4. Avoir 90 ans / mes grands-parents

 ____

5. Avoir peur des / Marie / araignées

 ____

6. Avoir froid / elle

 ____

7. Avoir sommeil / ce chien

 ____

8. Avoir honte de / elle / ses résultats

 ____

9. Il y a / de choix / beaucoup

 ____

10. Avoir du mal / mon fils / avec ses devoirs

 ____

EX. 1.20 *Choisissez entre **être** et **avoir** et conjuguez le verbe au présent.* AUDIO 7-8.8

1. Il ______________________________ sommeil.
2. J'______________________________ du mal à dormir.
3. Le train ______________________________ sur le point de partir.
4. Les voisins ______________________________ de retour.
5. Le professeur ______________________________ toujours raison.
6. Il y ______________________________ du jus dans le frigo.
7. L'avion ______________________________ en retard.

8. Ma colocataire ______________________________ suédoise.
9. Est-ce que tu ______________________________ au courant ?
10. On en ______________________________ marre du bruit.
11. Il ______________________________ toujours du bol.
12. Je ______________________________ d'accord avec lui.
13. La voiture ______________________________ encore en panne.
14. Tu ______________________________ l'air fatigué.
15. Elle ______________________________ mal au dos.

Aller

Aller is the only irregular verb ending in **-er**. The only forms that stay consistent are **nous** and **vous**.

Knowing this verb by heart is important to form the tense called "futur proche", the simplified tense used when talking about the future.

Aller To go AUDIO 9.1

Je **vais**	Nous **allons**
Tu **vas**	Vous **allez**
Il-Elle-On **va**	Ils-Elles **vont**

AUDIO 9.2

The common question "How are you?" in French uses the verb **aller**, not être:

Comment allez-vous ? How are you? (form.)
Comment ça va ? How are you? (inform.)

Other expressions and idioms with aller:

Aller + inf. To be going + inf.
Aller à pied To go on foot
Aller à quelqu'un To suit someone
Allez (filler word) Come on – Let's go

Aller is of course used as a verb of motion, To go somewhere. It's always followed by a preposition: AUDIO 9.3

Aller + à la Use **à la** when followed by a feminine noun (**à l'** when the noun starts with a vowel or a silent H)
Aller à la piscine To go to the pool
Aller à la librairie To go to the bookstore

Aller + au Use **au** when followed by a masculine noun
Aller au parc To go to the park
Aller au magasin To go to the store

Aller + aux Use **aux** when followed by a plural noun
Aller aux courses To go grocery shopping
Aller aux toilettes To go to the washroom

Aller + en Use **en** when followed by a feminine country
Aller en Belgique To go to Belgium
Aller en France To go to France

Aller + au Use **au** when followed by a masculine country
Aller au Canada To go to Canada
Aller au Portugal To go to Portugal

Aller + aux Use **aux** when followed by a plural country
Aller aux États-Unis To go to the United States
Aller aux Pays-Bas To go to the Netherlands

Aller + à Use **à** when followed by a city
Aller à Paris To go to Paris
Aller à Londres To go to London

Aller + chez Use **chez** when followed by a person, a business, a store
Aller chez le docteur To go to the doctor
Aller chez Paul To go to Paul's

EX. 1.21 *Traduisez les phrases suivantes.* AUDIO 9.4

1. I am going to the store.

___

2. They (m) are going to the United States.

___

3. She is going to church.

___

4. We are going to Barcelona.

___

5. You (pl) are going to Spain.

___

EX. 1.22 *Conjuguez le verbe **aller** au présent et ajoutez **à - au - aux - à l' - à la - en**.* AUDIO 9.5

1. Il / Canada
2. On / concert (m)
3. Nous / médecin (m)
4. Vous / pharmacie (f)
5. Tu / Philippines
6. Mes voisins / Paris
7. Le professeur / musée (m)
8. Luc et Julie / poste (f)
9. Elles / église (f)
10. Elle / Marie
11. Je / Allemagne
12. On / Japon
13. Ma femme / plage (f)
14. Son ami / coiffeur (m)
15. Amy / toilettes (f.pl)

Faire

The verb **faire** is probably the most versatile verb in French. We use it to talk about what we do, make, play, bake, to talk about the weather, and more!

Faire is also used as an impersonal verb.

Faire To do – To make AUDIO 10.1

Je **fais**	Nous **faisons**
Tu **fais**	Vous **faites**
Il-Elle-On **fait**	Ils-Elles **font**

Notes on pronunciation:

The conjugated verb with **nous** has a different pronunciation:

Nous f**ai**sons = **e**

Other verbs conjugated the same way contain the verb **faire**:

Re<u>faire</u> To redo
Dé<u>faire</u> To undo

AUDIO 10.2

Expressions with faire – à la maison:

Faire la cuisine To cook
Faire un gâteau To bake
Faire le ménage To do the housework
Faire la lessive To do the laundry
Faire les poussières To dust
Faire le repassage To iron
Faire la vaisselle To do the dishes
Faire son lit To make one's bed
Faire les courses To go grocery shopping

Expressions with faire – à l'école:

Faire ses devoirs To do one's homework
Faire des progrès To make progress
Faire des fautes To make mistakes

Expressions with faire – du sport:

Faire du sport To exercise
Faire du vélo To bike
Faire du patinage To ice skate
Faire du football To play soccer
Faire du judo To do judo
Faire du ski To ski
Faire de la natation To swim

Expressions with faire – les loisirs:

Faire une promenade To take a walk
Faire un voyage To take a trip

Expressions with faire – le temps:

Quel temps fait-il ? How is the weather?
Il fait chaud It's warm
Il fait froid It's cold
Il fait bon It's nice
Il fait mauvais It's bad
Il fait doux It's mild
Il fait soleil It's sunny
Il fait jour It's light out
Il fait nuit It's night out

Other expressions with faire:

Faire attention To pay attention
Faire la tête To be moody
Faire peur (à) To scare
Faire croire To make someone believe
Faire la queue To queue
Faire partie de To be a part of
Faire la grasse matinée To sleep in

EX. 1.23 *Trouvez les erreurs et corrigez-les.* AUDIO 10.3

1. Le clown faisons peur aux enfants. ____________________
2. Tu fais doux. ____________________
3. Ma nièce fais du piano. ____________________
4. Je font des progrès. ____________________
5. Ils fait attention. ____________________

EX. 1.24 *Ajoutez le verbe faire et conjuguez-le au présent.* AUDIO 10.4

1. Je / un gâteau

   ____

2. Les enfants / du ski

   ____

3. Il / le repassage

4. Nous / une promenade

5. Tu / la vaisselle

6. Il / nuit

7. Elle / des fautes

8. Mes cousines / la cuisine

9. Je / la grasse matinée

10. Il / bon

11. Les clients / la queue

12. Julian / ses devoirs

Jouer à - Jouer du - Faire de

Jouer à, jouer de and **faire** are often a struggle for French learners because they have similar uses.

> **Jouer à** is used for **sports and games**
> **Jouer de** is used for **musical instruments**
> **Faire de** is used for **sports and activities**

Let's look at each of them and see how the gender of the following noun impacts **à** and **de**.

Jouer à: AUDIO 11.1

Depending on whether the following noun is feminine, masculine, singular or plural, **à** is going to change into the following:

Jouer à + specific game
Jouer à la + feminine noun
Jouer au + masculine noun
Jouer aux + feminine – masculine noun but plural

A few examples with **jouer à** + specific game:

Jouer à cache-cache To play hide-and-seek
Jouer à Zelda To play Zelda
Jouer à Mario To play Mario

A few examples with **jouer à la** + feminine noun:

Jouer à la balle To play ball
Jouer à la marelle To play hopscotch
Jouer à la pétanque To play boules

A few examples with **jouer au** + masculine noun:

Jouer au basketball To play basketball
Jouer au billard To play pool
Jouer au golf To play golf
Jouer au football To play soccer
Jouer au tennis To play tennis
Jouer au loto To play the lotto
Jouer au hockey To play hockey

A few examples with **jouer aux** + plural noun:

Jouer aux cartes To play cards
Jouer aux dames To play checkers
Jouer aux échecs To play chess
Jouer aux dominos To play dominos

Jouer de: AUDIO 11.2

Depending on whether the following noun is feminine, masculine, singular or plural, **de** is going to change into the following:

Jouer de l' + feminine or masculine noun starting with a vowel or a silent h.
Jouer de la + feminine noun
Jouer du + masculine noun

A few examples with **jouer de l'** + feminine or masculine noun starting with a vowel or a silent h:

Jouer de l'harmonica To play the harmonica
Jouer de l'orgue To play the organ
Jouer de l'accordéon To play the accordion

A few examples with **jouer de la** + feminine noun:

Jouer de la batterie To play the drums
Jouer de la flûte To play the flute
Jouer de la guitare To play the guitar
Jouer de la trompette To play the trumpet

A few examples with **jouer du** + masculine noun:

Jouer du piano To play the piano
Jouer du violon To play the violin
Jouer du trombone To play the trombone
Jouer du saxophone To play the saxophone

Faire de: AUDIO 11.3

Depending on whether the following noun is feminine, masculine, singular or plural, **de** is going to change into the following:

Faire de l' + feminine or masculine noun starting with a vowel or a silent h.
Faire de la + feminine noun
Faire du + masculine noun

A few examples with **faire de l'** + feminine or masculine noun starting with a vowel or a silent h:

Faire de l'équitation To horseback ride
Faire de l'escalade To rock climb

A few examples with **faire de la** + feminine noun:

Faire de la boxe To box
Faire de la natation To swim
Faire de la plongée To go scuba diving

A few examples with **faire du** + masculine noun:

Faire du yoga To do yoga
Faire du cheval To horseback ride
Faire du vélo To cycle

Jouer à vs. Faire de AUDIO 11.4

In some cases, we can use **jouer à** and **faire de** for the same sport/activity:

Jouer au tennis - Faire du tennis
Jouer au football - Faire du football
Jouer au golf - Faire du golf

Il joue de la batterie depuis longtemps. *He has been playing the drums for a long time.*
Nous avons joué aux cartes toute la soirée. *We played cards the whole evening.*

EX. 1.25 *Ajoutez le verbe et la préposition avant le nom.* AUDIO 11.5

1. ______________ ski
2. ______________ piano
3. ______________ trompette
4. ______________ tir à l'arc
5. ______________ roller
6. ______________ tennis
7. ______________ football
8. ______________ batterie
9. ______________ Tetris
10. ______________ flûte
11. ______________ yoga
12. ______________ cartes
13. ______________ guitare
14. ______________ dessin
15. ______________ saxophone
16. ______________ accordéon
17. ______________ judo
18. ______________ poker
19. ______________ danse
20. ______________ golf

Prendre

Prendre doesn't conjugate the same way as **attendre**. Its singular forms are similar to the endings for verbs ending in -re, but not the plural forms.

Prendre To take AUDIO 12.1

Je **prends**	Nous **prenons**
Tu **prends**	Vous **prenez**
Il-Elle-On **prend**	Ils-Elles **prennent**

AUDIO 12.2

Prendre translates to To take and shares most of the same uses with English (unless we are talking about food and drinks. See next point):

Prendre le train - le bus - l'avion To take the train - the bus - the plane
Prendre son temps To take your time
Prendre une photo To take a picture
Prendre la route - l'autoroute To take the road - the highway
Prendre des médicaments To take medicine

In French, we use the verb **prendre** to talk about consuming food and drinks. While in English, to have is commonly used.

Je prends un café tous les matins. *I have a coffee every morning.*
Nous prenons le petit déjeuner ensemble. *We are having breakfast together.*

Prendre can also be used to talk about directions:

Prenez la première à droite. *Take the first turn right.*

Other verbs conjugated the same way contain the verb **prendre**: AUDIO 12.3

Ap<u>prendre</u> To learn
Com<u>prendre</u> To understand
Entre<u>prendre</u> To undertake
Re<u>prendre</u> To take back
Sur<u>prendre</u> To surprise

Expressions and idioms with prendre and compounds: AUDIO 12.4

Apprendre la nouvelle To learn the news
Comprendre le français To understand French
Prendre ses jambes à son cou Take run for your life
Prendre froid To have a cold
Prendre peur To get scared

Prendre la fuite To escape
Prendre du poids To gain weight
Prendre l'air To get some air
Prendre un rendez-vous To make an appointment
Prendre une décision To make a decision
Reprendre le travail To go back to work
Surprendre quelqu'un To surprise someone

EX. 1.26 *Choisissez entre **prendre** – **apprendre** – **surprendre** – **reprendre** et conjuguez le verbe au présent.* AUDIO 12.5

1. Je / le bus

 ____

2. Vous / vos affaires

 ____

3. Elles / la nouvelle

 ____

4. Je / un rendez-vous

 ____

5. Nous / souvent un verre ensemble

 ____

6. Elle / ses amis

 ____

7. Il / toujours froid

 ____

8. Ma femme / le travail demain

 ____

9. Nous / l'air

 ____

10. J' / le français

 ____

Revision

EX. 1.27 *Choisissez entre **aller** – **faire** – **être** – **avoir** – **prendre** et conjuguez le verbe au présent.*

AUDIO 12.6

1. Je ______________________________ à la librairie.
2. Tu ______________________________ du vélo.
3. On ______________________________ en forme.
4. Nous ______________________________ chez le dentiste.
5. Ils ______________________________ le ménage.
6. J' ______________________________ trente-trois ans.
7. J' ______________________________ peur.
8. Elles ______________________________ aux courses.
9. Ils ______________________________ dans le doute.
10. Tu ______________________________ un café.
11. Nous ______________________________ en Belgique ce week-end.
12. Robyn ______________________________ à l'heure.
13. Il ______________________________ ses devoirs.
14. Tu ______________________________ l'air fatigué.
15. Vous ______________________________ à pied.
16. Ils ______________________________ une décision.
17. Vous ______________________________ besoin d'une nouvelle voiture.
18. Marc ______________________________ de la natation.
19. Nous ______________________________ le train.
20. Tu ______________________________ toujours en avance.

Negation

The regular **negation** is made up of two words in French: **ne** and **pas.**
Each word goes around the verb and after the pronoun/subject => **ne** + verb + **pas**
When the verb starts with a vowel or a silent h, **ne** becomes **n'.**

AUDIO 12.1.1

Je mange. *I eat.*
Je + **ne** + mange + **pas.** *I don't eat.*

Je mange beaucoup. *I eat a lot.*
Je **ne** mange **pas** beaucoup. *I don't eat much.*

When **pas** is followed by an indefinite article **un, une, des** or by a partitive article **du, de la, de l', des**, the article becomes **de.** De becomes **d'** before a word starting with a vowel or a silent h.

On a un chat. *We have a cat.*
On **n'**a **pas** de chat. *We don't have a cat.*

However, the definite articles **le, la, l', les** don't change.

Il aime le chocolat. *He likes chocolate.*
Il **n'**aime **pas** le chocolat. *He doesn't like chocolate.*

Negation in speech AUDIO 12.1.2

In everyday speech, **ne** tends to be left out and only **pas** is pronounced. But it's important to keep **ne** and **pas** when writing and in formal speech.

Writing:	Je **ne** vais **pas** au magasin. *I don't go to the store.*
Informal speech:	Je vais **pas** au magasin. *I don't go to the store.*

There are other ways to express **negation.**
A lot of words can replace the word **pas.** Here is the list:

ne + verb + **pas** — Not
ne + verb + **plus** — Not anymore – None left

J'ai de l'argent. *I have money.*

Writing:	Je **n'**ai **plus** d'argent. *I don't have money anymore.*
Informal speech:	J'ai **plus** d'argent. *I don't have money anymore.*

ne + verb + **que** — Only

Tu as 100 dollars. *You have 100 dollars.*

Writing:	Tu **n'**as **que** 100 dollars. *You only have 100 dollars.*
Informal speech:	Tu as **que** 100 dollars. *You only have 100 dollars.*

ne + verb + **jamais** Never

Il lit tous les jours. *He reads every day.*

Writing: Il **ne** lit **jamais.** *He never reads.*
Informal speech: Il lit **jamais.** *He never reads.*

ne + verb + **rien** Nothing

Elle veut tout essayer. *She wants to try everything.*

Writing: Elle **ne** veut **rien** essayer. *She wants to try nothing.*
Informal speech: Elle veut **rien** essayer. *She wants to try nothing.*

ne + verb + **pas encore** Not yet

Je suis là. *I am there.*

Writing: Je **ne** suis **pas encore** là. *I am not there yet.*
Informal speech: Je suis **pas encore** là. *I am not there yet.*

ne + verb + **personne** No one – Nobody – Anyone

Je vois quelqu'un. *I see someone.*

Writing: Je **ne** vois **personne.** *I don't see anyone.*
Informal speech: Je vois **personne.** *I don't see anyone.*

EX. 1.28 *Changez la phrase en phrase négative en utilisant (by using) la négation donnée entre parenthèses.* AUDIO 12.1.3

1. Je suis là. (ne ... pas)

   ___

2. Elle a des bonbons. (ne ... plus)

   ___

3. Nous sommes malades. (ne ... pas)

   ___

4. Il aime le fromage. (ne ... pas)

   ___

5. Il regarde seulement la télévision. (ne ... que)

   ___

6. Il y a quelqu'un dans la maison. (ne ... personne)

   ___

7. Ma sœur cuisine bien. (ne ... pas)

____

8. Ce vélo est le mien. (ne ... pas)

____

9. La réceptionniste est toujours là. (ne ... jamais)

____

10. Je vis au Canada. (ne ... pas)

____

11. Ce livre est noir. (ne ... pas)

____

12. Mon téléphone fonctionne encore. (ne ... plus)

____

13. Le chien veut sortir. (ne ... pas)

____

14. Il est souvent en retard. (ne ... jamais)

____

15. On veut tout voir. (ne ... rien)

____

EX. 1.29 *Conjuguez le verbe et formez une phrase affirmative (P) sur la première ligne, ajoutez la négation donnée entre parenthèses sur la deuxième ligne (N).* **AUDIO 12.1.4**

1. Vous / amener / une tarte (ne ... pas)

   P : ____

   N : ____

2. Il / avoir / 15 ans (ne ... plus)

   P : ____

   N : ____

3. Nous / parler / français (ne ... pas)

   P : ____

   N : ____

4. Vous / chercher / quelque chose (ne ... rien)

   P : ______________________________

   N : ______________________________

5. Je / être / riche (ne ... pas)

   P : ______________________________

   N : ______________________________

6. Il y / avoir / du vin (ne ... plus)

   P : ______________________________

   N : ______________________________

7. Pierre / être / pompier (ne ... pas)

   P : ______________________________

   N : ______________________________

8. Céline / manger / beaucoup / de fruits (ne ... jamais)

   P : ______________________________

   N : ______________________________

9. Je / aimer / le football (ne ... pas)

   P : ______________________________

   N : ______________________________

10. Ils / adopter / un chien (ne ... pas)

    P : ______________________________

    N : ______________________________

Battre and Mettre

The verbs **battre** and **mettre** have nothing in common other than ending in **-ttre.**

Battre To beat AUDIO 13.1

Je **bats**	Nous **battons**
Tu **bats**	Vous **battez**
Il-Elle-On **bat**	Ils-Elles **battent**

Other verbs conjugated the same way contain the verb **battre**:

Abattre To kill
Combattre To fight
Débattre To discuss

Mettre To put AUDIO 13.2

Je **mets**	Nous **mettons**
Tu **mets**	Vous **mettez**
Il-Elle-On **met**	Ils-Elles **mettent**

Other verbs conjugated the same way contain the verb **mettre**:

Admettre To admit
Commettre To commit
Permettre To allow
Promettre To promise

Expressions with mettre: AUDIO 13.3

Mettre de l'argent de côté To put money aside
Mettre ses mains dans les poches To put your hands in your pockets
Mettre son manteau To put on one's coat
Mettre la table To set the table
Mettre la télé – la radio To turn on the TV – the radio
Mettre à jour To update

Promettre la lune To promise the moon

EX. 1.30 *Conjuguez le verbe au présent et formez des phrases.* AUDIO 13.4

1. Il / admettre / son erreur

____

2. Le pont / permettre / d'aller plus vite

____

3. Je / promettre

___

4. Shirley / battre / toujours Eric aux échecs

___

5. Je / ne / mettre / pas / la table

___

Venir and Tenir

The verbs **venir** and **tenir** both follow the same pattern of conjugation. The singular forms turn into **-iens** and **-ient**. In the plural forms, **nous** and **vous**, **-ien** turns into **-enons** and **-enez**, **ils** and **elles** use **-iennent**.

Venir To come AUDIO 14.1

Je **viens**	Nous **venons**
Tu **viens**	Vous **venez**
Il-Elle-On **vient**	Ils-Elles **viennent**

Other verbs conjugated the same way contain the verb **venir**:

Devenir To become
Intervenir To intervene
Parvenir To reach
Prévenir To warn
Revenir To come back

Tenir To hold AUDIO 14.2

Je **tiens**	Nous **tenons**
Tu **tiens**	Vous **tenez**
Il-Elle-On **tient**	Ils-Elles **tiennent**

Other verbs conjugated the same way contain the verb **tenir**:

Appartenir To belong
Obtenir To obtain

The endings -**iens** and -**ient** are pronounced the same way.
The **E** in **venons** and **venez** is pronounced distinctively, with no nasal vowel.
The **E** in **viennent** is pronounced as an **È**.

Expressions with tenir and venir: AUDIO 14.3

Tenir à qqn To be attached to sb
Venir de To come from
Venir de + inf. To have just + inf.
Venir au monde To be born

EX. 1.31 *Traduisez les phrases en français.* AUDIO 14.4

1. The bag belongs to my mother.

   ____

2. He is coming back tomorrow.

   ____

3. My colleague is from Russia.

   ____

4. He is really attached to his dog.

   ____

5. We are coming now.

   ____

Irregular -ir Verbs

Irregular -ir verbs (besides the ones from the 2nd group) can be divided into the 3 following groups:

Group 1:

-ir verbs that take the same ending as **-er** verbs because of the last consonant of the stem, which is usually **R** or **L**.

Don't mix them up with regular verbs ending in **-ir** from the 2nd group.

Ouvrir To open AUDIO 15.1

J'**ouvre**	Nous **ouvrons**
Tu **ouvres**	Vous **ouvrez**
Il-Elle-On **ouvre**	Ils-Elles **ouvrent**

Other verbs conjugated the same way contain the verb **ouvrir**:

Couvrir To cover
Découvrir To discover

Offrir To offer AUDIO 15.2

J'**offre**	Nous **offrons**
Tu **offres**	Vous **offrez**
Il-Elle-On **offre**	Ils-Elles **offrent**

Other verbs conjugated the same way contain the end of the verb **Offrir**:

Souffrir To suffer

Accueillir To welcome AUDIO 15.3

J'**accueille**	Nous **accueillons**
Tu **accueilles**	Vous **accueillez**
Il-Elle-On **accueille**	Ils-Elles **accueillent**

Other verbs conjugated the same way contain the verb **cueillir**:

Cueillir To pick
Recueillir To gather

Group 2:

Dormir To sleep AUDIO 15.4

Je **dors**	Nous **dormons**
Tu **dors**	Vous **dormez**
Il-Elle-On **dort**	Ils-Elles **dorment**

Mentir To lie AUDIO 15.5

Je **mens**	Nous **mentons**
Tu **mens**	Vous **mentez**
Il-Elle-On **ment**	Ils-Elles **mentent**

Common verbs with the same conjugation as **mentir**:

Partir To leave
Repartir To leave again
Sentir To smell – To feel
Sortir To go out

*Remember to **download the audio** and to **watch the videos** – see Preface*

Servir To serve AUDIO 15.6

Je **sers**	Nous **servons**
Tu **sers**	Vous **servez**
Il-Elle-On **sert**	Ils-Elles **servent**

Group 3:

The 3rd and last group of verbs ending in **-ir** with an irregular conjugation.
The stem ends with **-r**, so the endings are **-s, -s, -t, -ons, -ez,** and **-ent.**

Courir To run AUDIO 15.7

Je **cours**	Nous **courons**
Tu **cours**	Vous **courez**
Il-Elle-On **court**	Ils-Elles **courent**

Recourir To resort has the same conjugation as **courir**.

The stem of **mourir** is **meur-** for all forms except **nous** and **vous.**

Mourir To die AUDIO 15.8

Je **meurs**	Nous **mourons**
Tu **meurs**	Vous **mourez**
Il-Elle-On **meurt**	Ils-Elles **meurent**

Expressions with **mourir:**

Mourir de rire To die of laughter
Mourir de faim To be very hungry

EX. 1.32 *Conjuguez les verbes en* ***-ir*** *entre parenthèses au présent. Attention, les 3 types de verbes irréguliers en -ir sont mélangés dans cet exercice.* AUDIO 15.9

1. (Ouvrir) Le magasin ______________________ à 9 heures.
2. (Mentir) Cet élève ______________________ sans cesse.
3. (Partir) Nous ______________________ ce soir.
4. (Mourir) Je ______________________ de faim.
5. (Servir) Les serveurs ______________________ les clients.
6. (Dormir) On ______________________ toujours tôt.

7. (Accueillir) Nous ______________________________ nos invités.
8. (Offrir) Il ______________________________ un cadeau à sa femme.
9. (Découvrir) Le docteur ______________________________ découvre la cause de la maladie.
10. (Courir) Je ______________________________ tous les matins.

Irregular -indre Verbs

Among verbs ending in **-dre**, some end in **-aindre**, **-eindre** and **-oindre**. The conjugation is regular for the singular forms, but the **n** from the stem turns into **gn** in the plural forms.

Craindre To fear AUDIO 15.1.1

Je **crains**	Nous **craignons**
Tu **crains**	Vous **craignez**
Il-Elle-On **craint**	Ils-Elles **craignent**

Common verbs with the same conjugation as **craindre**:

Contraindre To force
Plaindre To pity

Éteindre To turn off AUDIO 15.1.2

J'**éteins**	Nous **éteignons**
Tu **éteins**	Vous **éteignez**
Il-Elle-On **éteint**	Ils-Elles **éteignent**

Common verbs with the same conjugation as **éteindre**:

Atteindre To reach
Feindre To feign
Peindre To paint
Teindre To dye

Joindre To join AUDIO 15.1.3

Je **joins**	Nous **joignons**
Tu **joins**	Vous **joignez**
Il-Elle-On **joint**	Ils-Elles **joignent**

Rejoindre To rejoin has the same conjugation as **joindre**.

EX. 1.33 *Trouvez les erreurs et corrigez-les.* AUDIO 15.1.4

1. Le chat craignent l'eau.

2. Il atteins son but.

3. Nous peignez les murs de l'appartement.

4. Ils rejoins leurs amis ce soir.

5. Je plaint ses voisins !

Verbs With a Stem Including V

In this group of verbs, the singular forms stay the same besides adding **S** and **T** to differentiate **je** - **tu** and **il** - **elle** - **on**.

The stem of the plural forms includes the letter **v** before the endings **-ons -ez -ent**.

Boire To drink AUDIO 15.1.5

Je **bois**	Nous **buvons**
Tu **bois**	Vous **buvez**
Il-Elle-On **boit**	Ils-Elles **boivent**

Savoir To know AUDIO 15.1.6

Je **sais**	Nous **savons**
Tu **sais**	Vous **savez**
Il-Elle-On **sait**	Ils-Elles **savent**

Écrire To write AUDIO 15.1.7

J'**écris**	Nous **écrivons**
Tu **écris**	Vous **écrivez**
Il-Elle-On **écrit**	Ils-Elles **écrivent**

Recevoir To receive AUDIO 15.1.8

Je **reçois**	Nous **recevons**
Tu **reçois**	Vous **recevez**
Il-Elle-On **reçoit**	Ils-Elles **reçoivent**

Common verbs with the same conjugation as **recevoir**:

Apercevoir To see
Décevoir To disappoint

Suivre To follow AUDIO 15.1.9

Je **suis**	Nous **suivons**
Tu **suis**	Vous **suivez**
Il-Elle-On **suit**	Ils-Elles **suivent**

Vivre To live has the same conjugation as **Suivre** but has a different past participle.

EX. 1.34 *Choisissez le bon verbe et conjuguez-le.* AUDIO 15.1.10

boire - savoir - écrire - recevoir - décevoir - suivre - vivre

1. Tu ______________________________ tout.
2. Elle ______________________________ une lettre.
3. Nous ______________________________ un colis.
4. Je ______________________________ beaucoup de café.
5. Ils ______________________________ les informations.

Verbs With a Stem Including S

For verbs ending in **-ire**, the singular forms stay the same besides adding **S** and **T** to **i**. The stem of the plural forms includes the letter **s** before the endings **-ons -ez -ent**.

Conduire To drive AUDIO 15.1.11

Je **conduis**	Nous **conduisons**
Tu **conduis**	Vous **conduisez**
Il-Elle-On **conduit**	Ils-Elles **conduisent**

Common verbs with the same conjugation as **conduire**:

Construire To build
Déduire To deduct
Détruire To destroy
Instruire To instruct
Introduire To introduce
Nuire To harm
Produire To produce
Reconduire To drive someone back
Traduire To translate

Lire To read AUDIO 15.1.12

Je **lis**	Nous **lisons**
Tu **lis**	Vous **lisez**
Il-Elle-On **lit**	Ils-Elles **lisent**

Other verbs conjugated the same way contain the verb **lire**:

Relire To read again
Élire To elect

EX. 1.35 *Conjuguez le verbe donné entre parenthèses :* AUDIO 15.1.13

1. (Traduire) Le traducteur ______________________ le livre.
2. (Détruire) Les insectes ______________________ les plantes.
3. (Relire) Je ______________________ souvent le même livre.
4. (Conduire) Elle ______________________ les enfants à l'école.
5. (Produire) L'usine ______________________ des pneus.
6. (Introduire) Il ______________________ sa petite amie.
7. (Nuire) La cigarette ______________________ à la santé.
8. (Lire) Le papa ______________________ une histoire aux enfants.
9. (Déduire) Je ______________________ que tu as raison.
10. (Élire) Les habitants ______________________ le maire.

Verbs Ending in -aître

With verbs ending in **-aître**, only **-tre** is removed before adding the ending **S** and **T** in the singular forms.
The stem of the plural forms includes the double letter **ss** before the endings **-ons -ez -ent**.
All the forms turn Î into I, except **il** - **elle** -**on**.

Connaître To know AUDIO 15.1.14

Je **connais**	Nous **connaissons**
Tu **connais**	Vous **connaissez**
Il-Elle-On **connaît**	Ils-Elles **connaissent**

Common verbs with the same conjugation as **connaître**:

Apparaître To appear
Disparaître To disappear
Paraître To seem
Reconnaître To recognize

Differences between savoir and connaître: AUDIO 15.1.15

Savoir and **connaître** both translate to To know in English.
Here are the main differences between them:

Savoir To know – To be able to do something – To know how + inf.
Connaître To know – To be familiar with something/someone

Examples with **savoir**:

Je sais cuisiner. *I know how to cook.*
Il sait rouler à vélo. *He knows how to ride a bike.*

⇨ In French, we don't translate "To know how", only To know.

Examples with **connaître**:

Je connais bien mes collègues. *I know my colleagues well.*
Il connaît la recette par cœur. *He knows the recipe by heart.*

EX. 1.36 *Choisissez entre **savoir** et **connaître** et conjuguez le verbe au présent.* AUDIO 15.1.16

1. Il ne ________________ pas cuisiner.
2. Le marchand ________________ bien ses clients.
3. Elle ________________ toujours tout sur tout le monde.
4. Je ________________ ce quartier comme ma poche.
5. Tu ________________ Marc depuis longtemps ?

Verbs With a Stem Including Y

This group of verbs doesn't have the same endings, but they turn **i** into **y** with the forms **nous** and **vous**.

Croire To believe AUDIO 15.1.17

Je **crois**	Nous **croyons**
Tu **crois**	Vous **croyez**
Il-Elle-On **croit**	Ils-Elles **croient**

Common verbs with the same conjugation as **croire**:

Voir To see
Prévoir To predict
Revoir To see again

Fuir To flee AUDIO 15.1.18

Je **fuis**	Nous **fuyons**
Tu **fuis**	Vous **fuyez**
Il-Elle-On **fuit**	Ils-Elles **fuient**

EX. 1.37 *Traduisez le pronom et le verbe.* AUDIO 15.1.19

1. I believe – ______
2. She flees – ______
3. We predict – ______
4. You see again (pl) – ______
5. They see (m) – ______

Verbs With a Stem Including QU

Vaincre has a very specific conjugation with unusual endings for verbs in French.
The singular forms end with **c** and only **s** is added to **je** and **tu**.
In the plural forms, **c** turns into **qu**.

Vaincre To overcome AUDIO 15.1.20

Je **vaincs**	Nous **vainquons**
Tu **vaincs**	Vous **vainquez**
Il-Elle-On **vainc**	Ils-Elles **vainquent**

Convaincre To convince has the same conjugation as **vaincre**.

Devoir - Vouloir - Pouvoir

Devoir, vouloir and **pouvoir** are irregular but you should still study them together.

Devoir To owe – Must – To have to AUDIO 16.1

Je **dois**	Nous **devons**
Tu **dois**	Vous **devez**
Il-Elle-On **doit**	Ils-Elles **doivent**

Vouloir To want AUDIO 16.2

Je **veux**	Nous **voulons**
Tu **veux**	Vous **voulez**
Il-Elle-On **veut**	Ils-Elles **veulent**

Pouvoir To be able to - Can AUDIO 16.3

Je **peux**	Nous **pouvons**
Tu **peux**	Vous **pouvez**
Il-Elle-On **peut**	Ils-Elles **peuvent**

Devoir - Vouloir - Pouvoir + infinitive verb

Devoir, vouloir and **pouvoir** are often followed by an infinitive verb as a complement.

AUDIO 16.4

Je dois terminer mon projet. *I must finish my project.*
Elle doit aller au magasin. *She must go to the store.*

Ils veulent partir en vacances. *They want to go on vacation.*
Je veux acheter un nouveau sac à main. *I want to buy a new handbag.*

Tu peux aller jouer. *You can go play.*
Est-ce que je peux avoir un jus d'orange ? *Can I have an orange juice?*

EX. 1.38 *Conjuguez le verbe entre parenthèses au présent.* AUDIO 16.5

1. (Devoir) Je ______________________ y aller.
2. (Pouvoir) Il ne ______________________ pas manger de fraises.
3. (Vouloir) Le chat ______________________ sortir.
4. (Devoir) Nous ______________________ aller chez le dentiste.
5. (Pouvoir) On ______________________ terminer demain.

*Remember to **download the audio** and to **watch the videos** - see Preface*

6. (Vouloir) Je ______________________ une nouvelle montre.
7. (Devoir) Paul ______________________ travailler plus.
8. (Pouvoir) Est-ce que tu ______________________ t'en occuper ?
9. (Vouloir) Je sais ce que je ______________________ faire.
10. (Vouloir) Vous ______________________ un peu plus de café ?

A Few Other Verbs

Dire To tell – To say AUDIO 17.1

Je **dis**	Nous **disons**
Tu **dis**	Vous **dites**
Il-Elle-On **dit**	Ils-Elles **disent**

Rire To laugh AUDIO 17.2

Je **ris**	Nous **rions**
Tu **ris**	Vous **riez**
Il-Elle-On **rit**	Ils-Elles **rient**

Sourire To smile has the same conjugation as **rire**.

Valoir To be worth AUDIO 17.3

Je **vaux**	Nous **valons**
Tu **vaux**	Vous **valez**
Il-Elle-On **vaut**	Ils-Elles **valent**

Revision

EX. 1.39 *Choisissez le bon verbe entre parenthèses et conjuguez-le au présent.* AUDIO 17.4

1. (Lire / Mettre / Changer)

   Je ______________________ un nouveau livre tous les mois.

2. (Essayer / Mettre / Pendre)

   Marc ______________________ de vendre sa voiture.

3. (Aller / Changer / Quitter)

   Bec ______________________ de travail bientôt.

4. (Avoir / Aller / Être)

Nous ______________________________ en retard.

5. (Tenir / Venir / Avoir)

On ______________________________ de partir.

6. (Suivre / Prendre / Aimer)

Elles ______________________________ le temps de se connaître.

7. (Mettre / Lancer / Brosser)

Charles ______________________________ son manteau.

8. (Devoir / Avoir / Revoir)

Nous ______________________________ finir le projet.

9. (Recevoir / Décevoir / Passer)

Je ______________________________ toujours des cadeaux.

10. (Craindre / Sentir / Adorer)

Les chats ______________________________ l'eau.

11. (Vouloir / Avoir / Être)

Est-ce que tu ______________________________ faim ?

12. (Nettoyer / Fermer / Ouvrir)

J' ______________________________ la fenêtre pour aérer la pièce.

13. (Payer / Valoir / Acheter)

Ce pull ne ______________________________ pas 150 dollars.

14. (Faire / Conduire / Aller)

Nous ______________________________ du vélo en famille.

15. (Écrire / Répéter / Être)

Les élèves ______________________________ la pièce de théâtre.

16. (Aller / Devoir / Marcher)

Ils ______________________________ au marché tous les samedis.

17. (Planifier / Achever / Voyager)

On ______________________________ de planifier notre voyage.

18. (Ranger / Aller / Avoir)

Tu peux jouer si tu ______________________________ ta chambre.

19. (Croire / Penser / Changer)

Nous ________________________________ qu'il ne dit pas la vérité.

20. (Tenir / Venir / Regarder)

Il ________________________________ la corde des deux mains.

21. (Aimer / Apprécier / Pouvoir)

Je n' ________________________________ pas la couleur jaune.

22. (Surprendre / Offrir / Acheter)

Elle ________________________________ son amie pour son anniversaire.

23. (Pousser / Cueillir / Arroser)

Nous ________________________________ des fleurs dans le jardin.

24. (Promettre / Être / Arriver)

Il ________________________________ d'être là.

25. (Être / Savoir / Avoir)

Je ________________________________ que ce n'est pas vrai.

EX. 1.40 *Faites une phrase avec* ***Depuis, Il y a – que*** *et* ***Ça fait – que****. Si la phrase n'est pas possible, ajoutez /.* AUDIO 17.5

Exemple :
Il / habite / à Paris / 3 ans
Depuis : Il habite à Paris **depuis** 3 ans.
Il y a : **Il y a** 3 ans **qu'**il habite à Paris.
Ça fait : **Ça fait** 3 ans **qu'**il habite à Paris.

1. Il / dormir / une heure

   Depuis : ________________________________

   Il y a : ________________________________

   Ça fait : ________________________________

2. Elle / travailler / deux mois

   Depuis : ________________________________

   Il y a : ________________________________

   Ça fait : ________________________________

3. Ils / parler / une heure

Depuis : ____

Il y a : ____

Ça fait : ____

4. J' / attendre / cinq minutes

Depuis : ____

Il y a : ____

Ça fait : ____

5. Le chauffeur / conduire / ce matin

Depuis : ____

Il y a : ____

Ça fait : ____

6. Elle / aimer / la banane / qu'elle est petite

Depuis : ____

Il y a : ____

Ça fait : ____

7. Nous / gagner / plus d'argent / janvier

Depuis : ____

Il y a : ____

Ça fait : ____

8. Vous / connaître / Jean / 10 ans

Depuis : ____

Il y a : ____

Ça fait : ____

9. Ali / être en forme / ne pas / quelques temps

Depuis : ____

Il y a : ____

Ça fait : ____

10. Elle / avoir mal la tête / hier soir

Depuis : ____

Il y a : ____

Ça fait : ____

EX. 1.41 *Changez les phrases du pronom* ***TU*** *au pronom* ***VOUS****, et ajoutez la négation donnée.*
AUDIO 17.6

Exemple:
Tu es à l'heure.
Vous : **Vous êtes** à l'heure.
Ne ... jamais : Vous **n'**êtes **jamais** à l'heure.

1. Tu achèves le morceau de gâteau.
   Vous : ______________________________
   Ne ... pas : ______________________________
2. Tu prends toujours l'avion pour venir en France.
   Vous : ______________________________
   Ne ... jamais : ______________________________
3. Tu as chaud.
   Vous : ______________________________
   Ne ... pas : ______________________________
4. Tu veux encore du thé ?
   Vous : ______________________________
   Ne ... plus : ______________________________
5. Tu appelles le docteur pour prendre rendez-vous.
   Vous : ______________________________
   Ne ... pas : ______________________________

EX. 1.42 *Changez les phrases du pronom* ***ON*** *au pronom* ***NOUS****, et enlevez la négation.*
La phrase reste la même s'il n'y a pas d'indications. La phrase change s'il y a une indication entre parenthèses. AUDIO 17.7

Exemple :
On n'est jamais ensemble pendant le week-end.
Nous : **Nous** ne **sommes** jamais ensemble pendant le week-end.
(Toujours) : Nous sommes **toujours** ensemble pendant le week-end.

1. On ne part pas en vacances demain matin.
   Nous : ______________________________
   ____

2. On ne regarde pas les étoiles filantes.

Nous : ____

____

3. On ne peut pas tout avoir.

Nous : ____

____

4. On ne voit rien de bizarre.

Nous : ____

(Quelque chose) ____

5. On ne va pas manger au restaurant.

Nous : ____

____

Questions

There are many ways to ask a question in French. In this course, we are going to focus on 6 different ways.

3 ways for yes/no questions:

⇨ By raising your voice at the end of the question
⇨ By using est-ce que
⇨ By using inversion

And 3 ways to get an answer about location, time, etc.

⇨ By using an interrogative adverb
⇨ By using an interrogative pronoun
⇨ By using an interrogative adjective

AUDIO **17.1.1**

1. For yes – no questions, the easiest way and the most common one in everyday French is simply to raise your voice at the end of the sentence to turn it into a question. This is what you will encounter the most.

   Tu es prête ?
   → **Oui**, je suis prête.

   Tu es libre ce week-end ?
   → **Non**, je ne suis pas libre ce week-end.

   Le dîner est prêt ?
   → **Oui**, le dîner est prêt.

2. Now that you know how to make a question by simply raising your voice at the end of the question, the next step is to add est-ce que in front of the subject. This is also a yes – no question.

   Tu es prête ? => Est-ce que tu es prête ?
   → **Non**, je ne suis pas prête.

   Est-ce qu'il a réussi son examen ?
   → **Oui**, il a réussi son examen.

   Est-ce que vous avez faim ?
   → **Oui**, on a faim.

3. Using inversion is the most formal way to ask a question. The verb is placed before the pronoun and a hyphen joins the two.

   Elle boit du thé.
   → **Boit-elle du thé ?**

   Vous allez à Londres.
   → **Allez-vous à Londres ?**

   Tu parles français.
   → **Parles-tu français ?**

Note that when the verb ends with a vowel and the pronoun starts with a vowel, we add **-t-** between the verb and the pronoun. **-t-** doesn't have any meaning. We add it only for phonetic reasons.

Elle aime le thé.
→ **Aime-t-elle le thé ?**

Il habite à Londres.
→ **Habite-t-il à Londres ?**

Elle parle français.
→ **Parle-t-elle français ?**

4. Asking a question by using an interrogative adverb requires mastering points 2. and 3.

AUDIO 17.1.2

Here is the list of the interrogative adverbs:

Quand	When
Comment	How
Pourquoi	Why
Où	Where
Combien (de)	How many – How much

To use an interrogative adverb, you have two possibilities. The first and easiest is to use **est-ce que** after the interrogative adverb; the second is to use **inversion**:

Quand When

When are you going on vacation?

Quand est-ce que tu vas en vacances ?
Quand vas-tu en vacances ?

Comment How

How are we going to school?

Comment allons-nous à l'école ?
Comment est-ce que nous allons à l'école ?

Pourquoi Why

Why did you buy those shoes?

Pourquoi est-ce que tu as acheté ces chaussures ?
Pourquoi as-tu acheté ces chaussures ?

Où Where

Where are you going?

Où est-ce que tu vas ?
Où vas-tu ?

Combien How many - How much

How many candies do you want?

Combien est-ce que vous voulez de bonbons ?
Combien voulez-vous de bonbons ?

5. Asking a question by using an interrogative pronoun also requires mastering points 2. and 3.

   Here is the list of the interrogative pronouns:

Qui	Who – Whom
Que – qu'	What
Qu'est-ce que – qu'	What
De – à – avec - ... quoi	What

   Like interrogative adverbs, you can use the interrogative pronouns before **est-ce que** or use **inversion**.

   Only **qui** is the subject or object of the question. AUDIO 17.1.3

Qui Who – Whom

Who is there?

Qui est là ?

Que What

What do you want?

Que veux-tu ?

Qu'est-ce que What

What do you want?

Qu'est-ce que tu veux ?

De quoi What

What are you talking about?

De quoi parles-tu ?
De quoi est-ce que tu parles ?

À quoi What

What are you thinking about?

À quoi penses-tu ?
À quoi est-ce que tu penses ?

Avec quoi What

What are you cooking with?

Avec quoi cuisines-tu ?
Avec quoi est-ce que tu cuisines ?

EX. 1.43 *Changez la question en incluant **Est-ce que** ou une **inversion**.* AUDIO 17.1.4

Exemple:
Tu es là ?
Est-ce que : **Est-ce que** tu es là ?
Inversion : **Es-tu** là ?

1. Les prix augmentent chaque année ?

   Est-ce que : ______________________________

2. Tu notes les informations importantes ?

   Inversion : ______________________________

3. Les policiers interrogent le suspect ?

   Est-ce que : ______________________________

4. Tu es arrivé ?

   Inversion : ______________________________

5. Mes amis viennent avec nous.

   Est-ce que : ______________________________

6. Tu parles à qui ?

   Inversion : ______________________________

7. Que veux-tu ?

   Est-ce que : ______________________________

8. Tu aimes la citrouille ?

   Inversion : ______________________________

9. Avez-vous ce pantalon en noir ?

   Est-ce que : ______________________________

10. Vous partez en vacances bientôt ?

    Est-ce que : ______________________________

11. Est-ce que tu peux faire moins de bruit ?

    Inversion : ______________________________

12. As-tu vu mon sac à dos ?

    Est-ce que : ______________________________

13. Est-ce que tu connais Tex ?

    Inversion : ______________________________

14. Le chat est dans la boîte.

    Est-ce que : ____________________

15. Est-ce que tu as faim ?

    Inversion : ____________________

Impersonal Verbs

Impersonal verbs are verbs that refer to no one or nothing in particular. They are all regular verbs as well, besides **falloir** and **pleuvoir**.

As impersonal verbs, they are all conjugated with **il**, sometimes **ça – c'**.

AUDIO **18.1**

Impersonal verbs used to talk about general subjects:

Avoir	**Il y a** There is – There are
Être + time	**Il est deux heures** It's two o'clock
Être	**Il est temps** It's time
Être	**C'est** It is – This is
Faire	**Il fait jour** It's daylight
Falloir	**Il faut** We have to
Manquer	**Il manque** There is – There are ... missing
Paraître	**Il paraît que** It appears that
Rester	**Il reste** There is ... left
Sembler	**Il semble** It seems that
Valoir	**Il vaut mieux** It's better that

Impersonal verbs used to talk about the weather

Faire	**Il fait chaud** It's hot
Geler	**Il gèle** It's freezing
Neiger	**Il neige** It's snowing
Pleuvoir	**Il pleut** It's raining

AUDIO **18.2**

Il **pleut** depuis ce matin. *It has been raining since this morning.*
Il **reste** trois jus d'oranges. *There are three orange juices left.*
C'**est** trop tard. *It's too late.*
Il **est** l'heure de partir. *It's time to leave.*
Il y **a** un cerf dans le jardin. *There is a deer in the yard.*

EX. 1.44 *Choisissez un verbe de la liste ci-dessus et conjuguez-les au présent. Ils sont tous impersonnels, à part Remonter.* AUDIO 18.3

Aujourd'hui, c' ________________ mardi. Il ________________ froid mais il y ________________ un peu de soleil. Il ________________ depuis plusieurs semaines ici. On ________________ hâte que les températures ________________ (remonter). Il ________________ quelques semaines avant le printemps. Au printemps, il ________________ toujours plus chaud et il y ________________ moins de pluie et de neige.

COD & DOP

COD means **Complément d'Objet Direct** (direct object), **DOP** means **Direct Object Pronoun.**

Subject + verb + direct object

The **direct object** is placed directly after the verb and is found by asking the direct question **Quoi** What – **Qui** Who.
AUDIO 18.1.1

Quoi ?

Je mange une orange. *I am eating an orange.*
Je mange quoi ? *What am I eating?*
Une orange – An orange
Une orange is the direct object

Elle regarde un film. *She is watching a movie.*
Elle regarde quoi ? *What is she watching?*
Un film – A movie
Un film is the direct object

Qui ?

Il appelle Paul. *He is calling Paul.*
Il appelle qui ? *Who is he calling?*
Paul
Paul is the direct object

Nous attendons Jack. *We are waiting for Jack.*
Nous attendons qui ? *Who are we waiting for?*
Jack
Jack is the direct object

A direct object can be replaced by a **Direct Object Pronoun (DOP)**. The **DOP** is always placed before the verb in French.

Subject + direct object pronoun + verb

Why knowing the **Direct Object Pronouns** is important:

If we look at the 2 sentences that we used before in English, but this time we change the Direct Object with a pronoun:

I eat an apple	I eat **it**
He calls his sister	He calls **her**

The Direct Object Pronoun replaces the Direct Object when the object is known in the conversation and avoids repetition, especially when answering a question including a Direct Object.

Here is the list of **direct object pronouns.** Study them by heart: AUDIO 18.1.2

Singular		Plural	
Me - m'	me	**Nous**	us
Te - t'	you	**Vous**	you
Le - l'	him - it	**Les**	them
La - l'	her - it		

AUDIO 18.1.3

Je mange une orange. *I am eating an orange.*
Je la mange. *I am eating it.*

Elle regarde un film. *She is watching a movie.*
Elle le regarde. *She is watching it.*

Il appelle Paul. *He is calling Paul.*
Il l'appelle. *He is calling him.*

Nous attendons Jack. *We are waiting for Jack.**
Nous l'attendons. *We are waiting for him.*

Il regarde la télévision. *He is watching television.*
Il la regarde. *He is watching it.*

Elle apprend la nouvelle. *She is learning the news.*
Elle l'apprend. *She is learning it.*

*As you see, some verbs such as **attendre**, take a direct object in French but a preposition in English such as for, at, to. Remember these verbs as **REDCAP.** AUDIO 18.1.4

Regarder qqch – qqn	To look at sth – sb
Écouter qqch – qqn	To listen to sth – sb
Demander qqch – qqn	To ask for sth – sb

Chercher qqch - qqn	To search for sth – sb
Attendre qqch - qqn	To wait for sth – sb
Payer qqch	To pay for sth

Direct object pronouns and negation

In the case of a negative sentence, the direct object pronoun is placed immediately before the verb.

Subject + ne + direct object pronoun + verb + pas

AUDIO **18.1.5**

Est-ce que tu aimes les champignons ? Non, je ne les aime pas.
Do you like mushrooms? No, I don't like them.

Est-ce que tu attends ton avocat ? Non, je ne l'attends pas.
Are you waiting for your lawyer? No, I am not waiting for him.

EX. 1.45 *Changez le COD en pronom :* ***me - te - le - la - nous - vous - les.*** AUDIO **18.1.6**

1. Mes sœurs : ____________________
2. Marie : ____________________
3. Le chat : ____________________
4. Moi : ____________________
5. Le cahier : ____________________
6. La brosse : ____________________
7. Les affaires : ____________________
8. La tasse : ____________________
9. Les chocolats : ____________________
10. Julian et Pauline : ____________________

EX. 1.46 *Faites une phrase en conjuguant le verbe au présent, soulignez le COD. Changez le COD en pronom (DOP) sur la deuxième ligne.* AUDIO **18.1.7**

Exemple:
Il / regarder / un film
Il regarde un film.
Il le regarde.

1. Marie / oublier / toujours sa veste

COD : ____

DOP : ____

2. Le chat / manger / ses croquettes

COD : ____

DOP : ____

3. Kurt / offrir / un collier à Jeanne

COD : ____

DOP : ____

4. J' / écrire / un livre

COD : ____

DOP : ____

5. Nous / préparer / nos valises

COD : ____

DOP : ____

6. Nous / attendre / nos collègues

COD : ____

DOP : ____

7. Elles / garder / le chien de la voisine

COD : ____

DOP : ____

8. Le serveur / choisir / le vin

COD : ____

DOP : ____

9. Elle / porter / une robe bleue

COD : ____

DOP : ____

10. Nous / préparer / le dîner

COD : ____

DOP : ____

11. Elle / montrer / sa chambre

COD : ______________________________

DOP : ______________________________

12. Le facteur / apporter / le courrier

COD : ______________________________

DOP : ______________________________

13. Je / faire / un gâteau aux pommes

COD : ______________________________

DOP : ______________________________

14. J' / adorer / Douglas

COD : ______________________________

DOP : ______________________________

15. La banquière / accepter / le chèque

COD : ______________________________

DOP : ______________________________

COI & IOP

COI means **Complément d'Objet Indirect** (indirect object), **IOP** means **Indirect Object Pronoun.**

Subject + verb + indirect object

The **indirect object** can be placed after the verb or after the direct object and is found by asking the indirect question **À qui** To who, for who. Most of the time, the indirect object starts with **à**.

AUDIO **18.2.1** 🔊

À qui

Il donne un livre à son élève. => Il donne un livre à qui ?
He gives a book to his student.
À qui = à son élève
Je rends visite à mes parents. => Je rends visite à qui ?
I visit my parents.
À qui = à mes parents

*Remember to **download the audio** and to **watch the videos** – see Preface*

Finding **à** in a sentence is easy, but this preposition sometimes takes other forms:

à la	+	feminine noun starting with a consonant or an H aspiré
à l'	+	feminine noun starting with a vowel or an H muet
au	+	masculine noun starting with a consonant or an H aspiré
à l'	+	masculine noun starting with a vowel or an H muet
aux	+	masculine or feminine noun but plural

An indirect object can be replaced by an **Indirect Object Pronoun (IOP).** The **IOP** is always placed before the verb.

Subject + indirect object pronoun + verb

Let's look at the sentence that we used before, but this time we change the Indirect Object with a pronoun:

Il donne un livre à son élève => Il donne quoi à qui ?
Il **lui** donne un livre.

The Indirect Object Pronouns replace the Indirect Object when the object is known in the conversation and avoids repetition, especially when answering a question including a Direct Object.

Here is the list of **indirect object pronouns.** Study them by heart: AUDIO 18.2.2

Singular		Plural	
Me - m'	me	**Nous**	us
Te - t'	you	**Vous**	you
Lui	him – her – it	**Leur**	them

Elle **me** téléphone — She is calling **me**
Elle **te** téléphone — She is calling **you**
Elle **lui** téléphone — She is calling **him - her**
Elle **nous** téléphone — She is calling **us**
Elle **vous** téléphone — She is calling **you**
Elle **leur** téléphone — She is calling **them**

Indirect object pronouns and negation

In the case of a negative sentence, the indirect object pronoun is placed immediately before the verb, just like the direct object pronouns.

Subject + ne + indirect object pronoun + verb + pas

AUDIO 18.2.3

Est-ce que tu offres souvent des fleurs **à ta femme** ? Non, je ne **lui** offre jamais de fleurs.
Do you often give flowers to your wife? No, I never give her flowers.

A few verbs that take à : AUDIO 18.2.4

Acheter à	To buy for
Emprunter à	To borrow from
Prêter à	To lend to
Offrir à	To give to
Rendre à	To give back to
Donner à	To give to
Vendre à	To sell to
Parler à	To talk to
Demander à	To ask for
Dire à	To say - To tell
Téléphoner à	To call
Écrire à	To write to

Like the RECAP verbs, some verbs take an indirect object in French but no preposition in English. AUDIO 18.2.5

Assister à qqch	To assist sth
Conseiller à qqn	To advise sb
Dire à qqn	To say - To tell
Demander à qqn	To ask sb
Obéir à qqn - qqch	To obey sth - sb
Rendre visite à qqn	To visit sb
Répondre à qqn	To answer sth - sb
Ressembler à qqn - qqch	To ressemble sth - sb
Téléphoner à qqn	To call sb

EX. 1.47 *Trouvez le COI ou le IOP dans les phrases suivantes.* AUDIO 18.2.6

1. Je conseille à ma sœur une nouvelle télévision. ____________________
2. Nous offrons un cadeau à mes parents. ____________________
3. Ils nous appellent. ____________________
4. Elle me donne un cadeau. ____________________
5. Vous me souhaitez un joyeux anniversaire. ____________________
6. Tu téléphones à ton cousin. ____________________
7. Je le cherche depuis midi. ____________________
8. Tu ressembles tellement à ta mère. ____________________
9. Je t'achète un café. ____________________
10. Cela plaît beaucoup à mon mari. ____________________

DOP & IOP together

Direct and Indirect object pronouns have a lot of similarities. Let's compare them: AUDIO 18.3.1

DOP		IOP	
Me - m'	me	Me – m'	me
Te - t'	you	Te – t'	you
Le - l'	**him – it**	**Lui**	**him – it**
La - l'	**her – it**	**Lui**	**her – it**
Nous	us	Nous	us
Vous	you	Vous	you
Les	them	**Leur**	them

Only 3 of them are different. **Me, te, nous** and **vous** stay the same in both direct and indirect object pronouns.

In what order to use them? AUDIO 18.3.2

1st		2nd		3rd	
Me – m'	me	**Le – l'**	him – it	**Lui**	him – her – it
Te – t'	you	**La – l'**	her – it	**Leur**	them
Nous	us	**Les**	them		
Vous	you				

Since many of them are the same, knowing the order in which to use them only requires 3 steps.
A good way to remember it is the **selfish rule.**

Me First
Object second
Other people third

AUDIO 18.3.3

Elle explique .... la leçon. *She explains the lesson.*

ME	Elle **m'**explique la leçon.	Elle **me l'**explique.
TE	Elle **t'**explique la leçon.	Elle **te l'**explique.
NOUS	Elle **nous** explique la leçon.	Elle **nous l'**explique.
VOUS	Elle **vous** explique la leçon.	Elle **vous l'**explique.
LUI	Elle **lui** explique la leçon.	Elle **la lui** explique.
LEUR	Elle **leur** explique la leçon.	Elle **la leur** explique.

EX. 1.48 *Trouvez le COI dans la phrase et transformez-le en IOP. Faites la même chose avec le COD et DOP sur la troisième ligne. S'il n'y a pas de COI ou COD, ajoutez /.* **AUDIO 18.3.4**

Exemple:
J'achète un cadeau à mon ami.
IOP : Je **lui** achète un cadeau.
DOP : Je **le lui** achète.

1. Le professeur accompagne les élèves à la bibliothèque.

   IOP : ______________________________

   DOP : ______________________________

2. Il emprunte un stylo à son camarade de classe.

   IOP : ______________________________

   DOP : ______________________________

3. Nous écrivons une lettre à notre famille.

   IOP : ______________________________

   DOP : ______________________________

4. Je raconte une histoire aux enfants.

   IOP : ______________________________

   DOP : ______________________________

5. Elle envoie la lettre au juge.

   IOP : ______________________________

   DOP : ______________________________

6. Ils enseignent la leçon aux étudiants.

   IOP : ______________________________

   DOP : ______________________________

7. J'envoie un bouquet de fleurs à ma grand-mère.

   IOP : ______________________________

   DOP : ______________________________

8. Il prend le jouet des mains du garçon.

   IOP : ______________________________

   DOP : ______________________________

9. Elle prend le temps d'expliquer le problème au policier.

   IOP : ______________________________

   DOP : ______________________________

10. Léa montre un schéma aux élèves.

   IOP : ______________________________

   DOP : ______________________________

Reflexive Verbs

What is a reflexive verb?

A reflexive verb in French is a verb indicating that the action is being performed on the subject. There are similar verbs in English such as *To burn oneself.*

In French, a reflexive verb is called **un verbe pronominal** because it includes a pronoun (pronom). The infinitive of a reflexive verb is always **SE + verb**, or **S' + verb** if the verb starts with a vowel or a silent h. **SE** is the pronoun.

Differences between a regular and a reflexive verb: AUDIO 19.1

Regular verb: **Laver** – To wash
Il **lave** la fenêtre. *He washes the window.*

Reflexive verb: **Se laver** – To wash oneself
Il **se lave** tous les soirs. *He washes himself every night.*

Many reflexive verbs and regular verbs have the same meaning, just that the reflexive verb refers to the person or the object. Some of them have very different meanings and can be incredibly confusing. We will see them in the next point.

How to conjugate a reflexive verb?

When a reflexive verb is conjugated, it's a bit of a mix of a simple verb with a direct object pronoun. If you remember, the direct object pronoun is always placed before the verb. This is the same here.

The verb part is conjugated the same way as the regular verb, with the pronoun before the verb.

The pronouns are: AUDIO 19.2

Subject pronouns	Reflexive pronouns
Je	**Me - m'**
Tu	**Te - t'**
Il-Elle-On	**Se - s'**
Nous	**Nous**
Vous	**Vous**
Ils-Elles	**Se - s'**

Remember that in the case of **me**, **te** and **se**, if the verb starts with a vowel or a silent h, we use **m'**, **t'**, **s'**.

And here is the complete conjugation: AUDIO 19.3

Regular verb:

Laver To wash

Je **lave**	Nous **lavons**
Tu **laves**	Vous **lavez**
Il-Elle-On **lave**	Ils-Elles **lavent**

Reflexive verb:

Se laver To wash oneself

Je **me lave**	Nous **nous lavons**
Tu **te laves**	Vous **vous lavez**
Il-Elle-On **se lave**	Ils-Elles **se lavent**

Regular reflexive verbs: AUDIO 19.4

S'adapter To adapt
S'adresser (à) To address – To speak to
S'amuser To have fun
S'apprêter (à) To get ready (to)
S'approcher (de) To approach
S'arrêter (de) To stop oneself
S'énerver To get mad
S'entendre (avec) To get along (with)
S'épiler To pluck – To wax
S'excuser To apologize
S'habiller To get dressed
S'habituer (à) To get used to

S'imaginer To imagine
S'intéresser (à) To be interested in
S'attendre To expect
S'occuper (de) To take care of
Se baigner To go swimming
Se brosser To brush (one's hair – one's teeth)
Se cacher To hide
Se casser To break (one's leg – one's arm)
Se coiffer To do one's hair
Se comporter To behave
Se coucher To go to bed – To lay down
Se couper To cut oneself

Se débrouiller To manage
Se demander To wonder
Se dépêcher (de) To hurry (to)
Se déshabiller To get undressed
Se détendre To relax
Se disputer To argue
Se doucher To take a shower
Se fâcher To get angry
Se fatiguer To get tired
Se laver To wash oneself
Se limer (les ongles) To file one's nails
Se maquiller To put on makeup
Se marier To get married
Se moquer (de) To make fun of
Se moucher To blow one's nose
Se passer To happen
Se peigner To comb one's hair
Se perdre To get lost
Se raser To shave
Se regarder To look at oneself
Se relaxer To relax
Se rendre compte (de) To realize
Se reposer To rest
Se réveiller To wake up
Se soûler To get drunk
Se terminer To come to an end
Se tromper To make a mistake

EX. 1.49 *Conjuguez le verbe entre parenthèses au présent. N'oubliez pas de changer le pronom réflexif.* AUDIO 19.5

1. (Se détendre) Elle ______________________ seulement en vacances.
2. (Se tromper) Il ______________________ de sortie.
3. (S'excuser) Je ______________________.
4. (S'habiller) Je ______________________ et je suis prête.
5. (Se laver) On ______________________ toujours le soir.
6. (S'adapter) Le chat ______________________ bien avec le chiot.
7. (S'imaginer) Paul ______________________ plus intelligent qu'il ne l'est.
8. (Se couper) Elle ______________________ les cheveux à la maison.
9. (Se demander) Je ______________________ s'il a réussi.
10. (Se marier) Ils ______________________ l'année prochaine.

What about irregular verbs and verbs with spelling changes?

Reflexive verbs can also be irregular. Only the verb itself changes, just like regular verbs.

If we look at **Appeler** To call **vs S'appeler** To call oneself: AUDIO 19.6

Irregular verb :

Appeler To call

J'**appelle**	Nous **appelons**
Tu **appelles**	Vous **appelez**
Il-Elle-On **appelle**	Ils-Elles **appellent**

Reflexive verb :

S'appeler To call oneself

Je **m'appelle**	Nous **nous appelons**
Tu **t'appelles**	Vous **vous appelez**
Il-Elle-On **s'appelle**	Ils-Elles **s'appellent**

Irregular reflexive verbs: AUDIO 19.7

S'appeler To be called - To be named
S'appuyer To lean
S'asseoir To sit down
S'endormir To fall asleep
S'ennuyer To be bored
S'inquiéter To worry
S'inscrire To enroll
S'apercevoir (de) To notice
S'en aller To leave
Se changer To get changed
Se conduire To behave
Se faire To make something for oneself
Se fiancer To get engaged
Se lever To get up - To rise
Se mettre à + inf To begin to + inf
Se noyer To drown
Se plaindre To complain
Se promener To (take a) walk
Se rappeler To remember
Se sécher To dry off
Se sentir To feel
Se servir (de) To use
Se souvenir To remember

S'appeler is conjugated like **appeler**
S'appuyer is conjugated like **appuyer**
See notes
S'endormir is conjugated like **endormir**
S'ennuyer is conjugated like **ennuyer**
S'inquiéter is conjugated like **inquiéter**
S'inscrire is conjugated like **inscrire**
S'apercevoir is conjugated like **recevoir**
S'en aller is conjugated like **aller**
Se changer is conjugated like **changer**
Se conduire is conjugated like **conduire**
Se faire is conjugated like **faire**
Se fiancer is conjugated like **commencer**
Se lever is conjugated like **lever**
Se mettre is conjugated like **mettre**
Se noyer is conjugated like **noyer**
Se plaindre is conjugated like **plaindre**
Se promener is conjugated like **promener**
Se rappeler is conjugated like **appeler**
Se sécher is conjugated like **sécher**
Se sentir is conjugated like **sentir**
Se servir is conjugated like **servir**
Se souvenir is conjugated like **venir**

The verb **s'asseoir** has two possible conjugations: AUDIO 19.8

1. **S'asseoir** To sit down

Je m'ass**ois**	Nous nous ass**oyons**
Tu t'ass**ois**	Vous vous ass**oyez**
Il-Elle-On s'ass**oit**	Ils-Elles s'ass**oient**

2. **S'asseoir** To sit down

Je m'ass**ieds**	Nous nous ass**eyons**
Tu t'ass**ieds**	Vous vous ass**eyez**
Il-Elle-On s'ass**ied**	Ils-Elles s'ass**eyent**

*Remember to **download the audio** and to **watch the videos** - see Preface*

EX. 1.50 *Conjuguez le verbe entre parenthèses au présent. N'oubliez pas de changer le pronom réflexif.* AUDIO 19.9

1. (Se promener) On ______________________________ autour du lac.
2. (Se sentir) Il ______________________________ mieux que jamais.
3. (Se souvenir) Est-ce que tu ______________________________ de lui ?
4. (Se changer) Nous ______________________________ avant de partir.
5. (S'inquiéter) Tu ______________________________ pour rien.
6. (S'asseoir) Il ______________________________ sur la chaise.
7. (S'appeler) Je ______________________________ Léo.
8. (Se lever) On ______________________________ tôt.
9. (Se rappeler) On ______________________________ bien de cette histoire.
10. (S'en aller) On ______________________________ dans 5 minutes.

Focus on Se mettre (à): AUDIO 19.10

Se mettre en colère To get angry
Se mettre sur son 31 To dress up to the nines
Se mettre d'accord To come to an agreement
Se mettre à table To sit down at the table
Se mettre au vert To move to the countryside
Se mettre à la lecture To start reading
Se mettre à rire To start laughing

Focus on Se faire: AUDIO 19.11

Se faire un sandwich To make yourself a sandwich
Se faire faire quelque chose To have someone make you something
Se faire couper les cheveux To have someone cut your hair
Se faire servir To have someone to serve you
Se faire mal To hurt yourself

EX. 1.51 *Choisissez entre* ***Se mettre*** *et* ***Se faire****. Conjuguez le verbe au présent.* AUDIO 19.12

1. Elle ______________________________ sur son 31.
2. Je ______________________________ un café.
3. On ______________________________ d'accord sur la date de la réunion.
4. Nous ______________________________ couper les cheveux demain.
5. Ils ______________________________ en colère facilement.

Reflexive verbs and body parts:

A big difference between French and English is that in French, we don't use possessive adjectives (my, your, etc.) to talk about body parts. Instead, definite articles **le, la, les** (the) are used.

The reason behind this rule is pretty simple, reflexive verbs already refer to the subject. Adding possessive adjectives would result in a double possessive.

AUDIO 19.13

Examples:

Je **me** brosse **les** dents. *I am brushing **my** teeth.*

Se brosser les cheveux. To brush one's hair.
Se brosser les dents. To brush one's teeth.
Se peigner la barbe. To comb one's beard.
Se raser la moustache. To shave one's mustache.
Se casser la jambe. To break one's leg.
Se laver les mains. To wash one's hands.
S'essuyer les pieds. To wipe one's feet.
Se limer les ongles. To file one's nails.
Se couper les ongles. To cut one's nails.
S'épiler les sourcils. To pluck one's eyebrows.
Se sécher les cheveux. To dry one's hair.

EX. 1.52 *Choisissez le bon verbe pour parler des parties du corps. Plusieurs possibilités possibles.* AUDIO 19.14

1. Je ______________________ les ongles.
2. Tu ______________________ les mains.
3. Il ______________________ les cheveux.
4. Elle ______________________ les sourcils.
5. On ______________________ la barbe.
6. Nous ______________________ les dents.
7. Vous ______________________ la jambe.
8. Ils ______________________ la moustache.
9. Elles ______________________ les pieds.

Uses of the infinitive of reflexive verbs:

Just like in English, French uses verbs in the infinitive in sentences as well. In the case of reflexive verbs, the pronoun **se – s'** will agree with the subject while the verb itself remains infinitive.

AUDIO 19.15

Tu dois **te** changer avant de partir. *You have to get changed before leaving.*
Je vais **me** raser. *I am going to shave.*
Vous allez bien **vous** amuser. *You are going to have fun.*

Reflexive verbs and negation:

When adding negation to a sentence with a reflexive verb, think of the reflexive verb as one verb that cannot be split. Refer to the list we saw in chapter 1. Negation goes:

- **Around** the verb when the verb is conjugated
- **Before** the verb when the verb is infinitive

A few examples: AUDIO 19.16

ne + reflexive verb + **pas** Not

Est-ce que tu te rappelles de moi ? *Do you remember me?*
Non, je **ne** me rappelle **pas** de toi. *No, I don't remember you.*

ne + reflexive verb + **plus** Not anymore - None left

Cela **ne** me fait **plus** mal. *It doesn't hurt anymore.*

EX. 1.53 *Répondez aux questions négativement en incluant les informations entre parenthèses.*

AUDIO 19.17

Exemple:
Est-ce que tu te rappelles ?
Non, je **ne** me rappelle **pas.**

1. Est-ce que cela se fait facilement ?

   Non, ______________________________

2. Tu t'amuses bien ?

   Non, ______________________________

3. Est-ce qu'elle s'épile les sourcils ?

   Non, ______________________________

4. Il se conduit toujours de cette façon ?

   Non, ______________________________

5. Est-ce que tu te changes maintenant ?

   Non, ______________________________

6. Où est-ce qu'il se cache ? (dans le placard)

   ____

7. Tu te moques de moi ? (de toi)

   Non, ______________________________

8. Vous vous douchez maintenant ?

   Non, ______________________________

9. Est-ce que tu t'appelles Jeanne ?

   Non, ______________________________

10. Est-ce que tu t'attends à cette surprise ?

    Non, ______________________________

Reflexive verbs in a question:

Just like for negation, the sentence moves around the reflexive verb. Let's see an example for each type of question:

AUDIO 19.18

⇨ By **raising your voice** at the end of the question
Tu **te sens** mieux ? *Are you feeling better?*

⇨ By using **est-ce que**
Est-ce que tu **te brosses** les dents tous les matins ? *Do you brush your teeth every morning?*

⇨ By using an **inversion**
Te promènes-tu souvent au parc ? *Do you often go for a walk in the park?*

The other way is to get an answer about location, time, etc.

⇨ By using a **question word**
Quand **te douches-tu** ? *When are you showering?*
Quand est-ce que tu **te douches** ? *When are you showering?*

EX. 1.54 *Formez une question négative avec les morceaux de phrases et la négation donnés. N'oubliez pas de conjuguer le verbe au présent.* AUDIO 19.19

Exemple:
Est-ce que tu ne vas pas bien ?
Non, je **ne** vais **pas** bien.

1. Tu / se sentir / bien ?

   Ne ... pas : ______________________________

2. Est-ce qu'il / se laver / les mains / avant le repas ?

   Ne ... pas : ______________________________

3. Vous / s'endormir / toujours vite ?

   Ne ... jamais : ______________________________

4. De quoi / est-ce qu'il / se plaindre ?

   Ne ... pas : ______________________________

5. Ils / se marier / cette année ?

   Ne ... pas : ______________________________

When reflexive verbs and regular verbs don't match: AUDIO 19.20

Most of the time, regular verbs and reflexive verbs have the same meaning (Laver vs Se laver). But sometimes, the meaning is very different. Here is the list of the most common ones:

Agir - S'agir

Agir To act

Il **agit** sans réfléchir.
He acts without thinking.

S'agir To be about

De quoi **s'agit**-il ?
What is this about?

Appeler - S'appeler

Appeler To call

Le banquier **appelle** son client.
The banker is calling their client.

S'appeler To be called - To be named

Je **m'appelle** Laura.
My name is Laura.

Appuyer sur - S'appuyer sur

Appuyer sur To push

L'enfant **appuie** sur le bouton.
The child pushes the button.

S'appuyer sur To rely on - To lean on

Cette étude **s'appuie** sur des faits.
This study relies on facts.

Attendre - S'attendre

Attendre To wait

On **attend** le train.
We are waiting for the train.

S'attendre To expect

Il ne **s'attend** pas à ça !
He doesn't expect that!

Conduire - Se conduire

Conduire To drive

Elle apprend à **conduire.**
She is learning to drive.

Se conduire To behave

Il **se conduit** toujours bien.
He always behaves well.

Demander - Se demander

Demander To ask

Il **demande** un renseignement.
He is asking for information.

Se demander To wonder

Je **me demande** où il est.
I wonder where he is.

Ennuyer - S'ennuyer

Ennuyer To bother

Elle **ennuie** toujours son frère.
She always bothers her brother.

S'ennuyer To be bored

On **s'ennuie.**
We are bored.

Entendre - S'entendre

Entendre To hear

Est-ce que tu **entends** ce bruit ?
Do you hear that noise?

S'entendre To get along

Le chien et le chat **s'entendent** bien.
The dog and the cat get along.

Installer - S'installer

Installer To install

Ils **installent** la cuisine aujourd'hui.
They're installing the kitchen today.

S'installer To move in - To settle in

Nous **nous installons** doucement.
We are slowly moving in.

Mettre - Se mettre (à)

Mettre To put – To put on

Il **met** sa veste.
He is putting on his jacket.

Se mettre (à) To take something up

Il **se met** à la peinture.
He is taking up painting.

Occuper - S'occuper (de)

Occuper To occupy – To keep busy

Ce jeu **occupe** les enfants.
This game keeps the kids busy.

S'occuper de To take care of

Luc **s'occupe** toujours de sa sœur.
Luc always takes care of his sister.

Passer - Se passer - Se passer (de)

Passer du temps To spend time

Vous **passez** trop de temps ensemble.
You spend too much time together.

Se passer To happen

Qu'est-ce qu'il **se passe ?**
What is happening?

Se passer de To go without

J'essaye de **me passer de** sucre.
I try to go without sugar.

Plaindre - Se plaindre

Plaindre To pity

Je le **plains.**
I pity him.

Se plaindre To complain

Elle **se plaint** du bruit.
She complains about the noise.

Plaire - Se plaire

Plaire To please

Fais ce qu'il te **plaît.**
Do what pleases you.

Se plaire To enjoy

Nous **nous plaisons** bien ici.
We enjoy it here.

Rappeler - Se rappeler

Rappeler To call back

N'oublie pas de **rappeler** Charlotte.
Don't forget to call Charlotte back.

Se rappeler To remember

Je ne **me rappelle** pas de ça.
I don't remember that.

Rendre - Se rendre - Se rendre compte de

Rendre To give back

Il **rend** son test au professeur.
He gives his test back to the teacher.

Se rendre To go

Nous **nous rendons** chez ma tante.
We are going to my aunt's place.

Se rendre compte de To realize

Je **me rends compte de** mon erreur.
I realize my mistake.

Reposer - Se reposer

Reposer To put back - down

Il **repose** le livre sur la table.
He puts the book back on the table.

Se reposer To rest

Il **se repose** un petit peu.
He is resting a little bit.

Saisir - Se saisir de

Saisir To seize

L'huissier **saisit** la maison.
The bailiff is seizing the house.

Se saisir de To take on

L'avocat **se saisit** de cette affaire.
The lawyer takes on this case.

Sentir - Se sentir

Sentir To feel - To smell

Est-ce que ça **sent** le gaz ?
Does it smell like natural gas?

Se sentir To feel

Il ne **se sent** pas bien.
He is not feeling well.

Servir - Se servir de

Servir To serve

Ils **servent** du champagne au petit déjeuner.
They serve champagne for breakfast.

Se servir de To use

Tu ne **te sers** jamais **de** ta voiture ?
Do you never use your car?

Tromper - Se tromper

Tromper To cheat

Il **trompe** sa femme depuis des années.
He has been cheating on his wife for years.

Se tromper To make a mistake

Tout le monde peut **se tromper.**
Everyone can make mistakes.

Trouver - Se trouver

Trouver To find

Elle ne **trouve** pas ce qu'elle veut.
She can't find what she wants.

Se trouver To be

La clé **se trouve** sur la table.
The key is on the table.

Reflexive pronoun = Each other

French uses three of the reflexive pronouns to indicate that people do something to each other. Because more than one person is involved, only the plural reflexive pronouns are used: **nous, vous, se - s'**.

AUDIO 19.21

Nous **nous** téléphonons tous les jours.	*We call **each other** every day.*
Est-ce que vous **vous** connaissez ?	*Do you know **each other**?*
Ils **se** parlent souvent.	*They talk to **each other** often.*
Le chien et le chat **s'**aiment bien.	*The dog and the cat like **each other**.*

Passive reflexive

Passive reflexive in French requires the use of a non-reflexive verb with the reflexive pronoun **se – s'**. The verb is conjugated in the third person singular or plural.

AUDIO **19.22**

Le français ne **s'**apprend pas facilement.	*French isn't learned easily.*
Cela **se** voit.	*It can be seen – It's visible.*
Ce gâteau **se** cuit au four.	*This cake is baked(cooked) in the oven.*
Les ordonnances **s'**obtiennent chez le docteur.	*Prescriptions are delivered at the doctor.*

Past Tenses – Les Temps du Passé

In French, we have 5 tenses to talk about the past. Out of the 5, we use 3 of them daily.

Le passé composé	The perfect tense
L'imparfait	The imperfect
Le passé récent	The recent past

These three tenses have very specific conjugations and very specific timelines.

Here is how to build them:

Le passé composé = **J'ai mangé** — **I ate – I have eaten – I did eat**
Avoir (présent) + past participle
Être (présent) + past participle

L'imparfait = **Je mangeais** — **I was eating – I ate**
Stem + ais – ais – ait – ions – iez – aient

Le passé récent = **Je viens de manger** — **I have just eaten – I just ate**
Venir (présent) + de + infinitive

The **passé composé** is used to talk about the past, mostly actions that took place in the past and were completed in the past.

The **imparfait** is used to talk about the past, mostly actions and situations without a specific timeframe, that happened an unspecified number of times or were in progress when something else happened.

The **passé récent** is used to talk about things that just happened.

The 2 other verbs are the **plus-que-parfait** and the **passé simple**.

The **passé simple** is only used in literature. You should be able to recognize it, but you don't need to learn it.

The **plus-que-parfait** is a compound tense of the past, seen in chapter 12.

CHAPTER 2

The Perfect Tense
Le Passé Composé

The Perfect Tense - Le Passé Composé

The perfect tense, called **passé composé** in French, is one of the 2 tenses mainly used to talk about the past. It is a compound tense with the auxiliaries **avoir** (to have) and **être** (to be) conjugated in the **present tense** followed by a **participe passé**.

It doesn't follow a specific translation between English and French, but it has similarities with the present perfect, the simple past, and the emphatic past.

The present perfect	*I have eaten*
The simple past	*I ate*
The emphatic past	*I did eat*

In French, the **passé composé** can replace these three conjugations: **J'ai mangé**

> The **passé composé** is used to talk about the past, mostly actions that took place in the past and were completed in the past.

Building the Passé Composé

Since the **passé composé** is a compound tense, it requires a conjugated auxiliary followed by a past participle.

Most of the verbs conjugated in the passé composé are built with the auxiliary **avoir** in the present tense:

AUDIO 20.1

Avoir To have

J'**ai**	Nous **avons**
Tu **as**	Vous **avez**
Il-Elle-On **a**	Ils-Elles **ont**

A list of specific verbs, as well as all reflexive verbs, are conjugated in the passé composé with the auxiliary **être** in the present tense:

Être To be

Je **suis**	Nous **sommes**
Tu **es**	Vous **êtes**
Il-Elle-On **est**	Ils-Elles **sont**

The Past Participle

Before seeing the different verbs conjugated in the **passé composé**, we need to see the different past participles.

The past participle changes depending on the group of verbs and if the verb is irregular or not. We can find the same in English with regulars: searched, painted, called, and irregulars: ate, brought, etc.

AUDIO 20.2 🔊

⇨ 1st group **-er** verbs change from the ending **er** to the ending **é** Chant**er** => chant**é**

All verbs ending in **-er** take **é.** Even the irregular ones keep the same spelling as the infinitive:

Infinitive	**Past participle**
Ending in **-cer** and **-ger**:	
Annonc**er**	annonc**é**
Mang**er**	mang**é**
Ending in **-yer**:	
Essay**er**	essay**é**
Nettoy**er**	nettoy**é**
Essuy**er**	essuy**é**
Ending in **-eler** and **-eter** (double letters):	
Appel**er**	appel**é**
Jet**er**	jet**é**
Ending in **-eler**, **-ener**, **-eser**, **-eter** and **-ever** (change of accent):	
Gel**er**	gel**é**
Amen**er**	amen**é**
Pes**er**	pes**é**
Achet**er**	achet**é**
Achev**er**	achev**é**
Ending in **-éder**, **-érer**, **-éter**, and **-ébrer** (change of accent):	
Céd**er**	céd**é**
Espér**er**	espér**é**
Répét**er**	répét**é**
Célébr**er**	célébr**é**
Even the only fully irregular **-er**:	
All**er**	all**é**

⇨ 2nd group **-ir** verbs change from the ending **ir** to the ending **i** Fin**ir** => fin**i**

⇨ 3rd group **-re** verbs change from the ending **re** to the ending **u** Attend**re** => attend**u**

Many French verbs are irregulars and most of them also have irregular past participles. Remember to keep verbs of the same kind grouped, so it's easier to remember.

AUDIO 20.3

Infinitive	Past participle	Similar verbs
Accueillir	**accueilli**	Cueillir – Recueillir
Avoir	**eu**	
Battre	**battu**	Abattre – Débattre
Boire	**bu**	
Conduire	**conduit**	
Connaître	**connu**	Apparaître – Disparaître – ...
Courir	**couru**	Recourir
Craindre	**craint**	Contraindre – Plaindre
Croire	**cru**	Voir – Prévoir – ...
Devoir	**dû**	
Dire	**dit**	
Dormir	**dormi**	
Écrire	**écrit**	
Éteindre	**éteint**	Éteindre – Feindre – ...
Être	**été**	
Faire	**fait**	Défaire – Refaire
Falloir	**fallu**	
Fuir	**fui**	
Joindre	**joint**	Rejoindre
Lire	**lu**	Relire – Élire
Mentir	**menti**	Partir – Repartir – ...
Mettre	**mis**	Admettre – Commettre – ...
Mourir	**mort**	
Naître	**né**	
Offrir	**offert**	Souffrir
Ouvrir	**ouvert**	Couvrir – Découvrir
Pleuvoir	**plu**	
Pouvoir	**pu**	
Prendre	**pris**	Apprendre – Comprendre – ...
Recevoir	**reçu**	Apercevoir – Décevoir
Rire	**ri**	
Savoir	**su**	
Servir	**servi**	
Suivre	**suivi**	
Tenir	**tenu**	Appartenir – Obtenir – ...
Vaincre	**vaincu**	Convaincre
Valoir	**valu**	
Venir	**venu**	Devenir – Intervenir – ...
Vivre	**vécu**	
Vouloir	**voulu**	

EX. 2.1 *Donnez le participe passé des verbes suivants.* AUDIO 20.4

1. Faire ______
2. Donner ______
3. Décevoir ______
4. Cueillir ______
5. Boire ______
6. Voir ______
7. Prendre ______
8. Savoir ______
9. Finir ______
10. Avoir ______
11. Admettre ______
12. Peser ______
13. Éteindre ______
14. Télécharger ______
15. Être ______
16. Découvrir ______
17. Venir ______
18. Grandir ______
19. Lire ______
20. Vouloir ______

Passé Composé with Avoir

The **passé composé** of verbs conjugated with **avoir** combines the conjugation of the verb **avoir** in the **present tense** followed by the **past participle** of the verb.

The past participle doesn't agree with the subject in gender and number.

> Note:
> Remember that **Je** becomes **J'** when followed by a verb starting with **a vowel** or a **silent h.**

Regarder To look	Past participle: ***regardé*** AUDIO 21.1
J'ai regardé	I looked – I have looked – I did look
Tu as regardé	You looked – You have looked – You did look
Il a regardé	He looked – He has looked – He did look
Elle a regardé	She looked – She has looked – She did look
On a regardé	We looked – We have looked – We did look
Nous avons regardé	We looked – We have looked – We did look
Vous avez regardé	You looked – You have looked – You did look
Ils ont regardé	They looked – They have looked – They did look
Elles ont regardé	They looked – They have looked – They did look

A few other ones:

Grandir To grow up	Past participle: ***grandi***
J'ai grandi	Nous avons grandi
Tu as grandi	Vous avez grandi
Il-Elle-On a grandi	Ils-Elles ont grandi

AUDIO 21.2

Entendre To hear	Past participle: ***entendu***
J'ai entendu	Nous avons entendu
Tu as entendu	Vous avez entendu
Il-Elle-On a entendu	Ils-Elles ont entendu

AUDIO 21.3

Tenir To hold	Past participle: ***tenu***
J'ai tenu	Nous avons tenu
Tu as tenu	Vous avez tenu
Il-Elle-On a tenu	Ils-Elles ont tenu

AUDIO 21.4

EX. 2.2 *Conjuguez les verbes suivants au passé composé.* AUDIO 21.5

1. Avoir

   J'____________________

   Tu ____________________

   Il-Elle-On ____________________

   Nous ____________________

   Vous ____________________

   Ils-Elles ____________________

2. Écrire

   J'____________________

   Tu ____________________

   Il-Elle-On ____________________

   Nous ____________________

   Vous ____________________

   Ils-Elles ____________________

3. Nettoyer

   J'____________________

   Tu ____________________

   Il-Elle-On ____________________

   Nous ____________________

   Vous ____________________

   Ils-Elles ____________________

EX. 2.3 *Traduisez le verbe et le pronom.* AUDIO 21.6

1. I drank ____________________
2. You had (s) ____________________
3. They sang (m) ____________________
4. She did ____________________
5. We spelled ____________________
6. They looked ____________________
7. We bought ____________________
8. I read ____________________
9. You slept (pl) ____________________
10. He studied ____________________

A few sentences including passé composé with avoir: AUDIO 21.7

Elle **a expliqué** le problème au professeur. *She explained the problem to the teacher.*
On **a réservé** le restaurant pour samedi. *We booked the restaurant for Saturday.*
Est-ce que tu **as réussi** ? *Have you succeeded?*
J'**ai** déjà **mangé.** *I already ate.*

EX. 2.4 *Conjuguez le verbe entre parenthèses au passé composé.* AUDIO 21.8

1. (Ranger) J' ____________________ ma chambre.
2. (Jouer) Il ____________________ ce week-end.
3. (Réparer) Les techniciens ____________________ le circuit.
4. (Tenir) Le gentleman ____________________ la porte pour la dame.

5. (Vouloir) Nous ______________________________ bien faire.
6. (Appeler) L'agent immobilier ______________________________ pour faire une offre.
7. (Mentir) Tu ______________________________ à ton professeur.
8. (Convaincre) J' ______________________________ mon ami de venir avec moi.
9. (Signer) Ils ______________________________ les documents lundi dernier.
10. (Cueillir) Elle ______________________________ des fleurs dans le jardin.
11. (Dormir) Mes parents ______________________________ ici hier.
12. (Vivre) Tu ______________________________ des expériences incroyables.
13. (Faire) Vous ______________________________ les démarches pour le permis ?
14. (Oublier) J' ______________________________ de fermer la porte !
15. (Brosser) Il ______________________________ le chien ce matin.

EX. 2.5 *Réécrivez chaque phrase au passé composé.* AUDIO 21.9

1. Vous gardez les enfants.

   ____

2. Le policier exige que le suspect s'arrête.

   ____

3. Je cherche ce livre partout.

   ____

4. Mon père conduit sa voiture au garage.

   ____

5. Elle court un marathon.

   ____

6. Je prends le bus pour aller au travail.

   ____

7. Il aime la soupe que je fais pour lui.

   ____

8. Elle reçoit un collier pour Noël.

   ____

9. Ils jouent dans le jardin tout l'après-midi.

____

10. Le livreur apporte les colis.

____

Passé Composé with Être

The **passé composé** of verbs conjugated with **être** combines the conjugation of the verb **être** in the **present tense** followed by the **past participle** of this verb.

> The **past participle** of verbs conjugated with **être** agrees in gender and number with the subject.

AUDIO 22.1

Not many verbs are conjugated with **être.** To remember them, remember the rule of **DR & MRS VANDERTRAMPP,** each letter corresponding to a verb conjugated with **être.**

Infinitive	Translation	Past participle
Devenir	To become	**Devenu**
Revenir	To come back	**Revenu**
&		
Monter	To go up	**Monté**
Rester	To stay	**Resté**
Sortir	To go out	**Sorti**
Venir	To come	**Venu**
Aller	To go	**Allé**
Naître	To be born	**Né**
Descendre	To go down	**Descendu**
Entrer	To enter	**Entré**
Rentrer	To go home	**Rentré**
Tomber	To fall	**Tombé**
Retourner	To return	**Retourné**
Arriver	To arrive	**Arrivé**
Mourir	To die	**Mort**
Partir	To leave	**Parti**
Passer	To pass by	**Passé**

Let's see how the agreement changes the endings of the past participle:

AUDIO 22.2 🔊

Devenir To become

Past participle: ***Devenu***		**M.sing.**	**F.sing.**	**M.plu.**	**F.plu.**
Je	suis	devenu	devenu**e**	–	–
Tu	es	devenu	devenu**e**	–	–
Il	est	devenu	–	–	–
Elle	est	–	devenu**e**	–	–
On	est	–	–	devenu**s**	devenu**es**
Nous	sommes	–	–	devenu**s**	devenu**es**
Vous	êtes	devenu	devenu**e**	devenu**s**	devenu**es**
Ils	sont	–	–	devenu**s**	–
Elles	sont	–	–	–	devenu**es**

We can see that depending on the subject, if the subject is masculine or feminine, singular or plural, the past participle will take a -**e, -s, -es** or nothing at all if the subject is masculine singular.

What about ON?

When **on** translates to **WE**, the past participle agrees with the subject in gender and number, but the verb is still conjugated like **il** and **elle**.

AUDIO 22.3 🔊

On **est entrées** dans le magasin. *We entered the store.*
On **est arrivés** à l'aéroport. *We arrived at the airport.*

EX. 2.6 *Conjuguez les verbes suivants au passé composé.* AUDIO 22.4 🔊

Ajoutez le féminin entre parenthèses avec Je, Tu, On, Nous, Vous => Je suis allé(e)

1. Venir

Je ______________________________

Tu ______________________________

Il ______________________________

Nous ______________________________

Vous ______________________________

Ils ______________________________

2. Passer

Je ______________________________

Tu ______________________________

Elle ______________________________

Nous ______________________________

Vous ______________________________

Elles ______________________________

3. Naître

Je ______________________________

Tu ______________________________

On ______________________________

Nous______________________________

Vous ______________________________

Elles ______________________________

EX. 2.7 *Conjuguez le verbe avec le pronom correspondant au passé composé.* AUDIO 22.5

Ajoutez le féminin entre parenthèses avec Je, Tu, On, Nous, Vous => Je suis allé(e)

1. Revenir => Il ______________________________
2. Sortir => Nous ______________________________
3. Aller => Nous ______________________________
4. Partir => Je ______________________________
5. Mourir => Ils ______________________________
6. Tomber => Nous ______________________________
7. Descendre => Il ______________________________
8. Devenir => Vous ______________________________
9. Arriver => Nous ______________________________
10. Monter => Ils ______________________________

Agreement - Passé Composé with Avoir

As we saw before, the past participle of verbs conjugated with **avoir** doesn't agree in gender and number with the subject.

However, it agrees in gender and number with the **direct object if the direct object is before the verb.**

Direct object + avoir + past participle + e.s.es

The direct object can be:

⇨ A direct object pronoun = **Le, La, Les, L', Nous, ...** AUDIO 23.1

Elle a envoyé **une lettre.** [1]	*She sent a letter.*
Elle **l'**a envoy**ée.** [2]	*She sent it.*

[1] In the first sentence, **Une lettre** is the direct object, but it's placed after the verb. Therefore nothing changes.
[2] But if we transform **Une lettre** into a direct object pronoun, **LA**, it will be placed before the verb and change the gender of the past participle.

J'ai reçu **les colis du voisin.**	*I got the neighbor's packages.*
Je **les** ai reçu**s.**	*I got them.*
Il **nous** a appelé**s.**	*He called us.*

EX. 2.8 *Trouvez le COD et transformez la phrase avec un objet direct.* AUDIO 23.2

1. Tu as pris les bouteilles d'eau.

____

2. J'ai écouté la nouvelle chanson.

____

3. Nous avons loué un chalet pour les vacances.

____

4. Philipe a mis sa veste.

____

5. Elle a appris la nouvelle leçon.

____

6. Tu as mangé la pomme.

____

7. Il a bientôt fini son examen.

____

8. La mariée a choisi sa robe.

____

9. Le groupe d'élèves a visité les musées.

____

10. J'ai nettoyé la voiture.

____

⇨ The relative pronoun **Que – Qu'** AUDIO 23.3

The relative pronoun replaces the direct object.

Elle a envoyé **une lettre.**	*She sent a letter.*
La lettre **qu'**elle a envoyé**e.**	*The letter (that) she sent.*
J'ai reçu **les colis du voisin.**	*I got the neighbor's packages.*
Les colis du voisin **que** j'ai reçu**s.**	*The neighbor's packages (that) I got.*

If it's easier for you, remember only the direct object which you can still find easily in the sentence instead of remembering the relative pronoun.

> The pronouns **lui** and **leur** are not direct pronouns but **indirect pronouns**. Therefore the past participle doesn't change if **lui** or **leur** are before the conjugated verb.

EX. 2.9 *Complétez les phrases après QUE.* AUDIO 23.4

1. J'ai conseillé un livre à Paul.

   Le livre que ____

2. Nous avons réservé une croisière.

   La croisière que ____

3. Vous avez fait une promenade.

   La promenade que ____

4. Elle a acheté une jolie maison.

   La jolie maison qu' ____

5. Tu as oublié ton portefeuille.

   Le portefeuille que ____

6. Il a commandé une bouteille d'eau.

   La bouteille d'eau qu' ______________________________

7. Mandy a préparé son sac de sport.

   Le sac de sport que ______________________________

8. J'ai fait mon devoir.

   Le devoir que ______________________________

9. L'infirmière a fait une piqûre.

   La piqûre que ______________________________

10. On a fermé les portes de la maison.

    Les portes de la maison qu' ______________________________

When to Use the Passé Composé

The **passé composé** is used in these situations:

⇨ To describe something that took place in the past at a very specific moment. Usually, the sentence will indicate some time references indicating that the action is completed.

Here is a list of words frequently used with passé composé: AUDIO 24.1

Avant-hier	The day before yesterday
Ce matin	This morning
Hier	Yesterday
Hier soir	Yesterday evening
Il y a deux jours	Two days ago
L'année dernière	Last year
L'été dernier	Last summer
La semaine dernière	Last week
Le mois dernier	Last month
Mercredi dernier	Last Wednesday

Il **est arrivé** ce matin. *He arrived this morning.*
Je t'**ai appelé** il y a deux jours. *I called you two days ago.*
Il **a plu** la semaine dernière. *It rained last week.*

EX. 2.10 *Créez une phrase avec le verbe conjugué au passé composé et ajoutez une référence de temps de votre choix.*

1. Chercher ______________________________
2. Revenir ______________________________
3. Sentir ______________________________
4. Savoir ______________________________
5. Pleuvoir ______________________________
6. Avoir ______________________________
7. Faire ______________________________
8. Être ______________________________
9. Partir ______________________________
10. Aller ______________________________

⇨ To describe an event that usually only happens once. The verbs used in this case show that the action is not repeated.

Here is a list of verbs frequently used with passé composé: AUDIO 24.2

Mourir	To die
Naître	To be born
Se marier	To get married
Se fiancer	To get engaged
Divorcer	To get divorced
Avorter	To abort
Avoir ... ans	To turn ... years old

Il **est mort** l'année dernière. *He died last year.*
Elles **se sont mariées** cet été. *They got married this summer.*
Ma fille **est née**. *My daughter was born.*
J'**ai** récemment **eu** 30 ans. *I recently turned 30 years old.*

EX. 2.11 *Faites des phrases et conjuguez le verbe au passé composé.* AUDIO 24.3

1. Mes parents / divorcer / récemment.

   ____

2. Ma fille / naître / la semaine dernière.

   ____

3. Le voisin / mourir / hier.

   ____

⇨ To talk about something that happened repeatedly or at least a few times: AUDIO 24.4

J'**ai visité** le Canada deux fois. *I visited Canada twice.*
Elle vous **a appelé** plusieurs fois. *She called you several times.*

EX. 2.12 *Conjuguez le verbe **ALLER** au passé composé et ajoutez la préposition adéquate.*

AUDIO 24.5

Ajoutez le féminin entre parenthèses avec Je, Tu, On, Nous, Vous => Je suis allé(e)

1. Nous / aller / Allemagne / deux fois.

   ____

2. Elle / aller / magasin / trois fois cette semaine.

   ____

3. Il / aller / Mexique / une seule fois.

   ____

4. Ma famille / aller / Londres / plusieurs fois.

   ____

⇨ To indicate something that happened suddenly: AUDIO 24.6

Here is a list of words frequently used for sudden actions:

Soudainement	Suddenly
Immédiatement	Immediately
Tout à coup	All of a sudden
Tout de suite	Right away
Au moment où	At the moment when
Juste quand	Just when

La police **est arrivée** tout de suite. *The police arrived right away.*
Le magicien **a disparu** tout à coup. *The magician disappeared all of a sudden.*

EX. 2.13 *Conjuguez le verbe entre parenthèses au passé composé.*

Ajoutez le féminin entre parenthèses avec Je, Tu, On, Nous, Vous => Je suis allé(e), si nécessaire.

AUDIO 24.7

Au moment où je ____________ (entrer), il ____________ (cacher) ses affaires et il ____________ (commencer) à mentir. Je lui ____________ (demander) pourquoi, il ____________ (répondre) que cela ne me regardait pas.

⇨ To talk about a series of actions taking place successively: AUDIO 24.8

Here is a list of words frequently used for stories with successive actions:

D'abord	First
Enfin	Finally
Ensuite	Then
Puis	Then
Quand	When

D'abord, j'**ai essayé** de l'appeler au bureau, puis j'**ai appelé** son téléphone portable.
Enfin, j'**ai téléphoné** à sa secrétaire.
First, I tried to call him at work, then I called his cellphone. Finally, I called his secretary.

EX. 2.14 *Conjuguez le verbe entre parenthèses au passé composé.* AUDIO 24.9

D'abord, j' ____________________ (mélanger) la farine et le beurre, puis j' ____________________ (ajouter) le lait. Je pense que j' ____________________ (mettre) trop de beurre car la pâte ____________________ (devenir) très grasse. Ce n'est pas grave, au moins j' ____________________ (essayer).

Verbs with Avoir and Être

A few verbs can be conjugated with the auxiliaries **avoir** and **être**. The meaning of the sentence will be different depending on the auxiliary. With **avoir**, the verb will act as a **transitive verb** (which allows a direct object). With **être**, the verb is **intransitive**.

AUDIO 24.10

Descendre To go down

Être descendu

Je **suis descendu.**
I went downstairs.

Avoir descendu

J'**ai descendu** la poubelle.
I took the garbage downstairs.

Monter To go up

Être monté

Il **est monté.**
I went upstairs.

Avoir monté

Il **a monté** la valise au grenier.
He took the luggage to the attic.

Passer To pass (by)

Être passé

Nous **sommes passés** au bureau.
We passed by the office.

Avoir passé

Nous **avons passé** nos examens.
We passed on our exams.

Rentrer To go home

Être rentré

Elle **est rentrée** à la maison.
She went home.

Avoir rentré

Elle **a rentré** la voiture.
She took the car in.

Retourner To return

Être retourné

Il **est retourné** en train.
He returned by train.

Avoir retourné

Il **a retourné** le chapeau.
He sent back the hat.

Sortir To go out – To take out

Être sorti

Vous **êtes sortis** dehors.
You went outside.

Avoir sorti

Vous **avez sorti** le chien.
You took the dog out.

EX. 2.15 *Conjuguez le verbe entre parenthèses au passé composé, choisissez si le verbe est conjugué avec* ***être*** *ou avoir* ***avoir.*** AUDIO 24.11

1. (Retourner) Nous ______________________________ au même hôtel.
2. (Sortir) J' ______________________________ la poubelle trop tard.
3. (Rentrer) Est-ce que tu ______________________________ les chaises de jardin ?
4. (Monter) Ils ______________________________ il y a quelques minutes.

The Passé Composé of Reflexive Verbs

Reflexive verbs are always conjugated with the auxiliary **être**, which means that the past participle will agree in gender and number with the direct object.

> In most cases, the **direct object** is the **reflexive pronoun: me, te, se, nous, vous.**

The past participles are the same as the regular verbs.

S'adapter To adapt AUDIO 25.1

Past participle: ***adapté***			M.sing.	F.sing.	M.plu.	F.plu.
Je	me	suis	adapté	adapté**e**	–	–
Tu	t'	es	adapté	adapté**e**	–	–
Il	s'	est	adapté	–	–	–
Elle	s'	est	–	adapté**e**	–	–
On	s'	est	–	–	adapté**s**	adapté**es**
Nous	nous	sommes	–	–	adapté**s**	adapté**es**
Vous	vous	êtes	adapté	adapté**e**	adapté**s**	adapté**es**
Ils	se	sont	–	–	adapté**s**	–
Elles	se	sont	–	–	–	adapté**es**

A few other ones, including irregulars:

Se sentir To feel — Past participle: ***senti*** AUDIO 25.2

Je me suis senti(e)	Nous nous sommes senti(e)s
Tu t'es senti(e)	Vous vous êtes senti(e)s
Il-Elle-On s'est senti(e.s)	Ils-Elles se sont senti(e)s

Se souvenir To remember — Past participle: ***souvenu*** AUDIO 25.3

Je me suis souvenu(e)	Nous nous sommes souvenu(e)s
Tu t'es souvenu(e)	Vous vous êtes souvenu(e)s
Il-Elle-On s'est souvenu(e.s)	Ils-Elles se sont souvenu(e)s

S'asseoir To sit down — Past participle: ***assis*** AUDIO 25.4

Je me suis assis(e)	Nous nous sommes assis(es)
Tu t'es assis(e)	Vous vous êtes assis(es)
Il-Elle-On s'est assis(e.s)	Ils-Elles se sont assis(es)

However, if a direct object follows the reflexive verb, the reflexive pronoun becomes an indirect object. Therefore, the past participle agrees in gender and number with the direct object.

Reflexive pronoun + être + past participle + direct object

This is a common type of sentence with reflexive verbs and body parts. 25.5

Elle **s'est coupée.** [1]	*She cut herself.*
Elle s'est coupé **la main.** [2]	*She cut her hand.*
Elle se **l'**est coupée. [2]	*She cut it.*

[1] In the first sentence, **se (s')** is the direct object. Since it's placed before the verb, the past participle agrees.
[2] In the second sentence, **le doigt** is the direct object. Since it's placed after the verb, the past participle doesn't agree.

EX. 2.16 *Conjuguez les verbes suivants au passé composé, n'oubliez pas d'ajouter le féminin et pluriel.* **AUDIO 25.6**

1. Se détendre

   Je ______

   Tu ______

   Il ______

   Elle ______

   On ______

   Nous ______

   Vous ______

   Ils ______

   Elles ______

2. Se raser

   Je ______

   Tu ______

   Il ______

   Elle ______

   On ______

   Nous ______

   Vous ______

   Ils ______

   Elles ______

EX. 2.17 *Conjuguez le verbe entre parenthèses au passé composé, n'oubliez pas d'ajouter le féminin et pluriel.* **AUDIO 25.7**

1. (Se doucher) Je ______ ce matin.
2. (S'occuper) Elle ______ de cela ce week-end.
3. (Se tromper) Il ______ sur la question numéro 3.
4. (S'inscrire) Nous ______ pour décembre.
5. (Se faire) Je ______ un sandwich.

6. (S'asseoir) Vous ______________________________ au premier rang.
7. (Se couper) Elle ______________________________ les cheveux elle-même.
8. (Se mettre) Nous ______________________________ d'accord assez vite.
9. (S'essuyer) Ils ______________________________ les pied savant d'entrer.
10. (Se casser) Elle ______________________________ la jambe.
11. (Se brosser) Ils ______________________________ les dents.
12. (Se rappeler) Je ______________________________ de cette histoire récemment.
13. (S'amuser) Ils ______________________________ à l'anniversaire.
14. (Se sentir) Elle ______________________________ mieux après le dîner.
15. (S'imaginer) Tu ______________________________ cette histoire.

Passé Composé and Negation

Negation in the case of the **passé composé** follows a specific order. **Ne** is placed before the auxiliary and **pas** is placed before the past participle.

Pronoun + ne – n' + avoir – être + pas + past participle

Of course, other negations follow the same order: **ne ... rien, ne ... jamais**, etc.

AUDIO 26.1

⇨ Ne ... pas

Je **n'**ai **pas** dit ça. *I didn't say that.*

⇨ Ne ... rien

Nous **n'**avons **rien** reçu. *We didn't receive anything.*

⇨ Ne ... jamais

Elle **n'**est **jamais** partie. *She never left.*

But in ne ... personne, **personne** is placed after the past participle.

⇨ Ne ... personne

Je **n'**ai vu **personne**. *I didn't see anyone.*

When the verb is reflexive, **ne** is placed before the reflexive pronoun and **pas** is placed before the past participle.

Ne + reflexive pronoun + être + pas + past participle

Other negations follow the same order as well: **ne ... rien**, **ne ... jamais**, etc.

AUDIO 26.2 🔊

⇨ Ne ... pas

Je **ne** me suis **pas** inscrite. *I didn't register.*

⇨ Ne ... rien

Elle **ne** s'est **rien** demandée. *She asked herself nothing.*

⇨ Ne ... jamais

Nous **ne** nous sommes **jamais** demandé(e)s pourquoi. *We never asked ourselves why.*

EX. 2.18 *Ajoutez la négation donnée à chaque phrase.* AUDIO 26.3 🔊

1. Nous avons reçu la livraison ce matin.

   Ne ... pas ______________________________

2. Elles sont passées par là.

   Ne ... jamais ______________________________

3. J'ai vidé la bouteille dans l'évier.

   Ne ... pas ______________________________

4. Tu as oublié.

   Ne ... rien ______________________________

5. Cet hôtel est devenu populaire.

   Ne ... jamais ______________________________

6. Le professeur a annulé sa classe de yoga.

   Ne ... pas ______________________________

7. Le fermier a acheté une deuxième ferme.

   Ne ... pas ______________________________

8. J'ai décidé de lire tous les jours un chapitre.

   Ne ... jamais ______________________________

9. Le directeur a accepté ses congés.

   Ne ... pas ______________________________

10. Elle a aidé sa sœur à faire la vaisselle.

    Ne ... pas ______________________________

11. Elles sont arrivées il y a quelques heures.

    Ne ... pas ______________________________

12. Il a convaincu ses parents de le conduire.

    Ne ... pas ______________________________

13. Les élèves ont étudié dur pour l'examen.

    Ne ... pas ______________________________

14. Elles se sont disputées à propos de la facture.

    Ne ... pas ______________________________

15. Nous avons manqué son récital de danse.

    Ne ... pas ______________________________

Questions Using the Passé Composé

Using the **passé composé** to ask questions is slightly different than regular conjugation with only one verb. But the question types are the same, you can ask a question by:

AUDIO 26.4 🔊

⇨ Raising your voice at the end of the question:

Tu **es** déjà **parti(e)** ? *Have you already left?*
Ils **ont célébré** son augmentation ? *Have they celebrated his raise?*

Tu t'**es lavé** les cheveux ? *Have you washed your hair?*

⇨ Using **est-ce que:**

Est-ce que tu **es** déjà **parti(e)** ? *Have you already left?*
Est-ce qu'ils **ont célébré** son augmentation ? *Have they celebrated his raise?*

Est-ce que tu t'**es lavé** les cheveux ? *Have you washed your hair?*

⇨ Using **inversion:**

Es-tu déjà **parti(e)** ? *Have you already left?*
Ont-ils **célébré** son augmentation ? *Have they celebrated his raise?*
A-t-elle **été** en Australie ? *Did she go to Australia?*

⇨ When using inversion, the auxiliary is placed first, then the pronoun, and finally the past participle. For **il** and **elle**, add a **-t-** between the pronoun and the auxiliary.

T'es-tu **lavé** les cheveux ? *Have you washed your hair?*

⇨ For reflexive verbs, the reflexive pronoun is placed first, followed by the auxiliary, then the pronoun, and finally the past participle.

EX. 2.19 *Changez la phrase du présent au passé composé sur la première ligne. Sur la deuxième ligne, changez la phrase en question en utilisant l'inversion.* **AUDIO 26.5**

Exemple:
Elle conseille le client.
Elle a conseillé le client.
A-t-elle conseillé le client ?

1. Tu changes de travail.

____

____

2. On boit du thé au déjeuner.

____

____

3. Il fume plusieurs cigarettes.

____

____

4. Elle veut organiser une surprise.

____

____

5. Ils viennent tous ce soir.

____

____

6. Il doute de ses compétences.

____

____

7. Nous espérons gagner à la loterie.

____

____

8. Vous vous connaissez.

____

____

9. Il prend une décision rapidement.

____

____

10. Elle fait un gâteau aux pommes.

____

____

EX. 2.20 *Formez une question au passé composé en utilisant **est-ce que** sur la première ligne. Sur la deuxième ligne, répondez à la question avec **oui** ou **non**.* **AUDIO 26.6**

Exemple:
Elle / montrer / la réponse.
Est-ce qu'elle a montré la réponse ?
Oui, elle a montré la réponse.

1. Tu / réserver / un traitement au spa.

   ____

   Non, ____

2. Il / respecter / ses parents.

   ____

   Oui, ____

3. Tu / faire / du vélo.

   ____

   Non, ____

4. Je / voir / ce film au cinéma.

____

Oui, ______________________________

5. Tu / se lever / tôt.

____

Non, ______________________________

6. Le docteur / dire / de rester au lit.

____

Oui, ______________________________

7. Tu / trouver / un appartement.

____

Non, ______________________________

8. Elle / entendre / la conversation.

____

Oui, ______________________________

9. Il / travailler / trop.

____

Non, ______________________________

10. Ils / aller / au stade.

____

Oui, ______________________________

CHAPTER 3

The Imperfect Tense
L'Imparfait

The Imperfect Tense - L'Imparfait

The imperfect tense, called **imparfait** in French, is the other tense mainly used to talk about the past. It's not a compound tense like the **passé composé.**

The imperfect tense is translated into English with the past progressive and the simple past.

The past progressive *I was eating*
The simple past *I ate*
As well as *I used to eat* **or** *I would eat*

In French, the **imparfait** can be used to translate these conjugations: **Je mangeais.**

The **imparfait** is used to talk about the past, mostly actions and situations without a specific timeframe that happened an unspecified number of times or were in progress when something else happened.

Building the Imparfait

To form the **imparfait**, we need to find the stem of the verb. To do this, we will look at the **verb conjugated in the present tense with nous**, remove the **-ons** and add the endings for the imparfait:

-ais, -ais, -ait, -ions, iez and **-aient. Être** is the only verb not following the stem rule.

Regular **-er** verbs:

Donner To give Nous donn~~**ons**~~ **Stem: donn** AUDIO 27.1

Pr.	Stem + Endings	Conjugated verb	Translation
Je	donn - **ais**	Je donn**ais**	I gave – I was giving
Tu	donn - **ais**	Tu donn**ais**	You gave – You were giving
Il	donn - **ait**	Il donn**ait**	He gave – He was giving
Elle	donn - **ait**	Elle donn**ait**	She gave – She was giving
On	donn - **ait**	On donn**ait**	We gave – We were giving
Nous	donn - **ions**	Nous donn**ions**	We gave – We were giving
Vous	donn - **iez**	Vous donn**iez**	You gave – You were giving
Ils	donn - **aient**	Ils donn**aient**	They gave – They were giving
Elles	donn - **aient**	Elles donn**aient**	They gave – They were giving

Regular **-ir** verbs:

Finir To finish   Nous finiss**~~ons~~**   **Stem: finiss**   AUDIO 27.2

Pr.	Stem + Endings	Conjugated verb	Translation
Je	finiss - **ais**	Je finiss**ais**	I finished – I was finishing
Tu	finiss - **ais**	Tu finiss**ais**	You finished – You were finishing
Il	finiss - **ait**	Il finiss**ait**	He finished – He was finishing
Elle	finiss - **ait**	Elle finiss**ait**	She finished – She was finishing
On	finiss - **ait**	On finiss**ait**	We finished – We were finishing
Nous	finiss - **ions**	Nous finiss**ions**	We finished – We were finishing
Vous	finiss - **iez**	Vous finiss**iez**	You finished – You were finishing
Ils	finiss - **aient**	Ils finiss**aient**	They finished – They were finishing
Elles	finiss - **aient**	Elles finiss**aient**	They finished – They were finishing

Regular **-re** verbs:

Attendre To wait   Nous attend**~~ons~~**   **Stem: attend**   AUDIO 27.3

Pr.	Stem + Endings	Conjugated verb	Translation
J'	attend - **ais**	J'attend**ais**	I waited – I was waiting
Tu	attend - **ais**	Tu attend**ais**	You waited – You were waiting
Il	attend - **ait**	Il attend**ait**	He waited – He was waiting
Elle	attend - **ait**	Elle attend**ait**	She waited – She was waiting
On	attend - **ait**	On attend**ait**	We waited – We were waiting
Nous	attend - **ions**	Nous attendions	We waited – We were waiting
Vous	attend - **iez**	Vous attend**iez**	You waited – You were waiting
Ils	attend - **aient**	Ils attend**aient**	They waited – They were waiting
Elles	attend - **aient**	Elles attend**aient**	They waited – They were waiting

The endings **-ais, -ait, -aient** have the same pronunciation.

The stem of verbs ending in **-cer** changes slightly:

Prononcer To pronounce   Nous prononç**ons**   **Stem: prononç**   AUDIO 27.4

Pr.	Stem + Endings	Conjugated verb
Je	prononç - **ais**	Je prononçais
Tu	prononç - **ais**	Tu prononçais
Il-Elle-On	prononç - **ait**	Il-Elle-On prononçait
Nous	prononc - **ions**	Nous prononcions
Vous	prononc - **iez**	Vous prononciez
Ils-Elles	prononç - **aient**	Ils-Elles prononçaient

The stem includes a **Ç** but changes back to a regular **C** with **nous** and **vous. C** followed by **i** will be pronounced as an **S.**

Verbs ending in **-ger** change the same way as verbs ending in **-cer**:

Bouger To move Nous bouge~~ons~~ **Stem: bouge** AUDIO 27.5

Pr.	Stem + Endings	Conjugated verb
Je	bouge - **ais**	Je bougeais
Tu	bouge - **ais**	Tu bougeais
Il-Elle-On	bouge - **ait**	Il-Elle-On bougeait
Nous	**boug** - **ions**	Nous bou**g**ions
Vous	**boug** - **iez**	Vous bou**g**iez
Ils-Elles	bouge - **aient**	Ils-Elles bougeaient

The stem includes an **E** after **G** but changes back to only **G** with **nous** and **vous**. **G** followed by **i** will be pronounced as a **J**.

Verbs with stem ending with **-i**:

Étudier To study Nous étudi~~ons~~ **Stem: étudi** AUDIO 27.6

Pr.	Stem + Endings	Conjugated verb
J'	étudi - **ais**	J'étudiais
Tu	étudi - **ais**	Tu étudiais
Il-Elle-On	étudi - **ait**	Il-Elle-On étudiait
Nous	étudi - **ions**	Nous étudiions
Vous	étudi - **iez**	Vous étudiiez
Ils-Elles	étudi - **aient**	Ils-Elles étudiaient

When conjugated with **nous** and **vous**, the verb takes a **double i**: nous **étudiions**, vous **étudiiez**.

Other irregular verbs from the 3 groups: AUDIO 27.7

Verb	Présent	Imparfait
Essayer To try	Nous **essay**ons	**J'essayais**
Nettoyer To clean	Nous **nettoy**ons	**Je nettoyais**
Essuyer To wipe	Nous **essuy**ons	**J'essuyais**
Appeler To call	Nous **appel**ons	**J'appelais**
Jeter To throw	Nous **jet**ons	**Je jetais**
Geler To freeze	Nous **gel**ons	**Je gelais**
Amener To bring	Nous **amen**ons	**J'amenais**
Acheter To buy	Nous **achet**ons	**J'achetais**
Peser To weigh	Nous **pes**ons	**Je pesais**
Achever To finish	Nous **achev**ons	**J'achevais**
Céder To yield	Nous **céd**ons	**Je cédais**
Espérer To hope	Nous **espér**ons	**J'espérais**
Répéter To repeat	Nous **répét**ons	**Je répétais**
Célébrer To celebrate	Nous **célébr**ons	**Je célébrais**
Avoir To have	Nous **av**ons	**J'avais**
Aller To go	Nous **all**ons	**J'allais**
Faire To do	Nous **fais**ons	**Je faisais**
Prendre To take	Nous **pren**ons	**Je prenais**

Ouvrir To open	Nous **ouvr**ons	**J'ouvrais**
Offrir To offer	Nous **offr**ons	**J'offrais**
Accueillir To welcome	Nous **accueill**ons	**J'accueillais**
Dormir To sleep	Nous **dorm**ons	**Je dormais**
Mentir To lie	Nous **ment**ons	**Je mentais**
Servir To serve	Nous **serv**ons	**Je servais**
Courir To run	Nous **cour**ons	**Je courais**
Mourir To die	Nous **mour**ons	**Je mourais**
Craindre To fear	Nous **craign**ons	**Je craignais**
Éteindre To turn off	Nous **éteign**ons	**J'éteignais**
Joindre To join	Nous **joign**ons	**Je joignais**
Battre To beat	Nous **batt**ons	**Je battais**
Mettre To put	Nous **mett**ons	**Je mettais**
Venir To come	Nous **ven**ons	**Je venais**
Tenir To hold	Nous **ten**ons	**Je tenais**
Boire To drink	Nous **buv**ons	**Je buvais**
Savoir To know	Nous **sav**ons	**Je savais**
Écrire To write	Nous **écriv**ons	**J'écrivais**
Recevoir To receive	Nous **recev**ons	**Je recevais**
Suivre To follow	Nous **suiv**ons	**Je suivais**
Conduire To drive	Nous **conduis**ons	**Je conduisais**
Lire To read	Nous **lis**ons	**Je lisais**
Connaître To know	Nous **connaiss**ons	**Je connaissais**
Croire To believe	Nous **croy**ons	**Je croyais**
Fuir To flee	Nous **fuy**ons	**Je fuyais**
Vaincre To overcome	Nous **vainqu**ons	**Je vainquais**
Devoir To have to	Nous **dev**ons	**Je devais**
Vouloir To want	Nous **voul**ons	**Je voulais**
Pouvoir To be able	Nous **pouv**ons	**Je pouvais**
Dire To tell	Nous **dis**ons	**Je disais**
Rire To laugh	Nous **ri**ons	**Je riais**
Valoir To be worth	Nous **val**ons	**Je valais**

The verb **être** is the only one that doesn't use the present tense stem:

Être To be AUDIO 27.8

J'**étais**	Nous **étions**
Tu **étais**	Vous **étiez**
Il-Elle-On **était**	Ils-Elles **étaient**

The impersonal verbs **falloir**, **pleuvoir** and **neiger** only exist with **il** and are conjugated as follow:
AUDIO 27.9

Falloir To be necessary	Il **fall**ait
Pleuvoir To rain	Il **pleuv**ait
Neiger To snow	Il **neige**ait

EX. 3.1 *Ajoutez le verbe conjugué au présent avec nous et à l'imparfait avec le pronom donné.*

AUDIO 27.10

	Verbe	*Présent*	*Imparfait*
1.	To be	Nous ______	Ils ______
2.	To have	Nous ______	J' ______
3.	To take	Nous ______	Tu ______
4.	To call	Nous ______	Nous ______
5.	To do	Nous ______	Vous ______
6.	To sleep	Nous ______	Ils ______
7.	To turn off	Nous ______	Elles ______
8.	To come	Nous ______	Je ______
9.	To write	Nous ______	Vous ______
10.	To build	Nous ______	On ______

EX. 3.2 *Traduisez le pronom et le verbe.* AUDIO 27.11

1. I turned ______
2. You seemed (s) ______
3. We prepared ______
4. She spent ______
5. They recommended (m) ______
6. You noticed (pl) ______
7. I forced ______
8. He walked ______
9. They went (f) ______
10. We brought ______
11. He traveled (m) ______
12. They sang ______
13. We watched ______
14. She fished ______
15. You shared (s) ______

EX. 3.3 *Conjuguez le verbe entre parenthèses à l'imparfait.* AUDIO 27.12

1. Elles ______________________ un poème. (écrire)
2. Nous ______________________ un verre de vin. (boire)
3. Il ______________________ beaucoup d'outils. (acheter)
4. L'ordinateur ne ______________________ plus. (fonctionner)
5. J' ______________________ au téléphone. (être)
6. L'auteur ______________________ beaucoup de livres. (vendre)
7. Vous ______________________ toujours en retard. (arriver)
8. Il ______________________ chaud. (faire)
9. Qu'est-ce que tu ______________________ ? (dire)
10. Mon grand-père ______________________ tellement bien. (cuisiner)

EX. 3.4 *Trouvez les erreurs et corrigez-les.* AUDIO 27.13

1. Nous habitiez en ville. ______________________
2. Je chantait au cabaret. ______________________
3. Tu restais souvent après moi. ______________________
4. Elle jouai avec le chien. ______________________
5. Elle se couchaient tôt. ______________________
6. Nous sommes là. ______________________
7. Je lis le journal. ______________________
8. Ils éteignait toujours les lampes. ______________________
9. Nous étudions tous les jours. ______________________
10. Je finissaient mes devoirs à la va-vite. ______________________
11. Il se trompait souvent de numéro. ______________________

*Remember to **download the audio** and to **watch the videos** – see Preface*

When to Use the Imparfait

The **imparfait** is used in these situations:

⇨ To describe **habits** and **repeated actions** in the past without being specific in terms of timing.

Here is a list of words frequently used with the **imparfait**: AUDIO 28.1

Autrefois	Formerly
Avant	Before
D'habitude	Usually
D'ordinaire	Usually
De temps à autre	From time to time
De temps en temps	From time to time
En ce temps-là	At that time
En général	Generally
Fréquemment	Frequently
Généralement	Generally
Habituellement	Usually
Jamais	Never
Le lundi, le mardi, ...	On Mondays, on Tuesdays

Autrefois, il **était** professeur. *Formerly, he was a teacher.*
Nous n'**étudiions** jamais. *We never studied.*

EX. 3.5 *Réécrivez les phrases en conjuguant le verbe à l'imparfait.* AUDIO 28.2

1. En général, on dépense 300 dollars par mois en nourriture.

____

2. Le lundi, je joue au football et j'ai cours de piano.

____

3. Il ne reconnaît jamais ses erreurs.

____

4. D'habitude, il est toujours à l'heure.

____

5. Il aime bien se détendre de temps à autre.

____

⇨ To talk about **repeated actions** in the past that you could translate to used to or would. Once again, without a specific timeframe.

Here is a list of words frequently used with the **imparfait**: AUDIO 28.3

Chaque année	Every year
Chaque jour	Every day
Chaque mois	Every month
Chaque saison	Every season
Chaque semaine	Every week
Parfois	Sometimes
Quelquefois	Sometimes
Souvent	Often
Toujours	Always
Tous les ans	Every year
Tous les jours	Every day
Tous les mois	Every month
Tout le temps	All the time

Ils **étaient** toujours en famille. *They used to always be with family.*
Je **jouais** au football tous les jours. *I used to play soccer every day.*
Il **dormait** souvent avec la fenêtre ouverte. *He often used to sleep with the window open.*

EX. 3.6 *Choisissez un verbe de la liste ci-dessous et conjuguez-le à l'imparfait.* AUDIO 28.4

permettre - être - faire - aller - adorer - déranger - rester

Chaque année, nous ________________ chez mes grands-parents pour les vacances. Ma grand-mère ________________ souvent des tartes et mon grand-père ________________ toujours dans le jardin. Mes frères et moi ________________ là-bas pendant plusieurs semaines. Cela ________________ à mes parents d'avoir un peu de temps pour eux. Cela ne ________________ pas mes grands-parents. Ils ________________ nous avoir à la maison.

⇨ To describe a **person**, a **property**, the **weather** or even a **physical state** or an **emotion**. AUDIO 28.5

Il **était** grand. *He was tall.*
La maison **se situait** au bout de la rue. *The house was situated at the end of the street.*
Il **pleuvait** beaucoup. *It rained a lot.*

Here are some verbs frequently used with the **imparfait** to talk about a physical state or an emotion:

Adorer	To adore
Aimer	To like
Avoir faim	To be hungry
Avoir froid	To be cold
Avoir soif	To be thirsty
Croire	To believe
Désirer	To wish
Détester	To hate
Espérer	To hope
Être fatigué(e)	To be tired
Être malade	To be sick
Penser	To think
Préférer	To prefer
Regretter	To regret
S'attendre	To expect
Savoir	To know
Se sentir	To feel
Sembler	To seem
Souhaiter	To wish
Vouloir	To want

J'**aimais** beaucoup le café. *I used to really like coffee.*
Il **souhaitait** réussir. *He wished to succeed.*
Nous **espérions** être là. *We were hoping to be there.*

EX. 3.7 *Décrivez les personnes à l'imparfait avec les informations données.* AUDIO 28.6

1. Elle / grande / yeux bleus / cheveux blonds.

____

2. Il / petit / yeux bruns / cheveux courts.

____

3. Elle / de taille moyenne / une chemise et des lunettes (porter).

____

⇨ To talk about actions happening at the same time. AUDIO 28.7

Elle **rangeait** la terrasse pendant que les enfants **jouaient**.
She was tidying up the patio while the kids were playing.
Il **travaillait** et elle **répondait** au téléphone.
He was working and she was answering the phone.

EX. 3.8 *Conjuguez les verbes donnés à l'imparfait.* AUDIO 28.8

1. Nous ______________ (faire) la vaisselle pendant qu'ils ______________ (préparer) le dessert.
2. Pendant qu'elle ______________ (accoucher), Il ______________ (être) dans les embouteillages.
3. J' ______________ (attendre) toujours le bus pendant qu'il ______________ (être) déjà à la maison.
4. Le marché ______________ (s'effondrer) pendant qu'il ______________ (voyager) en Europe.
5. Tu ______________ (étudier) pendant qu'elle ______________ (passer) son examen.

AUDIO 28.9

⇨ After **si**:

Si seulement j'**avais** plus de temps ! *If only I had more time!*

⇨ After **et si** as a suggestion:

Et si tu **venais** ce week-end ? *And what if you came this weekend?*
Et si on se **voyait** ce soir ? *What about we meet tonight?*

EX. 3.9 *Ajoutez la fin des phrases en imaginant que vous parlez à un ami.*

1. Et si tu ____ ?
2. Et si tu ____ ?
3. Et si tu ____ ?
4. Et si tu ____ ?
5. Et si tu ____ ?

Other Important Points About the Imparfait

AUDIO 28.10

⇨ **Aller + infinitive** To be going + infinitive

J'**allais** partir. *I was going to leave.*
Il **allait** la demander en mariage. *He was going to ask her to marry him.*

⇨ **Venir de + infinitive** To have just +

Il **venait** d'arriver. *He had just arrived.*

⇨ **Être en train de + infinitive** To be in the process of doing

Nous **étions** en train d'étudier. *We were (in the process) of studying.*

⇨ **Être sur le point de + infinitive** To be about to +

Ils **étaient** sur le point de divorcer. *They were about to get divorced.*

EX. 3.10 *Complétez les phrases avec les verbes entre parenthèses, conjuguez le verbe et ajoutez la négation (**ne ... pas - ne ... jamais**) si vous ne faisiez pas cela quand vous étiez petit - petite.* AUDIO 28.11

Quand j'étais petit - petite:

1. Je ______________________________ des légumes. (manger)
2. Je ______________________________ au football. (jouer)
3. Je ______________________________ du vélo. (faire)
4. J' ______________________________ tous les jours. (étudier)
5. Je ______________________________ avec mes parents. (se disputer)
6. J' ______________________________ le chocolat. (adorer)
7. J' ______________________________ bon à l'école. (être)
8. Je ______________________________ la télévision. (regarder)
9. Je ______________________________ toujours. (se salir)

CHAPTER 4

Passé Composé Imparfait

Perfect Tense vs Imperfect
Le Passé Composé vs l'Imparfait

One of the major difficulties for French learners is knowing **when to use the passé composé** or **when to use the imparfait.** Let's review when to use each:

> The **imparfait** is used to talk about the past, mostly actions and situations without a specific timeframe that happened an unspecified number of times or were in progress when *something else* happened.

> The **passé composé** is used to talk about the past, mostly actions that took place in the past and were completed in the past.

When having both definitions together, we can see that the ***something else*** that happens in the **imparfait** is indeed the **passé composé.**

The **passé composé** is the action that happens during the **imparfait.**

The **imparfait** is the big picture, while the **passé composé** can be measured in time.

AUDIO **29.1**

Je regardais la télévsion quand le téléphone **a sonné.**
I was watching TV when the phone rang.

Je regardais = Big picture = **imparfait**

Le téléphone a sonné = Something happens = **passé composé**

EX. 4.1 *Traduisez et conjuguez chaque verbe au passé composé et à l'imparfait.* AUDIO 29.2

	Verbe	*Passé composé*	*Imparfait*
1.	To participate	Nous ______	Nous ______
2.	To do	Nous ______	Nous ______
3.	To go	Nous ______	Nous ______
4.	To put	Nous ______	Nous ______
5.	To study	Nous ______	Nous ______
6.	To change	Nous ______	Nous ______
7.	To say	Nous ______	Nous ______
8.	To know	Nous ______	Nous ______
9.	To apply	Nous ______	Nous ______
10.	To wait	Nous ______	Nous ______

EX. 4.2 *Dans le texte ci-dessous, trouvez les verbes conjugués à l'imparfait et ceux conjugués au passé composé.* AUDIO 29.3

Il travaillait sur son ordinateur quand sa femme lui a demandé : « Est-ce que tu as réparé la machine à café ? ». Non, je n'ai pas eu le temps. Je devais préparer les documents pour la réunion.

Imparfait : ______

______

Passé composé : ______

______

EX. 4.3 *Conjuguez les verbes donnés au passé composé ou à l'imparfait.* AUDIO 29.4

1. J' ______ (étudier) le lundi.
2. Il ______ (renverser) le café sur la cliente.
3. Mon grand-père ______ (fumer) beaucoup.
4. Elle ______ (naître) il y a quelques jours.
5. En général, je ______ (faire) mes devoirs le soir.

6. Ma collègue ______________________ (être) sur le point de démissionner.
7. C' ______________________ (être) incroyable !
8. Ton père ______________________ (avoir) toujours de bonnes notes.
9. Mon frère ______________________ (acheter) un cadeau pour les enfants.
10. Mon patron m' ______________________ (croire).

EX. 4.4 *Traduisez les phrases en français, les verbes seront conjugués à l'imparfait ou au passé composé.* **AUDIO 29.5**

1. You never listened to me!

____

2. I took a coffee to go (à emporter).

____

3. There was a party at my house last night.

____

4. My dad used to work here.

____

5. My turtle died after 10 years.

____

6. I didn't take my umbrella.

____

7. This book was great!

____

8. We weren't here in January.

____

9. Have you read the book I recommended you?

____

10. I was really disappointed.

____

EX. 4.5 *Choisissez le bon verbe dans la liste et conjuguez-le au passé composé ou à l'imparfait.*

AUDIO 29.6

chanter - vérifier - se maquiller - regarder - aller - faire - être - avoir - fermer - boire voir - être

1. J' ______________________ de la poterie pendant plusieurs années.
2. Avant ma grossesse, je ______________________ un verre de vin à chaque repas.
3. Est-ce que tu ______________________ la porte ?
4. Elle ______________________ les cheveux noirs et les yeux bleus.
5. Mon père ______________________ toujours mes devoirs après moi.
6. Elle ______________________ avant de partir.
7. Tu ______________________ tellement bien.
8. Quand tu ______________________ petite, tu ne ______________________ jamais la télévision.
9. Est-ce qu'il ______________________ à la banque quand tu l' ______________________ ?
10. Mes cousins ______________________ très proches.

EX. 4.6 *Voici une lettre qui raconte mes vacances, conjuguez les verbes entre parenthèses à l'imparfait ou au passé composé.* AUDIO 29.7

Je ______________________ (rentrer) de vacances ce matin, c' ______________________ (être) super ! Le temps ______________________ (être) parfait, la nourriture ______________________ (être) bonne et l'hôtel ______________________ (être) magnifique. L'eau de la piscine ______________________ (être) un petit peu froide mais après quelques minutes cela ______________________ (aller).

Le premier jour nous ______________________ (aller) en excursion autour du lac, et nous ______________________ (manger) dans un restaurant italien. Après cela, nous ______________________ (avoir) quelques jours de repos jusqu'au vendredi où nous ______________________ (aller) à la montagne pour le week-end. Nous ______________________ (rester) dans un petit chalet, le chalet ______________________ (être) très mignon. Il ______________________ (faire) beaucoup plus chaud qu'à la mer où nous ______________________ (rester) pendant la semaine. Nous ______________________ (faire) de la randonnée, j' ______________________ aussi ______________________ (essayer) l'escalade mais je ______________________ (ne pas aimer). Le dernier jour, nous ______________________ (manger) tous ensemble avant de préparer nos valises. Le bus ______________________ (avoir) deux heures de retard mais nous ______________________ (jouer) à des jeux en attendant.

J'espère y retourner l'année prochaine car je ______________________ (se faire) beaucoup de nouveaux amis.

À bientôt,
Dylane.

EX. 4.7 *Racontez vos propres vacances.*

____

____

____

____

____

____

____

____

____

EX. 4.8 *Dans ces phrases, choisissez si le verbe doit être conjugué à l'imparfait ou au passé composé.* AUDIO 29.8

1. Je ____________________ (se préparer) à aller au lit quand soudain, la tempête ____________________ (commencer).
2. Elle ____________________ (vouloir) te dire au revoir mais tu ____________________ (partir) trop vite.
3. Quand il ____________________ (se réveiller), il ____________________ (être) déjà en retard.
4. La voisine ____________________ (surprendre) son mari qui ____________________ (être) avec une autre femme.
5. Au moment où le professeur ____________________ (entrer) dans la classe, Paul ____________________ (jouer) avec son téléphone.
6. J' ____________________ (essayer) de faire mes devoirs mais je n' ____________________ (avoir) pas mon cahier.
7. Nous ____________________ (aller) en Espagne quand nous ____________________ (être) jeunes mariés.
8. Le téléphone ____________________ (fonctionner) puis soudainement, il ____________________ (s'éteindre).
9. Quand les pompiers ____________________ (arriver), la maison ____________________ (être) complètement en feu.
10. Elle ____________________ (penser) réussir mais elle ____________________ (devoir) repasser son examen d'anglais.

EX. 4.9 *Trouvez l'objet direct et transformez-le en pronom direct. N'oubliez pas d'accorder le participe passé si nécessaire.* **AUDIO 29.9**

1. J'avais mes lunettes en mains il y a quelques secondes.

   ____

2. Tu as déposé mes chaussures chez le cordonnier ?

   ____

3. Il faisait ses achats l'après-midi.

   ____

4. Le pâtissier a préparé une tarte.

   ____

5. Elle rangeait sa chambre tous les soirs.

   ____

6. Est-ce que tu as pris le train ce matin ?

   ____

7. C'est comme ça que je portais mon sac quand j'étais jeune.

   ____

8. Elle a goûté ta sauce et elle a adoré !

   ____

9. Il choisissait toujours cette série.

   ____

10. J'ai déposé les chèques ce matin.

   ____

CHAPTER 5

The Recent Past
Le Passé Récent

The Recent Past - Le Passé Récent

After learning the passé composé and the imparfait, the **recent past** is going to be incredibly easy!

The recent past is called **passé récent** in French, simply because it just happened.

To build the **passé récent**, all you need to do is conjugate the verb **venir** in the present tense and add **de** and the infinitive verb of the action you want to describe. It's also common to have **juste** between **venir** and **de.**

Note that **venir de + location** translates to coming from + location. Here we add the infinitive after the verb **venir.**

> **Je viens de** + infinitive = I have just done – I just did
> **Je viens juste de** + infinitive = I have just done – I just did

The verb **venir** - present tense: AUDIO 30.1

Je **viens**	Nous **venons**
Tu **viens**	Vous **venez**
Il-Elle-On **vient**	Ils-Elles **viennent**

De becomes **d'** when followed by an infinitive verb starting with a vowel or a silent h.

AUDIO 30.2

Je **viens juste de** le voir. *I just saw him.*
Marie **vient de** m'appeler. *Marie just called me.*
Nous **venons d'**arriver. *We just arrived.*
Le bébé **vient juste de** se réveiller. *The baby just woke up.*

Venir de - Imparfait

We can also use the **passé récent** with the imparfait to talk about something that just happened before the main action in the past. Usually, we will find this construction in sentences to describe a recent action when something else happened. Because the verb is conjugated in the **imparfait,** the second verb is conjugated in the **passé composé.**

> **Je venais de** + infinitive = I had just done
> **Je venais juste de** + infinitive = I had just done

The verb **venir** – imparfait: AUDIO 30.3

Je **venais**	Nous **venions**
Tu **venais**	Vous **veniez**
Il-Elle-On **venait**	Ils-Elles **venaient**

AUDIO 30.4

Je **venais juste de** traverser la rue quand l'ambulance **est passée.**
I had just crossed the street when the ambulance passed by.

Nous **venions de** nous réveiller quand elle **est arrivée.**
We had just woken up when she arrived.

Elle **venait juste d'**acheter cette voiture quand elle **est tombée en panne.**
She had just bought this car when it broke down.

Les clients **venaient de** terminer le plat principal quand le serveur **a amené** le dessert.
The customers had just finished their main dish when the waiter brought the dessert.

EX. 5.1 *Traduisez les phrases en français.* AUDIO 30.5

1. I just arrived 5 minutes ago.

 ____

2. He just lost his (son) phone.

 ____

3. We just learned the news!

 ____

4. The children just came back from school.

 ____

5. The letter just arrived.

 ____

EX. 5.2 *Formez des phrases avec les informations données. Attention de placer "juste" au bon endroit.* AUDIO 30.6

1. Il / venir de / juste / répéter / la question.

 ____

2. Je / venir de / déposer / le colis à la poste.

 ____

3. L'artiste / venir de / finir / sa nouvelle peinture.

4. On / venir de / juste / faire / les courses.

5. Je / venir de / prendre / mes somnifères.

EX. 5.3 *Conjuguez la première phrase à l'imparfait et la deuxième phrase au passé composé. Connectez les deux phrases ensemble en utilisant l'adverbe quand.* **AUDIO 30.7**

1. Il vient de partir. Tu arrives.
   Quand :

2. Le chien vient de vomir. Il revient de la promenade.
   Quand :

3. Elle vient de manger. Elle commence à se sentir mal.
   Quand :

4. Mon père vient de réserver un vol. Son patron annule le voyage.
   Quand :

5. Ils viennent d'adopter un enfant. Elle tombe enceinte.
   Quand :

Future Tenses – Les Temps du Futur

Three tenses represent the future in French.

Le futur simple	The future tense
Le futur proche	The near future
Le futur antérieur	The future perfect

Here is how to build them:

Le futur simple – Je ferai **I will do**

Stem + ai – as – a – ons – ez – ont

Le futur proche - Je vais faire **I am going to do**

Aller (présent) + infinitive

Le futur antérieur – J'aurai fait **I will have done**

Avoir (futur) + past participle
Être (futur) + past participle

The three of them are very different in terms of conjugation and use. We'll look at the first two in the following two chapters, while the **futur antérieur** will be explained in one of the last chapters.

CHAPTER 6

The Future Tense
Le Futur Simple

The Future Tense - Le Futur Simple

The future tense, called **futur simple** in French, is the equivalent of will in English. In English, you add will in front of the verb, but we add endings to the infinitive verb in French. We don't use the stem (unless a verb is irregular), we add the ending right after verbs ending in **-er** and **-ir**.

> The **futur simple** is used to talk about future plans and intentions.

Building the Futur Simple

As mentioned in the last paragraph, to form the **futur simple**, we don't need to know the stem of the verb. We simply add the endings to the infinitive for verbs ending in **-er** and **-ir**. The endings for the **futur simple** are: **-ai, -as, -a, -ons, ez** and **-ont**.

> The endings **-ai, -ez,** have the same pronunciation = **é**
> The endings **-as, -a,** have the same pronunciation = **a**
> The endings **-ons, -ont,** have the same pronunciation = **on**
>
> *depending on the area, -ai can also be pronounced è.

Regular verbs ending in **-er**:

Ranger To tidy AUDIO 31.1

Pr.	Stem + Endings	Conjugated verb	Translation
Je	ranger -**ai**	Jeranger**ai**	I will tidy
Tu	ranger -**as**	Tu ranger**as**	You will tidy
Il	ranger -**a**	Il ranger**a**	He will tidy
Elle	ranger -**a**	Elle ranger**a**	She will tidy
On	ranger -**a**	On ranger**a**	We will tidy
Nous	ranger -**ons**	Nous ranger**ons**	We will tidy
Vous	ranger -**ez**	Vous ranger**ez**	You will tidy
Ils	ranger -**ont**	Ils ranger**ont**	They will tidy
Elles	ranger -**ont**	Elles ranger**ont**	They will tidy

Including irregular verbs endings in: AUDIO 31.2

-cer	Lancer	Je lancer**ai** – Nous lancer**ons** – Ils lancer**ont**
-ger	Manger	Je manger**ai** – Nous manger**ons** – Ils manger**ont**
-éder	Céder	Je céder**ai** – Nous céder**ons** – Ils céder**ont**
-érer	Espérer	J'espérer**ai** – Nous espérer**ons** – Ils espérer**ont**
-éter	Répéter	Je répéter**ai** – Nous répéter**ons** – Ils répéter**ont**
-ébrer	Célébrer	Je célébrer**ai** – Nous célébrer**ons** – Ils célébrer**ont**

Irregular verbs ending in **-er**:

For verbs ending in -**ayer**, **-oyer**, **-uyer**, **Y** becomes **I** in all forms.

Nettoyer To clean AUDIO 31.3

Je **nettoierai**	Nous **nettoierons**
Tu **nettoieras**	Vous **nettoierez**
Il-Elle-On **nettoiera**	Ils-Elles **nettoieront**

Other irregular verbs following the same rule:

-ayer	Essayer	J'essaier**ai** – Nous essaier**ons** – Ils essaier**ont**
-uyer	Essuyer	J'essuier**ai** – Nous essuier**ons** – Ils essuier**ont**

The verbs **appeler** and **jeter** (and compounds) double the **L** and the **T** in all forms.

Appeler To call AUDIO 31.4

J'**appellerai**	Nous **appellerons**
Tu **appelleras**	Vous **appellerez**
Il-Elle-On **appellera**	Ils-Elles **appelleront**

Jeter To throw AUDIO 31.5

Je **jetterai**	Nous **jetterons**
Tu **jetteras**	Vous **jetterez**
Il-Elle-On **jettera**	Ils-Elles **jetteront**

For verbs ending in -**eler**, -**ener**, -**eser**, -**eter**, -**ever**, **E** becomes **È** in all forms.

Geler To freeze AUDIO 31.6

Je **gèlerai**	Nous **gèlerons**
Tu **gèleras**	Vous **gèlerez**
Il-Elle-On **gèlera**	Ils-Elles **gèleront**

Other irregular verbs following the same rule:

-ener	Amener	J'amèner**ai** – Nous amèner**ons** – Ils amèner**ont**
-eser	Peser	Je pèser**ai** – Nous pèser**ons** – Ils pèser**ont**
-eter	Acheter	J'achèter**ai** – Nous achèter**ons** – Ils achèter**ont**
-ever	Achever	J'achèver**ai** – Nous achèver**ons** – Ils achèver**ont**

EX. 6.1 *Réécrivez ces phrases au futur simple.* AUDIO 31.7

1. La caissière compte l'argent avant de partir.

   ____

2. Mes parents s'inquiètent si je ne rentre pas.

   ____

3. J'amène une bouteille de vin.

   ____

4. Le film commence bientôt.

   ____

5. Nous passons dire bonjour à nos voisins.

   ____

6. On ferme le restaurant à 22 heures ce soir.

   ____

7. Ils gardent les enfants pendant que les parents seront au cinéma.

   ____

8. Elle achète le cadeau pour ses enfants ce week-end.

   ____

9. Ma famille visite Rome en janvier prochain.

   ____

10. Je porte une robe bleue au mariage.

   ____

Regular **-ir** verbs:

Accomplir To accomplish AUDIO 31.8

Pr.	Stem + Endings	Conjugated verb	Translation
J'	accomplir - **ai**	J'accomplir**ai**	I will accomplish
Tu	accomplir - **as**	Tu accomplir**as**	You will accomplish
Il	accomplir - **a**	Il accomplir**a**	He will accomplish
Elle	accomplir - **a**	Elle accomplir**a**	She will accomplish
On	accomplir - **a**	On accomplir**a**	We will accomplish
Nous	accomplir - **ons**	Nous accomplir**ons**	We will accomplish
Vous	accomplir - **ez**	Vous accomplir**ez**	You will accomplish
Ils	accomplir - **ont**	Ils accomplir**ont**	They will accomplish
Elles	accomplir - **ont**	Elles accomplir**ont**	They will accomplish

Including irregular verbs endings in -ir: AUDIO 31.9

Ouvrir	J'ouvrir**ai** – Nous ouvrir**ons** – Ils ouvrir**ont**
Offrir	J'offrir**ai** – Nous offrir**ons** – Ils offrir**ont**
Accueillir	J'accueiller**ai** – Nous accueiller**ons** – Ils accueiller**ont**
Dormir	Je dormir**ai** – Nous dormir**ons** – Ils dormir**ont**
Mentir	Je mentir**ai** – Nous mentir**ons** – Ils mentir**ont**
Servir	Je servir**ai** – Nous servir**ons** – Ils servir**ont**
Fuir	Je fuir**ai** – Nous fuir**ons** – Ils fuir**ont**

EX. 6.2 *Choisissez un des verbes irréguliers ci-dessus et conjuguez-le au futur simple.*

AUDIO 31.10

1. Le magasin ______________________ bientôt.
2. Le détenu ______________________ devant les gardes qui le rattrapent.
3. Nous ______________________ nos premiers clients la semaine prochaine.
4. Je pense qu'il ne ______________________ plus jamais.
5. On ______________________ du caviar au mariage.

What about verbs ending in **-re**?

For regular verbs ending in **-re**, the stem isn't exactly the infinitive but the infinitive verb without its final **e.** This means that the stem ends with **r-** and we can add the endings right after it.

Pendre To hang AUDIO 31.11

Pr.	Stem + Endings	Conjugated verb	Translation
Je	pendr - **ai**	Je pendr**ai**	I will hang
Tu	pendr - **as**	Tu pendr**as**	You will hang
Il	pendr - **a**	Il pendr**a**	He will hang
Elle	pendr - **a**	Elle pendr**a**	She will hang
On	pendr - **a**	On pendr**a**	We will hang
Nous	pendr - **ons**	Nous pendr**ons**	We will hang
Vous	pendr - **ez**	Vous pendr**ez**	You will hang
Ils	pendr - **ont**	Ils pendr**ont**	They will hang
Elles	pendr - **ont**	Elles pendr**ont**	They will hang

Including irregular verbs endings in **-re**: AUDIO 31.12

Prendre	Je prendr**ai** – Nous prendr**ons** – Ils prendr**ont**
Craindre	Je craindr**ai** – Nous craindr**ons** – Ils craindr**ont**
Éteindre	J'éteindr**ai** – Nous éteindr**ons** – Ils éteindr**ont**
Joindre	Je joindr**ai** – Nous joindr**ons** – Ils joindr**ont**
Battre	Je battr**ai** – Nous battr**ons** – Ils battr**ont**
Mettre	Je mettr**ai** – Nous mettr**ons** – Ils mettr**ont**
Boire	Je boir**ai** – Nous boir**ons** – Ils boir**ont**
Écrire	J'écrir**ai** – Nous écrir**ons** – Ils écrir**ont**
Suivre	Je suivr**ai** – Nous suivr**ons** – Ils suivr**ont**
Conduire	Je conduir**ai** – Nous conduir**ons** – Ils conduir**ont**
Croire	Je croir**ai** – Nous croir**ons** – Ils croir**ont**
Dire	Je dir**ai** – Nous dir**ons** – Ils dir**ont**
Rire	Je rir**ai** – Nous rir**ons** – Ils rir**ont**

EX. 6.3 *Conjuguez ces phrases au futur simple.* AUDIO 31.13

1. Tu mets le lait au frigo avant de partir.

   ____

2. Je conduis les enfants au tournoi de football.

   ____

3. Nous prenons toutes les précautions nécessaires.

   ____

4. Je lui dis que tu ne peux pas venir à la réunion.

____

5. Il nous rejoint dès qu'il aura fini.

____

Other irregular verbs and compounds are also irregular when conjugated in the **futur simple**:

AUDIO 31.14

Aller	J'**ir**ai – Nous **ir**ons – Ils **ir**ont
Avoir	J'**aur**ai – Nous **aur**ons – Ils **aur**ont
Courir	Je **courr**ai – Nous **courr**ons – Ils **courr**ont
Devoir	Je **devr**ai – Nous **devr**ons – Ils **devr**ont
Envoyer	J'**enverr**ai – Nous **enverr**ons – Ils **enverr**ont
Être	Je **ser**ai – Nous **ser**ons – Ils **ser**ont
Faire	Je **fer**ai – Nous **fer**ons – Ils **fer**ont
Mourir	Je **mourr**ai – Nous **mourr**ons – Ils **mourr**ont
Pouvoir	Je **pourr**ai – Nous **pourr**ons – Ils **pourr**ont
Recevoir	Je **recevr**ai – Nous **recevr**ons – Ils **recevr**ont
Savoir	Je **saur**ai – Nous **saur**ons – Ils **saur**ont
Tenir	Je **tiendr**ai – Nous **tiendr**ons – Ils **tiendr**ont
Valoir	Je **vaudr**ai – Nous **vaudr**ons – Ils **vaudr**ont
Venir	Je **viendr**ai – Nous **viendr**ons – Ils **viendr**ont
Vouloir	Je **voudr**ai – Nous **voudr**ons – Ils **voudr**ont

The impersonal verbs:

Falloir To be necessary	Il **faudr**a
Pleuvoir To rain	Il **pleuvr**a

Il y a:

Il y aura There will be

EX. 6.4. *Construisez des phrases personnelles avec les verbes irréguliers ci-dessus.*

1. Savoir ____
2. Il y a ____
3. Courir ____
4. Avoir ____
5. Faire ____

When to Use the Futur Simple

The **futur simple** is used in these situations:

⇨ To simply talk about something that is going to happen in the future.

Here is a list of words frequently used with the **futur simple**: AUDIO 31.15

Bientôt	Soon
Ce soir	Tonight
Demain	Tomorrow
La semaine prochaine	Next week
Le mois prochain	Next month
Lundi, mardi, ...	On Monday, on Tuesday, ...
Dans quelques jours	In a few days
Dans une semaine	In a week
Dans deux ans	In two years
À l'avenir	In the future
Un jour	One day

Nous **serons** bientôt là. *We will be there soon.*
Un jour, je **visiterai** l'Australie. *One day, I will visit Australia.*

EX. 6.5 *Faites de phrases avec les éléments donnés. Conjuguez le verbe au futur simple.*
AUDIO 31.16

1. Lundi / je / être / aux Bahamas.

____

2. Demain / nous / aller / chez mes parents.

____

3. Nous / recevoir / les clés / dans quelques jours.

____

4. Un jour / ils / venir / nous voir.

____

5. Dans deux ans / je / avoir / 35 ans.

____

⇨ To make suppositions about the future: AUDIO 31.17

Je pense qu'il **arrivera** en retard. *I think he will arrive late.*
Tu ne **seras** pas prêt pour ce soir. *You won't be ready for tonight.*

EX. 6.6 *Conjuguez le verbe au futur simple.* AUDIO 31.18

1. Je pense que tu (devenir) ______________________________ acteur.
2. Nous pensons que le ministre (être) ______________________ président.
3. Tu penses que tu (pouvoir) ____________________________ venir ?

⇨ After conjunctions of time: AUDIO 31.19

English uses the present tense after a conjunction of time in the subordinate clause, even when it's understood that the action will happen in the future. In French, a subordinate clause following a conjunction of time is always conjugated in the **futur simple**.

Quand	When
Lorsque – Lorsqu'	When
Aussitôt que – qu'	As soon as
Dès que – qu'	As soon as
Après que – qu'	After

Appelle-moi quand tu **recevras** l'invitation.
Call me when you get the invitation.

Vois avec elle dès qu'elle **sera** de retour.
See that with her when she is back.

Je commencerai à nettoyer aussitôt que tu **partiras.**
I will start cleaning as soon as you leave.

EX. 6.7 *Traduisez ces phrases en français.* AUDIO 31.20

1. The desk will arrive tomorrow.

____

2. I will be at the office to sign the contract.

____

3. They will be there.

____

4. My parents will visit (rendre visite) us this summer.

5. The cleaning lady will start next month.

6. We will hire more people (de gens) as soon as we can.

7. I hope he will survive the surgery!

8. We will probably watch this movie this weekend.

9. The theater will open soon!

10. The students will graduate (être diplômé) in June.

EX. 6.8 *Changez les phrases du futur proche au futur simple.* AUDIO 31.21

1. Je vais être en retard.

2. Mon mari va chercher les enfants à l'école.

3. Nous allons vivre à l'étranger pendant quelques années.

4. Il va être docteur à la fin de ses études.

5. Il va couler un bain pour sa femme.

6. Nous allons téléphoner pour avoir plus de nouvelles.

7. Quand il va recevoir le paquet, il va être surpris !

____

8. La province va commencer à recycler le plastique en 2022.

____

9. Les oiseaux vont manger les graines du jardin.

____

10. Il ne va pas se souvenir de tous ces beaux paysages.

____

CHAPTER 7

The Near Future
Le Futur Proche

The Near Future - Le Futur Proche

The near future is called **futur proche** in French, simply because it's going to happen in the **near future**.

To build the **futur proche,** all you need to do is to conjugate the verb **aller** in the present tense and add the infinitive verb of the action you want to describe.

Je vais + infinitive = I am going to + infinitive

The verb **aller** - present tense: AUDIO 32.1

Je **vais**	Nous **allons**
Tu **vas**	Vous **allez**
Il-Elle-On **va**	Ils-Elles **vont**

We use the **futur proche** to talk about an action that is going to happen in the near future or to talk about a planned action in the near future. AUDIO 32.2

On **va nager**. *We are going to swim.*
Elles **vont apprendre** la cuisine. *They are going to learn to cook.*

When the infinitive verb (second verb) is reflexive, the reflexive pronoun agrees with the subject. AUDIO 32.3

Je **vais <u>me</u> faire** un café. *I am going to make myself a coffee.*
Tu **vas <u>te</u> faire** un café. *You are going to make yourself a coffee.*
Il **va <u>se</u> faire** un café. *He is going to make himself a coffee.*
Nous **allons <u>nous</u> faire** un café. *We are going to make ourselves a coffee.*

EX. 7.1 *Faites une phrase en conjuguant le verbe au futur proche.* AUDIO 32.4

1. Tu / manger / une pomme.

    ____

2. Je sais / que / tu / réussir.

    ____

3. Il / pleuvoir.

    ____

4. Nous / rester / à la maison.

    ____

5. Ce créateur / essayer / de gagner / de l'argent.

____

6. Je / voir.

____

7. Le peintre / repeindre / la façade.

____

8. Est-ce que / tu / chercher / les enfants ?

____

9. Les habitants / recevoir / un chèque.

____

10. Tu penses / qu'il / neiger / ce soir ?

____

Futur Proche and Negation

As we saw before, **negation** is made of two words in French: **ne ... pas, ne ... plus, ne ... rien, etc.**

In the **futur proche**, **ne** is placed after the subject, while **pas - plus - rien** are placed after the verb aller => **ne** + aller + **pas** + infinitive.

AUDIO 32.5

> Je + **ne** + vais + **pas** + infinitive

On va nager. *We are going to swim.*
On + **ne** + va + **pas** nager
⇨ **On ne va pas nager.** *We are not going to swim.*

When the second verb is reflexive, the pronoun and the verb stay together

=> **ne** + aller + **pas + infinitive reflexive verb.**

> Je + **ne** + vais + **pas** + infinitive reflexive verb

Je vais me faire un café. *I am going to make myself a coffee.*
Je + **ne** + vais + **pas** me faire un café
⇨ **Je ne vais pas me faire un café.** *I am not going to make myself a coffee.*

EX. 7.2 *Transformez ces phrases en phrases négatives.* AUDIO 32.6

1. Il va prendre le train.

   ____

2. Je vais ramener le livre à la bibliothèque.

   ____

3. Elle va appeler le dentiste pour prendre rendez-vous.

   ____

4. On va s'occuper des enfants.

   ____

5. Le train va arriver en gare.

   ____

6. Tu vas te laver maintenant ?

   ____

7. Mon ami va aller à l'université.

   ____

8. Tu vas être en retard !

   ____

9. Il va se couper s'il ne fait pas attention.

   ____

10. Tu vas te brosser les dents ?

    ____

EX. 7.3 *Listez 5 activités que vous allez faire dans un futur proche.*

1. Aujourd'hui, je vais ______________________________ .
2. Ce matin, je vais ______________________________ .
3. Je vais ______________________________ maintenant.
4. Je vais ______________________________ dans 5 minutes.
5. Ce soir, je vais ______________________________ .

CHAPTER 8

The Conditional
Le Conditionnel

The Present Conditional
Le Conditionnel Présent

The present conditional, called **conditionnel présent** in French, is the equivalent of would + infinitive in English. When in English you add would in front of the verb, we add endings to the infinitive verb.

We use it to **ask something politely, to express a wish or to talk about something that would happen "if", about a possibility.**

> The **conditionnel** is used in a similar way as in English.

Building the Conditional

To form the **conditionnel présent**, we are going to **add the endings of the imparfait to the stem used with the futur simple.**

The endings of the imparfait are: **-ais, -ais, -ait, -ions, iez and -aient.**

> The endings **-ais, -ait, -aient** have the same pronunciation.

Regular verbs ending in **-er**:

Ranger To tidy AUDIO 33.1

Futur simple	Stem + imp. endings	Conditionnel	Translation
Je rangerai	ranger - **ais**	Je ranger**ais**	I would tidy
Tu rangeras	ranger - **ais**	Tu ranger**ais**	You would tidy
Il rangera	ranger - **ait**	Il ranger**ait**	He would tidy
Elle rangera	ranger - **ait**	Elle ranger**ait**	She would tidy
On rangera	ranger - **ait**	On ranger**ait**	We would tidy
Nous rangerons	ranger - **ions**	Nous ranger**ions**	We would tidy
Vous rangerez	ranger - **iez**	Vous ranger**iez**	You would tidy
Ils rangeront	ranger - **aient**	Ils ranger**aient**	They would tidy
Elles rangeront	ranger - **aient**	Elles ranger**aient**	They would tidy

Including irregular verbs endings in: AUDIO 33.2

-cer	Lancer	Je lancer**ais** – Nous lancer**ions** – Ils lancer**aient**
-ger	Manger	Je manger**ais** – Nous manger**ions** – Ils manger**aient**
-éder	Céder	Je céder**ais** – Nous céder**ions** – Ils céder**aient**
-érer	Espérer	J'espérer**ais** – Nous espérer**ions** – Ils espérer**aient**
-éter	Répéter	Je répéter**ais** – Nous répéter**ions** – Ils répéter**aient**
-ébrer	Célébrer	Je célébrer**ais** – Nous célébrer**ions** – Ils célébrer**aient**

Irregular verbs ending in **-er**:

For verbs ending in **-ayer**, **-oyer**, **-uyer**, **Y** becomes **I** in all forms.

Nettoyer To clean AUDIO 33.3

Je **nettoierais**	Nous **nettoierions**
Tu **nettoierais**	Vous **nettoieriez**
Il-Elle-On **nettoierait**	Ils-Elles **nettoieraient**

Other irregular verbs following the same rule:

-ayer	Essayer	J'essaier**ais** – Nous essaier**ions** – Ils essaier**aient**
-uyer	Essuyer	J'essuier**ais** – Nous essuier**ions** – Ils essuier**aient**

The verbs **appeler** and **jeter** (and compounds) double the **L** and the **T** in all forms.

Appeler To call AUDIO 33.4

J'**appellerais**	Nous **appellerions**
Tu **appellerais**	Vous **appelleriez**
Il-Elle-On **appellerait**	Ils-Elles **appelleraient**

Jeter To throw AUDIO 33.5

Je **jetterais**	Nous **jetterions**
Tu **jetterais**	Vous **jetteriez**
Il-Elle-On **jetterait**	Ils-Elles **jetteraient**

For verbs ending in **-eler**, **-ener**, **-eser**, **-eter**, **-ever**, **E** becomes **È** in all forms.

Geler To freeze AUDIO 33.6

Je **gèlerais**	Nous **gèlerions**
Tu **gèlerais**	Vous **gèleriez**
Il-Elle-On **gèlerait**	Ils-Elles **gèleraient**

Other irregular verbs following the same rule: AUDIO 33.7

-ener	Amener	J'amèner**ais** – Nous amèner**ions** – Ils amèner**aient**
-eser	Peser	Je pèser**ais** – Nous pèser**ions** – Ils pèser**aient**
-eter	Acheter	J'achèter**ais** – Nous achèter**ions** – Ils achèter**aient**
-ever	Achever	J'achèver**ais** – Nous achèver**ions** – Ils achèver**aient**

EX. 8.1 *Traduisez ces phrases en français.* AUDIO 33.8

1. I would not try. ______________________________
2. She would help. ______________________________
3. You would freeze. ______________________________
4. I would bring. ______________________________
5. He would clean. ______________________________

Regular **-ir** verbs:

Accomplir To accomplish AUDIO 33.9

Futur simple	Stem + imp. endings	Conditionnel	Translation
J'accomplirai	accomplir - **ais**	J'accompli**rais**	I would accomplish
Tu accompliras	accomplir - **ais**	Tu accompli**rais**	You would accomplish
Il accomplira	accomplir - **ait**	Il accompli**rait**	He would accomplish
Elle accomplira	accomplir - **ait**	Elle accompli**rait**	She would accomplish
On accomplira	accomplir - **ait**	On accompli**rait**	We would accomplish
Nous accomplirons	accomplir - **ions**	Nous accompli**rions**	We would accomplish
Vous accomplirez	accomplir - **iez**	Vous accompli**riez**	You would accomplish
Ils accompliront	accomplir - **aient**	Ils accompli**raient**	They would accomplish
Elles accompliront	accomplir - **aient**	Elles accompli**raient**	They would accomplish

Including irregular verbs endings in -ir: AUDIO 33.10

Ouvrir	J'ouvrir**ais** – Nous ouvrir**ions** – Ils ouvrir**aient**
Offrir	J'offrir**ais** – Nous offrir**ions** – Ils offrir**aient**
Accueillir	J'accueiller**ais** – Nous accueiller**ions** – Ils accueiller**aient**
Dormir	Je dormir**ais** – Nous dormir**ions** – Ils dormir**aient**
Mentir	Je mentir**ais** – Nous mentir**ions** – Ils mentir**aient**
Servir	Je servir**ais** – Nous servir**ions** – Ils servir**aient**
Fuir	Je fuir**ais** – Nous fuir**ions** – Ils fuir**aient**

EX. 8.2 *Choisissez un des verbes irréguliers ci-dessus et conjuguez-le au conditionnel présent.*

AUDIO 33.11

1. Nous ______________________________ un compte en banque.
2. Elle ______________________________ toute la journée.
3. On ______________________________ un cadeau.
4. Je ______________________________ des nouilles au tofu.
5. Les hôtesses ______________________________ les nouveaux clients.

What about verbs ending in **-re**?

Pendre To hang AUDIO 33.12

Futur simple	Stem + imp. endings	Conditionnel	Translation
Je pendrai	pendr - **ais**	Je pendr**ais**	I would hang
Tu pendras	pendr - **ais**	Tu pendr**ais**	You would hang
Il pendra	pendr - **ait**	Il pendr**ait**	He would hang
Elle pendra	pendr - **ait**	Elle pendr**ait**	She would hang
On pendra	pendr - **ait**	On pendr**ait**	We would hang
Nous pendrons	pendr - **ions**	Nous pendr**ions**	We would hang
Vous pendrez	pendr - **iez**	Vous pendr**iez**	You would hang
Ils pendront	pendr - **aient**	Ils pendr**aient**	They would hang
Elles pendront	pendr - **aient**	Elles pendr**aient**	They would hang

Including irregular verbs endings in **-re**: AUDIO 33.13

Prendre	Je prendr**ais** – Nous prendr**ions** – Ils prendr**aient**
Craindre	Je craindr**ais** – Nous craindr**ions** – Ils craindr**aient**
Éteindre	J'éteindr**ais** – Nous éteindr**ions** – Ils éteindr**aient**
Joindre	Je joindr**ais** – Nous joindr**ions** – Ils joindr**aient**
Battre	Je battr**ais** – Nous battr**ions** – Ils battr**aient**
Mettre	Je mettr**ais** – Nous mettr**ions** – Ils mettr**aient**
Boire	Je boir**ais** – Nous boir**ions** – Ils boir**aient**
Écrire	J'écrir**ais** – Nous écrir**ions** – Ils écrir**aient**
Suivre	Je suivr**ais** – Nous suivr**ions** – Ils suivr**aient**
Conduire	Je conduir**ais** – Nous conduir**ions** – Ils conduir**aient**
Croire	Je croir**ais** – Nous croir**ions** – Ils croir**aient**
Dire	Je dir**ais** – Nous dir**ions** – Ils dir**aient**
Rire	Je rir**ais** – Nous rir**ions** – Ils rir**aient**

EX. 8.3 *Conjuguez ces phrases au conditionnel présent.* AUDIO 33.14

1. Je prends des nouvelles de mes parents.

____

2. Il bat ses adversaires à chaque fois.

____

3. Ils suivent les indications du chemin.

____

4. Elle écrit avec une plume au lieu d'un stylo.

____

5. Nous pendrons les habits à l'extérieur.

____

Irregular verbs and compounds are also irregular when conjugated in **conditionnel présent**:

AUDIO 33.15

Aller	J'**ir**ais – Nous **ir**ions – Ils **ir**aient
Avoir	J'**aur**ais – Nous **aur**ions – Ils **aur**aient
Courir	Je **courr**ais – Nous **courr**ions – Ils **courr**aient
Envoyer	J'**enverr**ais – Nous **enverr**ions – Ils **enverr**aient
Être	Je **ser**ais – Nous **ser**ions – Ils **ser**aient
Faire	Je **fer**ais – Nous **fer**ions – Ils **fer**aient
Mourir	Je **mourr**ais – Nous **mourr**ions – Ils **mourr**aient
Recevoir	Je **recevr**ais – Nous **recevr**ions – Ils **recevr**aient
Savoir	Je **saur**ais – Nous **saur**ions – Ils **saur**aient
Tenir	Je **tiendr**ais – Nous **tiendr**ions – Ils **tiendr**aient
Valoir	Je **vaudr**ais – Nous **vaudr**ions – Ils **vaudr**aient
Venir	Je **viendr**ais – Nous **viendr**ions – Ils **viendr**aient

The impersonal verbs:

Falloir To be necessary	Il **faudr**ait
Pleuvoir To rain	Il **pleuvr**ait

Il y a:

Il y aurait There would be

I purposely removed the verbs **devoir, vouloir and pouvoir** from the irregular verbs list because they have a specific meaning when conjugated in the **conditionnel**. These 3 verbs are often followed by an infinitive verb.

- **Devoir** = je **devrais** — I should
- **Vouloir** = je **voudrais** — I would like
- **Pouvoir** = je **pourrais** — I could

Devoir - Should AUDIO 33.16

Je **devrais**	Nous **devrions**
Tu **devrais**	Vous **devriez**
Il-Elle-On **devrait**	Ils-Elles **devraient**

Je **devrais** partir maintenant. *I should leave now.*
Tu **devrais** étudier plus. *You should study more.*

Vouloir – Would like AUDIO 33.17

Je **voudrais**	Nous **voudrions**
Tu **voudrais**	Vous **voudriez**
Il-Elle-On **voudrait**	Ils-Elles **voudraient**

Je **voudrais** devenir actrice. *I would like to become an actress.*
Il **voudrait** parler français. *He would like to speak French.*

Pouvoir – Could AUDIO 33.18

Je **pourrais**	Nous **pourrions**
Tu **pourrais**	Vous **pourriez**
Il-Elle-On **pourrait**	Ils-Elles **pourraient**

Nous **pourrions** peut-être aider. *We could maybe help.*
Pourriez-vous vous inscrire ? *Could you register?*

EX. 8.4 *Faites des phrases personnelles avec ce que vous devriez faire, pourriez faire et voudriez faire.*

1. ______________________________
2. ______________________________
3. ______________________________
4. ______________________________
5. ______________________________

When to Use the Conditional

The **conditionnel présent** is used in these situations:

⇨ To talk about something that would happen "if", a possibility. AUDIO 33.19

Ça **serait** mieux de partir maintenant. *It would be better to leave now.*
On **pourrait** y aller demain. *We could go there tomorrow.*

EX. 8.5 *Réécrivez ces phrases au conditionnel pour que la phrase soit incertaine.* AUDIO 33.20

1. C'est bien de faire comme ça.

   ____

2. Cela vaut plus que 10 euros.

   ____

3. Il arrivera dans l'après-midi.

   ____

4. Nous serons diplômés en septembre.

   ____

5. Il dit qu'il ne peut pas venir.

   ____

⇨ To ask something politely: AUDIO 33.21

Pourrais-tu me donner son numéro ? *Could you give me his number?*
Sauriez-vous où je peux trouver un taxi ? *Would you know where I could find a taxi?*

EX. 8.6 *Demandez les informations suivantes en conjuguant le verbe au conditionnel avec le sujet donné. Conservez l'ordre du verbe et du pronom.* AUDIO 33.22

1. Pouvoir / je / avoir / un café ?

   ____

2. Pouvoir / tu / nous / aider / à déménager ?

   ____

3. Savoir / vous / nous / indiquer / la gare ?

____

4. Pouvoir / vous / nous / laisser / un peu de place ?

____

5. Savoir / tu / m'aider / à changer / de numéro de téléphone ?

____

⇨ To express a wish: AUDIO 33.23

Here is a list of verbs frequently used to express a wish. Verbs are often followed by an infinitive:

Aimer	To like
Vouloir	To want
Désirer	To desire
Souhaiter	To wish - To like

Je **souhaiterais** gagner à la loterie. *I would like to win the lottery.*
Aimerais-tu aller au cinéma ? *Would you like to go to the movie theater?*

⇨ In sentences with **si**: AUDIO 33.24

To talk about a hypothetical situation, we are going to use **si** (if).

Si is always followed by the **imparfait**, while the second part of the sentence is conjugated with the **conditionnel présent**.

Si je gagnais à la loterie, j'achèterais une maison.
If I won the lottery, I would buy a house.

Depending on the sentence, **si** can also be in the middle of the sentence, but even then, **si** is always followed by the **imparfait**.

J'achèterais une maison si je gagnais à la loterie.
I would buy a house, if I won the lottery.

Remember to ***download the audio*** *and to* ***watch the videos*** *- see Preface*

EX. 8.7 *Formez une phrase avec ces deux phrases et conjuguez les verbes à l'imparfait et au conditionnel présent. Conservez l'ordre des phrases.* **AUDIO 33.25**

1. Je suis là. Si tu n'es pas là.

   ____

2. S'ils paient les factures. La société finit la maison.

   ____

3. Je vais à l'école. Si je me sens mieux.

   ____

4. Tu n'as pas mal à la tête. Si tu bois plus d'eau.

   ____

5. Si tu as 21 ans. Tu peux boire de l'alcool.

   ____

6. Si j'ai du temps. Je fais du sport.

   ____

7. Elle va. Si elle a envie.

   ____

8. Si elle marche plus. Elle se sent plus en forme.

   ____

9. Si on a de l'argent. On travaille moins.

   ____

10. Si vous fumez moins. Vous vivez plus longtemps.

    ____

CHAPTER 9

The Imperative
L'Impératif

The Imperative - L'Impératif

The imperative, called **impératif** in French, is the tense used to give orders and advice.

It's used the same way as in English. AUDIO 34.1

Mange Eat
Dors Sleep
Attends Wait

The **impératif** is only used with **tu**, **nous** and **vous**.

Building the Imperative

To form the **impératif**, take the verb conjugated in the present tense with **tu**, **nous** and **vous**, and don't use the subject pronouns.

Verbs ending in **-er** and other verbs that end in **-es** in the **tu** form, only take **-e** with **tu**, without the **s**.

Regarder To look AUDIO 34.2

Present tense	Imperative	
Tu regardes	Regarde	Look
Nous regardons	Regardons	Let's look
Vous regardez	Regardez	Look

Finir To finish AUDIO 34.3

Present tense	Imperative	
Tu finis	Finis	Finish
Nous finissons	Finissons	Let's finish
Vous finissez	Finissez	Finish

Attendre To wait AUDIO 34.4

Present tense	Imperative	
Tu attends	Attends	Wait
Nous attendons	Attendons	Let's wait
Vous attendez	Attendez	Wait

Verbs with a spelling change conserve it in the **impératif.**

Changeons - Appelle - Achète - ...

Only **avoir, être, savoir** and **vouloir** are irregular. The only form used for **vouloir** is **Veuillez.**

Avoir To have	**Être** To be	**Savoir** To know	**Vouloir** To want
Aie	Sois	Sache	*Veuille*
Ayons	Soyons	Sachons	*Veuillons*
Ayez	Soyez	Sachez	Veuillez
AUDIO 34.5	AUDIO 34.6	AUDIO 34.7	AUDIO 34.8

EX. 9.1 *Conjuguez les verbes suivants à l'impératif.* AUDIO 34.9

Jeter	Dire	Prendre	Tenir
________	________	________	________
________	________	________	________
________	________	________	________

EX. 9.2 *Traduisez ces phrases en français en utilisant tu.* AUDIO 34.10

1. Come here! ____________________
2. Be here! ____________________
3. Look! ____________________
4. Leave! ____________________
5. Listen! ____________________
6. Call! ____________________
7. Read! ____________________
8. Take! ____________________
9. Close the door! ____________________
10. Turn off the TV! ____________________

The Imperative and Negation

Negation is added around the conjugated verb, with **ne** being placed before the verb and the second part of the negation (**pas, plus, rien, etc.**) placed after. AUDIO 34.11

Ne regarde pas.	Don't look.
Ne partez pas.	Don't leave.
Ne bouge plus.	Don't move anymore – Stop moving.

When a verb is followed by a preposition such as **à** or **de**, it's common to have it included before the second part of the negation:

Ne touche à rien. Don't touch anything.

EX. 9.3 *Traduisez ces phrases en français avec* ***vous.*** AUDIO 34.12

1. Don't look. ______
2. Don't drink my coffee. ______
3. Don't ask that. ______
4. Don't touch the dog. ______
5. Don't let the cat out. ______
6. Don't forget the money. ______
7. Don't answer the question. ______
8. Don't sleep late. ______
9. Don't use this tool. ______
10. Don't forget to save. ______

The Imperative and Object Pronouns

Object pronouns are placed right after the verb and are attached to the verb with a **hyphen.**

AUDIO 35.1

The object pronouns **me** becomes **moi**, and **te** becomes **toi.**

Demande-moi.	Ask me.
Regarde-toi.	Look at you.
Demandez-lui.	Ask him – her.

Regardez-les.	Look at them.
Demande-nous.	Ask us.
Allons-y.	Let's go.
Prends-en.	Take some.

The pronouns **moi** and **toi** becomes **me** and **te** in the negation:

Ne te dérange pas.	Don't move – don't bother.
Ne me parle pas.	Don't talk to me.

For verbs ending in **-er** and other verbs ending in **e** with **tu**, if the pronoun is **en** or **y**, we add an **s** as well as a liaison **[z]**.

Commandes-en.	Order some.
Restes-y.	Stay there.

EX. 9.4 *Traduisez ces phrases en français avec* ***vous.*** AUDIO 35.2

1. Look at me. ______________________________
2. Bring me the remote. ______________________________
3. Don't leave me. ______________________________
4. Take the picture. ______________________________
5. Give me the book. ______________________________
6. Tell him that. ______________________________
7. Pay them soon. ______________________________
8. Don't scare me (faire peur). ______________________________
9. Forget us. ______________________________
10. Order me a coffee. ______________________________

If the sentence requires a **direct object pronoun** and an **indirect object pronoun**, the direct object pronoun comes first and is followed by the indirect object pronoun:

The order is as follow: AUDIO 35.3

Le – L'	**Moi – M'**	**Nous**	**Y**
La – L'	**Toi – T'**	**Vous**	**En**
Les		**Lui**	
		Leur	

The object pronoun **me** becomes **moi**, and **te** becomes **toi.**

Donne le jouet au chien.	Give the toy to the dog.
Donne-le au chien.	Give it to the dog.
Donne-le-lui.	Give it to him.

The correct grammar would require the use of **m'en**, but spoken French uses **moi** followed by **en** and adds a [z] sound:

Donne-m'en.	Give me some.
Donne-moi(z)en.	Give me some.

In the negation, the order of pronouns changes and we remove the hyphen. AUDIO 35.4

The order is as follow:

Me - M'	**Le - L'**	**Lui**	**Y**
Te - T'	**La - L'**	**Leur**	**En**
Se - S'	**Les**		
Nous			
Vous			

Ne le lui donne pas.	Don't give it to him.
Ne t'en fais pas.	Don't worry.
Ne m'y rejoignez pas.	Don't meet me there.
Ne l'appelle pas.	Don't call her – him.

The Imperative of Reflexive Verbs

AUDIO 36.1

In the case of a reflexive verb, the reflexive pronoun is added after the verb and is attached to the verb by a hyphen. **Te** also becomes **toi.**

Dépêche-toi.	Hurry up.
Dépêchons-nous.	Let's hurry.
Dépêchez-vous.	Hurry up.

In the negative form, the reflexive pronoun stays **te** and is placed before the verb.

Ne te dépêche pas.	Don't hurry.
Ne nous dépêchons pas.	Let's not hurry.
Ne vous dépêchez pas.	Don't hurry.

EX. 9.5 *Faites des phrases à l'impératif avec* ***tu.*** AUDIO 36.2

1. Venir au magasin avec moi.

___

2. Ne pas boire de vin.

___

3. Mettre tes chaussures dans l'armoire.

___

4. Savoir que je suis là.

___

5. Réserver une table pour nous deux.

___

6. Aider les patients à trouver la chambre.

___

7. Ne pas rester à la maison.

___

8. Faire un gâteau pour demain.

___

9. Ne pas poser de questions.

___

10. Ne pas attendre trop longtemps.

___

EX. 9.6 *Transformez ces phrases à l'impératif.* AUDIO 36.3

1. Tu te réveilles à 6 heures du matin.

___

2. Nous sommes là pour le dîner.

___

3. Vous lisez le journal en silence.

___

Remember to ***download the audio*** *and to* ***watch the videos*** *– see Preface*

4. Tu réfléchis avant d'agir.

____

5. Nous prenons les vélos pour aller au magasin.

____

6. Vous nous attendez avant de partir.

____

7. Tu pratiques la calligraphie souvent.

____

8. Nous partons sans lui.

____

9. Vous mangez ensemble à midi.

____

10. Tu écoutes la chanson sans faire de bruit.

____

EX. 9.7 *Faites des phrases à l'impératif avec **nous**.* AUDIO 36.4

1. Être ponctuels pour le rendez-vous.

____

2. Construire une nouvelle maison.

____

3. Aller à la campagne ce week-end.

____

4. Télécharger des musiques pour le trajet.

____

5. Voir si on peut faire ça.

____

6. Applaudir l'artiste à la fin du spectacle.

____

7. Demander l'autorisation à nos parents.

____

8. Essayer de ne pas perdre d'argent dans la transaction.

____

9. Attendre que l'orage passe.

____

10. Se promener au bord du lac.

____

EX. 9.8 *Conjuguez le verbe à l'impératif et transformez l'objet direct et indirect en pronom direct et indirect.* AUDIO 36.5

1. Passer le sel à Jean.

   (tu) ____

2. Rendre le sac à sa propriétaire.

   (vous) ____

3. Lire un livre à notre petite fille.

   (nous) ____

4. Accorder moi le crédit.

   (vous) ____

5. Prêter des livres à mes amis.

   (tu) ____

6. Acheter une voiture à Kurt.

   (nous) ____

7. Lire moi le message.

   (vous) ____

8. Connecter le modem.

   (tu) ____

9. Prendre le train maintenant.

   (nous) ____

10. Regarder les bateaux arriver au port.

    (vous) ____

CHAPTER 10

Infinitive & Prepositions
Infinitif & Prépositions

Infinitive & Prepositions – Infinitif & Prépositions

Here are all the points explained in this chapter:

- **The types of infinitives**
- **Verb + infinitive**
- **Verb + à + infinitive**
- **Verb + à + noun (for information)**
- **Verb + de + infinitive**
- **Verb + de + noun (for information)**
- **Prepositions + infinitive**
- **Faire + infinitive – causative**
- **Verb + de quoi + infinitive**
- **Être + en train + de + infinitive**
- **Être + sur le point + de + infinitive**
- **Être + adjective + de + infinitive**
- **Être + adjective – past participle + à + infinitive**
- **Il est + adjective + de + infinitive**
- **C'est + adjective + de + infinitive (Informal)**
- **C'est + adjective + à + infinitive**
- **... seul_ + à + infinitive**
- **Ordinal number + à + infinitive**
- **Il faut + infinitive**
- **The past infinitive**
- **The negative infinitive**
- **Merci de + infinitive**

> Note:
>
> We already saw with **Devoir**, **Vouloir** and **Pouvoir** that the three of them can be followed by an infinitive verb.

The types of infinitives

The **present infinitive** is the unconjugated form of a verb. In English, the infinitive begins with "to". In French, infinitive verbs have specific endings depending on the group of verbs:. AUDIO 37.1

- Verbs ending in **-er** — **Chanter** To sing
- Verbs ending in **-ir** — **Finir** To finish
- Verbs ending in **-re** — **Attendre** To wait

Plus, all the irregular verbs: **Être** To be, **Avoir** To have, **Prendre** To take, **Dire** To say, etc.

Verb + infinitive

When two verbs follow each other, the **second verb** is always infinitive (unless in specific conjugations such as the *passé composé*). It happens the same way as in English, **J'aime chanter** I like to sing.

Some verbs are followed by an infinitive verb without a preposition between them.

Here are the most common French verbs with no preposition: AUDIO 37.2

Adorer faire qqch	To love doing sth
Aimer faire qqch	To like – enjoy doing sth
Aimer mieux faire qqch	To rather do sth
Aller faire qqch	To be going to do sth
Avouer faire qqch	To admit to do sth
Compter faire qqch	To intend to do sth
Courir faire qqch	To run to do sth
Désirer faire qqch	To want to do sth
Détester faire qqch	To hate to do sth
Devoir faire qqch	To have to do sth
Écouter (qqn) faire qqch	To listen (someone) do sth
Emmener (qqn) faire qqch	To take (someone) to do sth
Envoyer (qqn) faire qqch	To send (someone) to do sth
Espérer faire qqch	To hope to do sth
Être censé faire qqch	To be supposed to do sth
Faire faire qqch	To have sth done
Falloir faire qqch	Must do sth about it
Laisser faire qqch	To allow – let sth to be done
Oser faire qqch	To dare to do sth
Penser faire qqch	To consider doing sth
Pouvoir faire qqch	To be able to do sth
Préférer faire qqch	To prefer to do sth
Prétendre faire qqch	To pretend to do sth
Regarder (qqn) faire qqch	To watch someone do sth
Savoir faire qqch	To know *how* to do sth
Sembler faire qqch	To seem to be doing sth
Souhaiter faire qqch	To wish to do sth
Venir faire qqch	To come to do sth
Vouloir faire qqch	To want to do sth

J'**aime cuisiner** quand j'ai le temps. *I like to cook when I have time.*
Il **semble oublier** ses propres erreurs. *He seems to forget his own mistakes.*
Elle **souhaite s'inscrire** aux cours. *She wishes to register for classes.*
Nous **espérons partir** en vacances bientôt. *We hope to go on vacation soon.*
Le plombier **vient réparer** la chaudière. *The plumber is coming to fix the furnace.*

*Remember to **download the audio** and to **watch the videos** – see Preface*

EX. 10.1 *Traduisez les phrases suivantes.* AUDIO 37.3

1. He is pretending to listen to the teacher.

____

2. He wants to leave now.

____

3. I love playing with Lego.

____

4. We have to pay the bills today.

____

5. He hopes to succeed with his new idea.

____

6. She considers selling her house.

____

7. I prefer sleeping in my bed.

____

8. He doesn't dare to jump.

____

9. She knows how to study fast.

____

10. We want to buy a new couch.

____

Verb + à + infinitive

In this case, the preposition **à** is required before adding the infinitive verb. These verbs don't follow a specific rule, so keep this list and refer to it when needed.

Here is the list of French verbs followed by à and an infinitive verb: AUDIO 37.4

Aider à faire qqch	To help to do sth
S'amuser à faire qqch	To have fun doing sth
Apprendre à faire qqch	To learn how to do sth
Arriver à faire qqch	To manage – succeed in doing sth
Aspirer à faire qqch	To aspire to do sth
S'attendre à faire qqch	To expect to do sth

S'autoriser à faire qqch	To allow oneself to do sth
Avoir à faire qqch	To have to – be obliged to do sth
Chercher à faire qqch	To attempt to do sth
Commencer à faire qqch	To begin to do sth
Consentir à faire qqch	To agree to do sth
Continuer à faire qqch	To continue to do sth
Se décider à faire qqch	To make up one's mind to do sth
Encourager qqn **à** faire qqch	To encourage sb to do sth
S'engager à faire qqch	To commit to do sth
S'épuiser à faire qqch	To exhaust oneself doing sth
Forcer qqn **à** faire qqch	To force sb to do sth
S'habituer à faire qqch	To get used to doing sth
Hésiter à faire qqch	To hesitate to do sth
Inviter qqn **à** faire qqch	To invite sb to do sth
Se mettre à faire qqch	To start doing sth
Obliger qqn **à** faire qqch	To force sb to do sth
Parvenir à faire qqch	To succeed in doing sth
Passer du temps **à** faire qqch	To spend time doing sth
Perdre du temps **à** faire qqch	To waste time doing sth
Persister à faire qqch	To persist in doing sth
Pousser qqn **à** faire qqch	To push sb to do sth
Se préparer à faire qqch	To prepare oneself to do sth
Recommencer à faire qqch	To start doing sth again
Réfléchir à faire qqch	To think of doing sth
Renoncer à faire qqch	To give up doing sth
Résister à faire qqch	To resist doing sth
Réussir à faire qqch	To succeed in doing sth
Servir à faire qqch	To be used to do sth
Songer à faire qqch	To think of doing sth
Tenir à faire qqch	To insist on doing sth
En **venir à** faire qqch	To come to do sth

Il **est parvenu à perdre** du poids. *He succeeded in losing weight.*
Nous **invitons** les voisins **à dîner**. *We invite the neighbors for dinner.*
Ils **se sont engagés à régler** le problème. *They are committed to fixing the problem.*
Nous **commençons à réaliser** le problème. *We are starting to realize the problem.*
Cet outil **sert à couper** du bois. *This tool is used to cut wood.*

EX. 10.2 *Complétez les phrases avec la préposition **à** et ajoutez la fin de votre choix.*

1. Il a recommencé ____________________
2. Tu renonces ____________________
3. Je tiens ____________________
4. Elle se met ____________________
5. Le piéton hésite ____________________

6. Elle est arrivée ______________________________

7. Il a recommencé ______________________________

8. Tu continues ______________________________

9. Le public encourage ______________________________

10. On passe l'après-midi ______________________________

Verb + à + noun

Just for your information and to make sure you don't mix up the verbs that we just saw, here is the list of French verbs followed by **à** and **a noun**: AUDIO 37.5

Acheter qqch **à** qqn	To buy sth from or for sb
Arracher qqch **à** qqn	To tear away from sb
Aller à qqn	To suit sb
Assister qqn **à** qqch	To assist sb to do sth
S'attendre à qqch	To expect sth
Croire à qqch	To believe sth
Conseiller qqch **à** qqn	To advise sb
Convenir à qqn	To be suitable for sb
Demander qqch **à** qqn	To ask sth to sb
Défendre à qqn	To forbid sb
Désobéir à qqn	To disobey sb
Dire qqch **à** qqn	To tell sb
Donner qqch **à** qqn	To give to sb
Écrire à qqn	To write to sb
Emprunter qqch **à** qqn	To borrow sth from sb
Envoyer qqch **à** qqn	To send to sb
Être à qqn	To belong to sb
Faire attention **à** qqn	To pay attention to – be careful with sb
Faire confiance **à** qqn	To trust sb
Faire mal **à** qqn	To hurt sb
Se fier à qqn – qqch	To trust sb – sth
Goûter à qqch	To taste sth
S'habituer à qqn	To get used to sb
Interdire qqch **à** qqn	To forbid sb
S'intéresser à qqn	To be interested by sb
Jouer à qqch	To play sth
Manquer à qqn	To miss sb
Nuire à qqn	To harm sb
Obéir à qqn	To obey sb
S'opposer à qqn	To oppose sb
Ordonner à qqn	To order sb
Pardonner à qqn	To forgive sb
Parler à qqn	To talk to sb

Penser à qqn – qqch	To think about sb – sth
Permettre à qqn	To allow sb
Plaire à qqn	To please sb
Profiter à qqn	To benefit sb
Promettre à qqn	To promise sb
Raconter qqch **à** qqn	To tell sth to sb
Rappeler qqch **à** qqn	To remind sth to sb
Réfléchir à qqch	To consider – reflect upon sth
Rendre visite **à** qqn	To visit sb
Répondre à qqn	To answer sb
Reprocher qqch **à** qqn	To reproach sb for sth
Résister à qqn	To resist sb
Ressembler à qqn	To look like sb
Servir à qqn	To be useful for sb
Songer à qqn – qqch	To dream of – To think of sb – sth
Sourire à qqn	To smill to sb
Succéder à qqn	To take over from sb
Survivre à qqn	To outlive sb
Téléphoner à qqn	To call sb
Voler qqch **à** qqn	To steal sth from sb

Verb + de + infinitive

Just like the last point, **de** is required before adding the infinitive verb.

Here is the list of French verbs followed by de and an infinitive verb: AUDIO 37.6

Accepter de faire qqch	To accept to do sth
Accuser qqn **de** faire qqch	To accuse sb of doing sth
Achever de faire qqch	To finish doing sth
Arrêter de faire qqch	To stop doing sth
Attendre de faire qqch	To wait to do sth
Avoir besoin **de** faire qqch	To need to do sth
Avoir envie **de** faire qqch	To feel like doing sth
Avoir l'air **de** faire qqch	To seem to be doing sth
Avoir l'intention **de** faire qqch	To intend to do sth
Avoir peur **de** faire qqch	To be afraid of doing sth
Avoir raison **de** faire qqch	To be right to do sth
Avoir tort **de** faire qqch	To be wrong to do sth
Cesser de faire qqch	To cease doing sth
Choisir de faire qqch	To choose to do sth
Commander à qqn **de** faire qqch	To order sb to do sth
Conseiller de faire qqch	To advise to do sth
Se contenter de faire qqch	To be happy to do sth
Continuer de faire qqch	To keep doing sth
Convaincre qqn **de** faire qqch	To convince sb to do sth
Convenir de faire qqch	To agree to do sth

Craindre de faire qqch	To fear doing sth
Décider de faire qqch	To decide to do sth
Défendre à qqn **de** faire qqch	To forbid sb to do sth
Se dépêcher de faire qqch	To hurry to do sth
Demander à qqn **de** faire qqch	To ask sb to do sth
Dire à qqn **de** faire qqch	To tell sb to do sth
S'efforcer de faire qqch	To try hard to do sth
Empêcher qqn **de** faire qqch	To keep – prevent sb from doing sth
S'empresser de faire qqch	To hurry to do sth
Envisager de faire qqch	To contemplate doing sth
Essayer de faire qqch	To try to do sth
Être en train de faire qqch	To be in the process of doing sth
Être sur le point de faire qqch	To be about to do sth
Éviter de faire qqch	To avoid doing sth
S'excuser de faire qqch	To apologize for doing sth
Faire semblant **de** faire qqch	To pretend to do sth
Feindre de faire qqch	To feign to – To pretend to do sth
Finir de faire qqch	To finish doing sth
Se hâter de faire qqch	To hurry to do sth
Interdire à qqn **de** faire qqch	To forbid sb to do sth
Manquer de faire qqch	To neglect doing sth
Menacer qqn **de** faire qqch	To threaten sb to do sth
Mériter de faire qqch	To deserve to do sth
Offrir de faire qqch	To offer to do sth
Oublier de faire qqch	To forget to do sth
Parler de faire qqch	To talk about doing sth
(Se) permettre de faire qqch	To allow sb to do sth
Persuader qqn **de** faire qqch	To convince sb to do sth
Se plaindre de faire qqch	To complain about doing sth
Prier de faire qqch	To beg to do sth
Projeter de faire qqch	To plan on doing sth
Promettre de faire qqch	To promise to do sth
Proposer de faire qqch	To suggest doing sth
Refuser de faire qqch	To refuse to do sth
Regretter de faire qqch	To regret doing sth
Remercier de faire qqch	To thank (sb) for doing sth
Reprocher à qqn **de** faire qqch	To reproach sb for doing sth
Rêver de faire qqch	To dream of doing sth
Risquer de faire qqch	To risk doing sth
Soupçonner qqn **de** faire qqch	To suspect sb of doing sth
Se souvenir de faire qqch	To remember doing sth
Supplier de faire qqch	To beg to do sth
Tâcher de faire qqch	To try to do sth
Venir de faire qqch	To have just done sth

Elle **a oublié de sortir** les poubelles. *She forgot to take out the trash.*
Je **m'efforce d'écouter** la leçon. *I am trying hard to listen to the lesson.*
Julie **accepte de rester** tard au travail. *Julie agrees to stay late at work.*
Le patron **dit** à ses employés **de vider** le camion. *The boss tells his employees to empty the truck.*

EX. 10.3 *Complétez les phrases avec un verbe de la liste et la préposition* ***de****. Conjuguez le verbe au temps qui convient.* AUDIO 37.7

1. Mon fils me ________________________ lui acheter un cadeau.
2. Il ________________________ partir.
3. Le policier ________________________ le suspect ______ parler.
4. Cet homme ________________________ aider la vieille dame.
5. Nous ________________________ déménager en Australie.
6. L'enfant ________________________ semblant ______ dormir.
7. Il ________________________ étudier il y a quelques heures.
8. La radio ________________________ fonctionner.
9. Le banquier ________________________ investir plus.
10. Je ________________________ tondre la pelouse.

Verb + de + noun

Just for your information and to make sure you don't mix up the verbs that we just saw, here is the list of French verbs followed by **de** and **a noun**: AUDIO 37.8

Descendre de qqch	To get off – down from sth
S'agir de qqn – qqch	To be about sb – sth
S'apercevoir de qqch	To notice sth
S'approcher de qqn – qqch	To approach sb – sth
Arriver de + endroit	To arrive from + place
Avoir besoin **de** qqn – qqch	To need sb – sth
Avoir envie **de** qqch	To want sth
Avoir l'air **de** qqn	To look like sb
Avoir peur **de** qqn – qqch	To be afraid of sb – sth
Changer de + qqch	To change + sth
Dépendre de qqn – qqch	To depend on sb – sth
Douter de qqn – qqch	To doubt sb – sth
S'emparer de qqn – qqch	To grab sb – sth
S'étonner de qqn – qqch	To be amazed by sb – sth
Être responsable **de** qqn –qqch	To be responsible for sb
Hériter **de** qqn – qqch	To inherit (sth) from sb – To inherit sth
Jouer du + instrument	To play + instrument
Manquer de qqch	To lack sth
Se méfier de qqn	To mistrust sb
Se moquer de qqn	To make fun of sb
S'occuper de qqn – qqch	To take care of sb – sth

Parler de qqn – qqch	To talk about sb – sth
Partir de + endroit	To leave + place
Se passer de qqn – qqch	To do without sb – sth
Penser de qqn – qqch	To think of sb – sth
Se plaindre de qqn – qqch	To complain about sb – sth
Profiter de qqn – qqch	To take advantage of sb – sth
Raffoler de qqch	To be crazy of sth
Rêver de qqn – qqch	To dream of sb – sth
Rire de qqn – qqch	To laugh at sb – sth
Se servir de qqn – qqch	To use sb – sth
Se souvenir de qqn – qqch	To remember sb – sth
Se tromper de + objet	To take the wrong – To buy the wrong + object
Tenir qqch **de** qqn	To take sth after sb
Vivre de qqch	To live on sth

EX. 10.4 *Complétez les phrases avec la préposition adéquate : **à** – **de** – /.* AUDIO 37.9

1. Il commence ________ faire meilleur.
2. Nous parlons ________ changer de rideaux.
3. Anna vient ________ chercher ses affaires.
4. Le principal accepte ________ revoir son dossier.
5. Il cherche ________ plaire à ses beaux-parents
6. Est-ce que tu as dit à Jean ________ prendre ses clés ?
7. Les clients doivent ________ évacuer le magasin.
8. On risque ________ manquer notre train.
9. Le coach encourage les enfants ________ se dépasser.
10. J'ai envoyé Shirley ________ chercher le courrier.
11. Il doit ________ arriver ________ faire ses devoirs tout seul.
12. Le chiot n'ose pas ________ sauter du canapé.
13. Les enfants apprennent ________ écrire aux alentours de 6 ans.
14. Le gouvernement envisage ________ changer les règles d'immigration.
15. Continue ________ chanter, tu as une très belle voix.
16. C'est permis ________ partir plus tôt.
17. Il compte ________ finir ses études en 2 ans.
18. Nous réfléchissons ________ adopter un enfant.
19. L'avocat essaye ________ prouver que son client est innocent.
20. Elle désire ________ devenir ingénieure.

Prepositions + infinitive

In French, we can find the infinitive after the prepositions: **avant de** before, **au lieu de** instead of, **loin de** far from, **sans** without, **pour** to, **afin de** in order to, and **de peur de** for fear of. In English, the verb used is the -ing form, but not after **pour** and **afin de**.

AUDIO 38.1

Afin de In order to

L'investigation continue **afin de trouver** le coupable.
The investigation continues in order to find the culprit.

Au lieu de Instead of

Nous restons à la maison **au lieu de voyager.**
We are staying home instead of traveling.

Avant de Before

Ferme la porte **avant de partir.**
Close the door before leaving.

De peur de For fear of

Ils partent plus tôt **de peur de râter** l'avion.
They leave early for fear of missing the plane.

Pour To

Nous téléphonons **pour prendre** rendez-vous.
We are calling to make an appointment.

Loin de Far from

Il est **loin de terminer** le projet.
He is far from finishing the project.

Sans Without

Elle traverse la rue **sans regarder**.
She crosses the street without looking.

EX. 10.5 *Ajoutez les prépositions :* AUDIO 38.2

avant de - au lieu de - loin de - sans - pour - afin de - de peur de

1. Ils apprennent à se connaître __________________ se marier.
2. J'ai ouvert un compte épargnes __________________ économiser de l'argent.
3. Il est __________________ se rendre compte de ses problèmes.

4. Les politiciens tentent de cacher leurs erreurs __________ perdre la prochaine élection.
5. Ils montent les escaliers __________ faire de bruit.
6. Elle engage une baby-sitter __________ garder les enfants.
7. Il faut tester le terrain __________ déterminer la stabilité.
8. Il prend les escaliers __________ prendre l'ascenseur.
9. Lisez le manuel __________ commencer.
10. Vous recevrez le document __________ faire une demande.
11. Ils ont besoin de plus d'indices __________ trouver la solution.
12. Elle débarrasse le plan de travail __________ faire la pâte.
13. Il ne faisait pas de bruit __________ réveiller les enfants.
14. Tu devrais voyager __________ commencer à étudier.
15. Utilisez la clé __________ entrer dans la maison.

Faire + infinitive = Causative

The verb **Faire + infinitive** is used to explain that the subject doesn't perform the action but makes someone else or something else do it. It can be translated into English as To make someone do something.

A reminder of the conjugation of **Faire** in the present tense:

Faire To do – To make AUDIO 38.3

Je **fais**	Nous **faisons**
Tu **fais**	Vous **faites**
Il-Elle-On **fait**	Ils-Elles **font**

AUDIO 38.4

Faire entrer qqn	To let sb in
Faire sortir qqn	To let sb out
Faire attendre qqn	To keep sb waiting
Faire boire qqn	To make sb drink
Faire faire les devoirs à qqn	To make sb do their homework
Faire laver qqch	To get sth washed
Faire manger qqn	To make sb eat
Faire pousser qqch	To make sth grow
Faire remarquer qqch à qqn	To make sb notice sth
Faire savoir qqch à qqn	To make sb know sth
Faire venir qqn	To make sb come
Faire voir qqch à qqn	To show sth to sb

Je **fais réparer** la cheminée. *I am getting the chimney fixed.*
Il **fait laver** sa voiture. *He is getting his car washed.*
Nous **faisons nettoyer** nos vêtements. *We are getting our clothes washed.*
Ils **ont fait attendre** le bus. *They kept the bus waiting.*
L'hôpital **fait venir** le chirurgien. *The hospital makes the surgeon come.*

Expressions with **faire + infinitive**:

Faire chanter qqn	To blackmail sb
Faire marcher qqn	To pull sb's leg
En faire voir à qqn	To give someone a hard time

Use **Se faire + infinitive (reflexive causative)** to specify that the subject is getting something done to himself or for himself. AUDIO 38.5

Se faire accompagner	To get sb to go with you
Se faire avoir	To get taken advantage of
Se faire comprendre	To make oneself understood
Se faire couper les cheveux	To get a haircut
Se faire écraser	To get run over
Se faire entendre	To be heard
Se faire faire les ongles	To get a manicure
Se faire faire un vêtement	To have a piece of clothing made
Se faire gronder	To get yelled at
Se faire mettre à la porte	To get kicked out – fired
Se faire opérer	To get a surgery
Se faire payer	To get paid
Se faire prendre	To get caught
Se faire prier	To be begged
Se faire remarquer	To get noticed
Se faire rembourser	To get paid back
Se faire renverser	To get run over by a car
Se faire renvoyer	To get fired
Se faire rouler	To get cheated
Se faire soigner	To get medical treatment
Se faire tuer	To get killed

Il **s'est fait renverser** devant la maison. *He got run over by a car in front of the house.*
Elle **se fait** toujours **avoir.** *She always gets taken advantage of.*
Le personnage **se fait tuer** à la fin du film. *The character gets killed at the end of the movie.*
Le touriste n'arrive pas à **se faire comprendre**. *The tourist can't make himself understood.*

> Note:
> Even if the reflexive verb stays infinitive, the reflexive pronoun agrees with the subject of the sentence.

EX. 10.6 *Conjuguez les verbes entre parenthèses au présent de l'indicatif si nécessaire (look at the prepositions or the first verb).* AUDIO 38.6

1. Il ______________________ (faire entrer) l'accusé dans le tribunal.
2. Cet employé ______________________ (se faire payer) tous les 15 jours.
3. Le professeur lève la voix pour ______________________ (se faire entendre).
4. L'avocat ______________________ (faire savoir) au juge que son client est malade.
5. Elle ______________________ (faire chanter) son ex-mari depuis des mois.
6. Il m' ______________________ (en faire voir) de toutes les couleurs.
7. J'essaye de ______________________ (se faire couper) les cheveux tous les 6 mois.
8. Tu dois ______________________ (se faire opérer) d'urgence.
9. Le patron demande à ______________________ (faire laver) sa voiture demain matin.
10. Il aime ______________________ (se faire remarquer) en classe.

Verb + de quoi + infinitive

In this case, **de quoi** means something – enough. It underlines that the subject has enough of something to do. AUDIO 38.7

Avoir de quoi manger	To have enough to eat
Avoir de quoi s'occuper	To have enough to keep busy

EX. 10.7 *Traduisez les phrases en français.* AUDIO 38.8

1. Do you have enough to read ?

____

2. I took enough to drink for the walk.

____

3. My brothers have enough to play with.

____

Être + en train + de + infinitive

Since there is no equivalent of the English continuous present, if you want to emphasize an ongoing action, you can use **Être + en train + de + infinitive.** It translates to To be + in the process + of but the easiest translation is To be ____ing.

Train is also the word for "train," but this expression has nothing to do with trains and rails.

AUDIO 38.9

Je **suis en train de** lire. *I am reading.*
Nous **sommes en train de** partir. *We are leaving.*
Tu **es en train de** regarder la télévision. *You are watching TV.*

Être + sur le point + de + infinitive

Être + sur le point + de + infinitive translates to To be about to.

AUDIO 38.10

J'**étais sur le point de** partir. *I was about to leave.*
La société **est sur le point de** fermer. *The company is about to close.*
Il **est sur le point de** plonger. *He is about to dive.*

EX. 10.8 *Traduisez ces phrases en utilisant **être sur le point de.*** AUDIO 38.11

1. He is about to move the car.

   ____

2. I am about to call the police.

   ____

3. This couple is about to get divorced.

   ____

4. This TV show (série télévisée) is about to be canceled.

   ____

5. She is about to take notes.

   ____

Être + adjective + de + infinitive

Être + adjective + de + infinitive is a common way to express feelings. It translates almost word by word to To be + adjective + to. (Except for To be sure of, To be tired of, To be proud of)

In French, the adjective agrees in gender and number with the subject. The feminine version is added after the masculine form of the adjective.

Here is the list of commonly used expressions: AUDIO 38.12

Être anxieux (anxieuse) de	To be anxious to
Être content (contente) de	To be happy to
Être désolé (désolée) de	To be sorry to
Être enchanté (enchantée) de	To be delighted to
Être fatigué (fatiguée) de	To be tired of
Être fier (fière) de	To be proud of
Être heureux (heureuse) de	To be happy to
Être impatient (impatiente) de	To be impatient to
Être libre de	To be free to
Être obligé (obligée) de	To be obligated to
Être ravi (ravie) de	To be delighted to
Être reconnaissant (reconnaissante) de	To be thankful to
Être satisfait (satisfaite) de	To be satisfied to
Être sûr (sûre) de	To be sure to
Être surpris (surprise) de	To be surprised to
Être triste de	To be sad to

Elle **est triste de quitter** son amie. *She is sad to leave her friend.*
Nous **sommes fatigués de travailler.** *We are tired of working.*
Je **suis** fier **de te connaître.** *I am proud to know you.*

EX. 10.9 *Conjuguez le verbe être entre parenthèses au présent de l'indicatif, attention de changer l'adjectif si nécessaire.* AUDIO 38.13

1. Nous (f) ____________________ (être heureux de) être ici.
2. Est-ce que tu ____________________ (être sûr de) pouvoir venir ?
3. La scientifique ____________________ (être ravi de) être nominée.
4. Il ____________________ (être anxieux de) prendre l'avion.
5. Nous ____________________ (être désolé de) être en retard.
6. Jeff ____________________ (être triste de) apprendre la nouvelle.

7. Je (f) ______________________________ (être impatient de) arriver.
8. Ma mère ______________________________ (être surpris de) te voir.
9. Il ______________________________ (être ravi de) recevoir ta lettre.
10. Emma ______________________________ (être content de) participer au jeu.

Être + Adjective – Past Participle + à + Infinitive

Être + adjective – past participle + à + infinitive is used to describe the state of someone or something, not feelings.

In French, the adjective agrees in gender and number with the subject, the feminine version is added after the masculine form of the adjective.

AUDIO 38.14

Here is the list of commonly used expressions:

Être prêt (prête) à	To be ready to
Être autorisé (autorisée) à	To be authorized to
Être habitué (habituée) à	To be used to
Être occupé (occupée) à	To be busy with
Être déterminé (déterminée) à	To be determined to

Je **suis prête à partir.** *I am ready to leave.*
Nous **sommes habitués à dormir** avec la fenêtre ouverte. *We are used to sleeping with the window open.*
Elle **est déterminée à réussir.** *She is determined to succeed.*

EX. 10.10 *Conjuguez le verbe être entre parenthèses au présent de l'indicatif, attention de changer l'adjectif si nécessaire.* AUDIO 38.15

1. Je ______________________________ (être déterminé à) payer mes dettes.
2. Nous ______________________________ (être habitué à) dormir tard.
3. Elles ______________________________ (être occupé à) regarder la télévision.
4. Le directeur ______________________________ (être autorisé à) signer.
5. Elle ______________________________ (être prêt à) changer.

Il est + Adjective + de + Infinitive

Il est + adjective + de + infinitive is a formal way to speak in French. The informal way is explained in the next point.

Here **être** is an impersonal verb, therefore the adjective stays masculine – singular.

Here is the list of commonly used expressions: AUDIO 39.1

Il est bon de	It's good to
Il est dangereux de	It's dangerous to
Il est défendu de	It's forbidden to
Il est interdit de	It's forbidden to
Il est difficile de	It's difficult to
Il est dur de	It's hard to
Il est facile de	It's easy to
Il est important de	It's important to
Il est nécessaire de	It's necessary to
Il est impossible de	It's impossible to
Il est possible de	It's possible to
Il est utile de	It's useful to
Il est inutile de	It's useless to

Il est interdit de fumer à l'intérieur. *It's forbidden to smoke inside.*
Il est impossible de réparer cette voiture. *It's impossible to fix this car.*
Il est dangereux de jouer avec le feu. *It's dangerous to play with fire.*

C'est + Adjective + de + Infinitive

C'est + adjective + de + infinitive is the informal way to talk, as opposed to **il est**.

Here **être** is an impersonal verb, therefore the adjective stays masculine – singular.

Here is the list of commonly used expressions: AUDIO 39.2

C'est interdit de	It's forbidden to
C'est difficile de	It's difficult to
C'est bien de	It's good to
C'est dommage de	It's a shame to

C'est bien de changer d'air. *It's good to change air.*
C'est difficile de se détendre. *It's difficult to relax.*

EX. 10.11 *Ajoutez un verbe infinitif de votre choix après il est et c'est.*

1. Il est utile de ____________________
2. C'est interdit de ____________________
3. Il est bon de ____________________
4. C'est bien de ____________________
5. Il est important de ____________________
6. C'est dommage de ____________________
7. Il est défendu de ____________________
8. Il est facile ____________________

C'est + Adjective + à + Infinitive

C'est + adjective + à + infinitive is used to refer to something previously mentioned in the conversation.

Here **être** is an impersonal verb, therefore the adjective stays masculine - singular.

Here is the list of commonly used expressions: AUDIO 39.3

C'est bon à savoir.	*It's good to know.*
C'est difficile à dire.	*It's difficult to say.*
C'est impossible à dire.	*It's impossible to say.*

... seul + à + Infinitive

In this case, much like ordinal numbers in the next point, we don't have a verb before the preposition **à**. **Le seul** is a pronoun and will change depending on whether the subject is masculine, feminine, singular, or plural. The change in gender and number doesn't affect the verb that follows since it's infinitive.

It also happens with **nombreux**, which will change to **nombreuses** when feminine. **Nombreux** and **nombreuses** are always plural.

Here are the 6 possibilities with different gender and number: AUDIO 39.4

Le seul à (m)	The only one who
La seule à (f)	The only one who
Les seuls à (m)	The only ones who
Les seules à (f)	The only ones who
Nombreux à (m)	Many are
Nombreuses à (f)	Many are

Il est **le seul à comprendre** son écriture. *He is the only one who understands his writing.*

Les seules à avoir la réponse sont ses tantes. *The only ones who have the answer are her aunts.*

Ils sont **nombreux à attendre** des nouvelles. *Many are waiting for news.*
Elles sont **nombreuses à arrêter** leurs études. *Many are stopping their studies.*

EX. 10.12 *Complétez les phrases avec :* AUDIO 39.5

seul - seule - seuls - seules - nombreux - nombreuses

1. C'est le ________________________ à être venu.
2. Ils étaient ________________________ à attendre le chanteur.
3. Amélia et moi étions les ________________________ à prendre des nouvelles.
4. Je suis la ________________________ à être diplômée dans ma famille.
5. Les ________________________ à être là pour moi sont mon mari et mes frères.
6. Les petites filles sont ________________________ à vouloir être princesses.

Ordinal Number + à + Infinitive

Just like the last point, we don't have a verb before the preposition **à. Ordinal numbers** will change depending on whether the subject is masculine, feminine, singular, or plural. The change in gender and number doesn't affect the verb that follows since it's infinitive.

Here are a few possibilities with different gender and number: AUDIO 39.6

Le premier à (m)	The first one to
La première à (f)	The first one to
Les premiers à (m)	The first ones to
Les premières à (f)	The first ones to
Le deuxième à (m)	The second one to
La deuxième à (f)	The second one to
Les deuxièmes à	The second ones to

Le dernier à (m)	The last one to
La dernière à (f)	The last one to
Les derniers à (m)	The last ones to
Les dernières à (f)	The last ones to

Il est **le premier à aller** à l'université. *He is the first one to go to university.*
Elles sont **les deuxièmes à** me **dire** ça. *They are the second ones telling me that.*

EX. 10.13 *Complétez les phrases avec : **dernier** – **première** – **premier** – **dernières*** AUDIO 39.7

1. Elle est toujours la ________________________ à quitter le travail.
2. Je pense qu'elles étaient les ________________________ à sortir du bâtiment.
3. Le ________________________ à entrer gagne un voyage à Mexico.
4. Il est le ________________________ à arriver.

Il faut + Infinitive

Il faut is an impersonal verb and is only conjugated with **il**. It translates to To have to, to be necessary, must, to need to in English. It doesn't require a preposition before adding the infinitive.

AUDIO 39.8

Il faut partir maintenant. *We must leave now.*
Il faut aller faire des courses. *We have to go grocery shopping.*

EX. 10.14 *Complétez les phrases avec :* AUDIO 39.9

aller – commander – regarder – remplir – connaître – dormir – penser

1. Il faut ________________________ moins la télévision.
2. Il faut ________________________ les différences entre savoir et connaître.
3. Il faut ________________________ plus vite.
4. Il faut ________________________ du papier.
5. Il faut ________________________ plus tôt.
6. Il faut ________________________ à payer ses factures.
7. Il faut ________________________ ce document avant de l'envoyer.

The Past Infinitive

The past infinitive is a compound form. It requires the verb **avoir** or **être** present infinitive present + **participle past.**

To know when to use **avoir** or **être**, refer to the lesson about the **passé composé**.

avoir + past participle
être + past participle

Infinitif présent	**Infinitif passé** AUDIO 39.10
Chanter	Avoir chanté
Partir	Être parti
Se préparer	S'être préparé

Nous vous remercions d'**être venus.** We thank you for coming.

⇨ After the preposition **après**, the infinitive is always a past infinitive.

Je suis partie **après avoir rendu** les clés. *I left after giving back the keys.*
Il est fatigué **après avoir mangé.** *He is tired after eating.*
Ils sont allés au restaurant **après être arrivés.** *They went to the restaurant after arriving.*

⇨ After the verbs **se rappeler de** and **se souvenir de**, the infinitive is always a past infinitive.

Je ne me rappelle pas d'avoir commandé ça. *I don't remember ordering that.*
Est-ce que tu te souviens d'avoir fermé la porte ? *Do you remember closing the door?*

The Negative Infinitive

AUDIO 39.11

When the verb is infinitive, present or past, the 2 parts of the negation: **ne pas, ne plus, ne jamais, ne rien**, etc, stay together and are placed before the verb.

J'essaye de ne pas fumer. *I try not to smoke.*
C'est sale de ne pas se laver les mains. *It's dirty to not wash your hands.*
Je préfère ne plus manger de viande. *I prefer not to eat meat anymore.*

In the case of a pronoun, the pronoun stays between the negation and the verb.

Je préfère ne pas y retourner. *I prefer to not go back (there).*
C'est difficile de ne pas le voir. *It's hard not to see it.*

Merci de + Infinitive

Merci de + infinitive is used to give an order and thank the person for following the rules at the same time.

AUDIO 39.12

Merci d'arriver tôt. *Thanks for arriving early.*
Merci de fermer les fenêtres. *Thanks for closing the windows.*
Merci d'être venu. *Thanks for coming.*
Merci de ne pas fumer. *Thanks for not smoking.*

CHAPTER 11

The Subjunctive
Le Subjonctif

The Subjunctive - Le Subjonctif

The subjunctive, called **subjonctif,** is the fourth and the last mood that we are going to look at in this book. We already saw the indicative, the conditional and the imperative.

This mood includes four different tenses, but we will only focus on the **subjonctif présent** and the **subjonctif passé.**

The **subjonctif** doesn't correspond to any rule in the English language.

> The **subjonctif** is used after **que**, mostly in the subordinate clause, and indicates a wish, regret, emotion, opinion, or doubt.

AUDIO 40.1

Il faut **que je parte** maintenant. *I must leave now.*
Je suis heureux **que tu sois** là. *I am happy that you are here.*

Building the Subjunctive

The **subjonctif présent** is formed by taking the verb conjugated in the **present tense** with **ils** and removing the **-ent.** That gives us the stem.
Then we add the endings for the **subjonctif présent**: **-e, -es, -e, -ions, iez** and **-ent.**

Être and **avoir** are the only verbs not following the stem rule.

Since the subjunctive is always preceded by **que,** we always use **que** in the conjugation as well.

AUDIO 40.2

Regular **-er** verbs:

Donner To give
Ils donn~~ent~~
Stem: donn

Que je donn**e**
Que tu donn**es**
Qu'il donn**e**
Qu'elle donn**e**
Qu'on donn**e**
Que nous donn**ions**
Que vous donn**iez**
Qu'ils donn**ent**
Qu'elles donn**ent**

AUDIO 40.3

Regular **-ir** verbs:

Finir To finish
Ils finiss~~ent~~
Stem: finiss

Que je finiss**e**
Que tu finiss**es**
Qu'il finiss**e**
Qu'elle finiss**e**
Qu'on finiss**e**
Que nous finiss**ions**
Que vous finiss**iez**
Qu'ils finiss**ent**
Qu'elles finiss**ent**

AUDIO 40.4

Regular **-re** verbs:

Attendre To wait
Ils attend~~ent~~
Stem: attend

Que j'attend**e**
Que tu attend**es**
Qu'il attend**e**
Qu'elle attend**e**
Qu'on attend**e**
Que nous attend**ions**
Que vous attend**iez**
Qu'ils attend**ent**
Qu'elles attend**ent**

> The endings **-e, -es, -ent** have the same pronunciation.

- Verbs ending in -**cer** and -**ger** don't need a **ç** or an **e** after **g.**
- When the stem ends with **i**, the **nous** and **vous** forms will take a **double ii.**
- Verbs with spelling changes in the stem in the present tense, especially with **nous** and **vous**, follow the same rule in the subjunctive. Here are a few:

AUDIO **40.5**

Essuyer To wipe
Ils essui~~**ent**~~
Stem: essui

Que j'essui**e**
Que tu essui**es**
Qu'il essui**e**
Qu'elle essui**e**
Qu'on essui**e**
Que nous essuy**ions**
Que vous essuy**iez**
Qu'ils essui**ent**
Qu'elles essui**ent**

AUDIO **40.6**

Peser To weigh
Ils pès~~**ent**~~
Stem: pès

Que je pès**e**
Que tu pès**es**
Qu'il pès**e**
Qu'elle pès**e**
Qu'on pès**e**
Que nous pes**ions**
Que vous pes**iez**
Qu'ils pès**ent**
Qu'elles pès**ent**

AUDIO **40.7**

Célébrer To celebrate
Ils célèbr~~**ent**~~
Stem: célèbr

Que je célèbr**e**
Que tu célèbr**es**
Qu'il célèbr**e**
Qu'elle célèbr**e**
Qu'on célèbr**e**
Que nous célébr**ions**
Que vous célébr**iez**
Qu'ils célèbr**ent**
Qu'elles célèbr**ent**

EX. 11.1 *Conjuguez les verbes suivants au subjonctif présent.* AUDIO **40.8**

1. Grandir

   Que je ______________________________

   Que tu ______________________________

   Qu'on ______________________________

   Que nous ______________________________

   Que vous ______________________________

   Qu'elles ______________________________

2. Entendre

   Que j' ______________________________

   Que tu ______________________________

   Qu'il ______________________________

   Que nous ______________________________

   Que vous ______________________________

   Qu'ils ______________________________

Irregular verbs with a regular subjonctif présent

Some irregular verbs (and compounds) in other tenses have a regular conjugation in the subjunctive. We will again take the verb conjugated with **ils** in the **present tense**, remove the ending **-ent,** and add the endings for the subjunctive.

Here is the list of verbs: AUDIO 40.9

Battre (Ils **batt**ent)	Que je **batte** – Que nous **battions** – Qu'ils **battent**
Mettre (Ils **mett**ent)	Que je **mette** – Que nous **mettions** – Qu'ils **mettent**
Conduire (Ils **conduis**ent)	Que je **conduise** – Que nous **conduisions** – Qu'ils **conduisent**
Lire (Ils **lis**ent)	Que je **lise** – Que nous **lisions** – Qu'ils **lisent**
Plaire (Ils **plais**ent)	Que je **plaise** – Que nous **plaisions** – Qu'ils **plaisent**
Dire (Ils **dis**ent)	Que je **dise** – Que nous **disions** – Qu'ils **disent**
Vivre (Ils **viv**ent)	Que je **vive** – Que nous **vivions** – Qu'ils **vivent**
Suivre (Ils **suiv**ent)	Que je **suive** – Que nous **suivions** – Qu'ils **suivent**
Écrire (Ils **écriv**ent)	Que j'**écrive** – Que nous **écrivions** – Qu'ils **écrivent**
Connaître (Ils **connaiss**ent)	Que je **connaisse** – Que nous **connaissions** – Qu'ils **connaissent**
Ouvrir (Ils **ouvr**ent)	Que j'**ouvre** – Que nous **ouvrions** – Qu'ils **ouvrent**
Courir (Ils **cour**ent)	Que je **coure** – Que nous **courions** – Qu'ils **courent**
Craindre (Ils **craign**ent)	Que je **craigne** – Que nous **craignions** – Qu'ils **craignent**
Rire (Ils **ri**ent)	Que je **rie** – Que nous **riions** – Qu'ils **rient**
Partir (Ils **part**ent)	Que je **parte** – Que nous **partions** – Qu'ils **partent**

EX. 11.2 *Corrigez les conjugaisons suivantes.* AUDIO 40.10

1. Que j'écrives __________
2. Que tu pars __________
3. Qu'il crainde __________
4. Que nous ditions __________
5. Que vous riez __________
6. Qu'ils batent __________
7. Que je conduis __________
8. Que tu cours __________
9. Qu'il vives __________
10. Que nous suivons __________

Irregular verbs with 2 different stems

Some verbs (and compounds) have two different stems in the **subjonctif présent**.
The first one will be used for: **je, tu, il, elle, on, ils, elles.**

The second will be used for: **nous, vous.**

Memorize one of each to be more efficient. Here we are going to see **je** and **nous**:

AUDIO **40.11**

Boire	Que je **boiv**e	Que nous **buv**ions
Devoir	Que je **doiv**e	Que nous **dev**ions
Envoyer	Que j'**envoi**e	Que nous **envoy**ions
Mourir	Que je **meur**e	Que nous **mourr**ions
Recevoir	Que je **reçoiv**e	Que nous **recev**ions
Tenir	Que je **tienn**e	Que nous **ten**ions
Venir	Que je **vienn**e	Que nous **ven**ions
Voir	Que je **voi**e	Que nous **voy**ions

EX. 11.3 *Conjuguez les verbes suivants au subjonctif présent.* AUDIO **40.12**

1. Revenir

   Que je ______________________

   Que tu ______________________

   Qu'on ______________________

   Que nous ______________________

   Que vous ______________________

   Qu'elles ______________________

2. Renvoyer

   Que je ______________________

   Que tu ______________________

   Qu'il ______________________

   Que nous ______________________

   Que vous ______________________

   Qu'ils ______________________

Irregular verbs with an irregular stem

These verbs and compounds have an irregular stem which is the same for all forms, except **valoir** and **vouloir**:

AUDIO 40.13

Faire To do
Que je fass**e**
Que tu fass**es**
Qu'il fass**e**
Qu'elle fass**e**
Qu'on fass**e**
Que nous fass**ions**
Que vous fass**iez**
Qu'ils fass**ent**
Qu'elles fass**ent**

AUDIO 40.14

Savoir To know
Que je sach**e**
Que tu sach**es**
Qu'il sach**e**
Qu'elle sach**e**
Qu'on sach**e**
Que nous sach**ions**
Que vous sach**iez**
Qu'ils sach**ent**
Qu'elles sach**ent**

AUDIO 40.15

Pouvoir To be able to
Que je puiss**e**
Que tu puiss**es**
Qu'il puiss**e**
Qu'elle puiss**e**
Qu'on puiss**e**
Que nous puiss**ions**
Que vous puiss**iez**
Qu'ils puiss**ent**
Qu'elles puiss**ent**

AUDIO 40.16

Aller To go
Que j'aill**e**
Que tu aill**es**
Qu'il aill**e**
Qu'elle aill**e**
Qu'on aill**e**
Que nous all**ions**
Que vous all**iez**
Qu'ils aill**ent**
Qu'elles aill**ent**

AUDIO 40.17

Valoir To be worth
Que je vaill**e**
Que tu vaill**es**
Qu'il vaill**e**
Qu'elle vaill**e**
Qu'on vaill**e**
Que nous val**ions**
Que vous val**iez**
Qu'ils vaill**ent**
Qu'elles vaill**ent**

AUDIO 40.18

Vouloir To want
Que je veuill**e**
Que tu veuill**es**
Qu'il veuill**e**
Qu'elle veuill**e**
Qu'on veuill**e**
Que nous voul**ions**
Que vous voul**iez**
Qu'ils veuill**ent**
Qu'elles veuill**ent**

The impersonal verbs **falloir**, **pleuvoir** and **neiger** only exist with **il** and are conjugated as follow: AUDIO 40.19

Falloir To be necessary	Qu'il **faill**e
Pleuvoir To rain	Qu'il **pleuv**e
Neiger To snow	Qu'il **neig**e

Être and **avoir** are fully irregular. They are also used to form the subjunctive past, therefore they must be learned by heart.

AUDIO 40.20

Être To be
Que je **sois**
Que tu **sois**
Qu'il **soit**
Qu'elle **soit**
Qu'on **soit**
Que nous **soyons**
Que vous **soyez**
Qu'ils **soient**
Qu'elles **soient**

AUDIO 40.21

Avoir To have
Que j'**aie**
Que tu **aies**
Qu'il **ait**
Qu'elle **ait**
Qu'on **ait**
Que nous **ayons**
Que vous **ayez**
Qu'ils **aient**
Qu'elles **aient**

Building the Past Subjunctive

The **subjonctif passé** is formed with the **subjonctif présent** of the auxiliaries **être** and **avoir** and the past participle of the conjugated verb.

All rules followed by compound tenses apply to the subjonctif passé as well.

AUDIO 40.22	AUDIO 40.23	AUDIO 40.24
Demander To ask	**Partir** To leave	**Se trouver** To be (located)
Que j'**aie demandé**	Que je **sois parti(e)**	Que je **me sois trouvé(e)**
Que tu **aies demandé**	Que tu **sois parti(e)**	Que tu **te sois trouvé(e)**
Qu'il **ait demandé**	Qu'il **soit parti**	Qu'il **se soit trouvé**
Qu'elle **ait demandé**	Qu'elle **soit partie**	Qu'elle **se soit trouvée**
Qu'on **ait demandé**	Qu'on **soit parti(e)s**	Qu'on **se soit trouvé(e)s**
Que nous **ayons demandé**	Que nous **soyons parti(e)s**	Que nous **nous soyons trouvé(e)s**
Que vous **ayez demandé**	Que vous **soyez parti(e)s**	Que vous **vous soyez trouvé(e)s**
Qu'ils **aient demandé**	Qu'ils **soient partis**	Qu'ils **se soient trouvés**
Qu'elles **aient demandé**	Qu'elles **soient parties**	Qu'elles **se soient trouvées**

EX. 11.4 *Conjuguez le verbe donné au **subjonctif présent** et au **subjonctif passé**.*

AUDIO 40.25

1. **Nettoyer**

   Présent Que je ____________________

   Passé Que vous ____________________

2. **Faire**

   Présent Que je ____________________

   Passé Que vous ____________________

3. **Pouvoir**

   Présent Que je ____________________

   Passé Que vous ____________________

4. **Dire**

   Présent Que je ____________________

   Passé Que vous ____________________

*Remember to **download the audio** and to **watch the videos** – see Preface*

5. **Finir**

Présent Que je ______________________________

Passé Que vous ______________________________

6. **Avoir**

Présent Que j' ______________________________

Passé Que vous ______________________________

7. **Manger**

Présent Que je ______________________________

Passé Que vous ______________________________

8. **Aller**

Présent Que j' ______________________________

Passé Que vous ______________________________

9. **Être**

Présent Que je ______________________________

Passé Que vous ______________________________

10. **Aimer**

Présent Que j' ______________________________

Passé Que vous ______________________________

When to Use the Subjunctive

As mentioned before, the **subjonctif** is used after **que**, mostly in the subordinate clause, and indicates a **wish, emotion, regret, opinion**, or **doubt.** It's also used in **impersonal expressions.**

But what is a subordinate clause?

AUDIO **41.1**

A subordinate clause is the second part of the sentence after que. The first part is called the main clause. Remember that in English, que is not always translated.

Je veux que ce problème soit réglé. *I want this problem to be solved.*

Je veux = Main clause
Ce problème soit réglé = Subordinate clause

An important rule to understand is that the subject in the main clause must be different than the subject in the subordinate clause. **If the subjects are the same, we don't use the subjunctive but the infinitive of the verb.**

Je veux qu'elle parte aujourd'hui. *I want her to leave today.*

Je veux = Main clause
Elle parte aujourd'hui = Subordinate clause

⇨ Different subjects = Subjunctive

Je veux partir aujourd'hui. *I want to leave today.*

⇨ Only one subject = Infinitive

If the verb in the main clause is followed by **de** or **pour,** for example, and there is no que in the sentence, the next verb will be infinitive, not subjonctif.

Il attend de partir.	He is waiting to leave.

A good way to remember the different uses is with the acronym **WEIRDO**:

Wish
Emotions
Impersonal expressions
Regrets and **R**ecommendations
Doubts
Opinions

⇨ To express a **wish**: AUDIO 41.2

Here is a list of verbs used in the main clause followed by the subjunctive:

Aimer que	To like that
Aimer mieux que	To prefer that
Attendre que	To wait that
Désirer que	To desire that
Exiger que	To require that
S'attendre à ce que	To expect that
Avoir envie que	To want that
Demander que	To ask that
Insister pour que	To insist that
Souhaiter que	To wish that
Tenir à ce que	To want that
Vouloir que	To want that

J'aime qu'il prenne soin d'elle.
I like that he takes care of her.

Nous exigeons qu'il soit là demain.
We demand that he be there tomorrow.

Ils ne s'attendent pas à ce qu'il démissionne.
They don't expect him to quit.

J'insiste pour qu'elle reçoive un cadeau aussi.
I insist that she gets a gift as well.

Espérer requires the indicative form even after que:

J'espère que tu seras là.
I hope you will be there.

EX. 11.5 *Ajoutez **que**, formez des phrases avec les éléments donnés et conjuguez le verbe donné **au subjonctif** ou **à l'indicatif**.* AUDIO 41.3

1. Je souhaite / il / recevoir / son diplôme

   ____

2. Il espère / le bus / être / à l'heure

   ____

3. Nous aimerions mieux / vous / arriver / demain

   ____

4. Les enseignants tiennent à ce / les enfants / réussir

   ____

5. Le tuteur insiste pour / ils / faire / leurs devoirs

   ____

6. Je veux / les enfants / être / au lit / à 21 heures

   ____

7. Le client s'attend à ce / la chambre / être prête

   ____

8. Mes parents ont envie / ils / venir / avec nous

   ____

9. Le garde exige / les prisonniers / rester / silencieux

   ____

10. Le responsable espère / la livraison / arriver / bientôt

    ____

⇨ To express an **emotion**: AUDIO 41.4

Here is a list of verbs and expressions used in the main clause followed by the subjunctive:

Être content (contente) que	To be happy that
Être heureux (heureuse) que	To be happy that
Être ravi (ravie) que	To be delighted that
Être étonné (étonnée) que	To be surprised that
Être surpris (surprise) que	To be surprised that
Être malheureux (malheureuse) que	To be unhappy that
Être triste que	To be sad that
Être soulagé (soulagée) que	To be relieved that
Être déçu (déçue) que	To be disappointed that
Être désolé (désolée) que	To be sorry that
Avoir peur que (ne)	To be afraid that

Il était tellement content que tu sois venue.
He was so happy that you came.

Nous avons peur qu'elle n'arrive pas à temps.
We are afraid that she won't get here on time.

Je suis ravie que tu viennes pour le week-end.
I am delighted that you are coming for the weekend.

Nous sommes désolés que vous soyez malade.
We are sorry that you are sick.

The subjunctive is not used if the adjective is followed by an infinitive verb.

Nous sommes désolés d'apprendre la nouvelle.
We are sorry to learn this news.

EX. 11.6 *Finissez les phrases avec des idées personnelles. Attention de ne pas ajouter le même sujet deux fois.*

1. Je suis surpris(e) que ______________________________
2. Je suis ravi(e) que ______________________________
3. Je suis déçu(e) que ______________________________
4. Je suis soulagé(e) que ______________________________
5. J'ai peur que ______________________________

⇨ **Impersonal expressions** used to talk about obligations: AUDIO 41.5

Here is a list of impersonal expressions used in the main clause followed by the subjunctive:

Il faut que	It's necessary that/To have to
Il est important que	It's important that
Il est nécessaire que	It's necessary that

Il est essentiel que	It's essential that
Il est inévitable que	It's unavoidable that
Il vaut mieux que	It's better that
Il est préférable que	It's preferable that
Il est indispensable que	It's indispensable that
Il est temps que	It's about time that

Il faut que is the most used impersonal expression with the subjunctive.

Il faut que j'achète à manger.
I have to buy food.

Il faut que je te dise quelque chose.
I have to tell you something.

Il faut que tu prennes tes médicaments.
You have to take your medicine.

Il est indispensable que l'opération soit réalisée par un bon chirurgien.
It's indispensable that the surgery is done by a good surgeon.

Il vaut mieux que tu t'en ailles.
It's better that you leave.

EX. 11.7 *Complétez les phrases avec un de ces verbes et conjuguez-le au subjonctif présent.*

AUDIO 41.6

réserver – vérifier – se décider – prendre – couper – remplir – boire – être – venir

1. Il faut que je ______________________ la pression des pneus.
2. Il faut que je ______________________ ma déclaration d'impôts.
3. Il faut que je ______________________ à la banque.
4. Il faut que je ______________________ plus d'eau.
5. Il faut que je ______________________ rendez-vous.
6. Il faut que je ______________________ en forme.
7. Il faut que je ______________________.
8. Il faut que je ______________________ du bois.
9. Il faut que je ______________________ te voir.
10. Il faut que je ______________________ une table au restaurant.

EX. 11.8 *Écrivez un email à un collègue pour lui dire ce qu'il doit préparer pour la réunion avec les éléments suivants :*

imprimer les dossiers - acheter des pâtisseries - confirmer l'heure - réserver la salle de réunion - préparer une offre de prix

*Attention, si vous n'utilisez pas « **il faut que** » ou un autre élément avec que, le verbe ne sera pas conjugué au subjonctif.*

Il faut que vous ______________________________

____

____

____

____

____

____

____

⇨ To express **regret** or give **recommendations**: AUDIO 41.7

Here is a list of impersonal expressions and verbs used in the main clause followed by the subjunctive:

Recommander que	To recommend that
Regretter que	To regret that
Suggérer que	To suggest that

Le ministre recommande que les vaccins soient distribués au plus vite.
The minister recommends that the vaccines be distributed as soon as possible.

Je regrette que tu l'apprennes de cette façon.
I regret that you found it this way.

Le professeur suggère qu'il pratique plus la lecture.
The teacher suggests that he practice more reading.

EX. 11.9 *Conjuguez les verbes entre parenthèses au **subjonctif présent** ou **passé**.* AUDIO 41.8

1. Nous regrettons que ce (se passer) de cette façon.

____

2. L'agent de voyage a recommandé que nous (réserver) assez vite.

____

3. Le docteur a suggéré que nous (faire) plus de tests.

____

⇨ To express an uncertainty or a **doubt**: AUDIO 41.9

Here is a list of impersonal expressions and verbs used in the main clause followed by the subjunctive:

Il est possible que	It's possible that
Il est impossible que	It's impossible that
Il est incroyable que	It's incredible that
Il est douteux que	It's doubtful that
Douter que	To doubt that
Avoir l'impression que	To have the impression that
Il semble que	It seems that

Il est* can be replaced by **c'est.

Il semble que la tempête soit passée.
It seems that the storm has passed.

C'est impossible que tu aies raté ça !
It's impossible that you missed that!

The verbs **croire**, **penser** and **avoir l'impression** only take the subjunctive in a negative sentence and in questions with inversion:

Indicatif:	**Je crois qu'il sait cuisiner.** *I think he knows how to cook.*
Subjonctif:	**Je ne crois pas qu'il sache cuisiner.** *I don't think he knows how to cook.*
Indicatif:	**J'ai l'impression qu'elle est déçue.** *I feel like she is disappointed.*
Subjonctif:	**Je n'ai pas l'impression qu'elle soit déçue.** *I don't feel like she is disappointed.*
Indicatif:	**Je pense qu'il a du talent.** *I think he has talent.*
Subjonctif:	**Je ne pense pas qu'il ait du talent.** *I don't think he has talent.*

EX. 11.10 *Transformez ces phrases en question et en phrases négatives.* AUDIO 41.10

1. Nous croyons qu'il est bon pour nous de dormir tard.

   Croyons-nous qu'____ ?

   Nous ne croyons pas ____

2. Elle a l'impression que je fais de la natation tous les matins.

   A-t-elle l'impression que ____________________________________ ?

   Elle n'a pas l'impression pas __________________________________

3. Tu penses que cette artiste vient de France.

   Penses-tu que ____ ?

   Tu ne penses pas que ____

Expressions and verbs that **DON'T** express doubt and uncertainty are followed by the indicative:
AUDIO 41.11

Ne pas douter que	To not doubt that
Être sûr (sûre) que	To be sure that
Être certain (certaine) que	To be certain that
Il est certain que	It's certain that
Il est évident que	It's evident that
Il est vrai que	It's true that
Il paraît que	It appears that
Savoir que	To know that
Il n'y a pas de doute que	There is no doubt that

EX. 11.11 *Conjuguez les verbes entre parenthèses à l'indicatif ou au subjonctif.* AUDIO 41.12

1. Je ne doute pas que tu __________________________ le meilleur. (être)
2. Tu doutes que l'équipe __________________________ . (gagner)
3. Il paraît que tu ________________________________ d'Écosse. (revenir)
4. Il semble que les jours __________________________ . (rallonger)
5. On sait que les choses ne _________________________ pas toutes seules. (s'arranger)
6. C'est possible que tu ___________________________ un gâteau pour demain. (faire)
7. Il est vrai que la poterie _________________________ difficile. (sembler)
8. Il est incroyable que ce chien ______________________ . (survivre)
9. Il est évident que les parents ______________________ . (fatiguer)

*Remember to **download the audio** and to **watch the videos** – see Preface*

⇨ To express an **opinion**: AUDIO 41.13

Here is a list of impersonal expressions used in the main clause followed by the subjunctive:

Il est bien que	It's good that
Il est bon que	It's good that
Il est dommage que	It's unfortunate that
Il est juste que	It's fair that
Il est logique que	It makes sense that
Il est rare que	It's unusual that
Il est urgent que	It's urgent that
Il est utile que	It's useful that

*__Il est__ can be replaced by **c'est**.

*The gender of the adjective doesn't change after **il est**.

C'est dommage que vous ne puissiez pas venir.
It's unfortunate that you can't come.

C'est logique qu'il ait gagné.
It makes sense that he won.

Il est rare qu'on trouve des nouvelles espèces.
It's unusual to find new species.

EX. 11.12 *Conjuguez les verbes entre parenthèses au subjonctif.* AUDIO 41.14

1. Il est bien que tu ______________ le problème. (comprendre)
2. C'est bon que j'______________ depuis longtemps. (économiser)
3. Il est dommage que le temps ______________ si vite. (passer)
4. Il est juste qu'ils ______________ l'argent. (rendre)
5. C'est logique que ces produits ______________ en promotion. (être)
6. Il est rare qu'il ______________ beau en décembre. (faire)
7. C'est urgent qu'on ______________ un remède. (découvrir)
8. C'est utile qu'on ______________télécharger les documents en ligne. (pouvoir)

⇨ After some conjunctions: AUDIO 41.15

Here is a list of common conjunctions followed by the subjunctive:

À condition que	Provided that – if
À supposer que	Assuming that
Afin que	So that
Bien que	Although
De façon que	So that

De manière que	So that
De sorte que	So that
En attendant que	Until – while
Encore que	So that
Jusqu'à ce que	Until
Où que	Wherever
Pour que	So that
Pourvu que	Provided that
Qui que	Whoever
Quoi que	Whatever

Je suis d'accord à condition que tu te tiennes bien.
I agree if you behave.

Elle utilise son vieux téléphone jusqu'à ce qu'elle reçoive le nouveau.
She is using her old phone until she gets the new one.

Je pense à toi où que tu sois.
I think of you wherever you are.

EX. 11.13 *Ajoutez une des conjonctions de la liste ci-dessus.* AUDIO 41.16

1. Je le range ________________________ il ne le trouve pas.
2. Le directeur explique les problèmes ________________________ tout soit clair.
3. Nous mangerons tôt ________________________ tu te couches à l'heure.
4. Tu réussiras ________________________ tu étudies.
5. Le film commencera à l'heure ________________________ tout fonctionne.
6. ________________________ ça dure !
7. Elle cuisine le dîner ________________________ j'arrive.
8. J'ai mis la boîte sur le frigo ________________________ tu ne puisses pas l'attraper.

Some conjunctions take a **"ne"** after **que**. It's called the **ne explétif.** AUDIO 41.17

It's a little word that we use to draw attention to the first part of the sentence. It doesn't add any meaning and doesn't turn the sentence into a negative sentence either.

À moins que ... (ne)	Unless
Avant que ... (ne)	Before that
De crainte que ... (ne)	For fear that
De peur que ... (ne)	For fear that
Sans que ... (ne)	Without

*Remember to **download the audio** and to **watch the videos** – see Preface*

Il marche tout seul sans que je ne l'aide.
He walks alone without me helping him.

Prépare le dossier avant que je n'arrive.
Get the file ready before I arrive.

EX. 11.14 *Formez une phrase avec les éléments donnés et ajoutez le **ne explétif**.* AUDIO 41.18

1. Je vais acheter la maison / à moins que / il y a un problème.

   ____

2. Elle dormait / avant que / tu / arriver.

   ____

3. Il ne voulait pas te le dire / de crainte que / tu / être vexée.

   ____

4. Il a déjà préparé les papiers/ de peur que / la banque / refuse.

   ____

5. Il a préparé ses affaires / sans que / je lui / demander.

   ____

Other conjunctions with **que** take the indicative: AUDIO 41.19

Ainsi que	Just as
Alors que	While
Après que	After
Aussitôt que	As soon as
Bien sûr que	Of course
Depuis que	Since
Dès que	As soon as
En même temps que	At the same time that
Lorsque	When
Parce que	Because
Pendant que	While
Plutôt que	Instead of
Puisque	Since
Tandis que	While

⇨ The superlative is often followed by the subjunctive: AUDIO 41.20

Le seul - La seule ... qui - que - dont The only one that

C'est le seul qui sache faire fonctionner cette machine.
He is the only one who knows how to operate this machine.

Le premier - La première ... qui - que The first that

La première qui arrive gagne le gros lot.
The first one who arrives wins the big prize.

Le meilleur - La meilleure ... qui - que The best that

C'est la meilleure tarte que j'aie jamais mangée.
It's the best pie that I have ever eaten.

Il n'y a que ... qui - que There is only ... that

Il n'y a que l'argent qui compte pour toi.
There is only money for you.

Il y a peu de ... qui - que There aren't many ... that

Il y a peu d'oisillons qui survivent le premier mois.
There aren't many chicks that survive the first months.

EX. 11.15 *Réécrivez les phrases en ajoutant **que** et en transformant un des verbes au **subjonctif**.*

AUDIO 41.21

1. Je suis surprise, tu es déjà là.

___

2. On trouve une solution au plus vite, c'est important.

___

3. Ma grand-mère est heureuse, nous allons lui rendre visite.

___

4. Ils sont tristes, ils doivent rester à la maison.

___

5. Elle veut participer, je m'en doute.

___

6. J'ai assez d'argent, c'est probable.

___

7. Il peut encore faire du cinéma, c'est incroyable.

____

8. Lave-toi les mains, cela vaut mieux.

____

9. Il a dix-huit ans, c'est étonnant.

____

10. Vous savez la vérité, je ne crois pas.

____

Compound Tenses
Les Temps Composés

In French, the **passé composé** is not the only compound tense but it is the one that we use the most. Now that you know all the rules, it will be easy for you to understand how to use the three other compound tenses:

Le plus-que-parfait	The pluperfect
Le futur antérieur	The future perfect
Le conditionnel passé	The conditional perfect.

These three compound tenses follow the same rules as the passé composé, including the use of avoir and être.

Here is how to build them:

Plus-que-parfait = J'avais fait **I had done**

Avoir (imparfait) + past participle
Être (imparfait) + past participle

Le futur antérieur = J'aurai fait **I will have done**

Avoir (futur) + past participle
Être (futur) + past participle

Le conditionnel passé = J'aurais fait **I would have done**

Avoir (conditionnel présent) + past participle
Être (conditionnel présent) + past participle

You can see that the only difference with the **passé composé** is that the passé composé is built with the conjugation of **avoir** and **être** in the **present tense**. This is the only difference.

A few Rules to Remember

⇨ Verbs conjugated with **avoir** and **être** are conjugated with the same auxiliary as with the **passé composé.**

⇨ When a verb is conjugated with the auxiliary **être**, including reflexive verbs, the past participle agrees in gender and number with the subject.

⇨ When a verb is conjugated with the auxiliary **avoir**, the past participle agrees in gender and number with the direct object.

⇨ Negation and questions are made the exact same way as in the **passé composé**.

CHAPTER 12

The Pluperfect
Le Plus-Que-Parfait

The Pluperfect – Le Plus-Que-Parfait

In English, the **plus-que-parfait** corresponds to the past perfect tense: I had done
The **plus-que-parfait** is very similar in formation and in uses.

Building the Plus-Que-Parfait

Most of the verbs conjugated in the **plus-que-parfait** are built with the auxiliary **avoir** in the imparfait:

Avoir To have AUDIO 42.1

J'**avais**	Nous **avions**
Tu **avais**	Vous **aviez**
Il-Elle-On **avait**	Ils-Elles **avaient**

A list of specific verbs as well as all reflexive verbs are conjugated in the **plus-que-parfait** with the auxiliary **être** in the imparfait:

Être To be AUDIO 42.2

J'**étais**	Nous **étions**
Tu **étais**	Vous **étiez**
Il-Elle-On **était**	Ils-Elles **étaient**

Let's see the complete conjugation of a verb conjugated with **avoir**, a verb conjugated with **être** and a reflexive verb:

Téléphoner To call AUDIO 42.3

J'**avais téléphoné**
Tu **avais téléphoné**
Il **avait téléphoné**
Elle **avait téléphoné**
On **avait téléphoné**
Nous **avions téléphoné**
Vous **aviez téléphoné**
Ils **avaient téléphoné**
Elles **avaient téléphoné**

Partir To leave AUDIO 42.4

J'**étais parti(e)**
Tu **étais parti(e)**
Il **était parti**
Elle **était partie**
On **était parti(e)s**
Nous **étions parti(e)s**
Vous **étiez parti(e)s**
Ils **étaient partis**
Elles **étaient parties**

Se changer To get changed AUDIO 42.5

Je **m'étais changé(e)**
Tu **t'étais changé(e)**
Il **s'était changé**
Elle **s'était changée**
On **s'était changé(e)s**
Nous **nous étions changé(e)s**
Vous **vous étiez changé(e)s**
Ils **s'étaient changés**
Elles **s'étaient changées**

When to Use the Plus-Que-Parfait

We use the **plus-que-parfait** to talk about an action or situation that happened before another past action. It's often used in the same sentence as other past tenses, such as the **imparfait** or **passé composé**. If used by itself, we understand that we are referring to something previously mentioned about the past.

> The **plus-que-parfait** is used to talk about an action or a situation that happened before another past action.

AUDIO 42.6

J'avais compris quand le téléphone a sonné.
I had understood when the phone rang.

Il s'était trompé dans son test mais le professeur ne l'a pas remarqué.
He had made a mistake on his test, but the professor didn't notice it.

Vous aviez déjà acheté votre nouvelle voiture à ce moment-là.
You had already bought your new car at that time.

Je pensais que tu n'avais jamais vu ce film.
I thought that you had never seen this movie.

Les soldats s'étaient cachés quand ils ont entendu les coups de feu.
The soldiers had hidden when they heard the shots.

Sa compagne avait appris le français il y a des années.
His partner had learned French many years ago.

EX. 12.1 *Conjuguez les verbes suivants au **plus-que-parfait**.* AUDIO 42.7

Ajoutez le féminin entre parenthèses avec Je, Tu, On, Nous, Vous => J'étais allé(e)

1. Avoir
   J' ____________________
   Tu ____________________
   Il ____________________
   Nous ____________________
   Vous ____________________
   Ils ____________________
2. Rentrer
   J' ____________________
   Tu ____________________
   Elle ____________________
   Nous ____________________
   Vous ____________________
   Elles ____________________
3. Se maquiller
   Je ____________________
   Tu ____________________
   On ____________________
   Nous ____________________
   Vous ____________________
   Elles ____________________

EX. 12.2 *Réécrivez chaque phrase au* ***plus-que-parfait.*** AUDIO 42.8

1. J'ai cherché mon stylo partout.

 ____

2. Son responsable l'a prévenu.

 ____

3. L'échelle est tombée toute seule.

 ____

4. Nous avons lavé la voiture au carwash.

 ____

5. Elle a encore oublié ses livres.

 ____

6. Martin a vaincu le cancer.

 ____

7. Ma tante a fait de la soupe.

 ____

8. J'ai reçu un collier pour mon anniversaire.

 ____

9. Il a plu toute la nuit.

 ____

10. L'application a arrêté de fonctionner.

 ____

Remember to ***download the audio*** *and to* ***watch the videos*** *– see Preface*

EX. 12.3 *Trouvez le* ***complément d'objet direct*** *et transformez-le en* ***pronom****. Accordez le participe passé en fonction.* AUDIO 42.9 🔊

1. Il avait attendu cette lettre pendant des semaines.

   ____

2. Les propriétaires avaient changé les serrures.

   ____

3. Elle s'était lavé les cheveux avant d'aller chez le coiffeur.

   ____

4. Le ministre avait envoyé ses cartes de vœux en avance.

   ____

5. Les étudiants avaient déjà acheté tous leurs manuels.

   ____

CHAPTER 13

The Future Perfect
Le Futur Antérieur

The Future Perfect - Le Futur Antérieur

In English, the **futur antérieur** corresponds to the future perfect tense: I will have done.
The **futur antérieur** is very similar in formation and uses.

Building the Futur Antérieur

Most of the verbs conjugated in the **futur antérieur** are built with the auxiliary **avoir** in the **futur simple**:

Avoir To have AUDIO 43.1

J'**aurai**	Nous **aurons**
Tu **auras**	Vous **aurez**
Il-Elle-On **aura**	Ils-Elles **auront**

A list of specific verbs as well as all reflexive verbs are conjugated in the **futur antérieur** with the auxiliary **être** in the **futur simple**:

Être To be AUDIO 43.2

Je **serai**	Nous **serons**
Tu **seras**	Vous **serez**
Il-Elle-On **sera**	Ils-Elles **seront**

Let's see the complete conjugation of a verb conjugated with **avoir**, a verb conjugated with **être** and a reflexive verb:

Manger To eat AUDIO 43.3

J'**aurai mangé**
Tu **auras mangé**
Il **aura mangé**
Elle **aura mangé**
On **aura mangé**
Nous **aurons mangé**
Vous **aurez mangé**
Ils **auront mangé**
Elles **auront mangé**

Descendre To go down AUDIO 43.4

Je **serai descendu(e)**
Tu **seras descendu(e)**
Il **sera descendu**
Elle **sera descendue**
On **sera descendu(e)s**
Nous **serons descendu(e)s**
Vous **serez descendu(e)s**
Ils **seront descendus**
Elles **seront descendues**

Se lever To get up AUDIO 43.5

Je **me serai levé(e)**
Tu **te seras levé(e)**
Il **se sera levé**
Elle **se sera levée**
On **se sera levé(e)s**
Nous **nous serons levé(e)s**
Vous **vous serez levé(e)s**
Ils **se seront levés**
Elles **se seront levées**

When to Use the Futur Antérieur

The **futur antérieur** is used to talk about an action or situation going to be completed before another action in the future.

AUDIO 43.6

Je serai rentrée quand tu arriveras.
I will have come home when you will arrive.

Quand j'aurai terminé ce dossier, je demanderai une augmentation.
When I (will) have finished this file, I will ask for a raise.

Elle vivra à l'étranger quand elle aura fini ses études.
She will live abroad when she is done with her studies.

Nous aurons bientôt terminé la rénovation.
We will be done soon with the renovation.

Quand il verra l'oiseau, il se sera envolé.
When he sees the bird, it will have flown away.

EX. 13.1 *Conjuguez les verbes suivants au futur antérieur.* AUDIO 43.7

Ajoutez le féminin entre parenthèses avec Je, Tu, On, Nous, Vous => Je serai allé(e)

1. Regarder

   J' ______________________________

   Tu ______________________________

   Il ______________________________

   Nous ______________________________

   Vous ______________________________

   Ils ______________________________

2. Monter

   Je ______________________________

   Tu ______________________________

   Elle ______________________________

   Nous ______________________________

   Vous ______________________________

   Elles ______________________________

3. Se perdre

   Je ______________________________

   Tu ______________________________

   On ______________________________

   Nous ______________________________

   Vous ______________________________

   Elles ______________________________

EX. 13.2 *Conjuguez le verbe entre parenthèses au **futur antérieur**.* AUDIO 43.8

1. Ils (faire) ______________________ le changement.
2. Dans quelques jours, nous (partir) ______________________ .
3. Vous (boire) ______________________ tout le café.
4. Je (rester) ______________________ plus longtemps que prévu.
5. Demain, elles (présenter) ______________________ leurs dissertations.
6. L'architecte (finir) ______________________ les plans bientôt.
7. On (obtenir) ______________________ le permis d'ici là.
8. J' (terminer) ______________________ pour 18 heures.
9. Demain, il (recevoir) ______________________ ses résultats.
10. J'espère que nous (déménager) ______________________ avant décembre.

CHAPTER 14

The Conditional Perfect
Le Conditionnel Passé

The Conditional Perfect – Le Conditionnel Passé

In English, the **conditionnel passé** corresponds to the English: I would have done.
As we saw with the **conditionnel présent**, in French, the **conditionnel** conjugates the verb; we don't use would, should and could.

Building the Conditionnel Passé

Most of the verbs conjugated in the **conditionnel passé** are built with the auxiliary **avoir** in the **conditionnel présent**:

Avoir To have AUDIO 44.1

J'**aurais**	Nous **aurions**
Tu **aurais**	Vous **auriez**
Il-Elle-On **aurait**	Ils-Elles **auraient**

A list of specific verbs as well as all reflexive verbs are conjugated in the **conditionnel passé** with the auxiliary **être** in the **conditionnel présent**:

Être To be AUDIO 44.2

Je **serais**	Nous **serions**
Tu **serais**	Vous **seriez**
Il-Elle-On **serait**	Ils-Elles **seraient**

Let's see the complete conjugation of a verb conjugated with **avoir**, a verb conjugated with **être** and a reflexive verb:

Chercher To search AUDIO 44.3

J'**aurais cherché**
Tu **aurais cherché**
Il **aurait cherché**
Elle **aurait cherché**
On **aurait cherché**
Nous **aurions cherché**
Vous **auriez cherché**
Ils **auraient cherché**
Elles **auraient cherché**

Rester To stay AUDIO 44.4

Je **serais resté(e)**
Tu **serais resté(e)**
Il **serait resté**
Elle **serait restée**
On **serait resté(e)s**
Nous **serions resté(e)s**
Vous **seriez resté(e)s**
Ils **seraient restés**
Elles **seraient restées**

S'arrêter To stop oneself AUDIO 44.5

Je **me serais arrêté(e)**
Tu **te serais arrêté(e)**
Il **se serait arrêté**
Elle **se serait arrêtée**
On **se serait arrêté(e)s**
Nous **nous serions arrêté(e)s**
Vous **vous seriez arrêté(e)s**
Ils **se seraient arrêtés**
Elles **se seraient arrêtées**

When to Use the Conditionnel Passé

The **conditionnel passé** is used to talk about a past situation, uncertain information, a wish, or a regret.

AUDIO 44.6

D'après ce que l'on sait, les parents auraient abandonné l'enfant dans l'appartement.
From what we know, the parents would have left the child in the apartment.

Il aurait mis 10 jours pour arriver.
He would have taken 10 days to get here.

Je ne serais pas partie si j'avais su.
I wouldn't have left if I had known.

Elle aurait demandé plusieurs fois un médicament.
She would have asked for medicine several times.

EX. 14.1 *Conjuguez les verbes suivants au* ***conditionnel passé****.* AUDIO 44.7

Ajoutez le féminin entre parenthèses avec Je, Tu, On, Nous, Vous => Je serais allé(e)

1. Peser

   J' ______________________________

   Tu ______________________________

   Il ______________________________

   Nous ______________________________

   Vous ______________________________

   Ils ______________________________

2. Devenir

   Je ______________________________

   Tu ______________________________

   Elle ______________________________

   Nous ______________________________

   Vous ______________________________

   Elles ______________________________

3. Se conduire

   Je ______________________________

   Tu ______________________________

   On ______________________________

   Nous ______________________________

   Vous ______________________________

   Elles ______________________________

EX. 14.2 *Conjuguez le verbe entre parenthèses au* ***conditionnel passé.*** AUDIO **44.8**

1. On (passer) ____________________ de bonnes vacances si on n'était pas tombés malade.
2. Si vous (étudier) ____________________ vous (réussir) ____________________ votre examen.
3. Elle (avoir) ____________________ faim si elle n'avait pas mangé.
4. La société (perdre) ____________________ plusieurs millions.
5. Au cas où vous (oublier) ____________________, nous avons rendez-vous ce soir.
6. Je ne sais pas si elle (aimer) ____________________ cette idée.
7. De ce que j'ai entendu, le peintre (faire) ____________________ un travail incroyable.
8. Ils se (téléphoner) ____________________ il y a quelques jours.
9. Il (devoir) ____________________ faire plus attention.
10. Cela (être) ____________________ plus rapide si on était passés par là.

CHAPTER 15

The Present Participle – The Gerund
Le Participe Présent – Le Gérondif

The Present Participle – Le Participe Présent
The Gerund – Le Gérondif

The present participle, called **participe présent** in French, is used in French and English. However, both languages have specific uses and different rules around it.

It is a very formal way to speak. You can find it in the news, for example, or also in writing, like in newspapers and books.

When preceded by **en**, it's called **gérondif**.

Building the Participe Présent

All the French **participe présent** end with **-ant** and are **invariable.** To build them take the verb conjugated in the present tense with **nous**, remove the ending **-ons** and add **-ant**.

In English, the equivalent (but not always) is words ending in -ing: seeing, knowing, ...

AUDIO 45.1

Nous form	Participe présent	Translation
Nous **donn**~~ons~~	**Donnant**	Giving
Nous **finiss**~~ons~~	**Finissant**	Finishing
Nous **attend**~~ons~~	**Attendant**	Waiting
Nous **prononç**~~ons~~	**Prononçant**	Pronouncing
Nous **mange**~~ons~~	**Mangeant**	Eating
Nous **craign**~~ons~~	**Craignant**	Fearing
Nous **serv**~~ons~~	**Servant**	Serving
Nous **voul**~~ons~~	**Voulant**	Wanting
Nous **découvr**~~ons~~	**Découvrant**	Discovering

Only 3 verbs are irregular present participles:

Avoir	**Ayant**	Having
Être	**Étant**	Being
Savoir	**Sachant**	Knowing

EX. 15.1 *Traduisez en français.* AUDIO 45.2

1. Seeing ______________________
2. Drinking ______________________
3. Studying ______________________
4. Going ______________________
5. Being ______________________
6. Smiling ______________________
7. Adding ______________________
8. Telling ______________________
9. Waiting ______________________
10. Wishing ______________________
11. Hearing ______________________
12. Obligating ______________________
13. Buying ______________________
14. Working ______________________
15. Finishing ______________________
16. Snowing ______________________
17. Playing ______________________
18. Doing ______________________
19. Brushing ______________________
20. Believing ______________________

A **participe présent** can also be used as an adjective. In this case, the adjective agrees in gender and number with the noun. The spelling can be different from the **participe présent**.

AUDIO 45.3

Surprendre	**Surprenant(e)**	Une histoire **surprenante** A surprising story
Briller	**Brillant(e)**	Une étoile **brillante** A shinny star
Précéder	**Précédent(e)**	Le chapitre **précédent** The previous chapter

When to Use the Participe Présent

We use the **participe présent**: AUDIO 45.4

⇨ To modify a noun:

The **participe présent** refers to the noun. This form is similar to its use in English.

Voyant Karen, il a changé de direction.
Seeing Karen, he changed direction.

Habitant près de la gare, il est dérangé constamment par le bruit des trains.
Living by the train station, he is constantly bothered by the noise of trains.

La petite fille, regardant la télévision, était assise dans le canapé.
The little girl, watching TV, was sitting on the couch.

*Remember to **download the audio** and to **watch the videos** – see Preface*

The Uses of the Gérondif

AUDIO 45.5

Le **gérondif** is built with **en + participe présent**. We use it to:

⇨ To talk about an action related to the verb. It's usually about simultaneity and translates to while or upon.

J'écoute toujours de la musique en travaillant.
I always listen to music while working.

Nous avons rencontré Paul en mangeant au restaurant.
We met Paul while eating at the restaurant.

En arrivant au travail, elle a vu un accident.
Upon arriving at work, she saw an accident.

⇨ To talk about the cause and it mostly translates to by.

Elle a gagné 3 millions en jouant à la loterie.
She won 3 million by playing the lottery.

Il s'est fait mal en tombant de la chaise.
He hurt himself by falling from the chair.

Nous sommes devenus docteurs en étudiant tous les jours pendant des années.
We became doctors by studying every day for years.

⇨ To replace a relative clause (without en).

Most of the time, the relative clause includes **qui**:

Nous cherchons des guides **qui parlent** français.
Nous cherchons des guides parlant français.
We are looking for guides who speak French.

Les passagers **qui attendent** le train de 16 heures sont priés de changer de quai.
Les passagers attendant le train de 16 heures sont priés de changer de quai.
Passengers waiting for the 4 p.m. train are requested to change platform.

Participe Présent vs Gérondif

Let's look at similar sentences with a **participe présent** and a **gérondif**. AUDIO 45.6

J'ai vu Nicole traversant la rue.
I saw Nicole crossing the street.

Here **traversant** act as a **participe présent**. *It describes Nicole, who was crossing the street.*

J'ai vu Nicole en traversant la rue.
I saw Nicole while crossing the street.

En traversant is a **gérondif**. *It describes what I was doing when I saw Nicole.*

EX. 15.2 *Transformez le verbe en **gérondif** et liez les phrases ensemble.* AUDIO 45.7

Je m'endors souvent. Je regarde la télévision.
Je m'endors souvent en regardant la télévision.

1. Il a eu un accident. Il conduisait tard la nuit.

 ____

2. J'ai réveillé ma fille. Je chantais trop fort.

 ____

3. Il est arrivé à l'école. Il courait.

 ____

4. Mes parents se sont rencontrés. Ils voyageaient en Europe.

 ____

5. Pauline est sous la pluie. Elle attend le bus.

 ____

6. Il faut prendre ces médicaments. Il mange.

 ____

7. Il a gradué. Il avait 2 travails.

 ____

8. Nous sommes tombés amoureux de cette ville. Nous l'avons visitée l'année dernière.

 ____

9. Ils se sont mariés civilement. Ils attendent d'économiser pour célébrer.

____

10. Vous avez cherché une maison. Vous regardez sur internet.

____

EX. 15.3 *Ajoutez le bon verbe et changez-le en* ***participe présent.*** AUDIO 45.8

travailler - changer - regarder - sourire - réserver - faire - dire - vendre - marcher - savoir

1. En ____________________ cela, tu risques de perdre des amis.
2. En ____________________ de plus près, on voit bien les défauts.
3. En ____________________ ensemble, nous pouvons y arriver.
4. En ____________________ cela, je ne lui parlerai plus.
5. En ____________________ aux clients, les interactions se passent mieux.
6. En ____________________ la chaudière, on économise 300 euros par an.
7. En ____________________ des gros mots, tu vas t'attirer des ennuis.
8. En ____________________ des affaires d'occasion, ils ont doublé leurs ventes.
9. En ____________________ une heure par jour, tu diminues ton rythme cardiaque.
10. En ____________________ maintenant, nous aurons la meilleure chambre.

CHAPTER 16

The Passive Voice
La Voix Passive

The Passive Voice – La Voix Passive

The passive voice, called **voix passive** in French, is similar to the English one in formation and use. They both require the use of the verb **Être** To be.

> The **passive voice** is used to shift the focus of the sentence to the second character or the second action.

When a sentence is passive, the verb is always conjugated with **être**, regardless of the tense. Therefore, the past participle always agrees in gender and number with the subject.

AUDIO 46.1

Let's look at an active sentence turned into a passive one conjugated in the present tense.

Active **Le banquier appelle la cliente.**
The banker is calling the client.

Passive **La cliente est appelée par le banquier.**
The client is called by the banker.

In passé composé:

Active **Le banquier a appelé la cliente.**
The banker called the client.

Passive **La cliente a été appelée par le banquier.**
The client has been called by the banker.

In imparfait:

Active **Le banquier appelait la cliente.**
The banker called the client.

Passive **La cliente était appelée par le banquier.**
The client was called by the banker.

In futur simple:

Active **Le banquier appellera la cliente.**
The banker will call the client.

Passive **La cliente sera appelée par le banquier.**
The client will be called by the banker.

The agent can also be introduced by **de** when the verbs express a condition or an emotion.

Active **Tout le monde les aime.**
Everyone loves them.

Passive **Ils sont aimés de tous.**
They are loved by everyone.

The voix passive in French isn't used as much as in English. Another form that is used more than the regular passive voice is the use of **on** or even **ils.**

La voiture a été réparée = On a réparé la voiture = Ils ont réparé la voiture.
The car has been fixed = We fixed the car = They fixed the car.

Use **on** to talk about a generality, **ils** to talk about people without naming them.

EX. 16.1 *Transformez ces phrases actives en* ***phrases passives.*** AUDIO 46.2

1. Marie a vendu sa voiture.

____

2. La voiture a renversé le passant.

____

3. Le bûcheron coupe l'arbre avec sa tronçonneuse.

____

4. Le principal ferme l'école tous les soirs.

____

5. Ce vignoble produit un vin excellent.

____

6. Ce livre te changera la vie !

____

7. Le facteur dépose le courrier à la réception chaque matin.

____

8. Paul va acheter une tarte chez le boulanger.

____

9. Elle aurait entendu un bruit pendant la nuit.

____

10. C'est un enfant qui a écrit ce poème.

____

11. Maman t'a laissé de l'argent sur la table.

____

12. Le professeur donne une leçon intéressante.

____

CHAPTER 17

The Simple Past
Le Passé Simple

The Simple Past - Le Passé Simple

The **passé simple** is the tense that replaces the **passé composé** in formal writing. The **passé simple is never used in conversation.**

So why should you learn it?

I don't think you should. This tense has complicated endings and just adds confusion to the French past tenses. That being said, it's good to recognize it because it's still used in some newspapers and books. Let's see how to conjugate one verb from each group.

> The **passé simple** is the historical past.

Building the Passé Simple

The endings of the **passé simple** change depending on the group of verbs

For verbs ending in **-er**, the endings are: **-ai, -as, -a, -âmes, âtes** and **-èrent.**

Ajouter To add AUDIO 46.1.1

J'ajout**ai**	Nous ajout**âmes**
Tu ajout**as**	Vous ajout**âtes**
Il-Elle-On ajout**a**	Ils-Elles ajout**èrent**

For verbs ending in -**ir** and **-re**, the endings are: **-is, -is, -it, -îmes, îtes and -irent.**

Réussir To succeed AUDIO 46.1.2

Je réuss**is**	Nous réuss**îmes**
Tu réuss**is**	Vous réuss**îtes**
Il-Elle-On réuss**it**	Ils-Elles réuss**irent**

Répondre To answer AUDIO 46.1.3

Je répond**is**	Nous répond**îmes**
Tu répond**is**	Vous répond**îtes**
Il-Elle-On répond**it**	Ils-Elles répond**irent**

CHAPTER 18

Revision
Révision

EX. 18.1 *Traduisez les verbes suivants en français.* AUDIO R.1

1. I know ______
2. You (s) think ______
3. She saves ______
4. You (pl) forget ______
5. We throw ______
6. She hopes ______
7. I do ______
8. You (s) have to ______
9. They (m) offer ______
10. We (on) say ______

EX. 18.2 *Choisissez parmi les verbes de la liste et conjuguez-les au présent de l'indicatif.* AUDIO R.2

attendre – nettoyer – décider – s'appeler – voir – tenir – venir – falloir – être – avoir

1. Nous ______ en retard, comme d'habitude.
2. Je ______ l'océan de ma chambre.
3. Elle ______ la main de son amie.
4. Il ______ partir tout de suite.
5. Comment est-ce que tu ______ ?
6. Nous ______ toujours tout en dernière minute.
7. Je ______ du sud de la France.
8. J' ______ 14 ans, bientôt 15 ans.
9. Nous ______ la cuisine tous les soirs avant de nous coucher.
10. L'ambulance ______ les appels pour partir.

EX. 18.3 *Conjuguez les verbes entre parenthèses au présent de l'indicatif.* AUDIO R.3

1. On ______ (acheter) du beurre au marché tous les jeudis.
2. Nous ______ (prendre) le train pour aller à l'aéroport.
3. ______ (savoir)-tu que le voisin est décédé ?

4. Est-ce que tu ______________________ (connaitre) cette histoire ?
5. Je ne ______________________ (boire) pas assez d'eau durant la journée.
6. Il ______________________ (céder) ses parts à son fils.
7. Vous ______________________ (choisir) sans réfléchir.
8. Je ______________________ (chercher) un petit sac noir en cuir végétal.
9. Regarde ta facture, tu ______________________ (téléphoner) beaucoup trop.
10. Est-ce que tu ______________________ (vouloir) un café avant de partir ?

EX. 18.4 *Traduisez les phrases en français.* AUDIO R.4

1. We are moving out of the apartment next Saturday.

   ____

2. I have been working here since December.

   ____

3. We have been living here for 3 years.

   ____

4. I only drink filtered water.

   ____

5. You (s) are already at work.

   ____

6. The car is still not working.

   ____

7. We are getting changed before leaving for the restaurant.

   ____

8. Are you (s) watching TV every morning?

   ____

9. The dog is sleeping on the grass.

   ____

10. The landlord is selling the house.

    ____

EX. 18.5 *Choisissez parmi les verbes de la liste et conjuguez-les au présent de l'indicatif.*

AUDIO R.5

être en train de - être en retard - être dans la lune - être de - avoir mal à - avoir du mal à - avoir la pêche - avoir chaud - aller chez - aller au - faire du - faire la - il fait

1. Il ________________ vaisselle.
2. Elle ________________ , elle ne t'a pas entendu.
3. Le patient ________________ la tête.
4. Nous ________________ le docteur cet après-midi.
5. J' ________________ avec ce gros pull !
6. Nous ________________ chercher une nouvelle table.
7. Il ________________ faire ses lacets.
8. Le train ________________ de plusieurs minutes.
9. Je ________________ Londres, et toi ?
10. On ________________ ce matin !
11. Je ________________ marché acheter des légumes.
12. On ________________ vélo tous les samedis matin.
13. Il ________________ aujourd'hui !

EX. 18.6 *Ajoutez un verbe impersonnel et conjuguez-le au présent de l'indicatif.* AUDIO R.6

1. Il ________________ 6 heures du matin.
2. C' ________________ trop tôt.
3. Il y ________________ du lait dans le frigo.
4. Il ________________ mieux arriver quelques minutes plus tôt.
5. Il ________________ froid dans ma chambre.
6. Il ________________ que tu t'es marié.

EX. 18.7 *Changez le COD en pronom (DOP) sur la deuxième ligne.* AUDIO R.7

1. Elle reçoit une récompense pour son travail.

   DOP : ________________

2. Nous promenons nos chiens tous les matins à 8 heures.

   DOP : ________________

3. On aide mes parents à faire les courses.

   DOP : ______________________________

4. Elle connaît bien ses voisins.

   DOP : ______________________________

5. Ils adoptent un nouveau chat.

   DOP : ______________________________

6. Nous regardons un film d'horreur.

   DOP : ______________________________

7. Elle n'aime pas les légumes, surtout les tomates.

   DOP : ______________________________

8. Le directeur envoie les dossiers au client.

   DOP : ______________________________

9. Je fais une carte moi-même pour mon frère.

   DOP : ______________________________

10. Est-ce que tu comprends la leçon ?

    DOP : ______________________________

EX. 18.8 *Conjuguez le verbe entre parenthèses au présent. N'oubliez pas de changer le pronom réflexif.* **AUDIO R.8**

1. (Se souvenir) Elle ______________________ de toi.
2. (S'adapter) Les employés ______________________ doucement au nouveau programme.
3. (Se marier) Nous ______________________ le mois prochain.
4. (Se couper) La coiffeuse ______________________ les cheveux elle-même.
5. (S'asseoir) Il ______________________ toujours là.
6. (Se reposer) On ______________________ ce week-end.
7. (S'ennuyer) Les enfants ______________________ , il n'y a rien à faire.
8. (Se laver) Je ______________________ et je vais au lit.
9. (Se rappeler) Je ne ______________________ pas de cette leçon.
10. (Se fâcher) Ils ______________________ facilement quand ils sont fatigués.

EX. 18.9 *Corrigez les verbes et les pronoms dans les phrases suivantes.* AUDIO R.9

1. Nous s'amusons bien au parc aujourd'hui. ______
2. Tu ne vous laver pas les mains avant de cuisiner ? ______
3. On se brossent les dents avant d'aller au lit. ______
4. Mes voisins se réveille tôt et nous réveillent à chaque fois. ______
5. Je ne m'attens pas à ça ! ______
6. Tu te trompe toujours avec ce verbe. ______
7. Je m'appele Jeanne, et toi ? ______
8. Mon père se sers de cet outil pour couper du bois. ______
9. Elle se soucient pour ses enfants. ______
10. Nous nous mettont au judo. ______

EX. 18.10 *Donnez le participe passé des verbes suivants.* AUDIO R.10

1. Aller ______
2. Voir ______
3. Connaître ______
4. Devoir ______
5. Savoir ______
6. Manger______
7. Faire ______
8. Vouloir ______
9. Finir ______
10. Ouvrir ______
11. Sortir ______
12. Sentir ______
13. Pouvoir ______
14. Lire ______
15. Cuisiner ______
16. Cuire______
17. Être ______
18. Nourrir ______
19. Lire ______
20. Vendre ______

EX. 18.11 *Conjuguez le verbe entre parenthèses au passé composé.* AUDIO R.11

1. (Partir) Nous ______ tôt ce matin.
2. (Avoir) On ______ la grippe.
3. (Boire) J' ______ trop de café.
4. (Finir) Tu ______ ta présentation ?
5. (Aller) Nous ______ à la piscine hier.

6. (Manger) Nous ______________________________ dans ce restaurant.
7. (Fermer) Tu ______________________________ la porte ?
8. (Perdre) J' ______________________________ mes clés !
9. (Lire) Elles ______________________________ ta lettre.
10. (Apprendre) Est-ce que tu ______________________________ la nouvelle ?

EX. 18.12 *Conjuguez les phrases au **passé composé** en utilisant **être** ou **avoir**.* AUDIO R.12

1. J'achète cette lotion pour ma copine.

   ____

2. Elle signe cette facture pour la payer.

   ____

3. On rêve de partir au Mexique.

   ____

4. Tu prends tes affaires avant de partir ?

   ____

5. Le professeur répond aux questions.

   ____

6. Il nous parle de ses vacances.

   ____

7. Le chat a une opération pour se faire nettoyer les dents.

   ____

8. Nous terminons nos devoirs avant d'aller jouer.

   ____

9. Je vis à Lyon.

   ____

10. Elle sort de l'hôpital il y a quelques heures.

   ____

*Remember to **download the audio** and to **watch the videos** – see Preface*

EX. 18.13 *Complétez les phrases après* ***que****.* AUDIO R.13

1. Elle a mis la table.

   La table qu' ____________________

2. Nous avons acheté une nouvelle armoire.

   La nouvelle armoire que ____________________

3. J'ai pris l'ascenseur pour venir.

   L'ascenseur que ____________________

4. Le docteur m'a conseillé cette crème.

   Cette crème que ____________________

5. Il a félicité les élèves.

   Les élèves qu' ____________________

6. Nous leur avons prêté la tente.

   La tente que ____________________

7. Il a bu de très bons vins.

   Les très bons vins qu' ____________________

8. L'artiste a fini ses dernières créations.

   Les dernières créations qu' ____________________

9. L'infirmière a fait une piqûre.

   La piqûre que ____________________

10. Le patron a donné aux employés trois jours de congé.

    Les trois jours de congé qu' ____________________

EX. 18.14 *Conjuguez le verbe entre parenthèses au* ***passé composé****, n'oubliez pas d'ajouter le féminin et pluriel.* AUDIO R.14

1. (S'excuser) Nous ____________________ pour notre erreur.
2. (S'abonner) Je ____________________ au nouveau magazine.
3. (Se tromper) Il ____________________ sur la question numéro 3.
4. (S'amuser) Nous ____________________ à cette fête.
5. (S'arrêter) La voiture ____________________ au dernier moment.

6. (S'occuper) Vous ______________________________ du dîner ?
7. (S'intéresser) Elle ______________________________ à la poterie.
8. (S'endormir) Nous ______________________________ vite.
9. (Se mettre) Je ______________________________ à la méditation.
10. (Se faire) Elle ______________________________ une teinture.

EX. 18.15 *Changez la phrase du* ***présent*** *au* ***passé composé*** *sur la première ligne. Sur la deuxième ligne, ajoutez la* ***négation*** *donnée.* AUDIO R.15

1. J'arrive tout de suite.

   ____

   Ne ... pas : ______________________________
2. On joue au poker samedi.

   ____

   Ne ... jamais : ______________________________
3. Elle devient docteur.

   ____

   Ne ... pas : ______________________________
4. Cette personne appartient à un gang.

   ____

   Ne ... pas : ______________________________
5. Le pompier agit sans réfléchir.

   ____

   Ne ... pas : ______________________________
6. Je conduis les enfants à l'arrêt de bus.

   ____

   Ne ... pas : ______________________________
7. Elle ose prendre des risques.

   ____

   Ne ... jamais : ______________________________

8. Il essaye de changer sa réputation.

____

Ne ... plus : ____________________

9. Le vent souffle toute la nuit.

____

Ne ... pas : ____________________

10. Elle vit une vie complète et heureuse.

____

Ne ... pas : ____________________

EX. 18.16 *Traduisez les pronoms et les verbes.* AUDIO R.16

1. I got old – ____________________
2. You warned (s) – ____________________
3. We studied – ____________________
4. She moved – ____________________
5. They counted (m) – ____________________
6. She put back – ____________________
7. I knew – ____________________
8. He asked – ____________________
9. They accepted (f) – ____________________
10. We fired – ____________________
11. He found – ____________________
12. They poured – ____________________
13. We discovered – ____________________
14. She met – ____________________
15. You turned (s) – ____________________

EX. 18.17 *Conjuguez le verbe entre parenthèses à l'**imparfait**.* AUDIO R.17

1. Elles ______________________ toujours tard. (se réveiller)
2. Tu ______________________ sans cesse à ce jeu. (jouer)
3. Il ______________________ être là aujourd'hui. (devoir)
4. Le bruit ne me ______________________ pas. (déranger)
5. Je ______________________ une odeur de brûlé. (sentir)
6. Le contrat leur ______________________ de les utiliser. (permettre)
7. Vous ______________________ les devoirs des élèves. (corriger)
8. Il ______________________ trop vite. (conduire)
9. Elle ______________________ tout ce qui ne fonctionnait pas. (jeter)
10. L'inspecteur ______________________ le suspect. (interroger)

EX. 18.18 *Conjuguez les verbes donnés à l'**imparfait**.* AUDIO R.18

1. Le vendeur ______________ (attendre) pendant que les clients ______________ (prendre) une décision.
2. Elle ______________ (habiter) à Nice, ses parents ______________ (vivre) à Paris.
3. Parce qu'elle ______________ (prendre) le bus, elle ______________ (être) toujours en retard.
4. Il ______________ (parler) tout le temps pendant qu'on ______________ (regarder) un film.
5. La boulangère ______________ (demander) si on ______________ (vouloir) autre chose.
6. Le mécanicien ______________ (expliquer) le problème ______________ mais elle n' ______________ (écouter) rien.
7. Elle ______________ (perdre) 3 kilos par mois mais elle ______________ (manger) très équilibré.
8. Je ______________ (partir) quand il ______________ (arriver).
9. Elle ______________ (adorer) le pain mais ______________ (détester) les pâtes.
10. Il ______________ (chanter) pendant qu'il ______________ (se laver).

EX. 18.19 *Conjuguez les verbes donnés au passé composé ou à l'**imparfait**.* AUDIO R.19

1. Elle ____________________ (s'évanouir) soudainement.
2. Le soleil ____________________ (se lever) à l'arrière de la cabane.
3. Je ne sais pas s'il ____________________ (payer).
4. On ____________________ (se chauffer) au bois dans le temps.
5. Elle ____________________ (insister) pour te voir tout de suite.
6. Ma collègue ____________________ (apporter) des gâteaux pour son anniversaire.
7. L'hiver ____________________ (être) toujours froid.
8. Les passagers ____________________ (survivre) à l'accident.
9. Elle ____________________ (changer) de train.
10. Je ____________________ (lire) 10 pages par jour.

EX. 18.20 *Traduisez les phrases en français, les verbes seront conjugués à l'**imparfait** ou au **passé composé**.* AUDIO R.20

1. We called each other every Sunday.

   ____

2. We called each other this Sunday.

   ____

3. They (f) left this morning.

   ____

4. You paid too much money for this car.

   ____

5. We used to do the groceries in the city, now it's too expensive.

   ____

6. She had an incredible memory!

   ____

7. What did you do?

   ____

8. My wife ironed my shirt before my meeting.

____

9. Prices raised continually last year.

____

10. I gave my jacket away because it was too small.

____

EX. 18.21 *Corrigez les phrases ci-dessous.* AUDIO R.21

1. Je lisais ce livre, j'ai adoré l'histoire.

____

2. Tu s'est levée tôt ce matin !

____

3. Chaque jour, je suis allé acheter du pain à la boulangerie.

____

4. Il a regardé la télévision quand le téléphone sonnait.

____

5. Je visitais Paris en 2020.

____

6. Elle recevait ton email il y a quelques minutes.

____

7. Tu mangeais déjà ?

____

8. J'ai conduit quand tu appelais.

____

9. Il a été fatigué.

____

10. Mardi, Léa venait chez moi.

____

EX. 18.22 *Transformez les phrases ci-dessous au* ***passé récent (venir de - venir juste de).***

AUDIO R.22

1. Il s'endort dans le canapé.

____

2. Tu mets le lave-vaisselle en route.

____

3. Le client paye ses courses par carte de crédit.

____

4. Ce film passe à la télévision.

____

5. Ce building est démoli pour construire des nouvelles maisons.

____

6. Ce couple adopte une petite fille de 3 ans.

____

7. Il casse le vase mais il ne l'a pas fait exprès.

____

8. L'écrivain finit d'écrire son nouveau roman.

____

9. Ce café ouvre aujourd'hui.

____

10. La police prévient la famille de l'accident.

____

EX. 18.23 *Conjuguez la première phrase à l'****imparfait*** *et la deuxième phrase au* ***passé composé.*** *Connectez les deux phrases ensemble en utilisant les adverbes* ***quand, que.*** AUDIO R.23

1. On vient de survoler la ville. ______________________________

   L'avion commence à descendre. ______________________________

   Quand : ______________________________

   ____

2. Il vient de se rendre compte. ______________________________

Il oublie son portefeuille. ______________________________

Que : ______________________________

____

3. Tu viens d'éviter un accident. ______________________________

Tu arrives ici. ______________________________

Quand : ______________________________

____

4. La chaise vient de casser. ______________________________

Il veut s'asseoir. ______________________________

Quand : ______________________________

____

5. Il vient de finir son discours. ______________________________

Tu commences à douter. ______________________________

Quand : ______________________________

____

6. Il vient d'être enterré. ______________________________

Tu arrives. ______________________________

Quand : ______________________________

____

7. Nous venons de préparer le dîner. ______________________________

Les voisins arrivent. ______________________________

Quand : ______________________________

____

8. Elle vient d'arriver. ______________________________

L'avion part. ______________________________

Quand : ______________________________

____

9. Je viens de me faire renvoyer. ______________________________

J'achète une maison. ______________________________

Quand : ______________________________

____

10. Tu viens de frapper à la porte. ______

Je te téléphone. ______

Quand : ______

______

EX. 18.24 *Conjuguez ces verbes au **futur simple** en utilisant le pronom donné.* AUDIO R.24

1. Charger – Tu ______
2. Valoir – Il ______
3. Pouvoir – Je ______
4. Répondre – Elle ______
5. Souffrir – On ______
6. Verser – Ils ______
7. Peindre – Il ______
8. Hésiter – Nous ______
9. Avoir – Tu ______
10. Enlever – Vous ______
11. Écrire – J' ______
12. Craindre – Elle ______
13. Blanchir – On ______
14. Aller – Nous ______

EX. 18.25 *Transformez ces phrases de l'**imparfait** au **futur simple**.* AUDIO R.25

1. Nous allions au magasin en voiture.

   ______

2. On chantait une chanson au spectacle.

   ______

3. Il éteignait les lumières avant de partir.

   ______

4. Je partais quand je suis prête.

   ______

5. Il tondait la pelouse quand il avait du temps.

6. Tu vendais tes affaires sur internet.

7. Je finissais mon devoir avant d'aller dormir.

8. Nous payions notre repas à la serveuse.

9. Vous choisissiez entre ces deux appartements.

10. Elle devenait docteur après ses études.

EX. 18.26 *Traduisez ces phrases en français.* **AUDIO R.26**

1. I will be at the airport tonight.

2. He will tidy his room when he comes back.

3. They will call you (pl) back.

4. Will you bring a few glasses to dinner?

5. As soon as the flowers bloom, I will pick a few (quelques unes).

6. We will borrow the money from the bank.

7. The mother will try to breastfeed (allaiter).

8. I will iron my clothes tonight.

9. They (f) will translate the document next week.

10. I will see if I can come.

EX. 18.27 *Transformez ces phrases du **futur simple** au **futur proche**.* AUDIO R.27

1. On partira après le repas.

2. Je me marierai quand je suis prête.

3. Elles embarqueront le train avec leurs valises.

4. Tu feras la vaisselle quand tu as fini d'étudier.

5. Nous remplacerons la cuisine en mai.

6. Vous rassemblerez vos idées pour être plus efficace.

7. On arrivera d'ici quelques heures.

8. L'eau bouillira en quelques minutes.

9. Tu arrêteras de fumer dans quelques semaines.

10. On s'occupera du jardin ce week-end.

EX. 18.28 *Transformez ces phrases du **futur proche** au **futur simple**.* AUDIO R.28

1. Qu'est-ce que tu vas faire demain soir ?

2. Nous allons manger au restaurant.

3. Tu vas manger des pâtes ce soir.

____

4. Il va lire un livre dans le canapé.

____

5. Je vais parler aux enfants à propos du problème.

____

6. L'avion va atterrir à 17 heures.

____

7. Il faut aller remplir ce document à la mairie.

____

8. Nous allons voir Luc dans quelques jours.

____

9. Tu vas te rendre malade si tu manges trop.

____

10. Ils vont faire leurs devoirs pour demain.

____

EX. 18.29 *Conjuguez ces verbes au **conditionnel présent** en utilisant le pronom donné.*

AUDIO R.29

1. Prendre – Tu _______________________________
2. Faire – Il _______________________________
3. Avoir – Nous _______________________________
4. Savoir – Ils _______________________________
5. Tenir – On _______________________________
6. Finir – Elle _______________________________
7. Boire – Vous _______________________________
8. Lancer – Je _______________________________
9. Nettoyer – Elle _______________________________
10. Dormir – Tu _______________________________

EX. 18.30 *Choisissez parmi les verbes de la liste et conjuguez-les au* ***conditionnel présent.***

AUDIO R.30

cuisiner - aller (2) - prendre - venir - aimer - adopter - manger - aimer - pouvoir

1. Je ______________________________ bien un café.
2. Tu ______________________________ arriver plus tôt.
3. Elle ______________________________ avoir plus d'argent.
4. Nous ______________________________ plus de légumes si on avait plus d'argent.
5. Il ______________________________ si tu l'invitais.
6. SI j'avais du temps, je ______________________________ plus souvent.
7. Vous ______________________________ faire les magasins si c'était ouvert.
8. Je pensais que tu n' ______________________________ pas.
9. Nous ______________________________ venir.
10. Tu ______________________________ un chien si tu pouvais ?

EX. 18.31 *Traduisez ces phrases en français.* AUDIO R.31

1. I would be there if I had time.

   ____

2. If he was thirsty, he would drink water.

   ____

3. If we had money, we would buy a house for my parents.

   ____

4. You (pl) would go to the beach if the weather was better.

   ____

5. We would be delighted if you agreed.

   ____

6. I would like to know if that works for you.

   ____

7. What would I do without you!

   ____

8. If you studied more, you would have better grades.

____

9. It would be better if you added a little bit of salt.

____

10. If we had more space, we would paint more often.

____

EX. 18.32 *Corrigez les verbes suivants conjugués à l'**impératif**.* AUDIO R.32

Aller	**Avoir**	**Chercher**	**Finir**
Vas	Ai	Cherches	Finisse
Allons	Ayont	Cherchons	Finissons
Allez	Ayez	Cherchai	Finissez

EX. 18.33 *Traduisez en français en utilisant **tu**.* AUDIO R.33

1. Buy the clothes. ______________________
2. Answer the phone. ______________________
3. Finish your plate. ______________________
4. Leave now. ______________________
5. Let's go. ______________________
6. Ask the cashier. ______________________
7. Avoid this road. ______________________
8. Be yourself. ______________________
9. Pay the bill. ______________________
10. Save your document. ______________________

EX. 18.34 *Transformez ces phrases à l'**impératif**.* AUDIO R.34

1. Nous prenons le train.

____

2. Tu manges ces bananes.

____

*Remember to **download the audio** and to **watch the videos** – see Preface*

3. Vous accrochez la remorque à la voiture.

____

4. Nous prévenons les voisins de la fuite d'eau.

____

5. Tu attrapes la corde.

____

6. Nous écoutons le sermon du pasteur.

____

7. Vous traversez la route prudemment.

____

8. Nous suivons les flèches de la randonnée.

____

9. Tu déposes les papiers dans le coffre.

____

10. Nous ajoutons cet exercice à l'examen.

____

EX. 18.35 *Utilisez les phrases de l'exercice 18.34 et transformez les* ***COD*** *en* ***DOP****.* AUDIO R.35

1. ______________________________
2. ______________________________
3. ______________________________
4. ______________________________
5. ______________________________
6. ______________________________
7. ______________________________
8. ______________________________
9. ______________________________
10. ______________________________

EX. 18.36 *Traduisez ces phrases en français, faites attention à l'infinitif des verbes.* AUDIO R.36

1. I am thinking of leaving.

   ____

2. He lost time waiting for his wife.

   ____

3. You needed to leave to relax.

   ____

4. He is revising before taking his test.

   ____

5. She always trusts everyone without knowing them.

   ____

6. We always get paid on the first of the month.

   ____

7. They were about to call you.

   ____

8. I am sad to leave, but I will be back.

   ____

9. It's good to drink water throughout the day.

   ____

10. It's difficult to say.

    ____

EX. 18.37 *Complétez les phrases avec la préposition adéquate :* ***à - de - /.*** AUDIO R.37

1. Nous sommes heureux __________ t'aider.
2. Es-tu libre __________ venir ce week-end ?
3. Je me suis fait faire __________ les ongles.
4. Nous économisons au lieu __________ dépenser de l'argent.
5. Ils passent beaucoup de temps __________ se connaître.
6. Il faut faire attention __________ .
7. Pouvez-vous demander au jardinier __________ tailler les buissons ?

8. J'ai du travail __________ finir.
9. Nous adorons __________ faire du sport ensemble.
10. Les employés sont censés __________ revenir en septembre.
11. Tu sembles __________ oublier que tu me dois de l'argent.
12. Les habitants commencent __________ comprendre ce qu'il se passe.
13. Nous nous préparons __________ partir tôt demain matin.
14. J'ai décidé __________ commencer __________ étudier le français.
15. Tu risques __________ être en retard.

EX. 18.38 *Formez des phrases avec les éléments donnés, conjuguez le verbe au temps entre parenthèses.* AUDIO R.38

1. Avoir / manger / nous / de quoi (présent)

   ____

2. Arriver / à finir / je / ce puzzle (imparfait)

   ____

3. Aller / jouer / avec tes amis (impératif – tu)

   ____

4. Avoir besoin de / Il / aide / pour finir / la toiture (présent)

   ____

5. Devoir / arriver / nous / ce soir (conditionnel présent)

   ____

6. Essayer de / se reposer / elle (présent)

   ____

7. Se souvenir de / payer / la facture (impératif – tu)

   ____

8. Me dire de / mon responsable / vérifier / les numéros (passé composé)

   ____

9. Pardonner / c'est bien de / lui (présent)

   ____

10. Risquer de / le chien / te mordre (présent)

   ____

EX. 18.39 *Choisissez entre **faire** et **se faire** et conjuguez le verbe au temps donné.* AUDIO R.39

1. Il ______________________ attendre. (présent)
2. Elle ______________________ mettre à la porte car elle ne paie pas. (présent)
3. Cet homme ______________________ opérer d'urgence. (présent)
4. Nous ______________________ laver la voiture avant de partir en vacances. (présent)
5. Le piéton ______________________ renverser par une voiture. (présent)
6. ______________________ entrer les participants. (impératif - vous)
7. Tu ______________________ toujours renvoyer ! (présent)
8. Il faut ______________________ savoir aux clients de ne pas boire l'eau. (infinitif)
9. Nous ______________________ avoir ! (passé composé)
10. Les élèves aiment en ______________________ voir de toutes les couleurs. (infinitif)

EX. 18.40 *Choisissez parmi les choix de la liste et conjuguez le verbe être au **présent**. Attention d'ajouter le féminin ou pluriel si nécessaire.* AUDIO R.40

être obligé de – être désolé de – être heureux de – être triste de – être anxieux de – être fier de – être sûr de – être surpris de – être fatigué de – être libre de

1. Il ______________ toujours ______________ prendre l'avion.
2. Est-ce que tu ______________________ partir ?
3. Nous ______________________ annoncer la naissance de notre fille.
4. Il ______________________ ne pas te voir.
5. Est-ce que vous ______________________ vouloir partir ?
6. Elle ______________________ être grande sœur.
7. Ma grand-mère ______________________ travailler.
8. Nous ______________________ ce résultat.
9. Tu ______________________ partir si tu veux.
10. Elle ______________________ ne pas être présente pour toi.

*Remember to **download the audio** and to **watch the videos** – see Preface*

EX. 18.41 *Conjuguez les verbes suivants au* ***subjonctif présent.*** AUDIO R.41

1. Choisir

   Que je ______________________

   Que tu ______________________

   Qu'on ______________________

   Que nous ______________________

   Que vous ______________________

   Qu'elles ______________________

2. Vouloir

   Que je ______________________

   Que tu ______________________

   Qu'il ______________________

   Que nous ______________________

   Que vous ______________________

   Qu'ils ______________________

3. Être

   Que je ______________________

   Que tu ______________________

   Qu'il ______________________

   Que nous ______________________

   Que vous ______________________

   Qu'ils ______________________

EX. 18.42 *Finissez les phrases avec idées personnelles conjuguées au **subjonctif**.* AUDIO R.42

1. Je m'attends à ce que ______
2. Je suis triste que ______
3. Je suis désolé(e) que ______
4. J'ai honte que ______
5. J'apprécie que ______
6. C'est bizarre que ______
7. C'est dommage que ______
8. C'est important que ______
9. C'est rare que ______
10. Il vaut mieux que ______

EX. 18.43 *Complétez les phrases avec un de ces verbes et conjuguez-le au **subjonctif présent**.* AUDIO R.43

finir - croire - apprendre - partir - prendre - promener - nettoyer - gagner - savoir - voir

1. Il faut que je ______.
2. Il faut que je ______ ce concours.
3. Il faut que je ______ mes parents au plus vite.
4. Il faut que je ______ la vérité.
5. Il faut que je ______ le ukulélé.
6. Il faut que je ______ en moi
7. Il faut que je ______ le garage.
8. Il faut que je ______ le chien.
9. Il faut que je ______ du temps pour moi.
10. Il faut que je ______ ce dessin.

EX. 18.44 *Réécrivez chaque phrase au **plus-que-parfait**.* AUDIO R.44

1. Je suis allée au magasin ce matin.

______

2. Nous avons reçu notre lettre d'expulsion.

______

3. L'assistant a reçu les patients.

____

4. Elle a fini le livre difficilement.

____

5. Tu as fini ce livre ?

____

6. Le chien a attendu son maître toute la journée.

____

7. Le menuisier a réparé la cuisine.

____

8. J'ai arrosé les plantes.

____

9. Elle est venue pour accueillir les invités.

____

10. Nous sommes partis un peu après minuit.

____

EX. 18.45 *Conjuguez le verbe entre parenthèses au **futur antérieur**.* AUDIO R.45

1. Ils (acheter) ______________________ leurs alliances à ce moment-là.
2. Nous (partir) ______________________ avant le lever du soleil.
3. Vous (avoir) ______________________ assez de temps pour vous préparer.
4. Il (se peser) ______________________ avant le rendez-vous.
5. Nous (aller) ______________________ dans 25 pays différents.
6. Le technicien (réparer) ______________________ la fuite ce soir.
7. Elle (se préparer) ______________________ pour la danse.
8. L'Allemagne (recycler) ______________________ 18 tonnes de plastique d'ici là.
9. La sirène (signaler) ______________________ le danger.
10. Nous (déjeuner) ______________________ quand tu arriveras.

EX. 18.46 *Conjuguez le verbe entre parenthèses au* ***conditionnel passé.*** AUDIO R.46

1. On (se blesser) ______________________ si on n'avait pas fait attention.
2. Si vous aviez donné plus de votre temps, vous ______________________ moins de temps pour penser.
3. Ton chien (obéir) ______________________ si tu avais pris le temps de le dresser.
4. On (pouvoir) ______________________ gagner à la loterie !
5. Nous (s'arrêter) ______________________ si nous étions parties plus tôt.
6. J' (lire) ______________________ ce livre s'il avait été disponible en anglais.
7. Il (payer) ______________________ la facture si le travail avait été bien fait.
8. Ils (remplacer) ______________________ la pièce s'ils l'avaient reçue.
9. La voiture (ralentir) ______________________ si le panneau avait été visible.
10. Cela me (servir) ______________________ si je n'avais pas vendu la voiture.

EX. 18.47 *Transformez le verbe en* ***gérondif*** *et liez les phrases ensemble.* AUDIO R.47

Je m'endors souvent. Je regarde la télévision.
Je m'endors souvent en regardant la télévision.

1. Ferme la porte. Tu pars.

   ____

2. Tu n'arriveras à rien. Tu doutes de toi-même.

   ____

3. Peut-être que tu le trouveras. Tu cherches sous ton lit.

   ____

4. Va au magasin. Tu reviens de l'école.

   ____

5. Je me suis fait mal au dos. Je bouge le canapé.

   ____

6. Tu peux vraiment faire du mal. Tu te moques de tes camarades.

   ____

7. Prends cette boîte. Tu montes.

   ____

8. Mon mari regarde la télévision. Il repasse le linge.

9. Tu peux fermer l'arrivée d'eau. Tu tournes le robinet.

10. Nous réussirions mieux. Nous utilisons un dictionnaire.

EX. 18.48 *Transformez ces phrases actives en* ***phrases passives.*** AUDIO R.48

1. Les soldats ont trouvé un refuge dans ce village.

2. L'airbag a sauvé les passagers.

3. Cette présentation persuade presque tous les clients.

4. Il est interdit de marcher sur le gazon.

5. Nous devons inclure cette histoire dans le livre.

6. Cette employée a détourné les fonds.

7. Ce couple a choisi cet hôtel.

8. Le facteur apporte le courrier.

9. Les cuisiniers préparent les repas pendant la nuit.

10. La couturière rallonge la robe.

EX. 18.49 *Traduisez ces phrases. Attention, les verbes peuvent être conjugués à tous les temps.*

AUDIO R.49

1. We went to the store, but they didn't have any milk left.

____

2. I would like to stay longer in this city.

____

3. Can I ask you something?

____

4. Let me take your bag for you.

____

5. They are going to show you your new house.

____

6. They (m) just left!

____

7. This author received a prize for her last book.

____

8. She suffered from headaches when she was a teenager.

____

9. Should I leave my work?

____

10. Don't cross the street without looking both ways.

____

11. I study every day for at least (au moins) 5 hours.

____

12. She didn't help us at all.

____

13. They didn't leave on time this morning.

____

14. My classmates are making fun of me.

____

15. This movie was so boring, I fell asleep!

____

16. We will get up at 6 a.m. tomorrow morning.

____

17. I thought you were Paul's sister.

____

18. We will be there for you when you (pl) need us.

____

19. Did you find your wallet?

____

20. I don't know how to use this machine.

____

THE ANNEXE

The French Tenses
The Table of Verbs
Solutions

The French Tenses

AUDIO 48.1

Présent de l'indicatif

The **présent de l'indicatif** is used to talk about things that are happening now, things that happen all the time, habits, general actions, or states.

Je mange

Passé composé

The **passé composé** is used to talk about the past, mostly actions that took place in the past and were completed in the past.

J'ai mangé

Imparfait

The **imparfait** is used to talk about the past, mostly actions and situations without a specific timeframe, that happened an unspecified number of times or were in progress when something else happened

Je mangeais

Plus-que-parfait

The **plus-que-parfait** is used to talk about an action or situation that happened before another past action.

J'avais mangé

Passé récent

The **passé récent** is used to talk about things that just happened.

Je viens de manger

Passé simple

The **passé simple** is the historical past, used in literature.

Je mangeai

Futur simple

The **futur simple** is used to talk about plans and intentions in the future.

Je mangerai

Futur proche

The **futur proche** is used to talk about something that is going to happen in the near future.

Je vais manger

Futur antérieur

The **futur antérieur** is used to talk about an action or a situation that is going to be completed before another action in the future.

J'aurai mangé

Impératif

The **impératif** is used to give orders and advice.

Mange

Condtionnel présent

The **conditionnel présent** is used to ask something politely, to express a wish or to talk about something that would happen "if", about a possibility.

Je mangerais

Conditionnel passé

The **conditionnel passé** is used to talk about a past situation, uncertain information, a wish, or a regret.

J'aurais mangé

Subjonctif

The **subjonctif** is used after que, mostly in the subordinate clause, and indicates a wish, regret, emotion, opinion, or doubt.

Il faut que je mange

Accueillir – To welcome

Participe présent accueillant

Présent de l'indicatif

J'accueille	Nous accueillons
Tu accueilles	Vous accueillez
Il accueille	Ils accueillent
Elle accueille	Elles accueillent
On accueille	

Imparfait

J'accueillais	Nous accueillions
Tu accueillais	Vous accueilliez
Il accueillait	Ils accueillaient
Elle accueillait	Elles accueillaient
On accueillait	

Futur simple

J'accueillerai	Nous accueillerons
Tu accueilleras	Vous accueillerez
Il accueillera	Ils accueilleront
Elle accueillera	Elles accueilleront
On accueillera	

Conditionnel présent

J'accueillerais	Nous accueillerions
Tu accueillerais	Vous accueilleriez
Il accueillerait	Ils accueilleraient
Elle accueillerait	Elles accueilleraient
On accueillerait	

Impératif

Accueille !
Accueillons !
Accueillez !

Participe passé accueilli

Passé composé

J'ai accueilli	Nous avons accueilli
Tu as accueilli	Vous avez accueilli
Il a accueilli	Ils ont accueilli
Elle a accueilli	Elles ont accueilli
On a accueilli	

Plus-que-parfait

J'avais accueilli	Nous avions accueilli
Tu avais accueilli	Vous aviez accueilli
Il avait accueilli	Ils avaient accueilli
Elle avait accueilli	Elles avaient accueilli
On avait accueilli	

Futur antérieur

J'aurai accueilli	Nous aurons accueilli
Tu auras accueilli	Vous aurez accueilli
Il aura accueilli	Ils auront accueilli
Elle aura accueilli	Elles auront accueilli
On aura accueilli	

Conditionnel passé

J'aurais accueilli	Nous aurions accueilli
Tu aurais accueilli	Vous auriez accueilli
Il aurait accueilli	Ils auraient accueilli
Elle aurait accueilli	Elles auraient accueilli
On aurait accueilli	

Subjonctif présent

Que j'accueille	Que nous accueillions
Que tu accueilles	Que vous accueilliez
Qu'il accueille	Qu'ils accueillent
Qu'elle accueille	Qu'elles accueillent
Qu'on accueille	

Common verbs with the same conjugation: **Cueillir** To pick – **Recueillir** To gather

Acheter – To buy

Participe présent achetant

Participe passé acheté

Présent de l'indicatif

J'achète	Nous achetons
Tu achètes	Vous achetez
Il achète	Ils achètent
Elle achète	Elles achètent
On achète	

Passé composé

J'ai acheté	Nous avons acheté
Tu as acheté	Vous avez acheté
Il a acheté	Ils ont acheté
Elle a acheté	Elles ont acheté
On a acheté	

Imparfait

J'achetais	Nous achetions
Tu achetais	Vous achetiez
Il achetait	Ils achetaient
Elle achetait	Elles achetaient
On achetait	

Plus-que-parfait

J'avais acheté	Nous avions acheté
Tu avais acheté	Vous aviez acheté
Il avait acheté	Ils avaient acheté
Elle avait acheté	Elles avaient acheté
On avait acheté	

Futur simple

J'achèterai	Nous achèterons
Tu achèteras	Vous achèterez
Il achètera	Ils achèteront
Elle achètera	Elles achèteront
On achètera	

Futur antérieur

J'aurai acheté	Nous aurons acheté
Tu auras acheté	Vous aurez acheté
Il aura acheté	Ils auront acheté
Elle aura acheté	Elles auront acheté
On aura acheté	

Conditionnel présent

J'achèterais	Nous achèterions
Tu achèterais	Vous achèteriez
Il achèterait	Ils achèteraient
Elle achèterait	Elles achèteraient
On achèterait	

Conditionnel passé

J'aurais acheté	Nous aurions acheté
Tu aurais acheté	Vous auriez acheté
Il aurait acheté	Ils auraient acheté
Elle aurait acheté	Elles auraient acheté
On aurait acheté	

Impératif

Achète !
Achetons !
Achetez !

Subjonctif présent

Que j'achète	Que nous achetions
Que tu achètes	Que vous achetiez
Qu'il achète	Qu'ils achètent
Qu'elle achète	Qu'elles achètent
Qu'on achète	

*Remember to **download the audio** and to **watch the videos** – see Preface*

Achever – To finish

Participe présent achevant

Participe passé achevé

Présent de l'indicatif

J'achève	Nous achevons
Tu achèves	Vous achevez
Il achève	Ils achèvent
Elle achève	Elles achèvent
On achève	

Passé composé

J'ai achevé	Nous avons achevé
Tu as achevé	Vous avez achevé
Il a achevé	Ils ont achevé
Elle a achevé	Elles ont achevé
On a achevé	

Imparfait

J'achevais	Nous achevions
Tu achevais	Vous acheviez
Il achevait	Ils achevaient
Elle achevait	Elles achevaient
On achevait	

Plus-que-parfait

J'avais achevé	Nous avions achevé
Tu avais achevé	Vous aviez achevé
Il avait achevé	Ils avaient achevé
Elle avait achevé	Elles avaient achevé
On avait achevé	

Futur simple

J'achèverai	Nous achèverons
Tu achèveras	Vous achèverez
Il achèvera	Ils achèveraient
Elle achèvera	Elles achèveraient
On achèvera	

Futur antérieur

J'aurai achevé	Nous aurons achevé
Tu auras achevé	Vous aurez achevé
Il aura achevé	Ils auront achevé
Elle aura achevé	Elles auront achevé
On aura achevé	

Conditionnel présent

J'achèverais	Nous achèverions
Tu achèverais	Vous achèveriez
Il achèverait	Ils achèveront
Elle achèverait	Elles achèveront
On achèverait	

Conditionnel passé

J'aurais achevé	Nous aurions achevé
Tu aurais achevé	Vous auriez achevé
Il aurait achevé	Ils auraient achevé
Elle aurait achevé	Elles auraient achevé
On aurait achevé	

Impératif

Achève !
Achevons !
Achevez !

Subjonctif présent

Que j'achève	Que nous achevions
Que tu achèves	Que vous acheviez
Qu'il achève	Qu'ils achèvent
Qu'elle achève	Qu'elles achèvent
Qu'on achève	

Common verbs with the same conjugation:
Élever To raise – **Enlever** To remove – **Lever** To get up – **Relever** To lift up

Aller – To go

Participe présent	allant

Participe passé	allé

Présent de l'indicatif

Je vais	Nous allons
Tu vas	Vous allez
Il va	Ils vont
Elle va	Elles vont
On va	

Passé composé

Je suis allé(e)	Nous sommes allé(e)s
Tu es allé(e)	Vous êtes allé(e)s
Il est allé	Ils sont allés
Elle est allée	Elles sont allées
On est allé(e)s	

Imparfait

J'allais	Nous allions
Tu allais	Vous alliez
Il allait	Ils allaient
Elle allait	Elles allaient
On allait	

Plus-que-parfait

J'étais allé(e)	Nous étions allé(e)s
Tu étais allé(e)	Vous étiez allé(e)s
Il était allé	Ils étaient allés
Elle était allée	Elles étaient allées
On était allé(e)s	

Futur simple

J'irai	Nous irons
Tu iras	Vous irez
Il ira	Ils iront
Elle ira	Elles iront
On ira	

Futur antérieur

Je serai allé(e)	Nous serons allé(e)s
Tu seras allé(e)	Vous serez allé(e)s
Il sera allé	Ils seront allés
Elle sera allée	Elles seront allées
On sera allé(e)s	

Conditionnel présent

J'irais	Nous irions
Tu irais	Vous iriez
Il irait	Ils iraient
Elle irait	Elles iraient
On irait	

Conditionnel passé

Je serais allé(e)	Nous serions allé(e)s
Tu serais allé(e)	Vous seriez allé(e)s
Il serait allé	Ils seraient allés
Elle serait allée	Elles seraient allées
On serait allé(e)s	

Impératif

Va !
Allons !
Allez !

Subjonctif présent

Que j'aille	Que nous allions
Que tu ailles	Que vous alliez
Qu'il aille	Qu'ils aillent
Qu'elle aille	Qu'elles aillent
Qu'on aille	

Amener – To bring

Participe présent	amenant

Participe passé	amené

Présent de l'indicatif

J'amène	Nous amenons
Tu amènes	Vous amenez
Il amène	Ils amènent
Elle amène	Elles amènent
On amène	

Passé composé

J'ai amené	Nous avons amené
Tu as amené	Vous avez amené
Il a amené	Ils ont amené
Elle a amené	Elles ont amené
On a amené	

Imparfait

J'amenais	Nous amenions
Tu amenais	Vous ameniez
Il amenait	Ils amenaient
Elle amenait	Elles amenaient
On amenait	

Plus-que-parfait

J'avais amené	Nous avions amené
Tu avais amené	Vous aviez amené
Il avait amené	Ils avaient amené
Elle avait amené	Elles avaient amené
On avait amené	

Futur simple

J'amènerai	Nous amènerons
Tu amèneras	Vous amènerez
Il amènera	Ils amèneront
Elle amènera	Elles amèneront
On amènera	

Futur antérieur

J'aurai amené	Nous aurons amené
Tu auras amené	Vous aurez amené
Il aura amené	Ils auront amené
Elle aura amené	Elles auront amené
On aura amené	

Conditionnel présent

J'amènerais	Nous amènerions
Tu amènerais	Vous amèneriez
Il amènerait	Ils amèneraient
Elle amènerait	Elles amèneraient
On amènerait	

Conditionnel passé

J'aurais amené	Nous aurions amené
Tu aurais amené	Vous auriez amené
Il aurait amené	Ils auraient amené
Elle aurait amené	Elles auraient amené
On aurait amené	

Impératif

Amène !
Amenons !
Amenez !

Subjonctif présent

Que j'amène	Que nous amenions
Que tu amènes	Que vous ameniez
Qu'il amène	Qu'ils amènent
Qu'elle amène	Qu'elles amènent
Qu'on amène	

Common verbs with the same conjugation: **Emmener** To take – **Mener** To lead – **Promener** To walk

Appeler – To call

Participe présent appelant

Présent de l'indicatif

J'appelle	Nous appelons
Tu appelles	Vous appelez
Il appelle	Ils appellent
Elle appelle	Elles appellent
On appelle	

Imparfait

J'appelais	Nous appelions
Tu appelais	Vous appeliez
Il appelait	Ils appelaient
Elle appelait	Elles appelaient
On appelait	

Futur simple

J'appellerai	Nous appellerons
Tu appelleras	Vous appellerez
Il appellera	Ils appelleront
Elle appellera	Elles appelleront
On appellera	

Conditionnel présent

J'appellerais	Nous appellerions
Tu appellerais	Vous appelleriez
Il appellerait	Ils appelleraient
Elle appellerait	Elles appelleraient
On appellerait	

Impératif

Appelle !
Appelons !
Appelez !

Participe passé appelé

Passé composé

J'ai appelé	Nous avons appelé
Tu as appelé	Vous avez appelé
Il a appelé	Ils ont appelé
Elle a appelé	Elles ont appelé
On a appelé	

Plus-que-parfait

J'avais appelé	Nous avions appelé
Tu avais appelé	Vous aviez appelé
Il avait appelé	Ils avaient appelé
Elle avait appelé	Elles avaient appelé
On avait appelé	

Futur antérieur

J'aurai appelé	Nous aurons appelé
Tu auras appelé	Vous aurez appelé
Il aura appelé	Ils auront appelé
Elle aura appelé	Elles auront appelé
On aura appelé	

Conditionnel passé

J'aurais appelé	Nous aurions appelé
Tu aurais appelé	Vous auriez appelé
Il aurait appelé	Ils auraient appelé
Elle aurait appelé	Elles auraient appelé
On aurait appelé	

Subjonctif présent

Que j'appelle	Que nous appelions
Que tu appelles	Que vous appeliez
Qu'il appelle	Qu'ils appellent
Qu'elle appelle	Qu'elles appellent
Qu'on appelle	

Common verbs with the same conjugation: **Épeler** To spell – **Rappeler** To call back

Avoir – To have

Participe présent ayant

Participe passé eu

Présent de l'indicatif

J'ai	Nous avons
Tu as	Vous avez
Il a	Ils ont
Elle a	Elles ont
On a	

Passé composé

J'ai eu	Nous avons eu
Tu as eu	Vous avez eu
Il a eu	Ils ont eu
Elle a eu	Elles ont eu
On a eu	

Imparfait

J'avais	Nous avions
Tu avais	Vous aviez
Il avait	Ils avaient
Elle avait	Elles avaient
On avait	

Plus-que-parfait

J'avais eu	Nous avions eu
Tu avais eu	Vous aviez eu
Il avait eu	Ils avaient eu
Elle avait eu	Elles avaient eu
On avait eu	

Futur simple

J'aurai	Nous aurons
Tu auras	Vous aurez
Il aura	Ils auront
Elle aura	Elles auront
On aura	

Futur antérieur

J'aurai eu	Nous aurons eu
Tu auras eu	Vous aurez eu
Il aura eu	Ils auront eu
Elle aura eu	Elles auront eu
On aura eu	

Conditionnel présent

J'aurais	Nous aurions
Tu aurais	Vous auriez
Il aurait	Ils auraient
Elle aurait	Elles auraient
On aurait	

Conditionnel passé

J'aurais eu	Nous aurions eu
Tu aurais eu	Vous auriez eu
Il aurait eu	Ils auraient eu
Elle aurait eu	Elles auraient eu
On aurait eu	

Impératif

Aie !
Ayez !
Ayons !

Subjonctif présent

Que j'aie	Que nous ayons
Que tu aies	Que vous ayez
Qu'il ait	Qu'ils aient
Qu'elle ait	Qu'elles aient
Qu'on ait	

Battre – To beat

Participe présent battant

Participe passé battu

Présent de l'indicatif

Je bats	Nous battons
Tu bats	Vous battez
Il bat	Ils battent
Elle bat	Elles battent
On bat	

Passé composé

J'ai battu	Nous avons battu
Tu as battu	Vous avez battu
Il a battu	Ils ont battu
Elle a battu	Elles ont battu
On a battu	

Imparfait

Je battais	Nous battions
Tu battais	Vous battiez
Il battait	Ils battaient
Elle battait	Elles battaient
On battait	

Plus-que-parfait

J'avais battu	Nous avions battu
Tu avais battu	Vous aviez battu
Il avait battu	Ils avaient battu
Elle avait battu	Elles avaient battu
On avait battu	

Futur simple

Je battrai	Nous battrons
Tu battras	Vous battrez
Il battra	Ils battront
Elle battra	Elles battront
On battra	

Futur antérieur

J'aurai battu	Nous aurons battu
Tu auras battu	Vous aurez battu
Il aura battu	Ils auront battu
Elle aura battu	Elles auront battu
On aura battu	

Conditionnel présent

Je battrais	Nous battrions
Tu battrais	Vous battriez
Il battrait	Ils battraient
Elle battrait	Elles battraient
On battrait	

Conditionnel passé

J'aurais battu	Nous aurions battu
Tu aurais battu	Vous auriez battu
Il aurait battu	Ils auraient battu
Elle aurait battu	Elles auraient battu
On aurait battu	

Impératif

Bats !
Battons !
Battez !

Subjonctif présent

Que je batte	Que nous battions
Que tu battes	Que vous battiez
Qu'il batte	Qu'ils battent
Qu'elle batte	Qu'elles battent
Qu'on batte	

Common verbs with the same conjugation:
Abattre To kill – **Combattre** To fight – **Débattre** To discuss

Boire – To drink

Participe présent buvant

Participe passé bu

Présent de l'indicatif

Je bois	Nous buvons
Tu bois	Vous buvez
Il boit	Ils boivent
Elle boit	Elles boivent
On boit	

Passé composé

J'ai bu	Nous avons bu
Tu as bu	Vous avez bu
Il a bu	Ils ont bu
Elle a bu	Elles ont bu
On a bu	

Imparfait

Je buvais	Nous buvions
Tu buvais	Vous buviez
Il buvait	Ils buvaient
Elle buvait	Elles buvaient
On buvait	

Plus-que-parfait

J'avais bu	Nous avions bu
Tu avais bu	Vous aviez bu
Il avait bu	Ils avaient bu
Elle avait bu	Elles avaient bu
On avait bu	

Futur simple

Je boirai	Nous boirons
Tu boiras	Vous boirez
Il boira	Ils boiront
Elle boira	Elles boiront
On boira	

Futur antérieur

J'aurai bu	Nous aurons bu
Tu auras bu	Vous aurez bu
Il aura bu	Ils auront bu
Elle aura bu	Elles auront bu
On aura bu	

Conditionnel présent

Je boirais	Nous boirions
Tu boirais	Vous boiriez
Il boirait	Ils boiraient
Elle boirait	Elles boiraient
On boirait	

Conditionnel passé

J'aurais bu	Nous aurions bu
Tu aurais bu	Vous auriez bu
Il aurait bu	Ils auraient bu
Elle aurait bu	Elles auraient bu
On aurait bu	

Impératif

Bois !
Buvons !
Buvez !

Subjonctif présent

Que je boive	Que nous buvions
Que tu boives	Que vous buviez
Qu'il boive	Qu'ils boivent
Qu'elle boive	Qu'elles boivent
Qu'on boive	

Céder – To give

Participe présent cédant

Participe passé cédé

Présent de l'indicatif

Je cède	Nous cédons
Tu cèdes	Vous cédez
Il cède	Ils cèdent
Elle cède	Elles cèdent
On cède	

Passé composé

J'ai cédé	Nous avons cédé
Tu as cédé	Vous avez cédé
Il a cédé	Ils ont cédé
Elle a cédé	Elles ont cédé
On a cédé	

Imparfait

Je cédais	Nous cédions
Tu cédais	Vous cédiez
Il cédait	Ils cédaient
Elle cédait	Elles cédaient
On cédait	

Plus-que-parfait

J'avais cédé	Nous avions cédé
Tu avais cédé	Vous aviez cédé
Il avait cédé	Ils avaient cédé
Elle avait cédé	Elles avaient cédé
On avait cédé	

Futur simple

Je céderai	Nous céderons
Tu céderas	Vous céderez
Il cédera	Ils céderont
Elle cédera	Elles céderont
On cédera	

Futur antérieur

J'aurai cédé	Nous aurons cédé
Tu auras cédé	Vous aurez cédé
Il aura cédé	Ils auront cédé
Elle aura cédé	Elles auront cédé
On aura cédé	

Conditionnel présent

Je céderais	Nous céderions
Tu céderais	Vous céderiez
Il céderait	Ils céderaient
Elle céderait	Elles céderaient
On céderait	

Conditionnel passé

J'aurais cédé	Nous aurions cédé
Tu aurais cédé	Vous auriez cédé
Il aurait cédé	Ils auraient cédé
Elle aurait cédé	Elles auraient cédé
On aurait cédé	

Impératif

Cède !
Cédons !
Cédez !

Subjonctif présent

Que je cède	Que nous cédions
Que tu cèdes	Que vous cédiez
Qu'il cède	Qu'ils cèdent
Qu'elle cède	Qu'elles cèdent
Qu'on cède	

Common verb with the same conjugation: **Posséder** To own – To possess

Célébrer – To celebrate

Participe présent célébrant

Participe passé célébré

Présent de l'indicatif

Je célèbre	Nous célébrons
Tu célèbres	Vous célébrez (es)
Il célèbre	Ils célèbrent
Elle célèbre	Elles célèbrent
On célèbre	

Passé composé

J'ai célébré	Nous avons célébré
Tu as célébré	Vous avez célébré
Il a célébré	Ils ont célébré
Elle a célébré	Elles ont célébré
On a célébré	

Imparfait

Je célébrais	Nous célébrions
Tu célébrais	Vous célébriez
Il célébrait	Ils célébraient
Elle célébrait	Elles célébraient
On célébrait	

Plus-que-parfait

J'avais célébré	Nous avions célébré
Tu avais célébré	Vous aviez célébré
Il avait célébré	Ils avaient célébré
Elle avait célébré	Elles avaient célébré
On avait célébré	

Futur simple

Je célébrerai	Nous célébrerons
Tu célébreras	Vous célébrerez
Il célébrera	Ils célébreront
Elle célébrera	Elles célébreront
On célébrera	

Futur antérieur

J'aurai célébré	Nous aurons célébré
Tu auras célébré	Vous aurez célébré
Il aura célébré	Ils auront célébré
Elle aura célébré	Elles auront célébré
On aura célébré	

Conditionnel présent

Je célébrerais	Nous célébrerions
Tu célébrerais	Vous célébreriez
Il célébrerait	Ils célébreraient
Elle célébrerait	Elles célébreraient
On célébrerait	

Conditionnel passé

J'aurais célébré	Nous aurions célébré
Tu aurais célébré	Vous auriez célébré
Il aurait célébré	Ils auraient célébré
Elle aurait célébré	Elles auraient célébré
On aurait célébré	

Impératif

Célèbre !
Célébrons !
Célébrez !

Subjonctif présent

Que je célèbre	Que nous célébrions
Que tu célèbres	Que vous célébriez
Qu'il célèbre	Qu'ils célèbrent
Qu'elle célèbre	Qu'elles célèbrent
Qu'on célèbre	

Conduire – To drive

Participe présent	conduisant	**Participe passé**	conduit

Présent de l'indicatif

Je conduis	Nous conduisons
Tu conduis	Vous conduisez
Il conduit	Ils conduisent
Elle conduit	Elles conduisent
On conduit	

Passé composé

J'ai conduit	Nous avons conduit
Tu as conduit	Vous avez conduit
Il a conduit	Ils ont conduit
Elle a conduit	Elles ont conduit
On a conduit	

Imparfait

Je conduisais	Nous conduisions
Tu conduisais	Vous conduisiez
Il conduisait	Ils conduisaient
Elle conduisait	Elles conduisaient
On conduisait	

Plus-que-parfait

J'avais conduit	Nous avions conduit
Tu avais conduit	Vous aviez conduit
Il avait conduit	Ils avaient conduit
Elle avait conduit	Elles avaient conduit
On avait conduit	

Futur simple

Je conduirai	Nous conduirons
Tu conduiras	Vous conduirez
Il conduira	Ils conduiront
Elle conduira	Elles conduiront
On conduira	

Futur antérieur

J'aurai conduit	Nous aurons conduit
Tu auras conduit	Vous aurez conduit
Il aura conduit	Ils auront conduit
Elle aura conduit	Elles auront conduit
On aura conduit	

Conditionnel présent

Je conduirais	Nous conduirions
Tu conduirais	Vous conduiriez
Il conduirait	Ils conduiraient
Elle conduirait	Elles conduiraient
On conduirait	

Conditionnel passé

J'aurais conduit	Nous aurions conduit
Tu aurais conduit	Vous auriez conduit
Il aurait conduit	Ils auraient conduit
Elle aurait conduit	Elles auraient conduit
On aurait conduit	

Impératif

Conduis !
Conduisons !
Conduisez !

Subjonctif présent

Que je conduise	Que nous conduisions
Que tu conduises	Que vous conduisiez
Qu'il conduise	Qu'ils conduisent
Qu'elle conduise	Qu'elles conduisent
Qu'on conduise	

Common verbs with the same conjugation:
Construire To build – **Déduire** To deduct – **Détruire** To destroy – More P.61

Connaître – To know

Participe présent connaissant

Participe passé connu

Présent de l'indicatif

Je connais	Nous connaissons
Tu connais	Vous connaissez
Il connaît	Ils connaissent
Elle connaît	Elles connaissent
On connaît	

Passé composé

J'ai connu	Nous avons connu
Tu as connu	Vous avez connu
Il a connu	Ils ont connu
Elle a connu	Elles ont connu
On a connu	

Imparfait

Je connaissais	Nous connaissions
Tu connaissais	Vous connaissiez
Il connaissait	Ils connaissaient
Elle connaissait	Elles connaissaient
On connaissait	

Plus-que-parfait

J'avais connu	Nous avions connu
Tu avais connu	Vous aviez connu
Il avait connu	Ils avaient connu
Elle avait connu	Elles avaient connu
On avait connu	

Futur simple

Je connaîtrai	Nous connaîtrons
Tu connaîtras	Vous connaîtrez
Il connaîtra	Ils connaîtront
Elle connaîtra	Elles connaîtront
On connaîtra	

Futur antérieur

J'aurai connu	Nous aurons connu
Tu auras connu	Vous aurez connu
Il aura connu	Ils auront connu
Elle aura connu	Elles auront connu
On aura connu	

Conditionnel présent

Je connaîtrais	Nous connaîtrions
Tu connaîtrais	Vous connaîtriez
Il connaîtrait	Ils connaîtraient
Elle connaîtrait	Elles connaîtraient
On connaîtrait	

Conditionnel passé

J'aurais connu	Nous aurions connu
Tu aurais connu	Vous auriez connu
Il aurait connu	Ils auraient connu
Elle aurait connu	Elles auraient connu
On aurait connu	

Impératif

Connais !
Connaissons !
Connaissez !

Subjonctif présent

Que je connaisse	Que nous connaissions
Que tu connaisses	Que vous connaissiez
Qu'il connaisse	Qu'ils connaissent
Qu'elle connaisse	Qu'elles connaissent
Qu'on connaisse	

Common verbs with the same conjugation:
Apparaître To appear – **Disparaître** To disappear – **Paraître** To seem – **Reconnaître** To recognize

Courir – To run

Participe présent courant

Participe passé couru

Présent de l'indicatif

Je cours	Nous courons
Tu cours	Vous courez
Il court	Ils courent
Elle court	Elles courent
On court	

Passé composé

J'ai couru	Nous avons couru
Tu as couru	Vous avez couru
Il a couru	Ils ont couru
Elle a couru	Elles ont couru
On a couru	

Imparfait

Je courais	Nous courions
Tu courais	Vous couriez
Il courait	Ils couraient
Elle courait	Elles couraient
On courait	

Plus-que-parfait

J'avais couru	Nous avions couru
Tu avais couru	Vous aviez couru
Il avait couru	Ils avaient couru
Elle avait couru	Elles avaient couru
On avait couru	

Futur simple

Je courrai	Nous courrons
Tu courras	Vous courrez
Il courra	Ils courront
Elle courra	Elles courront
On courra	

Futur antérieur

J'aurai couru	Nous aurons couru
Tu auras couru	Vous aurez couru
Il aura couru	Ils auront couru
Elle aura couru	Elles auront couru
On aura couru	

Conditionnel présent

Je courrais	Nous courrions
Tu courrais	Vous courriez
Il courrait	Ils courraient
Elle courrait	Elles courraient
On courrait	

Conditionnel passé

J'aurais couru	Nous aurions couru
Tu aurais couru	Vous auriez couru
Il aurait couru	Ils auraient couru
Elle aurait couru	Elles auraient couru
On aurait couru	

Impératif

Cours !
Courons !
Courez !

Subjonctif présent

Que je coure	Que nous courions
Que tu coures	Que vous couriez
Qu'il coure	Qu'ils courent
Qu'elle coure	Qu'elles courent
Qu'on coure	

Common verb with the same conjugation: **Recourir** To run

Craindre – To fear

Participe présent craignant

Participe passé craint

Présent de l'indicatif

Je crains	Nous craignons
Tu crains	Vous craignez
Il craint	Ils craignent
Elle craint	Elles craignent
On craint	

Passé composé

J'ai craint	Nous avons craint
Tu as craint	Vous avez craint
Il a craint	Ils ont craint
Elle a craint	Elles ont craint
On a craint	

Imparfait

Je craignais	Nous craignions
Tu craignais	Vous craigniez
Il craignait	Ils craignaient
Elle craignait	Elles craignaient
On craignait	

Plus-que-parfait

J'avais craint	Nous avions craint
Tu avais craint	Vous aviez craint
Il avait craint	Ils avaient craint
Elle avait craint	Elles avaient craint
On avait craint	

Futur simple

Je craindrai	Nous craindrons
Tu craindras	Vous craindrez
Il craindra	Ils craindront
Elle craindra	Elles craindront
On craindra	

Futur antérieur

J'aurai craint	Nous aurons craint
Tu auras craint	Vous aurez craint
Il aura craint	Ils auront craint
Elle aura craint	Elles auront craint
On aura craint	

Conditionnel présent

Je craindrais	Nous craindrions
Tu craindrais	Vous craindriez
Il craindrait	Ils craindraient
Elle craindrait	Elles craindraient
On craindrait	

Conditionnel passé

J'aurais craint	Nous aurions craint
Tu aurais craint	Vous auriez craint
Il aurait craint	Ils auraient craint
Elle aurait craint	Elles auraient craint
On aurait craint	

Impératif

Crains !
Craignons !
Craignez !

Subjonctif présent

Que je craigne	Que nous craignions
Que tu craignes	Que vous craigniez
Qu'il craigne	Qu'ils craignent
Qu'elle craigne	Qu'elles craignent
Qu'on craigne	

Common verbs with the same conjugation: **Contraindre** To force – **Plaindre** To pity

Croire – To believe

Participe présent croyant

Participe passé cru

Présent de l'indicatif

Je crois	Nous croyons
Tu crois	Vous croyez
Il croit	Ils croient
Elle croit	Elles croient
On croit	

Passé composé

J'ai cru	Nous avons cru
Tu as cru	Vous avez cru
Il a cru	Ils ont cru
Elle a cru	Elles ont cru
On a cru	

Imparfait

Je croyais	Nous croyions
Tu croyais	Vous croyiez
Il croyait	Ils croyaient
Elle croyait	Elles croyaient
On croyait	

Plus-que-parfait

J'avais cru	Nous avions cru
Tu avais cru	Vous aviez cru
Il avait cru	Ils avaient cru
Elle avait cru	Elles avaient cru
On avait cru	

Futur simple

Je croirai	Nous croirons
Tu croiras	Vous croirez
Il croira	Ils croiront
Elle croira	Elles croiront
On croira	

Futur antérieur

J'aurai cru	Nous aurons cru
Tu auras cru	Vous aurez cru
Il aura cru	Ils auront cru
Elle aura cru	Elles auront cru
On aura cru	

Conditionnel présent

Je croirais	Nous croirions
Tu croirais	Vous croiriez
Il croirait	Ils croiraient
Elle croirait	Elles croiraient
On croirait	

Conditionnel passé

J'aurais cru	Nous aurions cru
Tu aurais cru	Vous auriez cru
Il aurait cru	Ils auraient cru
Elle aurait cru	Elles auraient cru
On aurait cru	

Impératif

Crois !
Croyons !
Croyez !

Subjonctif présent

Que je croie	Que nous croyions
Que tu croies	Que vous croyiez
Qu'il croie	Qu'ils croient
Qu'elle croie	Qu'elles croient
Qu'on croie	

Common verbs with the same conjugation: **Voir** To see – **Prévoir** To predict – **Revoir** To see again

Devoir – To owe – Must – To have to

Participe présent devant

Participe passé dû

Présent de l'indicatif

Je dois	Nous devons
Tu dois	Vous devez
Il doit	Ils doivent
Elle doit	Elles doivent
On doit	

Passé composé

J'ai dû	Nous avons dû
Tu as dû	Vous avez dû
Il a dû	Ils ont dû
Elle a dû	Elles ont dû
On a dû	

Imparfait

Je devais	Nous devions
Tu devais	Vous deviez
Il devait	Ils devaient
Elle devait	Elles devaient
On devait	

Plus-que-parfait

J'avais dû	Nous avions dû
Tu avais dû	Vous aviez dû
Il avait dû	Ils avaient dû
Elle avait dû	Elles avaient dû
On avait dû	

Futur simple

Je devrai	Nous devrons
Tu devras	Vous devrez
Il devra	Ils devront
Elle devra	Elles devront
On devra	

Futur antérieur

J'aurai dû	Nous aurons dû
Tu auras dû	Vous aurez dû
Il aura dû	Ils auront dû
Elle aura dû	Elles auront dû
On aura dû	

Conditionnel présent

Je devrais	Nous devrions
Tu devrais	Vous devriez
Il devrait	Ils devraient
Elle devrait	Elles devraient
On devrait	

Conditionnel passé

J'aurais dû	Nous aurions dû
Tu aurais dû	Vous auriez dû
Il aurait dû	Ils auraient dû
Elle aurait dû	Elles auraient dû
On aurait dû	

Impératif

Dois !
Devons !
Devez !

Subjonctif présent

Que je doive	Que nous devions
Que tu doives	Que vous deviez
Qu'il doive	Qu'ils doivent
Qu'elle doive	Qu'elles doivent
Qu'on doive	

Dire – To say – To tell

Participe présent disant

Participe passé dit

Présent de l'indicatif

Je dis	Nous disons
Tu dis	Vous dites
Il dit	Ils disent
Elle dit	Elles disent
On dit	

Passé composé

J'ai dit	Nous avons dit
Tu as dit	Vous avez dit
Il a dit	Ils ont dit
Elle a dit	Elles ont dit
On a dit	

Imparfait

Je disais	Nous disions
Tu disais	Vous disiez
Il disait	Ils disaient
Elle disait	Elles disaient
On disait	

Plus-que-parfait

J'avais dit	Nous avions dit
Tu avais dit	Vous aviez dit
Il avait dit	Ils avaient dit
Elle avait dit	Elles avaient dit
On avait dit	

Futur simple

Je dirai	Nous dirons
Tu diras	Vous direz
Il dira	Ils diront
Elle dira	Elles diront
On dira	

Futur antérieur

J'aurai dit	Nous aurons dit
Tu auras dit	Vous aurez dit
Il aura dit	Ils auront dit
Elle aura dit	Elles auront dit
On aura dit	

Conditionnel présent

Je dirais	Nous dirions
Tu dirais	Vous diriez
Il dirait	Ils diraient
Elle dirait	Elles diraient
On dirait	

Conditionnel passé

J'aurais dit	Nous aurions dit
Tu aurais dit	Vous auriez dit
Il aurait dit	Ils auraient dit
Elle aurait dit	Elles auraient dit
On aurait dit	

Impératif

Dis !
Disons !
Dites !

Subjonctif présent

Que je dise	Que nous disions
Que tu dises	Que vous disiez
Qu'il dise	Qu'ils disent
Qu'elle dise	Qu'elles disent
Qu'on dise	

Donner – To give

Participe présent donnant

Participe passé donné

Présent de l'indicatif

Je donne	Nous donnons
Tu donnes	Vous donnez
Il donne	Ils donnent
Elle donne	Elles donnent
On donne	

Passé composé

J'ai donné	Nous avons donné
Tu as donné	Vous avez donné
Il a donné	Ils ont donné
Elle a donné	Elles ont donné
On a donné	

Imparfait

Je donnais	Nous donnions
Tu donnais	Vous donniez
Il donnait	Ils donnaient
Elle donnait	Elles donnaient
On donnait	

Plus-que-parfait

J'avais donné	Nous avions donné
Tu avais donné	Vous aviez donné
Il avait donné	Ils avaient donné
Elle avait donné	Elles avaient donné
On avait donné	

Futur simple

Je donnerai	Nous donnerons
Tu donneras	Vous donnerez
Il donnera	Ils donneront
Elle donnera	Elles donneront
On donnera	

Futur antérieur

J'aurai donné	Nous aurons donné
Tu auras donné	Vous aurez donné
Il aura donné	Ils auront donné
Elle aura donné	Elles auront donné
On aura donné	

Conditionnel présent

Je donnerais	Nous donnerions
Tu donnerais	Vous donneriez
Il donnerait	Ils donneraient
Elle donnerait	Elles donneraient
On donnerait	

Conditionnel passé

J'aurais donné	Nous aurions donné
Tu aurais donné	Vous auriez donné
Il aurait donné	Ils auraient donné
Elle aurait donné	Elles auraient donné
On aurait donné	

Impératif

Donne !
Donnons !
Donnez !

Subjonctif présent

Que je donne	Que nous donnions
Que tu donnes	Que vous donniez
Qu'il donne	Qu'ils donnent
Qu'elle donne	Qu'elles donnent
Qu'on donne	

Common verbs with the same conjugation:
Accepter To accept – **Adorer** To adore – **Chercher** To search – **Chanter** To sing – More P. 12

Dormir – To sleep

Participe présent dormant

Présent de l'indicatif

Je dors	Nous dormons
Tu dors	Vous dormez
Il dort	Ils dorment
Elle dort	Elles dorment
On dort	

Imparfait

Je dormais	Nous dormions
Tu dormais	Vous dormiez
Il dormait	Ils dormaient
Elle dormait	Elles dormaient
On dormait	

Futur simple

Je dormirai	Nous dormirons
Tu dormiras	Vous dormirez
Il dormira	Ils dormiront
Elle dormira	Elles dormiront
On dormira	

Conditionnel présent

Je dormirais	Nous dormirions
Tu dormirais	Vous dormiriez
Il dormirait	Ils dormiraient
Elle dormirait	Elles dormiraient
On dormirait	

Impératif

Dors !
Dormons !
Dormez !

Participe passé dormi

Passé composé

J'ai dormi	Nous avons dormi
Tu as dormi	Vous avez dormi
Il a dormi	Ils ont dormi
Elle a dormi	Elles ont dormi
On a dormi	

Plus-que-parfait

J'avais dormi	Nous avions dormi
Tu avais dormi	Vous aviez dormi
Il avait dormi	Ils avaient dormi
Elle avait dormi	Elles avaient dormi
On avait dormi	

Futur antérieur

J'aurai dormi	Nous aurons dormi
Tu auras dormi	Vous aurez dormi
Il aura dormi	Ils auront dormi
Elle aura dormi	Elles auront dormi
On aura dormi	

Conditionnel passé

J'aurais dormi	Nous aurions dormi
Tu aurais dormi	Vous auriez dormi
Il aurait dormi	Ils auraient dormi
Elle aurait dormi	Elles auraient dormi
On aurait dormi	

Subjonctif présent

Que je dorme	Que nous dormions
Que tu dormes	Que vous dormiez
Qu'il dorme	Qu'ils dorment
Qu'elle dorme	Qu'elles dorment
Qu'on dorme	

Écrire – To write

Participe présent écrivant

Présent de l'indicatif

J'écris	Nous écrivons
Tu écris	Vous écrivez
Il écrit	Ils écrivent
Elle écrit	Elles écrivent
On écrit	

Imparfait

J'écrivais	Nous écrivions
Tu écrivais	Vous écriviez
Il écrivait	Ils écrivaient
Elle écrivait	Elles écrivaient
On écrivait	

Futur simple

J'écrirai	Nous écrirons
Tu écriras	Vous écrirez
Il écrira	Ils écriront
Elle écrira	Elles écriront
On écrira	

Conditionnel présent

J'écrirais	Nous écririons
Tu écrirais	Vous écririez
Il écrirait	Ils écriraient
Elle écrirait	Elles écriraient
On écrirait	

Impératif

Écris !
Écrivons !
Écrivez !

Participe passé écrit

Passé composé

J'ai écrit	Nous avons écrit
Tu as écrit	Vous avez écrit
Il a écrit	Ils ont écrit
Elle a écrit	Elles ont écrit
On a écrit	

Plus-que-parfait

J'avais écrit	Nous avions écrit
Tu avais écrit	Vous aviez écrit
Il avait écrit	Ils avaient écrit
Elle avait écrit	Elles avaient écrit
On avait écrit	

Futur antérieur

J'aurai écrit	Nous aurons écrit
Tu auras écrit	Vous aurez écrit
Il aura écrit	Ils auront écrit
Elle aura écrit	Elles auront écrit
On aura écrit	

Conditionnel passé

J'aurais écrit	Nous aurions écrit
Tu aurais écrit	Vous auriez écrit
Il aurait écrit	Ils auraient écrit
Elle aurait écrit	Elles auraient écrit
On aurait écrit	

Subjonctif présent

Que j'écrive	Que nous écrivions
Que tu écrives	Que vous écriviez
Qu'il écrive	Qu'ils écrivent
Qu'elle écrive	Qu'elles écrivent
Qu'on écrive	

Entendre – To hear

Participe présent entendant

Participe passé entendu

Présent de l'indicatif

J'entends	Nous entendons
Tu entends	Vous entendez
Il entend	Ils entendent
Elle entend	Elles entendent
On entend	

Passé composé

J'ai entendu	Nous avons entendu
Tu as entendu	Vous avez entendu
Il a entendu	Ils ont entendu
Elle a entendu	Elles ont entendu
On a entendu	

Imparfait

J'entendais	Nous entendions
Tu entendais	Vous entendiez
Il entendait	Ils entendaient
Elle entendait	Elles entendaient
On entendait	

Plus-que-parfait

J'avais entendu	Nous avions entendu
Tu avais entendu	Vous aviez entendu
Il avait entendu	Ils avaient entendu
Elle avait entendu	Elles avaient entendu
On avait entendu	

Futur simple

J'entendrai	Nous entendrons
Tu entendras	Vous entendrez
Il entendra	Ils entendront
Elle entendra	Elles entendront
On entendra	

Futur antérieur

J'aurai entendu	Nous aurons entendu
Tu auras entendu	Vous aurez entendu
Il aura entendu	Ils auront entendu
Elle aura entendu	Elles auront entendu
On aura entendu	

Conditionnel présent

J'entendrais	Nous entendrions
Tu entendrais	Vous entendriez
Il entendrait	Ils entendraient
Elle entendrait	Elles entendraient
On entendrait	

Conditionnel passé

J'aurais entendu	Nous aurions entendu
Tu aurais entendu	Vous auriez entendu
Il aurait entendu	Ils auraient entendu
Elle aurait entendu	Elles auraient entendu
On aurait entendu	

Impératif

Entends !
Entendons !
Entendez !

Subjonctif présent

Que j'entende	Que nous entendions
Que tu entendes	Que vous entendiez
Qu'il entende	Qu'ils entendent
Qu'elle entende	Qu'elles entendent
Qu'on entende	

Common verbs with the same conjugation:
Attendre To wait – **Fondre** To melt – **Pendre** To hang – **Vendre** To sell – More P. 32

Espérer – To hope

Participe présent espérant

Participe passé espéré

Présent de l'indicatif

J'espère	Nous espérons
Tu espères	Vous espérez
Il espère	Ils espèrent
Elle espère	Elles espèrent
On espère	

Passé composé

J'ai espéré	Nous avons espéré
Tu as espéré	Vous avez espéré
Il a espéré	Ils ont espéré
Elle a espéré	Elles ont espéré
On a espéré	

Imparfait

J'espérais	Nous espérions
Tu espérais	Vous espériez
Il espérait	Ils espéraient
Elle espérait	Elles espéraient
On espérait	

Plus-que-parfait

J'avais espéré	Nous avions espéré
Tu avais espéré	Vous aviez espéré
Il avait espéré	Ils avaient espéré
Elle avait espéré	Elles avaient espéré
On avait espéré	

Futur simple

J'espérerai	Nous espérerons
Tu espéreras	Vous espérerez
Il espérera	Ils espéreront
Elle espérera	Elles espéreront
On espérera	

Futur antérieur

J'aurai espéré	Nous aurons espéré
Tu auras espéré	Vous aurez espéré
Il aura espéré	Ils auront espéré
Elle aura espéré	Elles auront espéré
On aura espéré	

Conditionnel présent

J'espérerais	Nous espérerions
Tu espérerais	Vous espéreriez
Il espérerait	Ils espéreraient
Elle espérerait	Elles espéreraient
On espérerait	

Conditionnel passé

J'aurais espéré	Nous aurions espéré
Tu aurais espéré	Vous auriez espéré
Il aurait espéré	Ils auraient espéré
Elle aurait espéré	Elles auraient espéré
On aurait espéré	

Impératif

Espère !
Espérons !
Espérez !

Subjonctif présent

Que j'espère	Que nous espérions
Que tu espères	Que vous espériez
Qu'il espère	Qu'ils espèrent
Qu'elle espère	Qu'elles espèrent
Qu'on espère	

Common verbs with the same conjugation:
Préférer To prefer – **Exagérer** To exaggerate – **Considérer** To consider

Essayer – To try

Participe présent essayant

Participe passé essayé

Présent de l'indicatif

J'essaye	Nous essayons
Tu essayes	Vous essayez
Il essaye	Ils essayent
Elle essaye	Elles essayent
On essaye	

Passé composé

J'ai essayé	Nous avons essayé
Tu as essayé	Vous avez essayé
Il a essayé	Ils ont essayé
Elle a essayé	Elles ont essayé
On a essayé	

Imparfait

J'essayais	Nous essayions
Tu essayais	Vous essayiez
Il essayait	Ils essayaient
Elle essayait	Elles essayaient
On essayait	

Plus-que-parfait

J'avais essayé	Nous avions essayé
Tu avais essayé	Vous aviez essayé
Il avait essayé	Ils avaient essayé
Elle avait essayé	Elles avaient essayé
On avait essayé	

Futur simple

J'essayerai	Nous essayerons
Tu essayeras	Vous essayerez
Il essayera	Ils essayeront
Elle essayera	Elles essayeront
On essayera	

Futur antérieur

J'aurai essayé	Nous aurons essayé
Tu auras essayé	Vous aurez essayé
Il aura essayé	Ils auront essayé
Elle aura essayé	Elles auront essayé
On aura essayé	

Conditionnel présent

J'essayerais	Nous essayerions
Tu essayerais	Vous essayeriez
Il essayerait	Ils essayeraient
Elle essayerait	Elles essayeraient
On essayerait	

Conditionnel passé

J'aurais essayé	Nous aurions essayé
Tu aurais essayé	Vous auriez essayé
Il aurait essayé	Ils auraient essayé
Elle aurait essayé	Elles auraient essayé
On aurait essayé	

Impératif

Essaye !
Essayons !
Essayez !

Subjonctif présent

Que j'essaye	Que nous essayions
Que tu essayes	Que vous essayiez
Qu'il essaye	Qu'ils essayent
Qu'elle essaye	Qu'elles essayent
Qu'on essaye	

Common verbs with the same conjugation:
Balayer To sweep – **Effrayer** To frighten – **Égayer** To entertain – **Payer** To pay

Essuyer – To wipe

Participe présent essuyant

Participe passé essuyé

Présent de l'indicatif

J'essuie	Nous essuyons
Tu essuies	Vous essuyez
Il essuie	Ils essuient
Elle essuie	Elles essuient
On essuie	

Passé composé

J'ai essuyé	Nous avons essuyé
Tu as essuyé	Vous avez essuyé
Il a essuyé	Ils ont essuyé
Elle a essuyé	Elles ont essuyé
On a essuyé	

Imparfait

J'essuyais	Nous essuyions
Tu essuyais	Vous essuyiez
Il essuyait	Ils essuient
Elle essuyait	Elles essuient
On essuyait	

Plus-que-parfait

J'avais essuyé	Nous avions essuyé
Tu avais essuyé	Vous aviez essuyé
Il avait essuyé	Ils avaient essuyé
Elle avait essuyé	Elles avaient essuyé
On avait essuyé	

Futur simple

J'essuierai	Nous essuierons
Tu essuieras	Vous essuierez
Il essuiera	Ils essuieront
Elle essuiera	Elles essuieront
On essuiera	

Futur antérieur

J'aurai essuyé	Nous aurons essuyé
Tu auras essuyé	Vous aurez essuyé
Il aura essuyé	Ils auront essuyé
Elle aura essuyé	Elles auront essuyé
On aura essuyé	

Conditionnel présent

J'essuierais	Nous essuierions
Tu essuierais	Vous essuieriez
Il essuierait	Ils essuieraient
Elle essuierait	Elles essuieraient
On essuierait	

Conditionnel passé

J'aurais essuyé	Nous aurions essuyé
Tu aurais essuyé	Vous auriez essuyé
Il aurait essuyé	Ils auraient essuyé
Elle aurait essuyé	Elles auraient essuyé
On aurait essuyé	

Impératif

Essuie !
Essuyons !
Essuyez !

Subjonctif présent

Que j'essuie	Que nous essuyions
Que tu essuies	Que vous essuyiez
Qu'il essuie	Qu'ils essuient
Qu'elle essuie	Qu'elles essuient
Qu'on essuie	

Common verbs with the same conjugation: **Appuyer** To press – To lean – **Ennuyer** To bore – To annoy

Éteindre – To turn off

Participe présent éteignant

Participe passé éteint

Présent de l'indicatif

J'éteins	Nous éteignons
Tu éteins	Vous éteignez
Il éteint	Ils éteignent
Elle éteint	Elles éteignent
On éteint	

Passé composé

J'ai éteint	Nous avons éteint
Tu as éteint	Vous avez éteint
Il a éteint	Ils ont éteint
Elle a éteint	Elles ont éteint
On a éteint	

Imparfait

J'éteignais	Nous éteignions
Tu éteignais	Vous éteigniez
Il éteignait	Ils éteignaient
Elle éteignait	Elles éteignaient
On éteignait	

Plus-que-parfait

J'avais éteint	Nous avions éteint
Tu avais éteint	Vous aviez éteint
Il avait éteint	Ils avaient éteint
Elle avait éteint	Elles avaient éteint
On avait éteint	

Futur simple

J'éteindrai	Nous éteindrons
Tu éteindras	Vous éteindrez
Il éteindra	Ils éteindront
Elle éteindra	Elles éteindront
On éteindra	

Futur antérieur

J'aurai éteint	Nous aurons éteint
Tu auras éteint	Vous aurez éteint
Il aura éteint	Ils auront éteint
Elle aura éteint	Elles auront éteint
On aura éteint	

Conditionnel présent

J'éteindrais	Nous éteindrions
Tu éteindrais	Vous éteindriez
Il éteindrait	Ils éteindraient
Elle éteindrait	Elles éteindraient
On éteindrait	

Conditionnel passé

J'aurais éteint	Nous aurions éteint
Tu aurais éteint	Vous auriez éteint
Il aurait éteint	Ils auraient éteint
Elle aurait éteint	Elles auraient éteint
On aurait éteint	

Impératif

Éteins !
Éteignons !
Éteignez !

Subjonctif présent

Que j'éteigne	Que nous éteignions
Que tu éteignes	Que vous éteigniez
Qu'il éteigne	Qu'ils éteignent
Qu'elle éteigne	Qu'elles éteignent
Qu'on éteigne	

Common verbs with the same conjugation:
Atteindre To reach – **Feindre** To feign – **Peindre** To paint – **Teindre** To dye

Être – To be

Participe présent étant

Participe passé été

Présent de l'indicatif

Je suis	Nous sommes
Tu es	Vous êtes
Il est	Ils sont
Elle est	Elles sont
On est	

Passé composé

J'ai été	Nous avons été
Tu as été	Vous avez été
Il a été	Ils ont été
Elle a été	Elles ont été
On a été	

Imparfait

J'étais	Nous étions
Tu étais	Vous étiez
Il était	Ils étaient
Elle était	Elles étaient
On était	

Plus-que-parfait

J'avais été	Nous avions été
Tu avais été	Vous aviez été
Il avait été	Ils avaient été
Elle avait été	Elles avaient été
On avait été	

Futur simple

Je serai	Nous serons
Tu seras	Vous serez
Il sera	Ils seront
Elle sera	Elles seront
On sera	

Futur antérieur

J'aurai été	Nous aurons été
Tu auras été	Vous aurez été
Il aura été	Ils auront été
Elle aura été	Elles auront été
On aura été	

Conditionnel présent

Je serais	Nous serions
Tu serais	Vous seriez
Il serait	Ils seraient
Elle serait	Elles seraient
On serait	

Conditionnel passé

J'aurais été	Nous aurions été
Tu aurais été	Vous auriez été
Il aurait été	Ils auraient été
Elle aurait été	Elles auraient été
On aurait été	

Impératif

Sois !
Soyons !
Soyez !

Subjonctif présent

Que je sois	Que nous soyons
Que tu sois	Que vous soyez
Qu'il soit	Qu'ils soient
Qu'elle soit	Qu'elles soient
Qu'on soit	

Faire – To do – To make

Participe présent faisant

Participe passé fait

Présent de l'indicatif

Je fais	Nous faisons
Tu fais	Vous faites
Il fait	Ils font
Elle fait	Elles font
On fait	

Passé composé

J'ai fait	Nous avons fait
Tu as fait	Vous avez fait
Il a fait	Ils ont fait
Elle a fait	Elles ont fait
On a fait	

Imparfait

Je faisais	Nous faisions
Tu faisais	Vous faisiez
Il faisait	Ils faisaient
Elle faisait	Elles faisaient
On faisait	

Plus-que-parfait

J'avais fait	Nous avions fait
Tu avais fait	Vous aviez fait
Il avait fait	Ils avaient fait
Elle avait fait	Elles avaient fait
On avait fait	

Futur simple

Je ferai	Nous ferons
Tu feras	Vous ferez
Il fera	Ils feront
Elle fera	Elles feront
On fera	

Futur antérieur

J'aurai fait	Nous aurons fait
Tu auras fait	Vous aurez fait
Il aura fait	Ils auront fait
Elle aura fait	Elles auront fait
On aura fait	

Conditionnel présent

Je ferais	Nous ferions
Tu ferais	Vous feriez
Il ferait	Ils feraient
Elle ferait	Elles feraient
On ferait	

Conditionnel passé

J'aurais fait	Nous aurions fait
Tu aurais fait	Vous auriez fait
Il aurait fait	Ils auraient fait
Elle aurait fait	Elles auraient fait
On aurait fait	

Impératif

Fais !
Faisons !
Faites !

Subjonctif présent

Que je fasse	Que nous fassions
Que tu fasses	Que vous fassiez
Qu'il fasse	Qu'ils fassent
Qu'elle fasse	Qu'elles fassent
Qu'on fasse	

Common verbs with the same conjugation: **Refaire** To redo – **Défaire** To undo

Finir – To finish

Participe présent finissant

Participe passé fini

Présent de l'indicatif

Je finis	Nous finissons
Tu finis	Vous finissez
Il finit	Ils finissent
Elle finit	Elles finissent
On finit	

Passé composé

J'ai fini	Nous avons fini
Tu as fini	Vous avez fini
Il a fini	Ils ont fini
Elle a fini	Elles ont fini
On a fini	

Imparfait

Je finissais	Nous finissions
Tu finissais	Vous finissiez
Il finissait	Ils finissaient
Elle finissait	Elles finissaient
On finissait	

Plus-que-parfait

J'avais fini	Nous avions fini
Tu avais fini	Vous aviez fini
Il avait fini	Ils avaient fini
Elle avait fini	Elles avaient fini
On avait fini	

Futur simple

Je finirai	Nous finirons
Tu finiras	Vous finirez
Il finira	Ils finiront
Elle finira	Elles finiront
On finira	

Futur antérieur

J'aurai fini	Nous aurons fini
Tu auras fini	Vous aurez fini
Il aura fini	Ils auront fini
Elle aura fini	Elles auront fini
On aura fini	

Conditionnel présent

Je finirais	Nous finirions
Tu finirais	Vous finiriez
Il finirait	Ils finiraient
Elle finirait	Elles finiraient
On finirait	

Conditionnel passé

J'aurais fini	Nous aurions fini
Tu aurais fini	Vous auriez fini
Il aurait fini	Ils auraient fini
Elle aurait fini	Elles auraient fini
On aurait fini	

Impératif

Finis !
Finissons !
Finissez !

Subjonctif présent

Que je finisse	Que nous finissions
Que tu finisses	Que vous finissiez
Qu'il finisse	Qu'ils finissent
Qu'elle finisse	Qu'elles finissent
Qu'on finisse	

Common verbs with the same conjugation:
Agir To act – **Guérir** To heal – **Salir** To soil – **Unir** To join – More P. 30

Fuir – To flee

Participe présent fuyant

Participe passé fui

Présent de l'indicatif

Je fuis	Nous fuyons
Tu fuis	Vous fuyez
Il fuit	Ils fuient
Elle fuit	Elles fuient
On fuit	

Passé composé

J'ai fui	Nous avons fui
Tu as fui	Vous avez fui
Il a fui	Ils ont fui
Elle a fui	Elles ont fui
On a fui	

Imparfait

Je fuyais	Nous fuyions
Tu fuyais	Vous fuyiez
Il fuyait	Ils fuyaient
Elle fuyait	Elles fuyaient
On fuyait	

Plus-que-parfait

J'avais fui	Nous avions fui
Tu avais fui	Vous aviez fui
Il avait fui	Ils avaient fui
Elle avait fui	Elles avaient fui
On avait fui	

Futur simple

Je fuirai	Nous fuirons
Tu fuiras	Vous fuirez
Il fuira	Ils fuiront
Elle fuira	Elles fuiront
On fuira	

Futur antérieur

J'aurai fui	Nous aurons fui
Tu auras fui	Vous aurez fui
Il aura fui	Ils auront fui
Elle aura fui	Elles auront fui
On aura fui	

Conditionnel présent

Je fuirais	Nous fuirions
Tu fuirais	Vous fuiriez
Il fuirait	Ils fuiraient
Elle fuirait	Elles fuiraient
On fuirait	

Conditionnel passé

J'aurais fui	Nous aurions fui
Tu aurais fui	Vous auriez fui
Il aurait fui	Ils auraient fui
Elle aurait fui	Elles auraient fui
On aurait fui	

Impératif

Fuis !
Fuyons !
Fuyez !

Subjonctif présent

Que je fuie	Que nous fuyions
Que tu fuies	Que vous fuyiez
Qu'il fuie	Qu'ils fuient
Qu'elle fuie	Qu'elles fuient
Qu'on fuie	

Geler – To freeze

Participe présent gelant

Participe passé gelé

Présent de l'indicatif

Je gèle	Nous gelons
Tu gèles	Vous gelez
Il gèle	Ils gèlent
Elle gèle	Elles gèlent
On gèle	

Passé composé

J'ai gelé	Nous avons gelé
Tu as gelé	Vous avez gelé
Il a gelé	Ils ont gelé
Elle a gelé	Elles ont gelé
On a gelé	

Imparfait

Je gelais	Nous gelions
Tu gelais	Vous geliez
Il gelait	Ils gelaient
Elle gelait	Elles gelaient
On gelait	

Plus-que-parfait

J'avais gelé	Nous avions gelé
Tu avais gelé	Vous aviez gelé
Il avait gelé	Ils avaient gelé
Elle avait gelé	Elles avaient gelé
On avait gelé	

Futur simple

Je gèlerai	Nous gèlerons
Tu gèleras	Vous gèlerez
Il gèlera	Ils gèleront
Elle gèlera	Elles gèleront
On gèlera	

Futur antérieur

J'aurai gelé	Nous aurons gelé
Tu auras gelé	Vous aurez gelé
Il aura gelé	Ils auront gelé
Elle aura gelé	Elles auront gelé
On aura gelé	

Conditionnel présent

Je gèlerais	Nous gèlerions
Tu gèlerais	Vous gèleriez
Il gèlerait	Ils gèleraient
Elle gèlerait	Elles gèleraient
On gèlerait	

Conditionnel passé

J'aurais gelé	Nous aurions gelé
Tu aurais gelé	Vous auriez gelé
Il aurait gelé	Ils auraient gelé
Elle aurait gelé	Elles auraient gelé
On aurait gelé	

Impératif

Gèle !
Gelons !
Gelez !

Subjonctif présent

Que je gèle	Que nous gelions
Que tu gèles	Que vous geliez
Qu'il gèle	Qu'ils gèlent
Qu'elle gèle	Qu'elles gèlent
Qu'on gèle	

Common verb with the same conjugation: **Peler** To peel

Jeter – To throw

Participe présent	jetant

Participe passé	jeté

Présent de l'indicatif

Je jette	Nous jetons
Tu jettes	Vous jetez
Il jette	Ils jettent
Elle jette	Elles jettent
On jette	

Passé composé

J'ai jeté	Nous avons jeté
Tu as jeté	Vous avez jeté
Il a jeté	Ils ont jeté
Elle a jeté	Elles ont jeté
On a jeté	

Imparfait

Je jetais	Nous jetions
Tu jetais	Vous jetiez
Il jetait	Ils jetaient
Elle jetait	Elles jetaient
On jetait	

Plus-que-parfait

J'avais jeté	Nous avions jeté
Tu avais jeté	Vous aviez jeté
Il avait jeté	Ils avaient jeté
Elle avait jeté	Elles avaient jeté
On avait jeté	

Futur simple

Je jetterai	Nous jetterons
Tu jetteras	Vous jetterez
Il jettera	Ils jetteront
Elle jettera	Elles jetteront
On jettera	

Futur antérieur

J'aurai jeté	Nous aurons jeté
Tu auras jeté	Vous aurez jeté
Il aura jeté	Ils auront jeté
Elle aura jeté	Elles auront jeté
On aura jeté	

Conditionnel présent

Je jetterais	Nous jetterions
Tu jetterais	Vous jetteriez
Il jetterait	Ils jetteraient
Elle jetterait	Elles jetteraient
On jetterait	

Conditionnel passé

J'aurais jeté	Nous aurions jeté
Tu aurais jeté	Vous auriez jeté
Il aurait jeté	Ils auraient jeté
Elle aurait jeté	Elles auraient jeté
On aurait jeté	

Impératif

Jette !
Jetons !
Jetez !

Subjonctif présent

Que je jette	Que nous jetions
Que tu jettes	Que vous jetiez
Qu'il jette	Qu'ils jettent
Qu'elle jette	Qu'elles jettent
Qu'on jette	

Common verbs with the same conjugation: **Rejeter** To reject – **Projeter** To project

Joindre – To join

Participe présent joignant

Participe passé joint

Présent de l'indicatif

Je joins	Nous joignons
Tu joins	Vous joignez
Il joint	Ils joignent
Elle joint	Elles joignent
On joint	

Passé composé

J'ai joint	Nous avons joint
Tu as joint	Vous avez joint
Il a joint	Ils ont joint
Elle a joint	Elles ont joint
On a joint	

Imparfait

Je joignais	Nous joignions
Tu joignais	Vous joigniez
Il joignait	Ils joignaient
Elle joignait	Elles joignaient
On joignait	

Plus-que-parfait

J'avais joint	Nous avions joint
Tu avais joint	Vous aviez joint
Il avait joint	Ils avaient joint
Elle avait joint	Elles avaient joint
On avait joint	

Futur simple

Je joindrai	Nous joindrons
Tu joindras	Vous joindrez
Il joindra	Ils joindront
Elle joindra	Elles joindront
On joindra	

Futur antérieur

J'aurai joint	Nous aurons joint
Tu auras joint	Vous aurez joint
Il aura joint	Ils auront joint
Elle aura joint	Elles auront joint
On aura joint	

Conditionnel présent

Je joindrais	Nous joindrions
Tu joindrais	Vous joindriez
Il joindrait	Ils joindraient
Elle joindrait	Elles joindraient
On joindrait	

Conditionnel passé

J'aurais joint	Nous aurions joint
Tu aurais joint	Vous auriez joint
Il aurait joint	Ils auraient joint
Elle aurait joint	Elles auraient joint
On aurait joint	

Impératif

Joins !
Joignons !
Joignez !

Subjonctif présent

Que je joigne	Que nous joignions
Que tu joignes	Que vous joigniez
Qu'il joigne	Qu'ils joignent
Qu'elle joigne	Qu'elles joignent
Qu'on joigne	

Common verb with the same conjugation: **Rejoindre** To rejoin

Lancer – To throw

Participe présent	lançant

Présent de l'indicatif

Je lance	Nous lançons
Tu lances	Vous lancez
Il lance	Ils lancent
Elle lance	Elles lancent
On lance	

Imparfait

Je lançais	Nous lancions
Tu lançais	Vous lanciez
Il lançait	Ils lançaient
Elle lançait	Elles lançaient
On lançait	

Futur simple

Je lancerai	Nous lancerons
Tu lanceras	Vous lancerez
Il lancera	Ils lanceront
Elle lancera	Elles lanceront
On lancera	

Conditionnel présent

Je lancerais	Nous lancerions
Tu lancerais	Vous lanceriez
Il lancerait	Ils lanceraient
Elle lancerait	Elles lanceraient
On lancerait	

Impératif

Lance !
Lançons !
Lancez !

Participe passé	lancé

Passé composé

J'ai lancé	Nous avons lancé
Tu as lancé	Vous avez lancé
Il a lancé	Ils ont lancé
Elle a lancé	Elles ont lancé
On a lancé	

Plus-que-parfait

J'avais lancé	Nous avions lancé
Tu avais lancé	Vous aviez lancé
Il avait lancé	Ils avaient lancé
Elle avait lancé	Elles avaient lancé
On avait lancé	

Futur antérieur

J'aurai lancé	Nous aurons lancé
Tu auras lancé	Vous aurez lancé
Il aura lancé	Ils auront lancé
Elle aura lancé	Elles auront lancé
On aura lancé	

Conditionnel passé

J'aurais lancé	Nous aurions lancé
Tu aurais lancé	Vous auriez lancé
Il aurait lancé	Ils auraient lancé
Elle aurait lancé	Elles auraient lancé
On aurait lancé	

Subjonctif présent

Que je lance	Que nous lancions
Que tu lances	Que vous lanciez
Qu'il lance	Qu'ils lancent
Qu'elle lance	Qu'elles lancent
Qu'on lance	

Common verbs with the same conjugation:
Agacer To annoy – **Forcer** To force – **Remplacer** To replace – **Placer** To put – More P. 18

Lire – To read

Participe présent lisant

Participe passé lu

Présent de l'indicatif

Je lis	Nous lisons
Tu lis	Vous lisez
Il lit	Ils lisent
Elle lit	Elles lisent
On lit	

Passé composé

J'ai lu	Nous avons lu
Tu as lu	Vous avez lu
Il a lu	Ils ont lu
Elle a lu	Elles ont lu
On a lu	

Imparfait

Je lisais	Nous lisions
Tu lisais	Vous lisiez
Il lisait	Ils lisaient
Elle lisait	Elles lisaient
On lisait	

Plus-que-parfait

J'avais lu	Nous avions lu
Tu avais lu	Vous aviez lu
Il avait lu	Ils avaient lu
Elle avait lu	Elles avaient lu
On avait lu	

Futur simple

Je lirai	Nous lirons
Tu liras	Vous lirez
Il lira	Ils liront
Elle lira	Elles liront
On lira	

Futur antérieur

J'aurai lu	Nous aurons lu
Tu auras lu	Vous aurez lu
Il aura lu	Ils auront lu
Elle aura lu	Elles auront lu
On aura lu	

Conditionnel présent

Je lirais	Nous lirions
Tu lirais	Vous liriez
Il lirait	Ils liraient
Elle lirait	Elles liraient
On lirait	

Conditionnel passé

J'aurais lu	Nous aurions lu
Tu aurais lu	Vous auriez lu
Il aurait lu	Ils auraient lu
Elle aurait lu	Elles auraient lu
On aurait lu	

Impératif

Lis !
Lisons !
Lisez !

Subjonctif présent

Que je lise	Que nous lisions
Que tu lises	Que vous lisiez
Qu'il lise	Qu'ils lisent
Qu'elle lise	Qu'elles lisent
Qu'on lise	

Common verbs with the same conjugation: **Relire** To read again – **Élire** To elect

Manger – To eat

Participe présent mangeant

Participe passé mangé

Présent de l'indicatif

Je mange	Nous mangeons
Tu manges	Vous mangez
Il mange	Ils mangent
Elle mange	Elles mangent
On mange	

Passé composé

J'ai mangé	Nous avons mangé
Tu as mangé	Vous avez mangé
Il a mangé	Ils ont mangé
Elle a mangé	Elles ont mangé
On a mangé	

Imparfait

Je mangeais	Nous mangions
Tu mangeais	Vous mangiez
Il mangeait	Ils mangeaient
Elle mangeait	Elles mangeaient
On mangeait	

Plus-que-parfait

J'avais mangé	Nous avions mangé
Tu avais mangé	Vous aviez mangé
Il avait mangé	Ils avaient mangé
Elle avait mangé	Elles avaient mangé
On avait mangé	

Futur simple

Je mangerai	Nous mangerons
Tu mangeras	Vous mangerez
Il mangera	Ils mangeront
Elle mangera	Elles mangeront
On mangera	

Futur antérieur

J'aurai mangé	Nous aurons mangé
Tu auras mangé	Vous aurez mangé
Il aura mangé	Ils auront mangé
Elle aura mangé	Elles auront mangé
On aura mangé	

Conditionnel présent

Je mangerais	Nous mangerions
Tu mangerais	Vous mangeriez
Il mangerait	Ils mangeraient
Elle mangerait	Elles mangeraient
On mangerait	

Conditionnel passé

J'aurais mangé	Nous aurions mangé
Tu aurais mangé	Vous auriez mangé
Il aurait mangé	Ils auraient mangé
Elle aurait mangé	Elles auraient mangé
On aurait mangé	

Impératif

Mange !
Mangeons !
Mangez !

Subjonctif présent

Que je mange	Que nous mangions
Que tu manges	Que vous mangiez
Qu'il mange	Qu'ils mangent
Qu'elle mange	Qu'elles mangent
Qu'on mange	

Common verbs with the same conjugation:
Bouger To move – **Charger** To charge – **Corriger** To correct – **Songer** To think – More P. 18

Mentir – To lie

Participe présent mentant

Participe passé menti

Présent de l'indicatif

Je mens	Nous mentons
Tu mens	Vous mentez
Il ment	Ils mentent
Elle ment	Elles mentent
On ment	

Passé composé

J'ai menti	Nous avons menti
Tu as menti	Vous avez menti
Il a menti	Ils ont menti
Elle a menti	Elles ont menti
On a menti	

Imparfait

Je mentais	Nous mentions
Tu mentais	Vous mentiez
Il mentait	Ils mentaient
Elle mentait	Elles mentaient
On mentait	

Plus-que-parfait

J'avais menti	Nous avions menti
Tu avais menti	Vous aviez menti
Il avait menti	Ils avaient menti
Elle avait menti	Elles avaient menti
On avait menti	

Futur simple

Je mentirai	Nous mentirons
Tu mentiras	Vous mentirez
Il mentira	Ils mentiront
Elle mentira	Elles mentiront
On mentira	

Futur antérieur

J'aurai menti	Nous aurons menti
Tu auras menti	Vous aurez menti
Il aura menti	Ils auront menti
Elle aura menti	Elles auront menti
On aura menti	

Conditionnel présent

Je mentirais	Nous mentirions
Tu mentirais	Vous mentiriez
Il mentirait	Ils mentiraient
Elle mentirait	Elles mentiraient
On mentirait	

Conditionnel passé

J'aurais menti	Nous aurions menti
Tu aurais menti	Vous auriez menti
Il aurait menti	Ils auraient menti
Elle aurait menti	Elles auraient menti
On aurait menti	

Impératif

Mens !
Mentons !
Mentez !

Subjonctif présent

Que je mente	Que nous mentions
Que tu mentes	Que vous mentiez
Qu'il mente	Qu'ils mentent
Qu'elle mente	Qu'elles mentent
Qu'on mente	

Common verbs with the same conjugation:
Partir To leave – **Repartir** To leave again – **Sentir** To smell – To feel – **Sortir** To go out

Mettre – To put

Participe présent mettant

Présent de l'indicatif

Je mets	Nous mettons
Tu mets	Vous mettez
Il met	Ils mettent
Elle met	Elles mettent
On met	

Imparfait

Je mettais	Nous mettions
Tu mettais	Vous mettiez
Il mettait	Ils mettaient
Elle mettait	Elles mettaient
On mettait	

Futur simple

Je mettrai	Nous mettrons
Tu mettras	Vous mettrez
Il mettra	Ils mettront
Elle mettra	Elles mettront
On mettra	

Conditionnel présent

Je mettrais	Nous mettrions
Tu mettrais	Vous mettriez
Il mettrait	Ils mettraient
Elle mettrait	Elles mettraient
On mettrait	

Impératif

Mets !
Mettons !
Mettez !

Participe passé mis

Passé composé

J'ai mis	Nous avons mis
Tu as mis	Vous avez mis
Il a mis	Ils ont mis
Elle a mis	Elles ont mis
On a mis	

Plus-que-parfait

J'avais mis	Nous avions mis
Tu avais mis	Vous aviez mis
Il avait mis	Ils avaient mis
Elle avait mis	Elles avaient mis
On avait mis	

Futur antérieur

J'aurai mis	Nous aurons mis
Tu auras mis	Vous aurez mis
Il aura mis	Ils auront mis
Elle aura mis	Elles auront mis
On aura mis	

Conditionnel passé

J'aurais mis	Nous aurions mis
Tu aurais mis	Vous auriez mis
Il aurait mis	Ils auraient mis
Elle aurait mis	Elles auraient mis
On aurait mis	

Subjonctif présent

Que je mette	Que nous mettions
Que tu mettes	Que vous mettiez
Qu'il mette	Qu'ils mettent
Qu'elle mette	Qu'elles mettent
Qu'on mette	

Common verbs with the same conjugation:
Admettre To admit – **Commettre** To commit – **Permettre** To allow – **Promettre** To promise

Mourir – To die

Participe présent mourant

Présent de l'indicatif

Je meurs	Nous mourons
Tu meurs	Vous mourez
Il meurt	Ils meurent
Elle meurt	Elles meurent
On meurt	

Imparfait

Je mourais	Nous mourions
Tu mourais	Vous mouriez
Il mourait	Ils mouraient
Elle mourait	Elles mouraient
On mourait	

Futur simple

Je mourrai	Nous mourrons
Tu mourras	Vous mourrez
Il mourra	Ils mourront
Elle mourra	Elles mourront
On mourra	

Conditionnel présent

Je mourrais	Nous mourrions
Tu mourrais	Vous mourriez
Il mourrait	Ils mourraient
Elle mourrait	Elles mourraient
On mourrait	

Impératif

Meurs !
Mourons !
Mourez !

Participe passé mort

Passé composé

Je suis mort(e)	Nous sommes mort(e)s
Tu es mort(e)	Vous êtes mort(e)s
Il est mort	Ils sont morts
Elle est morte	Elles sont mortes
On est mort(e)s	

Plus-que-parfait

J'étais mort(e)	Nous étions mort(e)s
Tu étais mort(e)	Vous étiez mort(e)s
Il était mort	Ils étaient morts
Elle était morte	Elles étaient mortes
On était mort(e)s	

Futur antérieur

Je serai mort(e)	Nous serons mort(e)s
Tu seras mort(e)	Vous serez mort(e)s
Il sera mort	Ils seront morts
Elle sera morte	Elles seront mortes
On sera mort(e)s	

Conditionnel passé

Je serais mort(e)	Nous serions mort(e)s
Tu serais mort(e)	Vous seriez mort(e)s
Il serait mort	Ils seraient morts
Elle serait morte	Elles seraient mortes
On serait mort(e)s	

Subjonctif présent

Que je meure	Que nous mourions
Que tu meures	Que vous mouriez
Qu'il meure	Qu'ils meurent
Qu'elle meure	Qu'elles meurent
Qu'on meure	

Nettoyer – To clean

Participe présent	nettoyant	**Participe passé**	nettoyé

Présent de l'indicatif

Je nettoie	Nous nettoyons
Tu nettoies	Vous nettoyez
Il nettoie	Ils nettoient
Elle nettoie	Elles nettoient
On nettoie	

Passé composé

J'ai nettoyé	Nous avons nettoyé
Tu as nettoyé	Vous avez nettoyé
Il a nettoyé	Ils ont nettoyé
Elle a nettoyé	Elles ont nettoyé
On a nettoyé	

Imparfait

Je nettoyais	Nous nettoyions
Tu nettoyais	Vous nettoyiez
Il nettoyait	Ils nettoyaient
Elle nettoyait	Elles nettoyaient
On nettoyait	

Plus-que-parfait

J'avais nettoyé	Nous avions nettoyé
Tu avais nettoyé	Vous aviez nettoyé
Il avait nettoyé	Ils avaient nettoyé
Elle avait nettoyé	Elles avaient nettoyé
On avait nettoyé	

Futur simple

Je nettoierai	Nous nettoierons
Tu nettoieras	Vous nettoierez
Il nettoiera	Ils nettoieront
Elle nettoiera	Elles nettoieront
On nettoiera	

Futur antérieur

J'aurai nettoyé	Nous aurons nettoyé
Tu auras nettoyé	Vous aurez nettoyé
Il aura nettoyé	Ils auront nettoyé
Elle aura nettoyé	Elles auront nettoyé
On aura nettoyé	

Conditionnel présent

Je nettoierais	Nous nettoierions
Tu nettoierais	Vous nettoieriez
Il nettoierait	Ils nettoieraient
Elle nettoierait	Elles nettoieraient
On nettoierait	

Conditionnel passé

J'aurais nettoyé	Nous aurions nettoyé
Tu aurais nettoyé	Vous auriez nettoyé
Il aurait nettoyé	Ils auraient nettoyé
Elle aurait nettoyé	Elles auraient nettoyé
On aurait nettoyé	

Impératif

Nettoie !
Nettoyons !
Nettoyez !

Subjonctif présent

Que je nettoie	Que nous nettoyions
Que tu nettoies	Que vous nettoyiez
Qu'il nettoie	Qu'ils nettoient
Qu'elle nettoie	Qu'elles nettoient
Qu'on nettoie	

Common verbs with the same conjugation:
Employer To emoploy – **Tutoyer** To use tu – **Vouvoyer** To use vous

Offrir – To offer

Participe présent offrant

Participe passé offert

Présent de l'indicatif

J'offre	Nous offrons
Tu offres	Vous offrez
Il offre	Ils offrent
Elle offre	Elles offrent
On offre	

Passé composé

J'ai offert	Nous avons offert
Tu as offert	Vous avez offert
Il a offert	Ils ont offert
Elle a offert	Elles ont offert
On a offert	

Imparfait

J'offrais	Nous offrions
Tu offrais	Vous offriez
Il offrait	Ils offraient
Elle offrait	Elles offraient
On offrait	

Plus-que-parfait

J'avais offert	Nous avions offert
Tu avais offert	Vous aviez offert
Il avait offert	Ils avaient offert
Elle avait offert	Elles avaient offert
On avait offert	

Futur simple

J'offrirai	Nous offrirons
Tu offriras	Vous offrirez
Il offrira	Ils offriront
Elle offrira	Elles offriront
On offrira	

Futur antérieur

J'aurai offert	Nous aurons offert
Tu auras offert	Vous aurez offert
Il aura offert	Ils auront offert
Elle aura offert	Elles auront offert
On aura offert	

Conditionnel présent

J'offrirais	Nous offririons
Tu offrirais	Vous offririez
Il offrirait	Ils offriraient
Elle offrirait	Elles offriraient
On offrirait	

Conditionnel passé

J'aurais offert	Nous aurions offert
Tu aurais offert	Vous auriez offert
Il aurait offert	Ils auraient offert
Elle aurait offert	Elles auraient offert
On aurait offert	

Impératif

Offre !
Offrons !
Offrez !

Subjonctif présent

Que j'offre	Que nous offrions
Que tu offres	Que vous offriez
Qu'il offre	Qu'ils offrent
Qu'elle offre	Qu'elles offrent
Qu'on offre	

Common verb with the same conjugation: **Souffrir** To suffer

Ouvrir – To open

Participe présent ouvrant

Participe passé ouvert

Présent de l'indicatif

J'ouvre	Nous ouvrons
Tu ouvres	Vous ouvrez
Il ouvre	Ils ouvrent
Elle ouvre	Elles ouvrent
On ouvre	

Passé composé

J'ai ouvert	Nous avons ouvert
Tu as ouvert	Vous avez ouvert
Il a ouvert	Ils ont ouvert
Elle a ouvert	Elles ont ouvert
On a ouvert	

Imparfait

J'ouvrais	Nous ouvrions
Tu ouvrais	Vous ouvriez
Il ouvrait	Ils ouvraient
Elle ouvrait	Elles ouvraient
On ouvrait	

Plus-que-parfait

J'avais ouvert	Nous avions ouvert
Tu avais ouvert	Vous aviez ouvert
Il avait ouvert	Ils avaient ouvert
Elle avait ouvert	Elles avaient ouvert
On avait ouvert	

Futur simple

J'ouvrirai	Nous ouvrirons
Tu ouvriras	Vous ouvrirez
Il ouvrira	Ils ouvriront
Elle ouvrira	Elles ouvriront
On ouvrira	

Futur antérieur

J'aurai ouvert	Nous aurons ouvert
Tu auras ouvert	Vous aurez ouvert
Il aura ouvert	Ils auront ouvert
Elle aura ouvert	Elles auront ouvert
On aura ouvert	

Conditionnel présent

J'ouvrirais	Nous ouvririons
Tu ouvrirais	Vous ouvririez
Il ouvrirait	Ils ouvriraient
Elle ouvrirait	Elles ouvriraient
On ouvrirait	

Conditionnel passé

J'aurais ouvert	Nous aurions ouvert
Tu aurais ouvert	Vous auriez ouvert
Il aurait ouvert	Ils auraient ouvert
Elle aurait ouvert	Elles auraient ouvert
On aurait ouvert	

Impératif

Ouvre !
Ouvrons !
Ouvrez !

Subjonctif présent

Que j'ouvre	Que nous ouvrions
Que tu ouvres	Que vous ouvriez
Qu'il ouvre	Qu'ils ouvrent
Qu'elle ouvre	Qu'elles ouvrent
Qu'on ouvre	

Common verbs with the same conjugation: **Couvrir** To cover – **Découvrir** To discover

Peser – To weigh

Participe présent pesant

Participe passé pesé

Présent de l'indicatif

Je pèse	Nous pesons
Tu pèses	Vous pesez
Il pèse	Ils pèsent
Elle pèse	Elles pèsent
On pèse	

Passé composé

J'ai pesé	Nous avons pesé
Tu as pesé	Vous avez pesé
Il a pesé	Ils ont pesé
Elle a pesé	Elles ont pesé
On a pesé	

Imparfait

Je pesais	Nous pesions
Tu pesais	Vous pesiez
Il pesait	Ils pesaient
Elle pesait	Elles pesaient
On pesait	

Plus-que-parfait

J'avais pesé	Nous avions pesé
Tu avais pesé	Vous aviez pesé
Il avait pesé	Ils avaient pesé
Elle avait pesé	Elles avaient pesé
On avait pesé	

Futur simple

Je pèserai	Nous pèserons
Tu pèseras	Vous pèserez
Il pèsera	Ils pèseront
Elle pèsera	Elles pèseront
On pèsera	

Futur antérieur

J'aurai pesé	Nous aurons pesé
Tu auras pesé	Vous aurez pesé
Il aura pesé	Ils auront pesé
Elle aura pesé	Elles auront pesé
On aura pesé	

Conditionnel présent

Je pèserais	Nous pèserions
Tu pèserais	Vous pèseriez
Il pèserait	Ils pèseraient
Elle pèserait	Elles pèseraient
On pèserait	

Conditionnel passé

J'aurais pesé	Nous aurions pesé
Tu aurais pesé	Vous auriez pesé
Il aurait pesé	Ils auraient pesé
Elle aurait pesé	Elles auraient pesé
On aurait pesé	

Impératif

Pèse !
Pesons !
Pesez !

Subjonctif présent

Que je pèse	Que nous pesions
Que tu pèses	Que vous pesiez
Qu'il pèse	Qu'ils pèsent
Qu'elle pèse	Qu'elles pèsent
Qu'on pèse	

Pouvoir – To be able to – Must

Participe présent	pouvant

Participe passé	pu

Présent de l'indicatif

Je peux	Nous pouvons
Tu peux	Vous pouvez
Il peut	Ils peuvent
Elle peut	Elles peuvent
On peut	

Passé composé

J'ai pu	Nous avons pu
Tu as pu	Vous avez pu
Il a pu	Ils ont pu
Elle a pu	Elles ont pu
On a pu	

Imparfait

Je pouvais	Nous pouvions
Tu pouvais	Vous pouviez
Il pouvait	Ils pouvaient
Elle pouvait	Elles pouvaient
On pouvait	

Plus-que-parfait

J'avais pu	Nous avions pu
Tu avais pu	Vous aviez pu
Il avait pu	Ils avaient pu
Elle avait pu	Elles avaient pu
On avait pu	

Futur simple

Je pourrai	Nous pourrons
Tu pourras	Vous pourrez
Il pourra	Ils pourront
Elle pourra	Elles pourront
On pourra	

Futur antérieur

J'aurai pu	Nous aurons pu
Tu auras pu	Vous aurez pu
Il aura pu	Ils auront pu
Elle aura pu	Elles auront pu
On aura pu	

Conditionnel présent

Je pourrais	Nous pourrions
Tu pourrais	Vous pourriez
Il pourrait	Ils pourraient
Elle pourrait	Elles pourraient
On pourrait	

Conditionnel passé

J'aurais pu	Nous aurions pu
Tu aurais pu	Vous auriez pu
Il aurait pu	Ils auraient pu
Elle aurait pu	Elles auraient pu
On aurait pu	

Impératif

–
–
–

Subjonctif présent

Que je puisse	Que nous puissions
Que tu puisses	Que vous puissiez
Qu'il puisse	Qu'ils puissent
Qu'elle puisse	Qu'elles puissent
Qu'on puisse	

Prendre – To take

Participe présent prenant

Participe passé pris

Présent de l'indicatif

Je prends	Nous prenons
Tu prends	Vous prenez
Il prend	Ils prennent
Elle prend	Elles prennent
On prend	

Passé composé

J'ai pris	Nous avons pris
Tu as pris	Vous avez pris
Il a pris	Ils ont pris
Elle a pris	Elles ont pris
On a pris	

Imparfait

Je prenais	Nous prenions
Tu prenais	Vous preniez
Il prenait	Ils prenaient
Elle prenait	Elles prenaient
On prenait	

Plus-que-parfait

J'avais pris	Nous avions pris
Tu avais pris	Vous aviez pris
Il avait pris	Ils avaient pris
Elle avait pris	Elles avaient pris
On avait pris	

Futur simple

Je prendrai	Nous prendrons
Tu prendras	Vous prendrez
Il prendra	Ils prendront
Elle prendra	Elles prendront
On prendra	

Futur antérieur

J'aurai pris	Nous aurons pris
Tu auras pris	Vous aurez pris
Il aura pris	Ils auront pris
Elle aura pris	Elles auront pris
On aura pris	

Conditionnel présent

Je prendrais	Nous prendrions
Tu prendrais	Vous prendriez
Il prendrait	Ils prendraient
Elle prendrait	Elles prendraient
On prendrait	

Conditionnel passé

J'aurais pris	Nous aurions pris
Tu aurais pris	Vous auriez pris
Il aurait pris	Ils auraient pris
Elle aurait pris	Elles auraient pris
On aurait pris	

Impératif

Prends !
Prenons !
Prenez !

Subjonctif présent

Que je prenne	Que nous prenions
Que tu prennes	Que vous preniez
Qu'il prenne	Qu'ils prennent
Qu'elle prenne	Qu'elles prennent
Qu'on prenne	

Common verbs with the same conjugation:
Apprendre To learn – **Comprendre** To understand – **Reprendre** To take back – **Surprendre** To surprise

Recevoir – To receive

Participe présent	recevant	**Participe passé**	reçu

Présent de l'indicatif

Je reçois	Nous recevons
Tu reçois	Vous recevez
Il reçoit	Ils reçoivent
Elle reçoit	Elles reçoivent
On reçoit	

Passé composé

J'ai reçu	Nous avons reçu
Tu as reçu	Vous avez reçu
Il a reçu	Ils ont reçu
Elle a reçu	Elles ont reçu
On a reçu	

Imparfait

Je recevais	Nous recevions
Tu recevais	Vous receviez
Il recevait	Ils recevaient
Elle recevait	Elles recevaient
On recevait	

Plus-que-parfait

J'avais reçu	Nous avions reçu
Tu avais reçu	Vous aviez reçu
Il avait reçu	Ils avaient reçu
Elle avait reçu	Elles avaient reçu
On avait reçu	

Futur simple

Je recevrai	Nous recevrons
Tu recevras	Vous recevrez
Il recevra	Ils recevront
Elle recevra	Elles recevront
On recevra	

Futur antérieur

J'aurai reçu	Nous aurons reçu
Tu auras reçu	Vous aurez reçu
Il aura reçu	Ils auront reçu
Elle aura reçu	Elles auront reçu
On aura reçu	

Conditionnel présent

Je recevrais	Nous recevrions
Tu recevrais	Vous recevriez
Il recevrait	Ils recevraient
Elle recevrait	Elles recevraient
On recevrait	

Conditionnel passé

J'aurais reçu	Nous aurions reçu
Tu aurais reçu	Vous auriez reçu
Il aurait reçu	Ils auraient reçu
Elle aurait reçu	Elles auraient reçu
On aurait reçu	

Impératif

Reçois !
Recevons !
Recevez !

Subjonctif présent

Que je reçoive	Que nous recevions
Que tu reçoives	Que vous receviez
Qu'il reçoive	Qu'ils reçoivent
Qu'elle reçoive	Qu'elles reçoivent
Qu'on reçoive	

Common verbs with the same conjugation: **Apercevoir** To see – **Décevoir** To disappoint

Répéter – To repeat

Participe présent	répétant	**Participe passé**	répété

Présent de l'indicatif

Je répète	Nous répétons
Tu répètes	Vous répétez
Il répète	Ils répètent
Elle répète	Elles répètent
On répète	

Passé composé

J'ai répété	Nous avons répété
Tu as répété	Vous avez répété
Il a répété	Ils ont répété
Elle a répété	Elles ont répété
On a répété	

Imparfait

Je répétais	Nous répétions
Tu répétais	Vous répétiez
Il répétait	Ils répétaient
Elle répétait	Elles répétaient
On répétait	

Plus-que-parfait

J'avais répété	Nous avions répété
Tu avais répété	Vous aviez répété
Il avait répété	Ils avaient répété
Elle avait répété	Elles avaient répété
On avait répété	

Futur simple

Je répéterai	Nous répéterons
Tu répéteras	Vous répéterez
Il répétera	Ils répéteront
Elle répétera	Elles répéteront
On répétera	

Futur antérieur

J'aurai répété	Nous aurons répété
Tu auras répété	Vous aurez répété
Il aura répété	Ils auront répété
Elle aura répété	Elles auront répété
On aura répété	

Conditionnel présent

Je répéterais	Nous répéterions
Tu répéterais	Vous répéteriez
Il répéterait	Ils répéteraient
Elle répéterait	Elles répéteraient
On répéterait	

Conditionnel passé

J'aurais répété	Nous aurions répété
Tu aurais répété	Vous auriez répété
Il aurait répété	Ils auraient répété
Elle aurait répété	Elles auraient répété
On aurait répété	

Impératif

Répète !
Répétons !
Répétez !

Subjonctif présent

Que je répète	Que nous répétions
Que tu répètes	Que vous répétiez
Qu'il répète	Qu'ils répètent
Qu'elle répète	Qu'elles répètent
Qu'on répète	

Rire – To laugh

Participe présent riant

Présent de l'indicatif

Je ris	Nous rions
Tu ris	Vous riez
Il rit	Ils rient
Elle rit	Elles rient
On rit	

Imparfait

Je riais	Nous riions
Tu riais	Vous riiez
Il riait	Ils riaient
Elle riait	Elles riaient
On riait	

Futur simple

Je rirai	Nous rirons
Tu riras	Vous rirez
Il rira	Ils riront
Elle rira	Elles riront
On rira	

Conditionnel présent

Je rirais	Nous ririons
Tu rirais	Vous ririez
Il rirait	Ils riraient
Elle rirait	Elles riraient
On rirait	

Impératif

Ris !
Rions !
Riez !

Participe passé ri

Passé composé

J'ai ri	Nous avons ri
Tu as ri	Vous avez ri
Il a ri	Ils ont ri
Elle a ri	Elles ont ri
On a ri	

Plus-que-parfait

J'avais ri	Nous avions ri
Tu avais ri	Vous aviez ri
Il avait ri	Ils avaient ri
Elle avait ri	Elles avaient ri
On avait ri	

Futur antérieur

J'aurai ri	Nous aurons ri
Tu auras ri	Vous aurez ri
Il aura ri	Ils auront ri
Elle aura ri	Elles auront ri
On aura ri	

Conditionnel passé

J'aurais ri	Nous aurions ri
Tu aurais ri	Vous auriez ri
Il aurait ri	Ils auraient ri
Elle aurait ri	Elles auraient ri
On aurait ri	

Subjonctif présent

Que je rie	Que nous riions
Que tu ries	Que vous riiez
Qu'il rie	Qu'ils rient
Qu'elle rie	Qu'elles rient
Qu'on rie	

Common verb with the same conjugation: **Sourire** To smile

*Remember to **download the audio** and to **watch the videos** – see Preface*

Savoir – To know

Participe présent sachant

Participe passé su

Présent de l'indicatif

Je sais	Nous savons
Tu sais	Vous savez
Il sait	Ils savent
Elle sait	Elles savent
On sait	

Passé composé

J'ai su	Nous avons su
Tu as su	Vous avez su
Il a su	Ils ont su
Elle a su	Elles ont su
On a su	

Imparfait

Je savais	Nous savions
Tu savais	Vous saviez
Il savait	Ils savaient
Elle savait	Elles savaient
On savait	

Plus-que-parfait

J'avais su	Nous avions su
Tu avais su	Vous aviez su
Il avait su	Ils avaient su
Elle avait su	Elles avaient su
On avait su	

Futur simple

Je saurai	Nous saurons
Tu sauras	Vous saurez
Il saura	Ils sauront
Elle saura	Elles sauront
On saura	

Futur antérieur

J'aurai su	Nous aurons su
Tu auras su	Vous aurez su
Il aura su	Ils auront su
Elle aura su	Elles auront su
On aura su	

Conditionnel présent

Je saurais	Nous saurions
Tu saurais	Vous sauriez
Il saurait	Ils sauraient
Elle saurait	Elles sauraient
On saurait	

Conditionnel passé

J'aurais su	Nous aurions su
Tu aurais su	Vous auriez su
Il aurait su	Ils auraient su
Elle aurait su	Elles auraient su
On aurait su	

Impératif

Sache !
Sachons !
Sachez !

Subjonctif présent

Que je sache	Que nous sachions
Que tu saches	Que vous sachiez
Qu'il sache	Qu'ils sachent
Qu'elle sache	Qu'elles sachent
Qu'on sache	

Servir – To serve

Participe présent servant

Participe passé servi

Présent de l'indicatif

Je sers	Nous servons
Tu sers	Vous servez
Il sert	Ils servent
Elle sert	Elles servent
On sert	

Passé composé

J'ai servi	Nous avons servi
Tu as servi	Vous avez servi
Il a servi	Ils ont servi
Elle a servi	Elles ont servi
On a servi	

Imparfait

Je servais	Nous servions
Tu servais	Vous serviez
Il servait	Ils servaient
Elle servait	Elles servaient
On servait	

Plus-que-parfait

J'avais servi	Nous avions servi
Tu avais servi	Vous aviez servi
Il avait servi	Ils avaient servi
Elle avait servi	Elles avaient servi
On avait servi	

Futur simple

Je servirai	Nous servirons
Tu serviras	Vous servirez
Il servira	Ils serviront
Elle servira	Elles serviront
On servira	

Futur antérieur

J'aurai servi	Nous aurons servi
Tu auras servi	Vous aurez servi
Il aura servi	Ils auront servi
Elle aura servi	Elles auront servi
On aura servi	

Conditionnel présent

Je servirais	Nous servirions
Tu servirais	Vous serviriez
Il servirait	Ils serviraient
Elle servirait	Elles serviraient
On servirait	

Conditionnel passé

J'aurais servi	Nous aurions servi
Tu aurais servi	Vous auriez servi
Il aurait servi	Ils auraient servi
Elle aurait servi	Elles auraient servi
On aurait servi	

Impératif

Sers !
Servons !
Servez !

Subjonctif présent

Que je serve	Que nous servions
Que tu serves	Que vous serviez
Qu'il serve	Qu'ils servent
Qu'elle serve	Qu'elles servent
Qu'on serve	

*Remember to **download the audio** and to **watch the videos** – see Preface*

Suivre – To follow

Participe présent suivant

Participe passé suivi

Présent de l'indicatif

Je suis	Nous suivons
Tu suis	Vous suivez
Il suit	Ils suivent
Elle suit	Elles suivent
On suit	

Passé composé

J'ai suivi	Nous avons suivi
Tu as suivi	Vous avez suivi
Il a suivi	Ils ont suivi
Elle a suivi	Elles ont suivi
On a suivi	

Imparfait

Je suivais	Nous suivions
Tu suivais	Vous suiviez
Il suivait	Ils suivaient
Elle suivait	Elles suivaient
On suivait	

Plus-que-parfait

J'avais suivi	Nous avions suivi
Tu avais suivi	Vous aviez suivi
Il avait suivi	Ils avaient suivi
Elle avait suivi	Elles avaient suivi
On avait suivi	

Futur simple

Je suivrai	Nous suivrons
Tu suivras	Vous suivrez
Il suivra	Ils suivront
Elle suivra	Elles suivront
On suivra	

Futur antérieur

J'aurai suivi	Nous aurons suivi
Tu auras suivi	Vous aurez suivi
Il aura suivi	Ils auront suivi
Elle aura suivi	Elles auront suivi
On aura suivi	

Conditionnel présent

Je suivrais	Nous suivrions
Tu suivrais	Vous suivriez
Il suivrait	Ils suivraient
Elle suivrait	Elles suivraient
On suivrait	

Conditionnel passé

J'aurais suivi	Nous aurions suivi
Tu aurais suivi	Vous auriez suivi
Il aurait suivi	Ils auraient suivi
Elle aurait suivi	Elles auraient suivi
On aurait suivi	

Impératif

Suis !
Suivons !
Suivez !

Subjonctif présent

Que je suive	Que nous suivions
Que tu suives	Que vous suiviez
Qu'il suive	Qu'ils suivent
Qu'elle suive	Qu'elles suivent
Qu'on suive	

Tenir – To hold

Participe présent tenant

Présent de l'indicatif

Je tiens	Nous tenons
Tu tiens	Vous tenez
Il tient	Ils tiennent
Elle tient	Elles tiennent
On tient	

Imparfait

Je tenais	Nous tenions
Tu tenais	Vous teniez
Il tenait	Ils tenaient
Elle tenait	Elles tenaient
On tenait	

Futur simple

Je tiendrai	Nous tiendrons
Tu tiendras	Vous tiendrez
Il tiendra	Ils tiendront
Elle tiendra	Elles tiendront
On tiendra	

Conditionnel présent

Je tiendrais	Nous tiendrions
Tu tiendrais	Vous tiendriez
Il tiendrait	Ils tiendraient
Elle tiendrait	Elles tiendraient
On tiendrait	

Impératif

Tiens !
Tenons !
Tenez !

Participe passé tenu

Passé composé

J'ai tenu	Nous avons tenu
Tu as tenu	Vous avez tenu
Il a tenu	Ils ont tenu
Elle a tenu	Elles ont tenu
On a tenu	

Plus-que-parfait

J'avais tenu	Nous avions tenu
Tu avais tenu	Vous aviez tenu
Il avait tenu	Ils avaient tenu
Elle avait tenu	Elles avaient tenu
On avait tenu	

Futur antérieur

J'aurai tenu	Nous aurons tenu
Tu auras tenu	Vous aurez tenu
Il aura tenu	Ils auront tenu
Elle aura tenu	Elles auront tenu
On aura tenu	

Conditionnel passé

J'aurais tenu	Nous aurions tenu
Tu aurais tenu	Vous auriez tenu
Il aurait tenu	Ils auraient tenu
Elle aurait tenu	Elles auraient tenu
On aurait tenu	

Subjonctif présent

Que je tienne	Que nous tenions
Que tu tiennes	Que vous teniez
Qu'il tienne	Qu'ils tiennent
Qu'elle tienne	Qu'elles tiennent
Qu'on tienne	

Common verbs with the same conjugation: **Appartenir** To belong – **Obtenir** To obtain

Vaincre – To overcome

Participe présent vainquant

Participe passé vaincu

Présent de l'indicatif

Je vaincs	Nous vainquons
Tu vaincs	Vous vainquez
Il vainc	Ils vainquent
Elle vainc	Elles vainquent
On vainc	

Passé composé

J'ai vaincu	Nous avons vaincu
Tu as vaincu	Vous avez vaincu
Il a vaincu	Ils ont vaincu
Elle a vaincu	Elles ont vaincu
On a vaincu	

Imparfait

Je vainquais	Nous vainquions
Tu vainquais	Vous vainquiez
Il vainquait	Ils vainquaient
Elle vainquait	Elles vainquaient
On vainquait	

Plus-que-parfait

J'avais vaincu	Nous avions vaincu
Tu avais vaincu	Vous aviez vaincu
Il avait vaincu	Ils avaient vaincu
Elle avait vaincu	Elles avaient vaincu
On avait vaincu	

Futur simple

Je vaincrai	Nous vaincrons
Tu vaincras	Vous vaincrez
Il vaincra	Ils vaincront
Elle vaincra	Elles vaincront
On vaincra	

Futur antérieur

J'aurai vaincu	Nous aurons vaincu
Tu auras vaincu	Vous aurez vaincu
Il aura vaincu	Ils auront vaincu
Elle aura vaincu	Elles auront vaincu
On aura vaincu	

Conditionnel présent

Je vaincrais	Nous vaincrions
Tu vaincrais	Vous vaincriez
Il vaincrait	Ils vaincraient
Elle vaincrait	Elles vaincraient
On vaincrait	

Conditionnel passé

J'aurais vaincu	Nous aurions vaincu
Tu aurais vaincu	Vous auriez vaincu
Il aurait vaincu	Ils auraient vaincu
Elle aurait vaincu	Elles auraient vaincu
On aurait vaincu	

Impératif

Vaincs !
Vainquons !
Vainquez !

Subjonctif présent

Que je vainque	Que nous vainquions
Que tu vainques	Que vous vainquiez
Qu'il vainque	Qu'ils vainquent
Qu'elle vainque	Qu'elles vainquent
Qu'on vainque	

Common verb with the same conjugation: **Convaincre** To convince

Valoir – To be worth

Participe présent valant

Participe passé valu

Présent de l'indicatif

Je vaux	Nous valons
Tu vaux	Vous valez
Il vaut	Ils valent
Elle vaut	Elles valent
On vaut	

Passé composé

J'ai valu	Nous avons valu
Tu as valu	Vous avez valu
Il a valu	Ils ont valu
Elle a valu	Elles ont valu
On a valu	

Imparfait

Je valais	Nous valions
Tu valais	Vous valiez
Il valait	Ils valaient
Elle valait	Elles valaient
On valait	

Plus-que-parfait

J'avais valu	Nous avions valu
Tu avais valu	Vous aviez valu
Il avait valu	Ils avaient valu
Elle avait valu	Elles avaient valu
On avait valu	

Futur simple

Je vaudrai	Nous vaudrons
Tu vaudras	Vous vaudrez
Il vaudra	Ils vaudront
Elle vaudra	Elles vaudront
On vaudra	

Futur antérieur

J'aurai valu	Nous aurons valu
Tu auras valu	Vous aurez valu
Il aura valu	Ils auront valu
Elle aura valu	Elles auront valu
On aura valu	

Conditionnel présent

Je vaudrais	Nous vaudrions
Tu vaudrais	Vous vaudriez
Il vaudrait	Ils vaudraient
Elle vaudrait	Elles vaudraient
On vaudrait	

Conditionnel passé

J'aurais valu	Nous aurions valu
Tu aurais valu	Vous auriez valu
Il aurait valu	Ils auraient valu
Elle aurait valu	Elles auraient valu
On aurait valu	

Impératif

Vaux !
Valons !
Valez !

Subjonctif présent

Que je vaille	Que nous valions
Que tu vailles	Que vous valiez
Qu'il vaille	Qu'ils vaillent
Qu'elle vaille	Qu'elles vaillent
Qu'on vaille	

Venir – To come

Participe présent venant

Participe passé venu

Présent de l'indicatif

Je viens	Nous venons
Tu viens	Vous venez
Il vient	Ils viennent
Elle vient	Elles viennent
On vient	

Passé composé

Je suis venu(e)	Nous sommes venu(e)s
Tu es venu(e)	Vous êtes venu(e)s
Il est venu	Ils sont venus
Elle est venue	Elles sont venues
On est venu(e)s	

Imparfait

Je venais	Nous venions
Tu venais	Vous veniez
Il venait	Ils venaient
Elle venait	Elles venaient
On venait	

Plus-que-parfait

J'étais venu(e)	Nous étions venu(e)s
Tu étais venu(e)	Vous étiez venu(e)s
Il était venu	Ils étaient venus
Elle était venue	Elles étaient venues
On était venu(e)s	

Futur simple

Je viendrai	Nous viendrons
Tu viendras	Vous viendrez
Il viendra	Ils viendront
Elle viendra	Elles viendront
On viendra	

Futur antérieur

Je serai venu(e)	Nous serons venu(e)s
Tu seras venu(e)	Vous serez venu(e)s
Il sera venu	Ils seront venus
Elle sera venue	Elles seront venues
On sera venu(e)s	

Conditionnel présent

Je viendrais	Nous viendrions
Tu viendrais	Vous viendriez
Il viendrait	Ils viendraient
Elle viendrait	Elles viendraient
On viendrait	

Conditionnel passé

Je serais venu(e)	Nous serions venu(e)s
Tu serais venu(e)	Vous seriez venu(e)s
Il serait venu	Ils seraient venus
Elle serait venue	Elles seraient venues
On serait venu(e)s	

Impératif

Viens !
Venons !
Venez !

Subjonctif présent

Que je vienne	Que nous venions
Que tu viennes	Que vous veniez
Qu'il vienne	Qu'ils viennent
Qu'elle vienne	Qu'elles viennent
Qu'on vienne	

Common verbs with the same conjugation:
Devenir To become – **Intervenir** To intervene – **Parvenir** To reach – **Prévenir** To warn – **Revenir** To come back

Vouloir – To want

Participe présent voulant

Participe passé voulu

Présent de l'indicatif

Je veux	Nous voulons
Tu veux	Vous voulez
Il veut	Ils veulent
Elle veut	Elles veulent
On veut	

Passé composé

J'ai voulu	Nous avons voulu
Tu as voulu	Vous avez voulu
Il a voulu	Ils ont voulu
Elle a voulu	Elles ont voulu
On a voulu	

Imparfait

Je voulais	Nous voulions
Tu voulais	Vous vouliez
Il voulait	Ils voulaient
Elle voulait	Elles voulaient
On voulait	

Plus-que-parfait

J'avais voulu	Nous avions voulu
Tu avais voulu	Vous aviez voulu
Il avait voulu	Ils avaient voulu
Elle avait voulu	Elles avaient voulu
On avait voulu	

Futur simple

Je voudrai	Nous voudrons
Tu voudras	Vous voudrez
Il voudra	Ils voudront
Elle voudra	Elles voudront
On voudra	

Futur antérieur

J'aurai voulu	Nous aurons voulu
Tu auras voulu	Vous aurez voulu
Il aura voulu	Ils auront voulu
Elle aura voulu	Elles auront voulu
On aura voulu	

Conditionnel présent

Je voudrais	Nous voudrions
Tu voudrais	Vous voudriez
Il voudrait	Ils voudraient
Elle voudrait	Elles voudraient
On voudrait	

Conditionnel passé

J'aurais voulu	Nous aurions voulu
Tu aurais voulu	Vous auriez voulu
Il aurait voulu	Ils auraient voulu
Elle aurait voulu	Elles auraient voulu
On aurait voulu	

Impératif

Veuille !	
Veuillons !	Voulions !
Veuillez !	Vouliez !

Subjonctif présent

Que je veuille	Que nous voulions
Que tu veuilles	Que vous vouliez
Qu'il veuille	Qu'ils veuillent
Qu'elle veuille	Qu'elles veuillent
Qu'on veuille	

Neiger – To snow Falloir – To be necessary Pleuvoir – To rain

Participe présent neigeant – / – pleuvant

Participe passé neigé – fallu – plu

Présent de l'indicatif

Il neige
Il faut
Il pleut

Passé composé

Il a neigé
Il a fallu
Il a plu

Imparfait

Il neigeait
Il fallait
Il pleuvait

Plus-que-parfait

Il avait neigé
Il avait fallu
Il avait plu

Futur simple

Il neigea
Il faudra
Il pleuvra

Futur antérieur

Il aura neigé
Il aura fallu
Il aura plu

Conditionnel présent

Il neigerait
Il faudrait
Il pleuvrait

Conditionnel passé

Il aurait neigé
Il aurait fallu
Il aurait plu

Subjonctif présent

Qu'il neige
Qu'il faille
Qu'il pleuve

Solutions – Le présent de l'indicatif

EX. 1.1

1. Je **cuisine**
2. Il **étudie**
3. Nous **regardons**
4. Elle **lave**
5. Ils **enseignent**
6. Tu **verses**
7. Je **montre**
8. Nous **marchons**
9. Elles **séparent**
10. Je **parle**
11. Il **dépense**
12. Ils **chantent**
13. Nous **acceptons**
14. Il **pue**
15. Tu **rêves**

EX. 1.2

1. Eric **regarde** la télévision.
2. Elle **coupe** une pomme.
3. Nous **trouvons** une solution.
4. Le docteur **aide** le patient.
5. Elles **chantent** une chanson.
6. Jeff **reste** à l'hôtel.
7. Elle **ajoute** du sel.
8. Le valet **porte** la valise.
9. Il **accroche** son manteau.
10. Nous **préparons** le déjeuner.
11. Vous **évitez un** accident.
12. Les mariés **remercient** les invités.
13. L'avocat **donne** un conseil.
14. Les enfants **aiment** le chocolat.
15. Elle **casse** une tasse.

EX. 1.3

1. Nous **aimons** les pommes.
2. Elle **explique** la leçon.
3. Il **pousse** la porte.
4. Je **tape** le numéro.
5. Elles **écoutent** de la musique.
6. Tu **voles** un biscuit.
7. Il **téléphone** au client.
8. Il **montre** ses dessins.
9. Je **joue** aux cartes.
10. Nous **traversons** la route.
11. Elle **travaille** aujourd'hui.
12. Je **parle** français.
13. Elle **signe** le document.
14. J'**oublie** le mot de passe.
15. Il **pêche** un poisson.

EX. 1.4

1. J'**habite** à la campagne.
2. On **cuisine** un poulet.
3. Je **reste** au travail.
4. Il **amuse** le chien.
5. Elle **couche** les enfants.
6. Je **cherche** mon téléphone.
7. Ils **négocient** le contrat.
8. Vous **quittez** le travail.
9. Nous **invitons** des amis.
10. Tu **plantes** des légumes.
11. Je **termine** le film.
12. Elle **rencontre** ses parents.
13. Nous **plions** les linges.
14. Tu **vérifies** le numéro.
15. Elle **donne** un cadeau.

EX. 1.5

1. Nous **remplaçons**
2. Nous **jugeons**
3. Nous **chargeons**
4. Nous **annonçons**
5. Nous **partageons**
6. Nous **agaçons**
7. Nous **forçons**
8. Nous **téléchargeons**
9. Nous **songeons**
10. Nous **voyageons**
11. Nous **lançons**
12. Nous **nageons**
13. Nous **commençons**
14. Nous **plaçons**
15. Nous **bougeons**

EX. 1.6

1. Je **paie** – **paye**
2. Nous **nettoyons**
3. Elle **essuie**
4. Tu **effraies** – **effrayes**
5. Vous **essayez**
6. Ils **emploient**
7. On **balaie** – **balaye**
8. Il **appuie**

EX. 1.7

1. Nous **appelons**
2. Je **rejette**
3. Elle **jette**
4. Ils **projettent**
5. Nous **épelons**

EX. 1.8

1. Nous achevons => Il **achève**
2. Tu mènes => Nous **menons**
3. Elle pèse => Nous **pesons**
4. Vous promenez => Je **promène**
5. Nous élevons => Ils **élèvent**
6. On emmène => Nous **emmenons**
7. J'amène => Il **amène**
8. Il relève => Vous **relevez**
9. Tu achètes => Nous **achetons**
10. Nous enlevons => Ils **enlèvent**

EX. 1.9

1. Je **préfère**
2. Nous **célébrons**
3. Ils **considèrent**
4. Tu **répètes**
5. On **cède**

EX. 1.10

1. Il **écoute** de la musique.
2. L'architecte **trace** les plans.
3. Le client **achète** du pain.
4. Nous **séjournons** à l'hôtel.
5. Elles **regardent** la télévision.
6. L'ouvrier **signale** le chantier.
7. Tu **exagères** toujours.
8. Mes parents **marchent** deux fois par jour.
9. Tout le monde **télécharge** illégalement.
10. Sa sœur **possède** une voiture de collection.
11. Je **remplace** une ampoule.
12. Mon mari **balaie** – **balaye** la terrasse.
13. On **plante** des légumes.
14. J'**enlève** mon pull.
15. Nous **mangeons** avant de partir.

EX. 1.11

1. On rentre - **Rentrer** - Nous **rentrons**
2. On voyage - **Voyager** - Nous **voyageons**
3. On considère - **Considérer** - Nous **considérons**
4. On commande - **Commander** - Nous **commandons**
5. On enlève - **Enlever** - Nous **enlevons**
6. On lance - **Lancer** - Nous **lançons**
7. On jette - **Jeter** - Nous **jetons**
8. On paye - **Payer** - Nous **payons**
9. On admire - **Admirer** - Nous **admirons**
10. On mesure - **Mesurer** - Nous **mesurons**
11. On vote - **Voter** - Nous **votons**
12. On corrige - **Corriger** - Nous **corrigeons**
13. On chauffe - **Chauffer** - Nous **chauffons**
14. On déménage - **Déménager** - Nous **déménageons**
15. On tombe - **Tomber** - Nous **tombons**

EX. 1.12

1. Le patient **refuse** le traitement.
2. Je **promène** le chien.
3. Nous **voyageons** toujours en première classe.
4. Les enfants **préfèrent** le chocolat aux légumes.
5. Ils **collent** des stickers dans le livre.
6. Les jeunes mariés **remercient** les invités.
7. L'éducateur **dirige** les enfants vers le terrain de football.
8. Le garçon **appuie** sur le bouton.
9. J'**appelle** mes parents tous les soirs.
10. Les voisins **amènent** un apéritif.
11. Les étudiants **travaillent** après l'école.
12. On **regarde** la télé quand il pleut.
13. Le comptable **vérifie** les transactions.
14. La radio **annonce** une tempête.
15. J'**essaie** - **essaye** un nouveau pantalon.

EX. 1.13

1. (Laver / Casser) Le lave-vaisselle **lave** les assiettes.
2. (Achever / Adorer) Il **adore** se rouler dans l'herbe.
3. (Répéter / Téléphoner) La réceptionniste **répète** le numéro.
4. (Corriger / Effacer) Le professeur **corrige** les devoirs.
5. (Aimer / Dépêcher) J'**aime** le jus d'orange.
6. (Cacher / Siffler) Le chien **cache** un os.
7. (Effacer / Embrasser) La maman **embrasse** son enfant.
8. (Siffler / Pêcher) L'homme **siffle** en marchant.
9. (Changer / Nettoyer) Elles **nettoient** leur chambre.
10. (Partager / Enlever) Les enfants **partagent** leurs goûters.

EX. 1.14

1. Mon père **choisit** ce qu'il veut manger.
2. Elle **réunit** les papiers.
3. Les enfants **finissent** leurs goûters.
4. La maman **nourrit** son enfant.
5. Elles **vieillissent** vite.
6. La voiture **ralentit** avant de tourner.
7. Les habits blancs **jaunissent** facilement.
8. Je **finis** de préparer ma valise.
9. Il **agit** comme un enfant.
10. Je ne **maigris** pas beaucoup.
11. Mon frère **réussit** tous ses examens.
12. Tu **grandis** tellement vite.
13. Le couple **bâtit** une nouvelle maison.
14. Le constructeur **démolit** le bâtiment.
15. La maladie **affaiblit** les patients.

EX. 1.15

1. Tu saisis – **Saisir** – Vous **saisissez**
2. Tu trahis – **Trahir** – Vous **trahissez**
3. Tu fournis – **Fournir** – Vous **fournissez**
4. Tu subis – **Subir** – Vous **subissez**
5. Tu réfléchis – **Réfléchir** – Vous **réfléchissez**
6. Tu grossis – **Grossir** – Vous **grossissez**
7. Tu salis – **Salir** – Vous **salissez**
8. Tu unis – **Unir** – Vous **unissez**
9. Tu remplis – **Remplir** – Vous **remplissez**
10. Tu désobéis – **Désobéir** – Vous **désobéissez**

EX. 1.16

1. Nous **correspondons** par email.
2. Tu **réponds** au téléphone.
3. Le voisin **tond** la pelouse.
4. Le magasin **vend** des cartes.
5. Ils **attendent** le train.
6. Je **descends** les escaliers.
7. Le beurre **fond** dans la poêle.
8. Je **perds** toujours mes clés.
9. Il **rend** les clés au propriétaire.
10. Elle **confond** le rouge et le bleu.

EX. 1.17

1. Je **suis**
2. Tu **as**
3. Elles **ont**
4. Vous **êtes**
5. Il **est**

EX. 1.18

1. La machine **est** en panne.
2. Le client **est** en avance.
3. Le chat **est** de mauvaise humeur.
4. Je **suis** de Londres.
5. Il **est** de retour.
6. Ce sac **est** à cette dame.
7. Est-ce que tu **es** d'accord ?
8. Les élèves **sont** dans la lune.
9. Mon oncle n'**est** jamais en colère.
10. J'espère qu'il **est** en bonne santé.

EX. 1.19

1. Tu **as** mal au pied.
2. Il **a** besoin d'un nouveau manteau.
3. Nous **avons** hâte de partir en vacances.
4. Mes grands-parents **ont** 90 ans.
5. Marie **a** peur des araignées.
6. Elle **a** froid.
7. Ce chien **a** sommeil.
8. Elle **a** honte de ses résultats.
9. Il y **a** beaucoup de choix.
10. Mon fils **a** du mal avec ses devoirs.

EX. 1.20

1. Il **a** sommeil.
2. J'**ai** du mal à dormir.
3. Le train **est** sur le point de partir.
4. Les voisins **sont** de retour.
5. Le professeur **a** toujours raison.
6. Il y **a** du jus dans le frigo.
7. L'avion **est** en retard.
8. Ma colocataire **est** suédoise.
9. Est-ce que tu **es** au courant ?
10. On en **a** marre du bruit.
11. Il **a** toujours du bol.
12. Je **suis** d'accord avec lui.
13. La voiture **est** encore en panne.
14. Tu **as** l'air fatigué.
15. Elle **a** mal au dos.

EX. 1.21

1. Je **vais** au magasin.
2. Ils **vont** aux États-Unis.
3. Elle **va** à l'église.
4. Nous **allons** à Barcelone.
5. Vous **allez** en Espagne.

EX. 1.22

1. Il **va** au Canada.
2. On **va** au concert. (m)
3. Nous **allons** chez le médecin. (m)
4. Vous **allez** à la pharmacie. (f)
5. Tu **vas** aux Philippines.
6. Mes voisins **vont** à Paris.
7. Le professeur **va** au musée. (m)
8. Luc et Julie **vont** à la poste. (f)
9. Elles **vont** à l'église. (f)
10. Elle **va** chez Marie.
11. Je **vais** en Allemagne.
12. On **va** au Japon.
13. Ma femme **va** à la plage. (f)
14. Son ami **va** chez le coiffeur. (m)
15. Amy **va** aux toilettes. (f.pl)

EX. 1.23

1. Le clown **fait** peur aux enfants.
2. Il **fait** doux.
3. Ma nièce **fait** du piano.
4. Je **fais** des progrès.
5. Ils **font** attention.

EX. 1.24

1. Je **fais** un gâteau.
2. Les enfants **font** du ski.
3. Il **fait** le repassage.
4. Nous **faisons** une promenade.
5. Tu **fais** la vaisselle.
6. Il **fait** nuit.
7. Elle **fait** des fautes.
8. Mes cousines **font** la cuisine.
9. Je **fais** la grasse matinée.
10. Il **fait** bon.
11. Les clients **font** la queue.
12. Julian **fait** ses devoirs.

EX. 1.25

1. **Faire du** ski
2. **Jouer du** piano
3. **Jouer de la** trompette
4. **Faire du** tir à l'arc
5. **Faire du** roller
6. **Jouer au - Faire du** tennis
7. **Jouer au - Faire du** football
8. **Jouer de la** batterie
9. **Jouer à** Tetris
10. **Jouer de la** flûte
11. **Faire du** yoga
12. **Jouer aux** cartes
13. **Jouer de la** guitare
14. **Faire du** dessin
15. **Jouer du** saxophone
16. **Jouer de l'**accordéon
17. **Faire du** judo
18. **Jouer au** poker
19. **Faire de la** danse
20. **Jouer au - Faire du** golf

EX. 1.26

1. Je **prends** le bus.
2. Vous **reprenez** vos affaires.
3. Elles **apprennent** la nouvelle.
4. Je **prends** un rendez-vous.
5. Nous **prenons** souvent un verre ensemble.
6. Elle **surprend** ses amis.
7. Il **prend** toujours froid.
8. Ma femme **reprend** le travail demain.
9. Nous **prenons** l'air.
10. J'**apprends** le français.

EX. 1.27

1. Je **vais** à la librairie.
2. Tu **fais** du vélo.
3. On **est** en forme.
4. Nous **allons** chez le dentiste.
5. Ils **font** le ménage.
6. J'**ai** trente-trois ans.
7. J'**ai** peur.
8. Elles **vont** aux courses.
9. Ils **sont** dans le doute.
10. Tu **prends** un café.
11. Nous **allons** en Belgique ce week-end.
12. Robyn **est** à l'heure.
13. Il **fait** ses devoirs.
14. Tu **as** l'air fatigué.
15. Vous **êtes** à pied.
16. Ils **prennent** une décision.
17. Vous **avez** besoin d'une nouvelle voiture.
18. Marc **fait** de la natation.
19. Nous **prenons** le train.
20. Tu **es** toujours en avance.

EX. 1.28

1. Je ne **suis** pas là.
2. Elle n'**a** plus de bonbons.
3. Nous ne **sommes** pas malades.
4. Il n'**aime** pas le fromage.
5. Il ne **regarde** que la télévision.
6. Il n'y **a** personne dans la maison.
7. Ma sœur ne **cuisine** pas bien.
8. Ce vélo n'**est** pas le mien.
9. La réceptionniste n'**est** jamais là.
10. Je ne **vis** pas au Canada.
11. Ce livre n'**est** pas noir.
12. Mon téléphone ne **fonctionne** plus.
13. Le chien ne **veut** pas sortir.
14. Il n'**est** jamais en retard.
15. On ne **veut** rien voir.

EX. 1.29

1. P : Vous **amenez** une tarte.
   N : Vous n'**amenez** pas de tarte.
2. P : Il **a** 15 ans.
   N : Il n'**a** plus 15 ans.
3. P : Nous **parlons** français.
   N : Nous ne **parlons** pas français.
4. P : Vous **cherchez** quelque chose.
   N : Vous ne **cherchez** rien.
5. P : Je **suis** riche.
   N : Je ne **suis** pas riche.
6. P : Il y **a** du vin.
   N : Il n'y **a** plus de vin.
7. P : Pierre **est** pompier.
   N : Pierre n'**est** pas pompier.
8. P : Céline **mange** beaucoup de fruits.
   N : Céline ne **mange** jamais de fruits.
9. P : J'**aime** le football.
   N : Je n'**aime** pas le football.
10. P : Ils **adoptent** un chien.
    N : Ils n'**adoptent** pas de chien.

EX. 1.30

1. Il **admet** son erreur.
2. Le pont **permet** d'aller plus vite.
3. Je **promets**.
4. Shirley **bat** toujours Eric aux échecs.
5. Je ne **mets** pas la table.

EX. 1.31

1. Le sac **appartient** à ma mère.
2. Il **revient** maintenant.
3. Mon collègue **vient** de Russie.
4. Il **tient** beaucoup à son chien.
5. On **vient** tout de suite.

EX. 1.32

1. Le magasin **ouvre** à 9 heures.
2. Cet élève **ment** sans cesse.
3. Nous **partons** ce soir.
4. Je **meurs** de faim.
5. Les serveurs **servent** les clients.
6. On **dort** toujours tôt.
7. Nous **accueillons** nos invités.
8. Il **offre** un cadeau à sa femme.
9. Le docteur **découvre** la cause de la maladie.
10. Je **cours** tous les matins.

EX. 1.33

1. Le chat **craint** l'eau.
2. Il **atteint** son but.
3. Nous **peignons** les murs de l'appartement.
4. Ils **rejoignent** leurs amis ce soir.
5. Je **plains** ses voisins !

EX. 1.34

1. Tu **sais** tout.
2. Elle **écrit** une lettre.
3. Nous **recevons** un colis.
4. Je **bois** beaucoup de café.
5. Ils **suivent** les informations.

EX. 1.35

1. Le traducteur **traduit** le livre.
2. Les insectes **détruisent** les plantes.
3. Je **relis** souvent le même livre.
4. Elle **conduit** les enfants à l'école.
5. L'usine **produit** des pneus.
6. Il **introduit** sa petite amie.
7. La cigarette **nuit** à la santé.
8. Le papa **lit** une histoire aux enfants.
9. Je **déduis** que tu as raison.
10. Les habitants **élisent** le maire.

EX. 1.36

1. Il ne **sait** pas cuisiner.
2. Le marchand **connaît** bien ses clients.
3. Elle **sait** toujours tout sur tout le monde.
4. Je **connais** ce quartier comme ma poche.
5. Tu **connais** Marc depuis longtemps ?

EX. 1.37

1. Je **crois**
2. Elle **fuit**
3. Nous **prévoyons**
4. Vous **revoyez**
5. Ils **voient**

EX. 1.38

1. Je **dois** y aller.
2. Il ne **peut** pas manger de fraises.
3. Le chat **veut** sortir.
4. Nous **devons** aller chez le dentiste.
5. On **peut** terminer demain.
6. Je **veux** une nouvelle montre.
7. Paul **doit** travailler plus.
8. Est-ce que tu **peux** t'en occuper ?
9. Je **sais** ce que je veux faire.
10. Vous **voulez** un peu plus de café ?

EX. 1.39

1. Je **lis** un nouveau livre tous les mois.
2. Marc **essaie** / **essaye** de vendre sa voiture.
3. Bec **change** de travail bientôt.
4. Nous **sommes** en retard.

5. On **vient** de partir.
6. Elles **prennent** le temps de se connaître.
7. Charles **met** son manteau.
8. Nous **devons** finir le projet.
9. Je **reçois** toujours des cadeaux.
10. Les chats **craignent** l'eau.
11. Est-ce que tu **as** faim ?
12. J'**ouvre** la fenêtre pour aérer la pièce.
13. Ce pull ne **vaut** pas 150 dollars.
14. Nous **faisons** du vélo en famille.
15. Les élèves **répètent** la pièce de théâtre.
16. Ils **vont** au marché tous les samedis.
17. On **achève** de planifier notre voyage.
18. Tu **peux** jouer si tu ranges ta chambre.
19. Nous **pensons** qu'il ne dit pas la vérité.
20. Il **tient** la corde des deux mains.
21. Je n'**aime** pas la couleur jaune.
22. Elle **surprend** son amie pour son anniversaire.
23. Nous **cueillons** des fleurs dans le jardin.
24. Il **promet** d'être là.
25. Je **sais** que ce n'est pas vrai.

EX. 1.40

1. Depuis : Il dort depuis une heure.
   Il y a : Il y a une heure qu'il dort.
   Ça fait : Ça fait une heure qu'il dort.
2. Depuis : Elle travaille depuis deux mois.
   Il y a : Il y a deux mois qu'elle travaille.
   Ça fait : Ça fait deux mois qu'elle travaille.
3. Depuis : Ils parlent depuis une heure.
   Il y a : Il y a une heure qu'ils parlent.
   Ça fait : Ça fait une heure qu'ils parlent.
4. Depuis : J'attends depuis 5 minutes.
   Il y a : Il y a 5 minutes que j'attends.
   Ça fait : Ça fait 5 minutes que j'attends.
5. Depuis : Le chauffeur conduit depuis ce matin.
   Il y a : /
   Ça fait : /
6. Depuis : Elle aime la banane depuis qu'elle est petite.
   Il y a : /
   Ça fait : /
7. Depuis : Nous gagnons plus d'argent depuis janvier.
   Il y a : /
   Ça fait : /
8. Depuis : Vous connaissez Jean depuis 10 ans.
   Il y a : Il y a 10 ans que vous connaissez Jean.
   Ça fait : Ça fait 10 ans que vous connaissez Jean.
9. Depuis : Ali n'est pas en forme depuis quelques temps.
   Il y a : Il y a quelques temps qu'Ali n'est pas en forme.
   Ça fait : Ça fait quelques temps qu'Ali n'est pas en forme.
10. Depuis : Elle a mal à la tête depuis hier soir.
    Il y a : /
    Ça fait : /

EX. 1.41

1. Vous : Vous **achevez** le morceau de gâteau.
   Ne ... pas : Vous **n'achevez pas** le morceau de gâteau.
2. Vous : Vous **prenez** toujours l'avion pour venir en France.
   Ne ... jamais : Vous **ne prenez jamais** l'avion pour venir en France.
3. Vous : Vous **avez** chaud.
   Ne ... pas : Vous **n'avez pas** chaud.
4. Vous : Vous **voulez** encore du thé ?
   Ne ... plus : Vous **ne voulez plus** de thé ?
5. Vous : Vous **appelez** le docteur pour prendre rendez-vous.
   Ne ... pas : Vous **n'appelez pas** le docteur pour prendre rendez-vous.

EX. 1.42

1. Nous : **Nous** ne **partons** pas en vacances demain matin.
   Nous partons en vacances demain matin.

2. Nous : **Nous** ne **regardons** pas les étoiles filantes.
   Nous regardons les étoiles filantes.
3. Nous : **Nous** ne **pouvons** pas tout avoir.
   Nous pouvons tout avoir.
4. Nous : **Nous** ne **voyons** rien de bizarre.
   Nous voyons quelque chose de bizarre.
5. Nous : **Nous** n'**allons** pas manger au restaurant.
   Nous allons manger au restaurant.

EX. 1.43

1. Est-ce que : Est-ce que les prix augmentent chaque année ?
2. Inversion : Notes-tu les informations importantes ?
3. Est-ce que : Est-ce que les policiers interrogent le suspect ?
4. Inversion : Es-tu arrivé ?
5. Est-ce que : Est-ce que mes amis viennent avec nous ?
6. Inversion : À qui parles-tu ?
7. Qu'est-ce que : Qu'est-ce que tu veux ?
8. Inversion : Aimes-tu la citrouille ?
9. Est-ce que : Est-ce que vous avez ce pantalon en noir ?
10. Est-ce que : Est-ce que vous partez en vacances bientôt ?
11. Inversion : Peux-tu faire moins de bruit ?
12. Est-ce que : Est-ce que tu as vu mon sac à dos ?
13. Inversion : Connais-tu Tex ?
14. Est-ce que : Est-ce que le chat est dans la boîte ?
15. Inversion : As-tu faim ?

EX. 1.44

Aujourd'hui, c'**est** mardi. Il **fait** froid mais il y **a** un peu de soleil. Il **pleut** depuis plusieurs semaines ici. On **a** hâte que les températures **remontent** (remonter). Il **reste** quelques semaines avant le printemps. Au printemps, il **fait** toujours plus chaud et il y **a** moins de pluie et de neige.

EX. 1.45

1. Mes sœurs : **Les**
2. Marie : **La**
3. Le chat : **Le**
4. Moi : **Me**
5. Le cahier : **Le**
6. La brosse : **La**
7. Les affaires : **Les**
8. La tasse : **La**
9. Les chocolats : **Les**
10. Julian et Pauline : **Les**

EX. 1.46

1. COD : Marie oublie toujours **sa veste.**
   DOP : Marie **l'**oublie toujours.
2. COD : Le chat mange **ses croquettes.**
   DOP : Le chat **les** mange.
3. COD : Kurt offre **un collier** à Jeanne.
   DOP : Kurt **l'**offre à Jeanne.
4. COD : J'écris **un livre.**
   DOP : Je **l'**écris.
5. COD : Nous préparons **nos valises.**
   DOP : Nous **les** préparons.
6. COD : Nous attendons **nos collègues.**
   DOP : Nous **les** attendons.
7. COD : Elle garde **le chien de la voisine.**
   DOP : Elle **le** garde.
8. COD : Le serveur choisit **le vin.**
   DOP : Le serveur **le** choisit.
9. COD : Elle porte **une robe bleue.**
   DOP : Elle **la** porte.

10. COD : Nous préparons **le dîner**.
    DOP : Nous **le** préparons.
11. COD : Elle montre **sa chambre**.
    DOP : Elle **la** montre.
12. COD : Le facteur apporte **le courrier**.
    DOP : Le facteur **l'**apporte.
13. COD : Je fais **un gâteau aux pommes**.
    DOP : Je **le** fais.
14. COD : J'adore **Douglas**.
    DOP : Je **l'**adore.
15. COD : La banquière accepte **le chèque**.
    DOP : La banquière **l'**accepte.

EX 1.47

1. Je conseille **à ma sœur** une nouvelle télévision.
2. Nous offrons un cadeau **à mes parents**.
3. Ils **nous** appellent.
4. Elle **me** donne un cadeau.
5. Vous **me** souhaitez un joyeux anniversaire.
6. Tu téléphones **à ton cousin**.
7. Je **le** cherche depuis midi.
8. Tu ressembles tellement **à ta mère**.
9. Je **t'**achète un café.
10. Cela plaît beaucoup **à mon mari**.

EX 1.48

1. Le professeur accompagne les élèves à la bibliothèque.
   IOP: /
   DOP: Le professeur **les** accompagne à la bibliothèque.
2. Il emprunte un stylo à son camarade de classe.
   IOP: Il **lui** emprunte un stylo.
   DOP: Il **le** lui emprunte.
3. Nous écrivons une lettre à notre famille.
   IOP: Nous **leur** écrivons une lettre.
   DOP : Nous **la** leur écrivons.
4. Je raconte une histoire aux enfants.
   IOP : Je **leur** raconte une histoire.
   DOP : Je **la** leur raconte.
5. Elle envoie la lettre au juge.
   IOP : Elle **lui** envoie la lettre.
   DOP : Elle **la** lui envoie.
6. Ils enseignent la leçon aux étudiants.
   IOP : Ils **leur** enseignent la leçon.
   DOP : Ils **la** leur enseignent.
7. J'envoie un bouquet de fleurs à ma grand-mère.
   IOP : Je **lui** envoie un bouquet de fleurs.
   DOP : Je **le** lui envoie.
8. Il prend le jouet des mains du garçon.
   IOP : Il **lui** prend le jouet des mains.
   DOP : Il **le** lui prend des mains.
9. Elle prend le temps d'expliquer le problème au policier.
   IOP : Elle prend le temps de **lui** expliquer le problème.
   DOP : Elle prend le temps de **le** lui expliquer.
10. Léa montre un schéma aux élèves.
    IOP : Léa **leur** montre un schéma.
    DOP : Léa **le** leur montre.

EX. 1.49

1. Elle **se détend** seulement en vacances.
2. Il **se trompe** de sortie.
3. Je **m'excuse**.
4. Je **m'habille** et je suis prête.
5. On **se lave** toujours le soir.
6. Le chat **s'adapte** bien avec le chiot.
7. Paul **s'imagine** plus intelligent qu'il ne l'est.
8. Elle **se coupe** les cheveux à la maison.
9. Je **me demande** s'il a réussi.
10. Ils **se marient** l'année prochaine.

EX. 1.50

1. On **se promène** autour du lac.
2. Il **se sent** mieux que jamais.
3. Est-ce que tu **te souviens** de lui ?
4. Nous **nous changeons** avant de partir.
5. Tu **t'inquiètes** pour rien.
6. Il **s'assoit - s'assied** sur la chaise.
7. Je **m'appelle** Léo.
8. On **se lève** tôt.
9. On **se rappelle** bien de cette histoire.
10. On **s'en va** dans 5 minutes.

EX. 1.51

1. Elle **se met** sur son 31.
2. Je **me fais** un café.
3. On **se met** d'accord sur la date de la réunion.
4. Nous **nous faisons couper** les cheveux demain.
5. Ils **se mettent** en colère facilement.

EX. 1.52

1. Je **me coupe - me lime** les ongles.
2. Tu **te laves - t'essuies** les mains.
3. Il **se coupe - se lave - se sèche** les cheveux.
4. Elle **s'épile** les sourcils.
5. On **se rase - se peigne** la barbe.
6. Nous **nous brossons** les dents.
7. Vous **vous rasez - vous cassez** la jambe.
8. Ils **se rasent - se peignent** la moustache.
9. Elles **s'essuient - se lavent** les pieds.

EX. 1.53

1. Non, cela ne **se fait** pas facilement.
2. Non, je ne **m'amuse** pas bien.
3. Non, elle ne **s'épile** pas les sourcils.
4. Non, il ne **se conduit** jamais de cette façon.
5. Non, je ne **me change** pas maintenant.
6. Il ne **se cache** pas dans le placard.
7. Non, je ne **me moque** pas de toi.
8. Non, je ne **me douche** pas maintenant.
9. Non, je ne **m'appelle** pas Jeanne.
10. Non, je ne **m'attends** pas à cette surprise.

EX. 1.54

1. Ne ... pas: Tu ne **te sens** pas bien ?
2. Ne ... pas: Est-ce qu'il ne **se lave** pas les mains avant le repas ?
3. Ne ... jamais: Vous ne **vous endormez** jamais vite ?
4. Ne ... pas: De quoi est-ce qu'il ne **se plaint** pas ?
5. Ne ... pas: Ils ne **se marient** pas cette année ?

Solutions – Le passé composé

EX. 2.1

1. **Fait**
2. **Donné**
3. **Déçu**
4. **Cueilli**
5. **Bu**
6. **Vu**
7. **Pris**
8. **Su**
9. **Fini**
10. **Eu**
11. **Admis**
12. **Pesé**
13. **Éteint**
14. **Téléchargé**
15. **Été**
16. **Découvert**
17. **Venu**
18. **Grandi**
19. **Lu**
20. **Voulu**

EX. 2.2

1. **Avoir**
   J'ai eu
   Tu **as eu**
   Il-Elle-On **a eu**
   Nous **avons eu**
   Vous **avez eu**
   Ils-Elles **ont eu**
2. **Écrire**
   J'**ai écrit**
   Tu **as écrit**
   Il-Elle-On **a écrit**
   Nous **avons écrit**
   Vous **avez écrit**
   Ils-Elles **ont écrit**
3. **Nettoyer**
   J'**ai nettoyé**
   Tu **as nettoyé**
   Il-Elle-On **a nettoyé**
   Nous **avons nettoyé**
   Vous **avez nettoyé**
   Ils-Elles **ont nettoyé**

EX. 2.3

1. J'**ai bu**
2. Tu **as eu**
3. Ils **ont chanté**
4. Elle **a fait**
5. Nous **avons épelé**
6. Ils **ont regardé**
7. Nous **avons acheté**
8. J'**ai lu**
9. Vous **avez dormi**
10. Il **a étudié**

EX. 2.4

1. J'**ai rangé** ma chambre.
2. Il **a joué** ce week-end.
3. Les techniciens **ont réparé** le circuit.
4. Le gentleman **a tenu** la porte pour la dame.
5. Nous **avons voulu** bien faire.
6. L'agent immobilier **a appelé** pour faire une offre.
7. Tu **as menti** à ton professeur.
8. J'**ai convaincu** mon ami de venir avec moi.
9. Ils **ont signé** les documents lundi dernier.
10. Elle **a cueilli** des fleurs dans le jardin.
11. Mes parents **ont dormi** ici hier.
12. Tu **as vécu** des expériences incroyables.
13. Vous **avez fait les** démarches pour le permis ?
14. J'**ai oublié** de fermer la porte !
15. Il **a brossé** le chien ce matin.

EX. 2.5

1. Vous **avez gardé** les enfants.
2. Le policier **a exigé** que le suspect s'arrête.
3. J'**ai cherché** ce livre partout.
4. Mon père **a conduit** sa voiture au garage.
5. Elle **a couru** un marathon.
6. J'**ai pris** le bus pour aller au travail.
7. Il **a aimé** la soupe que j'ai fait pour lui.
8. Elle **a reçu** un collier pour Noël.
9. Ils **ont joué** dans le jardin tout l'après-midi.
10. Le livreur **a apporté** les colis.

EX. 2.6

1. **Venir**
   Je **suis venu(e)**
   Tu **es venu(e)**
   Il **est venu**
   Nous **sommes venu(e)s**
   Vous **êtes venu(e)s**
   Ils **sont venus**
2. **Passer**
   Je **suis passé(e)**
   Tu **es passé(e)**
   Elle **est passée**
   Nous **sommes passé(e)s**
   Vous **êtes passé(e)s**
   Elles **sont passées**
3. **Naître**
   Je **suis né(e)**
   Tu **es né(e)**
   On **est né(e)s**
   Nous **sommes né(e)s**
   Vous **êtes né(e)s**
   Elles **sont nées**

EX. 2.7

1. Revenir => Il **est revenu**
2. Sortir => Nous **sommes sorti(e)s**
3. Aller => Nous **sommes allé(e)s**
4. Partir => Je **suis parti(e)**
5. Mourir => Ils **sont morts**
6. Tomber => Nous **sommes tombé(e)s**
7. Descendre => Il **est descendu**
8. Devenir => Vous **êtes devenu(e)s**
9. Arriver => Nous **sommes arrivé(e)s**
10. Monter => Ils **sont montés**

EX. 2.8

1. Tu **les** as pris**es**.
2. Je **l'**ai écout**ée**.
3. Nous **l'**avons loué pour les vacances.
4. Philipe **l'**a mis**e**.
5. Elle **l'**a appris**e**.
6. Tu **l'**as mang**ée**.
7. Il **l'**a bientôt fini.
8. La mariée **l'**a chois**ie**.
9. Le groupe d'élèves **les** a visit**és**.
10. Je **l'**ai nettoy**ée**.

EX. 2.9

1. Le livre que **j'ai conseillé à Paul**.
2. La croisière que **nous avons réservée**.
3. La promenade que **nous avons faite**.
4. La jolie maison qu'**elle a achetée**.
5. Le portefeuille que **tu as oublié**.
6. La bouteille d'eau qu'**il a commandée**.
7. Le sac de sport que **Mandy a préparé**.
8. Le devoir que **j'ai fait**.
9. La piqûre que **l'infirmière a faite**.
10. Les portes de la maison qu'**on a fermées**.

EX. 2.10 Personnel

EX. 2.11

1. Mes parents **ont divorcé** récemment.
2. Ma fille **est née** la semaine dernière.
3. Le voisin **est mort** hier.

EX. 2.12

1. Nous **sommes allé(e)s** en Allemagne deux fois.
2. Elle **est allée** au magasin trois fois cette semaine.
3. Il **est allé** au Mexique une seule fois.
4. Ma famille **est allée** à Londres plusieurs fois.

EX. 2.13

Au moment où je **suis entré(e)**, il **a caché** ses affaires et il **a commencé** à mentir. Je lui **ai demandé** pourquoi, il **a répondu** que cela ne me regardait pas.

EX. 2.14

D'abord, j'**ai mélangé** la farine et le beurre, puis j'**ai ajouté** le lait. Je pense que j'**ai mis** trop de beurre car la pâte **est devenue** très grasse. Ce n'est pas grave, au moins j'**ai essayé**.

EX. 2.15

1. Nous **sommes retourné(e)s** au même hôtel.
2. J'**ai sorti** la poubelle trop tard.
3. Est-ce que tu **as rentré** les chaises de jardin ?
4. Ils **sont montés** il y a quelques minutes.

EX. 2.16

1. **Se détendre**
   Je **me suis détendu(e)**
   Tu **t'es détendu(e)**
   Il **s'est détendu**
   Elle **s'est détendue**
   On **s'est détendu(e)s**
   Nous **nous sommes détendu(e)s**
   Vous **vous êtes détendu(e)s**
   Ils **se sont détendus**
   Elles **se sont détendues**

2. **Se raser**
   Je **me suis rasé(e)**
   Tu **t'es rasé(e)**
   Il **s'est rasé**
   Elle **s'est rasée**
   On **s'est rasé(e)s**
   Nous **nous sommes rasé(e)s**
   Vous **vous êtes rasé(e)s**
   Ils **se sont rasés**
   Elles **se sont rasées**

EX. 2.17

1. Je **me suis douché(e)** ce matin.
2. Elle **s'est occupée** de cela ce week-end.
3. Il **s'est trompé** sur la question numéro 3.
4. Nous **nous sommes inscrit(e)s** pour décembre.
5. Je **me suis fait** un sandwich.
6. Vous **vous êtes assis(es)** au premier rang.
7. Elle **s'est coupé** les cheveux elle-même.
8. Nous **nous sommes mis(es)** d'accord assez vite.
9. Ils **se sont essuyé** les pied savant d'entrer.
10. Elle **s'est cassé** la jambe.
11. Ils **se sont brossé** les dents.
12. Je **me suis rappelé(e)** de cette histoire récemment.
13. Ils **se sont amusés** à l'anniversaire.
14. Elle **s'est sentie** mieux après le dîner.
15. Tu **t'es imaginé** cette histoire.

EX. 2.18

1. Nous n'**avons** pas **reçu** la livraison ce matin.
2. Elles ne **sont** jamais **passées** par là.
3. Je n'**ai** pas **vidé** la bouteille dans l'évier.
4. Tu n'**as** rien **oublié**.
5. Cet hôtel n'**est** jamais **devenu** populaire.
6. Le professeur n'**a** pas **annulé** sa classe de yoga.
7. Le fermier n'**a** pas **acheté** de deuxième ferme.
8. Je n'**ai** jamais **décidé** de lire tous les jours un chapitre.
9. Le directeur n'**a** pas **accepté** ses congés.
10. Elle n'**a** pas **aidé** sa sœur à faire la vaisselle.
11. Elles ne **sont** pas **arrivées** il y a quelques heures.
12. Il n'**a** pas **convaincu** ses parents de le conduire.
13. Les élèves n'**ont** pas **étudié** dur pour l'examen.
14. Elles ne **se sont** pas **disputées** à propos de la facture.
15. Nous n'**avons** pas **manqué** son récital de danse.

EX. 2.19

1. Tu **as changé** de travail.
2. **As-tu changé** de travail ?
3. On **a bu** du thé au déjeuner.
4. **A-t-on bu** du thé au déjeuner ?
5. Il **a fumé** plusieurs cigarettes.
6. **A-t-il fumé** plusieurs cigarettes ?
7. Elle **a voulu** organiser une surprise.
8. **A-t-elle voulu** organiser une surprise ?
9. Ils **sont** tous **venus** ce soir.
10. **Sont-ils** tous **venus** ce soir ?
11. Il **a douté** de ses compétences.
12. **A-t-il douté** de ses compétences ?
13. Nous **avons espéré** gagner à la loterie.
14. **Avons-nous espéré** gagner à la loterie ?
15. Vous **vous êtes connus**.
16. **Vous êtes-vous connus** ?
17. Il **a pris** une décision rapidement.
18. **A-t-il pris** une décision rapidement ?
19. Elle **a fait** un gâteau aux pommes.
20. **A-t-elle fait** un gâteau aux pommes ?

EX. 2.20

1. Est-ce que tu **as réservé** un traitement au spa ?
2. Non, je n'**ai** pas **réservé** de traitement au spa.
3. Est-ce qu'il **a respecté** ses parents ?
4. Oui, il **a respecté** ses parents.
5. Est-ce que tu **as fait** du vélo ?
6. Non, je n'**ai** pas **fait** de vélo.
7. Est-ce que j'**ai vu** ce film au cinéma ?
8. Oui, tu **as vu** ce film au cinéma.
9. Est-ce que tu **t'es levé** tôt ?
10. Non, je ne **me suis pas levé** tôt.
11. Est-ce que le docteur **a dit** de rester au lit ?
12. Oui, le docteur **a dit** de rester au lit.
13. Est-ce que tu **as trouvé** un appartement ?
14. Non, je n'**ai** pas **trouvé** d'appartement.
15. Est-ce qu'elle **a entendu** la conversation ?
16. Oui, elle **a entendu** la conversation.
17. Est-ce qu'il **a travaillé** trop ?
18. Non, il n'**a** pas **travaillé** trop.
19. Est-ce qu'ils **sont allés** au stade ?
20. Oui, ils **sont allés** au stade.

Solutions - L'imparfait

EX. 3.1

1. To be - Nous **sommes** - Ils **étaient**
2. To have - Nous **avons** - J'**avais**
3. To take - Nous **prenons** - Tu **prenais**
4. To call - Nous **téléphonons** - Nous **téléphonions**
5. To do - Nous **faisons** - Vous **faisiez**
6. To sleep - Nous **dormons** - Ils **dormaient**
7. To turn off - Nous **éteignons** - Elles **éteignaient**
8. To come - Nous **venons** - Je **venais**
9. To write - Nous **écrivons** - Vous **écriviez**
10. To build - Nous **construisons** - On **construisait**

EX. 3.2

1. Je **tournais**
2. Tu **semblais**
3. Nous **préparions**
4. Elle **dépensait**
5. Ils **recommandaient**
6. Vous **remarquiez**
7. Je **forçais**
8. Il **marchait**
9. Elles **allaient**
10. Nous **amenions**
11. Il **voyageait**
12. Ils **chantaient**
13. Nous **regardions**
14. Elle **pêchait**
15. Tu **partageais**

EX. 3.3

1. Elles **écrivaient** un poème.
2. Nous **buvions** un verre de vin.
3. Il **achetait** beaucoup d'outils.
4. L'ordinateur ne **fonctionnait** plus.
5. J'**étais** au téléphone.
6. L'auteur **vendait** beaucoup de livres.
7. Vous **arriviez** toujours en retard.
8. Il **faisait** chaud.
9. Qu'est-ce que tu **disais** ?
10. Mon grand-père **cuisinait** tellement bien.

EX. 3.4

1. Nous **habitions** en ville.
2. Je **chantais** au cabaret.
3. Tu **restais** souvent après moi.
4. Elle **jouait** avec le chien.
5. Elle **se couchait** tôt.
6. Nous **étions** là.
7. Je **lisais** le journal.
8. Ils **éteignaient** toujours les lampes.
9. Nous **étudiions** tous les jours.
10. Je **finissais** mes devoirs à la va-vite.
11. Il **se trompait** souvent de numéro.

EX. 3.5

1. En général, on **dépensait** 300 dollars par mois en nourriture.
2. Le lundi, je **jouais** au football et j'avais cours de piano.
3. Il ne **reconnaissait** jamais ses erreurs.
4. D'habitude, il **était** toujours à l'heure.
5. Il **aimait** bien se détendre de temps à autre.

EX. 3.6

Chaque année, nous **allions** chez mes grands-parents pour les vacances. Ma grand-mère **faisait** souvent des tartes et mon grand-père **était** toujours dans le jardin. Mes frères et moi **restions** là-bas pendant plusieurs semaines. Cela **permettait** à mes parents d'avoir un peu de temps pour eux. Cela ne **dérangeait** pas mes grands-parents. Ils **adoraient** nous avoir à la maison.

EX. 3.7

1. Elle **était** grande, elle **avait** les yeux bleus et les cheveux blonds.
2. Il **était** petit, il **avait** les yeux bruns et les cheveux courts.
3. Elle **était** de taille moyenne, elle **portait** une chemise et des lunettes.

EX. 3.8

1. Nous **faisions** la vaisselle pendant qu'ils **préparaient** le dessert.
2. Pendant qu'elle **accouchait**, Il **était** dans les embouteillages.
3. J'**attendais** toujours le bus pendant qu'il **était** déjà à la maison.
4. Le marché **s'effondrait** pendant qu'il **voyageait** en Europe.
5. Tu **étudiais** pendant qu'elle **passait** son examen.

EX. 3.9 Personnel

EX. 3.10

Quand j'étais petit – petite :

1. Je **mangeais** des légumes.
2. Je **jouais** au football.
3. Je **faisais** du vélo.
4. J'**étudiais** tous les jours.
5. Je **me disputais** avec mes parents.
6. J'**adorais** le chocolat.
7. J'**étais** bon à l'école.
8. Je **regardais** la télévision.
9. Je **me salissais** toujours.

Solutions - Le passé compose - L'imparfait

EX. 4.1

1. To participate - Nous **avons participé** - Nous **participions**
2. To do - Nous **avons fait** - Nous **faisions**
3. To go - Nous **sommes allé(e)s** - Nous **allions**
4. To put - Nous **avons mis** - Nous **mettions**
5. To study - Nous **avons étudié** - Nous **étudiions**
6. To change - Nous **avons changé** - Nous **changions**
7. To say - Nous **avons dit** - Nous **disions**
8. To know - Nous **avons su** - Nous **savions**
9. To apply - Nous **avons appliqué** - Nous **appliquions**
10. To wait - Nous **avons attendu** - Nous **attendions**

EX. 4.2

Il **travaillait** sur son ordinateur quand sa femme lui **a demandé** : « Est-ce que tu **as réparé** la machine à café ? ». Non, je n'**ai** pas **eu** le temps. Je **devais** préparer les documents pour la réunion.
Imparfait : travaillait - devais
Passé composé : a demandé – as réparé – ai eu

EX. 4.3

1. J'**étudiais** le lundi.
2. Il **a renversé** le café sur la cliente.
3. Mon grand-père **fumait** beaucoup.
4. Elle **est née** il y a quelques jours
5. En général, je **faisais** mes devoirs le soir.
6. Ma collègue **était** sur le point de démissionner.
7. C'**était** incroyable !
8. Ton père **avait** toujours de bonnes notes.
9. Mon frère **a acheté** un cadeau pour les enfants.
10. Mon patron m'**a cru(e)**.

EX. 4.4

1. Tu ne m'**écoutais** jamais.
2. J'**ai pris** un café à emporter.
3. Il y **avait** une fête chez moi hier soir.
4. Mon père **travaillait** ici.
5. Ma tortue **est morte** après 10 ans.
6. Je n'**ai** pas **pris** mon parapluie.
7. Ce livre **était** génial !
8. Nous n'**étions** pas là en janvier.
9. **As**-tu **lu** le livre que je t'**ai recommandé** ?
10. J'**étais** très déçue.

*Remember to **download the audio** and to **watch the videos** – see Preface*

EX. 4.5

1. J'**ai fait** de la poterie pendant plusieurs années.
2. Avant ma grossesse, je **buvais** un verre de vin à chaque repas.
3. Est-ce que tu **as fermé** la porte ?
4. Elle **avait** les cheveux noirs et les yeux bleus.
5. Mon père **vérifiait** toujours mes devoirs après moi.
6. Elle **s'est maquillée** avant de partir.
7. Tu **chantais** tellement bien.
8. Quand tu **étais** petite, tu ne **regardais** jamais la télévision.
9. Est-ce qu'il **allait** à la banque quand tu l'**as vu** ?
10. Mes cousins **étaient** très proches.

EX. 4.6

Je **suis rentrée** de vacances ce matin, c'**était** super ! Le temps **était** parfait, la nourriture **était** bonne et l'hôtel **était** magnifique. L'eau de la piscine **était** un petit peu froide mais après quelques minutes cela **allait**. Le premier jour nous **sommes allés** en excursion autour du lac, et nous **avons mangé** dans un restaurant italien. Après cela, nous **avons eu** quelques jours de repos jusqu'au vendredi où nous **sommes allés** à la montagne pour le week-end. Nous **sommes restés** dans un petit chalet, le chalet **était** très mignon. Il **faisait** beaucoup plus chaud qu'à la mer où nous **sommes restés** pendant la semaine. Nous **avons fait** de la randonnée, **j'ai** aussi **essayé** l'escalade mais je n'**ai** pas **aimé**. Le dernier jour, nous **avons mangé** tous ensemble avant de préparer nos valises. Le bus **avait** deux heures de retard mais nous **avons joué** à des jeux en attendant. J'espère y retourner l'année prochaine car je **me suis fait** beaucoup de nouveaux amis.
À bientôt,
Dylane.

EX. 4.7 Personnel

EX. 4.8

1. Je **me préparais** à aller au lit quand soudain, la tempête **a commencé**.
2. Elle **voulait** te dire au revoir mais tu **es parti(e)** trop vite.
3. Quand il **s'est réveillé**, il **était** déjà en retard.
4. La voisine **a surpris** son mari qui **était** avec une autre femme.
5. Au moment où le professeur **est entré** dans la classe, Paul **jouait** sur son téléphone.
6. J'**ai essayé** de faire mes devoirs mais je n'**avais** pas mon cahier.
7. Nous **sommes allé(e)s** en Espagne quand nous **étions** jeunes mariés.
8. Le téléphone **fonctionnait** puis soudainement, il **s'est éteint**.
9. Quand les pompiers **sont arrivés**, la maison **était** complètement en feu.
10. Elle **pensait** réussir mais elle **a dû** repasser son examen d'anglais.

EX. 4.9

1. Je **les** avais en mains il y a quelques secondes.
2. Tu **les** as déposées chez le cordonnier ?
3. Il **les** faisait l'après-midi.
4. Le pâtissier **l'**a préparée.
5. Elle **la** rangeait tous les soirs.
6. Est-ce que tu **l'**as pris ce matin ?
7. C'est comme ça que je **le** portais quand j'étais jeune.
8. Elle **l'**a goûté**e** et elle a adoré !
9. Il **la** choisissait toujours.
10. Je **les** ai déposé**s** ce matin.

Solutions - Le passé récent

EX. 5.1

1. Je **viens (juste) d'arriver** il y a 5 minutes.
2. Il **vient (juste) de perdre** son téléphone.
3. On **vient (juste) d'apprendre** la nouvelle.
4. Les enfants **viennent (juste) de rentrer** de l'école.
5. La lettre **vient (juste) d'arriver.**

EX. 5.2

1. Il **vient juste de répéter** la question.
2. Je **viens de déposer** le colis à la poste.
3. L'artiste **vient de finir** sa nouvelle peinture.
4. On **vient juste de faire** les courses.
5. Je **viens de prendre** mes somnifères.

EX. 5.3

1. Il **venait de partir** quand tu **es arrivé.**
2. Le chien **venait de vomir** quand Il **est revenu** de la promenade.
3. Elle **venait de manger** quand elle **a commencé** à se sentir mal.
4. Mon père **venait de réserver** un vol quand son patron **a annulé** le voyage.
5. Ils **venaient d'adopter** un enfant quand elle **est tombée** enceinte.

Solutions - Le futur simple

EX. 6.1

1. La caissière **comptera** l'argent avant de partir.
2. Mes parents **s'inquièteront** si je ne rentre pas.
3. J'**amènerai** une bouteille de vin.
4. Le film **commencera** bientôt.
5. Nous **passerons** dire bonjour à nos voisins.
6. On **fermera** le restaurant à 22 heures ce soir.
7. Ils **garderont** les enfants pendant que les parents **seront** au cinéma.
8. Elle **achètera** le cadeau pour ses enfants ce week-end.
9. Ma famille **visitera** Rome en janvier prochain.
10. Je **porterai** une robe bleue au mariage.

EX. 6.2.

1. Le magasin **ouvrira** bientôt.
2. Le détenu **fuira** devant les gardes qui le rattrapent.
3. Nous **accueillerons** nos premiers clients la semaine prochaine.
4. Je pense qu'il ne **mentira** plus jamais.
5. On **servira** du caviar au mariage.

EX. 6.3

1. Tu **mettras** le lait au frigo avant de partir.
2. Je **conduirai** les enfants au tournoi de football.
3. Nous **prendrons** toutes les précautions nécessaires.
4. Je lui **dirai** que tu ne peux pas venir à la réunion.
5. Il nous **rejoindra** dès qu'il aura fini.

EX. 6.4 Personnel

EX. 6.5

1. Lundi je **serai** aux Bahamas.
2. Demain nous **irons** chez mes parents.
3. Nous **recevrons** les clés dans quelques jours.
4. Un jour ils **viendront** nous voir.
5. Dans deux ans j'**aurai** 35 ans.

EX. 6.6

1. Je pense que tu **deviendras** acteur.
2. Nous **pensons** que le ministre sera président.
3. Tu penses que tu **pourras** venir ?

EX. 6.7

1. Le bureau **arrivera** demain.
2. Je **serai** au bureau pour signer le contrat.
3. Ils **seront** là.
4. Mes parents nous **rendront** visite cet été.
5. La femme de ménage **commencera** le mois prochain.
6. Nous **engagerons** plus de gens dès que possible.
7. J'espère qu'il **survivra** la chirurgie.
8. Nous **regarderons** probablement ce film ce week-end.
9. Le cinéma **ouvrira** bientôt.
10. Les étudiants **seront** diplômés en juin.

EX. 6.8

1. Je **serai** en retard.
2. Mon mari **ira** chercher les enfants à l'école.
3. Nous **vivrons** à l'étranger pendant quelques années.
4. Il **sera** docteur à la fin de ses études.
5. Il **coulera** un bain pour sa femme.
6. Nous **téléphonerons** pour avoir plus de nouvelles.
7. Quand il **recevra** le paquet, il sera surpris !
8. La province **commencera** à recycler le plastique en 2022.
9. Les oiseaux **mangeront** les graines du jardin.
10. Il ne **se souviendra** pas de tous ces beaux paysages.

Solutions - Le futur proche

EX. 7.1

1. Tu **vas manger** une pomme.
2. Je sais que tu **vas réussir**.
3. Il **va pleuvoir**.
4. Nous **allons rester** à la maison.
5. Ce créateur **va essayer** de gagner de l'argent.
6. Je **vais voir**.
7. Le peintre **va repeindre** la façade.
8. Est-ce que tu **vas chercher** les enfants ?
9. Les habitants **vont recevoir** un chèque.
10. Tu penses qu'il **va neiger** ce soir ?

EX. 7.2

1. Il ne **va** pas **prendre** le train.
2. Je ne **vais** pas **ramener** le livre à la bibliothèque.
3. Elle ne **va** pas **appeler** le dentiste pour prendre rendez-vous.
4. On ne **va** pas **s'occuper** des enfants.
5. Le train ne **va** pas **arriver** en gare.
6. Tu ne **vas** pas **te laver** maintenant ?
7. Mon ami ne **va** pas **aller** à l'université.
8. Tu ne **vas** pas **être** en retard !
9. Il ne **va** pas **se couper** s'il ne fait pas attention.
10. Tu ne **vas** pas **te brosser** les dents ?

EX. 7.3 Personnel

Solutions – Le conditionnel présent

EX. 8.1

1. Je n'**essaierais** pas
2. Elle **aiderait**
3. Tu **gèlerais**
4. J'**amènerais**
5. Il **nettoierait**

EX. 8.2

1. Nous **ouvririons** un compte en banque.
2. Elle **dormirait** toute la journée.
3. On **offrirait** un cadeau.
4. Je **servirais** des nouilles au tofu.
5. Les hôtesses **accueilleraient** les nouveaux clients.

EX. 8.3

1. Je **prendrais** des nouvelles de mes parents.
2. Il **battrait** ses adversaires à chaque fois.
3. Ils **suivraient** les indications du chemin.
4. Elle **écrivait** avec une plume au lieu d'un stylo.
5. Nous **pendrions** les habits à l'extérieur.

EX. 8.4 Personnel

EX. 8.5

1. Ça **serait** bien de faire comme ça.
2. Cela **vaudrait** plus que 10 euros.
3. Il **arriverait** dans l'après-midi.
4. Nous **serions** diplômés en septembre.
5. Il **dirait** qu'il ne peut pas venir.

EX. 8.6

1. **Pourrais**-je avoir un café ?
2. **Pourrais**-tu nous aider à déménager ?
3. **Sauriez**-vous nous indiquer la gare ?
4. **Pourriez**-vous nous laisser un peu de place ?
5. **Saurais**-tu m'aider à changer de numéro de téléphone ?

EX. 8.7

1. Je **serais** là si tu n'**étais** pas là.
2. S'ils **payaient** les factures, la société **finirait** la maison.
3. J'**irais** à l'école si je **me sentais** mieux.
4. Tu n'**aurais** pas mal à la tête si tu **buvais** plus d'eau.
5. Si tu **avais** 21 ans, tu **pourrais** boire de l'alcool.
6. Si j'**avais** du temps, je **ferais** du sport.
7. Elle **irait** si elle **avait envie.**
8. Si elle **marchait** plus, elle **se sentirait** plus en forme.
9. Si on **avait** de l'argent, on **travaillerait** moins.
10. Si vous **fumiez** moins, vous **vivriez** plus longtemps.

Solutions - L'impératif

EX. 9.1

Jeter	**Dire**	**Prendre**	**Tenir**
Jette	Dis	Prends	Tiens
Jetons	Disons	Prenons	Tenons
Jetez	Dites	Prenez	Tenez

EX. 9.2

1. **Viens** ici !
2. **Sois** là !
3. **Regarde** !
4. **Pars** !
5. **Écoute** !
6. **Appelle** !
7. **Lis** !
8. **Prends** !
9. **Ferme** la porte !
10. **Éteins** la TV !

EX. 9.3

1. Ne **regardez** pas.
2. Ne **buvez** pas mon café.
3. Ne **demandez** pas ça.
4. Ne **touchez** pas le chien.
5. Ne **laissez** pas sortir le chat.
6. N'**oubliez** pas l'argent.
7. Ne **répondez** pas à la question.
8. Ne **dormez** pas tard.
9. N'**utilisez** pas cet outil.
10. N'**oubliez** pas d'enregistrer.

EX. 9.4

1. **Regardez**-moi.
2. **Apportez**-moi la télécommande.
3. Ne me **quittez** pas.
4. **Prenez** la photo.
5. **Donnez**-moi le livre.
6. **Dites**-lui ça.
7. **Payez**-les bientôt.
8. Ne me **faites** pas peur.
9. **Oubliez**-nous.
10. **Commandez**-moi un café.

EX. 9.5

1. **Viens** au magasin avec moi.
2. Ne **bois** pas de vin.
3. **Mets** tes chaussures dans l'armoire.
4. **Sache** que je suis là.
5. **Réserve** une table pour nous deux.
6. **Aide** les patients à trouver la chambre.
7. Ne **reste** pas à la maison.
8. **Fais** un gâteau pour demain.
9. Ne **pose** pas de questions.
10. N'**attends** pas trop longtemps.

EX. 9.6

1. **Réveille-toi** à 6 heures du matin.
2. **Soyons** là pour le dîner.
3. **Lisez** le journal en silence.
4. **Réfléchis** avant d'agir.
5. **Prenons** les vélos pour aller au magasin.
6. **Attendez-nous** avant de partir.
7. **Pratique** la calligraphie souvent.
8. **Partons** sans lui.
9. **Mangez** ensemble à midi.
10. **Écoute** la chanson sans faire de bruit.

EX. 9.7

1. **Soyons** ponctuels pour le rendez-vous.
2. **Construisons** une nouvelle maison.
3. **Allons** à la campagne ce week-end.
4. **Téléchargeons** des musiques pour le trajet.
5. **Voyons** si on peut faire ça.
6. **Applaudissons** l'artiste à la fin du spectacle.
7. **Demandons** l'autorisation à nos parents.
8. **Essayons** de ne pas perdre d'argent dans la transaction.
9. **Attendons** que l'orage passe.
10. **Promenons-nous** au bord du lac.

EX. 9.8

1. Passe-**le**-**lui**.
2. Rendez-**le**-**lui**.
3. Lisons-**le**-**lui**.
4. Accordez-**le**-**moi**.
5. Prête-**les**-**leur**.
6. Achetons-**la**-**lui**.
7. Lisez-**le**-**moi**.
8. Connecte-**le**.
9. Prenons-**le** maintenant.
10. Regardez-**les** arriver au port.

Solutions - Infinitive & prépositions

EX. 10.1

1. Il **prétend écouter** le professeur.
2. Il **veut partir** maintenant.
3. J'**aime jouer** avec les Lego.
4. On **doit** / Nous **devons payer** les factures aujourd'hui.
5. Il **espère réussir** avec sa nouvelle idée.
6. Elle **pense vendre** sa maison.
7. Je **préfère dormir** dans mon lit.
8. Il n'**ose** pas **sauter**.
9. Elle **sait étudier** vite.
10. On **veut** / Nous **voulons acheter** un nouveau canapé.

EX. 10.2 Personnel

EX. 10.3

1. Mon fils me **demande de** lui acheter un cadeau.
2. Il **vient de** partir.
3. Le policier **persuade** le suspect **de** parler.
4. Cet homme **accepte d'**aider la vieille dame.
5. Nous avons **décidé de** déménager en Australie.
6. L'enfant **fait semblant de** dormir.
7. Il **a arrêté d'**étudier il y a quelques heures.
8. La radio **cesse de** fonctionner.
9. Le banquier **refuse d'**investir plus.
10. Je **finis de** tondre la pelouse.

EX. 10.4

1. Il commence **à** faire meilleur.
2. Nous parlons **de** changer de rideaux.
3. Anna vient **-** chercher ses affaires.
4. Le principal accepte **de** revoir son dossier.
5. Il cherche **à** plaire à ses beaux-parents
6. Est-ce que tu as dit à Jean **de** prendre ses clés ?
7. Les clients doivent **-** évacuer le magasin.
8. On risque **de** manquer notre train.
9. Le coach encourage les enfants **à** se dépasser.
10. J'ai envoyé Shirley **-** chercher le courrier.
11. Il doit **-** arriver à faire ses devoirs tout seul.
12. Le chiot n'ose pas **-** sauter du canapé.
13. Les enfants apprennent **à** écrire aux alentours de 6 ans.
14. Le gouvernement envisage **de** changer les règles d'immigration.
15. Continue **à** chanter, tu as une très belle voix.
16. C'est permis **de** partir plus tôt.
17. Il compte **-** finir ses études en 2 ans.
18. Nous réfléchissons **à** adopter un enfant.
19. L'avocat essaye **de** prouver que son client est innocent.
20. Elle désire **-** devenir ingénieure.

EX. 10.5

1. Ils apprennent à se connaître **avant de** se marier.
2. J'ai ouvert un compte épargnes **afin d' - pour** économiser de l'argent.

3. Il est **loin de** se rendre compte de ses problèmes.
4. Les politiciens tentent de cacher leurs erreurs **de peur de** perdre la prochaine élection.
5. Ils montent les escaliers **sans** faire de bruit.
6. Elle engage une baby-sitter **pour** garder les enfants.
7. Il faut tester le terrain **afin de** déterminer la stabilité.
8. Il prend les escaliers **au lieu de** prendre l'ascenseur.
9. Lisez le manuel **avant de** commencer.
10. Vous recevrez le document **pour - afin de** faire une demande.
11. Ils ont besoin de plus d'indices **afin de - pour** trouver la solution.
12. Elle débarrasse le plan de travail **avant de** faire la pâte.
13. Il ne faisait pas de bruit **de peur de** réveiller les enfants.
14. Tu devrais voyager **avant de** commencer à étudier.
15. Utilisez la clé **pour** entrer dans la maison.

EX. 10.6

1. Il **fait entrer** l'accusé dans le tribunal.
2. Cet employé **se fait payer** tous les 15 jours.
3. Le professeur lève la voix pour **se faire entendre.**
4. L'avocat **fait savoir** au juge que son client est malade.
5. Elle **fait chanter** son ex-mari depuis des mois.
6. Il m'**en fait voir** de toutes les couleurs.
7. J'essaye de **me faire couper** les cheveux tous les 6 mois.
8. Tu dois **te faire opérer** d'urgence.
9. Le patron demande à **faire laver** sa voiture demain matin.
10. Il aime **se faire remarquer** en classe.

EX. 10.7

1. Avez-vous **de quoi** lire ?
2. J'ai pris **de quoi** boire pour la marche.
3. Mes frères ont **de quoi** jouer.

EX. 10.8

1. Il **est sur le point de** bouger la voiture.
2. Je **suis sur le point d'**appeler la police.
3. Ce couple **est sur le point de** divorcer.
4. Cette série télévisée **est sur le point d'**être annulée.
5. Elle **est sur le point de** prendre (des) notes.

EX. 10.9

1. Nous **sommes heureuses d'**être ici.
2. Est-ce que tu **es sûr de** pouvoir venir ?
3. La scientifique **est ravie d'**être nominée.
4. Il **est anxieux de** prendre l'avion.
5. Nous **sommes désolés d'**être en retard.

6. Jeff **est triste d'**apprendre la nouvelle.
7. Je **suis impatiente d'**arriver.
8. Ma mère **est surprise de** te voir.
9. Il **est ravi de** recevoir ta lettre.
10. Emma **est contente de** participer au jeu.

EX. 10.10

1. Je **suis déterminé(e) à** payer mes dettes.
2. Nous **sommes habitué(e)s à** dormir tard.
3. Elles **sont occupées à** regarder la télévision.
4. Le directeur **est autorisé à** signer.
5. Elle **est prête à** changer.

EX. 10.11 Personnel

EX. 10.12

1. C'est le **seul** à être venu.
2. Ils étaient **nombreux** à attendre le chanteur.
3. Amélia et moi étions les **seules** à prendre des nouvelles.
4. Je suis la **seule** à être diplômée dans ma famille.
5. Les **seuls** à être là pour moi sont mon mari et mes frères.
6. Les petites filles sont **nombreuses** à vouloir être princesses.

EX. 10.13

1. Elle est toujours la **dernière** à quitter le travail.
2. Je pense qu'elles étaient les **premières** à sortir du bâtiment.
3. Le **premier** à entrer gagne un voyage à Mexico.
4. Il est le **dernier** à arriver.

EX. 10.14

1. Il faut **regarder** moins la télévision.
2. Il faut **connaître** les différences entre savoir et connaître.
3. Il faut **aller** plus vite.
4. Il faut **commander** du papier.
5. Il faut **dormir** plus tôt.
6. Il faut **penser** à payer ses factures.
7. Il faut **remplir** ce document avant de l'envoyer.

Solutions - Le subjonctif

EX. 11.1

1. **Grandir**
   Que je **grandisse**
   Que tu **grandisses**
   Qu'on **grandisse**
   Que nous **grandissions**
   Que vous **grandissiez**
   Qu'elles **grandissent**

2. **Entendre**
   Que j'**entende**
   Que tu **entendes**
   Qu'il **entende**
   Que nous **entendions**
   Que vous **entendiez**
   Qu'ils **entendent**

EX. 11.2

1. Que j'**écrive**
2. Que tu **partes**
3. Qu'il **craigne**
4. Que nous **disions**
5. Que vous **riiez**
6. Qu'ils **battent**
7. Que je **conduise**
8. Que tu **coures**
9. Qu'il **vive**
10. Que nous **suivions**

EX. 11.3

1. **Revenir**
   Que je **revienne**
   Que tu **reviennes**
   Qu'on **revienne**
   Que nous **revenions**
   Que vous **reveniez**
   Qu'elles **reviennent**

2. **Renvoyer**
   Que je **renvoie**
   Que tu **renvoies**
   Qu'il **renvoie**
   Que nous **renvoyions**
   Que vous **renvoyiez**
   Qu'ils **renvoient**

EX. 11.4

1. Nettoyer // Présent - Que je **nettoie** // Passé - Que vous **ayez nettoyé**
2. Faire // Présent - Que je **fasse** // Passé - Que vous **ayez fait**
3. Pouvoir // Présent - Que je **puisse** // Passé - Que vous **ayez pu**
4. Dire // Présent - Que je **dise** // Passé - Que vous **ayez dit**
5. Finir // Présent - Que je **finisse** // Passé - Que vous **ayez fini**
6. Avoir // Présent - Que j'**aie** // Passé - Que vous **ayez eu**
7. Manger // Présent - Que je **mange** // Passé - Que vous **ayez mangé**
8. Aller // Présent - Que j'**aille** // Passé - Que vous **soyez allé(e)s**
9. Être // Présent - Que je **sois** // Passé - Que vous **ayez été**
10. Aimer // Présent - Que j'**aime** // Passé - Que vous **ayez aimé**

EX. 11.5

1. Je souhaite qu'il **reçoive** son diplôme.
2. Il espère que le bus est à l'heure.
3. Nous aimerions mieux que vous **arriviez** demain.
4. Les enseignants tiennent à ce que les enfants **réussissent.**
5. Le tuteur insiste pour qu'ils **fassent** leurs devoirs.
6. Je veux que les enfants **soient** au lit à 21 heures.

*Remember to **download the audio** and to **watch the videos** - see Preface*

7. Le client s'attend à ce que la chambre **soit** prête.
8. Mes parents ont envie qu'ils **viennent** avec nous.
9. Le garde exige que les prisonniers **restent** silencieux.
10. Le responsable espère que la livraison **arrive** bientôt.

EX. 11.6 Personnel

EX. 11.7

1. Il faut que je **vérifie** la pression des pneus.
2. Il faut que je **remplisse** ma déclaration d'impôts.
3. Il faut que j'**aille** à la banque.
4. Il faut que je **boive** plus d'eau.
5. Il faut que je **prenne** rendez-vous.
6. Il faut que je **sois** en forme.
7. Il faut que je **me décide**.
8. Il faut que je **coupe** du bois.
9. Il faut que je **vienne** te voir.
10. Il faut que je **réserve** une table au restaurant.

EX. 11.8 Personnel

EX. 11.9

1. Nous regrettons que ce **se soit passé** de cette façon.
2. L'agent de voyage a recommandé que nous **réservions** assez vite.
3. Le docteur a suggéré que nous **fassions** plus de tests.

EX. 11.10

1. Nous croyons qu'il est bon pour nous de dormir tard.
   Croyons-nous qu'il **soit bon pour nous de dormir tard ?**
   Nous ne croyons pas **qu'il soit bon pour nous de dormir tard.**
2. Elle a l'impression que je fais de la natation tous les matins.
   A-t-elle l'impression que **je fasse de la natation tous les matins ?**
   Elle n'a pas l'impression **que je fasse de la natation tous les matins.**
3. Tu penses que cette artiste vient de France.
   Penses-tu que **cette artiste vienne de France ?**
   Tu ne penses pas **que cette artiste vienne de France.**

EX. 11.11

1. Je ne doute pas que tu **es** le meilleur.
2. Tu doutes que l'équipe **gagne**.
3. Il paraît que tu **reviens** d'Écosse.
4. Il semble que les jours **rallongent**.
5. On sait que les choses ne **s'arrangent** pas toutes seules.
6. C'est possible que tu **fasses** un gâteau pour demain.
7. Il est vrai que la poterie **semble** difficile.
8. Il est incroyable que ce chien **ait survécu**.
9. Il est évident que les parents **sont fatigués**.

EX. 11.12

1. Il est bien que tu **comprennes** le problème.
2. C'est bon que j'**économise** depuis longtemps.
3. Il est dommage que le temps **passe** si vite.
4. Il est juste qu'ils **rendent** l'argent.
5. C'est logique que ces produits **soient** en promotion.
6. Il est rare qu'il **fasse** beau en décembre.
7. C'est urgent qu'on **découvre** un remède.
8. C'est utile qu'on **puisse** télécharger les documents en ligne.

EX. 11.13

1. Je le range **de façon qu'**il ne le trouve pas.
2. Le directeur explique les problèmes **afin que** tout soit clair.
3. Nous mangerons tôt **afin que** tu te couches à l'heure.
4. Tu réussiras **à condition que** tu étudies.
5. Le film commencera à l'heure **à supposer que** tout fonctionne.
6. **Pourvu que** ça dure !
7. Elle cuisine le dîner **en attendant que** j'arrive.
8. J'ai mis la boîte sur le frigo **de sorte que** tu ne puisses pas l'attraper.

EX. 11.14

1. Je vais acheter la maison à moins qu'il **n'**y ait un problème.
2. Elle dormait avant que tu **n'**arrives.
3. Il ne voulait pas te le dire de crainte que tu **ne** sois vexée.
4. Il a déjà préparé les papiers de peur que la banque **ne** refuse.
5. Il a préparé ses affaires sans que je **ne** lui demande.

EX. 11.15

1. Je suis surprise **que** tu **sois** déjà là.
2. C'est important **qu'**on **trouve** une solution au plus vite.
3. Ma grand-mère est heureuse **que** nous **allions** lui rendre visite.
4. Ils sont tristes **qu'**ils **doivent** rester à la maison.
5. Je m'en doute **qu'**elle **veuille** participer.
6. C'est probable **que** j'**aie** assez d'argent.
7. C'est incroyable **qu'**il **puisse** encore faire du cinéma.
8. Cela vaut mieux **que** tu **te laves** les mains.
9. C'est étonnant **qu'**il **ait** dix-huit ans.
10. Je ne crois pas **que** vous **sachiez** la vérité.

Solutions - Le plus-que parfait

EX. 12.1

1. **Avoir**
   J'**avais eu**
   Tu **avais eu**
   Il **avait eu**
   Nous **avions eu**
   Vous **aviez eu**
   Ils **avaient eu**

2. **Rentrer**
   J'**étais rentré(e)**
   Tu **étais rentré(e)**
   Elle **était rentrée**
   Nous **étions rentré(e)s**
   Vous **étiez rentré(e)s**
   Elles **étaient rentrées**

3. **Se maquiller**
   Je **m'étais maquillé(e)**
   Tu **t'étais maquillé(e)**
   On **s'était maquillé(e)s**
   Nous **nous étions maquillé(e)s**
   Vous **vous étiez maquillé(e)s**
   Elles **s'étaient maquillées**

EX. 12.2

1. J'**avais cherché** mon stylo partout.
2. Son responsable l'**avait prévenu.**
3. L'échelle **était tombée** toute seule.
4. Nous **avions lavé** la voiture au carwash.
5. Elle **avait** encore **oublié** ses livres.
6. Martin **avait vaincu** le cancer.
7. Ma tante **avait fait** de la soupe.
8. J'**avais reçu** un collier pour mon anniversaire.
9. Il **avait plu** toute la nuit.
10. L'application **avait arrêté** de fonctionner.

EX. 12.3

1. Il **l'**avait attendu**e** pendant des semaines.
2. Les propriétaires **les** avaient changé**es.**
3. Elle se **les** était lavé**s** avant d'aller chez le coiffeur.
4. Le ministre **les** avait envoyé**es** en avance.
5. Les étudiants **les** avaient déjà acheté**s.**

Solutions – Le futur antérieur

EX. 13.1

1. **Regarder**
   J'**aurai regardé**
   Tu **auras regardé**
   Il **aura regardé**
   Nous **aurons regardé**
   Vous **aurez regardé**
   Ils **auront regardé**

2. **Monter**
   Je **serai monté(e)**
   Tu **seras monté(e)**
   Elle **sera montée**
   Nous **serons monté(e)s**
   Vous **serez monté(e)s**
   Elles **seront montées**

3. **Se perdre**
   Je **me serai perdu(e)**
   Tu **te seras perdu(e)**
   On **se sera perdu(e)s**
   Nous **nous serons perdu(e)s**
   Vous **vous serez perdu(e)s**
   Elles **se seront perdues**

EX. 13.2

1. Ils **auront fait** le changement.
2. Dans quelques jours, nous **serons parti(e)s**.
3. Vous **aurez bu** tout le café.
4. Je **serai resté(e)** plus longtemps que prévu.
5. Demain, elles **auront présenté** leurs dissertations.
6. L'architecte **aura fini** les plans bientôt.
7. On **aura obtenu** le permis d'ici là.
8. J'**aurai terminé** pour 18 heures.
9. Demain, il **aura reçu** ses résultats.
10. J'espère que nous **aurons déménagé** avant décembre.

*Remember to **download the audio** and to **watch the videos** – see Preface*

Solutions – Le conditionnel passé

EX. 14.1

1. **Peser**
   J'**aurais pesé**
   Tu **aurais pesé**
   Il **aurait pesé**
   Nous **aurions pesé**
   Vous **auriez pesé**
   Ils **auraient pesé**

2. **Devenir**
   Je **serais devenu(e)**
   Tu **serais devenu(e)**
   Elle **serait devenue**
   Nous **serions devenu(e)s**
   Vous **seriez devenu(e)s**
   Elles **seraient devenues**

3. **Se conduire**
   Je **me serais conduit(e)**
   Tu **te serais conduit(e)**
   On **se serait conduit(e)s**
   Nous **nous serions conduit(e)s**
   Vous **vous seriez conduit(e)s**
   Elles **se seraient conduites**

EX. 14.2

1. On **aurait passé** de bonnes vacances si on n'était pas tombés malade.
2. Si vous aviez étudié vous **auriez réussi** votre examen.
3. Elle **aurait eu** faim si elle n'avait pas mangé.
4. La société **aurait perdu** plusieurs millions.
5. Au cas où vous **auriez oublié**, nous avons rendez-vous ce soir.
6. Je ne sais pas si elle **aurait aimé** cette idée.
7. De ce que j'ai entendu, le peintre **aurait fait** un travail incroyable.
8. Ils **se seraient téléphonés** il y a quelques jours.
9. Il **aurait dû** faire plus attention.
10. Cela **aurait été** plus rapide si on était passés par là.

Solutions – Le participe passé et le gérondif

EX. 15.1

1. **Voyant**
2. **Buvant**
3. **Étudiant**
4. **Allant**
5. **Étant**
6. **Souriant**
7. **Ajoutant**
8. **Disant**
9. **Attendant**
10. **Souhaitant**
11. **Entendant**
12. **Obligeant**
13. **Achetant**
14. **Travaillant**
15. **Finissant**
16. **Neigeant**
17. **Jouant**
18. **Faisant**
19. **Brossant**
20. **Croyant**

EX. 15.2

1. Il a eu un accident **en conduisant** tard la nuit.
2. J'ai réveillé ma fille **en chantant** trop fort.
3. Il est arrivé à l'école **en courant.**
4. Mes parents se sont rencontrés **en voyageant** en Europe.
5. Pauline est sous la pluie **en attendant** le bus.
6. Il faut prendre ces médicaments **en mangeant.**
7. Il a gradué **en ayant** 2 travails.
8. Nous sommes tombés amoureux de cette ville **en** la **visitant** l'année dernière.
9. Ils se sont mariés civilement **en attendant** d'économiser pour célébrer.
10. Vous avez cherché une maison **en regardant** sur internet.

EX. 15.3

1. **En faisant** cela, tu risques de perdre des amis.
2. **En regardant** de plus près, on voit bien les défauts.
3. **En travaillant** ensemble, nous pouvons y arriver.
4. **En sachant** cela, je ne lui parlerai plus.
5. **En souriant** aux clients, les interactions se passent mieux.
6. **En changeant** la chaudière, on économise 300 euros par an.
7. **En disant** des gros mots, tu vas t'attirer des ennuis.
8. **En vendant** des affaires d'occasion, ils ont doublé leurs ventes.
9. **En marchant** une heure par jour, tu diminues ton rythme cardiaque.
10. **En réservant** maintenant, nous aurons la meilleure chambre.

*Remember to **download the audio** and to **watch the videos** – see Preface*

Solutions - La voix passive

EX. 16.1

1. La voiture **a été vendue** par Marie.
2. Le passant **a été renversé** par la voiture.
3. L'arbre **est coupé** par le bûcheron avec sa tronçonneuse.
4. L'école **est fermée** par le principal tous les soirs.
5. Un vin excellent **est produit** dans ce vignoble.
6. Ta vie **sera changée** par ce livre !
7. Le courrier **est déposé** par le facteur à la réception chaque matin.
8. Une tarte **va être** achetée par Paul chez le boulanger.
9. Un bruit **aurait été entendu** par elle pendant la nuit.
10. Ce poème **a été écrit** par un enfant.
11. L'argent **a été laissé** par maman sur la table.
12. Une leçon intéressante **est donnée** par le professeur.

Solutions - Revisions

EX. 18.1

1. Je **sais**
2. Tu **penses**
3. Elle **enregistre**
4. Vous **oubliez**
5. Nous **jetons**
6. Elle **espère**
7. Je **fais**
8. Tu **dois**
9. Ils **offrent**
10. On **dit**

EX. 18.2

1. Nous **sommes** en retard, comme d'habitude.
2. Je **vois** l'océan de ma chambre.
3. Elle **tient** la main de son amie.
4. Il faut **partir** tout de suite.
5. Comment est-ce que tu **t'appelles** ?
6. Nous **décidons** toujours tout en dernière minute.
7. Je **viens** du sud de la France.
8. J'**ai** 14 ans, bientôt 15 ans.
9. Nous **nettoyons** la cuisine tous les soirs avant de nous coucher.
10. L'ambulance **attend** les appels pour partir.

EX. 18.3

1. On **achète** du beurre au marché tous les jeudis.
2. Nous **prenons** le train pour aller à l'aéroport.
3. **Sais**-tu que le voisin est décédé ?
4. Est-ce que tu **connais** cette histoire ?
5. Je ne **bois** pas assez d'eau durant la journée.
6. Il **cède** ses parts à son fils.
7. Vous **choisissez** sans réfléchir.
8. Je **cherche** un petit sac noir en cuir végétal.
9. Regarde ta facture, tu **téléphones** beaucoup trop.
10. Est-ce que tu **veux** un café avant de partir ?

EX. 18.4

1. Nous **déménageons** de l'appartement samedi prochain.
2. Je **travaille** ici depuis décembre.
3. Nous **habitons** ici depuis 3 ans.
4. Je **bois** seulement de l'eau filtrée.
5. Tu **es** déjà au travail.
6. La voiture ne **fonctionne** toujours pas.
7. Nous nous **changeons** avant de partir pour le restaurant.
8. Est-ce que tu **regardes** la télévision chaque matin ?
9. Le chien **dort** dans l'herbe.
10. Le propriétaire **vend** la maison.

EX. 18.5

1. Il **fait** la vaisselle.
2. Elle **est dans la lune**, elle ne t'a pas entendu.
3. Le patient **a mal à** la tête.
4. Nous **allons chez** le docteur cet après-midi.
5. J'**ai chaud** avec ce gros pull !
6. Nous **sommes en train de** chercher une nouvelle table.
7. Il **a du mal à** faire ses lacets.
8. Le train **est en retard** de plusieurs minutes.
9. Je **suis de** Londres, et toi ?
10. On **a la pêche** ce matin !
11. Je **vais au** marché acheter des légumes.
12. On **fait du** vélo tous les samedis matin.
13. Il **fait chaud** aujourd'hui !

EX. 18.6

1. Il **est** 6 heures du matin.
2. C'**est** trop tôt.
3. Il y **a** du lait dans le frigo.
4. Il **vaut** mieux arriver quelques minutes plus tôt.
5. Il **fait** froid dans ma chambre.
6. Il **paraît** que tu t'es marié.

EX. 18.7

1. DOP : Elle **la** reçoit pour son travail.
2. DOP : Nous **les** promenons tous les matins à 8 heures.
3. DOP : On **les** aide à faire les courses.
4. DOP : Elle **les** connaît bien.
5. DOP : Ils **l'**adoptent.
6. DOP : Nous **le** regardons.
7. DOP : Elle ne **les** aime pas, surtout les tomates.
8. DOP : Le directeur **les** envoie au client.
9. DOP : Je **la** fais moi-même pour mon frère.
10. DOP : Est-ce que tu **la** comprends ?

EX. 18.8

1. Elle **se souvient** de toi.
2. Les employés **s'adaptent** doucement au nouveau programme.
3. Nous **nous marions** le mois prochain.
4. La coiffeuse **se coupe** les cheveux elle-même.
5. Il **s'assoit – s'assied** toujours là.
6. On **se repose** ce week-end.
7. Les enfants **s'ennuient**, il n'y a rien faire.
8. Je **me lave** et je vais au lit.
9. Je ne **me rappelle** pas de cette leçon.
10. Ils **se fâchent** facilement quand ils sont fatigués.

EX. 18.9

1. Nous nous amusons
2. Tu ne te laves pas
3. On se brosse
4. Mes voisins se réveillent
5. Je ne m'attends pas
6. Tu te trompes
7. Je m'appelle
8. Mon père se sert
9. Elle se soucie
10. Nous nous mettons

EX. 18.10

1. **Allé**
2. **Vu**
3. **Connu**
4. **Dû**
5. **Su**
6. **Mangé**
7. **Fait**
8. **Voulu**
9. **Fini**
10. **Ouvert**
11. **Sorti**
12. **Senti**
13. **Pu**
14. **Lu**
15. **Cuisiné**
16. **Cuit**
17. **Été**
18. **Nourri**
19. **Lu**
20. **Vendu**

EX. 18.11

1. Nous **sommes parti(e)s** tôt ce matin.
2. On **a eu** la grippe.
3. J'**ai bu** trop de café.
4. Tu **as fini** ta présentation ?
5. Nous **sommes allé(e)s** à la piscine hier.
6. Nous **avons mangé** dans ce restaurant.
7. Tu **as fermé** la porte ?
8. J'**ai perdu** mes clés !
9. Elles **ont lu** ta lettre.
10. Est-ce que tu **as appris** la nouvelle ?

EX. 18.12

1. J'**ai acheté** cette lotion pour ma copine.
2. Elle **a signé** cette facture pour la payer.
3. On **a rêvé** de partir au Mexique.
4. Tu **as pris** tes affaires avant de partir ?
5. Le professeur **a répondu** aux questions.
6. Il nous **a parlé** de ses vacances.
7. Le chat **a eu** une opération pour se faire nettoyer les dents.
8. Nous **avons terminé** nos devoirs avant d'aller jouer.
9. J'**ai vécu** à Lyon.
10. Elle **est sortie** de l'hôpital il y a quelques heures.

EX. 18.13

1. La table qu'**elle a mise.**
2. La nouvelle armoire que **nous avons achetée.**
3. L'ascenseur que **j'ai pris pour venir.**
4. Cette crème que **le docteur m'a conseillée.**
5. Les élèves qu'**il a félicités.**
6. La tente que **nous leur avons prêtée.**
7. Les très bons vins qu'**il a bus.**
8. Les dernières créations que **l'artiste a finies.**
9. La piqûre que **l'infirmière a faite.**
10. Les trois jours de congé que **le patron a donnés aux employés.**

EX. 18.14

1. Nous **nous sommes excusé(e)s** pour notre erreur.
2. Je **me suis abonné(e)** au nouveau magazine.
3. Il **s'est trompé** sur la question numéro 3.
4. Nous **nous sommes amusé(e)s** à cette fête.
5. La voiture **s'est arrêtée** au dernier moment.
6. Vous **vous êtes occupé(e)s** du dîner ?
7. Elle **s'est intéressée** à la poterie.
8. Nous **nous sommes endormi(e)s** vite.
9. Je **me suis mis(e)** à la méditation.
10. Elle **s'est fait** une teinture.

EX. 18.15

1. Je **suis arrivé(e)** tout de suite.
   Je **ne suis pas arrivé(e)** tout de suite.
2. On **a joué** au poker samedi.
   On **n'a jamais joué** au poker samedi.
3. Elle **est devenue** docteur.
   Elle **n'est pas devenue** docteur.
4. Cette personne **a appartenu** à un gang.
   Cette personne **n'a pas appartenu** à un gang.
5. Le pompier **a agi** sans réfléchir.
   Le pompier **n'a pas agi** sans réfléchir.
6. J'**ai conduit** les enfants à l'arrêt de bus.
   Je **n'ai pas conduit** les enfants à l'arrêt de bus.
7. Elle **a osé** prendre des risques.
   Elle **n'a jamais osé** prendre de risques.
8. Il **a essayé** de changer sa réputation.
   Il **n'a plus essayé** de changer sa réputation.
9. Le vent **a soufflé** toute la nuit.
   Le vent **n'a pas soufflé** toute la nuit.
10. Elle **a vécu** une vie complète et heureuse.
    Elle **n'a pas vécu** une vie complète et heureuse.

EX. 18.16

1. I got old – Je **vieillissais**
2. You warned (s) – Tu **prévenais**
3. We studied – Nous **étudiions**
4. She moved – Elle **déménageait**
5. They counted (m) – Elles **comptaient**
6. She put back – Elle **reposait**
7. I knew – Je **savais**
8. He asked – Il **demandait**
9. They accepted (f) – Elles **acceptaient**
10. We fired – Nous **renvoyions**
11. He found – Il **trouvait**
12. They poured – Ils **versaient**
13. We discovered – Nous **découvrions**
14. She met – Elle **rencontrait**
15. You turned (s) – Tu **tournais**

EX. 18.17

1. Elles **se réveillaient** toujours tard.
2. Tu **jouais** sans cesse à ce jeu.
3. Il **devait** être là aujourd'hui.
4. Le bruit ne **me dérangeait** pas.
5. Je **sentais** une odeur de brûlé.
6. Le contrat leur **permettait** de les utiliser.
7. Vous **corrigiez** les devoirs des élèves.
8. Il **conduisait** trop vite.
9. Elle **jetait** tout ce qui ne fonctionnait pas.
10. L'inspecteur **interrogeait** le suspect.

EX. 18.18

1. Le vendeur **attendait** pendant que les clients **prenaient** une décision.
2. Elle **habitait** à Nice, ses parents **vivaient** à Paris.
3. Parce qu'elle **prenait** le bus, elle **était** toujours en retard.
4. Il **parlait** tout le temps pendant qu'on **regardait** un film.
5. La boulangère **demandait** si on **voulait** autre chose.
6. Le mécanicien **expliquait** le problème mais elle n'**écoutait** rien.
7. Elle **perdait** 3 kilos par mois mais elle **mangeait** très équilibré.
8. Je **partais** quand il **arrivait.**
9. Elle **adorait** le pain mais **détestait** les pâtes.
10. Il **chantait** pendant qu'il **se lavait.**

EX. 18.19

1. Elle **s'est évanouie** soudainement.
2. Le soleil **se levait** à l'arrière de la cabane.
3. Je ne sais pas s'il **a payé.**
4. On **se chauffait** au bois dans le temps.
5. Elle **a insisté** pour te voir tout de suite.
6. Ma collègue **a apporté** des gâteaux pour son anniversaire.
7. L'hiver **était** toujours froid.
8. Les passagers **ont survécu** à l'accident.
9. Elle **a changé** de train.
10. Je **lisais** 10 pages par jour.

EX. 18.20

1. Nous **nous appelions** tous les dimanches.
2. Nous **nous sommes appelé(e)s** ce dimanche.
3. Ils **sont partis** ce matin.
4. Tu **as payé** trop d'argent pour cette voiture.
5. Nous **faisions** les courses en ville, maintenant c'est trop cher.
6. Elle **avait** une mémoire incroyable.
7. Qu'est-ce que tu **as fait** ?
8. Ma femme **a repassé** ma chemise avant ma réunion.
9. Les prix **ont augmenté** continuellement l'année dernière.
10. J'**ai donné** ma veste car elle **était** trop petite.

EX. 18.21

1. J'**ai lu** ce livre, j'**ai adoré** l'histoire.
2. Tu **t'es levée** tôt ce matin !
3. Chaque jour, j'**allais** acheter du pain à la boulangerie.
4. Il **regardait** la télévision quand le téléphone **a sonné.**
5. J'**ai visité** Paris en 2020.
6. Elle **a reçu** ton email il y a quelques minutes.
7. Tu **as** déjà **mangé** ?
8. Je **conduisais** quand tu **as appelé.**
9. Il **était fatigué.**
10. Mardi, Léa **est venue** chez moi.

EX. 18.22

1. Il **vient de s'endormir** dans le canapé.
2. Tu **viens de mettre** le lave-vaisselle en route.
3. Le client **vient de payer** ses courses par carte de crédit.
4. Ce film **vient de passer** à la télévision.
5. Ce building **vient d'être démoli** pour construire des nouvelles maisons.
6. Ce couple **vient d'adopter** une petite fille de 3 ans.
7. Il **vient de casser** le vase mais il ne l'a pas fait exprès.
8. L'écrivain **vient de finir** d'écrire son nouveau roman.
9. Ce café **vient d'ouvrir** aujourd'hui.
10. La police **vient de prévenir** la famille de l'accident.

EX. 18.23

1. On **venait** de survoler la ville quand l'avion **a commencé** à descendre.
2. Il **venait** de se rendre compte qu'il **a oublié** son portefeuille.
3. Tu **venais** d'éviter un accident quand tu **es arrivé** ici.
4. La chaise **venait** de casser quand il **a voulu** s'asseoir.
5. Il **venait** de finir son discours quand tu **as commencé** à douter.
6. Il **venait** d'être enterré quand tu **es arrivé.**
7. Nous **venions** de préparer le dîner quand les voisins **sont arrivés.**
8. Elle **venait** d'arriver quand l'avion **est parti.**
9. Je **venais** de me faire renvoyer quand j'**ai acheté** une maison.
10. Tu **venais** de frapper à la porte quand je t'**ai téléphoné.**

EX. 18.24

1. Tu **chargeras**
2. Il **vaudra**
3. Je **pourrai**
4. Elle **répondra**
5. On **souffrira**
6. Ils **verseront**
7. Il **peindra**
8. Nous **hésiterons**
9. Tu **auras**
10. Vous **enlèverez**
11. J'**écrirai**
12. Elle **craindra**
13. On **blanchira**
14. Nous **irons**

EX. 18.25

1. Nous **irons** au magasin en voiture.
2. On **chantera** une chanson au spectacle.
3. Il **éteindra** les lumières avant de partir.
4. Je **partirai** quand je suis prête.
5. Il **tondra** la pelouse quand il aura du temps.
6. Tu **vendras** tes affaires sur internet.
7. Je **finirai** mon devoir avant d'aller dormir.
8. Nous **payerons** notre repas à la serveuse.
9. Vous **choisirez** entre ces deux appartements.
10. Elle **deviendra** docteur après ses études.

EX. 18.26

1. Je serai à l'aéroport ce soir.
2. Il rangera sa chambre quand il revient.
3. Ils vous rappelleront.
4. Apporterez-vous quelques verres au dîner ?
5. Dès que les fleurs fleurissent, j'en cueillerai quelques-unes.
6. Nous emprunterons l'argent à la banque.
7. La maman essayera d'allaiter.
8. Je repasserai mes habits ce soir.
9. Elles traduiront le document la semaine prochaine.
10. Je verrai si je peux venir.

EX. 18.27

1. On **va partir** après le repas.
2. Je **vais me marier** quand je suis prête.
3. Elles **vont embarquer** le train avec leurs valises.
4. Tu **vas faire** la vaisselle quand tu as fini d'étudier.
5. Nous **allons remplacer** la cuisine en mai.
6. Vous **allez rassembler** vos idées pour être plus efficace.
7. On **va arriver** d'ici quelques heures.
8. L'eau **va bouillir** en quelques minutes.
9. Tu **vas arrêter** de fumer dans quelques semaines.
10. On **va s'occuper** du jardin ce week-end.

EX. 18.28

1. Qu'est-ce que tu **feras** demain soir ?
2. Nous **mangerons** au restaurant.
3. Tu **mangeras** des pâtes ce soir.
4. Il **lira** un livre dans le canapé.
5. Je **parlerai** aux enfants à propos du problème.
6. L'avion **atterrira** à 17 heures.
7. Il **faudra** aller remplir ce document à la mairie.
8. Nous **irons** voir Luc dans quelques jours.
9. Tu **te rendras** malade si tu manges trop.
10. Ils **feront** leurs devoirs pour demain.

EX. 18.29

1. Tu **prendrais**
2. Il **ferait**
3. Nous **aurions**
4. Ils **sauraient**
5. On **tiendrait**
6. Elle **finirait**
7. Vous **boiriez**
8. Je **lancerais**
9. Elle **nettoierait**
10. Tu **dormirais**

EX. 18.30

1. Je **prendrais** bien un café.
2. Tu **pourrais** arriver plus tôt.
3. Elle **aimerait** avoir plus d'argent.
4. Nous **mangerions** plus de légumes si on avait plus d'argent.
5. Il **viendrait** si tu l'invitais.
6. SI j'**avais** du temps, je cuisinerais plus souvent.
7. Vous **iriez** faire les magasins si c'était ouvert.
8. Je pensais que tu n'**irais** pas.
9. Nous **aimerions** venir.
10. Tu **adopterais** un chien si tu pouvais ?

EX. 18.31

1. Je serais là si j'avais le temps.
2. S'il avait soif, il boirait de l'eau.
3. Si nous avions de l'argent, nous achèterions une maison à mes parents.
4. Vous iriez à la plage si le temps était meilleur.
5. Nous serions ravi(e)s si vous acceptiez.
6. J'aimerais savoir si ça fonctionne pour vous.
7. Qu'est-ce que je ferais sans toi !
8. Si vous étudiiez plus, tu aurais des meilleures notes.
9. Ce serait meilleur si tu ajoutais un peu de sel.
10. Si nous avions plus de place, nous peindrions plus souvent.

EX. 18.32

Aller	**Avoir**	**Chercher**	**Finir**
Va	Aie	Cherche	Finis
Allons	Ayons	Cherchons	Finissons
Allez	Ayez	Cherchez	Finissez

EX. 18.33

1. Achète les vêtements.
2. Réponds au téléphone.
3. Finis ton assiette.
4. Pars maintenant.
5. Vas-y.
6. Demande au caissier.
7. Évite cette route.
8. Sois toi-même.
9. Paie la facture.
10. Enregistre ton document.

EX. 18.34

1. **Prenons** le train.
2. **Mange** ces bananes.
3. **Accrochez** la remorque à la voiture.
4. **Prévenons** les voisins de la fuite d'eau.
5. **Attrape** la corde.
6. **Écoutons** le sermon du pasteur.
7. **Traversez** la route prudemment.
8. **Suivons** les flèches de la randonnée.
9. **Dépose** les papiers dans le coffre.
10. **Ajoutons** cet exercice à l'examen.

EX. 18.35

1. Prenons-**le**.
2. Mange-**les**.
3. Accrochez-**la** à la voiture.
4. Prévenons-**les** de la fuite d'eau.
5. Attrape-**la**.
6. Écoutons-**le**.
7. Traversez-**la** prudemment.
8. Suivons-**les**.
9. Dépose-**les** dans le coffre.
10. Ajoutons-**le** à l'examen.

EX. 18.36

1. Je pense partir.
2. Il a perdu du temps à attendre sa femme.
3. Tu avais besoin de partir pour te détendre.
4. Il revoit avant de passer son test.
5. Elle fait toujours confiance à tout le monde sans les connaître.
6. Nous nous faisons toujours payer le premier du mois.
7. Ils étaient sur le point de te téléphoner.
8. Je suis triste de partir mais je reviendrai.
9. C'est bien de boire de l'eau durant la journée.
10. C'est difficile à dire.

EX. 18.37

1. Nous sommes heureux **de** t'aider.
2. Es-tu libre **de** venir ce week-end ?
3. Je me suis fait faire / les ongles.
4. Nous économisons au lieu **de** dépenser de l'argent.
5. Ils passent beaucoup de temps **à** se connaître.
6. Il faut faire attention / .
7. Pouvez-vous demander au jardinier **de** tailler les buissons ?
8. J'ai du travail **à** finir.
9. Nous adorons / faire du sport ensemble.
10. Les employés sont censés / revenir en septembre.

11. Tu sembles / oublier que tu me dois de l'argent.
12. Les habitants commencent **à** comprendre ce qu'il se passe.
13. Nous nous préparons **à** partir tôt demain matin.
14. J'ai décidé **de** commencer **à** étudier le français.
15. Tu risques **d'**être en retard.

EX. 18.38

1. Nous **avons** de quoi manger.
2. J'**arrivais** à finir ce puzzle.
3. Va **jouer** avec tes amis.
4. Il **a** besoin d'aide pour finir la toiture.
5. Nous **devrions** arriver ce soir.
6. Elle **essaye – essaie** de se reposer.
7. **Souviens-toi** de payer ta facture.
8. Mon responsable m'**a dit** de vérifier les numéros.
9. C'**est** bien de lui pardonner.
10. Le chien **risque** de te mordre.

EX. 18.39

1. Il **se fait** attendre.
2. Elle **se fait** mettre à la porte car elle ne paie pas.
3. Cet homme **se fait** opérer d'urgence.
4. Nous **faisons** laver la voiture avant de partir en vacances.
5. Le piéton **se fait** renverser par une voiture.
6. **Faites** entrer les participants.
7. Tu **te fais** toujours renvoyer !
8. Il faut **faire** savoir aux clients de ne pas boire l'eau.
9. Nous **nous sommes fait** avoir !
10. Les élèves aiment en **faire** voir de toutes les couleurs.

EX. 18.40

1. Il **est** toujours **anxieux** de prendre l'avion.
2. Est-ce que tu **es obligé(e)** de partir ?
3. Nous **sommes heureux** d'annoncer la naissance de notre fille.
4. Il **est triste** de ne pas te voir.
5. Est-ce que vous **êtes sûr(e)s** de vouloir partir ?
6. Elle **est fière** d'être grande sœur.
7. Ma grand-mère **est fatiguée** de travailler.
8. Nous **sommes surpris** de ce résultat.
9. Tu **es libre** de partir si tu veux.
10. Elle **est désolée** de ne pas être présente pour toi.

EX. 18.41

1. **Choisir**
   Que je **choisisse**
   Que tu **choisisses**
   Qu'on **choisisse**
   Que nous **choisissions**
   Que vous **choisissiez**
   Qu'elles **choisissent**

2. **Vouloir**
   Que je **veuille**
   Que tu **veuilles**
   Qu'il **veuille**
   Que nous **voulions**
   Que vous **vouliez**
   Qu'ils **veuillent**

3. **Être**
   Que je **sois**
   Que tu **sois**
   Qu'on **soit**
   Que nous **soyons**
   Que vous **soyez**
   Qu'elles **soient**

EX. 18.42 Personnel

EX. 18.43

1. Il faut que je **parte**.
2. Il faut que je **gagne** ce concours.
3. Il faut que je **voie** mes parents au plus vite.
4. Il faut que je **sache** la vérité.
5. Il faut que j'**apprenne** le ukulélé.
6. Il faut que je **croie** en moi
7. Il faut que je **nettoie** le garage.
8. Il faut que je **promène** le chien.
9. Il faut que je **prenne** du temps pour moi.
10. Il faut que je **finisse** ce dessin.

EX. 18.44

1. J'**étais allée** au magasin ce matin.
2. Nous **avions reçu** notre lettre d'expulsion.
3. L'assistant **avait reçu** les patients.
4. Elle **avait fini** le livre difficilement.
5. Tu **avais fini** ce livre ?
6. Le chien **avait attendu** son maître toute la journée.
7. Le menuisier **avait réparé** la cuisine.
8. J'**avais arrosé** les plantes.
9. Elle **était venue** pour accueillir les invités.
10. Nous **étions partis** un peu après minuit.

EX. 18.45

1. Ils **auront acheté** leurs alliances à ce moment-là.
2. Nous **serons parti(e)s** avant le lever du soleil.
3. Vous **aurez eu** assez de temps pour vous préparer.
4. Il **se sera pesé** avant le rendez-vous.
5. Nous **serons allé(e)s** dans 25 pays différents.
6. Le technicien **aura réparé** la fuite ce soir.
7. Elle **se sera préparée** pour la danse.
8. L'Allemagne **aura recyclé** 18 tonnes de plastique d'ici là.
9. La sirène **aura signalé** le danger.
10. Nous **aurons déjeuné** quand tu arriveras.

EX. 18.46

1. On **se serait blessé(e)s** si on n'avait pas fait attention.
2. Si vous aviez donné plus de votre temps, vous **auriez eu** moins de temps pour penser.
3. Ton chien **aurait obéi** si tu avais pris le temps de le dresser.
4. On **aurait pu** gagner à la loterie !
5. Nous **nous serions arrêté(e)s** si nous étions parties plus tôt.
6. J'**aurais lu** ce livre s'il avait été disponible en anglais.
7. Il **aurait payé** la facture si le travail avait été bien fait.
8. Ils **auraient remplacé** la pièce s'ils l'avaient reçue.
9. La voiture **aurait ralenti** si le panneau avait été visible.
10. Cela m'**aurait servi** si je n'avais pas vendu la voiture.

EX. 18.47

1. Ferme la porte **en partant**.
2. Tu n'arriveras à rien **en doutant** de toi-même.
3. Peut-être que tu le trouveras **en cherchant** sous ton lit.
4. Va au magasin **en revenant** de l'école.
5. Je me suis fait mal au dos **en bougeant** le canapé.
6. Tu peux vraiment faire du mal **en** te **moquant** de tes camarades.
7. Prends cette boîte **en montant**.
8. Mon mari regarde la télévision **en repassant** le linge.
9. Tu peux fermer l'arrivée d'eau **en tournant** le robinet.
10. Nous réussirions mieux **en utilisant** un dictionnaire.

EX. 18.48

1. Un refuge **a été trouvé** par les soldats dans ce village.
2. Les passagers **ont été sauvés** par l'airbag.
3. Presque tous les clients **sont persuadés** par cette présentation.
4. Marcher sur le gazon **est interdit**.
5. Cette histoire doit **être incluse** dans le livre.
6. Les fonds **ont été détournés** par cette employée.
7. Cet hôtel **a été choisi** par ce couple.
8. Le courrier **est apporté** par le facteur.
9. Les repas **sont préparés** par les cuisiniers pendant la nuit.
10. La robe **est rallongée** par la couturière.

EX. 18.49

1. Nous sommes allé(e)s au magasin mais il n'y avait plus de lait.
2. J'aimerais rester plus longtemps en ville.
3. Est-ce que je peux te demander quelque chose ?
4. Laisse-moi prendre ton sac pour toi.
5. Ils vont vous montrer votre nouvelle maison.
6. Ils viennent juste de partir.
7. Cet auteur a reçu un prix pour son dernier livre.
8. Elle souffrait de maux de tête quand elle était adolescente.
9. Est-ce que je devrais quitter mon travail ?
10. Ne traverse pas la rue sans regarder des deux côtés.
11. J'étudie tous les jours pendant au moins 5 heures.
12. Elle ne nous a pas aidé du tout.
13. Ils ne sont pas partis à temps ce matin.
14. Mes camarades de classe se moquent de moi.
15. Ce film était tellement ennuyant, je me suis endormi(e) !
16. On se lèvera à 6 heures demain matin.
17. Je pensais que tu étais la sœur de Paul.
18. Nous serons là pour vous quand vous aurez besoin de nous.
19. Est-ce que tu as trouvé ton portefeuille ?
20. Je ne sais pas comment utiliser cette machine.

Made in United States
Orlando, FL
14 October 2024

52636871R00243

DEPARTMENT FOR TRANSPORT

SCOTTISH EXECUTIVE AND WELSH ASSEMBLY

Transport Statistics Great Britain

2005

31st EDITION

October 2005

London: TSO

Department for Transport
Great Minster House,
76 Marsham Street
London SW1P 4DR
Telephone 020 7944 8300
Internet service http://www.dft.gov.uk/

ISBN: 0-11-552701X

Printed in Great Britain on material containing 75% post-consumer waste, and 25% ECF pulp.
October 2005

A National Statistics publication produced by Transport Statistics: DfT
National Statistics are produced to high professional standards set out in the National Statistics Code of Practice. They undergo regular quality assurance reviews to ensure that they meet customer needs.
The National Statistician maintains professional responsibility for all outputs comprising National Statistics. A Statistics Commission, independent of both Government and the producers of official statistics, publicly provides independent comment and advice on the National Statistics programme.
Contact Points: For general enquiries call the National Statistics Customer Enquiry Centre at: Room D115, ONS, Government Buildings, Cardiff Road, Newport, Gwent, NP10 8XG. ☎ +044 (0) 845 601 3034, fax +44 (0) 1633 652747 or E-mail: info@statistics.gov.uk

You can also obtain National Statistics through the internet – go to www.statistics.gov.uk. For information relating to Transport Statistics go to www.dft.gov.uk/transtat

Prepared for publication by;

Tajbar Gul
Shawn Weekes
Ahad Sayed
Jacqui Scully
Colin Brailsford

DfT is often prepared to sell unpublished data. Further information and queries concerning this publication should be directed to:
Transport Statistics, 2/17, Great Minster House, 76 Marsham Street, London SW1P 4DR
☎ 020 7944 3098, Fax 020 7944 2165, E-mail: publicationgeneral.enq@dft.gov.uk

Cover photographs courtesy of Highways Agency and Alamy Images

Contents

	Page
Transport Statistics Contacts	**2**
Introduction	**3**
Symbols and conventions	**4**
List of tables and charts	**5**
Section 1 - Modal comparisons	**9**
Notes and Definitions	
Tables	
Section 2 - Aviation	**29**
Notes and Definitions	
Tables	
Section 3 - Energy and the environment	**45**
Notes and Definitions	
Tables	
Section 4 - Freight	**59**
Notes and Definitions	
Tables	
Section 5 - Maritime	**73**
Notes and Definitions	
Tables	
Section 6 - Public transport	**99**
Notes and Definitions	
Tables	
Section 7 - Roads and traffic	**115**
Notes and Definitions	
Tables	
Section 8 - Transport accidents and casualties	**137**
Notes and Definitions	
Tables	
Section 9 - Vehicles	**151**
Notes and Definitions	
Tables	
Section 10 - International comparisons	**169**
Notes and Definitions	
Tables	
List of Abbreviations	**183**
Index	**185**
Transport Statistics Liaison Group	**192**
Transport Statistics Users Group	**Inside Back Cover**

Transport Statistics Contacts

Travel

Barbara Noble
Chief Statistician
☎020-7944 3079

Statisticians

Kerrick Macafee
Bus & coach statistics: supply & demand, income & subsidies, fares, operating costs; bus stock; taxi statistics; assaults on public road transport users & staff; channel tunnel statistics.

☎020-7944 4589
E-mail: bus.statistics@dft.gov.uk

Olivia Christophersen
National Travel Survey: employment; census data.

☎020-7944 6594
E-mail: national.travelsurvey@dft.gov.uk

Stephen Reynolds
Sub-national data.

☎020-7944 4746
E-mail: subnational.stats@dft.gov.uk

Tracey Budd
Statistical advisor & research co-ordinator for TSA; Public attitudes towards transport environmental issues.

☎020-7944 4892
E-mail: attitudes.stats@dft.gov.uk

Fax: 020-7944-2166

Logistics, Aviation, Maritime

Antonia Roberts
Chief Statistician
(Head of Profession)
☎020-7944 4280

Statisticians

Paul Swallow
National Statistics; GIS

☎020-7944 4411

Alan Brown
Maritime statistics; Flag analysis of UK seaborne trade, merchant fleet statistics; sea passenger statistics; port traffic, finance and manpower statistics; coastwise & inland waterways freight statistics.

☎020-7944 4441
E-mail: maritime.stats@dft.gov.uk

Eric Crane
Aviation & airport statistics; international passenger survey; transport indictors; energy and the environment.

☎020-7944 4276
E-mail: aviation.stats@dft.gov.uk

Dorothy Salathiel
Transport statistics for EC & other international bodies; international comparisons, survey control.

☎020-7944 4442
E-mail: inter.transport.comparisons@dft.gov.uk

Chris Overson
Road freight statistics; continuing survey of road goods transport; ad hoc surveys of vehicle transport data collection and processing unit;
Survey of international road haulage.

☎020-7944 3093
E-mail: roadfreight.stats@dft.gov.uk

Colin Brailsford
Transport statistics publications and website management; Local ICT management.

☎020-7944 4748
E-mail: publicationgeneral.enq@dft.gov.uk

Fax: 020-7944-2165

Roads & Traffic

Alan Oliver
Chief Statistician
☎020-7944 4270

Statisticians

Andy Lees
Road traffic statistics; national core census. Liaison with Highways Agency. Review of core census. Computing development. London core traffic census; weigh-in-motion.

☎020-7944 6573
Email: roadtraff.autocou@dft.gov.uk

John Garnsworthy
Road traffic statistics - Annual and quarterly traffic estimates; manual traffic counts and road lengths surveys.

☎020-7944 6396
E-mail: roadtraff.stats@dft.gov.uk

Drew Hird
Highway maintenance statistics; national road maintenance condition survey; investment; highway expenditure.

☎020-7944 6398
E-mail: roadmaintenance.stats@dft.gov.uk

Mouna Kehil
Vehicle stock & new registrations; statistical advice to DVLA; VED evasion studies; vehicle stock and new registrations; road track costs; environmental statistics; congestion monitoring and speed surveys.

☎020-7944 6399
E-mail: vehicles.stats@dft.gov.uk

Val Davies
Road accidents; vehicle speeds; car safety; inter modal passenger safety; international co-ordination.

☎020-7944 3078
E-mail: roadacc.stats@dft.gov.uk

Fax: 020-7944-2164

Internet address:
http://www.dft.gov.uk/transtat

Introduction

Welcome to the 31st edition of *Transport Statistics Great Britain.*

Transport Statistics Great Britain (TSGB) is a major publication within the scope of National Statistics and provides an accurate, comprehensive and meaningful picture of transport patronage in Great Britain.

All individual tables that make up TSGB are on the web-site in both PDF and EXCEL format, enabling users to manipulate the information to produce further tables or charts. The whole document is available as a PDF file (chapter by chapter) in a separate theme dedicated to TSGB (http://www.dft.gov.uk/transtat/tsgb).

The web-site also contains a great deal of other published statistical material, including (in PDF format) all of the recent bulletins produced by Transport Statistics. It also includes a list of forthcoming publications, their publication dates and a number of links to other useful (transport related) web-sites. In many cases, the bulletins produced during the course of the year provide the first release of data and these are subsequently consolidated into the TSGB tables.

I hope you find this publication useful and interesting. Any comments you may have on the contents and presentation would be welcome. Please send these to the address below or E-mail to publicationgeneral.enq@dft.gov.uk

Colin Brailsford
Transport Statistics, 2/17
Great Minster House
76 Marsham Street
London, SW1P 4DR

Symbols and conventions

On 3 July 2000, Transport for London (TfL) was formed with a role of supporting the London Mayor in providing an overview of transport in London. TfL is responsible for the London Transport Studies (LTS) model and for studies to assess London transport policies.

Following the General Election on 7 June 2001, changes have been made to the responsibilities of a number of government departments. The former DETR became The Department for Transport, Local Government and the Regions (DTLR), with the The Environmental Protection Group, The Drinking Water Inspectorate and The Wildlife and Countryside Division of the former DETR becoming part of the newly formed Department of Environment, Food and Rural Affairs (DEFRA). References to data produced since the recent change will be credited to DTLR. All references to data prior to that date are credited to the former DETR.

In June 2002 ministerial resignations led directly to further changes in the structure and responsibility of the former DTLR. The Department for Transport (DfT) has been created and Transport Statistics is now part of this Department. Tables and data produced following June 2002 will be credited to DfT.

Unless otherwise stated, all tables refer to **Great Britain**.

Metric units are generally used.

Conversion factors:

1 kilometre	= 0.6214 mile
1 tonne	= 0.9842 ton
1 tonne-km	= 0.6116 ton-mile
1 billion	= 1,000 million
1 Gallon	= 4.546 litres
1 litre	= 0.220 gallons

Rounding of figures. In tables where figures have been rounded to the nearest final digit, there may be an apparent slight discrepancy between the sum of the constituent items and the total as shown.

Symbols. The symbols to the right have been used throughout.

..	= not available
.	= not applicable
-	= Negligible (less than half the final digit shown)
0	= Nil
*	= Sample size too small for reliable estimates.
ow	= of which
{	= subsequent data is disaggregated
}	= subsequent data is aggregated
|	= break in the series
P	= provisional data
F	= forecast expenditure
e	= estimated outturn
n.e.s.	= not elsewhere specified
R	= Revised data

All statistics in this publication are National Statistics unless indicated otherwise on each table.

List of tables and charts

Note: *Page numbers are given in italics after the table number.*

Section 1 - Modal comparisons

Passenger transport

1.1 *13* Passenger transport: by mode
1.2 *14* Passenger journeys on public transport vehicles
1.3 *15* Average distance travelled per person per year by mode of travel
1.4 *15* Trips per person per year by main mode and purpose
1.5 *16* Trip distance per person per year by main mode and purpose
1.6 *16* People entering central London during the morning peak
1.7 *17* Passenger casualty rates by mode
1.8 *18* Main mode of transport to work by Government Office Region of workplace and mean time taken
1.9 *19* Time taken to travel to work by Government Office Region of workplace

Overseas passenger travel

1.10 *20* Overseas travel: visits to and from the United Kingdom
1.11 *20* Overseas travel by air: visits to and from the United Kingdom: by area and purpose
1.12 *21* Overseas travel by sea: visits to and from the United Kingdom by area, purpose and type of vehicle on board

Expenditure on transport

1.13 *22* Household expenditure on transport: United Kingdom
1.14 *23* Investment in transport
1.15 *24* Central and local government expenditure on transport

Employment in transport

1.16 *26* People in employment in transport related occupations
1.17 *26* Employee jobs in transport and related industries
1.18 *27* Employee jobs in transport and related industries by sex and employment status

Financial information

1.19 27 Retail Price Index: transport components:
1.20 *28* Gross domestic product and Retail Prices Index deflators

Section 2 - Aviation

2.1 *32* Activity at civil aerodromes: United Kingdom:
2.2 *33* Traffic at United Kingdom airports: by type of service and operator
2.3 *35* Punctuality at United Kingdom airports: percentage of flights on time (within 15 minutes)
2.4 *36* Main outputs of United Kingdom airlines: by type of service
2.5 *37* Forecasts of Air traffic demand
2.6 *38* United Kingdom airline fleet
2.7 *39* Activity at major airports
2.8 *40* United Kingdom international passenger movements by air: arrivals plus departures: by country of embarkation or landing
2.9 *42* Casualties caused by aviation accidents:
2.10 *42* Aircraft proximity (Airprox): number of incidents
2.11 *43* Employment by United Kingdom airlines worldwide
2.12 *43* Passenger traffic via major international airlines
2.13 *44* Major Airports in Great Britain (map)

Section 3 - Energy and the environment

Consumption and prices

3.1 *50* Petroleum consumption: by transport mode and fuel type: United Kingdom
3.2 *50* Energy consumption: by transport mode and source of energy: United Kingdom
3.3 *51* Petrol and diesel prices and duties per litre
3.4 *52* Average fuel consumption of cars: by age of car and type of fuel
3.5 *52* Average new car fuel consumption: (chart)

Emissions

3.6 *53* Emissions for road vehicles in urban conditions
3.7 *53* Forecast of United Kingdom Carbon Dioxide emissions
3.8 *54* Carbon dioxide emissions in the United Kingdom
3.9 *55* Pollutant emissions from transport and other end users in the United Kingdom

Aircraft noise

3.10 *57* Aircraft noise: population affected by noise around airports

Section 4 - Freight

4.1 *62* Domestic freight transport: by mode
4.2 *63* Domestic freight moved by commodity
4.3 *64* Domestic freight transport by mode

Freight transported by road

4.4 *65* Freight transport by road: goods moved by goods vehicles over 3.5 tonnes
4.5 *66* Freight transport by road: goods lifted by goods vehicles over 3.5 tonnes
4.6 *67* Freight transport by road: length of haul by goods vehicles over 3.5 tonnes

International road haulage

4.7 *68* International road haulage by United Kingdom registered powered vehicles over 3.5 tonnes gross vehicle weight: goods carried: by country of loading or unloading
4.8 *69* International road haulage by United Kingdom registered powered vehicles over 3.5 tonnes gross weight: by type of transport and commodity
4.9 *70* Bilateral traffic between the United Kingdom and

European Union countries in vehicles registered in the United Kingdom and the corresponding European Union country
4.10 *70* National railways: freight
Roll-on/Roll-off ferry traffic
4.11 *71* Roll-on/roll-off ferry and Channel Tunnel traffic: road goods vehicles outward to mainland Europe: by country of registration
4.12 *72* Roll-on/roll-off ferry and Channel Tunnel traffic: road goods vehicles outward to mainland Europe

Section 5 - Maritime

Ports
5.1 *77* All ports of Great Britain, foreign, coastwise and one-port traffic
5.2 *78* UK ports: foreign, coastwise and one-port traffic
5.3 *80* UK ports: foreign and domestic traffic by port group
5.4 *82* UK ports: foreign and domestic unitised traffic
5.5. *83* UK ports: foreign and domestic main freight units by port group
Accompanied passenger vehicles
5.6 *85* UK ports: accompanied passenger vehicles Foreign and coastwise routes
5.7 *86* UK ports: accompanied passenger vehicles by port - Foreign and coastwise routes
Domestic waterborne freight transport
5.8 *87* Waterborne transport within the United Kingdom
5.9 *88* United Kingdom principal ports and port groups, rivers and other inland waterway routes used for freight (map)
5.10 *89* Traffic on major rivers and other inland waterway routes

Sea passengers
5.11 90 United Kingdom international sea passenger movements: by country of embarkation or landing
5.12 *91* United Kingdom international sea passenger movements: by seaport group
Shipping
5.13 *92* United Kingdom and Crown Dependency registered trading vessels of 500 gross tons and over: summary of tonnage by type
5.14 *93* Shipping: United Kingdom and Crown Dependency registered trading vessels of 500 gross tons and over: summary of tonnage by type of vessel
5.15 *94* Shipping: United Kingdom owned trading vessels of 500 gross tons and over: summary of tonnage: by type of vessel
5.16 *95* United Kingdom shipping industry: international revenue and expenditure
Safety at sea
5.17 *96* Marine accident casualties
5.18 *97* HM coastguard statistics: search and rescue operations

Section 6 - Public Transport

National rail
6.1 *104* Rail: length of national rail route, and passenger travel by national rail and London Underground
6.2 *106* Railway systems summary
6.3 *108* National railways: receipts
6.4 *108* Passenger kilometres on national railways
6.5 *108* National railways: route & stations open for traffic at end of year
6.6 *109* National railways: passenger charter punctuality and reliability
6.7 *109* London Underground
6.8 *110* Channel Tunnel: traffic to and from Europe
6.9 *110* Bus and coach services: vehicle kilometres
6.10 *111* Bus and coach services: vehicle stock
6.11 *111* Bus and coach services: passenger receipts (Including concessionary fare reimbursement)
6.12 *111* Bus and coach services: staff employed
6.13 *112* Local bus services: passenger journeys by area
6.14 *112* Local bus services: Local authority support by area
6.15 *113* Local bus services: fare indices by area
6.16 *113* Local bus services: operating costs per vehicle kilometre 6.17
6.17 *114* Taxis: vehicles, drivers and fares: England and Wales

Section 7 - Roads and traffic

Road traffic
7.1 *121* Road traffic by type of vehicle
7.2 *122* Road traffic: by type of vehicle
7.3 *122* Motor vehicle traffic: by road class
7.4 *123* Road traffic: by type of vehicle and class of road
7.5 *123* Forecasts of road traffic in England & vehicles in GB (illustrating the impact of *The Ten Year Plan*): 2010
Road lengths
7.6 *124* Road lengths: Great Britain
Motorway network
7.7 *125* Motorway and Trunk road network of England, Scotland and Wales (map)
Road network
7.8 *126* Public road length: by road type
7.9 *127* Public road length: by class of road and country
Traffic speeds
7.10 *128* Vehicle speeds on non-urban roads by road type and vehicle type
7.11 *129* Vehicle speeds on urban roads by speed limit and vehicle type
7.12 *130* Average traffic speeds in London

Expenditure on roads
7.13 *131* Regional expenditure on roads
7.14 *131* Road construction tender price index
7.15 *132* Road taxation revenue classified by

vehicle taxation group
7.16 *132* New road construction & improvement: motorway and trunk roads: England
7.17 *133* Defects index of road condition: England and Wales (chart)
7.18 *134* Percentage contribution of defects to defect index: England and Wales (chart)
7.19 *135* Footways condition: England and Wales (chart)
7.20 *136* Percentage of verge area and kerb lengths affected by deterioration: England and Wales (chart)

Section 8 - Transport accidents and casualties

Road Accidents

8.1 *140* Road accidents and casualties
8.2 *141* Road accident casualties by road user type and severity
8.3 *142* Road accidents and accident rates: by road class and severity
8.4 *143* Casualties by hour of day (chart) weekdays and weekends
8.5 *144* Road accidents: breath tests performed on car drivers and motorcycle riders involved in injury accidents: Great Britain

Motor vehicle offences

8.6 *144* Motor vehicle offences: drinking and driving: summary of breath tests and blood or urine tests: England and Wales
8.7 *145* Motor vehicle offences: findings of guilt at all courts, fixed penalty notices and written warnings: by type of offence: England and Wales
8.8 *146* Collation of motor insurance figures

Railway accidents

8.9 *147* Railway accidents: casualties: by type of accident
8.10 *148* Railway movement accidents: passenger casualties and casualty rates
8.11 *149* Railway accidents: train accidents

Section 9 - Vehicles

9.1 *156* Motor vehicles currently licensed
9.2 *157* Motor vehicles registered for the first time
9.3 *158* Motor vehicles currently licensed at end of year: by type of vehicle
9.4 *158* Motor vehicles currently licensed by method of propulsion
9.5 *159* Body type cars currently licensed: by Government Office Region

Goods vehicles

9.6 *159* Goods vehicles over 3.5 tonnes currently licensed
9.7 *160* Goods vehicles over 3.5 tonnes currently licensed at end of year
9.8 *160* Goods vehicles over 3.5 tonnes gross weight: by axle configuration
9.9 *161* Trailer tests by axle type

Vehicle safety

9.10 *161* Road vehicle testing scheme (MOT): test results
9.11 *162* Road passenger service vehicle testing scheme (MOT)
9.12 *162* Goods vehicles over 3.5 tonnes testing scheme (MOT)
9.13 *163* Road vehicle testing scheme (MOT): percentage of vehicles failing: by type of defect:

Private motoring

9.14 *164* Households with regular use of car(s)
9.15 *165* Private motoring: households with regular use of cars
9.16 *166* Private motoring: full car driving licence holders
9.17 *166* Annual mileage of cars by type of car and trip purpose
9.18 *167* Private motoring: driving tests

Section 10 - International comparisons

10.1 *171* General statistics
10.2 *172* Road and rail infrastructure
10.3 *173* Road vehicles by type: at end of year:
10.4 *174* Road traffic on national territory
10.5 *175* Freight moved by mode on national territory
10.6 *176* Passenger transport by national vehicles on national territory
10.7 *177* Road deaths: OECD 30 day standard
10.8 *178* Petrol and diesel in the European Community: current retail prices
10.9 *180* Principal trading fleets by type of vessel and flag at mid-year
10.10 *181* Selected outputs of airlines
10.11 *181* Carbon dioxide emissions from transport by sources

Transport Statistics Great Britain has been complied by staff at DfT with contributions from the Scottish Executive, the Welsh Assembly and other Government Departments. Thanks go to those individuals and businesses who provided data for analysis in the tables.

Transport Statistics are able to provide considerably more statistics than those included in this annual compendium. Many of these are published separately in more specialised publications – these are listed on the inside front cover, (as well as being available via the DfT Internet site at: www.dft.gov.uk/transtat. A great number of unpublished material is available on request, as is a service (subject to availability of resources) providing customised analyses for clients. Potential customers should note that we do charge for these services and there are strict guidelines for maintaining confidentiality. Information can be supplied in paper, CD-ROM, diskette or via e-mail. Contact points for further details are shown at the bottom of each table.

1 Modal Comparisons:

Notes and Definitions

Passenger transport: 1.1

Buses and coaches: Passenger kilometres are derived from other survey data such as receipts, vehicle kilometres and patronage. Changes are estimated by deflating passenger receipts by the most appropriate price indices available. Because this proxy method has to be used, the series gives only a broad guide to trends.

Cars, vans, taxis, motor cycles and pedal cycles: Estimates for cars (which include taxis), motorcycles (which include mopeds and scooters), and pedal cycles are derived from the traffic series (vehicle kilometres) shown in Table 7.2 and average occupancy rates (persons per vehicle) from the National Travel Survey (NTS).

Minor revisions have been made to the 2002 to 2003 road traffic estimates (car/van/taxi, motorcycle, and pedal cycle) and vehicle occupancy rates (car/van/taxi) used in this table. None of them affect the underlying rate of growth (see the *Special Note* in Notes and Definitions to Part 7: Table 7.1). Because of changes in methodology figures for 1993 have been shown calculated on the new and the old basis.

A more consistent method has been introduced to estimate car occupancy figures from the National Travel Survey (NTS). Figures for cars, vans and taxis were revised back to 1993 in the previous edition of *Transport Statistics Great Britain*, and are a few per cent higher than previously. In 2004, the occupancy rates were 1.65 for cars and taxis and 1.08 for motorcycles. Estimates for personal use of light vans are derived from the NTS.

Rail: Rail figures include National Rail, London Underground, Glasgow Underground, public metro and light rail systems (see Table 6.2 for further details).

Air: The figures are revenue passenger kilometres on scheduled and non-scheduled services. They exclude air taxi services, private flying and passengers paying less than 25 per cent of the full fare on scheduled and non-scheduled services.

All modes: Figures exclude travel by water within the United Kingdom (including the Channel Islands), estimated at 0.7 billion passenger kilometres in 2000.

Passenger journeys on public transport: 1.2

The data in this table is derived from – Bus: Returns from operators to DfT; Rail: Strategic Rail Authority; London Underground: Transport for London; light rail and trams: operators; Air: Civil Aviation Authority.

Personal travel: 1.3, 1.4 and 1.5

These tables present some basic information from the National Travel Survey (NTS). The NTS records personal travel by residents of Great Britain along the public highway in Great Britain. It records the number of trips (a one-way course of travel for a single main purpose) and the distance travelled. All modes of transport are covered, including walking more than 50 yards.

In Tables 1.4 and 1.5, escort trips are those where the traveller has no purpose of his/her own, other than to escort or accompany another person, e.g. take a child to school.

In 2002, the drawn sample size for the NTS was nearly trebled compared with previous years, enabling key results to be presented on a single year basis for the first time since the survey became continuous. Changes to the methodology in 2002 mean that there are some inconsistencies with data for earlier years.

People entering Central London during the morning peak: 1.6

The area defined as Central London approximates to that defined as the Greater London Conurbation Centre in the Population Censuses. It is bounded by South Kensington and Paddington in the West, Marylebone Road/Euston Road in the North, Shoreditch and Aldgate in the East, Elephant and Castle and Vauxhall in the South, and includes all the main railway termini.

The survey is a count of the number of vehicle occupants (other than goods vehicles) on each road crossing the Central London cordon. The cordon is situated outside the Inner Ring Road and encloses a slightly larger area than the Central London Congestion Charging Zone. Counts are conducted for one day at each of the survey points during October/November.

Results for London Underground are derived from exit counts of people leaving the Underground stations within the Central area. Since 1996, these have been taken from automatic ticket gate data. Rail passengers are counted by observers at their last station stop before the Central London cordon. InterCity passengers are counted on arrival at Central London rail termini. Figures for Underground exclude people transferring from surface rail.

Casualty rates: 1.7

There have been a number of small revisions to this table but these have had little affect on the comparisons of the different modes.

The air passenger casualty rates for 1999 have been revised following notification from the Civil Aviation Authority of a downward revision to the air casualties in that year.

For rail, changes in reporting regulations mean that serious and minor injuries are no longer collected; only casualties taken from the scene of the accident to hospital are included in these figures.

The killed or seriously injured casualty rate for water transport has been revised for 2001 and 2002.

Casualty rates for motor vehicle users and pedestrians have been revised from 1993 to take account of revisions to road traffic data and mid year population estimates.

Passenger casualty rates given in the table can be interpreted as the risk a traveller runs of being injured, per billion kilometres travelled. The coverage varies for each mode of travel and the definitions of injuries and accidents are different. Thus care should be exercised in drawing comparisons between the rates for different modes.

The table provides information on passenger casualties and where possible travel by drivers and other crew in the course of their work has been excluded. Exceptions are for private journeys and those in company owned cars and vans where drivers are included.

Figures for all modes of transport exclude confirmed suicides and deaths through natural causes. Figures for air, rail and water exclude trespassers and rail excludes attempted suicides. Accidents occurring in airports, seaports and railway stations that do not directly involve the mode of transport concerned are also excluded; for example, injuries sustained on escalators or falling over packages on platforms.

The following definitions are used:

Air: Accidents involving UK registered airline aircraft in UK and foreign airspace. Fixed wing and rotary wing aircraft are included but air taxis are excluded. Accidents cover UK airline aircraft around the world not just in the UK.

Rail: Train accidents and accidents occurring through movement of railway vehicles in Great Britain. As well as national rail the figures include accidents on underground and tram systems, Eurotunnel and minor railways.

Water: Figures for travel by water include both domestic and international passenger carrying services of UK registered merchant vessels.

Road: Figures refer to Great Britain and include accidents occurring on the public highway (including footways) in which at least one road vehicle or a vehicle in collision with a pedestrian is involved and which becomes known to the police within 30 days of its occurrence. Figures include both public and private transport. More information and analyses on road accidents and casualties can be found in Part 4: Road traffic, freight, accidents and motor vehicle offences.

Bus or coach: Figures for work buses are included. From 1 January 1994, the casualty definition was revised to include only those vehicles equipped to carry 17 or more passengers regardless of use. Prior to 1994 these vehicles were coded according to construction, whether or not they were being used for carrying passengers. Vehicles constructed as buses that were privately licensed were included under 'bus and coach' but PSV licensed minibuses were included under cars.

Car: Includes taxis, invalid tricycles, three and four wheel cars and minibuses. Prior to 1999 motor caravans were also included.

Van: Vans mainly include vehicles of the van type constructed on a car chassis. From 1 January 1994 these are defined as those vehicles not over 3.5 tonnes maximum permissible gross vehicle weight. Prior to 1994 the weight definition was not over 1.524 tonnes unladen.

Two-wheeled motor vehicle: Mopeds, motor scooters and motor cycles (including motor cycle combinations).

Pedal cycle: Includes tandems, tricycles and toy cycles ridden on the carriageway.

Pedestrian: Includes persons riding toy cycles on the footway, persons pushing bicycles, pushing or pulling other vehicles or operating pedestrian controlled vehicles, those leading or herding animals, occupants of prams or wheelchairs, and people who alight safely from vehicles and are subsequently injured.

Travel to work: 1.8-1.9

Tables 1.8 and 1.9 use data from the Autumn (September to November) 2004 Labour Force Survey (LFS). The table is based on those people who are employed, and excludes those on Government New Deal schemes, those working from home or using their home as a working base, and those whose workplace or mode of travel to work were not known.

The questions on usual method of travel to work and usual time have been asked in each Autumn survey since 1992. Table 1.8b gives a time series of the results from these surveys for Great Britain.

The LFS is a survey of households living at private addresses in Great Britain. In spite of its large sample size (55 thousand responding households), data for some cells in Tables 1.8 and 1.9 are not shown because they fall below the 10 thousand LFS reliability threshold.

Overseas travel and tourism, and international passenger movements: 1.10-1.12

Tables 1.10-1.12 are derived from the International Passenger Survey (IPS). In this survey, which is carried out by the Office for National Statistics, a large sample of passengers is interviewed entering and leaving the United Kingdom on the principal air and sea routes and via the Channel Tunnel. These tables are based on IPS 'main flow' interviews, i.e. United Kingdom residents returning to, and overseas residents leaving the United Kingdom. The unit of measurement is therefore the visit and not the journey, and the mode of travel for the unit is that used by a United Kingdom resident returning or by an overseas resident departing (fly cruises are an exception to this rule as they are counted as 'sea' even though United Kingdom resident interviewed will have returned by air).

Up to 1998 the results of the IPS have been supplemented with estimates of travel between the United Kingdom and the Irish Republic provided by the Irish Central Statistics Office. In Table 1.10, estimates of road and rail visits across the land border with the Irish Republic have been included with sea trips. Since 1999, IPS interviewing has been expanded to cover trips between the United Kingdom and the Irish Republic and therefore these estimates have not been necessary. The figures given here are annual totals, but quarterly as well as annual analyses are published in *Business Monitor MQ6 (Overseas Travel and Tourism)* and *Travel Trends (report of the IPS)*, with detailed notes and definitions.

These publications are available from TSO, or through the ONS website. More details can be found at:
www.statistics.gov.uk/ssd/surveys/international_passenger_survey.asp

The "European Union" category in Tables 1.11 and 1.12 includes the ten countries that acceded to the European Union in May 2004. Other Western Europe in Tables 1.11 and 1.12 cover Iceland, Norway, Switzerland, (former) Yugoslavia (except Solvenia), Gibraltar, Turkey, the Faroes, and Liechtenstein. Other areas figures in Table 1.12 are mostly non-Europeans travelling from Europe.

Household Expenditure on Transport: 1.13

Data is shown to the nearest ten pence in line with usual Expenditure and Food Survey (EFS) practice. Data to the nearest penny may be obtained from the EFS contact point ☎ 020-7533 5756 or from www.statistics.gov.uk

The coding framework was changed for the 2001/02 survey onwards. The table has been amended to present data on the new European Standard Classification of Individual Consumption by Purpose (COICOP) basis. The main totals are shown on the old basis for comparison with previously published data. The Retail Price Index (RPI) deflator has been taken as the measure of general inflation by which to adjust the figures in this table to 2003/04 prices.

Investment in transport: 1.14

Several sources of information have been used in compiling this table – National Rail: Strategic Rail Authority; Road: Highways Agency, local authority returns and returns from DBFO contractors; Seaports: various company reports; Airports: Individual airport returns. The table attempts to define investment in a consistent manner for each mode but because of differences in the ways data are collected this is not always possible. Therefore, for some modes estimates have been made on the basis of limited or partial information. Some figures are subject to revision.

Figures for public investment in road infrastructure are for gross capital expenditure on national roads (i.e. motorways and trunk roads).

Private investment in road infrastructure includes investment under Design, Build, Finance and Operate (DBFO) contracts. Expenditure on bus garages, stops, etc is not included.

Investment in rail infrastructure includes track renewals, new routes and electrification, signalling, buildings, and plant and equipment.
Other public investment in rail infrastructure and other rail rolling stock covers London Underground, Docklands Light Railway, Croydon Tramlink, Glasgow Underground, Manchester Metrolink light rail system, Midland Metro, Nottingham Express Transit, South Yorkshire Supertram and Tyne and Wear Metro.

Eurotunnel PLC investment figures, including plant and materials, are included in other rail infrastructure. Similarly, Eurotunnel investment in rolling stock is included in other rail rolling stock.

The figures for other rail rolling stock also include a tentative allowance for investment in privately owned wagons of £30 million per annum.

Airport and air traffic control infrastructure investment covers private sector airports, local authority airports and Civil Aviation Authority investment in air traffic control including the National Air Traffic Control System. PFI investment in the Oceanic Flight Data Processing System is not included in the published figures.

There have been a number of changes to the figures in the table. These are largely a result of revisions to data for London Underground and Docklands Light Railway from 1990/91. Other changes relate to public road infrastructure investment from 1998/99.

Central and local government expenditure on transport: 1.15

This table was revised in 2002, largely to account for a move to resource accounting for English central government expenditure from 1998/99. Further details of these and other revisions and reclassifications are provided in the footnotes to the table.

As the table shows local government expenditure on transport, the grants and other financial support provided to local government to fund this expenditure have been excluded from central government expenditure.

The figures shown are compiled from various government departments. Central government expenditure in England data is compiled by the Department for Transport. Local government expenditure in England is compiled by the Office of the Deputy Prime Minister (ODPM). Expenditure in Wales comes from *Welsh Transport Statistics*, produced by the National Assembly for Wales. Expenditure in Scotland comes from *Scottish Transport Statistics*, a Scottish Executive publication.

Transport related employment: 1.16-1.18

Details of transport-related employment by occupation are available from the Labour Force Survey (LFS). Data shown in Table 1.16 are from the Spring quarter (March to May) 2005. The LFS is a survey of households living at private addresses in Great Britain. In spite of its large sample size (55 thousand responding households), data for some cells in Table 1.16 are not shown because they fall below the 10 thousand LFS reliability threshold. Table 1.16 includes people with both main and second jobs as an employee, the self-employed, those on Government employment and training programmes, and unpaid family workers. The industry totals include those working in the following industry classifications: transport via railways, other inland transport, water transport, air transport, supporting and auxiliary transport activities and the activities of travel agents, and exclude those whose occupation was not known.

By comparison, Table 6.22 relates to local bus services only, and incorporates revisions due to late returns.

The new Standard Occupational Classification (SOC2000) has been used instead of the previous 1990 classification for editions of *Transport Statistics Great Britain* from 2001 onwards. SOC2000 is not directly comparable with the 1990 classifications, and it is therefore not possible to make direct comparisons with earlier editions.

The data on the number of employee jobs in transport related industries (Tables 1.17 and 1.18) are based on information from The Annual Business Inquiry (ABI/1). The ABI/1 is a sample survey, which ran for the first time in 1998 and replaced the Annual Employment Survey and the Census of Employment. The ABI/1 is the only source of employment statistics for Great Britain analysed by local area and detailed industrial classification. The sample was drawn from the Inter-Departmental Business Register (IDBR) and in 1998 the ABI/1 sample size was approximately 78,500 enterprises. An enterprise is roughly defined as a combination of local units (i.e. individual workplaces with PAYE schemes or registered for VAT) under common ownership.

The ABI/1 results are used to benchmark the monthly/quarterly employment surveys (STES) which measure 'movements' (by region and industrial group) between the annual survey dates. Self-employed people, armed forces personnel and government supported trainees, in transport related occupations, are not included.

The fall in railway workforce jobs in Tables 1.17 and 1.18, from 1995, has mainly been due to some parts of the old British Rail group being reclassified to other sectors. These sectors are generally SIC 63 (other transport), SIC 64 (telecommunications), SIC 45 (construction), SIC 31-35 (manufacturing) and SIC 74 (business services). In Table 1.18, part-time is defined as not more than normally 30 hours a week; figures are actual numbers working part-time, rather than full-time equivalents.

Retail: Prices Index: transport components: 1.19

These indices are taken from the published *Retail Prices Index*, rebased to 1993=100 for convenience. The bus fares index includes fare changes on local and non-local buses and coaches.

Gross Domestic Product and Retail Prices Index deflators: 1.20

Gross Domestic Product deflators (at market prices) are calculated by reference to column YBGB of table A1 of the *Quarterly National Accounts*. Retail Prices Index deflators have been calculated directly from the published 'All Items' *Retail Prices Index*.

1.1 Passenger transport: by mode: 1952 - 2004

Billion passenger kilometres/percentage

Year	Road: Buses and coaches		Road: Cars, vans and taxis		Road: Motor cycles		Road: Pedal cycles		All road		Rail [1]		Air		All modes [2]	
1952	92	42	58	27	7	3	23	11	180	82	38	18	0.2	0.1	218	100
1953	93	41	64	29	7	3	21	9	185	83	39	17	0.2	0.1	225	100
1954	92	40	72	31	8	3	19	8	191	83	39	17	0.3	0.1	230	100
1955	91	38	83	35	8	3	18	8	200	84	38	16	0.3	0.1	239	100
1956	89	36	91	37	8	3	16	7	204	83	40	16	0.5	0.2	245	100
1957	84	34	92	38	9	4	16	7	201	83	42	17	0.5	0.2	244	100
1958	80	31	113	44	9	4	14	5	216	84	41	16	0.5	0.2	258	100
1959	81	30	126	46	11	4	14	5	232	85	41	15	0.6	0.2	273	100
1960	79	28	139	49	11	4	12	4	241	86	40	14	0.8	0.3	282	100
1961	76	26	167	53	11	4	11	4	255	86	39	13	1.0	0.3	295	100
1962	74	25	171	57	10	3	9	3	264	87	37	12	1.1	0.4	302	100
1963	73	23	185	59	8	3	8	3	274	88	36	12	1.3	0.4	312	100
1964	71	21	214	63	8	2	8	2	301	89	37	11	1.5	0.4	340	100
1965	67	19	231	66	7	2	7	2	312	89	35	10	1.7	0.5	349	100
1966	67	18	252	68	7	2	6	2	332	90	35	9	1.8	0.5	369	100
1967	66	17	267	70	6	2	6	2	345	91	34	9	1.9	0.5	381	100
1968	64	16	279	72	5	1	5	1	353	91	33	9	1.9	0.5	389	100
1969	63	16	286	72	5	1	5	1	359	91	35	9	1.9	0.5	395	100
1970	60	15	297	74	4	1	4	1	365	91	36	9	2.0	0.5	403	100
1971	60	14	313	75	4	1	4	1	381	91	35	9	2.0	0.5	419	100
1972	60	14	327	76	4	1	4	1	395	91	34	8	2.2	0.5	431	100
1973	61	14	345	76	4	1	4	1	414	92	35	8	2.4	0.5	452	100
1974	61	14	333	76	5	1	4	1	403	91	36	8	2.1	0.5	441	100
1975	60	14	331	76	6	1	4	1	401	92	36	8	2.1	0.5	438	100
1976	58	13	348	77	7	2	5	1	418	92	33	7	2.4	0.5	452	100
1977	58	13	354	77	7	1	6	1	425	92	34	7	2.2	0.5	461	100
1978	56	12	368	78	7	1	5	1	436	92	35	7	2.7	0.6	474	100
1979	56	12	365	77	7	2	5	1	433	92	35	7	3.0	0.6	471	100
1980	52	11	388	79	8	2	5	1	453	92	35	7	3.0	0.6	491	100
1981	48	10	394	80	10	2	5	1	458	93	34	7	2.8	0.6	495	100
1982	48	10	406	81	10	2	6	1	470	93	31	6	2.9	1.0	504	100
1983	48	9	411	80	9	2	6	1	474	93	34	7	3.0	1.0	511	100
1984	48	9	432	80	9	2	6	1	495	93	35	7	3.0	1.0	534	100
1985	49	9	441	81	8	1	6	1	504	93	36	7	3.6	0.7	544	100
1986	47	8	465	82	8	1	6	1	525	93	37	7	3.7	0.7	566	100
1987	47	8	500	83	7	1	6	1	560	93	39	6	4.0	0.7	603	100
1988	46	7	536	84	6	1	5	1	595	93	41	6	4.5	0.7	640	100
1989	47	7	581	85	6	1	5	1	639	94	39	6	4.9	0.7	683	100
1990	46	7	588	85	6	1	5	1	645	93	40	6	5.2	0.8	690	100
1991	44	6	582	86	6	1	5	1	637	94	39	6	4.8	0.7	681	100
1992	43	6	583	86	5	1	5	1	635	94	38	6	4.8	0.7	678	100
1993	44	6	584	86	4	1	4	1	636	94	37	5	5.1	0.8	677	100
1993	44	6	607	87	4	1	4	1	659	94	37	5	5.1	0.7	701	100
1994	44	6	614	87	4	1	4	1	666	94	35	5	5.5	0.8	706	100
1995	43	6	618	87	4	1	4	1	669	94	37	5	5.9	0.8	712	100
1996	43	6	625	87	4	1	4	1	676	94	39	5	6.3	0.9	721	100
1997	44	6	632	86	4	1	4	1	684	93	42	6	6.8	0.9	733	100
1998	45	6	635	86	4	1	4	1	688	93	44	6	7.0	1.0	738	100
1999	46	6	641	85	5	1	4	1	696	93	46	6	7.3	1.0	750	100
2000	47	6	639	85	5	1	4	1	695	93	47	6	7.6	1.0	749	100
2001	47	6	654	85	5	1	4	1	710	93	47	6	7.7	1.0	765	100
2002	47	6	678	86	5	1	4	1	734	93	48	6	8.5	1.1	791	100
2003	47	6	677	85	6	1	5	1	735	93	49	6	9.1	1.2	793	100
2004	48 P	6	679 P	85	6	1	4	1	736 P	92	51	6	9.8	1.2	797 P	100

1 Financial years. National Rail, urban metros and modern trams.

2 Excluding travel by water within the United Kingdom (including the Channel Islands), estimated at 0.7 billion passenger kilometres in 2000.

NB: See Notes and Definitions in Sections 1 and 7 for details of discontinuity in road passenger figures from 1993 onwards.

Bus & coach: ☎020-7944 3076
Car, m/cycle & pedal cycle: ☎020-7944 3097
Rail: ☎020-7944 3076
Air: ☎020-7944 3088

The rail and air figures in this table are outside the scope of National Statistics

Sources - Rail: ORR, formerly SRA, Air: CAA

1.2 Passenger journeys on public transport vehicles: 1950-2004/05

Millions

	All local services	Street running public transport				Rail systems [1]			Air [2]
Year	Bus, trolleybus, or tram	Local bus service	Non-local bus or coach	Trolley buses	Trams	National rail network	London Under-ground	Light rail, other rail & metros	Passengers on domestic flights
1950	16,445	12,734	260	1,961	1,750	1,010	695	..	..
1951	16,340	12,985	282	1,876	1,479	1,030	702	..	..
1952	16,039	13,049	297	1,783	1,207	1,017	670	..	0.7
1953	15,765	13,026	318	1,726	1,013	1,015	672	..	0.8
1954	15,597	13,059	293	1,663	875	1,020	671	..	1.0
1955	15,592	13,225	337	1,598	769	994	676	..	1.2
1956	15,169	13,059	341	1,503	607	1,029	678	..	1.4
1957	14,404	12,491	332	1,437	476	1,101	666	..	1.6
1958	13,513	11,879	337	1,257	377	1,090	692	..	1.5
1959	13,592	12,152	345	1,193	247	1,069	669	..	1.7
1960	13,313	12,166	367	990	157	1,037	674	..	2.2
1961	13,019	12,159	384	756	104	1,025	675	..	2.8
1962	12,648	12,045	382	557	46	965	668	..	3.3
1963	12,352	11,860	381	476	16	938	673	26	3.7
1964	11,881	11,497	386	368	16	928	674	27	4.2
1965	11,239	10,938	413	286	15	865	657	24	4.7
1966	10,609	10,407	419	188	14	835	667	24	5.1
1967	10,166	10,047	450	106	13	837	661	23	5.3
1968	9,779	9,699	455	68	12	831	655	21	5.0
1969	9,365	9,303	458	50	12	806	676	20	5.2
1970	8,687	8,643	467	34	10	824	672	18	5.4
1971	8,153	8,128	486	15	10	816	654	17	5.4
1972	7,912	7,901	512	1	10	754	655	16	5.9
1973	7,877	7,866	577	.	11	728	644	16	6.5
1974	7,716	7,706	597	.	10	733	636	15	6.1
1975	7,533	7,524	635	.	9	730	601	15	5.8
1976	7,149	7,141	648	.	8	702	546	11	6.1
1977	6,864	6,856	641	.	8	702	545	5	5.5
1978	6,625	6,617	680	.	8	724	568	3 [3]	6.4
1979	6,472	6,463	628	.	9	748	594	3 [3]	7.2
1980	6,224	6,216	559	.	8	760	559	13	7.2
1981	5,694	5,688	584	.	6	719	541	28	6.6
1982	5,518	5,512	579	.	6 [e]	630	498	51	7.0
1983	5,587	5,581	622	.	6	694	563	62	7.0
1984	5,650	5,644	587	.	6	702	672	70	8.0
1985/86	5,641	5,635	537	.	6	686	732	72	8.6
1986/87	5,341	5,335	572	.	6 [e]	738	769	60	9.3
1987/88	5,292	5,287	592	.	5	798	798	59	10.3
1988/89	5,215	5,210	563	.	5	822	815	66	11.6
1989/90	5,074	5,068	594	.	6	812	765	69	12.6
1990/91	4,851	4,845	619	.	6	809	775	66	13.1
1991/92	4,665	4,660	..	.	5	792	751	63	12.0
1992/93	4,480	4,475	..	.	5	770	728	68	12.0
1993/94	4,386	4,381	..	.	5	740	735	72	12.4
1994/95	4,409	4,403	..	.	5	735	764	78	13.3
1995/96	4,371	4,366	..	.	5	761	784	82	14.3
1996/97	4,338	4,333	..	.	5	801	772	87	15.3
1997/98	4,317	4,313	..	.	5	846	832	93	16.2
1998/99	4,235	4,231	..	.	4	892	866	100	16.9
1999/00	4,282	4,278	..	.	4	931	927	109	17.4
2000/01	4,324	4,319	..	.	4	957	970	134	18.2
2001/02	4,357	4,352	..	.	5	960	953	141	18.5
2002/03	4,449	4,444	..	.	4	976	942	150	20.2
2003/04	4,568	4,564	..	.	4	1,014	948	156	21.0
2004/05	4,613	4,609	..	.	4	1,088	976	168	22.1

1 Light rail and metros shown here are Glasgow Subway, Nexus (opened 1980), Docklands Light Railway (1987), Manchester Metrolink (1992), Stagecoach Supertram (1994), West Midlands Metro (1999) Croydon Tramlink (2000) and Nottingham NET (2004).

2 UK airlines, domestic passengers uplifted on scheduled and non-scheduled flights. Figures are for calendar years.

3 Glasgow Subway was closed for refurbishment in 1978 and 1979.

☎020-7944 3076

The rail and air figures in this table are outside the scope of National Statistics

Source - bus, coach, tram and rail operators

1.3 Average distance travelled per person per year by mode of travel and average trip length: 1992/94 - 2004

Miles/percentage

	1992/1994	1995/1997	1998/2000	2002	2003	2004	Percentage change from 1992/1994 to 2004
By mode (miles per person per year):							
Walking (including short walks)[1]	199	195	192	189	192	196	*-2*
Bicycle	38	39	39	33	34	36	*-6*
Private hire bus	110	105	107	124	135	131	*19*
Car/van driver	3,205	3,420	3,560	3,555	3,465	3,469	*8*
Car/van passenger	2,030	2,028	2,011	2,065	2,048	1,999	*-2*
Motorcycle/moped	32	30	30	33	36	34	*6*
Other private (including minibuses and motorcaravans, etc) [2]	43	40	26	20	27	22	*-49*
Bus in London	42	39	40	42	51	50	*18*
Other local bus	217	212	205	214	213	206	*-5*
Non-local bus [2]	96	93	99	58	86	75	*-22*
London Underground	50	51	57	62	54	51	*1*
Surface rail	298	294	371	373	347	384	*29*
Taxi/minicab	38	43	58	55	49	49	*27*
Other public (including air, ferries, light rail, etc.) [2]	41	75	45	56	96	64	*55*
All modes	6,439	6,666	6,840	6,879	6,833	6,762	*5*
Percentage of mileage accounted for by car (including van/lorry)	*81*	*82*	*81*	*82*	*81*	*81*	.
Average trip length (miles per trip)	6.1	6.3	6.6	6.8	6.9	6.8	*12*

1 Short walks believed to be under-recorded in 2002 and 2003 compared with earlier years

2 This estimate has a large sampling error because of the small samples involved

☎020-7944 3097

1.4 Trips per person per year by main mode[1] and purpose: 2004

Trips

	Walk	Bicycle	Car driver	Car passenger	Motor-cycle	Other private	Local bus	Surface rail/under ground	Other Public	All Modes
Commuting/business	20	6	111	17	2	1	12	11	2	181
Education/escort education	50	1	24	27	-	3	10	1	1	118
Shopping	51	1	79	41	-	1	17	2	2	193
Other escort	10	-	51	27	-	-	2	-	-	91
Personal business	28	1	41	24	-	1	5	1	1	102
Leisure	48	5	93	91	1	2	12	4	6	262
Other	39	-	-	-	-	-	-	-	-	40
All purposes	246	15	399	226	3	8	59	19	13	988

1 Main mode is that used for the longest part of the trip.

☎020-7944 3097

1.5 Trip distance per person per year by main mode[1] and purpose: 2004

Miles

	Walk	Bicycle	Car driver	Car passenger	Motor-cycle	Other private	Local bus	Surface rail/under ground	Other Public	All Modes
Commuting/business	17	14	1,372	162	17	18	64	241	46	1,950
Education/escort education	30	2	95	86	-	33	47	16	6	315
Shopping	30	2	410	273	1	5	64	24	8	818
Other escort	6	-	271	178	-	2	6	6	2	472
Personal business	16	2	248	129	2	9	19	21	8	454
Leisure	32	15	1,060	1,164	13	88	54	163	119	2,709
Other	39	-	5	-	-	-	-	-	-	45
All purposes	171	35	3,462	1,992	34	155	254	471	189	6,762

1 Main mode is that used for the longest part of the trip.

☎020-7944 3097

1.6 People entering central London during the morning peak:[1] 1994-2004

People (thousands)

	1994	1995	1996	1997	1998	1999	2000	2001	2002	2003	2004
Public transport:											
Surface rail	392	395	399	435	448	460	465	468	451	455	452
London Underground & Docklands Light Railway [2]	346	348	333	341	360	362	383	377	380	338	339
Bus	63	63	68	68	68	68	73	81	88	104	116
Coach/minibus [3]	23	21	20	20	17	15	15	10	10	10	9
All public transport	824	827	819	863	892	905	935	935	929	909	916
Private transport:											
Private car	145	145	143	142	140	135	137	122	105	88	86
Motor cycle	11	11	11	11	13	15	17	16	15	16	16
Pedal cycle	9	10	10	10	10	12	12	12	12	12	14
All private transport [4]	165	166	164	163	163	162	165	150	132	113	115
All transport [4]	989	993	983	1,026	1,055	1,066	1,100	1,086	1,061	1,021	1,031

1 0700 - 1000 hours. Surveys are conducted in October/November.
2 Excludes passengers transferring from surface rail services.
3 Includes commuter and tourist coaches.
4 Excludes commercial vehicles and taxis.

☎020-7941 4610
The figures in this table are outside the scope of National Statistics
Source - Transport for London

1.7 Passenger casualty rates by mode: 1994-2003[1]

Per billion passenger kilometres

	1994	1995	1996	1997	1998	1999	2000	2001	2002	2003	1994-03 average
Air [2]											
Killed	0.00	0.05	0.00	0.00	0.00	0.00	0.00	0.00	0.00	0.00	0.00
KSI	0.00	0.05	0.01	0.00	0.00	0.02	0.00	0.00	0.00	0.00	0.01
All	0.01	0.07	0.01	0.03	0.07	0.18	0.04	0.00	0.00	0.00	0.04
Rail [3,4]											
Killed	0.4	0.2	0.4	0.5	0.4	0.9	0.4	0.2	0.4	0.1	0.4
KSI	2.4	1.7	..	..	..	..	..	..	..	..	..
All	68.7	79.6	..	..	..	..	..	..	..	..	..
Injured	..	..	19.1	19.4	16.2	18.5	17.0	12.5	14.3	11.5	..
Water [5]											
Killed	0.0	0.0	0.8	0.0	0.7	0.4	0.4	0.4	0.0	0.0	0.3
KSI	33	39	39	33	41	28	52	54	49	61	43
Bus or coach											
Killed	0.5	0.8	0.2	0.3	0.4	0.2	0.3	0.2	0.4	0.2	0.3
KSI	17	17	15	12	13	12	11	11	11	10	13
All	214	197	198	196	199	202	195	191	173	175	194
Car [6]											
Killed	3.0	2.9	3.0	2.9	2.8	2.7	2.7	2.8	2.7	2.7	2.8
KSI	40	40	40	38	35	33	32	31	29	27	34
All	331	327	341	346	342	332	335	322	303	290	326
Van [6]											
Killed	1.1	1.2	1.0	1.0	1.0	0.9	0.9	0.9	1.0	0.9	1.0
KSI	19	19	16	14	14	13	12	11	11	10	14
All	131	121	117	115	113	104	100	102	96	89	108
Two wheeled motor vehicle [6]											
Killed	110	110	108	119	112	113	122	112	111	114	113
KSI	1651	1634	1529	1507	1452	1423	1493	1405	1367	1264	1458
All	6033	5809	5697	5724	5546	5395	5712	5539	5168	4606	5487
Pedal cycle											
Killed	43	51	50	45	40	42	31	33	29	25	39
KSI	996	958	929	880	838	779	666	632	555	534	771
All	6184	6023	6031	6036	5798	5599	4953	4512	3874	3775	5246
Pedestrian											
Killed	62	57	56	57	50	50	49	47	44	43	52
KSI	713	672	651	651	580	564	543	521	491	443	583
All	2684	2572	2606	2693	2484	2464	2404	2332	2207	2035	2448

Note: KSI = killed or seriously injured
All = Killed, seriously and slightly injured

☎ 020-7944 6395

1 Figures have been revised from those published in previous years, see Notes and Definitions for more details.
2 Passenger casualties in accidents involving UK registered airline aircraft in UK and foreign airspace.
3 Figures provided are for Financial years.
4 Passenger casualties involved in train accidents and accidents occuring through movement of railway vehicles. Reporting regulations changed on 1 April 1996. Since then figures are only available for passenger fatalities and injuries. The reporting trigger for an injury is the passenger being taken to hospital directly from the scene.
5 Passenger casualties on UK registered merchant vessels.
6 Driver and passenger casualties.

1.8 Main mode of transport to work and mean time taken by Government Office Region and country of workplace

a) Autumn 2004 — Percentage/thousands

Area of workplace	Car, van, minibus	Motor-cycle	Bicycle	Bus, coach	Rail: ow: National Rail	Rail: ow: Other rail [1]	Rail: All Rail	Walk	Number in employment
North East	73	*	2	10	*	2	3	11	977
Tyne and Wear	68	*	*	12	*	4	5	10	470
Rest of North East	77	*	*	7	*	*	*	12	507
North West	76	1	2	8	2	-	3	10	2,897
Greater Manchester	75	*	1	9	2	1	3	10	1,122
Merseyside	71	*	*	11	5	*	5	9	518
Rest of North West	78	1	3	5	1	*	1	11	1,257
Yorkshire and the Humber	73	1	3	10	2	*	2	11	2,142
South Yorkshire	72	*	*	11	*	*	*	12	512
West Yorkshire	72	*	*	13	3	*	3	11	949
Rest of Yorks and the Humber	74	*	6	5	*	*	*	11	680
East Midlands	78	1	3	6	*	*	1	11	1,730
West Midlands	78	1	2	8	2	*	2	10	2,263
Metropolitan County	74	*	1	12	3	*	3	9	1,129
Rest of West Midlands	81	1	2	4	*	*	*	11	1,134
East of England	79	1	4	3	2	*	2	10	2,279
London	40	1	3	14	18	15	33	8	3,419
Central London	12	2	3	13	38	28	66	4	1,095
Rest of inner London	36	2	4	17	14	17	31	10	871
Outer London	65	1	2	13	4	5	9	9	1,453
South East	78	1	3	4	3	*	3	11	3,469
South West	77	1	3	4	1	*	1	13	2,161
England	71	1	3	8	4	3	7	10	21,337
Wales	81	*	1	4	1	*	1	11	1,180
Scotland	70	1	1	12	3	*	3	12	2,219
Strathclyde	68	*	*	14	6	*	6	10	913
Rest of Scotland	71	*	2	10	1	*	2	14	1,306
Great Britain	71	1	3	8	4	2	6	11	24,736

b) Great Britain: Autumn 1994 - Autumn 2004 — Percentage/minutes

	Car, van, minibus	Motor-cycle	Bicycle	Bus, coach	Rail: ow: National Rail	Rail: ow: Other rail [1]	Rail: All Rail	Walk	Mean time (minutes)
Autumn 1994	68	1	4	9	3	2	6	12	23.6
Autumn 1995	68	1	4	8	4	2	6	12	23.8
Autumn 1996	70	1	4	8	3	2	5	12	23.8
Autumn 1997	71	1	4	8	3	2	6	11	24.4
Autumn 1998	71	1	3	8	4	2	6	11	24.6
Autumn 1999	70	1	3	8	4	2	6	11	24.9
Autumn 2000	70	1	3	8	4	2	6	11	25.3
Autumn 2001	70	1	3	8	4	3	7	11	25.4
Autumn 2002	71	1	3	8	4	2	6	11	25.4
Autumn 2003	71	1	3	8	4	2	6	10	25.5
Autumn 2004	71	1	3	8	4	2	6	11	25.9

1 Underground systems to 1995. From 1996 includes light railway systems and trams.

☎020-7944 3096
Labour Force Survey Helpline: ☎020-7533 6094
Source - Labour Force Survey, ONS

1.9 Time taken to travel to work by Government Office Region of workplace: Autumn 2004

Area of workplace	cumulative percentage				Mean time (minutes)
	<20 minutes	<40 minutes	<60 minutes	<90 minutes	
North East	50	85	94	99	22
Tyne and Wear	43	80	93	99	25
Rest of North East	58	89	96	99	19
North West and Merseyside	46	81	93	98	24
Greater Manchester	41	77	90	98	27
Merseyside	43	82	94	98	24
Rest of North West	51	85	94	98	22
Yorkshire and the Humber	47	82	92	98	24
South Yorkshire	43	83	93	99	23
West Yorkshire	44	79	91	98	25
Rest of Yorks and the Humber	54	86	93	98	22
East Midlands	50	85	94	98	22
West Midlands	47	82	92	98	24
Metropolitan County	39	76	89	98	27
Rest of West Midlands	56	89	95	99	20
Eastern	49	85	94	98	23
London	20	49	69	90	42
Central London	5	26	51	86	55
Rest of Inner London	20	49	70	91	42
Outer London	33	69	83	94	32
South East	50	82	92	97	24
South West	52	85	94	98	22
England	44	78	89	97	26
Wales	54	88	96	99	20
Scotland	46	81	91	98	25
Strathclyde	43	78	90	98	26
Rest of Scotland	49	83	92	98	24
Great Britain	45	78	89	97	26

☎020-7944 4746
Labour Force Survey Helpline: ☎020-7533 6094
Source - Labour Force Survey, ONS

1.10 Overseas travel: visits to and from the United Kingdom: 1994-2004

Thousands

	Visits to the United Kingdom [1]						Visits abroad by United Kingdom residents [2]					
		Sea/Channel Tunnel						Sea/Channel Tunnel				
	Air	With car [3]	With coach	Other [4]	Irish sea	All	Air	With car [3]	With coach	Other [4]	Irish sea	All
1994 0	14,465	2,102	1,828	1,699	700	6,329	27,624	6,033	2,489	2,055	1,430	12,007
1995 0	15,754	2,418	2,073	2,507	785	7,783	28,097	6,373	2,657	2,631	1,586	13,248
1996 0	16,279	2,709	2,431	3,067	676	8,884	27,907	7,196	2,509	2,726	1,713	14,144
1997 0	16,858	2,504	2,198	3,297	657	8,656	30,341	7,913	2,831	2,948	1,926	15,617
1998 0	17,479	2,324	2,047	3,207	688	8,266	34,283	8,575	2,751	3,202	2,061	16,589
1999 [5] 0	17,284	2,509	1,571	4,030	.	8,110	37,510	9,309	2,857	4,205	.	16,371
2000 0	17,831	1,902	1,411	4,065	.	7,378	41,392	8,453	2,627	4,364	.	15,445
2001 0	16,054	1,670	1,415	3,697	.	6,782	43,011	8,213	2,589	4,467	.	15,269
2002 0	17,098	1,901	1,336	3,845	.	7,082	43,990	7,999	3,049	4,339	.	15,387
2003 0	17,635	1,821	1,561	3,699	.	7,080	47,101	7,860	2,068	4,395	.	14,323
2004	20,002	1,967	1,720	4,067	.	7,753	50,435	7,125	2,290	4,344	.	13,759

1 Mode shown is that for departure from the United Kingdom.
2 Mode shown is that for return to the United Kingdom.
3 Includes motorcycles and scooters.
4 "Other" includes foot passengers, passengers with lorries and passengers with unknown vehicle type.
5 Prior to 1999, data for Irish Sea crossings were supplied by Irish Central Statistical Office. Since 1999, Irish Sea traffic covered by the IPS.

☎020-7944 3088
Source - International Passenger Survey, ONS

1.11 Overseas travel by air:[1] visits to and from the UK: by area and purpose: 2004

(a) Visits to the United Kingdom: overseas residents by area of residence — Thousands

	North America	European Union [2]	Other Western Europe	Other areas	All areas
Business visit	770	3,622	415	729	5,536
Holiday - Independent [3]	1,153	2,574	355	950	5,032
Holiday - Inclusive tour [4]	215	383	69	136	803
Visiting friends and relatives	1,158	3,535	355	1,242	6,290
Miscellaneous	546	1,141	211	443	2,341
Total	3,842	11,256	1,404	3,500	20,002

(b) Visits abroad by United Kingdom residents: by area visited — Thousands

	North America	European Union [2]	Other Western Europe	Other areas	All areas
Business visit	787	4,516	540	760	6,604
Holiday - Independent [3]	1,859	13,095	761	2,114	17,828
Holiday - Inclusive tour [4]	1,039	12,132	1,247	2,117	16,535
Visiting friends and relatives	969	4,478	512	2,220	8,179
Miscellaneous	122	865	62	240	1,289
Total	4,776	35,086	3,122	7,451	50,435

1 Excludes passengers changing planes at UK airports.
2 "European Union" includes the 10 states that joined the EU in May 2004.
3 Not on a package holiday.
4 Excludes fly-cruise package holidays, which are included under 'other areas' in Table 1.12.

☎020-7944 3088
Source - International Passenger Survey, ONS

1.12 Overseas travel by sea and Channel Tunnel: visits to and from the United Kingdom by area, purpose and type of vehicle on board: 2004

Thousands

	(a) Visits to the United Kingdom: overseas residents by area of residence				(b) Visits abroad by United Kingdom residents: by country visited			
	European Union [1]	Other Western Europe	Other areas	All areas	European Union [1]	Other Western Europe	Other areas	All areas
Business visit								
Without vehicle	355	10	64	429	544	0	1	544
Vehicle type:								
Car	208	4	4	216	464	4	2	470
Coach	161	0	5	167	173	0	2	175
Lorry	1,050	73	0	1,123	340	6	0	346
Motorcycle	0	0	0	0	2	0	0	2
Unknown	0	0	0	0	0	0	0	0
All	1,774	87	73	1,934	1,523	9	4	1,536
Holiday - Independent [2]								
Without vehicle	636	57	364	1,057	1,468	56	2	1,526
Vehicle type:								
Car	608	29	28	665	3,243	53	0	3,295
Coach	450	3	35	487	388	4	0	392
Lorry	2	0	0	2	2	0	0	2
Motorcycle	14	1	2	16	57	2	0	60
Unknown	14	5	0	19	7	0	0	7
All	1,723	95	427	2,245	5,164	115	2	5,281
Holiday Inclusive tour [3]								
Without vehicle	178	13	203	394	575	12	428	1,015
Vehicle type:								
Car	58	4	3	65	869	8	1	878
Coach	666	11	58	735	1,345	19	2	1,365
Lorry	0	0	0	0	0	0	0	0
Motorcycle	1	0	0	1	9	0	0	9
Unknown	-	0	0	-	0	0	0	0
All	903	27	264	1,195	2,798	39	430	3,268
Visiting friends and relatives								
Without vehicle	549	6	113	668	668	3	1	672
Vehicle type:								
Car	687	11	34	732	871	13	2	885
Coach	140	0	23	163	59	0	0	59
Lorry	0	0	0	0	0	0	0	0
Motorcycle	6	0	0	6	3	0	0	3
Unknown	0	0	2	2	1	0	0	1
All	1,382	17	171	1,570	1,602	16	3	1,620
Miscellaneous								
Without vehicle	240	42	44	326	214	2	1	216
Vehicle type:								
Car	254	5	3	262	1,510	0	1	1,511
Coach	153	7	8	169	296	0	3	299
Lorry	42	0	0	42	14	0	0	14
Motorcycle	3	1	0	4	12	0	0	12
Unknown	5	0	0	5	2	0	0	2
All	698	56	55	808	2,048	2	5	2,054
Total								
Without vehicle	1,958	127	788	2,874	3,468	73	432	3,973
Vehicle type:								
Car	1,815	54	71	1,940	6,957	78	5	7,040
Coach	1,570	21	128	1,720	2,260	23	7	2,290
Lorry	1,094	73	0	1,167	356	6	0	361
Motorcycle	23	2	2	27	83	2	0	85
Unknown	20	5	2	26	10	0	0	10
All	6,481	282	990	7,753	13,134	182	444	13,759

1 "European Union" includes the 10 states that joined the EU in May 2004.
2 Not on a package holiday.
3 Including UK residents on cruise and fly-cruise holidays under 'other areas'.

☎020-7944 3088
Source - International Passenger Survey, ONS

1.13 Household expenditure on transport: United Kingdom: 1996/97-2003/04

£ Per week/percentage/number

Transport (COICOP categories [1])	1996/97	1997/98	1998/99	1999/00	2000/01	2001/02	2002/03	2003/04
(a) Motoring and bicycle costs								
Purchase of vehicles	16.20	20.20	23.90	23.00	23.20	25.80	26.60	28.30
New cars and vans	4.70	5.80	7.40	7.90	10.60	10.70	11.30	11.40
Second-hand cars and vans	10.90	13.40	15.90	14.30	11.80	14.40	14.50	16.00
Motorcycles and scooters	0.30	0.60	0.40	0.50	0.60	0.50	0.90	0.70
Other vehicles (mainly bicycles)	..	..	..	..	..	0.20	0.20	0.20
Bicycle purchase	0.30	0.40	0.20	0.30	0.20	..	..	..
Spares, accessories, repairs and servicing	5.90	6.30	6.40	6.40	6.40	7.00	7.30	6.90
Car or van	5.60	5.90	6.10	6.20	6.00	6.80	6.90	6.60
Motorcycle	0.20	0.20	0.10	0.10	0.20	0.10	0.20	0.20
Bicycle	0.10	0.20	0.20	0.20	0.10	0.10	0.20	0.10
Petrol, diesel and other motor oils:	11.80	12.60	13.00	14.40	15.80	14.80	14.80	15.00
Petrol	10.60	11.30	11.50	12.80	14.00	12.70	12.70	12.40
Diesel	1.00	1.20	1.30	1.40	1.80	2.00	2.10	2.50
Other motor oils	0.10	0.10	0.10	0.10	0.10	0.10	0.10	0.10
Other motoring costs	1.70	1.80	1.90	1.90	1.80	1.80	1.90	1.90
All motoring and bicycle costs	35.70	40.90	45.20	45.70	47.20	49.40	50.70	51.90
(b) Transport services								
Rail and tube fares:	1.30	1.40	1.90	1.80	2.00	1.90	1.80	1.90
Season tickets	0.40	0.40	0.70	0.60	0.60	0.60	0.60	0.70
Other tickets	0.90	1.00	1.20	1.20	1.40	1.30	1.20	1.20
Bus and coach fares:	1.40	1.30	1.30	1.40	1.40	1.50	1.40	1.40
Season tickets	0.30	0.30	0.30	0.30	0.30	0.30	0.40	0.40
Other tickets	1.10	1.10	1.10	1.10	1.10	1.10	1.10	1.10
Combined tickets	0.50	0.60	0.70	0.90	0.90	1.00	0.80	0.70
Season tickets	0.40	0.40	0.60	0.70	0.70	0.80	0.60	0.50
Other tickets	0.10	0.10	0.10	0.20	0.20	0.20	0.20	0.10
Air and other travel and transport:	3.00	3.80	3.70	4.00	4.30	4.10	4.50	4.80
Air fares [2]	0.70	1.30	1.00	1.00	1.30	1.20	1.50	1.90
Other transport and travel	2.30	2.60	2.70	3.00	3.00	2.90	3.00	2.80
All transport services	6.20	7.10	7.60	8.10	8.60	8.40	8.50	8.80
All transport (excluding motor vehicle insurance and taxation and boat purchase and repairs - see below)	41.80	48.00	52.70	53.80	55.90	57.80	59.20	60.70
All household expenditure	309.10	328.80	352.20	359.40	385.70	398.30	406.20	418.10
Percentage of household expenditure on transport	*13.5*	*14.6*	*15.0*	*15.0*	*14.5*	*14.5*	*14.6*	*14.5*
Old FES categories								
Included under transport and travel but excluded above:								
Motor vehicle insurance and taxation	6.00	6.30	7.00	7.30	8.20	9.20	11.00	10.40
Vehicle taxation	2.10	2.20	2.40	2.40	2.50	2.40	2.40	2.50
Vehicle insurance	3.90	4.10	4.50	4.90	5.70	6.80	8.60	7.90
Boat purchase and repairs	0.80	0.50	0.30	0.60	0.50	0.40	0.60	0.30
Key transport expenditure totals:								
Motoring costs	41.20	46.60	51.80	52.60	55.10	58.50	61.70	62.40
Fares and other travel costs	7.50	8.10	8.30	9.20	9.50	9.50	9.70	9.60
All transport and travel	48.70	54.80	60.00	61.70	64.50	68.00	69.70	72.00
Adjusted for general inflation: 2003/04 prices								
Motoring costs [3]	50.00	54.30	57.60	57.60	58.70	60.80	63.40	62.40
Fares and other travel costs	9.10	9.90	9.20	10.10	10.10	9.80	10.00	9.60
All transport and travel	59.10	64.10	66.90	67.70	68.70	70.60	73.40	72.00

1 Data for 1996/97-2000/01 are based on old FES categories which include some items excluded under COICOP, eg, motor caravans, audio equipment, helmets. (See Notes and Definitions)

2 Excludes air fare component of package holidays abroad.

3 Includes expenditure on motorcycles, bicycles, boats and vehicle taxation and insurance.

Further details on *Family Spending: A Report on the 2003-2004 Expenditure and Food Survey are* available at www.statistics.gov.uk

☎ 020 7944 3097
Expenditure and Food Survey Helpline: ☎ 020 7533 5758

Source - Expenditure and Food Survey, ONS

1.14 Investment in transport: 1993/94-2003/04 [1]

£ Million (outturn prices)

	1993/94	1994/95	1995/96	1996/97	1997/98	1998/99	1999/00	2000/01	2001/02	2002/03	2003/04
Road infrastructure											
Public [2]	4,731	4,675	4,228	3,583	3,267	2,957	3,071	3,344	3,643	4,108	4,191
Private	81	86	102	375	251	278	63	47	45	39	40
Total	4,812	4,761	4,330	3,958	3,518	3,235	3,134	3,391	3,688	4,147	4,231
Road vehicles											
Cars and motor cycles: household	11,500	11,700	12,100	13,300	16,100	15,800	15,100	15,400	17,400	18,300	19,800
Cars and motor cycles: other	11,100	12,600	13,900	15,700	17,900	18,600	18,900	17,600	18,900	19,500	20,500
Cars and motor cycles: total	22,600	24,200	26,000	29,100	34,000	34,400	34,000	33,000	36,300	37,800	40,300
Other vehicles	4,300	5,700	6,200	6,200	6,900	7,100	7,300	7,400	7,800	7,500	8,400
Total	26,900	30,000	32,200	35,300	40,900	41,600	41,300	40,400	44,100	45,400	48,700
Rail infrastructure											
National Rail	762	890	900	1,178	1,430	1,823	2,012	2,404	3,148	3,756	4,722
Other rail	1,068	1,108	1,101	1,047	898	821	1,163	386	504	485	464
Total	1,830	1,998	2,001	2,225	2,328	2,644	3,175	2,790	3,652	4,241	5,186
Rail rolling stock											
National Rail	422	360	200	47	114	176	236	554	922	566	774
Other rail	357	269	121	148	82	85	84	75	75	45	147
Total	779	629	321	195	196	261	320	629	997	611	921
Ports infrastructure [3]	123	120	165	150	200	240	250	205	233	236	307
Airports and air traffic control											
Public [3]	225	205	140	171	216	140	161	163	57	71	70
Private [3]	279	434	443	463	565	542	511	566	630	784	1,384
Total	504	639	583	634	781	682	673	729	687	854	1,454

1 Some revisions have been made to the data since last year
2 Investment in road infrastructure includes all 'patching' but excludes local authority capital expenditure on car parks.
3 Partly based on figures for calendar years.

☎020-7944 3088
The figures in this table are outside the scope of National Statistics
Source - see Notes and Definitions

1.15 Central and local government expenditure on transport[1]: 2000/01 - 2004/05

£ million (outturn prices)

	2000/01	2001/02	2002/03	2003/04	2004/05[2]
England	**5,856**	**6,995**	**8,169**	**8,049**	**10,373**
Central government expenditure[3, 4]	**1,834**	**2,116**	**2,587**	**1,655**	**1,843**
Capital	**736**	**1,090**	**1,508**	**438**	**616**
Strategic roads[5]	410	607	736	438	616
London Regional Transport[6]	315	483	772	0	0
Other transport in London[7]	10	0	0	0	0
Current / resource	**1,098**	**1,026**	**1,079**	**1,217**	**1,227**
Strategic roads[5]	1,076	1,026	1,079	1,217	1,226
London Regional Transport[6]	0	0	0	0	0
Other transport in London[7]	22	0	0	0	1
Local government expenditure[8]	**4,022**	**4,879**	**5,582**	**6,394**	**8,530**
Capital	**1,406**	**1,858**	**2,450**	**2,540**	**3,139**
Roads	1,103	1,557	2,050	1,919	..
Car Parks	55	57	68	77	..
Public transport	234	229	320	534	..
Ports	10	12	9	7	..
Airport companies	4	3	3	2	..
Current / resource	**2,616**	**3,021**	**3,132**	**3,855**	**5,391**
Roads	1,782	1,969	2,011	2,381	2,640
Car Parks	-316	-343	-365	-410	-444
Revenue support to public transport	664	907	980	1,357	2,663
Concessionary fares	486	487	507	528	533
Scotland	**781**	**910**	**1,178**	**1,497**	**1,635**
Central government expenditure[9]	**278**	**388**	**574**	**773**	**859**
Capital - strategic roads	**84**	**53**	**107**	**139**	**154**
Current / resource	**194**	**335**	**467**	**634**	**705**
Strategic roads	82	99	139	160	174
Subsidies to transport industries	112	236	328	474	531
Local government expenditure[8]	**503**	**522**	**604**	**724**	**776**
Capital	**125**	**165**	**200**	**262**	**301**
Roads	102	127	140	165	213
Public transport	23	38	60	97	88
Current / resource	**378**	**357**	**404**	**462**	**475**
Roads	304	279	299	297	291
Car Parks	-21	-23	-27	-26	-25
Revenue support to public transport	55	62	67	99	115
Concessionary fares	40	39	65	91	94
Wales	**374**	**412**	**478**	**507**	**571**
Central government expenditure[10]	**118**	**137**	**162**	**160**	**171**
Capital - strategic roads	**72**	**78**	**99**	**87**	**97**
Current / resource - strategic roads	**46**	**58**	**62**	**73**	**74**
Local government expenditure[8]	**257**	**275**	**316**	**347**	**400**
Capital	**94**	**100**	**107**	**120**	**169**
Roads	81	86	88	98	..
Car Parks	2	2	5	5	..
Public transport	11	12	14	17	..
Current / resource	**163**	**175**	**209**	**226**	**231**
Roads	141	150	166	169	175
Car Parks	-6	-8	-8	-5	-6
Revenue support to public transport	16	20	21	23	25
Concessionary fares	11	13	30	39	37

1.15 (continued) Central and local government expenditure on transport[1]: 2000/01 - 2004/05

£ million (outturn prices)

	2000/01	2001/02	2002/03	2003/04	2004/05[2]
Great Britain [11]	**8,685**	**11,018**	**13,250**	**14,562**	**17,442**
Central government expenditure	**3,904**	**5,342**	**6,748**	**7,098**	**7,735**
Capital	**967**	**2,229**	**3,171**	**3,395**	**3,655**
Allocated to individual countries	**891**	**1,221**	**1,714**	**664**	**867**
Strategic roads [5]	566	738	942	664	867
Transport in London [6]	326	483	772	0	0
Not allocated to individual countries [4]	**76**	**1,008**	**1,457**	**2,731**	**2,788**
Rail	35	952	1,353	2,650	2,705
Other roads and traffic	16	25	16	59	19
Air and water transport	25	27	86	21	29
Other expenditure	0	4	2	1	35
Current / resource	**2,937**	**3,113**	**3,576**	**3,703**	**4,080**
Allocated to individual countries	**1,338**	**1,419**	**1,608**	**1,924**	**2,006**
Strategic roads[5]	1,204	1,183	1,280	1,450	1,474
Transport in London [6]	22	0	0	0	1
Subsidies in Scotland	112	236	328	474	531
Not allocated to individual countries [4]	**1,599**	**1,694**	**1,968**	**1,779**	**2,074**
Bus fuel duty rebates	300	304	317	342	358
Rail	993	1,033	1,334	1,091	1,430
Other roads and traffic	94	87	101	133	83
Air and water transport	144	188	116	139	130
Other expenditure	69	82	100	74	73
Local government expenditure	**4,782**	**5,676**	**6,502**	**7,464**	**9,707**
Capital	**1,625**	**2,123**	**2,757**	**2,922**	**3,609**
Roads	1,286	1,770	2,279	2,182	..
Car Parks	57	59	73	82	..
Public transport	268	279	394	648	..
Ports	10	12	9	7	..
Airport companies	4	3	3	2	..
Current / resource	**3,157**	**3,553**	**3,745**	**4,542**	**6,098**
Roads	2,227	2,398	2,476	2,847	3,106
Car Parks	-343	-374	-400	-441	-475
Revenue support to public transport	735	989	1,068	1,479	2,803
Concessionary fares	537	539	602	657	664

1 Some revisions have been made to the figures since last year
2 Includes provisional estimates.
3 Based on Departmental Expenditure Limits. Figures exclude grants to local authorities and credit approvals for roads, local transport, airports and ports.
4 Figures are on a resource accounting basis.
5 As part of the SR2002 Settlement, renewals maintenance on Strategic Roads was re-classified from Capital to Resource bringing it into line with the treatment in the Resource Accounts
6 LRT was the public corporation responsible for London Underground and bus services in London; TfL gained responsibility for bus services in July 2000 and Underground services in May 2003. From 2003/04, included with GLA transport grant under local government expenditure
7 These figures cover expenditure on Dockland Light Railway and Traffic Directors Office in London; these functions were transferred to TfL in July 2000. Includes PPP Arbiter costs in 2004/05
8 Figures are on an accruals basis.
9 Figures are on a cash plan basis until 2000/01 and on a resource accounting basis from 2001/02.
10 Figures are on a cash plan basis.
11 Great Britain total expenditure is not the sum of total expenditure for England, Scotland and Wales since it includes expenditure not allocated to individual countries.

☎020-7944 3088
The figures in this table are outside the scope of National Statistics
Sources - DfT; ODPM; Scottish Executive; National Assembly for Wales

1.16 People in employment in transport related occupations: Spring 2005

Thousands

SOC2000 [1] code	Occupation	Transport industries [2]	Other industries	All industries
1161	Transport and distribution managers	44	44	88
4134	Transport and distribution clerks	27	24	50
1232	Garage managers and proprietors	*	40	42
1226, 6212, 6219	Travel agencies and service occupations	62	13	75
3511, 3512, 8218	Air traffic controllers, pilots, operatives, etc	28	*	38
3513, 8217, 9141	Ship officers, seafarers, stevadores, dockers, etc	24	13	37
6213	Travel and tour guides	14	*	22
6214	Air travel assistants	28	*	29
6215, 8216, 3514	Rail travel assistants, operatives and train drivers	42	*	44
8213	Bus and coach drivers	101	13	114
8211	Heavy goods vehicle drivers	179	130	309
8212	Van drivers	24	187	212
8214	Taxi, cab drivers and chauffeurs	149	33	181
5231, 5233	Motor mechanics, auto engineers and electricians	17	209	225
5232, 5234	Vehicle body builders, painters and repairers	*	56	57
8135	Tyre, exhaust and windscreen fitters	*	*	10
8215	Driving instructors	*	32	35
8219	Other transport operatives	11	11	21
	Transport related occupations	758	834	1,592
	All in employment	1,307	27,106	28,413

1 Standard Occupation Classification 2000, see Notes and Definitions.
2 1992 Standard Industrial Classification (SIC92)
I Transport, storage & communication:
60.1 Transport via Railway
60.2 Other inland transport
61 Water Transport
62 Air transport
63 Supporting and auxiliary transport activities; activities of travel agencies.

☎020 7944 3096
Labour Force Survey Helpline: ☎020 7533 6094
Source - Labour Force Survey, ONS

1.17 Employee jobs in transport and related industries: March 1994-2005 [1]

Thousands

SIC 1992 code	Industry	1994	1995	1996	1997	1998	1999	2000	2001	2002	2003	2004	2005
60.1	Railways [2]	89	90	85	55	46	49	50	49	50	48	48	50
60.2, 60.3	Other land transport	417	422	399	435	443	459	455	454	460	450	459	466
61	Water transport	23	27	25	23	20	18	17	15	16	16	15	17
62	Air transport	59	56	59	68	78	85	93	90	85	88	90	85
63.1, 63.2, 63.4	Cargo handling, storage & other supporting activities	223	222	219	230	234	226	245	260	263	277	282	285
63.3	Travel agencies & tour operators	87	86	85	97	97	110	116	129	122	128	131	134
Total: transport industries		899	902	872	908	918	947	975	997	997	1,007	1,024	1,037
Manufacture of transport equipment:													
34	motor vehicles, trailers	180	209	228	229	236	227	221	212	206	202	197	193
35	other transport equipment	153	143	146	148	154	162	167	171	159	150	141	138
50.1, 50.3-50.5	Retail distribution & filling stations	398	392	397	413	407	411	390	384	391	386	375	370
50.2	Maintenance and repair of motor vehicles	170	167	172	170	150	155	164	161	171	165	169	170
Total: transport related industries		902	911	942	961	947	955	942	928	926	903	883	871
All transport and related industries and services		1,801	1,814	1,814	1,869	1,864	1,902	1,918	1,925	1,923	1,910	1,907	1,908

1 The data in this table differ from those previously published. This is due to benchmarking the Annual Business Enquiry (ABI/1). See the note on Tables 1.17 and 1.18 in the Notes and Definitions of Section 1.
2 See Notes and Definitions.

☎01633 812079
Source - Employment, Earnings & Productivity Division, ONS

1.18 Employee jobs in transport and related industries: by sex and employment status: March 1990-2005

Thousands

SIC 1992 code	Industry	March 1990 Male	March 1990 Female All	March 1990 Female Part-time	March 1995 Male	March 1995 Female All	March 1995 Female Part-time	March 2004[1] Male	March 2004[1] Female All	March 2004[1] Female Part-time	March 2005 Male	March 2005 Female All	March 2005 Female Part-time
60.1	Railways[2]	155	7	1	67	23	1	39	9	1	41	9	1
60.2, 60.3	Other land transport, and via pipelines	389	27	7	406	16	6	373	86	28	391	75	32
61	Water transport	42	4	0	23	3	0	10	5	1	11	6	2
62	Air transport	36	21	2	31	25	3	51	39	11	48	37	13
63	Miscellaneous transport and storage	216	84	8	219	89	8	257	156	32	264	155	31
Total: transport industries		838	143	18	746	156	18	729	295	73	755	282	78
Manufacture of transport equipment:													
34	motor vehicles, trailers	235	12	1	198	12	1	171	26	4	169	23	4
35	other transport equipment	211	18	1	133	10	1	126	15	2	124	15	3
50.1, 50.3-50.5	Retail distribution & filling stations	303	44	13	356	35	14	281	94	39	278	92	35
50.2	Maintenance & repair of motor vehicles	208	18	6	144	23	4	133	36	15	137	32	13
Total: Transport related industries		957	92	21	831	80	20	712	171	60	708	163	54
All transport and related industries and services		1,803	236	39	1,577	236	39	1,441	466	133	1,463	444	133

1 The data in this table differ from those previously published. This is due to benchmarking the Annual Business Enquiry (ABI/1).
See the note on Tables 1.18 and 1.19 in the Notes and Definitions of Section 1.
2 See Notes and Definitions.

☎01633 812079
Source - Employment, Earnings & Productivity Division, ONS

1.19 Retail Prices Index: transport components: 1994-2004

1994=100

	All items	Motor vehicles: Purchase	Motor vehicles: Mainten-ance	Motor vehicles: Petrol and oil	Motor vehicles: Tax and insurance	Motor vehicles: All motor	Rail fares	Bus fares	Fares & other travel costs
1994	100.0	100.0	100.0	100.0	100.0	100.0	100.0	100.0	100.0
1995	103.4	101.7	101.9	105.1	97.5	101.8	104.4	103.7	102.5
1996	105.9	105.0	106.5	110.5	94.3	104.9	108.3	107.5	105.6
1997	109.3	107.5	112.3	121.4	98.2	110.5	110.9	111.4	109.1
1998	113.0	106.3	116.9	127.5	106.8	113.9	115.4	115.0	111.5
1999	114.8	101.8	121.5	138.2	115.5	116.7	119.6	119.2	115.0
2000	118.1	96.3	126.5	156.4	127.8	121.1	121.7	124.0	118.8
2001	120.3	94.9	132.7	148.4	134.5	120.5	126.4	129.2	122.6
2002	122.2	93.1	139.6	143.7	136.6	119.5	129.2	133.2	126.0
2003	125.8	90.4	147.9	148.9	142.5	121.1	131.5	138.8	135.0
2004	129.5	87.6	156.8	157.2	143.1	122.2	136.5	145.9	139.7

☎020-7944 4276
Source - Consumer Prices and Inflation Division, ONS

1.20 Gross Domestic Product and Retail Price Index deflators: 1994-2004

Calendar years to 2004 price level			Fiscal years to 2004/05 price level			Calendar years to 2004/05 price level		
Year	GDP Factor	RPI Factor	Year	GDP Factor	RPI Factor	Year	GDP Factor	RPI Factor
1994	1.285	1.295	1994/95	1.286	1.294	1994	1.293	1.305
1995	1.252	1.252	1995/96	1.251	1.253	1995	1.260	1.262
1996	1.211	1.222	1996/97	1.209	1.224	1996	1.218	1.232
1997	1.177	1.185	1997/98	1.174	1.185	1997	1.184	1.195
1998	1.144	1.146	1998/99	1.144	1.149	1998	1.151	1.155
1999	1.120	1.129	1999/00	1.122	1.131	1999	1.127	1.138
2000	1.107	1.096	2000/01	1.108	1.098	2000	1.113	1.105
2001	1.082	1.077	2001/02	1.081	1.082	2001	1.088	1.085
2002	1.049	1.060	2002/03	1.048	1.060	2002	1.055	1.068
2003	1.020	1.030	2003/04	1.021	1.031	2003	1.026	1.038
2004	1.000	1.000	2004/05	1.000	1.000	2004	1.006	1.008

☎020-7944 4276

Sources - GDP: National Expenditure and Income Division, ONS

2 Aviation:

Notes and Definitions

Tables 2.2a - 2.2c, and 2.8 are derived from the Civil Aviation Authority (CAA) publication *United Kingdom Airports* (annual), thus;

TSGB table	CAA publication table N°
2.2a	4.1 and 5
2.2b	8, 10.1 and 10.2
2.2c	13.1 and 14
2.8	12

Table 2.3 is derived from the CAA *Punctuality Statistics, Table 92.*

Tables 2.4, 2.6 and 2.11 are derived from the CAA publication *United Kingdom Airlines* (annual) and earlier volumes. Thus;

TSGB table	CAA publication table N°
2.4	1.7.1/2/3 and 1.8.1/2/3
2.6	1.11.2
2.11	1.15

CAA compile the statistics from returns submitted by United Kingdom airlines.

Tables 2.7 and 2.12 are derived from the ICAO publication *Civil Aviation Statistics of the World,* thus;

TSGB table	ICAO publication table N°
2.7	4.1 and 4.2
2.12	3.1

Table 2.9 is derived from the CAA publication *Reportable Accidents to United Kingdom Registered Aircraft and to Foreign Registered Aircraft in United Kingdom Airspace* and from data supplied by the Civil Aviation Authority's Safety Data Unit. Table 2.10 is derived from the CAA publication *United Kingdom Airmisses Involving Commercial Air Transport.*

Traffic at United Kingdom airports: 2.2

The table shows air transport movements (landings and take-offs of aircraft engaged in commercial air transport), terminal passengers (arrivals and departures) and cargo handled (uplifted and set down).

Domestic traffic (movements, passengers and cargo) shown is half that published in the CAA Airport Annual Reports, to remove double counting at airport of arrival and departure. The figures for individual airports have not, however, been adjusted to eliminate double counting of domestic traffic.

Terms used in Table 2.2 are defined as follows:

Air transport movements: All scheduled movements (whether loaded or empty) and loaded charter movements, but excludes empty positioning flights by scheduled aircraft and empty charter movements.

International services: These services are flown between the United Kingdom, Isle of Man or Channel Islands and points in other countries.

Scheduled services: Those performed according to a published timetable, include-ing those supplementary thereto, available for use by members of the public.

Non-scheduled services: Air transport movement other than scheduled service.

Terminal passengers: Passengers joining or leaving an aircraft at a United Kingdom airport (a passenger who changes from one aircraft to another, carrying the same flight number, is counted as a terminal passenger both on arrival and departure). Transit passengers who arrive and depart on the same aircraft are not included.

All revenue and non-revenue passengers (who pay less than 25 per cent of the normal applicable fare) are counted as terminal passengers. Cargo excludes mail and passengers' and crews' permitted baggage, but all other property carried on an aircraft is included. Thus excess baggage is included, as are diplomatic bags. Cargo in transit through an airport on the same aircraft is excluded.

Punctuality at United Kingdom Airports: 2.3

London airports include Heathrow, Gatwick, Stansted and Luton, but not the City airport. Regional airports include Manchester, Birmingham and Glasgow. Newcastle and Edinburgh airports also began reporting from July 1996; the resulting discontinuity in the series is very small.

Main outputs of United Kingdom airlines: 2.4

Table 2.4 shows the carriage of revenue passengers, cargo and mail on services flown by United Kingdom airlines, scheduled and non-scheduled (but excluding air-taxi operations and sub-charter operations performed on behalf of United Kingdom airlines). Passenger kilometres are calculated by multiplying the number of revenue passengers carried on each flight stage by the stage distance. Passenger seat occupancy is calculated as passenger kilometres as a percentage of seat kilometres available.

Cargo and mail uplifted are calculated by counting each tonne of revenue cargo or mail on a particular journey once only and not repeatedly on each individual stage of the flight. Cargo and mail tonne kilometres are calculated by multiplying the number of tonnes of revenue load on each stage flight by the stage distance. Terms used in Table 2.4 are defined as follows:

Passengers: Travellers are counted as revenue passengers if they pay at least 25 per cent of the normal applicable fare. They are counted only once on a particular flight (with one flight number) and not for each stage of that flight.

International services: These services are flown between the United Kingdom, Isle of Man or Channel Islands and points in other countries.

Domestic services: Those entirely within the United Kingdom, Isle of Man and Channel Islands.

Scheduled services: Those performed according to a published timetable, including those supplementary thereto, available for use by members of the public.

Non-scheduled services: Air transport movements other than scheduled services.

Forecasts of air traffic demand: 2.5

These forecasts supersede those published in 1997. They are the seventh set of forecasts produced by the Department of Transport, Local Government and the Regions (or predecessor Departments) since 1984. They reflect the intention to monitor air traffic developments and to keep assumptions and methodologies under review, as set out in the 1985 White Paper *Airports Policy*.

The forecasts are for the demand for air travel by UK and foreign residents to and from UK airports up to year 2020, extending the forecast period five years beyond that in the 1997 forecasts. They are based on econometric equations, which specify a relationship between passenger traffic and a number of explanatory variables, which determine it. The key variables determining air traffic were found to be domestic and foreign economic growth (principally GDP); air fares; trade and exchange rates. The relationships derived from past years' data are applied to projections of future year values of the explanatory variables to calculate forecasts of air traffic. A range of forecasts is given in order to reflect the uncertainties inherent in long term forecasting.

United Kingdom airline fleet: 2.6

Table 2.6 gives information on the fleet size of selected larger United Kingdom airlines.

Activity at major airports: 2.7

Table 2.7 gives a comparison of the activity at some of the world's major airports. Airports are selected such that the largest 25 (as reported to the International Civil Aviation Organisation) by number of terminal passengers are included. The ranking is only a guide as 'non reporting' airports are excluded. Some airports which did not report in previous years have entered the table. A substantial proportion of the figures are estimated by ICAO on the basis of part-year data; the table is therefore of use only as a guide.

United Kingdom international passenger movements: 2.8

The table records the origin and destination of all revenue and non-revenue terminal passengers on air transport movement flights as reported to United Kingdom airport authorities by United Kingdom and foreign airlines. Passengers changing planes are recorded twice, on arrival and departure. Passengers carried in aircraft chartered by British government departments, HM and other armed forces travelling in the course of their duties, and oil rig traffic are excluded. Operators are required to report, in respect of each service operated, the points of uplift and discharge of each passenger. The figures record data for direct flights only, so they may not reflect a passenger's entire air journey: the point at which a passenger disembarks from a particular service may not represent the passenger's ultimate destination.

Although operators are asked to report all passenger journeys, in some cases the actual point of uplift or discharge is not recorded. In such cases, all passengers are allocated to the aircraft's origin or ultimate destination. All identifiable diversions are reallocated to the point of intended operation.

Casualties: 2.9

The table includes deaths, serious and minor injuries where an aircraft was engaged in airline, air taxi, general aviation (including private flights) and other commercial (including training) operations.

Terms used in Table 2.9 are defined as follows:

Airline: Public transport flights, which are subject to a United Kingdom Air Transport Licence. Also public transport flights which are not subject to a United kingdom Air Transport Licence, but which utilise aircraft having a maximum take-off weight of 15 tonnes or more. Positioning flights are excluded. There are no airline - rotary wing services by United Kingdom registered aircraft in foreign airspace, and no rotary wing or air taxi services by foreign registered aircraft in United Kingdom airspace.

Air Taxi: Public Transport flights which are not subject to a United Kingdom Air Transport Licence and which utilise aircraft having a maximum take-off weight of less than 15 tonnes. Positioning flights are excluded.

General Aviation: Includes executive, club and group, private and training flights, but does not include accidents to gliders, microlights, hang gliders or hot-air balloons.

Number of incidents: 2.10

Table 2.10 reflects the Civil Aviation Authority's practice, introduced in 1990, of including controller-reported incidents. Further, the term "airmiss" has been replaced by AIRPROX, meaning aircraft proximity hazard.

An AIRPROX is a situation in which, in the opinion of a pilot or controller, the distance between aircraft as well as their relative positions and speed have been such that the safety of the aircraft was or may have been compromised. AIRPROX can occur between various combinations of commercial, military and private aircraft. The numbers of AIRPROX incidents involving commercial transport aircraft are shown separately in the table.

All AIRPROX reports are assessed and, following guidelines given by the International Civil Aviation Organisation, the degrees of risk involved are categorised as 'risk of collision', 'safety not assured', 'no risk of collision', and 'risk not determined'.

Employment: 2.11

Table 2.11 shows the average number of personnel employed by United Kingdom airlines in the United Kingdom and overseas, in each of the years 1992 to 2001. Personnel employed by companies performing solely air-taxi operations are excluded.

Passenger traffic via major international airlines: 2.12

Table 2.12 gives a comparison of the major international airlines. Airlines are selected such that the largest 25 (as reported to ICAO) by passengers uplifted are included. The ranking is only a guide as 'non reporting' airlines are excluded.

2.1 Activity at civil aerodromes: United Kingdom:[1] 1950-2004

For greater detail of the years 1994-2004 see Table 2.2

	Air transport movements: aircraft landings or take-offs (thousands)	Terminal passengers (thousands)	Freight loaded plus unloaded (thousand tonnes)
1950	195	2,133	31
1951	187	2,471	44
1952	195	2,776	40
1953	214	3,419	64
1954	232	4,004	84
1955	259	4,831	113
1956	293	5,617	121
1957	329	6,600	139
1958	340	6,761	167
1959	358	7,867	226
1960	402	10,075	279
1961	447	12,249	313
1962	449	13,793	344
1963	458	15,506	360
1964	480	17,649	399
1965	508	19,918	418
1966	556	22,582	517
1967	566	24,003	488
1968	560	24,845	524
1969	591	28,064	585
1970	607	31,606	580
1971	630	34,934	532
1972	669	39,125	649
1973	719	43,125	699
1974	710	40,082	717
1975	701	41,846	638
1976	740	44,666	659
1977	759	45,927	705
1978	862	52,829	748
1979	924	56,992	797
1980	954	57,823	744
1981	927	57,771	724
1982	973	58,778	693
1983	1,019	61,109	726
1984	1,079	67,572	861
1985	1,097	70,434	850
1986	1,125	75,161	881
1987	1,193	86,041	976
1988	1,280	93,162	1,088
1989	1,375	98,913	1,151
1990	1,420	102,418	1,193
1991	1,369	95,770	1,126
1992	1,448	106,123	1,238
1993	1,484	112,277	1,376
1994	1,485	122,159	1,589
1995	1,551	129,369	1,703
1996	1,630	135,810	1,772
1997	1,703	146,657	1,943
1998	1,807	158,856	2,080
1999	1,899	168,363	2,189
2000	1,986	179,885	2,314
2001	2,030	181,231	2,146
2002	2,023	188,761	2,195
2003	2,088	199,950	2,208
2004	2,208	215,681	2,371

1 Includes double counting of domestic traffic, unlike table 2.2.

☎020-7944 3088

The figures in this table are outside the scope of National Statistics

Source - Civil Aviation Authority

2.2 Traffic at United Kingdom airports: by type of service and operator: 1994-2004

(a) Air transport movements (aircraft landings or take-offs) — Thousands

	1994	1995	1996	1997	1998	1999	2000	2001	2002	2003	2004
International (incl. traffic to/from UK oil rigs):											
UK operators											
Scheduled	323	334	366	405	440	478	517	536	529	514	545
Non-scheduled	201	211	204	215	225	219	221	214	223	215	203
Total	524	545	570	620	665	697	738	750	752	729	748
Foreign operators											
Scheduled	354	369	395	406	434	474	503	496	497	559	601
Non-scheduled	37	37	39	40	46	42	44	56	45	44	47
Total	391	406	434	446	480	516	547	552	542	603	648
Domestic: [1, 2]											
Scheduled	258	272	284	292	306	317	324	338	340	343	370
Non-scheduled	27	28	29	27	25	26	26	26	24	20	20
Total	285	300	313	319	331	343	350	364	363	363	390
UK operators total: [1, 2]											
Scheduled	581	606	650	697	746	795	841	874	869	857	915
Non-scheduled	228	239	233	242	250	245	247	240	247	235	223
Total	809	845	883	939	996	1,040	1,088	1,114	1,115	1,092	1,138
Foreign operators	391	406	434	446	480	516	547	552	542	603	648
All operators: [1]	1,200	1,251	1,317	1,385	1,476	1,556	1,635	1,666	1,657	1,695	1,786
Selected airports: [3]											
Gatwick	179	190	209	227	240	245	251	244	234	234	241
Heathrow	409	419	427	429	441	449	460	458	460	457	470
Luton	15	19	28	37	44	51	56	56	55	58	64
Stansted	54	63	75	82	102	132	144	151	152	169	177
Birmingham	71	74	77	80	88	98	108	111	112	116	109
Bristol	24	26	26	30	32	33	34	41	46	50	55
East Midlands	28	32	35	36	39	39	40	41	49	54	56
Manchester	143	146	141	146	162	169	178	182	178	192	208
Newcastle	36	35	39	41	41	42	43	46	44	42	50
Aberdeen	74	73	78	82	85	78	78	83	80	77	81
Edinburgh	57	60	66	69	72	81	86	98	105	105	112
Glasgow	74	74	75	79	83	86	88	91	87	88	92
Belfast International	29	37	33	32	37	43	41	46	38	40	43

1 Adjusted to eliminate double counting.
2 Includes movements by foreign operators on domestic routes.
3 Includes double counting.

☎020-7944 3088
The figures in this table are outside the scope of National Statistics
Source - Civil Aviation Authority

2.2 (continued) Traffic at United Kingdom airports: by type of service and operator: 1994-2004

(b) Terminal passengers (arrivals or departures) Millions

	1994	1995	1996	1997	1998	1999	2000	2001	2002	2003	2004
International (incl. traffic to/from oil rigs)											
UK operators											
Scheduled	32.1	34.8	37.8	41.8	46.8	50.1	54.5	53.6	54.3	56.4	63.2
Non-scheduled	27.5	27.9	26.3	28.7	31.6	32.6	33.2	34.0	33.9	33.4	32.2
Total	59.6	62.7	64.1	70.5	78.4	82.7	87.7	87.6	88.2	89.8	95.4
Foreign operators											
Scheduled	32.7	34.5	36.9	39.9	42.5	46.6	51.1	51.3	54.5	60.2	67.6
Non-scheduled	4.0	4.2	4.4	4.3	4.5	4.1	3.9	4.0	3.9	4.1	4.1
Total	36.7	38.7	41.3	44.2	47.0	50.7	55.0	55.3	58.4	64.3	71.7
Domestic: [1,2]											
Scheduled	12.6	13.7	15.0	15.7	16.5	17.3	18.4	18.9	20.8	22.4	23.7
Non-scheduled	0.3	0.3	0.2	0.3	0.2	0.2	0.2	0.2	0.2	0.2	0.2
Total	12.9	14.0	15.2	16.0	16.7	17.5	18.6	19.2	21.0	22.6	23.9
UK operators total: [1,2]											
Scheduled	44.7	48.4	52.8	57.5	63.3	67.4	72.9	72.5	75.1	78.8	86.9
Non-scheduled	27.8	28.2	26.5	29.0	31.8	32.8	33.4	34.2	34.1	33.8	32.4
Total	72.5	76.6	79.3	86.5	95.1	100.2	106.3	106.8	109.2	112.6	119.3
Foreign operators	36.7	38.7	41.3	44.2	47.0	50.7	55.0	55.3	58.4	64.3	71.7
All traffic: [1]	109.2	115.3	120.6	130.7	142.1	150.9	161.3	162.1	167.6	176.9	191.0
Selected airports:											
International:											
Gatwick	19.4	20.6	22.0	24.4	26.3	27.6	29.0	28.1	26.1	26.0	27.5
Heathrow	44.3	46.8	48.3	50.6	53.2	54.8	56.9	53.8	56.4	56.6	60.2
Luton	1.7	1.7	2.0	2.5	3.3	3.9	4.4	4.8	4.7	5.1	5.9
Stansted	2.8	3.1	3.8	4.2	5.6	8.0	10.4	11.6	13.6	16.0	18.2
Birmingham	3.9	4.3	4.4	4.8	5.4	5.8	6.3	6.5	6.7	7.5	7.5
Bristol	1.1	1.1	1.1	1.2	1.4	1.6	1.7	2.1	2.5	2.8	3.3
East Midlands	1.3	1.5	1.4	1.5	1.8	1.9	1.9	2.0	2.7	3.4	3.6
Manchester	12.1	12.1	12.0	13.3	14.6	14.7	15.5	16.3	15.9	16.4	17.7
Newcastle	1.7	1.7	1.6	1.8	2.0	2.0	2.2	2.4	2.2	2.5	3.0
Aberdeen	0.7	0.7	0.8	0.9	0.9	0.8	0.8	0.9	0.9	1.0	1.0
Edinburgh	0.6	0.7	0.8	0.9	1.0	1.3	1.5	1.8	1.8	2.0	2.2
Glasgow	2.9	2.6	2.4	2.8	3.0	3.3	3.4	3.4	3.5	3.5	3.9
Belfast	0.6	0.7	0.7	0.7	0.8	1.0	0.9	1.0	0.9	1.0	1.2
Domestic: [3]											
Gatwick	1.6	1.8	2.1	2.4	2.7	2.8	2.9	3.0	3.4	3.9	3.9
Heathrow	7.1	7.3	7.4	7.2	7.2	7.1	7.4	6.6	6.7	6.7	6.9
Luton	0.1	0.1	0.5	0.7	0.9	1.3	1.7	1.8	1.7	1.7	1.6
Stansted	0.5	0.8	1.0	1.2	1.2	1.5	1.4	2.0	2.5	2.7	2.7
Birmingham	0.8	0.9	1.0	1.0	1.2	1.1	1.2	1.2	1.2	1.4	1.3
Bristol	0.2	0.3	0.3	0.3	0.4	0.4	0.4	0.5	0.9	1.1	1.3
East Midlands	0.3	0.3	0.4	0.4	0.4	0.4	0.3	0.3	0.5	0.8	0.8
Manchester	2.2	2.3	2.4	2.4	2.6	2.7	2.8	2.8	2.7	3.1	3.3
Newcastle	0.7	0.7	0.8	0.8	0.9	0.9	1.0	1.0	1.2	1.5	1.7
Aberdeen	1.2	1.3	1.4	1.5	1.6	1.5	1.5	1.7	1.6	1.5	1.5
Edinburgh	2.4	2.6	3.0	3.2	3.5	3.7	4.0	4.3	5.1	5.5	5.8
Glasgow	2.6	2.8	3.0	3.2	3.4	3.5	3.6	3.8	4.3	4.6	4.6
Belfast	1.4	1.6	1.7	1.8	1.8	2.1	2.2	2.6	2.7	3.0	3.2
All traffic: [3]											
Gatwick	21.0	22.4	24.1	26.8	29.0	30.4	31.9	31.1	29.5	29.9	31.3
Heathrow	51.4	54.1	55.7	57.8	60.4	61.9	64.3	60.4	63.0	63.2	67.1
Luton	1.8	1.8	2.5	3.2	4.2	5.2	6.1	6.6	6.5	6.8	7.5
Stansted	3.3	3.9	4.8	5.4	6.8	9.5	11.8	13.6	16.0	18.7	21.0
Birmingham	4.7	5.2	5.4	5.8	6.6	6.9	7.5	7.7	7.9	8.9	8.8
Bristol	1.3	1.4	1.4	1.6	1.8	2.0	2.1	2.7	3.4	3.9	4.6
East Midlands	1.6	1.8	1.8	1.9	2.2	2.3	2.2	2.3	3.2	4.3	4.4
Manchester	14.3	14.4	14.4	15.7	17.2	17.4	18.3	19.1	18.6	19.5	21.0
Newcastle	2.4	2.4	2.4	2.6	2.9	2.9	3.2	3.4	3.4	3.9	4.7
Aberdeen	1.9	2.0	2.2	2.4	2.5	2.3	2.3	2.5	2.5	2.5	2.6
Edinburgh	3.0	3.3	3.8	4.1	4.5	5.0	5.5	6.0	6.9	7.5	8.0
Glasgow	5.5	5.4	5.4	6.0	6.4	6.8	7.0	7.2	7.8	8.1	8.6
Belfast	2.0	2.3	2.4	2.5	2.6	3.0	3.1	3.6	3.6	4.0	4.4

1 Adjusted to eliminate double counting.
2 Includes passengers travelling with foreign operators on domestic routes
3 Includes double counting.

☎020-7944 3088
The figures in this table are outside the scope of National Statistics
Source - Civil Aviation Authority

2.2 (continued) Traffic at United Kingdom airports: by type of service and operator: 1994-2004

(c) Cargo handled (excl. mail and passengers' luggage) — Thousand tonnes

	1994	1995	1996	1997	1998	1999	2000	2001	2002	2003	2004
International (incl. traffic to/from oil rigs)											
UK operators											
Scheduled	524	550	569	656	714	734	773	658	678	702	778
Non-scheduled	74	103	90	83	74	85	75	54	44	33	33
Total	598	653	659	739	788	819	848	712	722	735	811
Foreign operators											
Scheduled	781	818	855	954	997	1,053	1,091	1,043	1,090	1,115	1,210
Non-scheduled	100	106	138	148	200	216	265	279	275	240	226
Total	881	924	993	1,102	1,197	1,269	1,356	1,322	1,365	1,355	1,436
Domestic: [1]											
Scheduled	16	17	20	18	15	14	14	11	10	15	18
Non-scheduled	39	46	40	33	33	36	42	44	45	43	43
Total	55	63	59	50	47	50	56	55	55	58	61
UK operators total: [1, 2]											
Scheduled	540	567	589	674	728	748	787	669	688	718	796
Non-scheduled	113	149	130	116	107	121	117	98	89	75	76
Total	653	716	718	789	835	869	904	767	777	793	872
Foreign operators	881	924	993	1,102	1,197	1,269	1,356	1,322	1,365	1,355	1,436
All operators: [1]	1,534	1,640	1,711	1,891	2,032	2,138	2,260	2,089	2,142	2,148	2,308
Selected airports: [3]											
Gatwick	222	229	267	265	274	294	319	280	243	223	218
Heathrow	963	1,032	1,040	1,156	1,209	1,265	1,307	1,180	1,235	1,223	1,325
Luton	10	12	16	21	26	23	33	23	20	23	26
Stansted	83	89	103	126	179	174	166	166	184	199	226
Birmingham	19	21	19	20	18	29	9	12	13	12	10
East Midlands	55	81	104	126	123	128	178	195	219	227	253
Kent International	5	5	2	2	6	23	32	36	32	43	27
Liverpool	24	30	27	25	25	25	29	23	14	12	9
Manchester	91	80	79	94	101	108	117	106	113	123	149
Edinburgh	4	5	7	8	14	18	18	16	21	25	27
Glasgow	18	13	11	11	8	9	9	6	5	5	8
Prestwick	14	20	22	34	40	41	41	43	40	40	34
Belfast International	26	30	27	25	25	26	31	32	29	30	32

1 Adjusted to eliminate double counting.
2 Includes freight carried by foreign operators on domestic routes.
3 Includes double counting.

☎020-7944 3088
The figures in this table are outside the scope of National Statistics
Source - Civil Aviation Authority

2.3 Punctuality at United Kingdom Airports: Percentage of flights on time (within 15 minutes): 1994-2004

Percentage

	All reporting London airports		All reporting regional airports		All reporting airports	
	Scheduled	Charter	Scheduled	Charter	Scheduled	Charter
1994	*79*	*50*	*86*	*51*	*81*	*50*
1995	*77*	*51*	*85*	*56*	*79*	*53*
1996	*74*	*47*	*83*	*57*	*77*	*52*
1997	*71*	*46*	*80*	*56*	*74*	*51*
1998	*69*	*50*	*78*	*56*	*72*	*53*
1999	*69*	*49*	*76*	*53*	*71*	*51*
2000	*70*	*52*	*77*	*55*	*72*	*53*
2001	*71*	*60*	*77*	*58*	*73*	*58*
2002	*69*	*68*	*76*	*68*	*72*	*68*
2003	*75*	*73*	*79*	*74*	*76*	*74*
2004	*73*	*69*	*78*	*71*	*75*	*70*

☎020-7944 3088
The figures in this table are outside the scope of National Statistics
Source - Civil Aviation Authority

2.4 Main outputs of United Kingdom airlines: by type of service: 1994-2004

(a) Aircraft kilometres flown — Million kilometres

	1994	1995	1996	1997	1998	1999	2000	2001	2002	2003	2004
International:											
Scheduled	541	579	630	698	789	827	895	920	921	965	1,059
Non-scheduled	344	363	359	370	403	427	447	437	412	431	423
Total	885	942	988	1,068	1,192	1,254	1,342	1,357	1,333	1,396	1,483
Domestic:											
Scheduled	95	101	106	111	118	120	121	128	126	123	138
Non-scheduled	8	8	8	8	7	7	7	8	9	8	8
Total	103	109	114	119	125	127	129	136	135	131	146
All services:											
Scheduled	636	680	735	809	886	947	1,016	1,048	1,047	1,088	1,198
Non-scheduled	352	371	367	378	410	434	455	445	421	440	431
Total	988	1,051	1,102	1,187	1,297	1,381	1,471	1,493	1,468	1,528	1,629

(b) Passengers uplifted — Millions

	1994	1995	1996	1997	1998	1999	2000	2001	2002	2003	2004
International:											
Scheduled	31	34	36	40	45	48	52	51	52	56	64
Non-scheduled	27	27	26	28	31	32	33	34	34	33	32
Total	58	61	62	69	76	81	86	85	86	89	96
Domestic:											
Scheduled	13.0	14.0	15.0	15.9	16.6	17.1	18.0	18.2	19.8	20.8	22.5
Non-scheduled	0.4	0.4	0.3	0.3	0.3	0.2	0.2	0.3	0.3	0.3	0.2
Total	13.3	14.3	15.3	16.2	16.9	17.4	18.2	18.5	20.2	21.0	22.7
All services:											
Scheduled	44	47	51	56	62	65	70	69	72	76	86
Non-scheduled	27	27	26	28	31	33	33	34	34	34	32
Total	71	75	77	85	93	98	104	104	107	110	118

(c) Passenger kilometres flown — Billion kilometres

	1994	1995	1996	1997	1998	1999	2000	2001	2002	2003	2004
International:											
Scheduled	99	110	119	130	145	153	163	151	148	156	173
Non-scheduled	67	70	72	77	84	87	90	90	88	89	90
Total	166	179	191	206	229	240	253	241	236	245	263
Domestic:											
Scheduled	5.3	5.8	6.2	6.6	6.9	7.2	7.5	7.6	8.3	8.9	9.5
Non-scheduled	0.1	0.1	0.1	0.1	0.1	0.1	0.1	0.1	0.1	0.2	0.2
Total	5.5	5.9	6.3	6.8	7.0	7.3	7.6	7.7	8.5	9.1	9.8
All services:											
Scheduled	104	115	125	136	152	160	170	159	156	165	183
Non-scheduled	67	70	72	77	84	87	90	90	88	90	90
Total	171	185	197	213	236	248	261	249	244	254	273

(d) Passenger seat occupancy — Percentage

	1994	1995	1996	1997	1998	1999	2000	2001	2002	2003	2004
International:											
Scheduled	*71.2*	*73.7*	*73.5*	*72.6*	*71.9*	*71.1*	*72.6*	*70.9*	*74.5*	*74.8*	*75.8*
Non-scheduled	*90.1*	*89.0*	*88.7*	*89.6*	*89.7*	*89.4*	*89.5*	*89.9*	*90.4*	*89.2*	*89.9*
Total	*77.7*	*79.0*	*78.6*	*78.1*	*77.5*	*76.8*	*77.9*	*77.0*	*79.7*	*79.5*	*80.1*
Domestic:											
Scheduled	*61.9*	*63.3*	*64.0*	*64.1*	*62.0*	*60.6*	*64.2*	*61.8*	*66.0*	*70.5*	*68.0*
Non-scheduled	*66.1*	*69.0*	*68.1*	*68.9*	*69.2*	*66.4*	*62.2*	*62.3*	*60.6*	*66.0*	*61.8*
Total	*62.0*	*63.4*	*64.0*	*64.2*	*62.1*	*60.7*	*64.9*	*61.8*	*65.9*	*70.4*	*67.9*
All services:											
Scheduled	*70.6*	*73.1*	*73.0*	*72.2*	*71.3*	*70.6*	*72.2*	*69.9*	*74.0*	*74.5*	*75.3*
Non-scheduled	*90.0*	*89.0*	*88.6*	*89.5*	*89.7*	*89.3*	*89.4*	*89.9*	*90.3*	*89.1*	*89.8*
Total	*77.1*	*78.4*	*78.0*	*77.6*	*76.9*	*76.2*	*77.4*	*75.9*	*79.1*	*79.1*	*79.6*

2.4 Main outputs of United Kingdom airlines: by type of service: 1994-2004(continued)

(e) Cargo and mail uplifted — Thousand tonnes

	1994	1995	1996	1997	1998	1999	2000	2001	2002	2003	2004
International:											
Scheduled	585	610	655	752	800	834	873	723	752	783	879
Non-scheduled	106	119	119	96	161	178	151	114	101	105	122
Total	691	729	774	848	960	1,012	1,024	837	853	888	1,002
Domestic:											
Scheduled	33	34	35	31	32	26	25	13	17	17	15
Non-scheduled	66	70	65	69	66	71	72	75	70	64	56
Total	99	103	100	99	98	97	96	88	87	81	71
All services:											
Scheduled	618	643	691	783	831	860	897	736	769	801	895
Non-scheduled	172	189	184	165	227	249	223	189	170	169	178
Total	790	832	875	948	1,059	1,109	1,120	925	939	969	1,072

(f) Cargo and mail tonne-kilometres flown — Millions

	1994	1995	1996	1997	1998	1999	2000	2001	2002	2003	2004
International:											
Scheduled	3,512	3,705	3,994	4,614	4,829	5,068	5,330	4,643	4,991	5,235	5,693
Non-scheduled	304	356	472	357	413	460	533	519	295	343	331
Total	3,816	4,061	4,466	4,972	5,242	5,528	5,863	5,162	5,286	5,578	6,024
Domestic:											
Scheduled	13	14	14	12	12	10	10	8	6	6	5
Non-scheduled	22	23	22	23	22	24	24	26	25	24	23
Total	35	36	36	35	34	34	33	34	31	30	29
All services:											
Scheduled	3,525	3,718	4,008	4,626	4,841	5,078	5,339	4,651	4,997	5,242	5,698
Non-scheduled	326	379	494	380	434	484	557	545	320	367	354
Total	3,851	4,097	4,502	5,006	5,275	5,562	5,896	5,196	5,317	5,608	6,053

☎020-7944 3088

The figures in this table are outside the scope of National Statistics

Source - Civil Aviation Authority

2.5 Forecasts of air traffic demand:[1] 1998 - 2020

Million terminal passengers at UK airports

	1998	2005	2010	2015	2020
International: [2]					
Low	.	153	180	211	247
Mid	104	159	193	235	284
High	.	164	208	261	327
Domestic: [3]					
Low	.	41	47	54	62
Mid	34	42	50	60	71
High	.	44	54	67	82
Total:					
Low	.	221	257	300	349
Mid	160	229	276	333	401
High	.	237	297	371	461

1 Published in June 2000.

2 Figures are on a different basis from those in Table 2.2(b) because they exclude airside interliners (passengers flying into and out of an airport without passing through passport control) and miscellaneous traffic, such as passengers to and from oil rigs. These passengers are included in the overall total.

3 Figures are on a different basis from those in Table 2.2(b) because passengers are counted at the airports at both ends of the journey.

☎020-7944 4276

The figures in this table are outside the scope of National Statistics

Source - Economics, Aviation, Maritime and International Division: DfT

Further details on 2000 Air Traffic Forecasts, available at: http://www.dft.gov.uk/aviation

2.6 United Kingdom airline fleet: 1994-2004

Aircraft in service (at end of year)											Number
	1994	1995	1996	1997	1998	1999	2000	2001	2002	2003	2004
Total	695	700	722	758	837	850	889	928	903	921	945
ow:											
Atlantic Airlines	13	13	15	17	17	18	18	18	18	19	19
Aurigny Air Services	.	.	.	9	9	11	12	12	13	13	14
Bac Express Airlines Ltd	.	.	.	9	10	10	12	12	12	16	..
Britannia Airways	29	29	28	27	28	28	32	31	32	32	37
British Airways [1]	227	212	212	226	229	217	235	235	240	240	228
British Airways (Euro Ops) [1]	16	26	28	34	34	40	38	35	.	.	.
British Airways Citiexpress Ltd [2]	9	9	9	11	19	19	22	22	21	68	63
BMI British Midland [3]	34	34	34	34	37	40	45	46	43	43	31
Channel Express	13	15	14	13	15	15	14	14	15	21	26
City Flyer Express [4]	10	11	11	14	16	19	21	21	21	.	.
EasyJet Airline Company Ltd	.	.	.	6	9	15	17	22	32	69	94
Emerald Airways Ltd	8	8	10	11	16	15	15	16	16	26	28
European Air Charter	5	14	15	15	16	13	11	13	13	13	12
First Choice Airways Ltd [5]	14	18	17	16	22	25	27	29	31	32	30
Flybe British European [6,7]	17	16	17	18	24	28	31	31	31	33	35
GB Airways Ltd	.	.	.	7	9	9	10	10	11	13	13
KLM UK [8,9]	36	37	41	39	41	41	38	37	38	.	.
Loganair	14	14	13	6	11	12	14	15	16	15	16
Manx and British Regional [10]	26	23	29	39	37	43	49	50	45	.	.
Monarch	18	22	24	17	17	20	19	22	23	22	24
My Travel Airways UK [11]	14	19	18	20	21	24	31	31	34	35	31
Virgin Atlantic	13	12	15	20	25	29	32	34	35	38	35

1 BA Euro Ops became part of the BA mainline fleet from 28 March 2002.
2 Prior to April 2002 known as Brymon Airways Ltd
and British Regional operations merged in October 2002.
3 Prior to May 2001 known as British Midland.
4 Operations merged with those of British Airways Citiexpress Ltd since October 2003.
5 Prior to 2003 known as Air 2000.
6 Prior to 2000 known as Jersey European Airways (UK).
7 Prior to July 2002 British European.
8 Air UK until take over by KLM in November 1997.
9 Company ceased trading April 2003.
10 Manx name changed to BA Citiexpress (IOM) Ltd in September 2002
and British Regional Airlines Ltd cease trade in October 2002.
11 Prior to 2002 known as Airtours Intl Airways Ltd.

☎020-7944 3088
The figures in this table are outside
the scope of National Statistics
Source - Civil Aviation Authority

2.7 Activity at major airports: 2004

Country	Location	Name	Terminal passengers: All (millions)	Terminal passengers: ow: International (millions)	Freight loaded plus unloaded [1] Tonnes (thousands)	Commercial air transport movements: All [2] (thousands)	Commercial air transport movements: ow: International (thousands)
USA	Atlanta	Hartsfield	83	6	865	952	46
USA	Chicago	O'Hare International	76	11	1,532	981	91
UK	London	Heathrow	67	60	1,412	470	408
Japan	Tokyo	Haneda	62	-	774	302	3 [3]
USA	Los Angeles	Los Angeles International	61	17	1,903	638	105
USA	Dallas	Dallas-Ft.Worth International	59	5	755	798	66 [3]
Germany	Frankfurt	Frankfurt International	51	44	1,839	469	390
France	Paris	Charles De Gaulle	51	46	1,638	535	467
Netherlands	Amsterdam	Schiphol	42	42	1,467	403	395
USA	Denver	Denver International	42	1	318	556	8 [3]
USA	Las Vegas	Maccarran International	41	1	91	473	13 [3]
USA	Phoenix	Sky Harbor International	40	2	303	488	10 [3]
USA	New York	J. F. Kennedy International	39	17	1,683	311	115
Spain	Madrid	Barajas	38	20	374	395	203
USA	Minneapolis	Minneapolis-St Paul International	37	2	252	500	12 [3]
USA	Houston	G. Bush Intercontinental	37	6	405	502	51 [3]
Hong Kong SAR	Hong Kong	Hong Kong International	36	36	3,132	238	237
Thailand	Bangkok	Bangkok International	36	26	1,058	245	165
USA	Detroit	Wayne County	35	3	230 [3]	505	29 [3]
China	Beijing	Capital	33	8	669	286	67
USA	New York	Newark International	33	9	920	423	73
USA	San Francisco	San Francisco International	32	8	658 [3]	323	46
UK	London	Gatwick	31	28	227	241	194
USA	Orlando	Orlando International	31	2	203	295	14
USA	Miami	Miami International	30	14	1,779	381	172

1 Includes mail
2 All commercial movements including positioning and local movements.
3 Estimated

☎020-7944 3088
The figures in this table are outside the scope of National Statistics
Source - ICAO

2.8 United Kingdom international passenger movements by air: arrivals plus departures: by country of embarkation or landing: 1994-2004

Thousands

	1994	1995	1996	1997	1998	1999	2000	2001	2002	2003	2004
European Union: [1]											
Austria	1,143	1,173	1,160	1,151	1,191	1,201	1,257	1,278	1,443	1,508	1,749
Belgium	1,878	1,864	1,923	2,338	2,673	2,858	2,864	2,686	2,343	2,277	1,863
Denmark	1,277	1,386	1,593	1,668	1,691	1,780	1,965	1,988	2,070	2,013	2,186
France	7,245	6,556	6,385	6,428	7,059	7,580	8,235	8,435	9,657	10,232	10,941
Finland	418	493	618	603	604	666	770	753	659	702	813
Germany	6,188	6,536	6,937	7,123	7,454	8,107	8,717	8,432	8,651	9,571	10,283
Greece	4,963	4,578	3,589	3,773	4,435	5,248	5,912	6,410	6,246	6,204	5,840
Irish Republic	5,121	6,016	6,935	7,781	8,522	8,966	9,295	9,293	9,813	10,163	10,862
Italy	4,189	4,708	4,943	5,233	5,895	6,454	7,033	7,456	7,654	8,913	9,677
Luxembourg	160	161	161	190	215	224	224	203	184	159	173
Netherlands	4,005	4,277	4,933	5,766	6,477	6,777	7,096	7,313	7,804	7,780	7,933
Portugal & Madeira [2]	2,692	2,761	2,674	2,887	3,178	3,443	3,607	3,752	3,967	4,022	4,256
Spain & Canary Islands	17,644	18,265	17,793	19,559	22,089	23,803	25,923	27,576	28,952	32,230	33,478
Sweden	1,119	1,213	1,305	1,589	1,877	1,896	2,032	1,958	1,976	1,993	2,253
Cyprus	1,940	1,834	1,521	1,691	2,034	2,333	2,670	2,962	2,683	2,787	2,776
Czech Republic	288	335	425	490	520	541	654	736	916	1,296	2,069
Estonia	1	3	16	24	29	27	28	29	38	45	83
Hungary	246	273	314	325	357	398	403	383	360	375	701
Latvia	19	52	51	64	68	64	51	54	58	61	126
Lithuania	19	25	29	32	51	58	51	48	48	55	95
Malta	1,186	1,063	948	1,029	1,045	994	1,022	1,039	1,025	1,055	1,096
Poland	194	261	299	348	419	499	498	453	467	516	998
Slovak Republic	-	-	-	3	1	-	-	-	2	29	127
Slovenia	42	49	50	47	58	71	69	52	48	53	116
Total EU-15	58,042	59,987	60,949	66,089	73,360	79,003	84,930	87,534	91,419	97,768	102,308
Total EU-25	61,979	63,880	64,603	70,142	77,941	83,989	90,376	93,289	97,064	104,040	110,495
Rest of Europe:											
Norway	1,063	1,160	1,276	1,488	1,615	1,569	1,432	1,244	1,277	1,353	1,606
Switzerland	2,644	2,714	2,868	3,100	3,228	3,631	3,926	3,829	3,983	4,108	4,184
Gibraltar	147	167	158	166	183	197	208	215	227	264	309
Turkey	1,613	2,166	2,368	2,450	2,454	2,028	2,019	2,112	2,233	2,175	2,791
Former Yugoslavia [3]	50	83	123	204	231	151	222	269	309	351	433
Other Western Europe	112	128	161	211	240	272	329	340	268	332	403
Other Eastern Europe	356	307	294	335	353	311	282	297	393	518	728
Total Rest of Europe	5,985	6,725	7,249	7,953	8,304	8,159	8,419	8,306	8,690	9,099	10,455
Total Europe	67,964	70,605	71,852	78,095	86,245	92,149	98,795	101,595	105,754	113,139	120,950
Former USSR [4]	461	496	533	583	603	576	667	727	816	911	1,030
North Africa	1,079	1,149	1,149	1,296	1,140	1,322	1,554	1,598	1,511	1,506	2,016
Southern Africa	775	943	1,043	1,220	1,371	1,438	1,510	1,588	1,584	1,602	1,768
Rest of Africa	964	900	972	861	854	1,009	1,129	1,163	1,310	1,336	1,588
Israel	762	862	885	878	925	969	967	770	630	617	659
Persian Gulf States	329	362	364	344	377	382	404	390	431	481	534
Saudi Arabia	338	337	357	385	378	350	346	297	263	229	247
UAE	558	644	698	849	926	1,056	1,324	1,524	1,795	2,022	2,535
Rest of Near and Middle East	493	564	605	705	777	849	913	875	907	1,002	1,238
USA	12,173	13,248	14,403	15,652	17,153	18,251	19,208	17,060	16,879	16,584	18,004
Canada	2,096	2,292	2,543	2,868	3,140	3,249	3,301	3,133	2,961	2,894	3,308
South America	392	410	467	474	572	587	610	523	414	379	394
Central America	236	306	471	833	825	838	862	927	884	906	1,150
Caribbean	941	1,010	1,121	1,235	1,399	1,635	1,744	1,692	1,657	1,763	1,895
Australia	720	845	799	782	900	918	916	737	693	727	874
New Zealand	153	135	159	173	187	194	203	154	130	202	180
India	752	856	970	973	1,012	911	911	1,017	858	960	1,073
Pakistan	280	309	340	376	387	413	477	486	443	517	582
Rest of Indian sub-continent	394	424	449	503	536	635	713	681	682	770	856
Japan	1,186	1,241	1,348	1,462	1,440	1,325	1,416	1,131	1,209	1,046	1,189
Hong Kong	947	939	1,024	1,007	1,021	996	1,081	983	1,113	1,020	1,275
Singapore	585	604	765	828	863	1,011	1,144	1,209	1,203	1,150	1,169
Thailand	350	380	443	374	446	525	575	710	715	673	718
Rest of Asia	827	1,032	1,161	1,312	1,234	1,281	1,349	1,215	1,242	1,205	1,447
Total rest of world [5]	27,792	30,285	33,069	35,972	38,465	40,721	43,323	40,592	40,328	40,505	45,731
All international air passenger movements	95,754	100,893	104,921	114,068	124,712	132,868	142,120	142,187	146,082	153,644	166,681

1 Austria, Finland and Sweden joined the EU in 1995 but are included in the EU totals for all years. EU totals are given with (EU-25) and without (EU-15) the 10 states that joined the EU in May 2004.
2 Includes Azores and Cape Verde Islands.
3 Or former constituent states, excluding Slovenia.
4 Or former constituent states, excluding Estonia, Latvia and Lithuania.
5 Includes Greenland.

☎020-7944 3088

The figures in this table are outside the scope of National Statistics
Source - Civil Aviation Authority

2.9 Casualties caused by aviation accidents: 1994-2004

(a) Casualties caused by accidents involving United Kingdom registered aircraft in the United Kingdom airspace

	1994	1995	1996	1997	1998	1999	2000	2001	2002	2003	2004
Airline and air taxi:											
Fixed-wing:											
Crew:											
Fatal	1	3	1	0	0	2	1	2	0	0	0
Total	2	5	3	3	0	2	4	2	0	3	0
Passengers:											
Fatal	0	9	0	1	0	6	4	0	0	0	0
Total	2	14	2	3	1	10	4	0	0	0	0
Total fixed-wing [1]	4	20	6	6	1	12	8	2	0	3	0
Rotary wing:											
Crew:											
Fatal	0	0	1	1	1	0	0	0	2	0	0
Total	0	0	2	3	3	0	1	2	3	3	0
Passengers:											
Fatal	0	0	4	0	3	0	0	0	9	0	0
Total	0	0	6	0	5	0	2	3	11	0	0
Total rotary-wing [1]	1	0	8	3	8	0	3	6	14	3	0
Other (general aviation, etc.):											
Crew:											
Fatal	18	10	22	14	15	15	20	18	9	8	12
Total	37	32	49	44	37	53	40	50	42	46	41
Passengers:											
Fatal	9	7	7	4	6	11	7	5	3	7	7
Total	24	11	27	33	24	28	22	17	14	21	14
Total other [1]	61	44	78	79	61	82	63	68	58	68	55
Overall total [1]											
Fatal	28	29	35	20	25	34	32	25	23	15	19
Total	66	64	92	88	70	94	74	76	72	74	55

(b) Casualties caused by accidents involving United Kingdom registered aircraft in foreign airspace

	1994	1995	1996	1997	1998	1999	2000	2001	2002	2003	2004
Airline and air taxi:											
Fixed-wing:											
Crew:											
Fatal	0	0	0	0	0	2	3	0	0	0	0
Total	3	4	0	2	0	2	5	0	3	4	1
Passengers:											
Fatal	0	0	0	0	0	1	0	0	0	0	0
Total	0	0	0	4	15	43	14	0	1	1	3
Total fixed-wing [1]	3	4	1	7	15	45	19	1	4	5	4
Other (general aviation, etc.):											
Crew:											
Fatal	1	1	4	0	2	4	2	4	1	1	1
Total	2	4	4	2	2	8	3	7	1	2	3
Passengers:											
Fatal	0	0	3	0	1	1	1	2	3	1	1
Total	2	2	3	0	3	6	1	3	3	2	3
Total other [1]	4	6	7	2	5	14	4	10	4	4	6
Overall total [1]											
Fatal	1	1	8	0	3	8	6	7	4	2	2
Total	7	10	8	9	20	59	23	11	8	9	10

2.9 (continued) Casualties caused by aviation accidents: 1994-2004

(c) Casualties caused by accidents involving aircraft registered overseas in United Kingdom airspace

	1994	1995	1996	1997	1998	1999	2000	2001	2002	2003	2004
Airline and air taxi:											
Fixed-wing:											
Crew:											
Fatal	0	0	0	0	0	4	0	0	0	0	0
Total	0	0	2	0	0	5	0	0	0	0	0
Passengers:											
Fatal	0	0	0	0	0	0	0	0	0	0	0
Total	0	1	1	0	1	1	0	0	0	0	0
Total fixed-wing [1]	0	1	4	1	1	6	0	0	0	0	0
Other (general aviation, etc.)											
Crew:											
Fatal	7	0	2	1	2	0	2	5	2	4	1
Total	10	0	2	1	10	2	4	9	6	5	4
Passengers:											
Fatal	2	0	0	1	2	0	4	0	3	2	0
Total	3	0	3	1	10	1	6	4	6	5	2
Total other [1]	14	0	5	2	20	3	10	13	13	11	6
Overall total [1]											
Fatal	9	0	2	2	4	4	6	5	5	6	1
Total	14	1	9	3	21	9	10	13	13	11	6

1 These totals include 'third-party' casualties, not shown separately.
Note: Some figures revised in this table.

☎020-7944 3088
The figures in this table are outside the scope of National Statistics
Source - Civil Aviation Authority

2.10 Aircraft proximity (AIRPROX): number of incidents: 1994-2004

	1994	1995	1996	1997	1998	1999	2000	2001	2002	2003	2004
Total AIRPROX civil and military:											
Risk-bearing :											
Risk of collision	15	17	37	36	23	23	28	33	17	14	15
Safety not assured	62	57	58	64	43	49	44	42	68	58	53
Total	77	74	95	100	66	72	72	75	85	72	68
No risk of collision	134	130	113	105	132	134	123	115	129	108	131
Risk not determined	1	4	3	3	3	2	3	5	7	1	8
Total AIRPROX	212	208	211	208	201	208	198	195	221	181	207
ow:											
Commercial air transport:											
Risk-bearing:											
Risk of collision	5	3	6	9	1	4	6	0	1	0	1
Safety not assured	20	21	24	20	14	12	8	14	6	11	7
Total	25	24	30	29	15	16	14	14	7	11	8
No risk of collision	65	64	75	67	82	83	84	64	70	53	67
Risk not determined	1	3	2	0	1	0	1	4	4	0	4
Total commercial air transport	91	91	107	96	98	99	99	82	81	64	79
Commercial air transport aircraft in risk-bearing AIRPROX per 100,000 hours flown in UK airspace	*2.5*	*2.3*	*2.7*	*2.5*	*1.2*	*1.2*	*1.0*	*1.0*	*0.5*	*0.8*	*0.5*

☎020-7944 3088
The figures in this table are outside the scope of National Statistics
Source - UK Airprox Board

2.11 Employment by United Kingdom airlines: worldwide: 1994-2004

Number

	1994	1995	1996	1997	1998	1999	2000	2001	2002	2003	2004
Pilots and co-pilots	6,957	7,201	7,703	7,918	8,548	9,244	9,443	9,984	9,933	9,758	9,798
Other cockpit personnel	466	402	453	458	460	457	332	274	209	120	102
Cabin attendants	18,233	19,744	21,478	24,272	26,967	28,465	28,819	30,461	28,548	28,398	29,634
Maintenance and overhaul personnel	13,805	13,811	13,944	13,100	12,264	12,138	12,055	11,824	11,749	11,186	9,933
Tickets and sales personnel	6,693	7,004	7,644	8,369	8,929	9,643	9,100	10,062	9,074	8,168	7,706
All other personnel	26,033	27,148	28,320	29,355	30,663	32,755	31,764	31,279	27,921	27,265	26,399
Total	72,187	75,310	79,542	83,472	87,831	92,702	91,513	93,884	87,433	84,895	83,572

☎020-7944 3088
The figures in this table are outside the scope of National Statistics
Source - Civil Aviation Authority

2.12 Passenger traffic via major international airlines: 2004

		All scheduled traffic		International scheduled traffic		Charter traffic	
Country	Airline	Passengers uplifted (millions)	Passenger kilometres (billions)	Passengers uplifted (millions)	Passenger kilometres (billions)	All passenger kilometres (billions)	International passenger kilometres (billions)
United States	American	91.6	209.2	18.9	70.0	0.2	0.2
United States	Delta	86.8	157.7	7.5	40.3	0.4	0.2
United States	United	70.1	184.3	10.0	69.6	1.1	1.1
United States	Northwest	55.4	117.9	9.4	51.7	0.2	-
Japan	JAL	51.7	94.8	12.7	64.6	0.7	0.6
Germany	Lufthansa	48.3	109.5	34.4	103.9	-	-
Japan	All Nippon Airways	46.3	54.1	3.4	16.8	0.5	0.5
United States	US Airways	42.4	65.2	4.6	17.1	-	0.0
United States	Continental	40.6	101.7	9.1	40.0	0.3	0.2
France	Air France	39.5	105.3	22.2	84.2	-	-
United Kingdom	British Airways	31.6	103.7	26.3	101.2	0.1	0.1
Ireland	Ryanair	26.6	22.6	26.6	22.6	0.0	0.0
Spain	Iberia	26.3	45.8	11.4	35.9	-	-
Australia	Qantas	24.3	73.6	7.8	50.8	-	-
China	Air China	24.1	46.1	4.2	19.4	0.6	0.3
United Kingdom	Easyjet	22.3	20.4	15.9	17.5	-	-
Italy	Alitalia	22.0	30.2	11.5	26.2	0.2	0.2
China	China Southern Airlines	21.3	29.7	1.6	6.2	0.6	0.2
United States	America West	21.1	37.5	1.0	2.1	-	0.0
Republic Of Korea	Korean Air	21.1	45.6	9.9	41.3	1.1	1.1
Netherlands	KLM	20.4	63.0	20.3	63.0	-	-
Scandinavia	SAS	20.4	24.1	12.8	20.9	1.4	1.4
China	China Eastern Airlines	19.5	29.1	2.8	9.9	0.3	0.1
Thailand	Thai Airways	18.8	50.7	13.3	47.5	0.1	0.1
Malaysia	Malaysian Airlines	17.3	42.6	8.3	37.8	0.0	0.0

☎020-7944 3088
The figures in this table are outside the scope of National Statistics
Source - ICAO

2.13 Major Airports in Great Britain

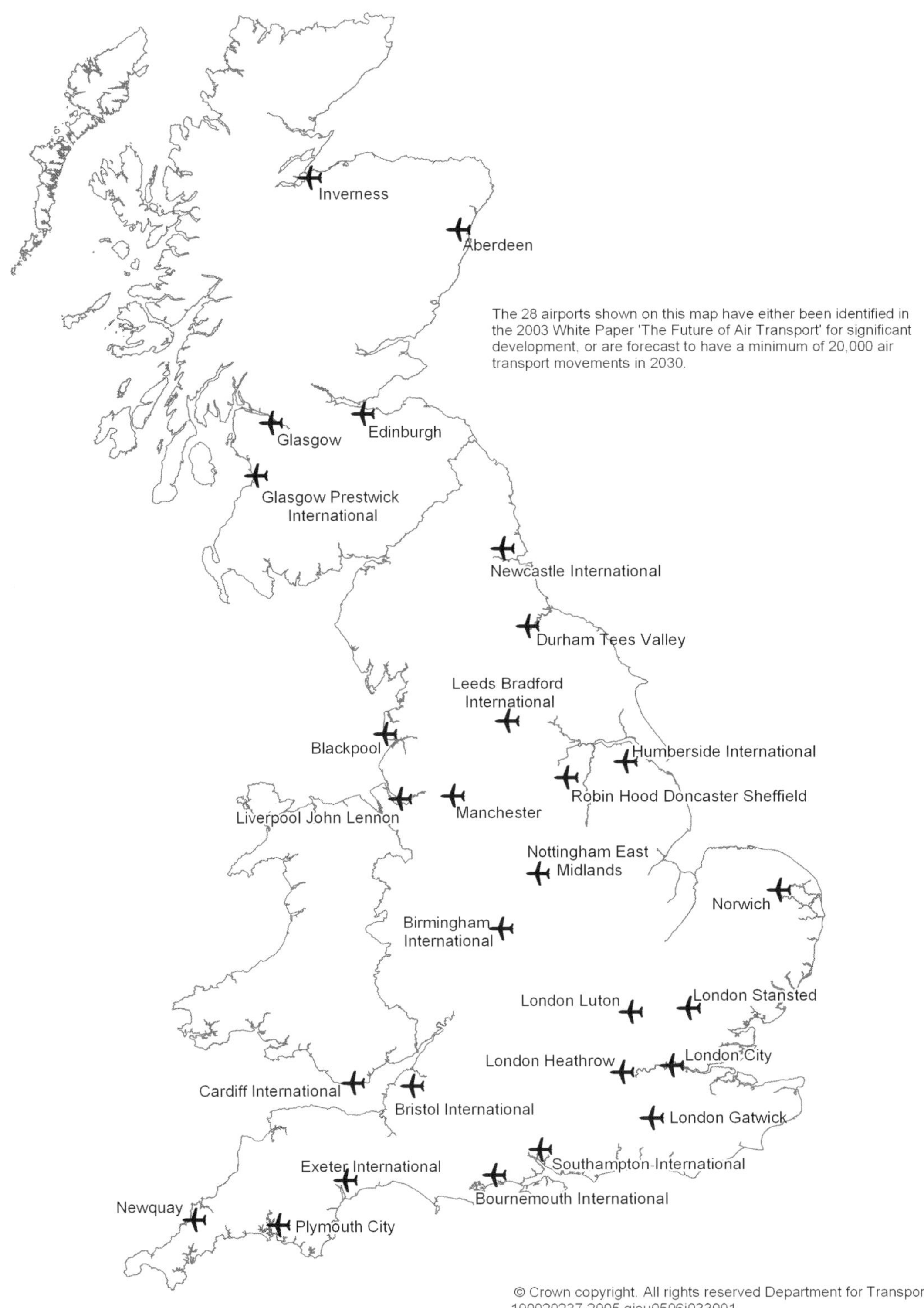

☎020-7944 3088

3 Energy and the Environment:

Notes and Definitions

Petroleum consumption by transport mode: 3.1

Motor spirit: One tonne = 300 gallons or 1,362 litres

Diesel: One tonne = 265 gallons or 1,203 litres

Figures for road vehicle classes are modelled by netcen using the mileage data from the road traffic estimates and fuel efficiency data from experimental testing and surveys. These are not yet available for 2004 and so the 2003 proportions have been used to estimate the 2004 split. A small proportion of motor spirit (estimated to be approximately 0.2 million tonnes per year) is not used by road vehicles, which is included in the total DTI publish for motor spirit used.

For railways, all fuel oil and some of the gas oil is used for heating premises; petroleum used in generating electricity for rail traction is not included. Water transport covers fuel used for fishing, coastal shipping including services between the UK and Eire, ports and inland waterways but excludes deliveries under international marine bunker contracts. Air figures cover fuel uplifted in the UK by domestic and international airlines, aircraft industry own use, private and business flying and armed services.

Total energy use includes use by refineries, power stations and gas works in addition to final users; non-energy use includes feedstock for chemicals, lubricating oils, bitumen and other.

Energy consumption by transport mode: 3.2

This is the energy content of fuels delivered to consumers. For electricity, it does not include the energy lost in generation and distribution. Detailed data for individual fuels are converted from original units to tonnes of oil equivalent using gross calorific values and conversion factors appropriate to each category of fuel.

1 tonne of oil equivalent (toe)
= 10^7 kilocalories
= 396.8 therms
= 41.87 gigajoules
= 11.63 megawatt hours

This unit should be regarded as a measure of energy content rather than a physical quantity. There is no intention to represent an actual physical tonne of oil, and indeed actual tonnes of oil will normally have measurements in tonnes of oil equivalent which differ from unity. Gross calorific values are reviewed each year in collaboration with the fuel industries. Estimated gross calorific values for petroleum and coal are as follows:

47.1 GJ per tonne of motor spirit
45.6 GJ per tonne of diesel

Water and aviation figures have the same coverage as for table 3.1. The total energy used by transport excludes international shipping; however, totals include some fuel for heating transport premises, data which are not included in the separate categories.

Petrol and diesel prices: 3.3

The price estimates are based on information provided by oil marketing companies and super/hypermarket chains and are representative of prices paid (inclusive of taxes) on or about the 15th of the month. Changes in fuel duty usually occur during the month in which a Budget is held. VAT is rebated to business users.

The figures in table 3.3 differ from those in table 10.8 because of the differences in availability and timing of data collection. The international comparisons in table 10.8 (supplied by DTI, and extracted from the weekly *EC Oil bulletin*), are based on averages over the year, whereas table 3.3 attempts to be as up to date as reasonably possible. The use of the term Tax in part (b) of table 10.8 is necessary because some other European countries impose other taxes and fees on fuel. For Great Britain this includes just fuel duty and VAT.

Average fuel consumption: 3.4

Passenger cars: These figures are based upon fuel consumption as recorded by participants in the National Travel Survey (NTS). This is estimated by recording the start and finish points of both the fuel gauge and the milometer, and the amount of fuel put in the vehicle in the travel week.

In 2002 the drawn sample size for the NTS was nearly trebled compared with previous years, enabling key results to be presented on a single year basis for the first time since the survey became continuous. Changes to the methodology in 2002 mean that there are some inconsistencies with data for earlier years. Data for earlier years are shown for a three year time period because of the smaller sample sizes for individual years.

HGVs: These figures are based on fuel consumption as recorded by participants in the Continuing Survey of Road Goods Transport (CSRGT). Respondents report the amount of fuel purchased during the survey week, with the amount of fuel at the start and end of the week assumed to balance out across the sample as a whole.

Unlike the NTS, the sample size is sufficient to report fuel consumption on a yearly basis for the whole time series. The fuel consumption figures have not been re-weighted to the population, so the figures may not be fully representative of the HGV fleet.

Registration-weighted new car fuel consumption (excluding diesels and 4wds): 3.5

Registrations have historically been recorded by engine size, not model. The registration-weighted new car fuel consumption figure is computed by grouping the models in the official new car fuel consumption list into 100cc engine size bands, calculating the average for each band, and then the overall average by applying a weighting based on the proportion of new cars registered in each band.

The figures are produced primarily to monitor trends in average petrol vehicle (excluding 4WD) fuel consumption from year to year. It is derived from figures obtained under carefully controlled conditions in order to ensure repeatability. The actual values achieved on the road will reflect many extraneous factors such as cold starts and different driving conditions. The data shown here represents fuel economy on the current standard of test (a drive cycle simulating urban and extra-urban driving).

Emissions for road vehicles: urban conditions: 3.6

This table takes into account emission factors for cars, light goods vehicles, heavy goods vehicles, buses and coaches and motorcycles of different ages, and indexes them against a baseline emissions from a pre-1993 petrol car without a three-way catalyst (=100). The emission factors, in units of grammes of pollutant per kilometre travelled (g/km), are from the National Atmospheric Emissions Inventory, maintained by netcen on behalf of DEFRA, and are based on the latest compilation of equations derived by the Transport Research Laboratory (TRL) relating emission factor to average vehicle speed. The equations are derived from a database of emissions measured from actual in-service vehicles, the measurements being carried out by different laboratories in the UK and the rest of Europe over different drive cycles. Particulate emissions (these are fine particles less than 10 micrometres or 0.01 millimetres diameter) are much lower from vehicles with petrol engines than they are from vehicles with diesel engines. For this pollutant, the index is against emissions from a pre-1993 diesel car (=100). Measurements have been made of emissions from vehicles of different sizes within each vehicle category. The figures shown here reflect average values of emission factors at a typical urban speed, weighted by the mix of sizes of vehicles in the fleet.

Since January 1993, all new cars have had to meet new EC emission standards. This resulted in the use of three way catalysts for petrol cars to meet those standards (EC Directive 91/441/EEC).

Projection of United Kingdom CO_2 emissions: 3.7

These projections are taken from the Department of Trade and Industry's *Updated Energy Projections* (UEP), published in November 2004. Projected emissions are for end users and therefore the transport emissions include emissions arising from the production of fuels used in the transport sector. The figures are based on a central growth assumption for GDP of an annual average of 2.25% in the long term and a central estimate of fuel prices.

These projections are on the IPCC basis and so total emissions are reported on a slightly different basis to those published in table 3.8, as the figures in table 3.7 include emissions from land use change. See the notes on table 3.8 below for further details.

These emissions are on the "by source" basis, in line with table 3.8a. Other transport includes railways, domestic aviation and shipping and other mobile sources and machinery.

The projections are based on the 2004 netcen emission estimates. They do not reflect revisions made to the emissions estimates for the release of the 2005 emissions estimates. The DTI forecasts for other transport also include emissions from the military, which are not included here.

The projections include estimated carbon savings from the fuel duty escalator to 1999. They also include the effect of the *10 Year Plan for Transport*, Sustainable Distribution initiatives and European-level voluntary agreements with car manufacturers to improve the average fuel efficiency of new cars by at least 25% on 1995 levels by 2008/09. Further details on these and other assumptions are available in the UEP and supporting papers, which can be accessed on the DTI's website:

http://www.dti.gov.uk/energy/sepn/uep.shtml

Emissions from greenhouse gases and other pollutants: 3.8 and 3.9

Emission figures, including more detail about the estimates and additional data are published in the *Digest of Environmental Statistics*, by the Department of the Environment, Food and Rural Affairs (DEFRA) at:

www.defra.gov.uk/environment/statistics/Index.htm

Further information on the UK atmospheric emissions estimates can be found at:

http://www.naei.org.uk

The figures in these tables are based on the United Nations Economic Commission for Europe (UNECE) definition of emissions. However, there are alternative definitions that are also used, based on guidelines from the Intergovernmental Panel on Climate Change (IPCC). From this year, both definitions now include all emissions from domestic aviation and shipping, but exclude international marine and aviation bunker fuels. These are however reported as memo items, excluded from the UK total but shown for information. The remaining difference between UNECE and IPCC systems is that UNECE excludes most land use change emissions while IPCC includes them.

Emissions from road transport are calculated either from a combination of total fuel consumption data and fuel properties or from a combination of drive related emission factors and road traffic data. Work continues to improve the methodology. UK national emissions estimates are updated annually and any developments in methodology are applied retrospectively to earlier years, resulting in some changes to estimates. Emissions for carbon dioxide are presented by emissions source, by end user and on the Environmental Accounts basis, while for other pollutants, emissions are given by source only.

Carbon dioxide: The data are expressed in terms of weight of carbon emitted. To convert the figures in the table to the weight of carbon dioxide emitted, the figures should be multiplied by 44/12.

Carbon dioxide is the most important greenhouse gas and is estimated to account for about two thirds of global warming. Although its global warming potential is much less per tonne than the other greenhouse gases it is present in the atmosphere in vastly greater quantities.

The main difference between source and end user emissions comes from the treatment of emissions from combustion of fossil fuels, the largest source of carbon dioxide in the UK. To derive emissions by end user, emissions from power stations and other fuel processing industries have been re-allocated to end users on an approximate basis according to their use of the fuel. Emissions by end user are subject to more uncertainty than emissions by source and should only be used to give a broad indication of emissions by sector.

Non-transport end users are composed of: domestic, industry, commercial & public service, agriculture, military, exports and other emissions. Exports are emissions arising from the production of secondary fuel which is then exported (including that which goes to international marine and aviation bunkers, and is therefore not within the scope of UNECE reporting when consumed). As there is no UK end user of this secondary fuel, these emissions are allocated to exports.

Carbon dioxide emissions are also presented on the Environmental Accounts basis. The Environmental Accounts are compiled by the Office for National Statistics to make data on environmental impacts directly comparable with Gross Domestic Product (GDP). More detail is available at:

http://www.statistics.gov.uk/statbase/Product.asp?vlnk=3698&More=n

In practice, there are two main differences between the source definition and the Environmental Accounts:

1. Emissions from commercial use are broken down depending on the main business of the owner. For example, emissions from an HGV owned by a road haulage company are attributed to road freight but emissions from an HGV owned by a supermarket are attributed to the retail sector. Personal use of vehicles is shown separately as "Household use of private vehicles".

2. Environmental Accounts emissions include those from UK residents and UK-registered companies, wherever the activity takes place. This means that private motoring overseas is included, but foreign motoring in the UK is not. Water and air transport include international activity, which is shown separately in the source breakdown.

Air pollutants: The selection of air pollutants in Table 3.9 has been updated in this edition to reflect the Public Service Agreement (PSA) target DfT took co-ownership of with Defra on air quality. Volatile organic compounds have been removed, and benzene, 1,3-butadiene and sulphur dioxide have been added. Data on other air pollutants are available from the Defra website. This year, all air pollutant emissions data are shown on the source basis.

Carbon monoxide: Derived from the incomplete combustion of fuels containing carbon. It is one of the most directly toxic of substances, interfering with respiratory bio-chemistry and can affect the central nervous and cardiovascular systems. Other pollutants can exacerbate the effects. The fitting of catalytic converters to all new petrol engine vehicles made after 1992 has reduced emissions of carbon monoxide from the 1992 level.

Nitrogen oxides (expressed as nitrogen dioxide equivalent): A number of nitrogen compounds including nitrogen dioxide and nitric oxide are formed in the combustion of fossil fuel. Nitrogen dioxide is directly harmful to human health causing respiratory problems and can reduce lung function. Nitrogen oxides also contribute to the formation of ozone which is a harmful secondary pollutant in the lower atmosphere and also an important greenhouse gas contributing to global warming (high levels of ozone increase susceptibility to respiratory disease and irritate the eyes, nose, throat and respiratory system). Oxides of nitrogen can also have adverse effects on plants, reducing growth. In addition they contribute to acid rain. Emissions of nitrogen oxides from petrol engined vehicles have been reduced from the 1992 level as new vehicles built from 1992 onwards must comply with EC standards (normally by the fitting of a suitable catalytic converter).

Particulates (PM10): Airborne particles may be measured in a number of ways. For quantifying the particles produced by transport (especially motor traffic), the most commonly used indicator relies on the use of a size-selective sampler which collects smaller particles preferentially, collecting more than 95 per cent of 5μm (0.005 millimetres) particles, 50 per cent of 10μm aerodynamic particles, and less than 5 per cent of 20μm particles. The resultant mass of material is known as PM10. The road transport figures include emissions from tyre and brake wear.

Benzene: A known human carcinogen, the main source of benzene is the combustion and distribution of petrol. Some benzene evaporates directly into the atmosphere. Benzene is also emitted in a number of industrial processes. The large reduction in benzene emissions in 2000 was due to a reduction in the benzene content of petrol.

1 3 –butadiene: A suspected human carcinogen, the main source of 1,3-butadiene is motor vehicle exhausts where 1,3-butadiene is formed from the cracking of higher olefines. 1,3-butadiene is also used in the production of synthetic rubber for tyres.

Lead: Of concern because of its effects on health, particularly that of children. The main sources of lead in air are from lead in petrol, coal combustion, and metal works. The maximum amount of lead permitted in petrol was reduced from 0.45 grams per litre to 0.40 in 1981 and then again in December 1985 to 0.15. A further step to reduce lead emissions from petrol was taken in 1986 when unleaded petrol was first sold in the United Kingdom. There was a rapid increase in the uptake of unleaded petrol in the 1990s followed by a ban on the general sale of leaded petrol at the end of 1999.

Sulphur dioxide: An acid gas, sulphur dioxide can affect health and vegetation. It affects the lining of the nose, throat and airways of the lung, in particular, among those who suffer from asthma and chronic lung disease. The United Nations Economic Commission for Europe's (UNECE) Second Sulphur Protocol sets reduction targets for total SO2 emissions of 50 per cent by the year 2000, 70 per cent by 2005 and 80 per cent by 2010 from a 1980 baseline. By 2000, the UK had achieved a 75 per cent reduction from 1980 baseline levels, 25 per cent ahead of the UNECE target level for that year. Road transport emissions have fallen by over 87 per cent since 1998 following a reduction in the sulphur content of fuel.

Aircraft noise: 3.10

The figures in this table are also published in the *Digest of Environmental Statistics*, produced by the Department for the Environment, Food and Rural Affairs. Air transport movements are landings or take-offs of aircraft engaged in transport of passengers or cargo on commercial terms. All scheduled service movements (whether loaded or empty) are included, as well as charter movements transporting passengers or cargo. Air taxi movements are excluded.

The equivalent continuous sound level (Leq) is an index of aircraft noise exposure. It is a measure of the equivalent continuous sound level averaged over a 16 hour day from 0700 to 2300 hours BST and is calculated during the peak summer months mid-June to mid-September.

The contours referred to are broadly comparable with the previous Noise and Number Index (NNI) - The change was announced by the Minister for Aviation on 4 September 1990. 57dBA Leq represents the approximate onset of significant community disturbance (comparable with 35 NNI at the time), 63dBA Leq moderate disturbance and 69dBA Leq high disturbance. Leq is correlated with community response to aircraft noise, but it is recognised that the reactions of different individuals to aircraft noise can vary considerably. Changes in wind direction from year to year influence the area affected by aircraft noise.

The methodology underlying the calculation of the aircraft noise Leq contours is published in The CAA Leq Aircraft Noise Contour Model: ANCON Version 1 (DORA Report DR 9120).

Following studies by DSEE and consideration by the Aircraft Noise Monitoring Advisory Committee, it was decided to include reverse thrust noise in the 1990 and subsequent contours, using the methodology adopted by the Society of Automotive Engineers. This is described in *The Modelling of Reverse Thrust Noise to the Side of Runways* (CS Report 9310). The contours for Manchester Airport also include reverse thrust.

All four reports are available from Documedia Solutions, Cheltenham (☎ 01242 235151, or visit their website at www.documedia.co.uk). Leq contours for 1990 to 2000 (transparent overlays scale 1:50000) for Heathrow, Gatwick and Stansted may be obtained from DfT, subject to availability. Contours for later years are available in dxf format or printed to 1:50,000 scale. Enquiries should be directed to AED4, 1st Floor, Great Minster House, 76 Marsham Street, London, SW1P 4DR (☎020-7944 5494).

Population figures for Heathrow, Gatwick and Stansted are based on 1991 census data (updated for the years 1999-2002) and on 2001 Census data for 2003 and 2004. Estimation errors for population increase proportionately with diminishing size of contour. Results are not given where the error is considered unacceptably large.

3.1 Petroleum Consumption: by transport mode and fuel type: United Kingdom: 1994-2004[1]

Million tonnes

	1994	1995	1996	1997	1998	1999	2000	2001	2002	2003	2004 [2]
Road transport:											
Motor spirit											
Cars & Taxis	20.75	20.08	20.61	20.55	20.23	20.35	20.10	19.76	19.74	18.96	18.54
Light goods	1.77	1.57	1.49	1.39	1.30	1.11	0.98	0.85	0.74	0.64	0.63
Motorcycles	0.12	0.11	0.12	0.12	0.12	0.13	0.13	0.14	0.14	0.13	0.13
Diesel											
Cars & Taxis	1.61	1.91	2.21	2.41	2.48	2.77	2.92	3.08	3.42	3.69	3.85
Light goods	2.58	2.70	2.91	3.17	3.27	3.48	3.65	3.93	4.16	4.51	4.71
Heavy goods	7.22	7.43	7.86	8.07	8.13	8.07	7.97	7.97	8.27	8.39	8.77
Buses & Coaches	1.49	1.41	1.37	1.32	1.25	1.18	1.09	1.07	1.07	1.12	1.17
All	35.55	35.21	36.57	37.03	36.79	37.10	36.84	36.80	37.54	37.43	37.80
Railways:											
Gas/diesel oil/fuel oil	0.59	0.59	0.57	0.46	0.47	0.45	0.43	0.41	0.33	0.30	0.16
Burning oil	0.01	0.01	0.01	0.01	0.01	-	0.01	0.01	0.01	0.01	0.01
All	0.60	0.60	0.58	0.48	0.48	0.46	0.44	0.42	0.35	0.31	0.17
Water transport:											
Gas/diesel oil	0.97	0.91	1.04	1.04	0.98	0.91	0.91	0.74	0.60	1.09	0.84
Fuel oil	0.18	0.20	0.16	0.13	0.10	0.07	0.04	0.03	0.04	0.05	0.27
All	1.15	1.11	1.20	1.16	1.09	0.98	0.95	0.78	0.65	1.14	1.11
Air:											
All aviation fuels	7.31	7.69	8.08	8.45	9.28	9.98	10.86	10.67	10.57	10.81	11.91
All petroleum used by transport	44.61	44.61	46.43	47.12	47.64	48.53	49.09	48.67	49.10	49.69	50.99
All petroleum use (energy and non-energy)	81.22	80.17	82.02	79.25	78.44	77.98	77.20	76.65	76.30	77.82	80.23
Transport as a percentage of all energy and non energy use	*55*	*56*	*57*	*59*	*61*	*62*	*64*	*63*	*64*	*64*	*64*

1 There are revisions to some of the earlier data
2 Figures for 2004 for road transport are estimated on 2003 ratios

☎020-7215 2712
Source - DTI

3.2 Energy consumption: by transport mode and source of energy: United Kingdom: 1994-2004[1]

Million tonnes of oil equivalent/percentage

	1994	1995	1996	1997	1998	1999	2000	2001	2002	2003	2004
Road transport											
Petroleum	39.69	39.27	40.78	41.26	41.02	41.40	41.07	41.10	41.94	41.82	42.22
Railways											
Petroleum	0.65	0.65	0.63	0.52	0.52	0.50	0.48	0.45	0.37	0.34	0.19
Water transport											
Petroleum	1.24	1.19	1.29	1.26	1.18	1.07	1.04	0.84	0.70	1.23	1.20
Aviation											
Petroleum	8.07	8.49	8.92	9.32	10.24	11.02	11.98	11.77	11.66	11.94	13.16
All modes											
Electricity [2]	0.60	0.64	0.64	0.72	0.73	0.74	0.74	0.76	0.73	0.71	0.69
ow: rail [3]	0.31	0.34	0.34	..	..	..	..	..	..	..	..
All energy used by transport	50.25	50.24	52.25	53.08	53.68	54.73	55.30	54.92	55.40	56.05	57.45
All energy used by final users	152.55	150.40	157.34	154.37	155.78	157.13	158.30	161.56	156.87	158.42	161.03
Energy used by transport as a percentage of all energy used by final users	*33*	*33*	*33*	*34*	*34*	*35*	*35*	*34*	*35*	*35*	*36*

1 There are revisions to some of the earlier data, for details see "Digest of UK Energy Statistics 2005" published by DTI
2 Includes consumption at transport premises
3 DTI have not been able to produce robust estimates of electricity used by rail since 1996

☎020-7215 2712
Source - DTI

3.3 Petrol and diesel prices and duties per litre: at April: 1995-2005

Pence/percentage

	April 1995	April 1996	April 1997	April 1998	April 1999	April 2000	April 2001	April 2002	April 2003	April 2004	April 2005
Lead replacement petrol [1]											
Price	60.1	60.4	64.6	72.4	77.8	84.5	78.2	77.8	81.4	81.3	88.5
Duty	36.1	39.1	41.7	49.3	52.9	50.9	46.8	48.8	48.8	47.1	47.1
VAT	9.0	9.0	9.6	10.8	11.6	12.6	11.7	11.6	12.1	12.1	13.2
All tax	45.1	48.1	51.3	60.0	64.5	63.5	58.5	60.4	61.0	59.2	60.3
All tax as a percentage of price	*75*	*80*	*79*	*83*	*83*	*75*	*75*	*78*	*75*	*73*	*68*
Unleaded petrol:											
Price	54.1	55.2	59.2	65.8	70.2	80.0	75.9	75.0	78.2	77.8	85.4
Duty	31.3	34.3	36.9	44.0	47.2	48.8	45.8	45.8	45.8	47.1	47.1
VAT	8.1	8.2	8.8	9.8	10.5	11.9	11.3	11.2	11.7	11.6	12.7
All tax	39.4	42.5	45.7	53.8	57.7	60.7	57.1	57.0	57.5	58.7	59.8
All tax as a percentage of price	*73*	*77*	*77*	*82*	*82*	*76*	*75*	*76*	*73*	*75*	*70*
Ultra low sulphur diesel [2]											
Price	54.7	56.4	60.2	66.8	73.2	81.1	77.3	76.9	80.9	79.2	89.6
Duty	31.3	34.3	36.9	45.0	50.2	48.8	45.8	45.8	45.8	47.1	47.1
VAT	8.2	8.4	9.0	10.0	10.9	12.1	11.5	11.5	12.0	11.8	13.3
All tax	39.5	42.7	45.8	54.9	61.1	60.9	57.3	57.3	57.9	58.9	60.4
All tax as a percentage of price	*72*	*76*	*76*	*82*	*83*	*75*	*74*	*74*	*72*	*74*	*67*

1 Prices prior to 2000 were for four star petrol
Pump prices are broadly the same.
2 Prices prior to 2000 were for diesel engined road vehicle fuel (DERV)
Pump prices are broadly the same.

☎020-7215 2722
Source - DTI

3.4 Average fuel consumption by age and type of vehicle and type of fuel: 1992/1994 to 2004

a) Passenger cars — Miles per gallon/litres per 100 km

	1992/1994	1995/1997	1998/2000	2002	2003	2004
Petrol cars						
Up to 2 years	32	32	30	31	31	32
Over 2 to 6 years	30	31	30	31	31	31
Over 6 to 10 years	29	30	29	31	30	30
Over 10 years	28	29	28	27	29	29
All petrol cars	30	31	29	30	30	30
Diesel cars [1]						
Up to 2 years	39	43	36	40	40	41
Over 2 years	40	43	39	37	38	39
All diesel cars	40	43	38	38	39	40
Company cars [1]	32	34	30	34	34	35
Private cars	30	32	31	31	32	32
All cars (miles/gallon)	31	32	31	32	32	32
All cars (litres/100 km)	9.2	8.8	9.3	8.9	8.9	8.8

b) HGVs — Miles per gallon

	1993	1996	1999	2002	2003	2004
Rigid vehicles	7.5	8.2	8.3	8.1	7.8	8.3
Articluated vehicles	6.9	7.3	7.7	7.6	7.5	7.9

1 These estimates have a large sampling error because of the small sample sizes involved.

Cars: ☎ 020 7944 3097
HGVs: ☎ 020 7944 4442
Sources - Passenger cars: National Travel Survey
HGVs: Survey of Road Goods Transport

3.5 Average New Car Fuel Consumption 1978-2004 (Registration-Weighted: petrol two wheel drive vehicles only)

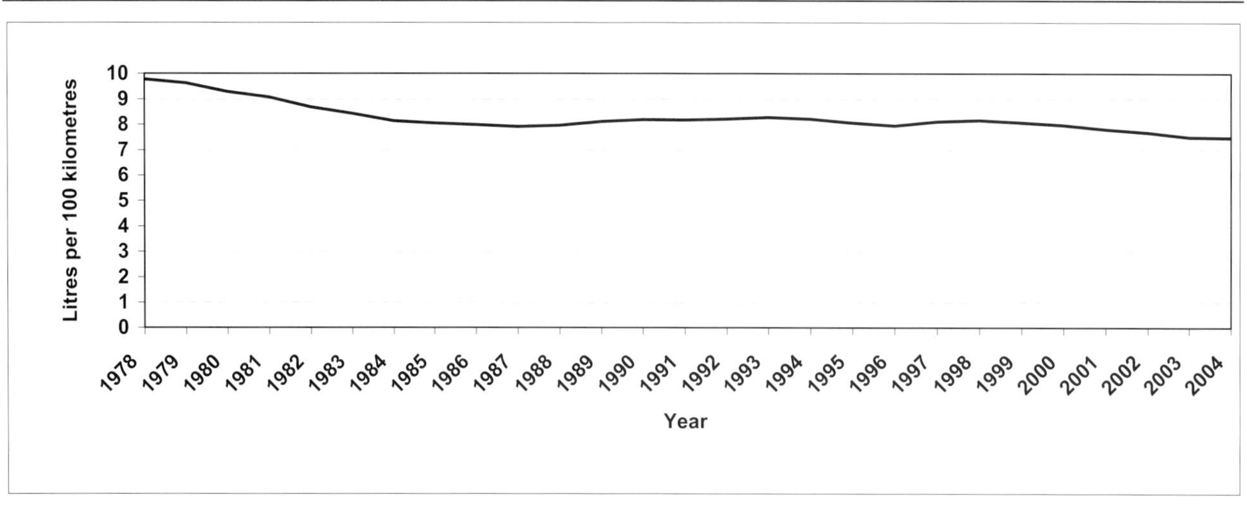

☎ 020-7944 3077
The figures in this graph are outside the scope of National Statistics
Source - Cleaner Fuels and Vehicles Division, DfT

3.6 Emissions for road vehicles (per vehicle kilometre) in urban conditions[1]

Index car without three-way catalyst: pre 1993 = 100[2]

		Carbon monoxide	Hydro-carbons[3]	Oxides of nitrogen	Particu-lates[4]	Carbon dioxide
Petrol car without three-way catalyst:	pre 1993	100	100	100	16	100
Petrol car with three-way catalyst:	1993-1996	10	2	13	2	98
Petrol car with three-way catalyst:	1997-2000	7	2	12	1	94
Petrol car with three-way catalyst:	2001-	6	1	5	1	89
Diesel car:	pre 1993	6	10	38	100	97
Diesel car:	1993-1996	3	5	33	37	95
Diesel car:	1997-2000	2	4	33	33	92
Diesel car:	2001-	1	3	33	20	82
Petrol light goods vehicle without three way catalyst:	pre 1994	136	96	94	19	111
Petrol light goods vehicle with three way catalyst:	1994-1997	20	3	19	2	140
Petrol light goods vehicle with three way catalyst:	1998-2000	5	2	17	1	143
Petrol light goods vehicle with three way catalyst:	2001-	4	1	7	1	136
Diesel light goods vehicle:	pre 1994	10	19	81	187	143
Diesel light goods vehicle:	1994-1997	4	9	63	52	143
Diesel light goods vehicle:	1998-2001	4	9	60	53	143
Diesel light goods vehicle:	2002-	3	7	45	37	131
Heavy goods vehicle - Rigid:	pre 1993	25	118	344	277	361
Heavy goods vehicle - Rigid:	1993-1996	14	43	437	143	361
Heavy goods vehicle - Rigid:	1997-2001	11	34	373	100	361
Heavy goods vehicle - Rigid:	2002-	8	23	258	72	361
Heavy goods vehicle - Articulated:	pre 1993	29	100	969	403	591
Heavy goods vehicle - Articulated:	1993-1996	40	107	1,159	375	523
Heavy goods vehicle - Articulated:	1997-2001	31	88	799	259	483
Heavy goods vehicle - Articulated:	2002-	21	60	554	187	483
Buses:	pre 1993	81	90	840	399	580
Buses:	1993-1996	25	67	674	202	479
Buses:	1997-2001	21	48	603	132	433
Buses:	2002-	14	33	418	95	433
Motorcycle (less than 50cc): two-stroke	pre 2000	236	854	2	26	37
Motorcycle (less than 50cc): two-stroke	2000-	24	188	1	26	16
Motorcycle (greater than 50cc): two-stroke	pre 2000	231	662	2	26	45
Motorcycle (greater than 50cc): two-stroke	2000-	119	458	2	26	37
Motorcycle (greater than 50cc): four-stroke	pre 2000	206	115	9	78	43
Motorcycle (greater than 50cc): four-stroke	2000-	69	48	13	78	37

1 These figures have been revised since last year
2 For diesel, particulates index is DERV car: pre 1993 =100
3 Figures based on non-methane hydrocarbons
4 Legislative standards exist only for diesel vehicles

☎020-7944 4276
The figures in this table are outside the scope of National Statistics
Source - netcen

3.7 Forecast of United Kingdom carbon dioxide emissions: by source: 1990-2020[1]

Million tonnes of carbon

	1990	1995	2000	2005	2010	2015	2020
Road transport	29.7	30.1	31.7	32.4	34.5	36.5	38.2
Other transport	2.3	2.2	2.1	1.8	1.9	2.0	2.1
Rest of the economy	133	121	119	118	106	104	104
Total	165	154	153	152	142	142	144

1 See Notes and Definitions for details of which policies and measures are included in these projections.

☎020-7944 4276
The figures in this table are outside the scope of National Statistics.
Source - Updated Energy Projections, DTI

3.8 Carbon dioxide emissions in the United Kingdom: 1993-2003[1]

	1993	1994	1995	1996	1997	1998	1999	2000	2001	2002	2003	Per cent of total in 2003
(a) By source category [2]								**Million tonnes of carbon/percentage**				
Transport:												
Road transport												
Passenger cars	19.8	19.4	19.2	19.9	20.0	19.8	20.1	20.1	20.0	20.3	19.8	*13*
Light duty vehicles	3.6	3.7	3.7	3.8	3.9	3.9	4.0	4.0	4.1	4.2	4.4	*3*
Buses	1.3	1.3	1.2	1.2	1.1	1.1	1.0	0.9	0.9	0.9	1.0	*1*
HGVs	5.8	6.2	6.4	6.8	7.0	7.0	7.0	6.9	6.9	7.1	7.2	*5*
Mopeds & motorcycles	0.1	0.1	0.1	0.1	0.1	0.1	0.1	0.1	0.1	0.1	0.1	-
Railways	0.5	0.5	0.5	0.5	0.4	0.4	0.4	0.4	0.4	0.3	0.3	-
Civil aircraft	0.4	0.3	0.4	0.4	0.4	0.4	0.5	0.5	0.6	0.6	0.6	-
Shipping	1.0	0.9	0.9	0.9	0.9	0.8	0.8	0.7	0.6	0.5	0.9	*1*
All domestic transport[3]	32.5	32.6	32.3	33.6	33.9	33.6	33.8	33.6	33.5	34.0	34.4	*23*
All sources	155	153	151	157	150	151	148	149	154	149	152	*100*
Memo items[4]:												
International aviation	5.0	5.2	5.5	5.8	6.2	6.9	7.5	8.2	8.0	7.9	8.1	*5*
International shipping	1.8	1.7	1.8	2.0	2.2	2.4	1.8	1.6	1.8	1.5	1.4	*1*
(b) By end user category[5]								**Million tonnes of carbon/percentage**				
Transport:												
Road transport	36.1	36.4	36.6	37.9	38.1	38.1	38.2	38.1	38.2	39.1	38.3	*25*
Railways[6]	1.9	1.8	1.8	1.7	1.6	1.6	1.5	1.5	1.6	1.4	1.5	*1*
Civil aircraft	0.4	0.4	0.4	0.5	0.5	0.5	0.6	0.6	0.7	0.7	0.7	-
Shipping	1.2	1.1	1.1	1.2	1.1	1.1	1.0	0.9	0.8	0.6	1.1	*1*
All domestic transport	39.6	39.7	39.9	41.3	41.3	41.3	41.3	41.2	41.2	41.8	41.6	*27*
All end users	155	153	151	157	150	151	148	149	154	149	152	*100*
(c) By Environmental Accounts industry code[7]								**Million tonnes of carbon/percentage**				
Transport industries:												
Railways	0.5	0.5	0.5	0.5	0.4	0.4	0.4	0.4	0.4	0.3	0.3	-
Buses and coaches	1.5	1.5	1.4	1.3	1.3	1.3	1.2	1.1	1.1	1.1	1.1	*1*
Tubes and trams	0.1	0.1	0.1	0.2	0.1	0.1	0.1	0.1	0.1	0.1	-	-
Taxis operation	0.4	0.4	0.4	0.4	0.4	0.5	0.5	0.5	0.5	0.5	0.5	-
Freight transport by road	4.4	4.8	5.0	5.4	5.6	5.7	5.7	5.6	5.8	5.7	5.8	*3*
Water transport	4.6	4.5	4.5	4.8	5.2	5.0	4.5	4.3	6.0	5.5	6.6	*4*
Air transport	6.6	6.4	7.0	7.6	8.2	9.2	10.0	11.2	10.7	10.5	10.6	*6*
All transport industries[8]	18.1	18.2	19.0	20.2	21.3	22.3	22.4	23.3	24.5	23.8	25.0	*15*
Household use of private vehicles	16.1	15.8	15.5	16.4	16.6	16.5	16.9	16.7	16.9	17.5	17.3	*10*
All industries	166	164	163	170	164	166	164	166	172	167	171	*100*

1 There are revisions to the series since last year

2 Source categories relate directly to the vehicle or other piece of equipment producing the emission. See Notes and Defintions for further details

3 Includes a small amount of emissions from other mobile sources and machinery

4 Categories not included in the national total reported to the UNECE

5 End user emissions for transport include a share of the emissions from combustion of fossil fuels at power stations and other fuel processing industries
See Notes and Definitions for further details

6 Rail emissions include stationary as well as mobile sources and electricity consumption by non-rail transport sector as well as railways

7 Industry categories based on the main business of the operator or, in the case of households, the purpose of travel
See Notes and Definitions for further details

8 Includes a small amount of emissions from transport via pipeline

020-7944 4276
Source - By source, end user: netcen
By Environmental Accounts industry code: ONS

3.9 Pollutant emissions from transport in the United Kingdom: by source: 1993-2003[1]

	1993	1994	1995	1996	1997	1998	1999	2000	2001	2002	2003	Per cent of total in 2003
(a) Carbon monoxide												Thousand tonnes/percentage
Transport:												
Road transport												
Passenger cars	3,888	3,656	3,452	3,321	3,024	2,733	2,463	1,888	1,532	1,325	1,112	*40*
Light duty vehicles	614	582	523	478	429	384	303	232	175	129	95	*3*
Buses	69	63	48	42	36	29	23	18	14	12	10	-
HGVs	70	69	70	70	68	66	64	60	57	54	50	*2*
Mopeds & motorcycles	91	90	90	90	95	99	108	96	90	85	78	*3*
Railways	5.6	5.2	5.7	5.5	4.5	4.5	4.3	4.2	3.9	3.3	2.5	-
Civil aircraft	28	31	31	34	39	39	47	54	59	51	47	*2*
Shipping[2]	8	8	7	8	8	7	6	6	5	4	8	-
All domestic transport[3]	4,774	4,505	4,227	4,049	3,703	3,362	3,019	2,359	1,937	1,662	1,402	*51*
All sources	7,300	6,889	6,341	6,188	5,727	5,288	4,972	4,117	3,820	3,336	2,768	*100*
Memo items[4]												
International aviation	14	13	14	14	15	16	17	18	17	17	17	*1*
International shipping[2]	16	15	16	17	19	21	15	13	15	12	12	-
(b) Nitrogen oxides												Thousand tonnes/percentage
Transport:												
Road transport												
Passenger cars	708	664	622	590	544	497	453	386	334	298	261	*17*
Light duty vehicles	76	77	75	75	75	75	72	70	69	66	65	*4*
Buses	72	69	63	61	58	56	53	48	46	43	42	*3*
HGVs	331	332	338	343	337	333	323	307	292	281	263	*17*
Mopeds & motorcycles	0.6	0.7	0.7	0.7	0.8	0.8	0.9	1.0	1.0	1.1	1.0	-
Railways	18	18	20	19	16	16	15	15	14	11	10	*1*
Civil aircraft	5	4	4	5	5	6	6	7	7	7	8	-
Shipping[2]	64	60	56	62	59	55	50	48	39	32	59	*4*
All domestic transport[3]	1,275	1,224	1,180	1,156	1,096	1,038	974	883	802	741	709	*45*
All sources	2,450	2,377	2,241	2,165	2,004	1,935	1,822	1,737	1,660	1,578	1,570	*100*
Memo items[4]												
International aviation	85	89	94	100	106	118	127	138	134	130	134	*9*
International shipping[2]	120	112	120	132	147	160	116	102	114	95	91	*6*
(c) Particulates (PM10)												Thousand tonnes/percentage
Transport:												
Road transport												
Passenger cars	15.5	14.8	14.1	13.5	12.7	11.5	10.5	8.2	8.0	7.8	7.4	*5*
Light duty vehicles	10.0	10.6	10.6	10.6	10.9	11.3	11.9	11.2	11.9	12.3	12.6	*9*
Buses	7.7	7.1	5.6	4.8	3.7	2.9	2.2	1.7	1.4	1.2	1.1	*1*
HGVs	17.0	16.2	15.5	14.3	12.0	11.2	10.2	9.0	8.1	7.5	6.9	*5*
Mopeds & motorcycles	0.4	0.4	0.4	0.4	0.4	0.4	0.5	0.5	0.5	0.5	0.5	-
Automobile tyre & brake wear	7.9	8.0	8.2	8.4	8.5	8.7	8.8	8.9	9.0	9.2	9.3	*7*
Railways	0.5	0.5	0.6	0.6	0.5	0.5	0.5	0.4	0.4	0.3	0.2	-
Civil aircraft	0.1	0.1	0.1	0.1	0.1	0.1	0.1	0.1	0.1	0.1	0.1	-
Shipping[2]	1.2	1.1	1.1	1.2	1.1	1.0	0.9	0.9	0.7	0.6	1.1	*1*
All domestic transport[3]	60.5	59.0	56.2	54.0	50.1	47.9	46.0	41.2	40.4	39.9	39.4	*28*
All sources	261	247	220	216	198	194	184	168	169	150	141	*100*
Memo items[4]												
International aviation	1.1	1.2	1.2	1.3	1.4	1.5	1.7	1.8	1.8	1.8	1.8	*1*
International shipping[2]	2.2	2.1	2.2	2.4	2.7	2.9	2.1	1.9	2.1	1.8	1.7	*1*
Road transport resuspension[5]	17.0	17.4	17.8	18.2	18.6	19.0	19.3	19.4	19.7	20.3	20.5	*15*
(d) Benzene												Thousand tonnes/percentage
Transport:												
Road transport												
Passenger cars	28.7	26.1	23.6	21.4	18.7	16.1	13.6	4.4	4.0	3.5	2.9	*19*
Light duty vehicles	2.3	2.1	1.9	1.7	1.5	1.3	1.1	0.3	0.3	0.3	0.2	*2*
Buses	-	-	-	-	-	-	-	-	-	-	-	-
HGVs	-	-	-	-	-	-	-	-	-	-	-	-
Mopeds & motorcycles	1.1	1.0	1.0	0.9	0.9	0.9	1.0	0.2	0.3	0.3	0.2	*2*
Gasoline evaporation	2.0	2.0	1.8	1.4	1.3	1.1	0.9	0.2	0.2	0.1	0.1	*1*
Railways	-	-	-	-	-	-	-	-	-	-	-	-
Civil aircraft	-	-	-	-	-	-	-	-	-	-	-	-
Shipping[2]	0.5	0.4	0.4	0.4	0.4	0.4	0.4	0.3	0.3	0.2	0.4	*3*
All domestic transport[3]	34.5	31.7	28.7	25.9	22.9	19.8	16.9	5.6	5.1	4.4	4.0	*26*
All sources	52.0	49.1	45.1	41.8	38.3	34.3	30.9	18.5	17.6	16.3	15.2	*100*
Memo items[4]												
International aviation	0.1	0.1	0.1	0.1	0.1	0.1	0.1	0.1	0.1	0.1	0.1	*1*
International shipping[2]	0.9	0.8	0.9	0.9	1.1	1.2	0.8	0.7	0.8	0.7	0.7	*4*

3.9 Pollutant emissions from transport in the United Kingdom: by source: 1993-2003[1]

	1993	1994	1995	1996	1997	1998	1999	2000	2001	2002	2003	Per cent of total in 2003
(e) 1,3-butadiene												**Thousand tonnes/percentage**
Transport:												
Road transport												
Passenger cars	6.0	5.4	4.9	4.4	3.8	3.3	2.7	2.2	1.8	1.4	1.1	*36*
Light duty vehicles	0.5	0.5	0.4	0.4	0.3	0.3	0.3	0.2	0.2	0.1	0.1	*4*
Buses	0.7	0.7	0.5	0.4	0.3	0.3	0.2	0.2	0.1	0.1	0.1	*3*
HGVs	1.7	1.5	1.4	1.3	1.2	1.1	1.0	0.9	0.8	0.8	0.7	*24*
Mopeds & motorcycles	0.2	0.2	0.2	0.2	0.2	0.2	0.2	0.2	0.2	0.2	0.2	*5*
Railways	0.1	0.1	0.1	0.1	0.1	0.1	0.1	0.1	-	-	-	*1*
Civil aircraft	-	-	-	-	-	-	-	-	-	-	-	*1*
Shipping[2]	0.0	0.0	0.0	0.0	0.0	0.0	0.0	0.0	0.0	0.0	0.0	*0*
All domestic transport[3]	9.2	8.4	7.4	6.8	6.0	5.2	4.5	3.8	3.2	2.7	2.2	*74*
All sources	10.9	10.0	9.0	8.1	7.2	6.4	5.9	4.8	4.1	3.5	3.0	*100*
Memo items[4]												
International aviation	0.1	0.1	0.1	0.1	0.1	0.1	0.1	0.1	0.1	0.1	0.1	*3*
International shipping[2]	0.0	0.0	0.0	0.0	0.0	0.0	0.0	0.0	0.0	0.0	0.0	*0*
(f) Lead												**Tonnes/percentage**
Transport:												
Road transport												
Passenger cars	1,381	1,174	971	830	730	537	284	1.5	1.3	1.2	1.2	*1*
Light duty vehicles	124	101	76.1	60.2	49.4	35	16	0.2	0.2	0.2	0.3	-
Buses HGVs	0.4	0.4	0.4	0.5	0.5	0.5	0.5	0.5	0.5	0.5	0.5	-
Mopeds & motorcycles	7.9	6.7	5.5	4.7	4.3	3.3	1.9	-	-	-	-	-
Railways	0.2	0.1	0.1	0.1	0.1	0.1	0.1	0.1	0.1	0.1	0.1	-
Civil aircraft	-	-	-	-	-	-	-	-	-	-	-	-
Shipping[2]	0.3	0.3	0.3	0.3	0.3	0.3	0.2	0.2	0.2	0.2	0.3	-
All domestic transport[3]	1,514	1,283	1,053	896	785	575	303	2.6	2.3	2.2	2.4	*2*
All sources	2,161	1,860	1,550	1,315	1,148	855	495	164	158	144	133	*100*
Memo items[4]												
International aviation	0.3	0.3	0.4	0.4	0.4	0.4	0.5	0.5	0.5	0.5	0.5	-
International shipping[2]	0.9	0.8	0.9	1.0	1.2	1.2	0.9	0.7	0.7	0.6	0.7	-
(g) Sulphur dioxide												**Thousand tonnes/percentage**
Transport:												
Road transport												
Passenger cars	17.5	23.0	19.6	14.7	16.4	11.8	11.2	4.7	2.2	1.9	1.8	-
Light duty vehicles	9.9	10.3	8.2	6.0	3.5	3.3	1.1	0.5	0.4	0.4	0.4	-
Buses	5.8	5.1	3.7	2.5	1.0	0.6	0.1	0.1	0.1	0.1	0.1	-
HGVs	25.4	24.5	19.3	14.1	6.5	6.8	1.2	0.6	0.6	0.7	0.7	-
Mopeds & motorcycles	0.1	0.1	0.1	0.1	0.1	0.1	0.1	-	-	-	-	-
Railways	2.4	2.1	1.7	1.6	1.3	1.3	1.2	1.1	1.0	0.9	0.9	-
Civil aircraft	0.3	0.4	0.3	0.4	0.5	0.5	0.4	0.5	0.5	0.4	0.5	-
Shipping[2]	27.5	27.2	27.0	27.3	24.8	22.4	19.6	18.0	14.4	12.4	21.9	*2*
All domestic transport[3]	89.0	92.8	79.9	66.7	54.2	46.9	34.9	25.5	19.3	16.9	26.4	*3*
All sources	3,098	2,663	2,354	2,014	1,653	1,598	1,219	1,194	1,118	1,002	979	*100*
Memo items[4]												
International aviation	4.6	6.0	5.1	5.4	7.2	8.0	6.1	6.9	7.5	6.1	7.2	*1*
International shipping[2]	89.7	79.4	91.1	98.8	116.9	116.8	83.1	69.4	70.0	60.8	63.1	*6*

1 Changes have been made to the basis of this table; see Notes and Definitions

2 Changes made to fuel use estimates have impacted the apportionment between domestic and international fuel use. As a result the 2003 estimates may not be directly comparable with earlier years

3 Includes a small amount of emissions from other mobile sources and machinery

4 Categories not included in the national total reported to the UNECE. As such, they do not contribute towards the total

5 Resuspension of particles caused by the turbulence of passing vehicles. Not included in totals for PM10 to avoid double-counting, but is important in reconcling roadside concentration measurements

☎020-7944 4276
Source - netcen

3.10 Aircraft noise: population affected by noise around airports: 1994-2004

(a) Heathrow	1994	1995	1996	1997	1998	1999	2000	2001	2002	2003	2004
Air transport movements (thousands)	408.9	418.9	426.7	429.2	441.2	449.5	459.7	457.6	460.3	457.1	469.8
Area (sq kms) within:											
57 Leq contour	175.5	169.2	164.7	158.3	163.7	155.6	135.6	117.4	126.9	126.9	117.4
63 Leq contour	60.3	58.3	56.0	53.8	55.4	53.9	48.2	41.2	43.8	43.8	40.3
69 Leq contour	27.5	26.1	23.8	23.2	22.8	21.9	19.0	14.1	16.4	15.6	13.3
Population (thousands) within:											
57 Leq contour	319.3	323.5	299.0	300.0	341.0	331.6	275.2	240.4	258.3	263.7	239.7
63 Leq contour	99.3	105.2	87.6	84.2	82.2	91.2	71.9	54.9	64.2	64.6	55.9
69 Leq contour	18.6	19.2	14.4	13.8	15.5	13.8	11.5	6.8	8.6	8.0	5.7
(b) Gatwick											
Air transport movements (thousands)	178.6	190.0	209.1	227.3	240.2	244.7	251.2	244.0	233.6	234.4	241.2
Area (sq kms) within:											
57 Leq contour	83.0	87.0	90.6	85.9	76.8	71.4	71.9	55.9	45.2	46.1	48.0
63 Leq contour	29.4	31.1	31.8	30.4	28.2	26.4	26.4	19.6	15.8	16.5	16.7
69 Leq contour	10.6	10.4	10.7	10.3	9.7	8.9	9.0	6.0	4.6	4.8	4.8
Population (thousands) within:											
57 Leq contour	14.6	15.5	14.9	12.6	9.0	7.8	8.7	5.2	3.5	4.2	4.5
63 Leq contour	2.4	2.7	2.2	2.0	1.4	1.4	1.4	0.8	0.5	0.6	0.6
69 Leq contour	0.4	0.5	0.4	0.4	0.3	0.3	0.2	0.1	0.1	0.1	0.1
(c) Stansted											
Air transport movements (thousands)	54.3	63.3	75.0	82.2	102.2	132.3	143.6	150.6	152.4	169.2	176.8
Area (sq kms) within:											
57 Leq contour	37.9	41.6	42.7	52.1	64.5	52.3	52.4	32.1	31.7	33.3	29.9
63 Leq contour	14.4	15.5	15.4	17.7	22.3	20.5	20.4	11.6	11.3	11.7	9.9
69 Leq contour	5.7	5.8	5.9	6.6	8.7	7.9	7.6	3.6	3.4	3.5	2.8
Population (thousands) within:											
57 Leq contour	3.4	3.7	3.8	6.0	7.6	4.4	5.7	2.3	2.0	2.3	2.9
63 Leq contour	0.7	0.8	0.8	0.9	1.3	1.4	1.3	0.4	0.3	0.5	0.3
69 Leq contour	0.2	0.2	0.2	0.2	0.3	0.2	0.2	0.1	0.1	0.1	0.1
(d) Manchester											
Air transport movements (thousands)	142.9	146.1	141.1	145.7	161.8	169.3	177.6	182.1	177.5	191.5	208.5
Area (sq kms) within:											
57 Leq contour	..	57.3	56.5	51.6	53.5	48.5	46.4	43.4	40.3	39.1	39.6
63 Leq contour	..	19.6	18.3	17.2	16.9	17.6	15.8	14.6	12.8	13.3	13.7
69 Leq contour	..	7.7	6.8	6.5	6.1	5.9	5.0	4.8	4.2	4.4	4.6
Population (thousands) within:											
57 Leq contour	..	50.7	46.2	45.6	44.7	53.5	48.4	44.9	38.7	40.6	40.9
63 Leq contour	..	10.4	9.7	9.5	10.1	11.9	9.4	6.4	4.5	5.8	5.1
69 Leq contour	..	3.0	2.9	2.4	2.0	1.9	1.2	0.5	0.5	0.6	0.6
(e) Birmingham											
Air transport movements (thousands)	70.9	74.3	76.6	79.8	88.2	98.4	108.4	111.0	112.3	116.0	109.2
Area (sq kms) within:											
57 Leq contour	..	..	44.2	..	35.3	..	19.0	..	14.8	..	16.2
63 Leq contour	..	..	15.9	..	12.3	..	6.2	..	4.4	..	5.1
69 Leq contour	..	..	7.2	..	4.5	..	1.7	..	1.2	..	1.3
Population (thousands) within:											
57 Leq contour	..	..	88.9	..	65.6	..	33.7	..	23.7	..	26.2
63 Leq contour	..	..	25.2	..	16.5	..	5.5	..	2.6	..	3.8
69 Leq contour	..	..	8.3	..	2.5	..	0.1	..	-	..	-
(f) Luton											
Air transport movements (thousands)	15.3	18.6	28.2	36.9	43.6	50.8	55.5	56.0	55.0	58.4	64.2
Area (sq kms) within:											
57 Leq contour	11.0	15.0	24.2	17.8	15.8	19.4	17.6	10.6	10.9	12.2	12.8
63 Leq contour	4.8	5.9	9.3	6.9	5.5	7.4	6.6	3.5	3.6	4.0	4.2
69 Leq contour	2.2	2.1	3.8	2.5	2.0	2.6	2.4	1.2	1.2	1.3	1.3
Population (thousands) within:											
57 Leq contour	3.6	5.6	9.8	5.5	5.8	7.4	8.1	2.3	2.4	3.2	3.8
63 Leq contour	0.8	1.5	2.9	1.2	1.1	1.2	1.7	-	0.1	0.1	0.1
69 Leq contour	0.0	0.0	0.0	0.0	0.0	0.0	0.0	0.0	0.0	0.0	0.0

☎020-7944 4276
The figures in this table are outside the scope of National Statistics
Sources - Noise contour data: Major UK airports
Air transport movements - Civil Aviation Authority

4 Freight:

Notes and Definitions

Freight transport by mode: 4.1

Rail: Figures up to 1962 include free-hauled (Departmental *i.e.* goods carried by British Rail for its own purposes) traffic on revenue-earning trains (the inclusion of this traffic in 1962 would have increased the figure). Figures for rail from 1991 are for each financial year.

Water: Figures from 1972 onwards are not comparable with earlier years. From 1972, water includes all UK coastwise and one-port freight movements by sea, and inland waterway traffic. Earlier years include only GB coastwise traffic and internal traffic on waterways controlled by British Waterways.

Pipeline: The increase between 1989 and 1990 is largely due to changes in coverage.

Domestic Freight Transport: 4.2 and 4.3

These figures include the activity of goods vehicles over 3.5 tonnes gross vehicle weight and light goods vehicles up to that weight. The estimates for heavy goods vehicles are derived from the Continuing Survey of Road Goods Transport (CSRGT) and, for light goods vehicles, surveys carried out in 1976, 1987, 1992/93, 2003 and 2004 and interpolation for the intervening and subsequent years. Pipeline estimates are for oil pipelines only (excluding offshore pipelines); data differ from those in the International Comparisons section as the latter exclude pipelines less than 50 kilometres long. Domestic air freight within the United Kingdom, while sometimes important in terms of speed of delivery, is insignificant in volume; in 2004, domestic air freight amounted to only 29 million tonne kilometres (see Table 2.4(f)).

All the activity of light goods vehicles has been assumed to be in 'other traffic' in Table 4.3 and in miscellaneous commodities (*Nomenclature Statistique de Transport* Chapter 9) in Table 4.2

Road freight transport by goods vehicles over 3.5 tonnes gross weight: 4.4-4.6

The data in these tables are derived from the Continuing Survey of Road Goods Transport.

Estimates are of domestic freight activity by GB-registered heavy goods vehicles over 3.5 tonnes gross vehicle weight. These vehicles pay the goods vehicle rates of Vehicle Excise Duty, are subject to goods vehicle 'plating' and annual testing, and require a goods operator's licence. They account for some 95 per cent of road freight activity, with the rest being carried by light goods vehicles up to 3.5 tonnes gross vehicle weight.

In Table 4.5, freight activity is measured in terms of the weight of goods (tonnes) handled, taking no account of the distance they are carried; this is termed 'goods lifted'. The measure in Table 4.4 is 'goods moved' (tonne kilometres) which does take account of distance. 'Goods moved', for each loaded journey, is the weight of the load multiplied by the distance it is carried. 'Goods moved' is therefore a better measure of the work done by heavy goods vehicles. In both tables activity is shown by 'mode of working', 'gross weight of vehicle' and 'commodity'.

In Tables 4.4 and 4.5 'Crude minerals' comprises *sand, gravel and clay and* other *crude minerals*. 'Building materials' comprises *cement* and *other building materials*.

The vehicle weight groups reflect some of the operating controls on goods vehicles. For rigid vehicles the maximum allowed gross vehicle weights are:

- 18 tonnes on 2 axles
- 26 tonnes on 3 axles
- 32 tonnes on 4 axles

For articulated vehicles the general limits are:

- 38 tonnes on 4 axles
- 40 tonnes on 5 axles
- 44 tonnes on 6 axles

'Mode of working' relates to whether goods are being carried on either a hire or reward or own account basis. The former relates to the carriage of goods owned by people other than the operator; the latter covers goods carried by operators in the course of their own trade or business.

The tonnes lifted and tonne kilometres estimates shown in these tables are not directly comparable to those of heavy goods vehicle kilometres derived from the traffic census in Table 7.2. Therefore, any analysis such as calculating average load (tonne kilometres/ vehicle kilometres) should use estimates published in *The Transport of Goods by Road in Great Britain 2004: Annual Report of the Continuing Survey of Road Goods Transport*, which is available from DfT, available at: http://www.transtat.dft.gov.uk

The estimates are derived from the Continuing Survey of Road Goods Transport (CSRGT) which in 2004 was based on an average weekly sample of some 330 heavy goods vehicles. The samples are drawn from the computerised vehicle licence records held by the Driver and Vehicle Licensing Agency (DVLA). Questionnaires are sent to the registered keepers of the sampled vehicles asking for a description of the vehicle and its activity during the survey week. The estimates are grossed to the vehicle population and, and at the overall national level have a two per cent margin of error (at 95 per cent confidence level). Further details are provided in the CSRGT annual report.

Methodological changes

A key component of National Statistics outputs is a programme of quality reviews carried out at least every five years to ensure that such statistics are fit for purpose and that their quality and value continue to improve. A quality review of the Department for Transport's road freight surveys, including the CSRGT, was carried out in 2003. A copy of the report can be accessed at

http://www.statistics.gov.uk/nsbase/methods_quality/quality_review/downloads/NSQR30FinalReport.doc

The quality review made a number of recommendations about the CSRGT. The main methodological recommendation was that, to improve the accuracy of survey estimates, the sample strata should be amended to reflect current trends in vehicle type, weight and legislative groups. These new strata are described more fully in Appendix C of the survey report. For practical and administrative reasons, changes were also made to the sample selection methodology (see Appendix B of the report). These changes have resulted in figures for 2004 not being fully comparable with those for 2003 and earlier years. Detailed comparisons should therefore be made with caution.

International Roads Goods Transport: 4.7-4.9

These tables show the international activity of United Kingdom registered vehicles. The statistics for GB registered vehicles are derived from the International Road Haulage Survey (IRHS), which has been conducted by the Department for Transport (and its predecessors) since 1979 in order to comply with EC Regulation 1172/98 (which replaced EC Directive 78/546 and 89/462). The Regulation requires each member state to compile statistics of the international road haulage carried out by its own goods vehicles as well as national haulage (see Tables 4.4 and 4.5).

The IRHS is carried out by asking hauliers who undertake international work to report the details of recently completed international trips travelling to mainland Europe or the Irish Republic via roll-on/roll-off ferry services or through the Channel Tunnel. Details of the sampling scheme are available from DfT.

The sample is grossed up quarterly in stages: the results, by each ferry route, are grossed to total route traffic; figures are then re-grossed to the grand total of United Kingdom powered vehicles on all ferry routes and the Channel Tunnel, to allow for routes not sampled. The ferry totals are obtained from the associated 'quarterly ro-ro survey'. Vehicles registered to hauliers operating in Northern Ireland are covered by the CSRGT(NI). Since 2004, this survey has been expanded to cover international activity including that across the Irish land boundary. Details of this activity is shown in Table 4.9

A substantial amount of traffic goes by unaccompanied trailers (as well as in the foreign powered vehicles) for which statistics are not obtained in this survey. In particular, trade across the North Sea is mainly carried on unaccompanied trailers. Freight carried in foreign vehicles is not included in the IRHS (or CSRGT) tables. Other EU countries, being subject to the same Regulation, obtain comparable statistics which are published by Eurostat.

The goods classification, *Nomenclature Statistiques de Transport* (NST), the classification of commodities for transport statistics used in the European Union, is a hierarchical structure which divides the 176 headings of the classification into 10 chapters and 52 main groups. At present it is only practicable to disaggregate the IRHS data by 'chapter' - apart from showing separately the two main components of chapter 9.

In Table 4.9, only 'bilateral' traffic is shown, that is traffic between the United Kingdom and another country in either United Kingdom vehicles or in those registered in that other country. The figures exclude (a) 'cross trade', i.e. trade in vehicles registered other than in the country of loading or unloading and (b) cabotage where goods are both picked up and delivered in another country.

Freight Traffic: 4.10

This table summarises the performance of the freight business in terms of freight 'lifted' (measured in tonnes) and freight 'moved' (measured in tonne-kilometres). Freight 'moved' takes account of the distance the goods are carried.

Freight data exclude all parcels traffic by coaching trains (but see below) and all departmental traffic (i.e. goods carried by Network Rail for its own purposes) whether carried on revenue-earning trains or on special departmental trains.

Following the move of BR's bulk freight operations to the private sector there have been some changes in the way estimates of freight traffic have been compiled. In particular, the method of estimating tonne kilometres is different with the result that recent estimates are not consistent with those for earlier periods. Some revisions have been made to the series. The freight moved series now has a full commodity breakdown with the inclusion of parcels. The freight lifted series has also been revised, in this case from 1999/00. Further details can be found in *National Rail Trends* published each quarter, by the Office of Rail Regulation (previously published by the Strategic Rail Authority).

Roll-on/roll-off: 4.11 and 4.12

Statistics on the number of lorries and unaccompanied trailers travelling from Great Britain to mainland Europe and Ireland are compiled from quarterly returns provided by roll-on/roll-off ferry operators and Eurotunnel. The results are broken down by country of vehicle registration, by country of disembarkation and by GB port group. Separate figures are given for powered vehicles and unaccompanied trailers. The statistics presented in Tables 4.11 and 4.12 refer to vehicle travelling to mainland Europe only and exclude those to Ireland.

Powered vehicles comprise rigid vehicles, lorries with semi-trailers (articulated units) and lorries with drawbar trailers. (Some vehicles under 3.5 tonnes gross vehicle weight are also included.) Unaccompanied trailers are trailers and semi-trailers not accompanied on the ferry by a powered unit. Up to 1978 inward traffic was also recorded, but because it was similar to outward traffic the data requirement was discontinued to save respondent effort.

More detailed analyses are provided in the Department's quarterly publication "Road Goods Vehicles Travelling to Mainland Europe", available on the Department's website: www.dft.gov.uk/transtat.

4.1 Domestic freight transport: by mode: 1953-2004

For greater detail of the years 1994-2004 see Table 4.3

	Goods moved (billion tonne kilometres)					Goods lifted (million tonnes)				
Year	Road	Rail [1]	Water	Pipe-line	All modes	Road	Rail [1]	Water	Pipe-line	All modes
1953	32	37	20	0	89	889	294	52	2	1,237
1954	35	36	20	0	91	940	288	52	2	1,282
1955	38	35	20	0	93	1,013	279	50	2	1,344
1956	38	35	22	0	95	1,009	281	55	2	1,347
1957	37	34	21	0	92	985	279	55	2	1,321
1958	41	30	21	0	92	1,078	247	53	2	1,380
1959	46	29	21	0	96	1,164	238	53	3	1,458
1960	49	30	20	0	100	1,211	252	54	4	1,521
1961	53	29	22	1	105	1,260	242	56	6	1,564
1962	55	26	24	1	106	1,268	232	58	7	1,565
1963	57	25	25	1	108	1,407	239	60	15	1,721
1964	66	26	25	1	118	1,560	243	61	18	1,882
1965	69	25	25	1	120	1,590	232	62	26	1,910
1966	73	24	26	2	125	1,641	217	61	31	1,950
1967	75	21	25	2	123	1,651	204	57	32	1,944
1968	79	23	25	2	129	1,707	211	59	32	2,009
1969	83	23	24	3	133	1,658	211	59	36	1,964
1970	85	25	23	3	136	1,610	209	57	39	1,915
1971	86	22	22	4	134	1,582	198	52	49	1,881
1972	88	21	29 [2]	4	142	1,629	177	117 [2]	45	1,968
1973	90	23	31	5	149	1,660	196	122	50	2,028
1974	90	22	31	5	148	1,537	176	117	50	1,880
1975	92	21	28	6	147	1,511	175	108	52	1,846
1976	96	21	30	6	153	1,515	176	113	53	1,857
1977	98	20	41	9	168	1,429	171	122	75	1,797
1978	100	20	48	10	178	1,503	171	133	83	1,890
1979	103	20	56	10	189	1,499	169	140	85	1,893
1980	93	18	54	10	175	1,395	154	137	83	1,769
1981	94	18	53	9	173	1,299	154	129	75	1,657
1982	95	16	59	10	179	1,389	142	137	78	1,746
1983	96	17	60	10	183	1,358	145	143	82	1,728
1984	100	13	60	10	183	1,400	79	140	88	1,707
1985	103	15	58	11	187	1,452	122	142	89	1,805
1986	105	17	55	10	187	1,473	140	144	79	1,836
1987	113	17	54	11	195	1,542	141	142	83	1,908
1988	130	18	59	11	219	1,758	150	156	99	2,163
1989	138	17	58	10	223	1,812	146	155	93	2,206
1990	136	16	56	11 [3]	219	1,749	140	152	121 [3]	2,162
1991	130	15	58	11	214	1,600	136	144	105	1,985
1992	127	15	55	11	208	1,555	122	140	106	1,923
1993	135	14	51	12	211	1,615	103	134	125	1,977
1994	144	13	52	12	221	1,689	97	140	161	2,087
1995	150	13	53	11	227	1,701	101	143	168	2,113
1996	154	15	55	12	236	1,730	102	142	157	2,131
1997	157	17	48	11	233	1,740	105	142	148	2,135
1998	160	17 [4]	57	12	245	1,727	102	149	153	2,131
1999	157	18	59	12	245	1,661	92 [4]	144	155	2,052
2000	158	18	67	11	255	1,689	95	137	151	2,072
2001	157	19	59	12	247	1,660	94	131	151	2,037
2002	157	19	67	11	254	1,708	87	139	146	2,080
2003	159	19	61	11	250	1,725	89	133	141	2,088
2004	160 [5]	21	..	11	..	1,831 [5]	102 [6]	..	158	..

1 From 1991 figures for rail are for financial years 1991/92 etc.
2 Figures from 1972 onwards are not comparable with earlier years. From 1972, water includes all UK coastwise and one-port freight movements by sea, and inland waterway traffic. Earlier years inlcude only GB coastwise traffic and internal traffic on BWB waterways.
3 The increase compared to the corresponding figure for 1989 is largely due to changes in coverage.
4 Figures for goods moved by rail are on a new basis from 1998. Figures for goods lifted by rail have a break in the series from 1999.
5 See footnote 2 Table 4.4.
6 Break in the series, increase largely due to changes in coverage.

Rail: ☎020-7944 4977
Road & pipeline: ☎020-7944 4261
Water: ☎020-7944 4443
The rail figures in this table are outside the scope of National Statistics
Sources - Rail: ORR, previously SRA
Pipeline: DTI

4.2 Domestic freight moved: by commodity: 2004

Billion tonne kilometres/percentage

Commodity group (NST Chapter)	NST[2] Chapter	Road[1] Billion tonne-kms	Road[1] Percentage	Rail[3] Billion tonne-kms	Rail[3] Percentage	Pipeline Billion tonne-kms	Pipeline Percentage
Agricultural products and live animals	0	15.0	*9*	..	..	0	*0*
Food stuffs and animal fodder	1	32.9	*21*	..	..	0	*0*
Solid mineral fuels	2	1.2	*1*	7	*34*	0	*0*
Petroleum products	3	5.7	*4*	1.2	*6*	10.7	*100*
Ores and metal waste	4	1.6	*1*	..	..	0	*0*
Metal products	5	5.4	*3*	2.6	*13*	0	*0*
Minerals and building materials	6	24.2	*15*	2.8	*14*	0	*0*
Fertilisers	7	0.8	*1*	..	..	0	*0*
Chemicals	8	8.0	*5*	..	..	0	*0*
Machinery, transport, equipment, manufactured articles and miscellaneous articles	9	65.1	*41*	..	..	0	*0*
All commodities		159.8	*100*	20.7	*100*	10.7	*100*

1 All goods vehicles, including those upto 3.5 tonnes gross vehicle weight
2 EC standard goods classification for transport statistics
3 Rail catagories do not all match those recorded by SRA, so the components do not sum to the total

Rail: ☎020-7944 4977
Road & pipeline: ☎020-7944 4261
The rail figures in this table are outside the scope of National Statistics
Sources - Rail: ORR, previously SRA: Pipeline: DTI

4.3 Domestic freight transport: by mode: 1994-2004

(a) Goods moved — Billion tonne kilometres/percentage

	1994	1995	1996	1997	1998	1999	2000	2001	2002	2003	2004
Petroleum products											
Road [1]	5.1	5.7	6.1	5.8	5.2	5.0	6.4	5.8	5.2	5.5	5.7
Rail [2]	1.8	1.8	..	..	1.6	1.5	1.4	1.2	1.1	1.2	1.2
Water [3]	43.0	42.5	45.9	38.3	45.2	48.6	52.7	43.5	51.7	46.9	..
ow: coastwise	28.9	31.4	38.7	33.8	36.4	33.3	26.0	23.1	24.2	23.3	..
Pipeline	12.0	11.1	11.6	11.2	11.7	11.6	11.4	11.5	10.9	10.5	10.7
All modes	61.9	61.1	63.6 [4]	55.3 [4]	63.6	66.6	71.9	62.0	68.9	64.1	..
Coal and coke											
Road [1]	2.9	2.7	2.5	2.7	2.0	2.2	1.5	2.1	1.5	1.5	1.2
Rail [2]	3.3	3.6	3.8	4.4	4.5	4.8	4.8	6.2	5.7	5.8	7.0
Water [3]	1.4	2.3	0.6	0.6	0.5	0.5	0.2	0.5	0.3	0.5	..
All modes	7.6	8.6	6.9	7.7	7.0	7.5	6.5	8.8	7.5	7.8	..
Other traffic											
Road [1]	135.7	141.2	145.3	148.6	152.4	149.6	150.2	149.0	150.6	152.4	153.0
Rail [2]	7.9	7.9	11.3	12.5	11.2	11.9	11.9	12.0	11.9	11.9	12.4
Water [3]	7.8	8.3	8.7	9.2	11.2	9.6	14.6	14.8	15.2	13.5	..
All modes	151.4	157.4	165.3	170.3	174.8	171.1	176.5	175.8	177.7	177.8	..
All traffic											
Road [1]	143.7	149.6	153.9	157.1	159.5	156.7	158.0	156.9	157.3	159.3	159.8 [5]
Rail [2]	13.0	13.3	15.1	16.9	17.3	18.2	18.1	19.4	18.7	18.9	20.7
Water [3]	52.2	53.1	55.3	48.1	56.9	58.7	67.4	58.8	67.2	60.9	..
Pipeline	12.0	11.1	11.6	11.2	11.7	11.6	11.4	11.5	10.9	10.5	10.7
All modes	220.9	227.1	235.9	233.3	245.4	245.2	254.9	246.6	254.1	249.6	..
Percentage of all traffic											
Road [1]	*65*	*66*	*65*	*67*	*65*	*64*	*62*	*64*	*62*	*64*	..
Rail [2]	*6*	*6*	*6*	*7*	*7*	*7*	*7*	*8*	*7*	*8*	..
Water [3]	*24*	*23*	*23*	*21*	*23*	*24*	*26*	*24*	*26*	*24*	..
Pipeline	*5*	*5*	*5*	*5*	*5*	*5*	*4*	*5*	*4*	*4*	..
All modes	*100*	*100*	*100*	*100*	*100*	*100*	*100*	*100*	*100*	*100*	..

(b) Goods lifted — Million tonnes/percentage

	1994	1995	1996	1997	1998	1999	2000	2001	2002	2003	2004
Petroleum products											
Road [1]	68	71	75	73	61	61	75	74	59	64	67
Rail [2]	8	6	..	..	..	..	..	..	..	..	..
Water [3]	70	72	71	69	76	72	72	60	67	64	..
ow: coastwise	43	47	54	52	55	52	40	34	36	35	..
Pipeline	161	168	157	148	153	155	151	151	146	141	158
All modes	307	317	303 [4]	290 [4]	290 [4]	288 [4]	298 [4]	285 [4]	272 [4]	269 [4]	..
Coal and coke											
Road [1]	42	34	32	37	26	28	22	21	17	22	14
Rail [2]	43	45	52	50	45	44	46	46	41	42	52 [6]
Water [3]	4	4	3	4	3	3	3	3	2	2	..
All modes	89	83	87	91	70	75	71	70	60	66	..
Other traffic											
Road [1]	1,579	1,596	1,623	1,630	1,646	1,572	1,593	1,565	1,632	1,639	1,750
Rail [2]	47	50	50	55	57	48	50	48	46	47	50 [6]
Water [3]	66	67	67	69	70	70	62	68	70	67	..
All modes	1,692	1,713	1,740	1,754	1,773	1,690	1,705	1,681	1,748	1,753	..
All traffic											
Road [1]	1,689	1,701	1,730	1,740	1,733	1,661	1,689	1,660	1,708	1,725	1,831 [5]
Rail [2]	97	101	102	105	102	92	95	94	87	89	102 [6]
Water [3]	140	143	142	142	149	144	137	131	139	133	..
Pipeline	161	168	157	148	153	155	151	151	146	141	158
All modes	2,087	2,113	2,131	2,135	2,131	2,052	2,072	2,037	2,080	2,088	..
Percentage of all traffic											
Road [1]	*81*	*80*	*81*	*81*	*81*	*81*	*81*	*81*	*82*	*83*	..
Rail [2]	*5*	*5*	*5*	*5*	*5*	*4*	*5*	*5*	*4*	*4*	..
Water [3]	*7*	*7*	*7*	*7*	*7*	*7*	*7*	*6*	*7*	*6*	..
Pipeline	*8*	*8*	*7*	*7*	*7*	*8*	*7*	*7*	*7*	*7*	..
All modes	*100*	*100*	*100*	*100*	*100*	*100*	*100*	*100*	*100*	*100*	..

1 All goods vehicles, including those up to 3.5 tonnes gross vehicle weight.
2. Figures for rail are for financial years eg 1994/95 etc
3 Figures for water are for UK traffic.
4 Excludes rail.
5 See footnote 2 Table 4.4.
6 See footnote 6 Table 4.1

Rail: ☎020-7944 4977
Road & pipeline: ☎020-7944 4261
Water: ☎020-7944 4443
The rail figures in this table are outside the scope of National Statistics.
Source - Rail: ORR, previously SRA
Pipeline: Department of Trade and Industry

4.4 Freight transport by road: goods moved by goods vehicles over 3.5 tonnes[1] : 1994-2004

Billion tonne-kilometres

(a) By mode of working	1994	1995	1996	1997	1998	1999	2000	2001	2002	2003	2004 [2]
Mainly public haulage	100.8	106.5	109.1	112.2	114.3	110.9	113.0	114.7	110.6	114.3	110.8
Mainly own account	37.0	37.2	37.7	37.4	37.6	38.3	37.5	34.7	39.2	37.4	41.4
All modes	137.8	143.7	146.8	149.6	151.9	149.2	150.5	149.4	149.8	151.7	152.2
(b) By gross weight of vehicle											
Rigid vehicles:											
Over / Not over											
3.5 tonnes / 17 tonnes	19.9	18.7	19.5	19.2	17.8	17.9	15.8	13.1	11.9	10.1	9.1
17 tonnes / 25 tonnes	6.1	5.6	5.3	4.7	4.2	4.3	4.8	5.7	6.3	6.8	7.9
25 tonnes	12.4	13.3	13.5	14.3	14.7	15.3	15.4	15.6	17.3	18.3	18.9
All rigids	38.4	37.5	38.3	38.1	36.6	37.5	36.0	34.5	35.6	35.2	35.9
Articulated vehicles:											
Over / Not over											
3.5 tonnes / 33 tonnes	16.9	15.9	15.9	14.3	14.4	14.0	14.0	12.8	9.9	8.8	7.0
33 tonnes	82.5	90.2	92.6	97.1	100.9	97.7	100.4	102.1	104.4	107.7	109.4
All artics	99.4	106.1	108.5	111.4	115.3	111.7	114.4	114.9	114.3	116.5	116.4
All vehicles:											
Over / Not over											
3.5 tonnes / 25 tonnes	26.6	24.7	25.3	24.3	22.5	22.7	21.3	19.3	18.7	17.3	17.3
25 tonnes	111.2	119.0	121.5	125.2	129.4	126.5	129.2	130.1	131.1	134.4	134.9
All weights	137.8	143.7	146.8	149.6	151.9	149.2	150.5	149.4	149.8	151.7	152.2
(c) By commodity											
Food, drink and tobacco	36.5	37.5	39.3	40.8	42.5	41.5	44.3	41.4	43.1	42.2	41.7
Wood, timber and cork	3.3	3.2	3.8	3.5	3.6	3.8	3.7	3.9	3.8	4.1	4.5
Fertiliser	1.3	1.4	1.5	1.3	1.2	1.4	1.2	1.2	1.2	1.2	0.8
Crude minerals	14.1	13.5	13.5	13.6	13.3	12.7	12.4	13.0	13.9	13.8	14.1
Ores	1.4	1.5	1.3	1.7	1.1	1.3	1.2	1.2	1.1	1.2	1.4
Crude materials	2.0	1.9	2.1	2.1	2.6	2.6	2.6	2.3	2.7	2.3	3.3
Coal and coke	2.9	2.7	2.5	2.7	2.0	2.2	1.5	2.1	1.5	1.5	1.2
Petrol and petroleum products	5.1	5.7	6.1	5.8	5.2	5.0	6.4	5.8	5.2	5.5	5.7
Chemicals	8.1	7.4	7.7	8.2	7.9	7.4	6.8	7.2	6.5	6.8	6.3
Building materials	10.0	10.7	9.6	11.1	10.7	10.6	10.6	11.7	10.9	12.0	12.1
Iron and steel products	6.7	7.8	7.2	7.9	7.7	6.8	6.8	5.7	5.3	5.4	5.4
Other metal products n.e.s.	2.0	1.7	1.7	1.5	1.7	1.7	1.7	1.4	1.5	1.5	1.9
Machinery and transport equipment	6.8	7.4	7.7	8.4	9.1	8.7	9.1	8.9	8.5	8.7	8.9
Miscellaneous manufactures n.e.s.	13.4	13.3	14.2	14.2	15.9	15.7	15.1	15.4	16.2	15.8	16.3
Miscellaneous transactions n.e.s. (incl. commodity not known)	24.3	27.8	28.4	26.8	27.5	27.9	27.1	28.2	28.4	29.5	28.8
All commodities	137.8	143.7	146.8	149.6	151.9	149.2	150.5	149.4	149.8	151.7	152.2

1 Rigid vehicles or articulated vehicles (tractive unit and trailer) with gross vehicle weight over 3.5 tonnes.

2 Figures for 2004 are not fully comparable with those for 2003 and earlier years. Detailed comparisons should therefore be made with caution. See Notes and Definitions.

☎020-7944 3093

4.5 Freight transport by road: goods lifted by goods vehicles over 3.5 tonnes:[1] 1994-2004

Million tonnes

(a) By mode of working		1994	1995	1996	1997	1998	1999	2000	2001	2002	2003	2004[2]
Mainly public haulage		980	987	1,011	1,044	1,041	991	1,038	1,052	1,019	1,053	1,101
Mainly own account		618	622	618	599	589	576	556	529	608	590	643
All modes		1,597	1,609	1,628	1,643	1,630	1,567	1,593	1,581	1,627	1,643	1,744
(b) By gross weight of vehicle												
Rigid vehicles:												
Over	Not over											
3.5 tonnes	17 tonnes	317	298	306	294	268	254	229	203	188	159	160
17 tonnes	25 tonnes	202	162	133	120	106	86	87	86	90	100	113
25 tonnes		332	373	371	380	401	408	424	443	491	506	539
All rigids		852	833	811	793	776	748	741	733	768	765	812
Articulated vehicles:												
Over	Not over											
3.5 tonnes	33 tonnes	142	139	138	124	125	113	107	97	81	69	60
33 tonnes		604	637	679	726	729	706	746	751	778	809	872
All artics		746	776	817	850	854	819	852	848	859	878	932
All vehicles:												
Over	Not over											
3.5 tonnes	25 tonnes	527	467	447	419	382	346	325	294	283	265	277
25 tonnes		1,070	1,142	1,181	1,224	1,248	1,221	1,268	1,287	1,343	1,378	1,467
All weights		1,597	1,609	1,628	1,643	1,630	1,567	1,593	1,581	1,627	1,643	1,744
(c) By commodity												
Food, drink and tobacco		302	308	326	342	346	333	346	321	339	333	351
Wood, timber and cork		24	24	27	26	27	28	26	28	28	32	42
Fertiliser		10	11	13	10	9	11	10	9	11	12	7
Crude minerals		355	319	320	329	327	297	308	298	333	327	364
Ores		18	18	18	25	18	20	16	16	17	21	22
Crude materials		16	16	18	17	20	20	18	20	21	19	25
Coal and coke		42	34	32	37	26	28	22	21	17	22	14
Petrol and petroleum products		68	71	75	73	61	61	75	74	59	64	67
Chemicals		51	50	51	53	53	47	49	50	41	47	46
Building materials		156	161	142	156	161	159	165	165	167	165	185
Iron and steel products		47	54	52	55	54	48	49	44	39	41	43
Other metal products n.e.s.		17	17	15	16	18	17	16	14	14	16	19
Machinery and transport equipment		57	61	59	71	73	67	69	70	68	66	70
Miscellaneous manufactures n.e.s.		84	85	88	90	96	91	97	97	105	98	111
Miscellaneous transactions n.e.s. (incl. commodity not known)		351	379	393	343	342	340	328	353	367	379	378
All commodities		1,597	1,609	1,628	1,643	1,630	1,567	1,593	1,581	1,627	1,643	1,744

1 Rigid vehicles or articulated vehicles (tractive unit and trailer) with gross vehicle weight over 3.5 tonnes.

2 Figures for 2004 are not fully comparable with those for 2003 and earlier years. Detailed comparisons should therefore be made with caution. See Notes and Definitions.

☎020-7944 3093

4.6 Freight transport by road: length of haul by goods vehicles over 3.5 tonnes[1]: 1994-2004

Million tonnes

(a) Goods lifted		1994	1995	1996	1997	1998	1999	2000	2001	2002	2003	2004 [2]
Not over 100 kilometres		1,158	1,145	1,148	1,157	1,132	1,073	1,093	1,083	1,129	1,132	1,230
Over 100 kilometres		439	464	480	487	497	494	501	496	498	509	514
All distances		1,597	1,609	1,628	1,643	1,630	1,567	1,593	1,581	1,627	1,643	1,744
(b) Goods moved												Billion tonne - kilometres
Not over 100 kilometres		38.1	38.6	38.6	39.7	38.6	36.9	38.1	36.8	38.8	39.4	42.3
Over 100 kilometres		99.7	105.1	108.2	109.9	113.3	112.3	112.4	112.6	111.0	112.0	109.9
All distances		137.8	143.7	146.8	149.6	151.9	149.2	150.5	149.4	149.8	151.7	152.2
(c) Average length of haul by gross weight of vehicle												Kilometres
Rigid vehicles:												
Over	Not over											
3.5 tonnes	17 tonnes	61	63	64	65	66	68	69	65	63	63	57
17 tonnes	25 tonnes	30	34	40	39	40	50	56	67	70	68	70
25 tonnes		37	36	36	38	37	37	36	35	35	36	35
All rigids		45	45	47	48	47	50	49	47	46	46	44
Articulated vehicles:												
Over	Not over											
3.5 tonnes	33 tonnes	119	115	115	116	115	124	131	132	122	128	118
33 tonnes		137	142	136	134	138	138	135	136	134	133	125
All artics		133	137	133	131	135	136	134	136	133	133	125
All vehicles:		86	89	90	91	93	95	94	94	92	92	87

1 Rigid vehicles or articulated vehicles (tractive unit and trailer) with gross vehicle weight over 3.5 tonnes.

2 Figures for 2004 are not fully comparable with those for 2003 and earlier years. Detailed comparisons should therefore be made with caution. See Notes and Definitions

☎020-7944 3093

4.7 International road haulage by United Kingdom registered powered vehicles over 3.5[1] tonnes gross vehicle weight: goods carried: by country of loading or unloading: 2004

	Outward journey [2]				Inward journey [2]			
Country	Tonnes (thousand)	Per cent	Tonne-kms (million)	Per cent	Tonnes (thousand)	Per cent	Tonne-kms (million)	Per cent
Austria	19	*0*	34	*1*	11	*0*	16	*0*
Belgium and Luxembourg	1,033	*16*	509	*9*	1,537	*20*	750	*12*
Denmark	16	*0*	22	*0*	11	*0*	11	*0*
Finland	2	*0*	5	*0*	1	*0*	1	*0*
France	1,942	*31*	1,358	*24*	2,516	*33*	1,526	*24*
Germany	901	*14*	833	*15*	1,065	*14*	991	*16*
Greece	29	*0*	95	*2*	5	*0*	15	*0*
Irish Republic	232	*4*	90	*2*	100	*1*	35	*1*
Italy	604	*10*	957	*17*	682	*9*	1,073	*17*
Netherlands	719	*11*	378	*7*	1,002	*13*	559	*9*
Portugal	33	*1*	72	*1*	29	*0*	58	*1*
Spain	438	*7*	812	*14*	528	*7*	996	*16*
Sweden	5	*0*	10	*0*	4	*0*	3	*0*
EU15 (excl. United Kingdom)	5,971	*95*	5,171	*91*	7,490	*97*	6,034	*95*
Cyprus	0	*0*	0	*0*	0	*0*	0	*0*
Czech Republic	6	*0*	8	*0*	0	*0*	0	*0*
Estonia	0	*0*	0	*0*	1	*0*	1	*0*
Hungary	11	*0*	21	*0*	9	*0*	17	*0*
Latvia	0	*0*	0	*0*	0	*0*	0	*0*
Lithuania	0	*0*	0	*0*	0	*0*	0	*0*
Malta	6	*0*	7	*0*	5	*0*	7	*0*
Poland	0	*0*	0	*0*	1	*0*	1	*0*
Slovakia	3	*0*	4	*0*	0	*0*	0	*0*
Slovenia	0	*0*	0	*0*	0	*0*	0	*0*
NMS10[3]	25	*0*	41	*1*	16	*0*	26	*0*
European Union	5,996	*96*	5,212	*92*	7,506	*97*	6,060	*95*
Switzerland	169	*3*	211	*4*	164	*2*	198	*3*
Norway	1	*0*	1	*0*	0	*0*	0	*0*
Other countries	109	*2*	255	*4*	51	*1*	108	*2*
All countries	6,275	*100*	5,679	*100*	7,721	*100*	6,366	*100*

1 Rigid vehicles or articulated vehicles (tractive unit and trailer) with gross vehicle weight over 3.5 tonnes.

2 Excludes vehicles travelling between Northern Ireland and the Republic of Ireland only, i.e. where the whole journey is confined to the island of Ireland.

3 New Member State countries that joined the EU on 1 May 2004. Data are for the whole of 2004

☎0117-372 8484

4.8 International road haulage by United Kingdom registered powered vehicles over 3.5[1] tonnes gross weight by type of transport and commodity: 2004

(a) Outward journey [2]

NST [3] chapter	Total traffic				*ow:* Hire or reward			
	Tonnes (thousand)	Per cent	Tonne-kms (million)	Per cent	Tonnes (thousand)	Per cent	Tonne-kms (million)	Per cent
0 Agricultural products	278	*4*	346	*6*	270	*5*	332	*6*
1 Foodstuffs	1,031	*16*	964	*17*	958	*17*	913	*17*
2 Fuels	16	*0*	9	*0*	16	*0*	9	*0*
3 Petroleum products	29	*0*	20	*0*	29	*1*	20	*0*
4 Metal ore & waste	13	*0*	6	*0*	13	*0*	6	*0*
5 Metal products	264	*4*	275	*5*	258	*4*	270	*5*
6 Building materials	161	*3*	122	*2*	158	*3*	121	*2*
7 Fertilizers	0	*0*	0	*0*	0	*0*	0	*0*
8 Chemicals	842	*13*	784	*14*	790	*14*	747	*14*
9 Miscellaneous	2,007	*32*	1,695	*30*	1,836	*32*	1,563	*29*
ow:								
Machinery & engines	966	*15*	885	*16*	873	*15*	813	*15*
Leather & textiles	824	*13*	639	*11*	752	*13*	585	*11*
All unclassified	1,634	*26*	1,458	*26*	1,477	*25*	1,345	*25*
All commodities	6,275	*100*	5,679	*100*	5,805	*100*	5,326	*100*

(b) Inward journey [2]

NST [3] chapter	Tonnes (thousand)	Per cent	Tonne-kms (million)	Per cent	Tonnes (thousand)	Per cent	Tonne-kms (million)	Per cent
0 Agricultural products	712	*9*	604	*9*	668	*9*	568	*9*
1 Foodstuffs	2,087	*27*	1,375	*22*	1,955	*27*	1,294	*22*
2 Fuels	46	*1*	25	*0*	41	*1*	23	*0*
3 Petroleum products	67	*1*	46	*1*	67	*1*	46	*1*
4 Metal ore & waste	7	*0*	5	*0*	7	*0*	5	*0*
5 Metal products	161	*2*	146	*2*	161	*2*	146	*2*
6 Building materials	153	*2*	124	*2*	148	*2*	120	*2*
7 Fertilizers	19	*0*	12	*0*	19	*0*	12	*0*
8 Chemicals	515	*7*	384	*6*	494	*7*	373	*6*
9 Miscellaneous	1,984	*26*	1,937	*30*	1,829	*25*	1,811	*30*
ow:								
Machinery & engines	996	*13*	837	*13*	904	*13*	767	*13*
Leather & textiles	624	*8*	592	*9*	566	*8*	542	*9*
All unclassified	1,971	*26*	1,709	*27*	1,829	*25*	1,614	*27*
All commodities	7,721	*100*	6,366	*100*	7,217	*100*	6,010	*100*

1 Rigid vehicles or articulated vehicles (tractive unit and trailer) with gross vehicle weight over 3.5 tonnes.

2 Excludes vehicles travelling between Northern Ireland and the Republic of Ireland only, i.e. where the whole journey is confined to the island of Ireland.

3 Standard EC classification for transport. See Notes.

☎0117-372 8484

4.9 Bilateral[1] traffic, between the United Kingdom and European Union countries, in vehicles registered in the United Kingdom and the corresponding European Union country: 2004[2]

Thousand tonnes /percentage

Country of loading/unloading	Goods loaded in the United Kingdom: In UK vehicles	In vehicles registered in the country of unloading	UK hauliers' share (percentage)	Goods unloaded in the United Kingdom: In UK vehicles	In vehicles registered in the country of loading	UK hauliers' share (percentage)
Austria	19	235	*7*	11	318	*3*
Belgium and Luxembourg	1,033	582	*64*	1,537	1,145	*57*
Denmark	16	45	*26*	11	113	*9*
Finland	2	.	*100*	1	.	*100*
France	1,942	1,804	*52*	2,516	3,166	*44*
Germany	901	899	*50*	1,065	1,790	*37*
Greece	29	..	..	5	..	..
Ireland	7,554	5,143	*59*	3,009	4,227	*42*
Italy	604	380	*61*	682	911	*43*
Netherlands	719	526	*58*	1,002	1,307	*43*
Portugal	33	72	*31*	29	180	*14*
Spain	438	697	*39*	528	1,521	*26*
Sweden	5	.	*100*	4	16	*18*
Total	13,293	10,383	*56*	10,399	14,694	*41*

1 Excluding 'cross trade', i.e. trade in vehicles registered elsewhere than in the country of loading or unloading. ☎0117-372 8484

2 Figures for goods carried in UK vehicles are for 2004; and those for goods carried in other countries' vehicles are for 2003 (the most recent available).

4.10 National railways freight: 1994/95-2004/05

(a) Freight moved by commodity[1] — Billion tonne-kilometres

	1994/95	1995/96	1996/97	[2]1997/98	1998/99	1999/00	2000/01	2001/02	2002/03	2003/04	2004/05
Coal	3.3	3.6	3.9	4.4	4.5	4.8	4.8	6.2	5.7	5.8	7.0
Metals	1.7	1.7	..	..	2.1	2.2	2.1	2.4	2.7	2.4	2.6
Construction	2.5	2.3	..	..	2.1	2.0	2.4	2.8	2.6	2.7	2.8
Oil and petroleum	1.8	1.8	..	..	1.6	1.5	1.4	1.2	1.1	1.2	1.2
Other traffic	3.8	3.9	11.2	12.5	7.1	7.6	7.4	6.7	6.5	6.8	7.0
All traffic	13.0	13.3	15.1	16.9	17.3	18.2	18.1	19.4	18.7	18.9	20.7

(b) Freight lifted by commodity[3] — Million tonnes

	1994/95	1995/96	1996/97	1997/98	1998/99	1999/00	2000/01	2001/02	2002/03	2003/04	2004/05
Coal	42.5	45.2	52.2	50.3	45.3	44.3	45.7	46.1	40.7	42.0	51.7[4]
Metals	16.9	15.1	..	..	..	..	..	..	..	..	..
Construction	16.8	11.5	..	..	..	..	..	..	..	..	..
Oil and petroleum	8.1	6.3	..	..	..	..	..	..	..	..	..
Other traffic	13.0	22.6	49.6	55.1	56.8	47.6	49.7	48.3	46.4	46.9	50.2[4]
All traffic	97.3	100.7	101.8	105.4	102.1	91.9	95.4	94.4	87.0	88.9	101.9[4]

1 Revised series on new basis from 1998/99, see Notes and Definitions.

2 Owing to changes in the way freight traffic has been estimated following privatisation data since 1996/97 are not comparable to those for previous years. Freight excludes parcels and materials carried for rail infrastructure, see Notes and Definitions.

3 Break in series from 1999/2000, see Notes and Definitions.

4 Break in series, increase largely due to changes in coverage

☎020-7944 4977

The figures in this table are outside the scope of National Statistics.

Source - ORR, previously SRA

4.11 Roll-on/roll-off ferry and Channel Tunnel traffic; road goods vehicles outward to mainland Europe: by country of registration: 1994-2004

Thousands

	1994	1995	1996	1997	1998	1999	2000	2001	2002	2003	2004
Powered vehicles:											
United Kingdom	453.1	486.0	531.1	543.2	544.3	562.7	544.8	517.6	493.3	473.9	493.1
Austria	.	9.7	8.6	5.4	10.2	14.9	17.0	42.0	45.8	42.9	30.0
Belgium/Luxembourg	37.1	45.7	41.0	53.6	74.5	96.7	114.1	119.3	121.4	104.3	112.4
Denmark	5.0	4.5	4.6	5.5	7.3	8.7	9.5	12.0	16.9	13.7	17.1
Finland	.	0.3	0.2	0.1	0.6	0.7	0.9	3.1	2.0	1.1	0.1
Germany	28.1	28.0	30.4	39.3	52.4	73.1	111.5	132.0	148.2	155.7	164.7
France	163.2	154.9	181.7	234.2	272.4	319.1	338.8	352.4	363.1	363.2	388.0
Greece	1.3	1.8	2.1	2.6	1.9	2.6	2.9	2.6	2.8	3.6	4.0
Irish Republic	32.4	31.0	30.1	32.3	38.8	44.7	48.5	46.6	44.6	30.8	27.6
Italy	22.7	29.3	28.8	30.4	35.3	45.8	67.8	91.1	127.8	132.4	120.1
Netherlands	76.3	84.6	87.2	107.0	125.4	153.3	185.1	187.5	186.3	210.2	252.1
Spain	35.2	38.4	39.4	45.1	56.3	67.7	81.8	93.9	102.2	105.9	109.8
Sweden	.	0.7	0.9	8.9	10.3	1.0	1.4	1.8	1.8	1.4	1.4
Portugal	3.7	3.4	3.1	5.1	6.7	9.2	10.7	10.2	11.0	9.4	8.9
EU15 (excluding United Kingdom)	405.2	432.2	458.1	569.5	692.1	837.3	990.0	1,094.5	1,173.9	1,174.6	1,236.2
Cyprus	..	..	..	..	..	0.1	0.2	0.1	0.2	0.2	0.2
Czech Republic	..	..	..	..	..	5.4	5.2	6.8	7.8	13.1	25.0
Estonia	..	..	..	..	..	0.0	0.1	0.2	0.3	0.3	0.8
Hungary	..	..	..	..	..	6.9	8.0	11.1	12.4	12.7	24.6
Latvia	..	..	..	..	..	0.3	0.3	0.1	0.2	0.2	0.2
Lithuania	..	..	..	..	..	0.9	1.4	1.0	0.7	1.6	2.9
Malta	..	..	..	..	..	0.2	0.3	0.3	0.3	0.2	0.1
Poland	..	..	..	..	..	7.0	10.4	12.5	12.0	14.2	31.0
Slovakia	..	..	..	..	..	0.2	0.2	0.4	1.0	2.4	8.0
Slovenia	..	..	..	..	..	1.5	1.9	3.5	4.7	4.7	10.0
NMS10[1]	..	..	..	..	..	22.5	28.0	36.2	39.5	49.5	102.9
Other countries in Europe and elsewhere	34.2	29.0	26.3	28.0	33.3	24.9	24.9	43.2	76.7	97.6	107.6
Unknown	4.0	3.0	2.2	5.7	4.8	6.3	17.7	20.5	18.1	19.1	17.0
All countries	896.5	950.2	1,017.7	1,146.4	1,274.8	1,453.7	1,605.4	1,711.9	1,801.5	1,814.7	1,956.8
Unaccompanied trailers	701.6	677.4	626.4	740.0	737.5	737.8	712.9	686.4	726.0	780.4	782.2
Powered vehicles and unaccompanied trailers	1,598.1	1,627.6	1,644.1	1,886.4	2,012.3	2,191.4	2,318.3	2,398.3	2,527.5	2,595.1	2,739.0

1 New Member State countries that joined the EU on 1 May 2004. There is no individual breakdown available before1999 for these countries.

☎0117-372 8484

4.12 Roll-on/roll-off ferry and Channel Tunnel traffic: road goods vehicles outward to mainland Europe: 1994-2004

(a) By country of disembarkation — Thousands

	1994	1995	1996	1997	1998	1999	2000	2001	2002	2003	2004
Powered vehicles:											
Belgium	157.1	147.1	147.7	168.8	132.4	132.3	152.3	144.1	143.6	76.4	89.1
France	646.5	707.1	767.9	854.2	1,024.4	1,209.5	1,330.3	1,435.2	1,520.4	1,601.4	1,710.1
Netherlands	86.9	90.4	96.7	110.1	102.9	107.4	118.5	124.7	128.5	129.5	149.5
Others	5.8	5.6	5.4	13.3	15.1	4.4	4.3	7.8	9.1	7.5	8.1
All countries	896.5	950.2	1,017.7	1,146.4	1,274.8	1,453.7	1,605.4	1,711.9	1,801.5	1,814.7	1,956.8
Unaccompanied trailers:											
Belgium	267.9	259.2	234.4	275.6	266.9	288.8	263.1	250.6	262.6	266.5	241.0
France	116.4	102.1	87.3	101.2	85.8	63.6	56.5	57.0	47.1	54.0	48.4
Netherlands	209.5	219.8	222.1	263.4	280.8	278.7	281.1	275.5	311.7	343.9	365.9
Others	107.8	96.4	82.6	99.9	104.0	106.6	112.1	103.4	104.5	116.1	126.9
All countries	701.6	677.4	626.4	740.0	737.5	737.8	712.9	686.4	726.0	780.4	782.2
All vehicles	1,598.1	1,627.6	1,644.1	1,886.4	2,012.3	2,191.4	2,318.3	2,398.3	2,527.5	2,595.1	2,739.0

(b) By Great Britain port area — Thousands

	1994	1995	1996	1997	1998	1999	2000	2001	2002	2003	2004
Powered vehicles:											
North Sea	108.3	110.9	114.5	141.5	132.4	129.0	144.1	151.7	154.5	157.5	175.6
Strait of Dover	643.7	705.8	771.6	890.8	1,017.9	1,207.4	1,349.5	1,446.0	1,531.2	1,525.1	1,648.1
English Channel	144.5	133.4	131.7	114.1	124.4	117.2	111.9	114.2	115.8	132.1	133.2
All ports	896.5	950.2	1,017.7	1,146.4	1,274.8	1,453.7	1,605.4	1,711.9	1,801.5	1,814.7	1,956.8
Unaccompanied trailers:											
North Sea	512.0	500.3	467.4	575.0	600.6	640.8	633.6	610.4	667.3	729.9	732.3
Strait of Dover	107.5	110.7	102.2	109.1	90.7	53.4	43.5	42.7	29.6	22.5	21.4
English Channel	82.1	66.5	56.9	55.9	46.1	43.6	35.8	33.3	29.1	28.0	28.5
All ports	701.6	677.4	626.4	740.0	737.5	737.8	712.9	686.4	726.0	780.4	782.2
All vehicles	1,598.1	1,627.6	1,644.1	1,886.4	2,012.3	2,191.4	2,318.3	2,398.3	2,527.5	2,595.1	2,739.0

☎0117-372 8484

5 Maritime:

Notes and Definitions

Ports traffic: 5.2 - 5.5, 5.6 and 5.7

These tables relate to foreign, coastwise and one-port traffic through ports in the United Kingdom, and are derived as follows:

(a) from 2000,

(i) detailed quarterly returns from shipping lines or their agents of all freight traffic at major UK ports;

(ii) quarterly returns of inwards and outwards weight and units by port authorities or other undertakings at major ports;

(iii) annual returns of inwards and outwards traffic only by port authorities or other undertakings at minor ports.

These returns were introduced by DfT in order to comply with regulations implementing an EC Maritime Statistics Directive (Council Directive 95/64/EC on statistical returns in respect of the carriage of goods and passengers by sea).

(b) prior to 2000,

(i) detailed annual traffic returns made by port authorities or other undertakings at major ports;

(ii) annual returns of inwards and outwards traffic from port authorities or other undertakings at minor ports

The major ports include all ports with cargo volumes of at least 1 million tonnes in 2001 (2 million tonnes under the previous system between 1995 and 1999) and a few other smaller ports. The breakdowns of traffic for 1995 and later years in the tables include major ports traffic and are supplemented by estimates for the minor ports.

Full statistics on port traffic in the United Kingdom in 2003, including detailed breakdowns of foreign and domestic traffic of the major ports, are available in the Transport Statistics Report *Maritime Statistics 2003* published by The Stationery Office. *Maritime Statistics 2004,* which will be published at the end of October 2005, will contain 2004 statistics.

Definitions of terms used in the tables are:

Port groups: For statistical purposes, ports of Great Britain are grouped geographically as shown in map 5.9.

Weights: All weights reported for port and waterborne freight statistics include crates and other packaging. The tare weights of containers and other items of transport equipment are excluded.

Foreign traffic: Traffic between ports in the United Kingdom (Great Britain and Northern Ireland), and foreign countries, that is countries outside Great Britain, Northern Ireland, the Isle of Man and the Channel Islands.

Domestic traffic: The sum of coastwise and one-port traffic.

Coastwise traffic: Goods loaded or unloaded at ports in the United Kingdom, and transported to or from another port in the United Kingdom.

One-port traffic: One-port traffic comprises:

- dredged sand, gravel, etc. landed at a port for commercial purposes;
- traffic to and from off-shore installations. Fuel shipped to oil rigs is included in 'Other traffic - outwards'; and
- material shipped for dumping at sea.

Container and roll-on traffic (commonly known as 'unitised traffic'): Includes road goods vehicles, unaccompanied trailers and other goods carried on roll-on/roll-off shipping services, containers carried on all types of shipping services and rail wagons and barges carried on ships. Goods carried on 'unitised' services constitute a subset of total traffic and are reported in tables 5.4 and 5.5.

Coastwise routes: Coastwise routes (table 5.6) are the ferry services between mainland Great Britain and Northern Ireland, the Isle of Man, the West of Scotland island of Lewis (between Ullapool and Stornoway), the Orkneys and Shetlands, and the Channel Islands. Short ferry routes between Scottish islands, and those across river estuaries and to the Isle of Wight are excluded. Only in the case of ferry routes between mainland Great Britain and the Orkneys and Shetlands is traffic counted at both ends of the route. In other cases, traffic is counted at the mainland Great Britain port only.

Domestic waterborne freight traffic: 5.8 and 5.10

These tables present estimates of goods lifted (tonnes) and goods moved (tonne -kilometres) in the United Kingdom by coastal shipping (coastwise and one-port traffic) and on inland waters. The data are based on annual studies for DfT by MDS- Transmodal.

Inland waters boundaries and traffic

The definition of inland waters was devised for the first survey of waterborne transport carried out in 1980. The definitions were produced from the perspective of measuring freight traffic travelling on inland waters, which could travel by another surface mode within the UK. There are two boundary definitions used to measure the amount of traffic:

Inland waterways: all water areas available for navigation that lie inland of a boundary defined as the most seaward point of any estuary which might reasonably be bridged or tunnelled - this is taken to be where the width of water surface area is both less than 3 km at low water and less than 5 km at high water on spring tides.

Inland waters: all waters within the summer boundary of the Partially Smooth Water Area (PSWA), which is generally much further seaward than the inland waterways boundary. The area between the inland waterways boundary and the PSWA line is termed "sheltered waters".

For the purpose of estimating tonnes and tonne-kilometres, all traffic *wholly within* inland waters (ie internal traffic) is counted. Tonnes is then simply tonnes lifted, and tonne-kilometres is tonnes lifted multiplied by the distance travelled.

Traffic which crosses the inland waters boundary and which also goes upstream of the inland waterways boundary, is counted as well; but traffic which is essentially *seagoing traffic* to and from major *seaboard* ports is specifically excluded.

Where traffic is included, tonnes is then tonnes lifted and tonne-kilometres is tonnes lifted multiplied by the distance travelled but calculated from the point at which the vessel crosses the *inland waterways* boundary.
Full detailed statistics for 2003 are available in the Statistics bulletin, *Waterborne Freight in the UK 2003*, published by DfT. *Waterborne Freight in the UK 2004*, which will be published by DfT later in 2005, will contain 2004 statistics.

United Kingdom International sea passenger movements: 5.11 and 5.12

These tables have been compiled from statistics collected monthly from shipping operators by DfT and cover travel between the UK and other countries. Domestic passengers are excluded. The figures include drivers of lorries, coaches and other vehicles.

United Kingdom and Crown Dependency registered trading vessels: 5.13

Until the end of 1986, United Kingdom registered fleet figures were derived from DfT records of trading vessels of 500 gross tons or over registered at ports in the United Kingdom, the Channel Islands and the Isle of Man. A different ship type classification was also in use. For 1986 only, for purposes of comparison, it shows figures from both sources giving the composition of the fleet on the basis of both the 'old' and 'new' ship type classifications.

The United Kingdom owned and registered merchant fleets: 5.14 and 5.15

The figures given in these tables are derived from Lloyd's Register-Fairplay data and cover trading vessels of 500 gross tons or above. Table 5.15 covers vessels owned by UK companies wherever the vessels are registered, while Table 5.14 covers vessels registered in the United Kingdom and Crown Dependencies (Isle of Man, Channel Islands), excluding those owned by the Government.

The figures for both fleets exclude offshore supply vessels, non-cargo vessels, tugs, fishing vessels, dredgers, river and other non seagoing vessels. For further background information and more detailed tables, see the Transport Statistics Report, *Maritime Statistics 2003*, available from The Stationery Office.

Gross tons: Under the International Convention on the Tonnage Measurement of Ships, 1969 gross tonnage (gt) is defined as the following function of the total volume of all enclosed spaces in the ship (V), in cubic metres:

GT = K1V
where K1 = 0.2 + 0.02 log 10 V.

Deadweight tonnes: The term deadweight tonnes, or 'dwt', is a measurement of the weight of cargo, stores, fuel, passengers and crew carried by the ship when loaded to her maximum summer loadline.

Tankers: Include oil, gas, chemical and other specialised tankers.

Bulk carriers: Large and small carriers including combination - ore/oil and ore/bulk/oil - carriers.

Specialised carriers: Includes vessels such as livestock carriers, car carriers and chemical carriers.

Fully cellular container: Figures include only container vessels of this type.

Ro-Ro: These are for passenger and cargo Ro-Ro vessels.

Other general cargo vessels: These include reefer vessels, general cargo/passenger vessels, and single and multi-deck general cargo vessels.

Passenger vessels: These are cruise liner and other passenger vessels.

United Kingdom shipping industry revenue and expenditure from international activities: 5.16

The revenue and expenditure figures in this table are derived from the results of annual inquiries carried out by the Chamber of Shipping (CoS). The United Kingdom shipping industry is defined as United Kingdom resident companies which own or operate ships irrespective of their flag of registry.

This includes companies, which are United Kingdom subsidiaries of overseas parent companies, and excludes overseas resident subsidiaries of United Kingdom companies.

This treatment arises from the primary purpose of the CoS inquiries, which is to provide estimates for the sea transport account of the United Kingdom Balance of Payments. In the Balance of Payments the revenue from overseas resident subsidiary companies is treated as investment income, not part of the sea transport account.

International activities cover the activities of ships either owned by the United Kingdom industry or operated by the industry on charter. The activities covered are:

- carriage of UK imports and exports;
- carriage of trade between two foreign countries (cross trades);
- carriage of passengers on international ferry routes and sea cruises;
- chartering ships to overseas operators.

The passenger revenue series includes revenue from overseas residents only and is consistent with data published in *The Pink Book* (United Kingdom Balance of Payments).
Associated expenditure includes:

- payment for bunkers uplifted abroad;
- disbursements in overseas ports: cargo handling, port dues, crews' expenses, agency fees, light dues etc.;
- charter payments to overseas ship owners.

Marine accident casualties: 5.17

The data refer to accidents to persons on UK registered merchant vessels of greater than or equal to 100gt only, including accidents during access.
The information is derived from incidents reported in compliance with the Merchant Shipping (Accident Reporting and Investigation) Regulations (SI 1999 No. 2567).

HM Coastguard Statistics: 5.18

HM Coastguard, part of the Maritime and Coastguard Agency MCA), continues to initiate and co-ordinate Civil Maritime Search and Rescue operations within the UK Search and Rescue Region (UKSRR), from 19 Rescue Centres strategically located around the UK coastline.

Machinery and equipment failure, the inability to cope when the weather deteriorates, diving incidents and failure to inform relatives or other agents ashore when likely to be overdue have been the major causes of SAR incidents.

HM Coastguard continues to tackle these issues both in its own SAR Prevention and Safety at Sea strategies, in conjunction with colleagues within the MCA, and with the RNLI, RYA, BMF, RoSPA and RLSS through the Safety on the Sea (SOS) Group, chaired by the RNLI.

Definitions of terms used are:

Commercial vessels: All Merchant Vessels (including ferries and cruise ships), tugs, barges, dredgers, offshore installations, tenders, supply vessels, support vessels, research vessels, cable layers, mega-yachts, hovercraft etc.

Fishing vessels: All registered fishing vessels.

Pleasure craft: Yachts (except mega-yachts), sailing dinghies, cabin cruisers, speedboats, diving support boats, sail training craft, square riggers, rowing boats and inflatable craft. From

1994 data also includes canoes/kayaks, sailboards and jet-skis (personal watercraft) previously included in 'others'.

Incidents to persons: Includes man-overboard, divers, swimmers, missing persons, persons cut off by tides, persons stuck on cliffs, etc.

Medical evacuations: Incidents where injured persons taken from vessels at sea to shore for medical treatment, or injured cliff walkers evacuated to hospital, etc.

Others: Includes incidents involving military vessels, military aircraft, civilian aircraft, animal rescue, etc.

Distress reports: Includes all Distress, Urgency, Pyrotechnic and EPIRB/ELT signals and those reports subsequently found to be false alarms or hoaxes.

5.1 All ports of United Kingdom[1], foreign, coastwise and one-port traffic: 1965-2003

For greater detail of the years 1993-2003 see Table 5.2

Million tonnes

	Foreign			Coastwise			One-port			Total		
Year	Imports	Exports	All	Inwards	Outwards	All	Inwards	Outwards [2]	All	Inwards	Outwards	All
Great Britain												
1965	153.4	35.7	189.1	54.1	60.4	114.5	7.2	8.5	15.7	214.7	104.6	319.2
1966	157.1	38.2	195.3	54.2	59.7	113.9	6.8	8.5	15.3	218.1	106.4	324.5
1967	161.7	38.0	199.7	53.1	56.9	110.0	6.6	8.5	15.1	221.4	103.4	324.8
1968	175.6	41.7	217.3	51.1	56.6	107.7	7.8	8.5	16.3	234.5	106.8	341.3
1969	185.5	43.3	228.8	52.1	56.9	109.0	8.3	8.5	16.8	245.9	108.7	354.6
1970	196.2	48.0	244.2	51.8	56.2	108.0	9.2	8.6	17.8	257.2	112.0	370.0
1971	202.0	48.7	250.7	46.0	52.0	98.0	10.9	8.6	19.5	258.9	109.3	368.2
1972	205.0	49.7	254.7	45.4	51.8	97.2	16.0	8.8	24.8	266.4	110.3	376.7
1973	219.5	53.5	273.0	46.4	57.3	103.7	13.9	8.9	22.8	279.8	119.7	399.5
1974	211.1	51.1	262.2	48.5	56.9	105.4	13.1	10.1	23.2	272.7	118.1	390.8
1975	175.3	50.2	225.5	41.5	48.9	90.4	13.0	11.2	24.2	229.8	110.3	340.1
1976	180.0	62.8	242.8	41.1	50.9	92.0	14.4	11.2	25.6	235.5	124.9	360.3
1977	158.2	77.6	235.8	44.1	56.3	100.4	21.7	12.3	34.0	224.0	146.2	370.2
1978	152.8	90.7	243.5	47.5	62.2	109.7	26.5	12.8	39.3	226.8	165.7	392.4
1979	157.1	107.5	264.6	52.7	67.0	119.7	29.5	12.9	42.4	239.3	187.5	426.8
1980	131.2	117.1	248.3	57.4	67.7	125.1	24.6	14.0	38.6	213.2	198.8	412.0
United Kingdom												
1980	133.4	117.5	250.8	64.8	69.8	134.6	24.6	14.0	38.6	222.8	201.3	424.1
1981	125.7	126.1	251.8	60.2	68.2	128.4	22.3	13.6	35.8	208.2	207.8	416.1
1982	122.9	130.7	253.6	67.2	71.3	138.5	24.6	13.4	37.9	214.7	215.4	430.1
1983	121.9	136.8	258.7	68.9	71.3	140.1	26.6	13.0	39.6	217.5	221.1	438.5
1984	143.5	142.1	285.5	64.2	66.3	130.5	28.5	12.3	40.9	236.3	220.7	456.9
1985	143.3	148.2	291.5	63.2	66.3	129.6	28.1	13.7	41.8	234.7	228.2	462.9
1986	150.6	150.7	301.3	60.9	63.7	124.6	27.2	13.4	40.6	238.7	227.8	466.5
1987	154.9	151.0	305.9	59.8	61.2	121.0	31.8	12.9	44.7	246.6	225.0	471.6
1988	169.7	142.2	311.9	66.3	65.1	131.3	34.2	14.6	48.8	270.2	221.9	492.1
1989	174.6	127.5	302.1	64.1	64.8	128.9	35.0	14.8	49.8	273.7	207.1	480.9
1990	183.5	136.2	319.6	61.0	61.5	122.3	34.1	15.9	50.0	278.4	213.6	492.0
1991	182.1	143.2	325.3	61.7	62.8	124.4	29.8	15.1	44.9	273.6	221.0	494.6
1992	182.6	150.2	332.8	58.2	60.8	119.0	29.0	14.9	43.9	269.8	225.9	495.7
1993	189.5	157.5	346.9	59.4	62.0	121.5	23.8	14.0	37.8	272.7	233.5	506.2
1994	190.1	179.0	369.1	63.3	64.8	128.1	28.6	12.4	41.0	281.9	256.2	538.1
1995	190.3	178.8	369.1	67.9	72.1	140.0	26.7	12.4	39.1	284.9	263.3	548.2
1996	192.7	175.8	368.5	69.9	75.3	145.2	25.1	12.4	37.5	287.7	263.5	551.2
1997	205.7	179.3	385.0	67.5	72.0	139.5	21.8	12.2	34.0	295.0	263.5	558.5
1998	209.3	181.7	390.9	70.7	71.9	142.7	26.1	8.8	34.9	306.1	262.4	568.5
1999	203.6	184.4	387.9	67.0	71.1	138.1	36.4	3.2	39.6	307.0	258.7	565.6
2000	220.9	193.1	414.0	57.4	61.9	119.3	38.0	1.7	39.8	316.3	256.7	573.1
2001	238.4	180.4	418.7	57.3	54.9	112.2	33.3	2.2	35.4	328.9	237.5	566.4
2002	220.9	178.2	399.1	58.2	57.3	115.5	41.7	2.0	43.7	320.8	237.5	558.3
2003	229.3	174.0	403.3	57.3	56.1	113.4	37.2	1.7	39.0	323.8	231.9	555.7

1 Great Britain only prior to 1980.
2 Prior to 1974, estimates only.

☎020-7944 3087

5.2 All ports: foreign, coastwise and one port traffic: by mode of appearance: 1993-2003

Thousand tonnes

	1993	1994	1995	1996	1997	1998	1999	2000	2001	2002	2003
Foreign traffic											
Liquid bulk traffic											
Imports	68,824	63,512	58,512	59,309	61,060	61,346	56,528	70,788	74,495	62,811	66,447
Exports	96,616	113,936	111,651	106,169	104,654	106,041	110,591	118,509	110,321	107,516	100,772
All	165,440	177,448	170,164	165,478	165,714	167,387	167,120	189,297	184,816	170,327	167,218
Dry bulk traffic											
Imports	58,053	58,297	62,121	63,905	68,208	68,333	65,219	65,652	77,360	67,575	72,644
Exports	18,546	19,652	19,632	19,549	19,596	20,840	18,905	19,739	17,206	18,026	20,559
All	76,598	77,949	81,753	83,454	87,805	89,173	84,124	85,391	94,565	85,600	93,203
Container and roll-on traffic											
Imports	45,519	49,930	51,668	52,008	58,822	61,191	64,272	64,753	65,721	68,371	69,199
Exports	36,079	38,942	41,694	43,711	48,805	49,029	49,616	49,323	47,334	47,313	47,291
All	81,598	88,873	93,362	95,719	107,628	110,220	113,889	114,076	113,054	115,685	116,490
Semi-bulk traffic											
Imports	15,145	16,988	16,445	15,987	16,097	16,878	15,967	17,174	17,059	18,523	17,284
Exports	5,183	5,349	4,891	5,267	5,142	4,897	4,519	4,411	3,737	3,613	3,848
All	20,329	22,337	21,337	21,253	21,239	21,775	20,486	21,584	20,796	22,136	21,131
Conventional traffic											
Imports	1,916	1,359	1,555	1,493	1,506	1,531	1,595	2,500	3,730	3,645	3,699
Exports	1,066	1,109	932	1,094	1,100	854	735	1,145	1,786	1,705	1,535
All	2,982	2,468	2,487	2,587	2,607	2,385	2,330	3,645	5,515	5,349	5,234
All foreign traffic											
Imports	189,457	190,087	190,302	192,702	205,694	209,279	203,581	220,866	238,364	220,924	229,273
Exports	157,490	178,988	178,801	175,790	179,298	181,661	184,367	193,127	180,383	178,173	174,003
All	346,947	369,075	369,103	368,492	384,992	390,940	387,948	413,993	418,747	399,097	403,276
Coastwise traffic											
Liquid bulk traffic											
Inwards	41,893	44,178	48,393	52,354	49,981	51,514	48,164	36,677	37,008	38,694	36,973
Outwards	44,557	46,135	51,459	57,146	53,753	52,622	51,966	41,696	36,049	37,535	35,371
All	86,450	90,313	99,852	109,501	103,734	104,136	100,131	78,373	73,058	76,229	72,344
Dry bulk traffic											
Inwards	8,433	9,098	9,352	7,613	6,678	7,599	6,792	8,243	8,032	7,245	79,563
Outwards	7,923	8,230	9,968	7,942	6,963	7,882	7,229	8,201	7,112	7,785	8,438
All	16,357	17,329	19,319	15,555	13,642	15,480	14,021	16,444	15,144	15,030	16,395
Container and roll-on traffic											
Inwards	8,754	9,542	9,820	9,623	10,522	11,236	11,542	12,186	11,797	11,854	11,788
Outwards	9,056	9,941	10,205	9,716	10,786	10,660	11,396	11,506	11,064	11,341	11,426
All	17,810	19,484	20,025	19,339	21,307	21,895	22,938	23,692	22,861	23,195	23,214
Semi-bulk traffic											
Inwards	234	199	172	187	166	176	203	247	364	324	373
Outwards	312	269	266	251	188	477	221	311	570	546	544
All	547	467	437	438	354	653	424	558	934	870	917
Conventional traffic											
Inwards	118	262	161	139	161	212	274	96	74	99	194
Outwards	177	224	238	261	314	306	285	139	131	124	368
All	295	486	399	400	475	518	559	236	206	223	562
All coastwise traffic											
Inwards	59,433	63,279	67,898	69,917	67,508	70,736	66,975	57,448	57,276	58,215	57,285
Outwards	62,027	64,799	72,134	75,316	72,004	71,946	71,098	61,853	54,926	57,331	56,147
All	121,460	128,078	140,032	145,233	139,512	142,682	138,073	119,302	112,202	115,546	113,432

☎020-7944 4121

5.2 (continued)All ports: foreign, coastwise and one port traffic: by mode of appearance: 1993-2003

Thousand tonnes

	1993	1994	1995	1996	1997	1998	1999	2000	2001	2002	2003
One-port traffic											
Liquid bulk traffic											
Inwards	10,063	13,725	10,848	10,861	6,871	10,587	20,220	24,937	18,245	25,886	22,328
Outwards	9,137	8,850	8,882	8,847	8,560	4,365	126	485	647	693	563
All	19,200	22,575	19,731	19,708	15,431	14,951	20,346	25,422	18,892	26,579	22,892
Dry bulk traffic											
Inwards	12,616	13,952	14,964	13,260	14,123	14,436	15,051	12,503	14,362	15,197	14,389
Outwards	1,126	312	105	98	106	98	41	41	68	67	70
All	13,743	14,263	15,069	13,357	14,229	14,534	15,092	12,544	14,430	15,264	14,460
Non-oil traffic with UK off-shore installations											
Inwards	1,123	900	914	984	851	1,063	1,136	589	643	606	490
Outwards	3,751	3,238	3,382	3,468	3,515	4,332	3,019	1,199	1,452	1,234	1,112
All	4,875	4,138	4,296	4,453	4,366	5,394	4,155	1,789	2,095	1,840	1,602
All one-port traffic											
Inwards	23,802	28,577	26,726	25,105	21,844	26,085	36,407	38,030	33,250	41,688	37,208
Outwards	14,015	12,400	12,369	12,413	12,181	8,794	3,186	1,725	2,167	1,994	1,745
All	37,818	40,977	39,095	37,518	34,026	34,880	39,593	39,755	35,417	43,682	38,953
Foreign and domestic traffic											
Liquid bulk traffic											
Inwards	120,780	121,415	117,754	122,524	117,912	123,446	124,913	132,402	129,748	127,391	125,748
Outwards	150,311	168,921	171,992	172,163	166,967	163,028	162,684	160,690	147,017	145,744	136,706
All	271,090	290,336	289,746	294,687	284,879	286,474	287,597	293,092	276,765	273,134	262,454
Dry bulk traffic											
Inwards	79,102	81,347	86,437	84,778	89,009	90,367	87,062	86,398	99,754	90,016	94,990
Outwards	27,596	28,194	29,705	27,588	26,666	28,820	26,175	27,981	24,386	25,878	29,067
All	106,698	109,542	116,141	112,366	115,675	119,187	113,237	114,379	124,140	115,894	124,057
Container and roll-on traffic											
Inwards	54,273	59,473	61,487	61,631	69,344	72,427	75,814	76,939	77,518	80,225	80,987
Outwards	45,136	48,884	51,899	53,427	59,591	59,689	61,013	60,829	58,398	58,654	58,717
All	99,409	108,357	113,387	115,058	128,935	132,115	136,827	137,768	135,915	138,879	139,704
Semi-bulk traffic											
Inwards	15,380	17,187	16,617	16,174	16,263	17,054	16,170	17,421	17,423	18,847	17,657
Outwards	5,496	5,618	5,157	5,518	5,330	5,374	4,740	4,721	4,307	4,159	4,392
All	20,876	22,805	21,774	21,692	21,593	22,428	20,910	22,142	21,730	23,006	22,049
Conventional traffic											
Inwards	2,034	1,621	1,716	1,632	1,667	1,744	1,869	2,596	3,804	3,744	3,893
Outwards	1,243	1,332	1,170	1,355	1,414	1,159	1,020	1,284	1,917	1,828	1,903
All	3,277	2,953	2,886	2,987	3,082	2,903	2,889	3,880	5,721	5,572	5,796
Non-oil traffic with UK off-shore installations											
Inwards	1,123	900	914	984	851	1,063	1,136	589	643	606	490
Outwards	3,751	3,238	3,382	3,468	3,515	4,332	3,019	1,199	1,452	1,234	1,112
All	4,875	4,138	4,296	4,453	4,366	5,394	4,155	1,789	2,095	1,840	1,602
All foreign and domestic traffic											
Inwards	272,692	281,943	284,926	287,724	295,046	306,100	306,963	316,344	328,890	320,828	323,766
Outwards	233,532	256,187	263,304	263,519	263,484	262,402	258,651	256,706	237,477	237,497	231,896
All	506,224	538,130	548,230	551,243	558,530	568,502	565,614	573,050	566,366	558,325	555,662

☎020-7944 4121

5.3 United Kingdom ports: foreign and domestic traffic by port: 1993-2003

Thousand tonnes

	1993	1994	1995	1996	1997	1998	1999	2000	2001	2002	2003
Aberdeen	3,800	3,479	3,644	3,992	4,013	3,786	3,368	3,377	3,845	3,645	3,233
Ayr	467	488	594	636	499	346	229	283	274	241	291
Barrow	264	284	274	247	261	275	247	231	225	279	241
Barry	618	498	424	405	384	433	445	597	586	547	457
Belfast	9,279	9,898	10,457	12,480	12,344	12,510	12,862	12,484	13,402	12,825	13,201
Berwick	101	157	169	191	143	139	135	146	110	89	134
Blyth	1,355	1,300	1,173	894	801	1,135	807	933	761	786	885
Boston	1,328	1,083	1,081	1,299	1,235	1,258	1,179	1,265	847	766	1,035
Bridgwater	80	77	80	88	69	67	59	84	104	86	101
Brightlingsea	141	236	111	154	153	140	142	65	248	76	125
Bristol	5,057	7,074	7,319	5,907	7,041	7,710	7,615	9,647	10,895	10,083	11,439
Cairnryan	1,234	1,233	1,991	2,025	2,227	2,504	2,437	2,283	2,014	2,099	2,328
Cardiff	2,280	2,484	2,369	2,541	2,857	2,452	2,661	2,699	2,739	2,209	2,287
Clyde (incl. Ardrossan)	4,527	6,781	7,573	7,201	7,494	8,127	8,495	7,224	11,069	9,733	9,214
Colchester	496	424	490	450	380	330	207	163	-	-	-
Coleraine	36	16	13	22	23	21	7	21	45	54	54
Cowes IOW	247	265	333	238	238	310	412	434	480	590	682
Cromarty Firth	1,187	2,470	2,264	4,328	3,971	4,456	2,336	2,329	2,145	2,658	3,501
Dover	13,773	14,115	12,671	13,224	19,073	17,690	19,387	17,434	19,074	20,212	18,796
Dundee	983	1,032	1,076	1,150	1,124	1,061	1,072	1,047	1,101	1,103	1,016
Exmouth (incl. Exeter)	57	38	38	43	46	52	-	-	-	-	-
Falmouth	417	378	504	461	431	484	398	598	471	406	438
Felixstowe	20,333	22,116	24,082	25,778	28,881	30,025	31,466	29,686	28,354	25,119	22,282
Fishguard	449	442	479	442	420	387	395	421	341	408	474
Fleetwood	1,442	1,198	1,236	1,288	1,362	1,106	1,368	1,530	1,608	1,521	1,624
Folkestone	204	411	73	34	347	634	462	560	251	-	112
Forth	26,374	44,359	47,083	45,583	43,102	44,400	45,396	41,143	41,607	42,202	38,752
Fowey	1,550	1,569	1,656	1,470	1,538	1,624	1,451	1,527	1,535	1,453	1,447
Garston	674	747	763	684	588	572	522	472	462	443	433
Glensanda	4,855	4,693	4,859	4,486	4,401	5,140	5,217	5,899	5,471	5,846	5,322
Gloucester and Sharpnes	393	310	398	373	414	410	427	598	541	564	552
Goole	1,706	2,048	2,304	2,435	2,760	2,648	2,650	2,711	2,633	2,265	1,913
Great Yarmouth	1,883	2,433	1,789	1,472	1,577	1,865	1,216	757	666	711	778
Grimsby and Immingham	41,290	42,866	46,790	46,813	47,991	48,387	49,757	52,501	54,831	55,731	55,931
Harwich	3,612	3,490	3,555	3,460	3,523	3,281	4,059	3,990	2,623	3,495	4,330
Heysham	2,205	2,809	2,708	3,124	4,069	3,585	3,370	3,723	3,824	3,705	4,083
Holyhead	1,017	1,052	2,307	2,541	2,951	3,407	3,437	3,444	3,229	3,288	3,329
Hull	8,966	10,181	9,998	9,721	10,047	10,249	10,119	10,722	10,586	10,298	10,529
Inverness	724	778	725	745	769	763	783	724	714	686	727
Ipswich	4,127	4,593	3,492	2,069	1,956	2,184	2,391	2,925	2,924	3,338	3,888
King's Lynn	1,057	1,059	954	1,002	855	883	945	1,069	873	1,019	1,052
Lancaster	141	148	129	129	121	126	112	135	117	130	156
Larne	4,334	4,604	4,673	3,452	3,153	3,389	4,032	4,508	3,520	4,295	4,319
Lerwick	909	883	901	800	687	559	486	521	979	653	616
Littlehampton	197	263	249	225	181	128	173	188	210	224	174
Liverpool	30,504	29,465	29,987	30,874	30,841	30,357	28,913	30,421	30,288	30,413	31,684
London	50,932	51,775	51,362	52,869	55,692	57,311	52,206	47,892	50,654	51,185	51,028
Londonderry	789	1,008	1,044	1,084	1,138	1,127	1,216	1,133	1,060	1,065	1,172
Lowestoft	595	497	520	653	378	269	456	439	319	309	370
Manchester	7,438	7,686	8,379	8,529	7,939	7,409	7,825	7,687	7,879	6,279	6,088
Medway	13,602	14,660	14,214	14,111	13,803	15,528	13,973	15,292	14,853	14,840	15,619
Milford Haven	35,740	34,294	32,473	36,587	34,518	28,783	32,187	33,768	33,792	34,543	32,737
Mistley Quay	279	247	245	214	217	217	144	150	163	116	116
Montrose	606	609	679	652	616	561	614	721	675	728	798
Mostyn	200	213	131	125	320	326	359	310	309	871	944
Neath	604	539	535	541	525	506	474	466	504	369	383
Newhaven	1,187	1,216	989	1,325	1,241	1,012	461	578	998	863	949
Newport	2,794	2,262	2,523	2,684	2,974	2,628	2,532	2,673	2,980	3,111	2,790
Orkneys	11,852	14,097	12,879	11,448	10,483	16,156	16,998	22,798	18,407	18,812	14,422
Par	688	696	695	610	605	549	605	558	485	479	348

☎020-7944 3087

Further details on *Maritime Statistics* are available at: *www.dft.gov.uk/transtat/maritime*

5.3 (continued) United Kingdom ports: foreign and domestic traffic by port: 1993-2003

Thousand tonnes

	1993	1994	1995	1996	1997	1998	1999	2000	2001	2002	2003
Perth	251	261	238	195	161	240	242	266	218	176	144
Peterhead	1,467	1,424	1,304	1,458	819	2,818	2,209	1,123	1,339	1,343	1,051
Plymouth	1,613	1,626	1,650	1,841	1,773	1,310	1,671	1,799	1,877	1,854	2,053
Poole	1,902	1,823	1,727	1,668	1,768	1,700	1,581	1,296	1,819	1,798	1,640
Port Talbot	10,127	11,092	11,028	12,208	13,050	13,302	11,821	11,725	8,271	4,971	7,819
Portsmouth	3,759	4,194	4,392	4,446	4,543	4,527	4,317	4,521	4,282	4,365	4,222
Ramsgate	4,209	4,701	4,829	3,681	2,208	1,869	1,207	1,237	1,432	1,848	1,789
River Ouse	534	515	557	601	582	412	247	302	197	181	236
River Trent	2,686	2,774	2,963	2,693	2,587	2,360	2,193	2,450	2,396	2,346	2,309
Rivers Hull and Humber	7,171	6,326	6,389	6,464	7,562	10,197	8,830	9,015	7,846	8,902	10,025
Seaham	508	519	570	511	608	521	493	506	536	314	459
Shoreham	1,837	2,159	2,030	1,598	1,812	1,811	1,708	1,762	1,804	1,786	1,725
Silloth	99	125	120	150	147	155	231	168	141	134	155
Southampton	30,939	31,537	32,383	34,193	33,053	34,259	33,289	34,773	35,689	34,156	35,773
Stranraer	1,717	1,813	1,868	1,646	1,794	1,780	1,690	1,506	1,404	1,273	1,274
Sullom Voe	39,374	38,592	38,335	38,162	32,082	31,109	37,680	38,204	31,166	29,376	26,360
Sunderland	2,079	1,117	1,188	1,219	1,305	999	1,037	934	1,021	928	1,020
Sutton Bridge	687	793	828	852	844	913	846	817	695	669	746
Swansea	5,370	4,382	3,989	4,139	3,674	3,137	1,650	1,014	1,261	1,069	848
Tees and Hartlepool	42,741	42,994	46,076	44,639	51,249	51,454	49,316	51,473	50,842	50,447	53,842
Teignmouth	634	628	691	586	665	665	654	657	660	641	641
Tyne	3,945	3,809	4,099	2,954	2,083	2,136	2,210	2,391	2,469	2,656	2,763
Wallasea	128	145	169	141	87	120	128	146	149	165	175
Warrenpoint	1,949	2,131	1,683	976	1,344	1,563	1,715	1,676	1,480	1,826	1,880
Whitby and Scarborough	78	75	86	63	75	65	62	39	-	-	-
Whitehaven	4	12	5	0	-	-	-	-	-	-	2
Whitstable	297	271	209	224	387	306	153	170	189	159	129
Wisbech	69	71	55	67	46	61	59	50	54	59	49
Workington	528	579	587	570	565	623	563	636	418	430	258
Other ports	5,544	5,512	5,671	4,891	3,864	4,313	4,118	4,412	5,014	4,589	4,543
England	326,071	336,032	343,878	342,500	361,563	367,560	357,652	363,212	366,645	362,786	370,540
Wales	60,069	58,220	57,160	63,212	62,307	56,150	56,578	57,892	54,734	52,020	52,613
Scotland	101,212	123,806	126,847	125,254	115,069	124,713	130,100	130,512	123,820	122,156	110,535
Great Britain	487,351	518,058	527,885	530,967	538,939	548,423	544,330	551,616	545,199	536,962	533,688
Northern Ireland	18,873	20,072	20,345	20,276	19,591	20,079	21,284	21,434	21,167	21,363	21,973
All UK ports	506,224	538,130	548,230	551,243	558,530	568,502	565,614	573,050	566,366	558,325	555,662

☎020-7944 3087

Further details on *Maritime Statistics* are available at: *www.dft.gov.uk/transtat/maritime*

5.4 United Kingdom ports: foreign and domestic unitised traffic:[1] 1993-2003

(a) Units — Thousands

	1993	1994	1995	1996	1997	1998	1999	2000	2001	2002	2003
Containers on Lo-Lo and conventional services [2]	2,740	2,975	3,264	3,295	3,518	3,722	3,918	4,325	4,464	4,506	4,533
Containers on Ro-Ro services [2]	373	389	372	465	514	528	550	-	-	-	-
Road goods vehicles	2,237	2,403	2,567	2,605	3,124	3,206	3,182	3,118	3,317	3,479	3,547
Unaccompanied trailers	2,089	2,260	2,081	2,058	2,304	2,312	2,533	2,742	2,687	2,760	2,781
Rail wagons, shipborne port-to-port trailers and barges [3]	28	29	20	-	-	-	-	361	344	348	374
All main freight units	7,467	8,056	8,304	8,423	9,459	9,769	10,182	10,546	10,811	11,094	11,235
Other unitised freight:											
Import/export vehicles	2,040	2,243	2,301	2,568	2,934	3,135	3,251	3,095	3,313	3,662	3,736
Other units	..	..	..	..	..	..	..	277	225	167	163
All freight units	9,507	10,299	10,605	10,991	12,393	12,904	13,433	13,918	14,349	14,923	15,133

(b) Tonnage — Thousand tonnes

	1993	1994	1995	1996	1997	1998	1999	2000	2001	2002	2003
Containers on Lo-Lo and conventional services [2]	35,740	38,527	42,541	42,753	45,442	46,680	49,600	51,613	51,814	51,178	51,413
Containers on Ro-Ro services [2]	4,910	5,159	5,045	7,241	7,884	8,830	8,800	-	-	-	-
Road goods vehicles [4]	54,506	59,649	61,194	60,790	71,057	71,802	73,519	35,852	37,706	39,434	39,089
Unaccompanied trailers	..	..	..	..	..	..	..	38,408	35,678	36,843	37,361
Rail wagons, shipborne port-to-port trailers and barges [3]	893	858	618	-	-	-	-	6,166	4,846	5,294	5,505
All main freight units	96,049	104,193	109,398	110,784	124,383	127,312	131,919	132,039	130,043	132,749	133,368
Other unitised freight:											
Import/export vehicles	2,424	2,770	2,896	3,268	3,503	3,812	3,965	4,083	4,023	4,693	4,839
Other unitised freight	935	1,394	1,093	1,006	1,050	992	942	1,646	1,849	1,437	1,497
All unitised traffic	99,409	108,357	113,387	115,058	128,935	132,115	136,827	137,768	135,915	138,879	139,704

1 Includes actual traffic for smaller ports up to and including 1994 and estimates from 1995 onwards
2 From 2000, containers on Ro-Ro services (essentially containers carried on by shipborne port-to-port trailers) are now included in "Rail wagons, shipborne port-to-port trailers and barges" or "Containers on Lo-Lo and conventional services".
3 Rail wagons only in 1992-1995.
4 Including unaccompanied trailers until 1999.

☎020-7944 3087

Further details on Maritime Statistics are available at: *www.dft.gov.uk/transtat/maritime*

5.5 United Kingdom ports: foreign and domestic main freight units[1] by port: 1993-2003 [2]

(a) Units — Thousands

	1993	1994	1995	1996	1997	1998	1999	2000	2001	2002	2003
Aberdeen	23	22	7	8	8	10	10	12	39	40	42
Belfast	241	248	272	390	419	448	456	471	444	422	448
Boston	33	24	20	21	22	20	16	17	4	3	7
Bristol	3	48	52	1	20	21	27	32	49	57	60
Cairnryan	111	112	126	144	142	170	171	157	165	179	193
Cardiff	-	2	11	17	23	25	24	29	29	24	28
Clyde	48	56	59	60	65	55	59	53	48	33	45
Cromarty Firth	4	4	4	4	5	6	5	4	1	-	-
Dover	1,132	1,181	1,071	1,064	1,593	1,499	1,652	1,625	1,774	1,856	1,786
Felixstowe	1,410	1,518	1,677	1,801	2,029	2,150	2,246	2,330	2,247	2,058	1,817
Fishguard	37	37	39	36	31	31	32	34	27	33	36
Fleetwood	107	94	90	99	92	91	108	116	125	120	126
Forth	53	58	58	59	64	63	66	79	90	117	143
Goole	22	29	41	46	69	67	68	70	70	51	18
Grimsby and Immingham	271	316	330	371	391	411	449	478	560	637	747
Harwich	228	216	220	205	219	212	215	246	199	258	323
Heysham	142	182	177	205	261	273	275	259	257	253	324
Holyhead	59	71	98	129	163	191	193	185	208	215	231
Hull	285	321	325	312	310	318	303	324	293	298	327
Ipswich	173	188	112	21	-	2	6	37	65	88	106
Larne	364	377	375	280	274	299	311	301	317	345	339
Liverpool	403	433	483	536	566	590	667	737	769	724	747
London	528	583	546	596	678	768	852	831	827	912	890
Manchester	-	-	10	15	1	1	-	1	-	-	-
Medway	200	187	231	255	260	333	326	324	310	325	314
Milford Haven	20	21	19	18	28	46	53	55	61	58	61
Newhaven	46	50	44	49	30	24	1	-	9	24	37
Newport	44	2	3	3	4	4	3	-	-	-	-
Orkneys	9	9	9	10	11	11	12	4	16	22	22
Plymouth	11	10	10	9	9	8	7	6	7	7	8
Poole	98	86	83	85	86	82	81	73	70	75	73
Portsmouth [3]	247	288	307	302	310	302	288	292	327	328	331
Ramsgate	229	267	281	221	128	100	60	83	95	135	147
Shoreham	-	-	1	-	-	-	-	-	-	-	-
Southampton [3]	368	427	486	561	593	559	604	713	745	793	849
Stranraer	141	140	143	126	148	146	146	155	139	122	117
Swansea	23	28	27	28	23	22	21	14	6	4	5
Tees and Hartlepool	165	191	282	230	235	237	207	234	213	219	228
Tyne	24	23	31	25	23	30	31	24	35	51	47
Warrenpoint	85	97	76	37	61	67	65	68	63	68	65
Other ports of UK	79	109	67	43	64	79	66	71	108	142	145
England	6,156	6,723	6,928	7,043	7,960	8,143	8,525	8,896	9,071	9,272	9,323
Wales	183	160	196	232	273	318	326	318	342	397	430
Scotland	438	451	456	441	473	493	499	492	574	590	628
Great Britain	6,777	7,334	7,581	7,716	8,705	8,955	9,350	9,706	9,987	10,259	10,382
Northern Ireland	690	722	723	707	754	814	832	840	824	835	853
All ports of UK	7,467	8,056	8,304	8,423	9,459	9,769	10,182	10,546	10,811	11,094	11,235

1 Includes containers, road goods vehicles, unaccompanied trailers, rail wagons, shipborne port to port trailers and shipborne barges only
2 Includes actuals for smaller ports up to 1994 and estimates for 1995 onwards
3 Excludes traffic to and from the Isle of Wight

☎020-7944 3087

Further details on *Maritime Statistics* are available at: *www.dft.gov.uk/transtat/maritime*

5.5 (continued) United Kingdom ports: foreign and domestic main freight units[1] by port: 1993-2003[2]

(b) Tonnage											Thousand tonnes of goods
	1993	1994	1995	1996	1997	1998	1999	2000	2001	2002	2003
Aberdeen	114	115	63	72	75	90	88	102	235	261	272
Belfast	2,860	3,101	3,383	5,046	5,580	5,928	6,068	5,727	5,944	5,658	5,926
Boston	397	302	303	350	342	270	238	229	47	39	87
Bristol	47	657	550	9	233	307	370	457	695	770	810
Cairnryan	1,224	1,226	1,991	2,025	2,225	2,502	2,436	2,116	1,834	1,915	2,138
Cardiff	-	18	124	185	259	283	239	290	307	247	205
Clyde	356	542	573	656	729	533	530	779	534	346	426
Cromarty Firth	34	36	37	37	40	44	45	30	10	-	-
Dover	13,151	13,516	12,004	12,400	18,587	17,162	18,782	17,017	18,627	19,694	18,261
Felixstowe	19,702	21,312	23,369	25,030	28,200	29,321	30,859	28,881	27,388	24,250	21,439
Fishguard	440	433	476	438	415	382	391	417	336	405	470
Fleetwood	1,442	1,198	1,236	1,288	1,362	1,106	1,368	1,469	1,542	1,470	1,561
Forth	795	888	896	858	940	900	985	607	832	1,687	2,077
Goole	252	346	544	766	1,215	1,071	980	966	920	684	294
Grimsby and Immingham	4,228	4,940	5,382	5,913	6,758	7,107	7,592	7,928	9,142	9,993	11,793
Harwich	2,963	2,584	2,682	2,523	2,587	2,485	3,211	3,121	1,992	2,858	3,517
Heysham	1,862	2,520	2,455	2,855	3,862	3,390	3,199	3,471	3,422	3,352	3,745
Holyhead	735	782	2,031	2,230	2,655	3,116	3,148	3,019	2,896	2,974	2,981
Hull	4,191	4,796	4,882	4,459	4,364	4,524	4,452	4,771	4,145	4,156	4,502
Ipswich	2,389	2,649	1,614	280	4	35	83	414	712	1,039	1,294
Larne	4,295	4,581	4,628	3,434	3,132	3,372	4,016	4,159	3,211	4,020	3,957
Liverpool	5,051	5,394	5,817	6,535	7,003	7,723	8,429	9,429	9,513	8,856	9,494
London	6382	7207	6620	7,713	8,631	10,444	10,282	10,711	10,986	12,015	12,233
Manchester	2	-	109	201	5	9	6	8	-	-	-
Medway	2,555	2,300	2,808	3,441	3,414	4,205	3,984	4,142	3,572	3,556	3,280
Milford Haven	260	268	256	236	370	567	712	717	797	760	794
Newhaven	599	565	520	625	587	326	20	-	251	300	450
Newport	522	16	25	32	39	37	44	-	-	1	9
Orkneys	78	82	83	90	144	101	105	91	84	129	69
Plymouth	124	115	148	161	160	118	92	78	76	69	78
Poole	1,264	1,102	1,049	1,014	1,077	1,043	1,012	602	1,048	1,118	902
Portsmouth [3]	3,065	3,580	3,720	3,746	3,764	3,765	3,639	3,771	3,549	3,400	3,312
Ramsgate	4,073	4,615	4,809	3,664	2,170	1,834	1,096	1,187	1,356	1,848	1,758
Shoreham	-	-	8	-	-	-	-	-	1	3	2
Southampton [3]	3,920	4,487	5,285	5,963	5,845	4,710	5,430	6,396	6,724	7,030	7,299
Stranraer	1,715	1,812	1,868	1,646	1,794	1,780	1,690	1,505	1,404	1,273	1,273
Swansea	207	233	236	237	186	174	159	100	31	39	50
Tees and Hartlepool	2,536	3,091	4,839	3,454	3,771	4,304	3,969	4,930	3,362	3,388	3,441
Tyne	146	146	218	276	261	322	333	433	434	510	518
Warrenpoint	1,456	1,654	1,274	548	945	1,033	1,088	1,160	1,046	1,196	1,205
Other ports of UK	618	982	484	351	655	889	749	808	1,039	1,441	1,449
England	80,717	88,160	91,227	92,798	104,606	106,247	109,933	111,006	109,789	110,435	110,150
Wales	2,169	1,749	3,147	3,358	3,924	4,559	4,693	4,543	4,498	5,179	5,337
Scotland	4,553	4,948	5,739	5,601	6,196	6,173	6,122	5,444	5,555	6,262	6,793
Great Britain	87,438	94,857	100,113	101,756	114,726	116,979	120,747	120,994	119,842	121,876	122,280
Northern Ireland	8,611	9,336	9,284	9,028	9,657	10,332	11,172	11,046	10,201	10,873	11,088
All ports of UK	96,049	104,193	109,398	110,784	124,383	127,312	131,919	132,039	130,043	132,749	133,368

1 Includes containers, road goods vehicles, unaccompanied trailers, rail wagons, shipborne port to port trailers and shipborne barges only
2 Includes actuals for smaller ports up to 1994 and estimates for 1995 onwards
3 Excludes traffic to and from the Isle of Wight

☎020-7944 3087

Further details on *Maritime Statistics* *are available at:* *www.dft.gov.uk/transtat/maritime*

5.6 United Kingdom ports: accompanied passenger vehicles Foreign and coastwise routes:[1] 1993-2003

Thousand vehicles

(a) Cars	1993	1994	1995	1996	1997	1998	1999	2000	2001	2002	2003
France	4,216	4,756	4,402	4,380	4,839	4,453	3,954	3,524	3,619	3,727	3,669
Belgium	413	404	400	279	235	87	244	260	115	120	111
Netherlands	410	328	331	353	337	351	405	422	383	420	390
Germany	44	48	46	46	43	44	40	22	27	32	19
Irish Republic	621	634	667	710	780	886	854	876	833	878	879
Denmark	32	39	34	27	24	25	27	23	26	27	22
Scandinavia and Baltic	53	42	49	54	52	52	36	26	15	36	44
of which:											
Norway	..	..	..	..	..	..	..	14	6	15	29
Swodon	..	..		..	..	..	..	11	8	20	15
Spain	70	79	79	82	84	83	84	83	93	104	80
All overseas routes	5,859	6,330	6,008	5,933	6,395	5,982	5,644	5,235	5,111	5,344	5,213
Coastwise routes by ship [2]:											
Northern Ireland [3]	977	1,060	1,178	1,101	1,175	1,179	1,282	1,108	1,078	1,082	1,104
Isle of Man	70	72	70	76	85	98	137	140	136	166	159
Orkneys and Shetlands [3]	99	103	107	119	120	122	127	128	104	125	155
Channel Islands	98	81	85	122	172	103	112	159	162	179	128
Other	31	29	30	35	35	34	34	36	39	42	44
All coastwise routes	1,275	1,344	1,470	1,453	1,588	1,536	1,692	1,570	1,520	1,594	1,591
All cars	7,133	7,674	7,477	7,385	7,982	7,518	7,336	6,806	6,631	6,939	6,804

(b) Buses and coaches	1993	1994	1995	1996	1997	1998	1999	2000	2001	2002	2003
France	167	184	182	175	178	166	167	157	153	155	141
Belgium	13	13	13	11	4	3	3	2	2	1	4
Netherlands	13	11	9	9	8	8	7	7	6	8	7
Germany	-	-	-	-	-	-	-	-	-	-	-
Irish Republic	12	14	15	17	18	19	18	19	16	17	16
Denmark	-	-	-	-	-	-	-	-	-	-	-
Scandinavia and Baltic	1	1	-	-	1	1	1	-	-	1	1
Spain	-	1	1	1	1	1	1	-	1	1	1
All overseas routes	207	224	221	214	211	198	196	187	178	183	169
Coastwise routes by ship [2]:											
Northern Ireland [3]	19	19	12	13	16	15	14	15	14	16	17
Isle of Man	-	-	-	1	1	1	1	1	1	1	1
Orkneys and Shetlands [3]	-	-	-	-	-	-	-	-	-	-	1
Channel Islands	-	-	-	-	-	-	-	-	-	-	-
Other	-	-	-	-	-	-	-	-	-	-	-
All coastwise routes	20	20	13	15	17	16	16	16	16	17	19
All buses and coaches	227	244	234	228	228	214	212	203	194	201	188

1 Includes actuals for smaller ports up to 1994 and estimates for 1995 onwards
2 Excludes traffic to the Isle of Wight
3 Includes vehicles counted at ports at both GB mainland and island ends of routes

☎020-7944 3087

Further details on *Maritime Statistics* are available at: *www.dft.gov.uk/transtat/maritime*

5.7 United Kingdom ports: accompanied passenger vehicles by port
Foreign and coastwise traffic:[1] 1993-2003

Thousand vehicles

	1993	1994	1995	1996	1997	1998	1999	2000	2001	2002	2003
Cars:											
Belfast	120	116	149	391	413	400	454	437	397	400	403
Cairnryan	104	147	155	115	169	183	182	151	140	153	139
Dover	2,796	3,045	2,731	2,894	3,332	3,047	2,758	2,433	2,396	2,466	2,418
Felixstowe	100	120	94	1	-	-	-	-	-	-	-
Fishguard	156	126	130	168	162	178	187	194	180	183	157
Harwich	285	281	267	269	282	256	273	285	272	280	254
Heysham	55	53	50	55	43	52	121	123	97	86	75
Holyhead	348	372	408	407	401	481	454	500	464	488	501
Hull	166	165	169	194	174	205	215	217	197	186	167
Larne	389	414	441	191	169	187	196	155	149	164	175
Liverpool	28	33	32	30	89	130	125	37	133	148	162
Medway	109	25	23	28	-	-	-	-	-	-	-
Milford Haven	70	81	77	79	143	124	119	130	114	117	118
Newhaven	187	162	161	156	152	136	78	73	76	78	90
Orkneys	38	40	42	46	47	49	51	50	40	49	62
Plymouth	171	167	169	157	180	178	178	175	176	192	187
Poole	157	130	133	104	274	202	163	176	200	234	216
Portsmouth	794	842	824	767	918	939	973	934	976	1,011	915
Ramsgate	262	453	471	367	282	21	-	-	-	-	-
Southampton	115	136	136	109	-	-	-	-	-	-	-
Stranraer	350	369	421	391	396	372	338	270	248	257	239
Swansea	47	55	51	56	48	48	45	41	38	41	41
Tyne	36	40	56	55	62	71	98	73	63	121	123
Other ports	250	302	286	352	245	260	326	351	274	286	362
All cars	7,133	7,674	7,477	7,385	7,982	7,518	7,336	6,806	6,631	6,939	6,804
Buses and coaches:											
Dover	149	157	158	154	165	154	157	148	145	148	125
Holyhead	6	7	9	11	12	13	12	13	12	12	12
Portsmouth	8	9	8	10	11	11	10	8	7	7	15
Other ports	65	71	59	54	40	36	33	33	30	33	35
All buses and coaches	227	244	234	228	228	214	212	203	194	201	188

1 Includes actuals for smaller ports up to 1994 and estimates for 1995 onwards.

☎020-7944 3087

Further details on *Maritime Statistics* are available at: *www.dft.gov.uk/transtat/maritime*

5.8 Waterborne transport within the United Kingdom: 1993-2003

(a) Goods moved											Billion tonne-kilometres
	1993	1994	1995	1996	1997	1998	1999	2000	2001	2002	2003
UK inland waters traffic											
Non-seagoing traffic											
Internal	0.2	0.2	0.2	0.2	0.2	0.2	0.2	0.2	0.2	0.2	0.2
Seagoing traffic (by route)											
Coastwise	0.3	0.3	0.2	0.2	0.2	0.2	0.2	0.2	0.2	0.2	0.2
Foreign	1.1	1.1	1.2	1.2	1.3	1.3	1.3	1.0	1.1	1.1	1.0
One-port	0.4	0.4	0.3	0.3	0.3	0.3	0.3	0.2	0.3	0.3	0.2
Total	2.0	2.1	1.0	1.0	1.9	2.0	1.9	1.7	1.8	1.7	1.6
Coastwise traffic between UK ports [1]	36.7	35.4	41.0	45.4	40.4	45.0	40.6	36.5	34.1	35.1	33.3
One-port traffic of UK ports [1]	12.5	14.7	10.2	7.9	5.7	10.0	16.2	29.7	23.3	30.8	26.4
All traffic [1 2]	51.2	52.2	53.1	55.3	48.1	56.9	58.7	67.4	58.8	67.2	60.9

(b) Goods lifted [1]											Million tonnes
	1993	1994	1995	1996	1997	1998	1999	2000	2001	2002	2003
UK inland waters traffic											
Non-seagoing traffic											
Internal	6.4	7.1	6.6	5.7	4.8	4.3	4.3	4.3	4.3	4.0	3.2
Seagoing traffic (by route)											
Coastwise	11.6	11.2	9.0	9.3	8.2	9.6	8.7	9.3	8.8	6.8	7.4
Foreign	31.2	32.1	32.7	32.0	34.6	35.3	33.9	30.8	33.4	32.0	31.8
One-port	10.5	11.6	12.5	10.2	10.9	8.2	7.0	4.5	7.0	6.2	5.0
Total	59.5	61.9	60.7	57.2	58.5	57.3	53.8	49.0	53.5	49.0	47.4
Coastwise traffic between UK ports [1]	60.2	61.2	67.7	70.9	71.1	77.3	73.0	63.1	58.5	59.5	58.5
One-port traffic of UK ports [1]	36.7	40.1	36.4	33.5	31.3	32.6	33.3	39.3	35.1	43.7	39.0
All traffic [1 2]	134.4	140.4	143.4	142.1	141.8	149.4	144.5	137.4	131.3	139.1	132.5

☎020-7944 3087

1 More accurate recording of the origin and destination of crude oil traffic from 2000 onwards has meant that figures for coastwise and one-port traffic are not directly comparable with previous years.
2 The 'All traffic' figures in table 1 (a) for all years and in table 1 (b) from 2000 onwards are calculated by the addition of the totals for coastwise traffic, one-port traffic, and the internal and foreign components of inland waters traffic.

Further details on *Waterborne Freight in the UK* are available at: *www.dft.gov.uk/transtat*

5.9 Principal ports, port groups and freight waterways

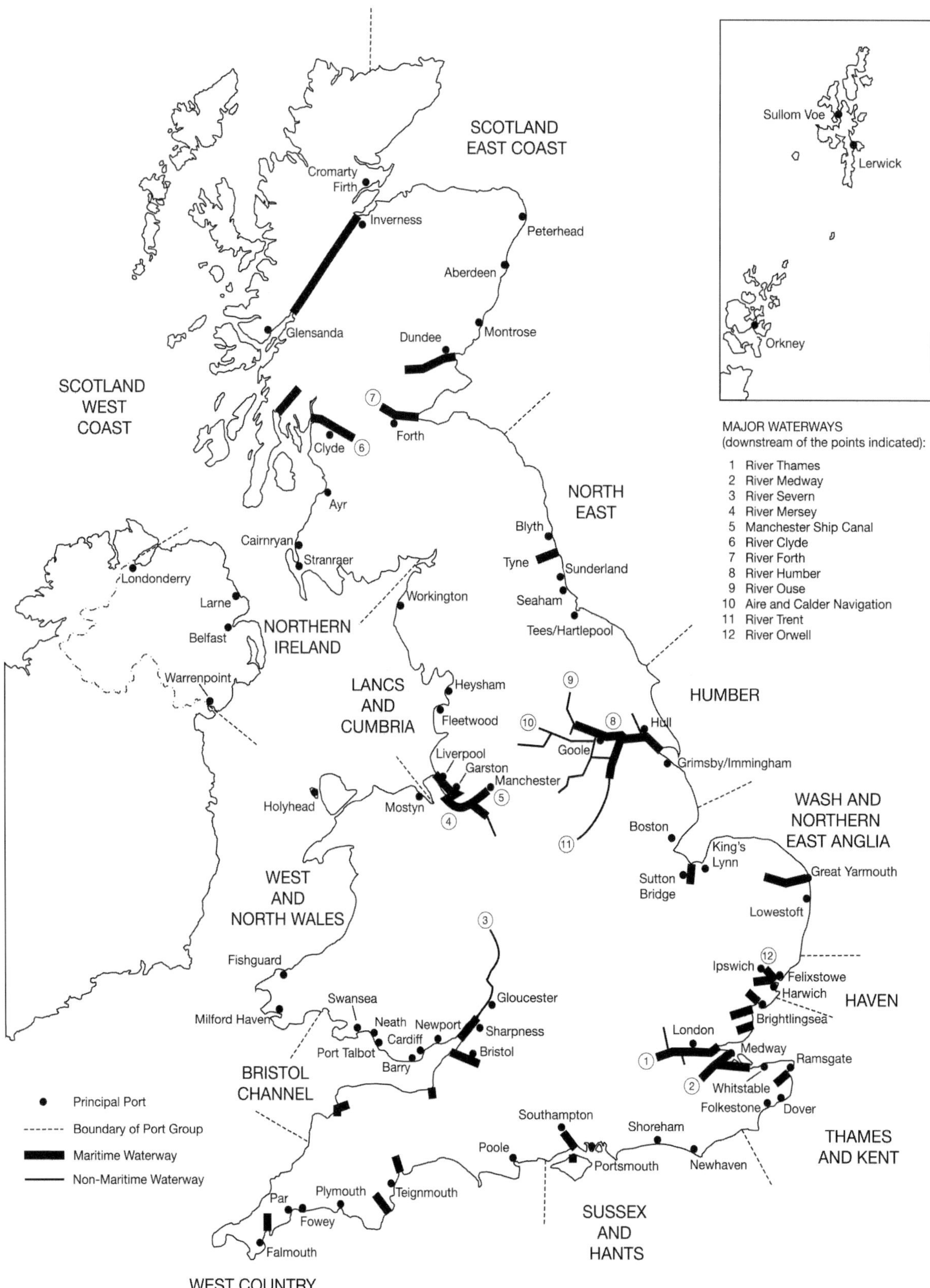

5.10 Traffic on major rivers and other inland waterway routes: 1998-2003

	Internal Traffic						Seagoing Traffic					
(a) Goods moved							Billion tonne-kilometres					
	1998	1999	2000	2001	2002	2003	1998	1999	2000	2001	2002	2003
River Thames	0.07	0.07	0.13	0.10	0.10	0.11	0.84	0.82	0.51	0.71	0.67	0.60
River Medway	-	-	-	-	-	-	0.06	0.06	0.03	0.04	0.04	0.05
River Severn	-	-	-	-	-	-	0.01	0.01	0.01	0.01	0.01	0.01
(incl Gloucester and Sharpness canal)												
River Mersey	-	-	-	-	-	-	0.11	0.11	0.13	0.12	0.09	0.09
Manchester Ship Canal	-	0.01	0.01	0.01	0.01	0.01	0.10	0.11	0.11	0.11	0.09	0.09
River Clyde	-	-	-	-	-	-	0.06	0.06	0.04	0.07	0.05	0.06
River Forth	-	-	-	-	-	-	0.19	0.17	0.23	0.20	0.18	0.18
River Humber	0.01	0.01	0.01	0.01	0.01	0.01	0.29	0.28	0.26	0.24	0.23	0.21
River Ouse	-	-	0.01	-	0.01	0.01	0.05	0.05	0.04	0.04	0.03	0.03
Aire and Calder Nav'n	0.02	0.02	0.03	0.03	0.02	0.01	-	-	-	-	-	-
River Trent	0.02	0.02	0.02	0.02	0.02	0.02	0.03	0.03	0.03	0.03	0.03	0.03
River Orwell	-	-	-	-	-	-	0.04	0.04	0.05	0.05	0.06	0.07
All above waterways	0.13	0.14	0.20	0.18	0.17	0.17	1.77	1.73	1.45	1.63	1.50	1.43
All waterways	0.15	0.16	0.21	0.19	0.18	0.18	1.80	1.76	1.47	1.65	1.51	1.44
(b) Goods lifted							Million tonnes					
River Thames	1.66	1.74	1.88	1.95	2.09	2.02	23.31	20.78	12.59	18.50	17.16	16.03
River Medway	0.26	0.34	0.19	0.47	0.58	0.56	2.68	2.89	1.45	2.01	2.38	2.74
River Severn	-	-	-	-	-	-	0.35	0.31	0.60	0.54	0.56	0.55
(incl Gloucester and Sharpness canal)												
River Mersey	0.03	0.15	0.33	0.28	0.23	0.22	6.33	6.46	7.68	6.99	5.51	5.08
Manchester Ship Canal	0.38	0.47	0.33	0.28	0.23	0.22	6.33	6.46	7.68	6.99	5.51	5.08
River Clyde	-	-	-	-	0.01	-	1.53	1.66	0.95	1.61	1.29	1.34
River Forth	-	-	-	-	-	-	8.56	7.54	11.02	9.59	8.53	8.58
River Humber	0.41	0.39	0.26	0.22	0.40	0.35	6.49	6.24	6.21	6.11	5.53	5.29
River Ouse	0.22	0.28	0.40	0.37	0.41	0.43	3.16	3.17	3.01	2.83	2.45	2.15
Aire and Calder Nav'n	1.72	1.61	1.64	1.57	1.06	0.50	-	-	-	-	-	-
River Trent	0.26	0.27	0.32	0.33	0.30	0.26	2.36	2.21	2.45	2.61	2.35	2.31
River Orwell	-	-	-	-	-	-	2.18	2.39	2.93	2.92	3.34	3.90
All waterways[1]	4.26	4.28	4.30	4.26	3.96	3.18	53.06	49.52	44.69	49.23	44.99	44.21

1 Where goods are carried on more than one inland waterway route, the tonnage lifted is counted on each route travelled. The 'All Waterways' figures exclude all such double counting.

☎020-7944 3087

Further details on *Waterborne Freight in the UK* are available at: *www.dft.gov.uk/transtat*

5.11 United Kingdom international sea passenger movements, by country of embarkation or landing: 1994-2004[1]

Thousands

	1994	1995	1996	1997	1998	1999	2000	2001	2002	2003	2004
Ro-Ro ferry passengers on short sea routes											
Belgium	2,878	2,480	2,053	2,075	1,749	1,592	1,507	1,379	1,129	740	739
Denmark	285	254	208	190	195	188	164	156	132	88	97
France	27,224	25,164	25,470	26,975	23,912	22,454	19,755	19,485	20,555	19,077	18,565
Germany	244	276	245	240	246	222	188	164	161	92	117
Irish Republic	3,443	3,598	3,859	4,066	4,606	4,343	4,234	3,882	3,880	3,802	3,656
Netherlands	1,987	1,847	1,956	1,961	1,769	1,939	2,031	2,026	2,209	2,094	2,002
Norway	138	166	179	172	188	208	225	230	241	235	231
Spain	367	353	367	388	373	346	320	355	341	308	310
Sweden	157	169	192	190	186	87	89	73	73	81	75
Other Europe	11	15	12	-	4	3	3	4	3	7	7
Total	36,733	34,321	34,543	36,258	33,226	31,381	28,517	27,753	28,726	26,523	25,799
Passengers on long sea journeys											
United States of America & Canada	31.1	29.9	20.4	26.9	23.1	24.7	24.8	26.3	29.5	24.3	39.5 P
Australia & New Zealand	1.3	1.4	1.4	0.7	-	-	0.1	0.1	-	-	-
Africa	0.8	0.7	0.5	0.7	0.1	0.7	0.6	0.4	2.0	0.4	0.1 P
Caribbean	-	-	0.3	0.7	-	-	-	-	-	-	-
Other countries	1.1	0.6	1.3	0.4	0.1	0.2	0.2	0.1	0.1	-	-
Total	34.2	32.6	23.9	29.4	23.4	25.6	25.7	26.9	31.5	24.7	39.6 P
Passengers on cruises beginning or ending at UK ports[2]	236	207	226	..	..	445	461	469	540	702	767 P
All international passengers[3]	37,002	34,562	34,792	36,288	33,249	31,852	29,003	28,249	29,298	27,250	26,605

1 For details of Channel Tunnel passenger numbers refer to table 6.18

2 Cruise passengers, like other passengers, are included at both departure and arrival if their journeys begin and end at a United Kingdom seaport.

3 Excluding cruise passengers in 1997 and 1998.

☎020-7944 4121

5.12 United Kingdom international sea passenger movements, by seaport group: 1994-2004 [1]

Thousands

	1994	1995	1996	1997	1998	1999	2000	2001	2002	2003	2004
Ro-Ro ferry passengers on short sea routes											
Thames and Kent											
London	-	-	-	-	12	16	15	14	13	11	14
Medway	194	78	81	-	-	-	-	-	-	-	-
Ramsgate	3,521	2,807	2,655	1,836	161	50	76	88	117	137	148
Dover	19,108	17,850	18,760	21,236	19,330	18,324	16,078	15,857	16,329	14,631	14,275
Folkestone	867	725	856	776	905	653	440	5	-	-	-
All Thames and Kent	23,690	21,460	22,352	23,848	20,408	19,043	16,609	15,964	16,459	14,780	14,437
South Coast											
Newhaven	1,175	979	841	750	621	337	313	337	379	397	361
Portsmouth	3,173	3,331	3,005	3,391	3,509	3,487	3,176	3,344	3,406	3,116	3,077
Southampton	554	533	461	1	-	-	-	-	-	-	5
Poole	542	373	376	418	414	472	455	586	620	623	520
Weymouth	-	-	-	-	53	56	60	-	8	15	20
Plymouth	702	582	562	649	642	627	583	583	631	603	617
Other ports	-	46	-	-	-	-	-	-	-	-	-
All South Coast	6,146	5,844	5,245	5,209	5,240	4,980	4,587	4,851	5,044	4,754	4,600
West Coast											
Swansea	183	163	172	150	158	133	124	122	121	118	116
Milford Haven	358	341	345	546	512	495	463	388	387	384	378
Fishguard	755	945	817	815	810	830	832	687	662	645	614
Holyhead	2,125	2,125	2,489	2,457	2,775	2,541	2,518	2,380	2,371	2,333	2,262
Mostyn	-	-	-	-	-	-	-	5	44	48	10
Liverpool	23	24	29	97	343	337	293	298	291	269	270
Fleetwood	-	-	7	1	-	-	-	-	-	-	-
Other ports	-	-	-	-	9	7	4	3	4	5	5
All West Coast	3,444	3,598	3,859	4,066	4,606	4,343	4,234	3,882	3,880	3,802	3,656
East Coast											
Lerwick	3	3	2	3	7	6	6	6	7	13	14
Forth	-	-	-	-	-	-	-	-	105	195	192
Tyne	259	406	337	365	466	626	667	745	816	829	767
Hull	945	961	1,013	1,006	1,027	1,022	972	1,006	1,041	994	976
Grimsby and Immingham	6	9	11	12	10	9	12	13	38	43	43
Ipswich	6	1	-	-	-	-	5	6	6	6	7
Felixstowe	515	447	62	77	77	78	86	80	58	19	19
Harwich	1,709	1,582	1,650	1,672	1,384	1,272	1,335	1,196	1,268	1,085	1,085
Other ports	9	11	12	-	2	2	3	4	3	3	3
All East Coast	3,452	3,420	3,087	3,134	2,973	3,016	3,086	3,056	3,342	3,188	3,106
All port areas	36,733	34,321	34,543	36,258	33,226	31,381	28,517	27,753	28,726	26,523	25,799
Passengers on long sea journeys	34	33	24	29	23	26	26	27	32	25	40 P
Passengers on cruises beginning and/or ending at UK ports [2]	236	207	226	..	..	445	461	469	540	702	767 P
of which											
Dover	..	..	..	..	..	136	119	100	120	139	154 P
Southampton	..	..	..	..	..	211	281	295	331	438	476 P
Harwich	..	..	..	..	..	70	43	68	69	97	91 P
All international passengers [3]	37,002	34,562	34,792	36,288	33,249	31,852	29,003	28,249	29,298	27,250	26,605

1 For details of Channel Tunnel passenger numbers refer to Table 6.8

☎020-7944 4121

2 Cruise passengers, like other passengers, are included at both departure and arrival if their journeys begin and end at a United Kingdom seaport.

3 Excluding cruise passengers in 1997 and 1998.

5.13 United Kingdom and Crown Dependency registered trading vessels of 500 gross tons and over: summary of tonnage by type on old classification: 1950 - 1986 and on new classification: 1986 - 2004

For greater detail of the years 1994-2004 see Table 5.14

End of year	Passenger 000 Gt	Cargo liners 000 Gt	Container 000 Gt	Tramps 000 Gt	Bulk carriers 000 Gt	Tankers 000 Gt	Total 000 Gt	Total Number [2]
1950	2,936	5,949	-	..	4,366	3,946	17,198	3,092
1951	2,992	5,933	-	..	4,084	4,187	17,196	3,056
1952	2,935	6,063	-	..	3,836	4,430	17,264	3,014
1953	2,825	6,066	-	..	3,939	4,637	17,467	3,016
1954	2,998	6,007	-	..	3,965	5,046	18,016	3,041
1955	3,012	6,080	-	..	3,979	5,138	18,208	3,041
1956	3,013	6,300	-	..	3,841	5,329	18,484	3,041
1957	2,958	6,540	-	..	3,696	5,638	18,833	3,031
1958	2,843	6,545	-	..	3,837	6,021	19,245	3,007
1959	2,749	6,605	-	..	3,706	6,745	19,805	2,950
1960	2,814	6,568	-	..	3,762	7,058	20,202	2,902
1961	2,771	6,294	-	..	4,143	7,288	20,497	2,808
1962	2,495	6,133	-	..	4,441	7,486	20,554	2,689
1963	2,342	5,939	-	..	4,328	7,788	20,396	2,538
1964	2,244	5,936	-	..	4,444	7,804	20,428	2,473
1965	2,115	5,894	-	..	4,687	7,685	20,382	2,401
1966	1,971	5,898	..	2,666	2,130	7,857	20,522	2,319
1967	1,709	5,576	..	2,521	2,661	7,908	20,375	2,181
1968	1,605	5,398	..	2,173	2,974	8,580	20,730	2,058
1969	1,245	5,452	194	1,904	3,265	10,215	22,274	2,002
1970	1,230	5,233	418	1,621	3,710	11,849	24,061	1,977
1971	1,101	4,444	683	1,425	4,219	13,304	25,177	1,875
1972	1,010	3,895	1,162	1,222	6,152	13,500	26,940	1,798
1973	920	3,749	1,346	1,060	7,366	14,665	29,106	1,776
1974	855	3,656	1,365	1,027	7,694	16,199	30,795	1,767
1975	748	3,330	1,363	958	8,022	17,069	31,489	1,682
1976	661	3,148	1,349	910	8,030	15,742	29,839	1,573
1977	654	2,923	1,624	882	8,181	15,797	30,061	1,545
1978	614	2,546	1,827	743	7,174	15,173	28,078	1,421
1979	606	2,248	1,651	613	6,555	13,558	25,232	1,305
1980	617	1,992	1,600	554	6,428	14,578	25,769	1,275
1981	604	1,589	1,600	470	5,985	11,870	22,117	1,118
1982	582	1,340	1,580	409	5,101	10,221	19,233	985
1983	602	1,099	1,543	372	3,911	8,367	15,894	866
1984	636	893	1,572	349	3,398	7,463	14,312	777
1985	616	728	1,489	335	2,851	6,191	12,208	693
1986	588	564	1,369	244	1,864	3,083	7,711	545

End of year	Passenger 000 Gt	Other cargo 000 Gt	Ro-Ro 000 Gt	Container 000 Gt	Specialised carriers 000 Gt	Bulk carriers 000 Gt	Tankers 000 Gt	Total 000 Gt	Total Number [2]
1986	259	510	561	1,369	95	2,003	3,249	8,046	546
1987	259	410	591	1,335	132	1,322	3,010	7,059	506
1988	259	332	586	1,335	128	1,301	2,661	6,603	482
1989	242	277	510	1,368	122	1,253	2,252	6,025	450
1990	269	257	555	1,275	118	828	2,210	5,512	427
1991	271	242	604	1,091	99	489	2,166	4,963	409
1992	276	174	632	1,015	100	446	2,188	4,831	363
1993	272	145	657	1,017	124	293	2,161	4,670	344
1994	281	212	874	1,236	110	294	2,481	5,488	360
1995	360	282	910	1,326	52	485	2,346	5,761	365
1996	360	269	1,068	1,110	49	819	2,383	6,057	377
1997	361	254	1,093	1,113	49	831	3,407	7,108	392
1998	358	307	1,123	1,379	49	854	2,977	7,048	416
1999	363	293	1,161	1,502	103	761	3,253	7,436	421
2000	762	321	1,332	2,140	151	844	3,971	9,521	471
2001	746	502	1,431	2,362	151	946	4,516	10,653	534
2002	945	570	1,617	3,303	100	1,491	4,472	12,497	610
2003	1,130	825	1,637	4,548	121	1,729	5,991	15,982	723
2004	711	830	1,608	5,072	165	2,302	6,214	16,902	754

1 See Notes for a brief explanation of change in classification.
2 Number of vessels (units).

Further details on Maritime Statistics are available at:. www.dft.gov.uk/transtat/maritime

☎020-7944 4443
The figures in this table are outside the scope of National Statistics

5.14 Shipping: United Kingdom and Crown Dependency registered trading vessels of 500 gross tons and over: summary of tonnage by type of vessel: 1994 - 2004 (end of year)

	1994	1995	1996	1997	1998	1999	2000	2001	2002	2003	2004
Number:											
Tankers	113	113	115	133	145	141	141	166	195	224	244
Bulk carriers	14	18	26	27	26	22	26	28	34	38	49
Specialised carriers	13	12	11	11	11	15	16	16	13	13	14
Fully cellular container	34	37	38	39	45	51	67	71	99	137	146
Ro-Ro (passenger & cargo)	84	83	88	89	92	94	105	110	118	120	118
Other general cargo	93	90	87	81	86	87	100	127	131	169	169
Passenger	9	12	12	12	11	11	16	16	20	22	14
All vessels	360	365	377	392	416	421	471	534	610	723	754
Gross tonnage (thousand tons):											
Tankers	2,481	2,346	2,383	3,407	2,977	3,253	3,971	4,516	4,472	5,991	6,214
Bulk carriers	294	485	819	831	854	761	844	946	1491	1729	2302
Specialised carriers	110	52	49	49	49	103	151	151	100	121	165
Fully cellular container	1,236	1,326	1,110	1,113	1,379	1,502	2,140	2,362	3,303	4,548	5,072
Ro-Ro (passenger & cargo)	874	910	1,068	1,093	1,123	1,161	1,332	1,431	1,617	1,637	1,608
Other general cargo	212	282	269	254	307	293	321	502	570	825	830
Passenger	281	360	360	361	358	363	762	746	945	1130	711
All vessels	5,488	5,761	6,057	7,108	7,048	7,436	9,521	10,653	12,497	15,982	16,902
Thousand deadweight tonnes:											
Tankers	4,576	4,289	4,347	6,119	5,163	5,737	7,069	7,885	7,567	9,446	9,660
Bulk carriers	528	884	1,501	1,519	1,563	1,404	1,545	1,738	2,782	3,245	4,375
Specialised carriers	76	31	29	29	29	47	65	65	44	48	59
Fully cellular container	1,253	1,358	1,212	1,224	1,543	1,682	2,365	2,597	3,691	5,124	5,663
Ro-Ro (passenger & cargo)	281	273	332	337	364	366	474	522	607	605	591
Other general cargo	299	375	360	335	414	402	430	706	799	1121	1126
Passenger	47	55	55	55	56	58	98	95	111	131	92
All vessels	7,061	7,266	7,835	9,618	9,132	9,695	12,045	13,608	15,602	19,719	21,566

☎020-7944 4443

Further details on Maritime Statistics are available at: www.dft.gov.uk/transtat

The figures in this table are outside the scope of National Statistics.
Source - Lloyds Register - Fairplay

5.15 Shipping: United Kingdom owned trading vessels of 500 gross tons and over: summary of tonnage by type of vessel: 1994 - 2004 (end of year)

	1994	1995	1996	1997	1998	1999	2000	2001	2002	2003	2004
Number:											
Tankers	145	139	129	123	127	124	133	114	113	124	145
Bulk carriers	41	41	42	35	29	29	29	38	35	43	51
Specialised carriers	22	22	19	11	10	14	10	10	10	9	9
Fully cellular container	48	52	54	60	62	57	73	77	72	92	78
Ro-Ro (passenger & cargo)	85	85	87	85	91	99	103	103	105	109	106
Other general cargo	177	187	168	156	148	153	139	116	115	124	138
Passenger	14	14	15	16	19	17	16	18	20	26	15
All vessels	532	540	514	486	486	493	503	476	470	527	542
Gross tonnage (thousand tons):											
Tankers	4,129	3,666	2,958	2,704	2,408	1,565	2,952	2,579	2,620	3,601	4,497
Bulk carriers	1,393	1,648	1,775	1,408	1,230	825	904	1,845	1,772	1,913	2,287
Specialised carriers	145	97	87	43	42	192	53	100	100	82	81
Fully cellular container	1,467	1,531	1,491	1,626	1,841	1,641	2,240	2,525	2,509	3,552	3,035
Ro-Ro (passenger & cargo)	724	780	834	827	991	1,145	1,260	1,355	1,423	1,589	1,472
Other general cargo	647	758	681	654	526	546	492	409	570	793	940
Passenger	401	455	484	548	541	585	604	636	725	1092	588
All vessels	8,906	8,935	8,309	7,809	7,577	6,499	8,505	9,449	9,720	12,622	12,900
Thousand deadweight tonnes:											
Tankers	7,735	6,856	5,538	5,048	4,411	2,662	5,205	4,646	4,690	5,529	6,687
Bulk carriers	2,502	3,011	3,255	2,575	2,254	1,479	1,636	3,495	3,377	3,594	4,300
Specialised carriers	88	44	40	30	29	80	32	45	45	42	40
Fully cellular container	1,470	1,555	1,519	1,672	1,948	1,774	2,433	2,734	2,785	3,993	3,349
Ro-Ro (passenger & cargo)	236	243	251	243	285	349	423	414	454	543	514
Other general cargo	893	1,010	928	887	713	735	660	569	807	1113	1323
Passenger	72	75	81	90	86	86	80	82	87	130	64
All vessels	12,996	12,793	11,611	10,546	9,727	7,164	10,469	11,985	12,245	14,945	16,277

☎020-7944 4443

The figures in this table are outside the scope of National Statistics

Source - Lloyds Register - Fairplay

5.16 United Kingdom shipping industry: international revenue and expenditure: 1994-2004

(a) Revenue — £ Million

	1994	1995	1996	1997	1998	1999	2000	2001	2002	2003	2004
Dry cargo and passenger vessels: (including ferries)											
Freight on:											
Imports	592	564	585	484	482	522	484	517 [1]	418 [1]	469	553
Exports	406	421	409	416	322	375	400	406	481	525	450
Cross-trades	1,272	1,354	1,345	1,614	1,602	1,511	1,453	1,609	1,844	2,069	2,776
Total freight revenue	2,270	2,339	2,339	2,514	2,406	2,408	2,337	2,532	2,743	3,063	3,779
Charter receipts	98	133	134	147	109	99	148	106	129	196	360
Passenger revenue	594	693	705	697	462	463	630	488	569	993	846
Total revenue	2,962	3,165	3,178	3,358	2,977	2,970	3,115	3,126	3,441	4,252	4,985
Wet (tankers and liquefied gas carriers):											
Freight on:											
Imports	56	49	113	24	29	20	3	34 [1]	34 [1]	37	48
Exports	66	64	71	68	60	59	98	82	96	126	173
Cross-trades	502	488	550	536	442	350	458	497	420	742	1,287
Total freight revenue	624	601	734	628	531	429	559	613	550	905	1,508
Charter receipts	128	139	120	68	70	87	104	336	162	247	454
Total revenue	752	740	854	696	601	516	663	949	712	1,152	1,962
All vessels:											
Freight on:											
Imports	648	613	698	508	511	542	487	551	452	506	601
Exports	472	485	480	484	382	434	498	488	577	651	623
Cross-trades	1,774	1,842	1,895	2,150	2,044	1,861	1,911	2,106	2,264	2,811	4,063
Total freight revenue	2,894	2,940	3,073	3,142	2,937	2,837	2,896	3,145	3,293	3,968	5,287
Charter receipts	226	272	254	215	179	177	252	442	291	443	814
Passenger revenue	594	693	705	697	462	463	630	488	569	993	846
Total revenue	3,714	3,905	4,032	4,054	3,578	3,486	3,778	4,075	4,153	5,404	6,947

(b) Expenditure — £ Million

	1994	1995	1996	1997	1998	1999	2000	2001	2002	2003	2004
Dry cargo operations:											
Bunkers	148	160	197	216	149	165	288	316	286	400	501
Other disbursements	1,094	1,194	1,447	1,780	1,367	1,060	1,143	1,285	1,627	1,626	1,959
Charter payments	191	200	215	282	239	146	173	335	255	235	342
Total expenditure	1,433	1,554	1,859	2,278	1,755	1,371	1,604	1,936	2,168	2,261	2,802
Wet cargo operations:											
Bunkers	89	91	118	100	70	81	141	105	94	145	212
Other disbursements	106	111	142	124	150	132	115	95	110	263	334
Charter payments	200	186	243	161	181	89	172	176	140	185	352
Total expenditure	395	388	503	385	401	302	428	376	344	593	898
All cargo operations:											
Bunkers	237	251	315	316	219	246	429	421	380	545	713
Other disbursements	1,200	1,305	1,589	1,904	1,517	1,192	1,258	1,380	1,737	1,889	2,293
Charter payments	391	386	458	443	420	235	345	511	395	420	694
Total expenditure	1,828	1,942	2,362	2,663	2,156	1,673	2,032	2,312	2,512	2,854	3,700

1 Estimate based on other related series

☎020-7944 4443

Source - Balance of Payments, ONS

5.17 Marine accident casualties: 1994-2004 (United Kingdom registered merchant vessels of 100 gt and over only)

(a) Deaths of passengers and crew members by cause — Number

	1994	1995	1996	1997	1998	1999	2000	2001	2002	2003	2004
Deaths from accidents to vessels	0	1	0	0	1	0	0	0	0	0	0
Deaths from accidents on board- other than accidents to vessels	1	2	2	2	1	2	2	1	4	1	3
Deaths Person overboard	1	1	3	3	2	3	2	3	1	2	1
Total	2	4	5	5	4	5	4	4	5	3	4
(b) Deaths and injuries to passengers by type of injury											
Death	0	0	2	0	2	1	1	1	0	0	0
Fractures	63	67	76	85	107	66	88	111	110	136	112
Cuts/lacerations	3	5	5	2	1	2	4	5	4	3	3
Bruising	4	8	1	2	1	2	5	6	3	7	5
Dislocations	0	3	3	3	2	3	4	4	10	9	7
Strains	3	4	2	2	1	3	1	3	0	10	4
Other Injuries	6	10	8	0	5	3	33	7	6	18	10
Total	79	97	97	94	119	80	136	137	133	183	141
(c) Deaths and injuries to crew members by type of injury											
Death	2	4	3	5	2	4	3	3	5	3	4
Major fractures	26	17	25	30	23	16	11	6	25	26	24
Other fractures	70	65	63	46	44	46	55	62	53	54	45
Strained back	55	28	52	44	55	47	23	28	29	36	45
Other strains, sprains, hernias etc	60	49	63	60	35	46	43	51	48	36	37
Bruising	73	50	59	34	54	24	39	34	33	42	43
Cuts/lacerations	45	39	39	50	28	32	41	40	39	35	40
Other injuries	105	93	96	56	84	70	85	68	70	57	70
Total	436	345	400	325	325	285	300	292	302	289	308

Further details on Marine Accidents are available at: www.maib.gov.uk

☎020-7944 4443
The figures in this table are outside the scope of National Statistics
Source - MAIB, DfT

5.18 HM Coastguard statistics: search and rescue operations:[1] United Kingdom: 1994-2004

Number

	1995	1996	1997	1998	1999	2000	2001	2002	2003	2004
Incidents involving vessels where assistance rendered:										
Commercial vessels	497	865	886	308	458	537	569	597	512	961
Fishing vessels	849	792	850	715	624	647	670	627	589	521
Pleasure craft	5,061	4,243	4,545	3,328	3,334	3,267	3,529	3,679	3,748	3,924
Incidents involving persons where assistance rendered:										
Incidents involving persons	2,274	2,131	2,365	1,359	1,202	1,693	1,872	2,241	2,436	2,169
Medical evacuations	992	946	958	370	427	403	473	460	585	481
Reports received:										
Distress reports	2,334	2,481	2,257	1,627	2,548	2,353	2,208	2,357	..	..
Hoaxes	..	..	..	269	258	221	206	260	232	301
Number of persons involved in incidents where assistance rendered:										
Persons assisted	19,152	19,235	16,884	14,366	17,535	14,717	16,487	19,984	25,118	21,929
Persons rescued	..	..	..	4,685	5,215	5,217	4,852	5,851	5,689	4,947
Lives lost	232	216	251	249	251	236	284	319	316	364
Total number of incidents where assistance rendered	..	..	..	6,328	6,581	6,703	7,242	7,604	8,070	8,056
Total number of incidents	..	..	..	11,553	12,220	12,016	12,514	13,395	13,849	14,240

1 HM Coastguard revised its statistical collection and collation procedures in 1998, so comparisons with previous years are difficult.

☎020-7944 3087
The figures in this table are outside the scope of National Statistics
Source - MCA

6 Public Transport:

Notes and Definitions

National Rail/London Underground passenger traffic: 6.1

The figures shown for national rail passenger traffic during 1919 and 1923 include all journeys on those 'London Railways' subsequently taken over by the London Passenger Transport Board in 1933. Additionally, in 1919 a journey using the services of more than one company was reported by each of them, with consequent duplication in the figures. The figures for journeys on the London Underground from 1948 include those originating on the former British Railways network (approximately 70 million journeys in 1948), and on those lines transferred to the London Transport Passenger Executive on 1 January 1948 (estimated at 62 million journeys in 1947).

Electrified route: Pre 1947 figures refer to track length, not route length, and include electrified sidings. In 1947, there were 3,370 electrified track kilometres.

National Railways passenger journeys and kilometres: Figures from 1986 are assessed on the All Purpose Ticket Issuing System (APTIS) and are not comparable with earlier years. The rail series for passenger data changes after privatisation in 1994, with possible double counting of some journeys where a route is shared with more than one operator. Both series have been revised from 1999/00.

London Underground passenger kilometres: From 1965 passenger kilometres are those actually travelled. Prior to 1965, a different method of estimation was used, leading to slight overestimates of the order of 0.1 billion passenger kilometres per year.

Rail systems: 6.2

National Rail

Data up to 1994/95 show services by the former British Rail. From 1995/96 data these show the transition to services provided by the privatised passenger train operators on the national network.

London Underground

Summary data are shown here. Further detail appears in Table 6.7.

Glasgow Underground

The series shown is for the underground loop line which serves Glasgow. Suburban rail services in Strathclyde PTE are excluded.

Docklands Light Railway

The series shows the growth of the DLR. The Lewisham extension under the Thames at Greenwich was completed in 1999. A new line for London City Airport and Woolwich Arsenal is currently under construction.

Nexus: Tyne and Wear Metro

The system has been extended in stages. Heworth to South Shields was opened on 24th March 1984. The extension from Bankfoot to Callerton and Newcastle Airport opened in November 1991. The 24km extension from Pelaw to Sunderland and South Hylton opened in March 2002. Part of that route shares some stations with national rail services.

Blackpool Trams

The traditional Victorian street-running tramway serving Blackpool Unitary Authority and Fleetwood, Lancashire.

Manchester Metrolink

Converted and extended from suburban rail, in 1991/92, 26 kilometres and 16 stations were transferred from the national network to the light rail system. It has a mix of segregated track and on-street running. Metrolink was opened in 1992, with the first section running between Bury and Manchester Victoria Station. The Eccles extension opened in 2000.

Stagecoach Supertram

The Supertram was opened in 1994 between Sheffield and Meadowhall. Further lines came into service from Malin Bridge to Halfway and Cathedral to Herdings Park. In December 1997 operations were transferred to Stagecoach Plc.

West Midlands Metro: Centro

This rapid transit system was constructed by the Altram consortium, making use of former rail alignments. The line from Wolverhampton to Birmingham Snow Hill opened in 1999.

Croydon Tramlink

A modern three line tram network in south London, opened in May 2000. It is operated by FirstGroup for TfL.

Nottingham Tram: NET

NET is a modern street running tram system running north-south through the city. It runs parallel to suburban rail north of the centre. It was opened in March 2004.

National Rail receipts and passenger traffic: 6.3 and 6.4

Passenger Revenue: Passenger revenue includes all ticket revenue and miscellaneous charges associated with passenger travel e.g. car park charges. For journeys involving some travel on London Underground, receipts have been apportioned appropriately. Revenue does not include government support or grants.

Passenger Kilometres: Estimates of passenger kilometres are made from ticket sales. Travel on season tickets assumes appropriate factors for the number of journeys per ticket. Results are compiled in respect of 13 four week periods per year, so quarterly figures are derived from these.

There is some underestimation of passenger kilometres from 1997/98. This is because, for technical reasons, the passenger kilometres represented by certain new ticket types were not being captured by the operators' ticket system.

The figures have therefore been revised to include current best estimates for this missing element.

The passenger kilometre and passenger journeys series for recent years been revised. Further details can be found in *National Rail Trends Yearbook,* published by ORR (previously the responsibility of the SRA).

Route and station/depots open to traffic: 6.5

In 1991/92, 16 stations transferred from the national network to Manchester Metrolink. From 1994/95 the number of stations shown include only those on the national network. Eighteen other stations, mainly on the London Underground, are included in the figures for earlier years.

Public Performance Measure (PPM): 6.6

The PPM was introduced in 2000 by the then Shadow Strategic Rail Authority, replacing the Passengers' Charter as a means of measuring passenger train performance. Unlike the Charter measure that only covered particular services, PPM covers all scheduled services and combines the previously individual punctuality and reliability results into a single performance measure. PPM is measured against the planned timetable, which makes allowance for specific delays (e.g. engineering works), which might differ from the previously published timetable. Table 6.6 shows the Charter results for years in which it applied, and also PPM results from the time it was introduced.

London Underground: 6.7

Data obtained from the London Underground Directors Report and Accounts each year up to 2002-03. Responsibility for the Underground transferred to Transport for London in July 2003. TfL's *Annual Report* provides further detail.

Traffic receipts data are provided by TfL in 13 four week periods per year. These include revenue from car parking and penalty fares. Season ticket journeys are those estimated to have been made in each year, irrespective of when the ticket was sold. The cost per train kilometre includes renewals and depreciation. It excludes reorganisation and restructuring costs within TfL.

Other income includes property rents received, and commercial advertising receipts.

The number of stations is for those currently owned and operated by London Underground. Some suburban stations on the national rail network in London are also served by London Underground trains but are managed by the local rail franchise holder.

Channel Tunnel: 6.8

The Channel Tunnel opened for traffic in 1994. Four different types of service operate through the Channel Tunnel as follows :

- *Freight Shuttles*: carrying road freight vehicles between Folkestone and Calais.
- *Tourist Shuttles*: carrying passenger vehicles between Folkestone and Calais.
- *Freight Trains*: through freight trains between Great Britain and Europe.
- *Eurostar Trains*: carrying passengers between London, France and Belgium.

Commercial traffic is fare-paying traffic using the tunnel. *Non-commercial traffic* is non-fare-paying traffic (e.g. staff and authorised agents). Figures for 1996-97 & 1997-98 were affected by a fire on 16 November 1996 which suspended services on both freight and tourist shuttles. Tourist shuttle resumed services on 10 December 1996 with full freight services resuming in June 1997.

Bus and coach industry: 6.9-6.16

Tables for the bus and coach industry refer to the activities of all holders of Public Service Vehicle (PSV) operators' licences. These vehicles are generally classified in the Bus Tax Class. An operator wishing to run bus or coach services is normally required to possess a PSV licence. However, certain vehicles and types of service are exempt from licensing and are excluded from the tables, such as community buses and local services operated by taxis. Taxis are generally classified in the Private Light Goods tax class, with private cars, so they are excluded from the PSV tables. Most of the information in these tables, which mainly refer to local bus services, is derived from annual returns made to DfT by a sample of holders of PSV operators' licences.

A local bus service is one available to the general public, where the route is registered with the Traffic Commissioner, where passengers pay separate, local fares.

Bus and coach services which comprise contract, private hire, tours, excursions and express journeys are generally classified as "non-local" or "other" work. Some services, such as long distance coach services, might contain a mixture of local work and non-local express work.

Some important changes have been made to the legal framework under which the industry operates.

Outside London:

- from 1 April 1986, the Passenger Transport Authorities in metropolitan areas were subjected to precept control
- local bus services outside London were deregulated on 26 October 1986, introducing on the road competition
- widespread privatisation of public sector bus operations took place from 1986. There are fewer bus operators in the public sector.

Within London:

- responsibility for London (Regional) Transport transferred from the former Greater London Council to the Secretary of State for Transport from 29 June 1984. On 1 April 1985, a separate operating subsidiary, London Buses Ltd, was established
- progressive tendering of local bus services in London was introduced in July 1985
- the former operating divisions of London Buses Ltd were privatised by the end of 1994
- from July 2000, Transport for London (TfL) was established as a successor body to London Transport, with strategic control of local buses through the Greater London Authority (GLA) under an elected Mayor of London.

Outside London, after bus deregulation in 1986, general subsidy was no longer feasible as most services were provided on a purely commercial basis, with on the road competition for routes.

Public transport support was restricted to unprofitable but socially necessary services, the operation of which was generally put out to tender.

In London, nearly all local bus services are operated by the private sector under contract to TfL. Bus routes, once awarded to a contractor after a tendering process, are then protected from on the road competition.

Bus and coach vehicle kilometres: 6.9

Service kilometres operated are measured by DfT's annual sample PSV survey of operators, and, for the bus contractors in London, by TfL. The majority of local bus service kilometres are run on a commercial basis. Subsidised local service kilometres are around a fifth of the local service total. Non-local service kilometres comprise long distance coaching, private hire, school contract work, excursions and tours.

Bus and coach stock: 6.10

After deregulation many large buses were replaced by smaller ones. In recent years, with the emphasis on passenger accessibility, more full size, low floor single deck buses have entered service. Operators have been buying more new vehicles, which has increased the fleet size and reduced the overall age of the PSV fleet.

Passenger receipts: 6.11

Receipts comprise amounts paid by, or for, all passengers carried. They include payments for season tickets and travel passes, and concessionary fare reimbursement from local authorities. Receipts exclude public transport support, Rural Bus Subsidy Grant (RBSG) and Bus Service Operator Grant (BSOG, formerly Fuel Duty Rebate).

Local authorities and passenger transport authorities run concessionary fare schemes for groups such as the elderly, the disabled and children. From mid 2001 the schemes in England must offer, as a minimum, half fare bus travel to elderly residents. Local authorities reimburse operators for revenue lost as a result of their participation in concessionary fare schemes after taking account of any income from the extra travel generated. The reimbursement should be seen as an incentive to the passenger to travel more. The operators should not lose, or gain, revenue through such schemes.

Staff employed: 6.12

There was a fall in staff employed in the mid 1990s reflecting the widespread use of driver-only buses and the contracting out of an increased proportion of activities such as fleet maintenance. In recent years, as the bus fleet has grown, staff numbers have increased. Staff members may have more than one role, so the tables show those classified according to their main occupation.

Local passenger journeys by area: 6.13

These are collected through DfT's annual sample PSV survey of operators and, for London, from TfL. They are a count of boardings of each vehicle, so a trip which requires a change from one bus to another would show two boardings. TfL obtains data on boardings from on-bus surveys. This information is useful as a check on DfT's annual PSV survey results for the capital. Over the last year, further bus patronage data have been obtained from local authorities, which they have used in their Local Transport Plans. This extra information has allowed DfT to revise its series of boardings. The main change has been an adjustment which gives a reduction in the allocation to London, with an increase in the surrounding counties.

Local authority support: 6.14

Public transport support, also known as "revenue support" covers forms of local authority current expenditure on public transport (not concessionary fare reimbursement). It includes payments to operators for the operation of subsidised services, and local authority administrative costs associated with bus operations, such as the tendering process itself and publicity. The Transport Act 1985 restricted support to unprofitable "socially necessary" services.

Subsidised bus services are run under contract to local transport authorities, usually following competitive tendering. Outside London, from 1998-99, Rural Bus Subsidy Grant (RBSG) has been paid by central government to many local authorities to encourage bus service provision in their more rural parts. RBSG is therefore included in the support table. In London, support takes a different form, as nearly all bus services are run on a commercial basis, under contract to TfL. Contracts for particular routes are awarded to operators after competitive tendering. The contract payments take into account the high level of service provision required in London, including services that run later in the evenings and at weekends.

Local bus fares indices: 6.15

Information required for the calculation of the index of local bus fares is obtained from a DfT survey of a panel of bus operators, who account for about 85 per cent of receipts from passengers on local bus services. Operators supply information about the size of each fare change, each quarter. Indices for groups of operators in different areas of GB are obtained by averaging changes, using weights based on receipts from passengers from DfT's PSV annual survey (receipts used for the index exclude concessionary fare reimbursement from local authorities). The DfT local bus fares index is a small part of the Retail Prices Index.

The index is intended to measure the change in the average cost to the fare-paying passenger. In practice, as the operators select the basket of fare changes to report each quarter and as cash-less transactions become more common (e.g. pre-paid travel passes) the index can only give a broad guide to fare changes. Also, fare changes outside London are frequent, so adjustments must be made to the index each quarter. Bus fare changes in London usually take place once a year, in January.

There is a trend towards simpler fare structures, with operators charging flat fares or zoned fares, and the use of pre-payment through stored value tickets, which speed up boarding.

Operating costs per local bus kilometre: 6.16

Costs per bus kilometre are higher in London and metropolitan areas than elsewhere. Greater traffic congestion, more frequent services and the need to use larger buses for busy services all contribute to higher costs.

Other costs, such as the cost of tendering and publicity associated with bus services, borne by local authorities or TfL rather than the operators, are not shown in this table.

Taxi industry: 6.17

A taxi, or hackney carriage, is a vehicle with fewer than 9 passenger seats which is licensed to "ply for hire" (i.e. it may stand at ranks or be hailed in the street by members of the public). This distinguishes taxis from Private Hire Vehicles (PHVs), which must be booked in advance through an operator and may not ply for hire (taxis may also be pre-booked). Taxis must normally be hired as a whole (i.e. separate fares are not charged to each passenger). However, taxis may charge separate fares when a sharing scheme is in operation, when they are run as a bus under a special PSV operators' licence or when pre-booked (PHV operators may also charge passengers separately if they share a journey).

In England and Wales taxis and PHVs are licensed by district or borough councils, unitary authorities or, in London, the Public Carriage Office (PCO) which is part of TfL. The licensing authority is usually the body which sets taxi fares, although fare changes may be requested by the taxi trade. PHV fares are set by the operator. TfL is implementing the Private Hire Vehicles (London) Act 1998 for the licensing of London PHV operators, drivers and vehicles. PHV operators in London must be licensed.

Taxi and PHV use has grown so there has been a large increase in the numbers of licensed taxis and PHVs.

The data on vehicles and drivers come from several sources. The London figures are from data held by TfL in the PCO. The statistics relating to provincial England and Wales come from surveys of district councils and unitary authorities.

6.1 Rail: length of national railway[1] route at year end, and passenger travel by national railway[1] and London Underground: 1900-2004/05

For greater detail of the years 1994/95-2004/05 see Table 6.2

	Length of National Rail route (kilometres)			National Rail		London Underground	
Year	Total route	Electrified[2] route	Open to Passenger traffic	Passenger journeys (million)	Passenger kilometres (billion)	Passenger journeys (million)	Passenger kilometres (billion)
1900	29,783	..	..	..	..	..	..
1919	32,420	1,321	..	2,064	..	..	..
1923	32,462	1,122	..	1,772	..	..	..
1928	32,565	1,901	..	1,250	..	..	..
1933	32,345	2,403	..	1,159	..	..	..
1938	32,081	3,378	..	1,237	30.6	492	..
1946	31,963	..	..	1,266	47.0	569	..
1947	31,950	1,455	..	1,140	37.0	554	5.4
1948	31,593	1,455	..	1,024	34.2	720	6.2
1949	31,500	1,489	..	1,021	34.0	703	6.1
1950	31,336	1,489	..	1,010	32.5	695	6.0
1951	31,152	1,487	..	1,030	33.5	702	5.6
1952	31,022	1,508	..	1,017	32.9	670	5.4
1953	30,935	1,508	..	1,015	33.1	672	5.4
1954	30,821	1,577	..	1,020	33.3	671	5.7
1955	30,676	1,577	23,820	994	32.7	676	5.6
1956	30,618	1,624	23,612	1,029	34.0	678	5.5
1957	30,521	1,621	23,532	1,101	36.4	666	5.4
1958	30,333	1,622	23,621	1,090	35.6	692	5.3
1959	29,877	1,799	22,632	1,069	35.8	669	5.1
1960	29,562	2,034	22,314	1,037	34.7	674	5.2
1961	29,313	2,234	22,043	1,025	33.9	675	5.1
1962	28,117	2,511	20,785	965	31.7	668	4.9
1963	27,330	2,556	20,328	938	30.9	674	4.9
1964	25,735	2,659	18,781	928	32.0	674	4.9
1965	24,011	2,886	17,516	865	30.1	657	4.7
1966	22,082	3,064	16,359	835	29.7	667	4.8
1967	21,198	3,241	15,904	837	29.1	661	4.8
1968	20,080	3,182	15,242	831	28.7	655	4.7
1969	19,470	3,169	15,088	805	29.6	676	5.0
1970	18,989	3,162	14,637	824	30.4	672	5.1
1971	18,738	3,169	14,484	816	30.1	654	5.2
1972	18,417	3,178	14,499	754	29.1	655	5.3
1973	18,227	3,462	14,375	728	29.8	644	5.2
1974	18,168	3,647	14,373	733	30.9	636	5.2
1975	18,118	3,655	14,431	730	30.9	601	4.8
1976	18,007	3,735	14,407	702	28.4	546	4.4
1977	17,973	3,767	14,413	702	29.3	545	4.3
1978	17,901	3,716	14,396	724	30.0	568	4.5
1979	17,735	3,718	14,412	748	30.7	594	4.5
1980	17,645	3,718	14,394	760	30.3	559	4.2
1981	17,431	3,729	14,394	719	29.7	541	4.1
1982	17,229	3,753	14,371	630	27.2	498	3.7
1983	16,964	3,750	14,375	695	29.5	563	4.3
1984/85	16,816	3,798	14,304	701	29.5	672	5.4
1985/86	16,752	3,809	14,310	686	30.4	732	6.0
1986/87	16,670	4,154	14,304	738[3]	30.8[3]	769	6.2
1987/88	16,633	4,207	14,302	798	32.4	798	6.3
1988/89	16,599	4,376	14,309	822	34.3	815	6.3
1989/90	16,587	4,546	14,318	812	33.3	765	6.0
1990/91	16,584	4,912	14,317	809	33.2	775	6.2

6.1 Rail: length of national railway [1] route at year end, and passenger travel by national railway [1] and London Underground: 1900-2004/05 (continued):

For greater detail of the years 1994/95-2004/05 see Table 6.2

	Length of National Rail route (kilometres)			National Rail		London Underground	
Year	Total route	Electrified [2] route	Open to Passenger traffic	Passenger journeys (million)	Passenger kilometres (billion)	Passenger journeys (million)	Passenger kilometres (billion)
1991/92	16,588	4,886	14,291	792	32.5	751	5.9
1992/93	16,528	4,910	14,317	770	31.7	728	5.8
1993/94	16,536	4,968	14,357	740	30.4	735	5.8
1994/95	16,542	4,970	14,359	735	28.7	764	6.1
1995/96	16,666	5,163	15,002	761	30.0	784	6.3
1996/97	16,666	5,176	15,034	801	32.1	772	6.2
1997/98	16,656	5,166	15,024	846	34.7	832	6.5
1998/99	16,659	5,166	15,038	892	36.3	866	6.7
1999/00	16,649	5,167	15,038	931 [4]	38.5 [4]	927	7.2
2000/01	16,652	5,167	15,042	957 [4]	38.2 [4]	970	7.5
2001/02	16,652	5,167	15,042	960	39.1	953	7.5
2002/03	16,652	5,167	15,042	976	39.7	942	7.4
2003/04	16,652	5,167	15,042	1,014	40.9	948	7.3
2004/05	16,116	5,200	14,328 [5]	1,088	42.4	976	7.6

1 From 1994/95 route length is for the former Railtrack.
From 1995/96 data are for National Rail, former British Rail and
Train Operating Companies. Excludes rail routes managed by PTEs.
2 Pre 1947 figures refer to track length, not route length,
and include electrified sidings. In 1947 electrified track kilometres totalled 3,370.
3 Break in series. From 1986/87 figures include an element of double counting,
as a journey involving more than one operator is scored against each operator.
This contrasts with former British Rail data for which a through ticket journey was counted only once.
4 Figures revised by Strategic Rail Authority.
5 Rail route length excludes the Merseyrail network operated by the Serco/Nedrail franchise.

☎Rail: 020-7944 4977
☎London Underground: 020-7944 3076
The figures in this table are outside the scope of National Statistics
Sources - SRA, London Underground

6.2 Rail systems: 1994/95-2004/05

(a) Passenger journeys — Millions

	1994/95	1995/96	1996/97	1997/98	1998/99	1999/00	2000/01	2001/02	2002/03	2003/04	2004/05
National Rail network [1,8]	735	761	801	846	892	931	957	960	976	1,014	1,088
London Undergound	764	784	772	832	866	927	970	953	942	948	976
Glasgow Underground	15	14	14	14	15	15	14	14	13	13	13
Docklands Light Railway	12	14	17	21	28	31	38	41	46	48	50
Nexus (Tyne & Wear Metro) [2]	37	36	35	35	34	33	33	33	37	38	37
Blackpool Trams [3]	5	5	5	5	4	4	4	5	4	4	4
Manchester Metrolink [4]	12	13	13	14	13	14	17	18	19	19	20
Stagecoach Supertram	2	5	8	9	10	11	11	11	12	12	13
West Midland Metro [5]	.	.	.	.	.	5	5	5	5	5	5
Croydon Tramlink [6]	.	.	.	.	.	.	15	18	19	20	22
Nottingham NET [7]	.	.	.	.	.	.	.	.	.	-	8
All light rail	68	73	78	84	89	99	124	131	142	147	159
All rail	1,582	1,632	1,665	1,776	1,862	1,972	2,065	2,058	2,074	2,122	2,236

(b) Passenger kilometres — Millions

	1994/95	1995/96	1996/97	1997/98	1998/99	1999/00	2000/01	2001/02	2002/03	2003/04	2004/05
National Rail network [1,8]	28,700	30,000	32,100	34,700	36,280	38,472	38,179	39,141	39,678	40,937	42,369
London Undergound	6,051	6,337	6,153	6,479	6,716	7,171	7,470	7,451	7,367	7,340	7,606
Glasgow Underground	43	41	40	45	47	47	46	44	43	43	43
Docklands Light Railway	55	70	86	103	144	172	200	207	232	235	245
Nexus (Tyne & Wear Metro)	271	261	254	249	238	230	229	238	275	284	283
Blackpool Trams	..	..	..	..	..	13	13	15	14	11	12
Manchester Metrolink	79	81	86	88	117	126	152	161	167	169	204
Stagecoach Supertram	8	20	29	34	35	37	38	39	40	42	44
West Midland Metro	.	.	.	.	.	50	56	50	50	54	52
Croydon Tramlink	.	.	.	.	.	.	96	99	100	105	112
Nottingham NET	.	.	.	.	.	.	.	.	.	2	37
Light rail	413	432	455	474	534	628	784	809	878	903	990
All rail	35,207	36,811	38,748	41,698	43,577	46,318	46,479	47,445	47,966	49,222	51,008

(c) Passenger revenue — £ million (at current prices)

	1994/95	1995/96	1996/97	1997/98	1998/99	1999/00	2000/01	2001/02	2002/03	2003/04	2004/05
National Rail network	2,171	2,379	2,573	2,821	3,089	3,368	3,413	3,548	3,663	3,901	4,158
London Undergound	718	765	797	899	977	1,058	1,129	1,151	1,138	1,161	1,241
Glasgow Underground	7	8	8	9	9	10	10	10	10	10	11
Docklands Light Railway	6	9	12	14	20	22	29	32	36	37	40
Nexus (Tyne & Wear Metro)	19	20	21	22	23	24	24	25	29	31	33
Blackpool Trams	4	5	4	5	4	4	4	5	5	4	4
Manchester Metrolink	10	11	13	14	..	..	18	20	20	21	22
Stagecoach Supertram	2	4	5	6	6	7	7	8	10	9	11
West Midland Metro	.	.	.	.	.	..	3	4	5	5	5
Croydon Tramlink	.	.	.	.	.	.	12	13	15	16	18
Nottingham NET	.	.	.	.	.	.	.	.	.	..	6
Light rail	41	49	55	61	53	57	97	107	120	122	140
All rail	2,937	3,201	3,433	3,790	4,128	4,493	4,649	4,815	4,930	5,195	5,550

(d) Route kilometres open for passenger traffic — Number

	1994/95	1995/96	1996/97	1997/98	1998/99	1999/00	2000/01	2001/02	2002/03	2003/04	2004/05
National Rail network	14,359	15,002	15,034	15,024	15,038	15,038	15,042	15,042	15,042	14,883	14,328
London Undergound	392	392	392	392	392	408	408	408	408	408	408
Glasgow Underground	11	11	11	11	11	11	11	11	11	11	11
Docklands Light Railway	22	22	22	22	22	26	26	26	26	26	26
Nexus (Tyne & Wear Metro)	59	59	59	59	59	59	59	78	78	78	78
Blackpool Trams	18	18	18	18	18	18	18	18	18	18	18
Manchester Metrolink	31	31	31	31	31	39	39	39	39	39	39
Stagecoach Supertram	22	29	29	29	29	29	29	29	29	29	29
West Midland Metro	.	.	.	.	.	.	20	20	20	20	20
Croydon Tramlink	.	.	.	.	.	.	28	28	28	28	28
Nottingham NET	.	.	.	.	.	.	.	.	.	14	14
Light rail	152	159	159	159	159	171	219	238	238	252	252
All rail	14,914	15,564	15,596	15,586	15,600	15,628	15,680	15,699	15,699	15,554	14,999

6.2 Rail systems: (continued)

(e) Stations or stops served — Number

	1994/95	1995/96	1996/97	1997/98	1998/99	1999/00	2000/01	2001/02	2002/03	2003/04	2004/05
National Rail network	2,489	2,497	2,498	2,495	2,499	2,503	2,508	2,508	2,508	2,507	2,508
London Undergound	245	245	245	245	246	253	253	253	253	253	253
Glasgow Underground	15	15	15	15	15	15	15	15	15	15	15
Docklands Light Railway	27	28	28	29	29	34	34	34	34	34	34
Nexus (Tyne & Wear Metro)	46	46	46	46	46	46	46	58	58	58	58
Blackpool Trams	124	124	124	124	124	124	124	124	124	124	124
Manchester Metrolink	26	26	26	26	26	36	36	36	37	37	37
Stagecoach Supertram	37	45	45	46	47	47	47	48	48	48	48
West Midland Metro	.	.	.	.	.	23	23	23	23	23	23
Croydon Tramlink	.	.	.	.	.	.	38	38	38	38	38
Nottingham NET	.	.	.	.	.	.	.	.	.	23	23
Light rail	260	269	269	271	272	310	348	361	362	385	385
All rail	3,009	3,026	3,027	3,026	3,032	3,081	3,124	3,137	3,138	3,160	3,161

(f) Loaded train or tram kilometres — Millions

	1994/95	1995/96	1996/97	1997/98	1998/99	1999/00	2000/01	2001/02	2002/03	2003/04	2004/05
National Rail network	357.1	372.2	375.0	376.3	405.1	418.4	427.2	435.9	443.3	446.2	456.0
London Undergound	54.8	57.2	58.6	62.1	61.2	63.1	63.8	65.4	65.9	68.5	69.5
Glasgow Underground	1.1	1.1	1.1	1.1	1.1	1.2	1.2	1.2	1.1	1.1	1.1
Docklands Light Railway	1.5	2.0	2.2	2.4	2.6	2.9	2.9	2.9	3.2	3.4	3.3
Nexus (Tyne & Wear Metro)	5.6	5.4	5.0	4.8	4.8	4.8	4.7	4.7	6.3	6.3	5.6
Blackpool Trams	1.4	1.3	1.3	1.2	1.2	1.2	1.2	1.3	1.1	0.9	0.8
Manchester Metrolink	2.1	2.1	2.3	3.2	3.4	3.6	4.4	4.5	4.6	4.6	4.4
Stagecoach Supertram	1.1	2.5	2.8	2.7	2.4	2.4	2.4	2.4	2.5	2.5	2.4
West Midland Metro	.	.	.	.	.	.	1.9	1.6	1.7	1.7	1.6
Croydon Tramlink	.	.	.	.	.	.	2.1	2.4	2.5	2.5	2.4
Nottingham NET	.	.	.	.	.	.	.	.	.	0.2	1.0
Light rail	11.7	13.3	13.6	14.3	14.4	14.9	19.6	19.8	21.9	22.1	21.7
All rail	424.7	443.8	448.3	453.8	481.8	497.6	511.8	522.3	532.2	537.9	548.2

(g) Passenger carriages or tramcars — Number

	1994/95	1995/96	1996/97	1997/98	1998/99	1999/00	2000/01	2001/02	2002/03	2003/04	2004/05
National Rail network[9]	11,483	8,504	..	..	..	..	..	..	..	..	..
London Undergound	3,923	3,923	3,867	3,886	3,923	3,954	3,954	3,954	3,954	3,959	3,959
Glasgow Underground	41	41	41	41	41	41	41	41	41	41	41
Docklands Light Railway	86	70	70	70	70	70	70	74	94	94	94
Nexus (Tyne & Wear Metro)	90	90	90	90	90	90	90	90	90	90	90
Blackpool Trams	81	77	77	77	77	75	81	75	76	76	76
Manchester Metrolink	26	26	26	26	26	32	32	32	32	32	32
Stagecoach Supertram	25	25	25	25	25	25	25	25	25	25	25
West Midland Metro	.	.	.	.	.	16	16	16	16	16	16
Croydon Tramlink	.	.	.	.	.	24	24	24	24	24	24
Nottingham NET	.	.	.	.	.	.	.	.	.	15	15
Light rail	308	288	288	288	288	332	338	336	357	372	372
All rail	15,755	12,756	..	..	..	..	..	..	..	..	..

1 Franchised train operating companies from February 1996 following rail privatisation.
2 Tyne & Wear Metro extension to Sunderland opened in March 2002.
3 Blackpool Trams shown as a self-contained system.
4 Transfer of 20 stations from the rail network to Manchester Metrolink.
5 West Midland Metro opened in 1999.
6 Croydon Tramlink opened in 2000.
7 Nottingham Express Transit opened in March 2004.
8 National Rail passenger journeys and passenger kilometres have been revised by the SRA.
9 No data available for National Rail leased rolling stock after rail privatisation.

☎020-7944 3076
The National Rail and Underground figures in this table are outside the scope of National Statistics
Sources: Network Rail, former Railtrack, SRA, TfL, light rail operators and PTEs

6.3 National railways: receipts:[1] 1994/95-2004/05

£ Million

	1994/95	1995/96	1996/97	1997/98	1998/99	1999/00	2000/01	2001/02	2002/03	2003/04	2004/05
All Passenger Operators											
Ordinary fares	1,559	1,720	1,870	2,048	2,242	2,463	2,463	2,585	2,693	2,893	3,078
Season tickets	611	660	702	773	847	905	950	964	970	1,009	1,081
All tickets (current prices)	2,171	2,379	2,573	2,821	3,089	3,368	3,413	3,548	3,663	3,901	4,158
All tickets (2004/05 prices)	2,803	2,986	3,123	3,339	3,554	3,792	3,800	3,851	3,843	3,986	4,158

1 Up to 1994/95 former British Rail. From 1995/96 includes British Rail services and those provided by private operators. Adjusted to 2004/05 prices using the GDP market price deflator.

☎020-7944 4977
The figures in this table are outside the scope of National Statistics
Source - ORR, formerly SRA

6.4 Passenger kilometres on national railways:[1] 1994/95-2004/05

Billions

	1994/95	1995/96	1996/97	1997/98	1998/99	1999/2000	2000/01	2001/02	2002/03	2003/04	2004/05
All Passenger Operators:											
Ordinary fare	20.7	22.2	23.4	25.3	26.4	28.0 [2]	27.2	28.1	28.4	29.1	30.0
Season ticket	8.0	7.9	8.7	9.3	9.8	10.4 [2]	10.9	11.0	11.3	11.8	12.4
All tickets	28.7	30.0	32.1	34.7	36.3	38.5 [2]	38.2	39.1	39.7	40.9	42.4

1 Estimates of passenger kilometres are derived from ticket sales. Travel on season tickets assumes appropriate factors for the number of journeys made per ticket.
2 Revisions to series made by the Strategic Rail Authority.

☎020-7944 4977
The figures in this table are outside the scope of National Statistics
Source - ORR, formerly SRA

6.5 National railways: route and stations open for traffic at end of year: 1994/95-2004/05

Kilometres/number

	1994/95	1995/96	1996/97	1997/98	1998/99	1999/00	2000/01	2001/02	2002/03	2003/04	2004/05
Route open for traffic:											
Electrified	4,970	5,163	5,176	5,166	5,166	5,167	5,167	5,167	5,167	5,167	5,200 [2]
Non-electrified	11,572	11,503	11,490	11,490	11,493	11,482	11,485	11,485	11,485	11,485	10,916 [2]
All routes:	16,542	16,666	16,666	16,656	16,659	16,649	16,652	16,652	16,652	16,652	16,116 [2]
Open for passenger traffic	14,359	15,002	15,034	15,024	15,038	15,038	15,042	15,042	15,042	15,042	14,328 [2]
Open for freight traffic only	2,183	1,664	1,632	1,632	1,621	1,610	1,610	1,610	1,610	1,610	1,788 [2]
Passenger stations [1]:	2,489	2,497	2,498	2,495	2,499	2,503	2,508	2,508	2,508	2,508	2,508

1 The number of stations shown are those on the national network. Metro stations and stations shared with London Underground are excluded.
2 Break in series is due to a change in methodology.

☎020-7944 4977
The figures in this table are outside the scope of National Statistics
Source - Network Rail, formerly Railtrack

6.6 National railways: punctuality and reliability: 1994/95-2004/05

Percentage

	1994/95	1995/96	1996/97	1997/98	1998/99	1999/00	2000/01	2001/02	2002/03	2003/04	2004/05
Public Performance Measure (PPM)[1]	..	..	..	*89.7*	*87.9*	*87.8*	*79.1*	*78.0*	*79.2*	*81.2*	*83.6*
Punctuality	*89.6*	*89.5*	*92.5*	*92.5*	*91.5*	*91.9*	..	..	..	..	..
Reliability	*98.7*	*98.8*	*99.1*	*98.9*	*98.8*	*98.8*	..	..	..	..	..

1 The PPM is a measure of the percentage of trains arriving on time, combining punctuality and reliability. It replaced the former Passenger's Charter measures from June 2000. Passenger Charter figures are displayed regularly by individual train operators.

☎020-7944 4977
The figures in this table are outside the scope of National Statistics
Source - ORR, formerly SRA

6.7 London Underground: 1994/95-2004/05

	1994/95	1995/96	1996/97	1997/98	1998/99	1999/00	2000/01	2001/02	2002/03	2003/04	2004/05
Passenger Journeys (millions)											
Ordinary [1]	398	416	418	448	463	477	486	491	495	491	486
Season ticket	366	368	354	384	403	450	484	462	446	457	490
All journeys	764	784	772	832	866	927	970	953	942	948	976
Passenger kilometres (millions)	6,051	6,337	6,153	6,479	6,716	7,171	7,470	7,451	7,367	7,340	7,606
Receipts (£ million)											
Ordinary [1]	396	430	449	510	547	579	610	636	628	625	663
Season ticket	322	335	348	389	430	479	519	515	510	536	578
Traffic receipts	718	765	797	899	977	1,058	1,129	1,151	1,138	1,161	1,241
Other income	47	51	56	62	69	91	100	101	107	115	..
All income (current prices)	765	816	854	961	1,045	1,149	1,229	1,251	1,244	1,277	..
All income at 2004/05 prices [2]	990	1,023	1,045	1,138	1,201	1,299	1,350	1,354	1,319	1,316	..
Costs (£ million)											
Rail Operations [3, 4]	626	612	629	681	869	962	1,115	1,341	1,628	..	..
Other operations	12	12	14	15	18	33	42	30	36	..	..
Depreciation, renewals, severance [3]	436	410	326	315	267	299	341	344	336	..	..
All costs (current prices)	1,073	1,034	970	1,010	1,154	1,294	1,497	1,715	2,000	..	..
All costs 2004/05 prices [2]	1,388	1,297	1,187	1,197	1,326	1,464	1,644	1,856	2,120	..	..
Loaded train kilometres (millions)	55	57	59	62	61	63	64	65	65	68	..
Passenger place kilometres (billions)	49	52	52	56	55	57	57	58	58	..	..
Receipts per journey (£)	0.94	0.98	1.03	1.08	1.13	1.14	1.16	1.21	1.21	1.22	1.27
Receipts per jny at 2004/05 prices [2]	1.22	1.22	1.26	1.28	1.30	1.29	1.28	1.31	1.28	1.26	1.27
Costs per train kilometre (£)	20	18	17	16	19	21	23	26	31	..	..
Costs per km at 2004/05 prices [2]	25	23	20	19	22	23	26	28	32	..	..
Average no. passengers per train	110	111	105	104	110	114	117	114	113	..	..
Loss before grants and tax (£ m)	308	218	116	50	109	145	268	464	756	..	..
Loss at 2004/05 prices [2]	399	273	142	59	125	164	294	502	802	..	..
Operational data (number)											
Rail staff	16,741	16,011	16,011	15,892	16,032	16,462	16,956	18,679	17,214	..	..
Stations	245	245	245	245	246	253	253	253	253	253	253
Rail carriages	3,923	3,923	3,867	3,886	3,923	3,954	3,954	3,954	3,954	3,959	3,959
Route kilometres	392	392	392	392	392	408	408	408	408	408	408

1 Ordinary journeys include daily travelcards and those where concessionary fares apply.
2 Adjustment to 2004/05 values using the RPI.
3 From 1998/99, following a change in London Underground's accounting policy, expenditure that had previously been treated as renewals was either charged to the cost of operations or capitalised as an addition to fixed assets.
4 The cost of rail operations includes most of the costs of London Underground's PFI and PPP contracts that are delivering a modernised tube network.

020-7944 3076
The figures in this table are outside the scope of National Statistics
Source - Transport for London

6.8 Channel Tunnel: traffic to and from Europe: 1996-2004

Thousands

	1996 [2]	1997 [2]	1998	1999	2000	2001	2002	2003	2004
Vehicles carried on Le Shuttle									
Passenger	2,135	2,383	3,448	3,342	2,864	2,605	2,408	2,351	2,165
Freight [1]	519	268	705	839	1,133	1,198	1,231	1,285	1,281
All vehicles	2,654	2,651	4,153	4,181	3,997	3,803	3,639	3,636	3,446
Passengers on Eurostar and Le Shuttle	12,809	14,653	18,405	17,550	17,018	16,313	15,252	14,699	15,064
Through-train freight tonnes	2,361	2,925	3,141	2,865	2,947	2,447	1,487	1,743	1,889

1 Opened for freight services in June 1994 and for through passenger services in November. Passenger shuttle services opened in December.
2 Figures for 1996 and 1997 were affected by a fire on 16 November 1996. Tourist shuttle resumed services on 10 Dec 1996 with full freight services resuming on 15 June 1997.

☎020-7944 4977
The figures in this table are outside the scope of National Statistics
Sources - Eurotunnel, Eurostar and EWS International

6.9 Bus and coach services: vehicle kilometres: 1994/95-2004/05

(a) Local bus services by area — Millions

	1994/95	1995/96	1996/97	1997/98	1998/99	1999/00	2000/01	2001/02	2002/03	2003/04	2004/05
London	356	353	342	362	358	366	373	379	406	474	470
English metropolitan areas	720	695	692	697	684	661	656	647	631	596	575
English other areas	1,080	1,102	1,116	1,083	1,123	1,160	1,134	1,102	1,082	1,063	1,088
England	2,156	2,150	2,150	2,142	2,165	2,186	2,164	2,128	2,119	2,133	2,133
Scotland	369	350	368	368	358	363	369	368	374	369	366
Wales	125	123	120	117	118	123	126	126	123	113	116
All Great Britain	2,650	2,623	2,638	2,628	2,642	2,673	2,659	2,622	2,616	2,615	2,614
All outside London	2,294	2,270	2,296	2,266	2,284	2,307	2,286	2,243	2,210	2,141	2,144

(b) Local bus services outside London by area — Millions

	2002/03			2003/04			2004/05		
	Commercial	Subsidised	Total	Commercial	Subsidised	Total	Commercial	Subsidised	Total
English metropolitan areas	550	82	631	509	87	596	491	85	575
English other areas	841	241	1,082	823	240	1,063	806	282	1,088
Scotland	311	63	374	302	67	369	309	56	366
Wales	89	35	123	85	28	113	84	32	116
All outside London	1,791	421	2,210	1,719	422	2,141	1,690	455	2,144

(c) All services — Millions

	1994/95	1995/96	1996/97	1997/98	1998/99	1999/00	2000/01	2001/02	2002/03	2003/04	2004/05
Local bus services	2,650	2,623	2,638	2,628	2,642	2,673	2,659	2,622	2,616	2,615	2,614
Other (non-local) services	1,428	1,482	1,503	1,558	1,590	1,448	1,504	1,469	1,335	1,399	1,335
All services	4,078	4,105	4,141	4,186	4,232	4,121	4,163	4,091	3,951	4,014	3,949

☎020-7944 3076

6.10 Bus and coach services: vehicle stock: 1994/95 - 2004/05

Thousands

	1994/95	1995/96	1996/97	1997/98	1998/99	1999/00	2000/01	2001/02	2002/03	2003/04	2004/05
Single deckers:											
up to 16 seats	9.3	8.8	10.0	10.5	10.9	11.5	10.8	11.3	11.7	14.2	14.5
17-35 seats	15.9	16.5	16.6	13.6	14.4	13.9	15.0	13.0	12.9	..	..
36 plus seats	30.4	30.8	30.5	34.9	36.4	37.5	37.5	39.2	37.9	..	..
All single deckers	55.6	56.1	57.1	59.0	61.7	62.9	63.3	63.5	62.5	63.6	64.0
All double deckers	19.7	19.6	18.6	17.1	17.0	16.8	16.0	16.0	16.3	16.5	16.6
All vehicles [1]	75.3	75.7	75.7	76.1	78.7	79.7	79.2	79.5	78.8	80.1	80.6

1 Public Service Vehicles in tax classes 34 and 38. Taken from DfT's annual surveys.

☎020-7944 3076

6.11 Bus and coach services: passenger receipts (Including concessionary fare reimbursement): 1993/94-2003/04

(a) Local bus services by area (current prices) — £ Million

Area	1993/94	1994/95	1995/96	1996/97	1997/98	1998/99	1999/00	2000/01	2001/02	2002/03	2003/04
London	464	492	520	561	599	626	652	674	695	715	767
English metropolitan areas	643	656	657	672	719	718	704	747	764	786	815
English other areas	800	830	838	866	906	930	972	1,038	1,074	1,135	1,281
England	1,907	1,978	2,015	2,099	2,224	2,274	2,328	2,459	2,533	2,635	2,863
Scotland	279	295	293	290	296	300	314	332	321	354	358
Wales	76	78	81	83	81	85	88	99	98	105	105
All Great Britain	2,262	2,351	2,389	2,472	2,601	2,659	2,731	2,890	2,952	3,094	3,326
All outside London	1,798	1,859	1,869	1,911	2,002	2,033	2,078	2,216	2,257	2,379	2,559
(b) All services at current prices											£ Million
Local bus services	2,262	2,351	2,389	2,472	2,601	2,659	2,731	2,890	2,952	3,094	3,326
Other (non-local) services	961	983	1,024	1,067	1,144	1,260	1,387	1,532	1,673	1,706	1,396
All services	3,223	3,334	3,413	3,539	3,745	3,919	4,118	4,422	4,625	4,800	4,722
(c) All services at 2004/05 prices [1]											£ Million
Local bus services	2,972	3,037	2,998	3,006	3,081	3,060	3,078	3,207	3,202	3,254	3,394
Other (non-local) services	1,258	1,269	1,285	1,295	1,355	1,450	1,562	1,706	1,816	1,790	1,420
All services	4,230	4,306	4,283	4,301	4,436	4,510	4,640	4,913	5,018	5,044	4,814

1 Data for 2004/05 not yet available. Prices for the series are adjusted for general inflation to 2004/05 prices, using the GDP market price deflator.

☎020-7944 3076

6.12 Bus and coach services: staff employed: 1994/95-2004/05

Thousands

Staff	1994/95	1995/96	1996/97	1997/98	1998/99	1999/00	2000/01	2001/02	2002/03	2003/04	2004/05
Drivers & crew	105.0	106.1	106.3	108.7	113.6	117.1	116.8	117.9	118.0	122.0	126.1
Maintenance	23.1	22.0	21.4	19.9	20.0	19.8	19.6	20.8	19.3	19.7	20.7
Other	20.2	17.8	18.0	17.3	18.1	17.9	19.5	21.5	17.9	20.7	20.1
All staff [1]	148.3	145.9	145.7	145.9	151.7	154.8	156.0	160.2	155.2	162.4	166.9

1 The full-time equivalents of all part time staff and all working proprietors are classified according to their main occupation.

☎020-7944 3076

6.13 Local bus services: passenger journeys by area: 1994/95-2004/05

Millions

Area	1994/95	1995/96	1996/97	1997/98	1998/99	1999/00	2000/01	2001/02	2002/03	2003/04	2004/05
London	1,155	1,193	1,230	1,281	1,266	1,294	1,347	1,422	1,527	1,692	1,782
English metropolitan areas	1,330	1,292	1,246	1,232	1,195	1,178	1,166	1,154	1,145	1,114	1,083
English other areas	1,273	1,260	1,260	1,243	1,242	1,250	1,247	1,222	1,210	1,189	1,167
England	3,758	3,745	3,736	3,755	3,702	3,722	3,761	3,798	3,882	3,995	4,032
Scotland	513	494	467	438	413	442	443	449	452	457	465
Wales	132	127	130	120	116	114	116	104	110	111	113
All Great Britain	4,403	4,366	4,333	4,313	4,231	4,278	4,319	4,352	4,444	4,564	4,609
All outside London	3,248	3,173	3,103	3,032	2,965	2,984	2,972	2,930	2,917	2,871	2,828

☎020-7944 3076

6.14 Local bus services: Local authority support by area: 1994/95-2004/05

(a) Concessionary fare reimbursement: by area (current prices) — £ Million

	1994/95	1995/96	1996/97	1997/98	1998/99	1999/00	2000/01	2001/02	2002/03	2003/04	2004/05
London	100	103	106	110	113	117	119	129	128	132	140
English metropolitan areas	177	177	174	176	176	175	183	183	181	185	191
English other areas	99	102	102	104	103	102	113	122	122	131	138
England	376	382	382	390	393	394	415	435	431	448	469
Scotland	41	40	40	39	42	41	40	39	45	86	82
Wales	8	9	9	8	8	10	11	13	13	13	14
All Great Britain	425	431	432	437	443	445	466	487	489	547	565
All outside London	325	328	326	327	330	328	347	358	361	415	425
(b) Public transport support: by area (current prices)											**£ Million**
London [1]	55	30	12	1	12	10	84	186	421	560	545
English metropolitan areas	100	100	106	98	109	109	120	121	106	113	117
English other areas	87	87	83	86	110	127	136	142	165	187	192
England	242	217	201	185	231	246	340	449	692	860	854
Scotland	22	25	26	23	22	25	28	33	35	36	38
Wales	8	9	8	9	11	14	16	17	17	17	18
All Great Britain	272	251	236	218	265	284	383	498	744	912	910
All outside London	217	221	224	217	253	274	299	312	323	352	365
(c) All Great Britain at 2004/05 prices [2]											**£ Million**
Concessionary fare reimbursement	549	541	524	517	510	501	519	528	513	556	565
Public transport support	351	315	287	258	305	320	426	540	780	928	910

1 London figures are affected by operational changes after the privatisation of London Transport Buses. From 1994/95, contracts with bus operators replaced the former support.

2 Adjusted for general inflation to 2004/05 prices.

☎020-7944 3076

6.15 Local bus services: fare indices by area: 1994/95-2004/05

1995=100

Area	1994/95	1995/96	1996/97	1997/98	1998/99	1999/00	2000/01	2001/02	2002/03	2003/04	2004/05
London	96.2	101.1	105.4	109.3	113.7	117.2	117.2	115.5	114.8	116.9	126.8
English metropolitan areas	96.4	101.5	106.9	113.3	118.7	124.6	129.9	137.4	142.7	148.0	154.2
English other areas	97.0	101.1	106.0	111.5	116.7	122.0	128.6	135.1	141.7	148.5	155.7
England	96.7	101.2	106.1	111.4	116.5	121.5	125.9	130.3	134.2	139.1	146.2
Scotland	96.9	100.8	108.0	116.5	121.8	125.3	129.9	131.8	134.5	136.8	140.4
Wales	97.4	100.7	104.4	110.1	116.3	122.2	127.5	133.5	139.5	145.5	152.4
All Great Britain	96.7	101.2	106.3	112.0	117.1	122.0	126.4	130.6	134.5	139.1	145.7
All outside London	96.8	101.2	106.6	112.8	118.2	123.4	129.2	135.3	140.8	146.3	152.5
Retail Prices Index	97.5	100.7	103.1	106.5	109.9	111.6	114.9	116.6	119.1	122.4	126.2

☎020-7944 3076

6.16 Local bus services: operating costs per vehicle-kilometre: 1993/94-2003/04

(a) At current prices — Pence per vehicle kilometre [1]

	1993/94	1994/95	1995/96	1996/97	1997/98	1998/99	1999/00	2000/01	2001/02	2002/03	2003/04
London [2]	160	147	141	154	152	155	157	168	178	203	216
English PTE areas	90	89	92	94	90	90	92	101	105	105	114
English other areas	75	76	76	74	76	79	81	87	94	89	99
England	94	92	92	91	92	94	96	105	111	114	123
Scotland	77	79	80	73	74	77	73	78	84	80	80
Wales	63	67	71	65	71	74	74	76	77	84	83
All Great Britain	90	89	89	88	89	91	92	100	105	108	120
All outside London	79	80	81	79	81	84	82	89	94	94	99

(b) At 2004/05 prices [3] — Pence per vehicle kilometre [1]

	1993/94	1994/95	1995/96	1996/97	1997/98	1998/99	1999/00	2000/01	2001/02	2002/03	2003/04
London [2]	210	190	177	188	180	178	178	184	193	215	216
English PTE areas	118	115	115	114	107	104	104	112	114	110	116
English other areas	98	98	95	90	90	91	91	97	102	93	101
England	123	119	115	110	109	108	108	117	120	120	129
Scotland	101	102	100	89	88	89	82	87	91	84	81
Wales	83	86	89	79	84	85	83	85	84	88	84
All Great Britain	118	115	112	107	105	105	104	111	114	113	120
All outside London	103	103	102	96	96	97	92	99	103	97	101

1 Net of fuel duty rebate. Includes depreciation of vehicles.
2 Routes operated under contract to Transport for London on the London bus network and other scheduled local services.
3 Adjusted for general inflation to 2004/05 prices using the Retail Prices Index.

☎020-7944 3076

6.17 Taxis: vehicles, drivers and fares: England and Wales: 1994-2004/05

Thousands/Index

	1994	1995	1996	1997	1998	1999	2000	2001	2002	2003/04	2004/05
London											
Number of licensed taxis [1]	18.3	18.3	18.7	18.9	19.4	19.2	20.9	20.5	20.5	20.8	20.8
Number of licensed drivers	21.6	22.0	22.1	22.3	22.7	23.3	23.7	24.5	24.5	24.8	24.9
Taxi fare index 1995=100 [2]	96	100	105	109	113	118	125	140	150	..	..
Private Hire Vehicles	..	..	..	..	..	..	..	..	..	..	40.0
Outside London											
Number of licensed taxis [1]	32.9	..	..	36.5	..	42.1	..	42.6	..	45.9	47.1
Number of licensed drivers [3]	79.3	..	..	83.2	..	98.2		96.4 |	..	48.0	47.7
Taxi fare index 1995=100 [2]	97	100	107	109	116	122	..	130	..	..	..
Private Hire Vehicles	56.4	..	..	66.2	..	..	..	..	..	80.8	..

1 Data for London are from TfL. Outside London they are from surveys of district councils and unitary authorities.

2 Fare changes are not collected each year. Fare rises usually take place in the spring in London, or at various times of the year outside London, so these indices can only give a guide.

3 Dual licensing of drivers for both taxis and PHVs may have overstated the figures from 1994 to 2001.

☎020-7944 3076

The figures in this table are outside the scope of National Statistics

Source - licensing authorities

7 Roads and Traffic:

Notes and Definitions

Road traffic: 7.1, 7.2, 7.3 and 7.4

Special Note

Road traffic

1. Some minor revisions have been made to the road traffic data for 2002 and 2003 because of:

(i) some time delays in taking account of traffic on recently built major roads or re-classified roads; these new links take time to be surveyed by Ordnance Survey whose OSCAR roads database is used for the Road Traffic Survey;
(ii) the inclusion of some tunnels (under the river Mersey and Aldwych, London) from 2002 onwards; and
(iii) resolution of some anomalies.

2. Revisions referred to in (i) above will continue to be made in future on an annual basis to the previous two years' figures for major roads prior because of the time lags in incorporating changes to the road network and associated traffic count data.

3. Improvements have been made to the methodology used to estimate minor roads traffic in 2004. From 2000 to 2003, trends in traffic flow, derived from a relatively small number of Automatic Traffic Counters, were used to update 1999 base-year estimates. For the 2004 estimates, the trends were derived from a set of some 4,200 manual traffic counts instead.

Road lengths

4. New information has enabled better estimates of minor road lengths, presented in sections 2 and 4, to be made in 2004. Road lengths are calculated using Ordnance Survey's roads information data and:

(a) data supplied by local authorities has been used to improve the accuracy of the minor road data set.
(b) amendments have been made to the data for roads in Scotland where some private roads (predominantly those for which the Forestry Commission is responsible) were previously incorrectly recorded as public roads (2,775 kilometres).

5. These changes represent 4,730 kilometres of minor roads (1.4 per cent of the previously published figure for total minor road length).

Quality Review

6. The Department is undertaking a *Quality Review* of its road traffic estimates, under National Statistics guidelines. The report of this *Quality Review* will be published on the Department for Transport website later in 2005.

Methodological Note

7. A revised short paper (*How National Traffic Estimates are Made*) outlining the full methodology used by the Department to calculate traffic estimates is now available from: Department for Transport, Transport Statistics Roads 2 Division, Zone 2/14, Great Minster House, 76 Marsham Street, London SW1P 4DR.

Local Authority level statistics

8. Estimates of road traffic statistics at local authority level, together with corresponding figures for casualties in road accidents, are available on the DfT web site.

They are provided to enable the calculation and monitoring of road casualty rates for individual local authorities. These traffic figures are less robust than the regional and national totals and are not classed as National Statistics.

End of Special Note

The total activity of traffic on the road network in Great Britain is measured in vehicle kilometres. In table 7.2 road traffic is given by vehicle class and year. The traffic for each year relates to the public road network in place in that year. Thus growth over time is the product of any change in the network (kilometres) and the change in traffic flow (vehicles).
For each link of the major road network, the Department produces estimates of annual average daily flow (AADF) and annual average weekday flow (AAWF). They are produced using 12-hour manual data counts from a large number of sites and traffic profiles derived from automatic counters at about 190 sites. These estimates can be supplied individually or as a whole set via various media such as Email, CD-Rom, or floppy disc. The definitions for the vehicle types included in the traffic census are given below:

All motor vehicles: All vehicles except pedal cycles.

Cars and taxis: Includes: estate cars, all light vans with windows to the rear of the driver's seat, passenger vehicles of less than 3.5 tonnes gross vehicle weight with 15 or fewer seats, three-wheeled cars, motorised invalid carriages, and Sports Utility Vehicles. Cars towing caravans or trailers are counted as one vehicle. The definition used for traffic statistics therefore differs from that used in the vehicle licensing statistics shown in tables 9.1-9.8.

Goods vehicles:

Rigid with two axles: Includes all rigid vehicles over 3.5 tonnes gross vehicle weight with two axles. Includes tractors (without trailers), road rollers, box vans and similar large vans. A two axle motor tractive unit without trailer is also included.

Rigid with three axles: Includes all non-articulated goods vehicles with three axles irrespective of the position of the axles. Excludes two axle rigid vehicles towing a single axle caravan or trailer. Three axle motor tractive units without a trailer are also included.

Rigid with four or more axles: Includes all non-articulated goods vehicles with four axles, regardless of the position of the axles. Excludes two or three axle rigid vehicles towing a caravan or trailer.

Articulated goods vehicles: When a goods vehicle is travelling with one or more axles raised from the road (sleeping axles or hobos) then the vehicle is classified into the class of the number of axles on the road, and not to the class of the total number of axles. Articulated goods vehicles with 3 and 4 axles are merged into one category, as they are not differentiated during manual traffic counts.

Articulated with three axles (or with trailer): Includes all articulated vehicles with three axles. The motor tractive unit will have two axles and the trailer one. Also included in this class are two axle rigid goods vehicles towing a single axle caravan or trailer.

Articulated with four axles (or with trailer): Includes all articulated vehicles with a total of four axles regardless of the position of the axles, i.e. two on the tractive unit with two on the trailer, or three on the tractive unit with one on the trailer. Also includes two axle rigid goods vehicles towing two axle close coupled or drawbar trailers.

Articulated with five or more axles (or with trailer): This includes all articulated vehicles with a total of five axles regardless of the position of the axles. Also includes rigid vehicles drawing close coupled or drawbar trailers where the total axle number equals five and articulated vehicles where the motor tractive unit has more than one trailer and the total axle number equals five.

Articulated with six or more axles (or with trailer): This includes all articulated vehicles with a total of six or more axles regardless of the position of the axles. Also includes rigid vehicles drawing close coupled or drawbar trailers where the total axle number equals six or more and articulated vehicles where the motor tractive unit has more than one trailer and the total axle number equals six or more.

Larger buses and coaches: Includes all public service vehicles and works buses over 3.5 tonnes gross vehicle weight.

Light vans: Includes all goods vehicles up to 3.5 tonnes gross vehicle weight. This includes all car delivery vans and those of the next larger carrying capacity such as transit vans. Included here are small pickup vans, three-wheeled goods vehicles, milk floats, ambulances and pedestrian controlled motor vehicles. Many of this group are delivery vans of one type or another.

Motor cycles etc: Includes motor cycles, scooters and mopeds and all motor cycle or scooter combinations.

Pedal cycles: Includes all non-motorised cycles.

Forecasts of Road Traffic: 7.5

The Government reviewed and updated its *10 Year Plan* in *The Future of Transport White Paper* published in July 2004. The forecasts in table 7.5 are derived from the supporting modelling and analytical work that informed the white paper. The forecasts show traffic growth in England, disaggregated by vehicle type. The figures in the table are based to 2000 = 100. Further details of the Department's National Transport Model can be found on the DfT web site.

Road network: 7.6, 7.8 and 7.9

The lengths of trunk roads, including motorways, in England are obtained from the Highways Agency and local authorities and for Scotland and Wales from the from the Scottish Executive and the National Assembly for Wales respectively. Lengths for other major non-trunk roads, (principal 'A' roads and principal motorways) are obtained from the major roads database maintained by the Department for Transport using information from the Government Offices, local authorities and Ordnance Survey. Road length information for minor B, C and unclassified roads are obtained from Ordnance Survey roads data, OSCAR Asset Manager. All figures given in tables 7.8 and 7.9

are road lengths at 1 April of each year. The road definitions are as follows:

Major roads: Include motorways and all class 'A' roads. These roads usually have high traffic flows and are often the main arteries to major destinations.

Motorways (built under the enabling legislation of the *Special Roads Act 1949,* now consolidated in the *Highways Acts of 1959 and 1980*): Are major roads of regional and urban strategic importance, often used for long distance travel. They are usually three or more lanes in each direction and generally have the maximum speed limit of 70mph.

'A' Roads: Can be **trunk** or **principal** roads. These are often described as the 'main' roads and tend to have heavy traffic flows though not as high as motorways.

Trunk roads (designated by the Trunk roads Acts 1936 and 1946): Major roads comprising the national network of through routes. The network contains both motorways (which legally are special roads reserved for certain classes of traffic), and all-purpose roads (which are open to all classes of traffic). All-purpose trunk roads are class 'A' roads as are most principal roads, see below. It is very common for inter-urban stretches of a given road to be classed as an all purpose trunk road, with one or more urban stretches of the same (with the same road number) classified as principal.
In England the trunk road highway authority is the Secretary of State for Transport, though certain responsibilities are delegated to the Highways Agency. The trunk road highway authority in Scotland is the Scottish Executive, and the highways authority in Wales is the National Assembly for Wales.

Non-trunk roads: Roads for which local authorities are highway authorities. The Secretary of State, the Scottish Executive, and the National Assembly for Wales the have power to classify non-trunk roads in agreement with the local highway authority. Non-trunk roads are therefore either classified or unclassified, the former being of two types, principal and non-principal. The classified principal roads are class 'A' roads, except for a few local authority motorways, and are of regional and urban strategic importance. The non-principal roads are those which distribute traffic to urban and regional localities. The non-principal roads are sub-divided into B and C classes. Unclassified roads are those in the least important categories, i.e. local distributor and access roads.

Minor Roads: These are 'B' and 'C' classified roads and unclassified roads (all of which are maintained by the local authorities), as referred to above. Class III (later 'C') roads were created in April 1946. Previously these roads were 'unclassified'. 'B' Roads in urban areas can have relatively high traffic flows, but are not regarded as being as significant as 'A' roads. They are useful distributor roads often between towns or villages. 'B' Roads in rural areas often have markedly low traffic flows compared with their 'A' road counterparts. 'C' Roads are regarded as of lesser importance than either 'B' or 'A' roads, and generally have only one carriageway of two lanes and carry less traffic. They can have low traffic flows in rural areas. Unclassified roads include residential roads both in urban and rural situations and rural lanes, the latter again normally having very low traffic flows. Most unclassified roads will have only two lanes, and in rural areas may only have one lane with "passing bays" at intervals to allow for two-way traffic flow.

Urban roads: Are major and minor roads within an urban area with a population of 10,000 or more. The definition is based on the 2001 ODPM definition of Urban Settlements. The definition for 'urban settlement' is in *Urban and rural area definitions* a user guide which can be found on the ODPM web site.

Rural roads: Are major and minor roads outside urban areas (these urban areas have a population of more than 10,000 people).

Private Roads: Are included in the major roads as these private roads (usually toll roads, tunnels or bridges) are accessible to the general public, whereas private minor roads, not usually being accessible to the general public, are not included.

Vehicle speeds: 7.10 and 7.11

The types of vehicle analysed in the urban and non-urban survey are motor cycles, cars, cars towing, LGVs, buses/coaches, rigid 2 axle HGVs, rigid 3 and rigid 4 axle HGVs, 4 axle articulated HGVs and 5 or more axle articulated HGVs. The automatic counters identify rigid 2 axle lorries but cannot distinguish between vehicles weighing less than 7.5 tonnes gross and those weighing more. The weight of this type of vehicle determines its speed limit on non-urban roads. Consequently it is impossible to tell how many rigid 2 axle HGVs are speeding. (For further details of speed limits for different types of vehicle on different classes of non-built up road, see Annex B of *Vehicle Speeds* bulletin, produced by Transport Statistics DfT).

Non-urban roads (Table 7.10): The speeds indicated are average traffic speeds from 27 motorway sites, 7 dual carriageway sites and 26 single carriageway sites.

Urban roads (Table 7.11): Speed measurements were taken from 26 sites with speed limits of 30 mph and from 10 sites with speed limits of 40 mph.

Regional expenditure on roads: 7.13

Whereas the figures in Table 1.15 relate to net expenditure, those in Table 7.13 relate to gross expenditure. For this reason, and because of certain differences in coverage (in particular the treatment of professional and technical services), England totals differ from those in Table 1.16.

The local roads figure for new construction/ improvement plus structural maintenance includes expenditure on technical surveys. These figures include both expenditure recorded on local authority capital expenditure returns and also structural maintenance recorded on the revenue returns. Structural maintenance includes reconstruction, overlay, resurfacing, patching, surface dressing, drainage, footways, bridges, earthworks and fences. Routine maintenance includes verge maintenance, sweeping, gullies, signals, signs and marking. Winter maintenance includes salting, snow clearance and the maintenance and operation of ice detection equipment.

Figures for motorways and trunk roads are not directly comparable with previously published data for years earlier than 2001/02, as the Highways Agency is now using a resource accounting system. The introduction of the new accounting systems has led to changes in categorisation and slight adjustments to the way some figures are calculated.

Road construction tender price index: 7.14

The overall index provides a measure of the change in tender prices for road construction in Great Britain. Since the end of June 1992, it has been based on bills of quantities for the winning tenders for new contracts with a works cost of £1 million or more. (Before that date the cut off was £250,000.) The index includes all HA national road - and local authority principal road - newbuild projects, and maintenance projects of appropriate value. The published annual figures are the derived from a quarterly series produced by the Construction Market Intelligence Division of the Department of Trade and Industry.

For each project a price relative is produced by re-pricing, using 1990 prices, after making an adjustment for preliminary and balancing items, the quantifiable items in the bill of quantities. Then the total adjusted cost of the quantifiable items at current prices is divided by their total adjusted cost at 1990 prices, over all contracts, in order to calculate the project price relative. A value-weighted index calculated by combining the price relatives of a single quarter's contracts, often relatively few in number, would be over-sensitive to tender prices of individual large schemes. For this reason a smoothed quarterly series is produced based on adjustment factors for type of work, location and contract size.

Road Tax Revenue: 7.15

Information on fuel tax revenues is collected by Customs and Excise. Fuel tax returns are initially allocated only from total petrol and diesel fuel sales. The allocation to different vehicle types is complicated, and relies on supplementary information on vehicle stocks fitted with petrol and diesel engines, and average annual vehicle mileages from a number of other surveys. Fuel tax allocations are therefore subject to considerable sampling and estimation error. Estimates are rounded to the nearest £5 million. The estimates of fuel duty from buses and coaches include all duty paid, although some is rebated to local operators.
Information on vehicle excise duty is collected by the Driver and Vehicle Licensing Agency (DVLA) and reported in financial returns and the motor tax account. These figures do not include revenues from trade plates but do include revenue from duties that are subsequently refunded. Vehicle numbers are averages based on quarterly analyses and therefore differ from the end year estimates given in section three.

Latest estimates on revenue loss from vehicle excise duty evasion is available from a DfT report – 'Vehicle Excise Duty Evasion 2004' or at www.dft.gov.uk/transtat

New road construction and improvements: 7.16

Start figures from 1996/97 onwards include schemes under Design, Build Finance and Operate (DBFO) contracts. These contracts, which are a part of the Private Finance Initiative, involve the private sector in the provision and improvement of sections of trunk road, or in a few cases of motorway, and in the management of both their own works and contiguous stretches of road over a lengthy period. The private sector provides the funding and is reimbursed by

Government through payments linked to usage and performance.

In 1997/98 there were no new starts for any national schemes (including PFI schemes see above) that involved the construction of additional lane kilometres. This reflected policy decisions taken by the previous and present governments. There were no completions in 2001/02.

Defects index of road condition: 7.17

The defects index is a composite measure of road condition produced by combining a number of carriageway physical defects visible at the surface; a higher value of the defects index representing worse condition. The index is derived by adding together individual defects weighted by their relative costs of repair at constant (1986/87) prices. For each road class the index is set at 100 for the base year (1977). The base year is simply the first for which results are available and does not represent a 'standard' or 'target'. As the index values are estimates based on a sample survey they are subject to uncertainty and have therefore been shown as a best estimate, which is the mid-point of a 90 per cent confidence interval i.e. a range which has a 9 in 10 chance of including the true value of the index. Motorways are excluded from the survey because of the expensive traffic control measures that would be required to carry out visual surveying of the carriageways on these roads.

Following a change in survey methodology, comparable results for all-purpose trunk roads, and hence all local roads, are not available from 2003.

Contribution of defects to defects index: 7.18

The defects index (see 7.17 above for description) is derived from a combination of extent, severity and cost of treatment for the defects listed below. The figure shows their estimated contributions to the road condition defects index.

Wheel-track Rutting: Wheel-track rutting does not necessarily indicate structural damage but it is undesirable because the ruts can hold water which can cause skidding, especially in Winter when the roads can become icy. The survey records the average depth of deformation in the near side wheel-track in millimetres.

Wheel-track Cracking: Most vehicles follow a similar path on a road, resulting in the formation of identifiable wheel-tracks. The significance of the wheel-tracks is that damage to the road structure, as well as the surface, is most serious there. In particular, cracking in the area of the wheel-tracks may indicate structural damage, especially if associated with the presence of a rut along the wheel-track. The survey records the average length of cracking present, per 100 metres of road and is weighted by an assessment of it severity.

Whole-carriageway Major Deterioration: The survey records the percentage of the carriageway area affected by cracking, coarse crazing or loss of aggregate, deformation or defective patches.

Whole-carriageway Minor Deterioration: The survey records the number of 20 metre lengths per 100 metres of road where fine crazing, loss of chippings from surface dressing or excess bitumen on the pavement surface show the need for a maintenance treatment.

Edge Deterioration: The survey records the length of carriageway edge with disintegration along the edge, erosion of verges or failed patching, per 100 metres of edge.

Other: The survey also records patching (the percentage of carriageway consisting of patches or reinstatements) and potholes (including broken, sunken or upstanding manhole covers and isolated depressions more than 25mm deep).

Footways condition: 7.19

The two measures of footway defects recorded by the survey (see 7.17 above for description) are shown below. Trends in these two measures are shown in the figures. As the defects values are estimates based on a sample survey they are subject to uncertainty and have therefore been shown as a best estimate, which is the mid-point of a 90 per cent confidence interval i.e. a range which has a 9 in 10 chance of including the true value of the index.

Footway Deterioration: The percentage of footway length subject to deterioration.

Footway Trips: The average number of spot conditions in every 100 metres, which constitute a specific danger to pedestrians. Where a surveyed site has a footway on both sides of the carriageway, the average condition of the two footways is used in the calculation of the national average.

Verges and kerbs affected by deterioration: 7.20

Trends in the percentage of verge area which is disintegrating or deformed, and the percentage of kerb length which needs replacing or resetting, are shown in the figures. As the defects values are estimates based on a sample survey they are subject to uncertainty and have therefore been shown as a best estimate, which is the mid-point of a 90 per cent confidence interval i.e. a range which has a 9 in 10 chance of including the true value of the index.

7.1 Road traffic by type of vehicle: 1938-2004

For greater detail for the years 1994-2004 see Table 7.2

Billion vehicle kilometres

Year	Cars and taxis	Motor cycles etc	Larger buses & coaches	Light vans [1]	Goods vehicles [2]	All motor vehicles	Pedal cycles
1938	27.8	3.1	3.1	12.7		46.7	27.5
1949	20.3	3.1	4.1	6.5	12.5	46.5	23.6
1950	25.6	4.4	4.1	7.8	11.2	53.1	19.9
1951	29.3	5.6	4.2	8.2	11.7	58.9	20.8
1952	30.6	6.0	4.2	8.7	11.3	60.8	22.9
1953	33.4	6.7	4.2	9.1	11.5	64.9	20.8
1954	37.2	6.9	4.2	9.3	12.2	69.7	18.8
1955	42.3	7.5	4.2	9.8	13.2	77.0	18.2
1956	46.2	7.4	4.2	10.0	13.0	80.8	16.2
1957	45.2	8.3	4.0	10.3	12.5	80.3	16.1
1958	55.4	8.4	3.9	11.9	13.5	93.0	14.1
1959	62.2	9.8	4.0	13.7	14.6	104.2	13.6
1960	68.0	10.0	3.9	15.0	15.3	112.3	12.0
1961	76.9	9.7	4.0	16.4	15.5	122.4	10.9
1962	83.7	8.7	4.0	16.6	15.4	128.3	9.3
1963	91.4	7.6	4.0	17.6	15.7	136.3	8.2
1964	105.7	7.5	4.0	17.7	17.4	152.3	8.0
1965	115.8	6.7	3.9	19.0	17.3	162.7	7.0
1966	126.5	6.0	3.9	19.0	17.5	172.9	6.3
1967	135.1	5.2	3.8	18.7	17.2	180.0	5.6
1968	142.7	4.7	3.8	18.9	17.6	187.7	5.0
1969	147.9	4.2	3.8	19.3	17.4	192.5	4.6
1970	155.0	4.0	3.6	20.3	17.6	200.5	4.4
1971	165.1	3.9	3.6	21.3	18.1	212.0	4.3
1972	174.7	3.7	3.6	22.2	18.4	222.5	3.9
1973	184.0	3.9	3.5	23.3	19.3	234.0	3.7
1974	180.0	4.2	3.3	23.6	18.6	229.7	3.8
1975	181.6	5.1	3.2	23.5	18.3	231.7	4.4
1976	190.4	6.3	3.3	24.2	19.2	243.5	5.0
1977	194.1	6.2	3.2	24.5	18.8	246.8	6.1
1978	202.4	6.1	3.3	25.2	19.5	256.5	5.1
1979	201.5	6.4	3.3	25.1	19.6	255.9	4.6
1980	215.0	7.7	3.5	26.1	19.7	271.9	5.1
1981	219.5	8.9	3.5	26.2	18.9	276.9	5.4
1982	227.3	9.2	3.5	26.0	18.4	284.5	6.4
1983	231.2	8.3	3.7	26.1	18.8	288.1	6.4
1984	244.0	8.1	3.9	27.5	19.6	303.1	6.4
1985	250.5	7.4	3.7	28.6	19.6	309.7	6.1
1986	264.4	7.1	3.7	30.0	20.1	325.3	5.5
1987	284.6	6.7	4.1	32.7	22.3	350.5	5.7
1988	305.4	6.0	4.3	36.2	23.8	375.7	5.2
1989	331.3	5.9	4.5	39.7	25.5	406.9	5.2
1990	335.9	5.6	4.6	39.9	24.9	410.8	5.3
1991	335.2	5.4	4.8	41.7	24.5	411.6	5.2
1992	338.0	4.5	4.6	41.2	23.8	412.1	4.7
1993 [3]	338.1	3.8	4.6	41.6	24.3	412.3	4.0
1994	345.0	3.8	4.6	43.3	24.8	421.5	4.0
1995	351.1	3.7	4.9	44.5	25.4	429.7	4.1
1996	359.9	3.8	5.0	46.2	26.2	441.1	4.1
1997	365.8	4.0	5.2	48.6	26.9	450.3	4.1
1998	370.6	4.1	5.2	50.8	27.7	458.5	4.0
1999	377.4	4.5	5.3	51.6	28.1	467.0	4.1
2000	376.8	4.6	5.2	52.3	28.2	467.1	4.2
2001	382.8	4.8	5.2	53.7	28.1	474.4	4.2
2002 [4]	392.9	5.1	5.2	55.0	28.3	486.5	4.4
2003 [4]	393.1	5.6	5.4	57.9	28.5	490.4	4.5
2004	398.1	5.2	5.2	60.8	29.4	498.6	3.9

1 Not exceeding 3,500 kgs gross vehicle weight.

2 Over 3,500 kgs gross vehicle weight.

3 There were some minor revisions, published in July 2004, to the traffic estimates for 1993 to 2002. Data for 1993 onwards are not directly comparable with the figures for 1992 and earlier.

4 Revisions have been made to the 2002 and 2003 figures for major roads, because of time lags in incorporating changes to the road network and associated traffic count data - See the 'Special Note' on Tables 7.1-7.4 in the Notes and Definitions of Section 7.

☎020-7944 3095

7.2 Road Traffic: by type of vehicle: 1994-2004[1]

Billion vehicle kilometres

	1994	1995	1996	1997	1998	1999	2000[2]	2001[3]	2002[4]	2003[4]	2004
Cars and taxis	345.0	351.1	359.9	365.8	370.6	377.4	376.8	382.8	392.9	393.1	398.1
Motor cycles etc	3.8	3.7	3.8	4.0	4.1	4.5	4.6	4.8	5.1	5.6	5.2
Larger buses and coaches	4.6	4.9	5.0	5.2	5.2	5.3	5.2	5.2	5.2	5.4	5.2
Light vans[5]	43.3	44.5	46.2	48.6	50.8	51.6	52.3	53.7	55.0	57.9	60.8
Goods vehicles[6]											
2 axles rigid	10.8	10.7	10.9	11.0	11.1	11.6	11.7	11.5	11.6	11.7	11.7
3 axles rigid	1.4	1.6	1.6	1.6	1.9	1.7	1.7	1.8	1.8	1.8	1.9
4 or more axles rigid	1.5	1.5	1.5	1.5	1.6	1.5	1.5	1.5	1.5	1.6	1.6
3 and 4 axles artic	3.6	3.3	3.3	3.2	3.0	3.0	2.7	2.5	2.3	2.2	2.2
5 axles artic	5.8	6.4	6.6	7.1	7.3	7.2	6.7	6.4	6.4	6.2	6.5
6 or more axles artic	1.8	2.0	2.3	2.5	2.9	3.3	4.1	4.5	4.8	5.0	5.4
All	24.8	25.4	26.2	26.9	27.7	28.1	28.2	28.1	28.3	28.5	29.4
All motor vehicles	421.5	429.7	441.1	450.3	458.5	467.0	467.1	474.4	486.5	490.4	498.6
Pedal cycles	4.0	4.1	4.1	4.1	4.0	4.1	4.2	4.2	4.4	4.5	3.9

1 There were some minor revisions, published in July 2004, to the traffic estimates for 1993 to 2002. ☎020-7944 3095
2 The decline in the use of cars and taxis in 2000 was due to the fuel dispute.
3 Figures affected by the impact of Foot and Mouth disease during 2001.
4 Revisions have been made to the 2002 and 2003 figures for major roads, because of time lags in incorporating changes to the road network and associated traffic count data - See the 'Special Note' on Tables 7.1-7.4 in the Notes and Definitions of Section 7.
5 Not exceeding 3,500 kgs gross vehicle weight.
6 Over 3,500 kgs gross vehicle weight.

7.3 Motor vehicle traffic: by road class: 1994-2004[1]

Billion vehicle kilometres

	1994	1995	1996	1997	1998	1999	2000[2]	2001[3]	2002[4]	2003[4]	2004
Motorways	70.7	73.9	78.3	82.1	85.7	87.8	88.4	90.8	92.6	93.0	96.6
Rural 'A' roads:[5]											
Trunk	56.5	57.9	60.4	62.5	63.3	64.7	64.2	65.9[7]	64.6	61.5	59.7
Principal	60.0	61.6	63.1	64.1	65.4	66.0	65.8	67.4[7]	71.8	77.7	81.6
All rural 'A' roads	116.5	119.5	123.5	126.6	128.7	130.7	130.0	133.3	136.4	139.3	141.3
Urban 'A' roads:[6]											
Trunk	13.8	13.8	13.9	13.8	13.8	14.0	14.0	7.6[7]	7.4	6.7	6.0
Principal	64.7	66.2	67.0	67.1	67.5	67.9	67.7	74.2[7]	74.8	75.1	76.8
All urban 'A' roads	78.5	80.1	80.9	80.9	81.3	81.9	81.7	81.8	82.2	81.7	82.8
All Major roads	265.8	273.5	282.7	289.6	295.7	300.4	300.0	305.9	311.2	314.0	320.7
Minor roads:											
Minor rural roads	57.6	57.8	58.9	60.0	60.4	61.3	61.5	61.6	64.5	64.4	65.9
Minor urban roads	98.1	98.5	99.6	100.7	102.4	105.3	105.5	106.9	110.8	111.9	112.0
All minor roads	155.7	156.2	158.5	160.7	162.8	166.6	167.0	168.5	175.3	176.4	177.9
All roads	421.5	429.7	441.1	450.3	458.5	467.0	467.1	474.4	486.5	490.4	498.6

1 There were some minor revisions, published in July 2004, to the traffic estimates for 1993 to 2002. ☎020-7944 3095
2 The decline in the use of cars and taxis in 2000 was due to the fuel dispute.
3 Figures affected by the impact of Foot and Mouth disease during 2001.
4. Revisions have been made to the 2002 and 2003 figures for major roads, because of time lags in incorporating changes to the road network and associated traffic count data - See the 'Special Note' on Tables 7.1-7.4 in the Notes and Definitions of Section 7.
5 Rural roads: Major and minor roads, from 1993 onwards, are defined as being outside an urban area.
6 Urban roads: Major and minor roads, from 1993 onwards, are defined as within an urban area with a population of 10,000 or more. These are based on the 2001 urban settlements. The definition for 'urban settlement' is in *Urban and rural area definitions: a user guide* which can be found on the ODPM web site at: http://www.odpm.gov.uk/stellent/groups/odpm_planning/documents/page/odpm_plan_609188.hcsp
7 Figures for trunk and principal 'A' roads in England, from 2001 onwards, are affected by the detrunking programme.

7.4 Road traffic: by type of vehicle and class of road: 2004

Billion vehicle kilometres

	Cars and taxis	Motor cycles etc.	Larger buses and coaches	Light vans [1]	Goods vehicles [2]: Rigid by number of axles: 2	3	4 or more	Articulated by number of axles: 3 + 4	5	6 or more	All Goods vehicles	All motor vehicles	Pedal cycles
Motorways:	72.6	0.39	0.46	11.00	3.37	0.48	0.42	1.07	3.96	2.90	12.2	96.6	.
Rural 'A' roads: [3]													
Trunk [4]	46.1	0.43	0.30	6.98	1.92	0.33	0.31	0.48	1.43	1.36	5.8	59.7	0.02
Principal [4]	66.1	0.87	0.58	9.51	2.11	0.39	0.40	0.32	0.65	0.62	4.5	81.6	0.12
All rural 'A' roads:	112.3	1.30	0.88	16.49	4.03	0.72	0.71	0.80	2.08	1.97	10.3	141.3	0.13
Urban 'A' roads: [5]													
Trunk [4]	4.9	0.04	0.03	0.67	0.17	0.03	0.03	0.03	0.08	0.08	0.4	6.0	0.01
Principal [4]	63.7	0.96	1.13	8.31	1.59	0.23	0.24	0.14	0.25	0.24	2.7	76.8	0.55
All urban 'A' roads:	68.6	1.00	1.16	8.98	1.76	0.26	0.26	0.18	0.33	0.32	3.1	82.8	0.56
Minor roads:													
Minor rural roads	52.2	0.77	0.70	10.45	1.18	0.27	0.16	0.07	0.07	0.11	1.9	65.9	0.79
Minor urban roads	92.5	1.70	2.03	13.88	1.42	0.20	0.08	0.05	0.04	0.09	1.9	112.0	2.39
All minor roads:	144.7	2.47	2.73	24.33	2.59	0.47	0.24	0.12	0.11	0.20	3.7	177.9	3.17
All roads:	398.1	5.16	5.23	60.80	11.75	1.92	1.64	2.16	6.48	5.40	29.4	498.6	3.86

1 Not exceeding 3.5 tonnes gross vehicle weight.

☎020-7944 3095

2 Over 3.5 tonnes gross vehicle weight.

3 Rural roads: Major and minor roads, from 1993 onwards, are defined as being outside an urban area.

4 Figures for trunk and principal 'A' roads in England, from 2001 onwards, are affected by the detrunking programme.

5 Urban roads: Major and minor roads, from 1993 onwards, are defined as within an urban area with a population of 10,000 or more. These are based on the 2001 urban settlements. The definition for 'urban settlement' is in *Urban and rural area definitions* : a user guide which can be found on the ODPM web site at: http://www.odpm.gov.uk/stellent/groups/odpm_planning/documents/page/odpm_plan_609188.hcsp

NB: Versions of this table for the years 1993 - 2003 are available from the DfT website at: http://www.dft.gov.uk/transtat/roadtraff

7.5 Forecasts of road traffic in England and vehicles in Great Britain: 2010

Index: 2000 = 100 [1]

Vehicle kilometres: England:	
Cars and taxis	*122-129*
Goods vehicles [2]	*110-111*
Light goods vehicles	*139-140*
Buses and coaches	*99*
All motor traffic (except two wheelers)	*123-129*
Car ownership: Great Britain:	
Cars per person	*115*
Number of cars	*118*

1 The range reflects key uncertainties in the modelling relating to forecasts of factors that influence travel, such as how people's choices are influenced by income growth.

2 Over 3.5 tonnes gross vehicle weight.

☎020-7944 6197

The figures in this table are outside of the scope of National Statistics

Source - Integrated Transport, Economics and Appraisal Division, DfT

7.6 Roads lengths: Great Britain: 1909- 2004

For greater detail for the years 1994-2004 see Table 7.8 or 7.9.

Kilometres

							ow: motorways		
Year	Trunk	Class 1 or principal	Class 2 or B	Class 3 or C	Unclassified	All	Trunk	Principal	Total
1909	.	..	..	.	..	282,380	.	.	.
1914	.	..	..	.	..	284,843	.	.	.
1923	.	37,383	23,720	.	224,265	285,369	.	.	.
1928	.	40,457	25,244	.	221,996	287,697	.	.	.
1933	.	42,784	26,786	.	215,842	285,412	.	.	.
1938	4,953	39,276	27,418	.	217,799	289,446	.	.	.
1943	7,176	37,305	28,532	.	..	..	.	.	.
1947	13,181	31,410	28,498	77,768	143,735	294,592	.	.	.
1951	13,275	31,435	28,481	78,346	145,929	297,466	.	.	.
1952	13,274	31,484	28,471	78,340	147,002	298,570	.	.	.
1953	13,284	31,464	28,485	78,364	148,161	299,758	.	.	.
1954	13,309	31,519	28,469	78,409	149,305	301,012	.	.	.
1955	13,309	31,553	28,479	78,505	150,863	302,710	.	.	.
1956	13,309	31,656	28,398	78,565	152,297	304,226	.	.	.
1957	13,311	31,762	28,333	78,615	153,998	306,018	.	.	.
1958	13,372	31,714	28,329	78,621	155,583	307,620	.	.	.
1959	13,401	31,744	28,329	78,653	158,573	310,700	13	.	13
1960	13,580	31,765	28,334	78,718	160,106	312,502	153	.	153
1961	13,628	31,780	28,357	78,740	161,667	314,171	209	10	219
1962	13,654	31,797	28,349	78,785	163,064	315,649	233	10	243
1963	13,745	31,860	28,337	78,829	166,611	319,382	312	10	322
1964	13,885	31,902	28,368	78,837	168,463	321,455	470	10	480
1965	13,993	31,971	28,392	78,855	170,357	323,568	557	10	566
1966	14,030	32,053	28,376	78,858	171,865	325,182	616	13	629
1967	14,159	32,543	..	279,479 [1]	..	326,180	747	11	761 [2]
1968	14,354	32,536	..	281,288 [1]	..	328,178	869	11	884 [2]
1969	14,439	32,533	107,254 [3]	..	166,089	320,315	946	18	964
1970	14,463	32,584	107,285 [3]	..	168,152	322,484	1,022	35	1,057
1971	14,668	32,737	107,388 [3]	..	169,872	324,665	1,235	35	1,270
1972	15,060	32,825	107,404 [3]	..	172,428	327,717	1,609	60	1,669
1973	15,011	32,859	27,409	79,791	172,060	327,131	1,660	70	1,730
1974	15,119	32,942	27,500	80,062	173,443	329,036	1,776	92	1,869
1975	15,240	33,088	27,606	80,156	173,949	330,039	1,881	94	1,975
1976	15,502	33,225	27,812	80,512	175,794	332,846	2,062	93	2,155
1977	15,223	33,598	27,875	80,693	177,874	335,263	2,131	106	2,237
1978	14,820	34,199	27,874	80,545	178,826	336,264	2,287	107	2,394
1979	14,805	34,430	27,866	80,599	180,278	337,978	2,340	116	2,455
1980	14,949	34,187	28,151	80,736	181,610	339,633	2,445	111	2,556
1981	14,915	34,656	28,232	80,398	184,119	342,320	2,524	123	2,647
1982	14,901	34,700	28,451	80,358	185,531	343,942	2,561	131	2,692
1983	14,972	34,819	28,537	80,327	187,121	345,776	2,609	132	2,741
1984	15,057	34,862	29,036	80,123	188,511	347,589	2,678	108	2,786
1985	15,014	34,908	29,042	80,460	189,276	348,699	2,705	108	2,813
1986	15,359	34,969	29,121	80,360	191,267	351,076	2,820	101	2,920
1987	15,394	35,089	29,766	80,004	192,442	352,695	2,874	101	2,975
1988	15,472	35,041	29,681	80,165	193,957	354,315	2,891	102	2,992
1989	15,618	35,131	29,706	80,542	195,606	356,602	2,903	92	2,995
1990	15,666	35,226	29,838	80,716	196,588	358,034	2,993	77	3,070
1991	15,356	35,649	30,106	81,073	197,783	359,966	3,033	68	3,102
1992	15,358	35,712	30,227	81,334	199,679	362,310	3,063	71	3,133
1993 [4]	14,819	34,514	30,229	83,816	221,461	384,839	3,139	72	3,211
1994	14,815	34,574	30,225	83,931	222,012	385,557	3,170	72	3,242
1995	14,840	34,732	30,221	84,046	222,562	386,401	3,197	72	3,269
1996	14,967	34,522	30,217	84,162	223,115	386,983	3,253	45	3,298
1997	15,131	34,603	30,213	84,277	223,668	387,893	3,333	45	3,378
1998	15,058	34,758	30,209	84,392	224,225	388,641	3,376	44	3,421
1999	15,102	34,916	30,205	84,509	224,783	389,515	3,404	45	3,449
2000	15,123	34,951	30,200	84,624	225,339	390,237	3,422	45	3,467
2001	14,800 [5]	35,330 [5]	30,196	84,742	225,901	390,969	3,431	45	3,476
2002	14,112	36,040	30,192	84,858	226,462	391,663	3,433	45	3,478
2003	13,047	37,083	30,188	84,976	227,048	392,342	3,432	46	3,478
2004	12,625	37,567	30,178 [6]	84,223 [6]	223,082 [6]	387,674 [6]	3,478	46	3,523

1 Includes 'B' and unclassified roads.

☎020-7944 3095

2 Includes other motorways ie those not at the time allocated to either the Department for Transport or local authorities.

3 Includes 'C' roads.

4 A number of minor revisions have been made to the lengths of major roads from 1993 onwards.

5 Figures for trunk and principal 'A' roads in England, from 2001 onwards, are affected by the detrunking programme.

6 Revisions have been made to the minor road length figures for 2004; see Special Note on Tables 7.1-7.4 . in the Notes and Definitions of Section 7.

7.7 Motorway and Trunk Road network of England, Scotland and Wales: 2005

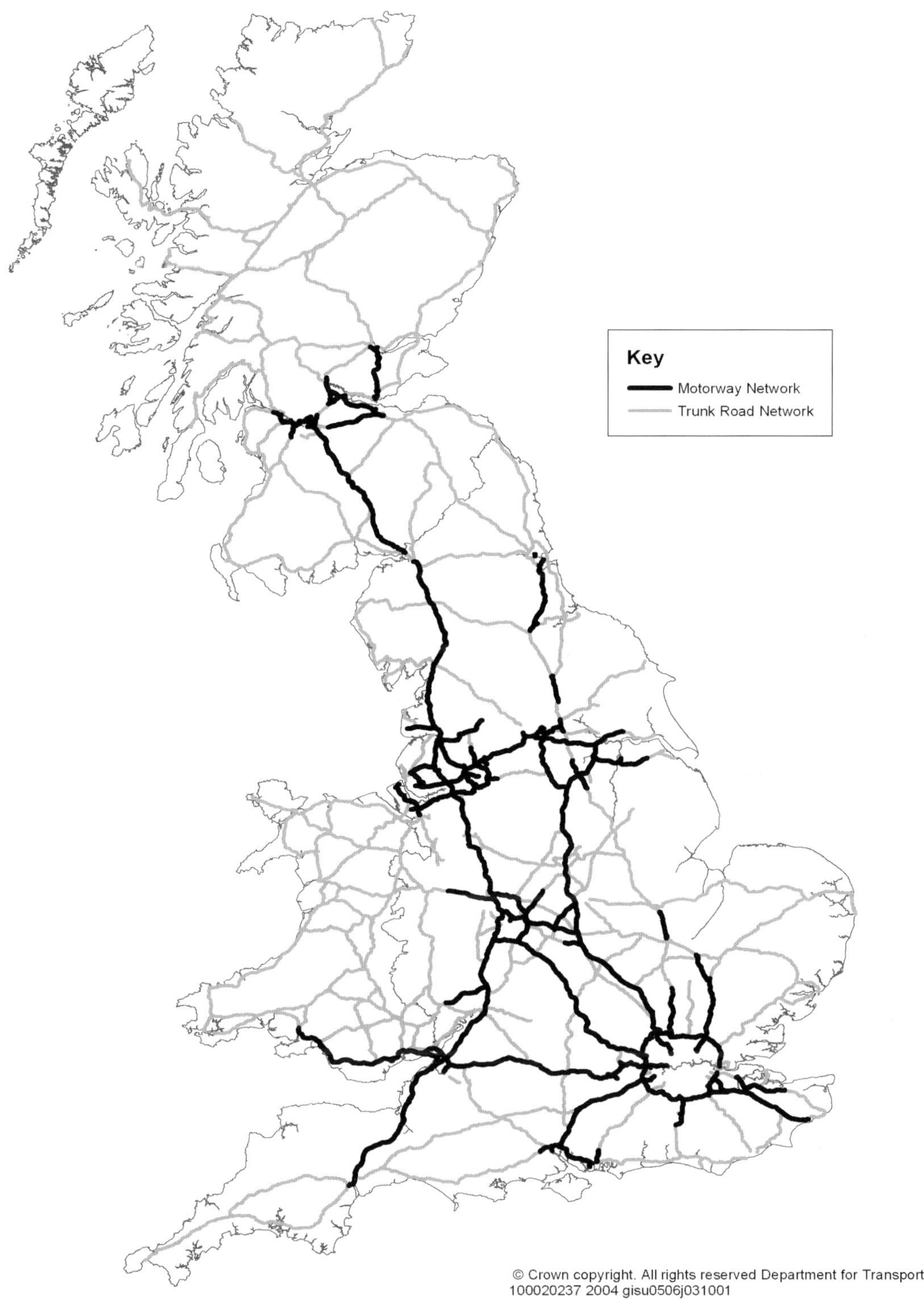

7.8 Public road length: by road type: 1994-2004 [1]

Kilometres

	1994	1995	1996	1997	1998	1999	2000	2001	2002	2003	2004
Trunk motorway	3,170	3,197	3,253	3,333	3,376	3,404	3,422	3,431	3,433	3,432	3,478
Principal motorway	72	72	45	45	44	45	45	45	45	46	46
Rural 'A' roads: [2]											
Trunk [3]	10,500	10,510	10,598	10,690	10,585	10,611	10,627	10,607	9,973	9,027	8,641
Principal [3]	24,609	24,759	24,592	24,636	24,783	24,852	24,866	24,915	25,559	26,498	26,889
All rural 'A' roads:	35,109	35,269	35,190	35,326	35,369	35,463	35,493	35,522	35,532	35,525	35,530
Urban 'A' roads: [4]											
Trunk [3]	1,146	1,133	1,117	1,108	1,096	1,087	1,074	762	705	587	506
Principal [3]	9,893	9,902	9,885	9,923	9,931	10,019	10,040	10,370	10,436	10,539	10,632
All urban 'A' roads:	11,039	11,035	11,002	11,031	11,027	11,106	11,114	11,132	11,141	11,127	11,138
Minor rural roads: [5]											
B roads	24,618	24,610	24,603	24,594	24,586	24,579	24,570	24,562	24,554	24,547	24,640
C roads	73,031	73,124	73,218	73,312	73,405	73,500	73,593	73,688	73,783	73,878	73,363
Unclassified	110,265	110,481	110,698	110,915	111,132	111,350	111,568	111,787	112,006	112,231	109,561
All minor rural roads	207,914	208,215	208,518	208,820	209,123	209,429	209,731	210,037	210,343	210,656	207,565
Minor urban roads: [5]											
B roads	5,608	5,611	5,615	5,618	5,622	5,626	5,630	5,633	5,638	5,641	5,538
C roads	10,900	10,922	10,943	10,966	10,986	11,009	11,031	11,054	11,076	11,098	10,859
Unclassified	111,747	112,081	112,417	112,754	113,093	113,432	113,772	114,114	114,456	114,816	113,520
All minor urban roads	128,254	128,614	128,975	129,338	129,702	130,068	130,432	130,802	131,169	131,556	129,917
All Major roads	49,389	49,572	49,490	49,735	49,816	50,018	50,074	50,130	50,152	50,130	50,192
All minor roads [5]	336,168	336,828	337,494	338,158	338,825	339,496	340,163	340,838	341,512	342,212	337,482
All roads	385,557	386,401	386,983	387,893	388,641	389,515	390,237	390,969	391,663	392,342	387,674

1 A number of minor revisions have been made to the lengths of major roads from 1993 onwards. ☎020-7944 3095

2 Rural roads: Major and minor roads, from 1993 onwards, are defined as being outside an urban area.

3 Figures for trunk and principal 'A' roads in England, from 2001 onwards, are affected by the detrunking programme.

4 Urban roads: Major and minor roads, from 1993 onwards, are defined as within an urban area with a population of 10,000 or more. These are based on the 2001 urban settlements. The definition for 'urban settlement' is in *Urban and rural area definitions* : a user guide which can be found on the ODPM web site at: http://www.odpm.gov.uk/stellent/groups/odpm_planning/documents/page/odpm_plan_609188.

5 Revisions have been made to the minor road length figures for 2004; see Special Note on Tables 7.1-7.4 in the Notes and Definitions of Section 7.

7.9 Public road length: by class of road and country: 2004[1]

Kilometres

	England	Wales	Scotland	Great Britain
Motorways:				
Trunk	2,950	141	386	3,478
Principal	46	.	.	46
Dual Carriageway:				
Trunk urban [2, 3]	240	19	50	308
Trunk rural [2, 4]	2,502	323	442	3,267
Principal urban [2, 3]	2,330	105	185	2,621
Principal rural [2, 4]	1,505	98	89	1,692
Single Carriageway:				
Trunk urban [2, 3]	131	29	38	198
Trunk rural [2, 4]	1,924	1,175	2,274	5,374
Principal urban [2, 3]	6,991	389	631	8,012
Principal rural [2, 4]	16,576	2,035	6,586	25,197
B roads [5]	19,854	2,986	7,337	30,178
C roads [5]	64,063	9,835	10,325	84,223
Unclassified roads [5]	178,668	16,044	28,370	223,082
Total	297,779	33,179	56,715	387,674

1 A number of minor revisions have been made to the lengths of major roads from 1993 onwards. ☎020-7944 3095

2 Figures for trunk and principal 'A' roads in England, from 2001 onwards, are affected by the detrunking programme.

3 Urban roads: Major and minor roads, from 1993 onwards, are defined as within an urban area with a population of 10,000 or more. These are based on the 2001 urban settlements. The definition for 'urban settlement' is in *Urban and rural area definitions: a user guide* which can be found on the ODPM web site at: http://www.odpm.gov.uk/stellent/groups/odpm_planning/documents/page/odpm_plan_609188.hcsp

4 Rural roads: Major and minor roads, from 1993 onwards, are defined as being outside an urban area.

5 Revisions have been made to the minor road length figures for 2004; see Special Note on Tables 7.1-7.4 in the Notes and Definitions of Section 7.

Table 7.10 Vehicle speeds on non-urban roads by road type and vehicle type: Great Britain: 2004

per cent/miles per hour/number of vehicles

						Heavy goods vehicles [5]				
						Rigid			Articulated	
(a) Motorways [1]	Motor-cycles	Cars	Cars towing	Light Goods [4]	Buses/ coaches	2 axle [6]	3 axle	4 axles	4 axles	5+ axles
Under 50 mph	4	3	16	4	5	7	12	13	8	8
50-60 mph	16	12	52	15	44	47	82	86	90	91
60-65 mph	9	12	18	13	42	15	6	1	1	1
65-70 mph	12	17	9	17	6	14	0	0	1	0
70-75 mph	16	20	4	19	2	9	0	0	0	0
75-80 mph	15	17	1	15	0	5	0	0	0	0
80-90 mph	20	16	0	14	0	3	0	0	0	0
90 mph and over	8	3	0	3	0	1	0	0	0	0
Speed limit	70	70	60	70	70	n/a	60	60	60	60
Percentage more than 10 mph over limit	28	19	5	17	0	n/a	0	0	0	0
Average speed	72	71	57	70	59	61	54	53	54	54
Number observed (thousands)	2,341	424,465	3,335	51,278	2,145	25,750	2,415	1,596	8,470	39,573
(b) Dual carriageways [2]										
Under 30 mph	0	0	1	0	0	0	0	0	1	0
30-40 mph	2	0	1	0	1	1	2	1	1	0
40-50 mph	11	3	18	4	10	10	21	21	18	12
50-60 mph	18	15	51	19	49	49	71	77	77	86
60-65 mph	9	15	17	15	33	15	3	1	2	1
65-70 mph	12	19	8	18	4	11	1	0	1	0
70-80 mph	27	34	4	31	2	11	2	0	0	0
80 mph and over	21	14	0	13	1	3	1	0	0	0
Speed limit	70	70	60	70	60	n/a	50	50	50	50
Percentage more than 10 mph over limit	21	14	5	13	3	n/a	6	1	3	1
Average speed	68	69	56	68	58	59	53	52	53	53
Number observed (thousands)	367	45,581	403	4,685	194	2,170	259	208	547	2,475
(c) Single carriageways [3]										
Under 20 mph	1	0	2	0	1	1	1	1	1	0
20-30 mph	6	2	5	3	3	3	6	9	6	2
30-40 mph	13	15	18	16	23	19	24	28	20	18
40-50 mph	28	42	51	41	49	47	51	45	51	50
50-60 mph	27	31	22	29	22	25	18	17	21	29
60-65 mph	9	6	2	6	2	3	0	0	0	1
65-70 mph	6	2	0	3	0	1	0	0	0	0
70 mph and over	10	2	0	2	0	1	0	0	0	0
Speed limit	60	60	50	60	50	n/a	40	40	40	40
Percentage more than 10 mph over limit	10	2	2	2	3	n/a	18	17	22	30
Average speed	51	48	44	48	45	46	43	42	44	46
Number observed (thousands)	469	47,953	599	5,017	316	2,176	325	213	450	2,201

1 Average vehicle speeds from 27 motorway sites.
2 Average vehicle speeds from 7 dual carriageway sites
3 Average traffic speeds from 26 single carriageway sites
4 Goods vehicles under 3.5 tonnes gross weight
5 Goods vehicles over 3.5 tonnes gross weight
6 Speed limit depends on loading which cannot be determined

☎020-7944 6397

Table 7.11: Vehicle speeds on urban roads by speed limit and vehicle type: Great Britain: 2004

(a) 30 mph speed limit roads [1] per cent/miles per hour/number of vehicles

	Motor-cycles [3]	Cars	Cars towing	Light goods [4]	Buses/ coaches	Heavy goods vehicles [5] Rigid 2 axle	Rigid 3 axle	Rigid 4 axle	Articulated 4 axles	Articulated 5+ axles
Under 20 mph	13	6	8	8	9	9	7	4	8	3
20-30 mph	40	41	46	39	63	44	46	42	45	43
30-35 mph	24	31	33	31	21	29	35	39	32	39
35-40 mph	13	16	11	16	6	14	10	13	12	13
40-45 mph	6	5	2	5	1	4	1	2	2	2
45-50 mph	3	1	0	1	0	1	0	0	0	0
50 mph and over	2	0	0	0	0	0	0	0	0	0
Percent over 35 mph	24	22	14	23	8	18	12	16	15	16
Average speed	30	31	29	30	27	29	29	30	29	31
Number observed (thousands)	908	67,413	174	5,691	514	1,837	135	121	101	203

(b) 40 mph speed limit roads [2] per cent/miles per hour/number of vehicles

	Motor-cycles [3]	Cars	Cars towing	Light goods [4]	Buses/ coaches	Heavy goods vehicles [5] Rigid 2 axle	Rigid 3 axle	Rigid 4 axle	Articulated 4 axles	Articulated 5+ axles
Under 20 mph	5	3	3	4	3	5	3	2	2	2
20 - 30 mph	13	11	16	11	16	14	14	10	11	10
30 - 35 mph	18	24	26	22	30	24	23	20	19	20
35 - 40 mph	26	34	36	33	38	34	41	42	42	44
40 - 45 mph	18	17	14	18	11	15	16	21	19	20
45 - 50 mph	10	7	4	7	2	5	3	4	5	4
50 - 60 mph	7	3	1	3	0	2	1	1	2	1
60 mph and over	2	0	0	1	0	0	0	0	0	0
Percent over 45 mph	19	10	4	11	3	7	4	5	6	5
Average speed	38	36	35	36	35	35	35	37	36	37
Number observed (thousands)	848	59,331	270	5,411	456	2,127	285	219	321	827

1 Speed measurements taken from 26 sites.
2 Speed measurements taken from 10 sites.
3 Motorcycles includes mopeds and other types of powered two wheeled vehicles.
4 Goods vehicles up to 3.5 tonnes gross weight.
5 Goods vehicles over 3.5 tonnes gross weight.

☎020-7944 6397

7.12 Average traffic speeds in London: 1968-2004

Miles per hour

Morning peak period:	Central area	Inner area	Outer area	All areas
1968 - 1970 cycle [1]	12.7	15.1	20.5	18.1
1971 - 1973 "	12.9	14.5	20.0	17.7
1974 - 1976 "	14.2	15.9	19.3	17.9
1977 - 1979 "	12.3	13.9	18.7	16.9
1980 - 1982 "	12.1	14.2	19.6	17.5
1983 - 1986 "	11.8	13.5	18.8	16.9
1986 - 1990 "	11.5	11.8	18.4	16.0
1990 - 1994 "	10.3	13.3	17.5	15.8
1994 - 1997 "	10.9	13.4	17.0	15.6
1997 - 2000 "	10.0	12.0	18.2	15.9
2000 - 2003 "	9.9	11.6	16.9	15.0
2003 - 2006 "	10.6	11.7		
Daytime off-peak period:				
1968 - 1970 cycle	12.1	18.3	26.5	21.3
1971 - 1973 "	12.6	18.6	26.2	21.6
1974 - 1976 "	12.9	18.6	26.1	21.7
1977 - 1979 "	12.6	17.3	25.0	20.9
1980 - 1982 "	11.6	17.2	24.9	20.6
1983 - 1986 "	11.9	16.3	25.3	20.9
1986 - 1990 "	11.0	14.6	22.7	18.9
1990 - 1994 "	10.6	15.8	22.8	19.3
1994 - 1997 "	10.9	15.0	22.7	19.1
1997 - 2000 "	10.0	14.8	21.9	18.5
2000 - 2003 "	9.0	13.7	21.4	17.7
2003 - 2006 "	10.5	14.1		
Evening peak period:				
1968 - 1970 cycle	11.8	15.2	21.9	18.6
1971 - 1973 "	12.7	14.5	21.5	18.3
1974 - 1976 "	13.2	15.5	20.7	18.3
1977 - 1979 "	11.9	13.5	20.1	17.2
1980 - 1982 "	12.2	14.1	20.5	18.0
1983 - 1986 "	11.5	13.1	20.1	17.2
1986 - 1990 "	11.0	11.6	19.8	16.5
1990 - 1994 "	10.3	13.2	19.7	17.0
1994 - 1997 "	10.8	12.8	19.0	16.6
1997 - 2000 "	10.2	11.4	19.1	16.2
2000 - 2003 "	9.6	11.3	18.4	15.7
2003 - 2006 "	10.6	12.3		

1 A cycle consists of a complete set of surveys on the three areas of London, beginning with the beginning with the central area and ending with the outer area.
The outer area survey for the 2003-2006 period is due to start in December 2004.

☎020-7941 3706
Source - TfL

7.13 Regional expenditure on roads: 2003/04

£ Million

	North East	Yorkshire and the Humber	North West	East Midlands	West Midlands	East of England	South East	London	South West	England
Motorways and trunk roads [1]:										
New construction/improvement and structural maintenance	34.1	76.9	116.3	96.0	118.1	121.7	164.2	11.6	117.4	856.3
Current maintenance, including routine & winter maintenance [2]	16.4	36.8	55.7	46.0	56.6	58.3	78.7	5.5	56.3	410.5
DBFO shadow tolls [3]	36.5	53.7	-	13.7	-	28.3	25.8	-	52.3	210.3
Local Roads [4]:										
New construction/Improvement for highways, lighting, road safety and structural maintenance [5]	125.2	222.5	333.8	207.9	235.5	283.3	317.3	414.1	239.2	2,378.8
Revenue expenditure on bridge structural maintenance & strengthening	2.9	4.2	6.6	2.2	4.9	4.6	6.6	22.6	6.0	60.6
Routine and winter maintenance	45.4	88.4	110.4	59.7	81.5	110.9	140.7	195.8	98.3	931.2
Revenue expenditure on road safety	5.6	12.3	23.1	14.3	13.3	18.8	24.8	165.6	10.8	288.7
Revenue expenditure on public lighting	20.2	33.6	53.2	24.8	30.1	26.7	40.5	42.4	27.0	298.4
All road expenditure	286.3	528.4	699.2	464.7	540.2	652.5	798.7	857.5	607.3	5,434.8

1 Figures are now collected on a resource accounting basis and cannot be compared with data prior to 2001/02. Until 2001/02, associated costs of investment (including depreciation and capital costs) were not included within these figures. Apportionment between the Government Office Regions involves an estimation process.

☎020-7944 3092

2 Until 2001/02 this table showed figures for 'routine and winter maintenance and public lighting'. Highways Agency is no longer able to separately identify this expenditure and this now falls within the wider category 'Current maintenance, including routine & winter maintenance.

3 Payments to contractors under Design, Build, Finance & Operate (DBFO) schemes.

4 Local authority expenditure excludes car parks.

5 Includes expenditure on 'patching'.

Sources - Highways Agency Financial Accounts and local authority returns to DfT

7.14 Road construction tender price index: 1994-2004

1990=100

Year	1994	1995	1996	1997	1998	1999	2000	2001	2002	2003	2004
All roads	111	125	122	124	123	125	142	146	151	149	149 [p]

☎020-7944 3092

The figures in this table are outside the scope of National Statistics

Source - DTI

7.15 Road taxation revenue in 2003/04 classified by vehicle taxation group

Vehicle class	Number of vehicles (thousand)	Road taxes (£million) Fuel tax	Vehicle excise duty	Total
Cars, light vans and taxis	27,887	17,304	4,516	21,820
Motorcycles	1,042	75	47	122
Buses and coaches	97	547	30	577
Goods vehicles over 3.5 tonnes gross weight	418	3,869	290	4,159
Other vehicles	1,982	766	54	820
All vehicles	31,427	22,561	4,937	27,498
of fuel taxes:-				
Petrol	.	12,713	.	.
Diesel	.	9,848	.	.

☎020-7944 6386
The road tax figures in this table are outside the scope of National Statistics
Sources - HM Customs and Excise; DVLA

7.16 New road construction and improvement: motorways and all purpose trunk roads: England: 1994/95-2004/05

	1994/95	1995/96	1996/97 [1]	1997/98	1998/99	1999/00	2000/01	2001/02	2002/03	2003/04	2004/05
(a) Starts											
Route kilometres	79	6	159	0 [2]	10	20	23	5	21	51	30
Lane kilometres	282	50	839	0 [2]	65	126	95	18	65	195	82
(b) Completions											
Route kilometres	77	151	74	133	96	40	38	0 [2]	56	113	49
Lane kilometres	327	514	204	657	559	160	197	0 [2]	191	446	172

1 Starts and completions for 1996/97 onwards include DBFO schemes.
2 See comments on Table 7.16 in the Notes and Definitions of Section 7.

☎020-7944 3092
The figures in this table are outside the scope of National Statistics
Source - Highways Agency

7.17 Defects index of road condition [1]: England and Wales: 1977-2004

Index 1977 = 100

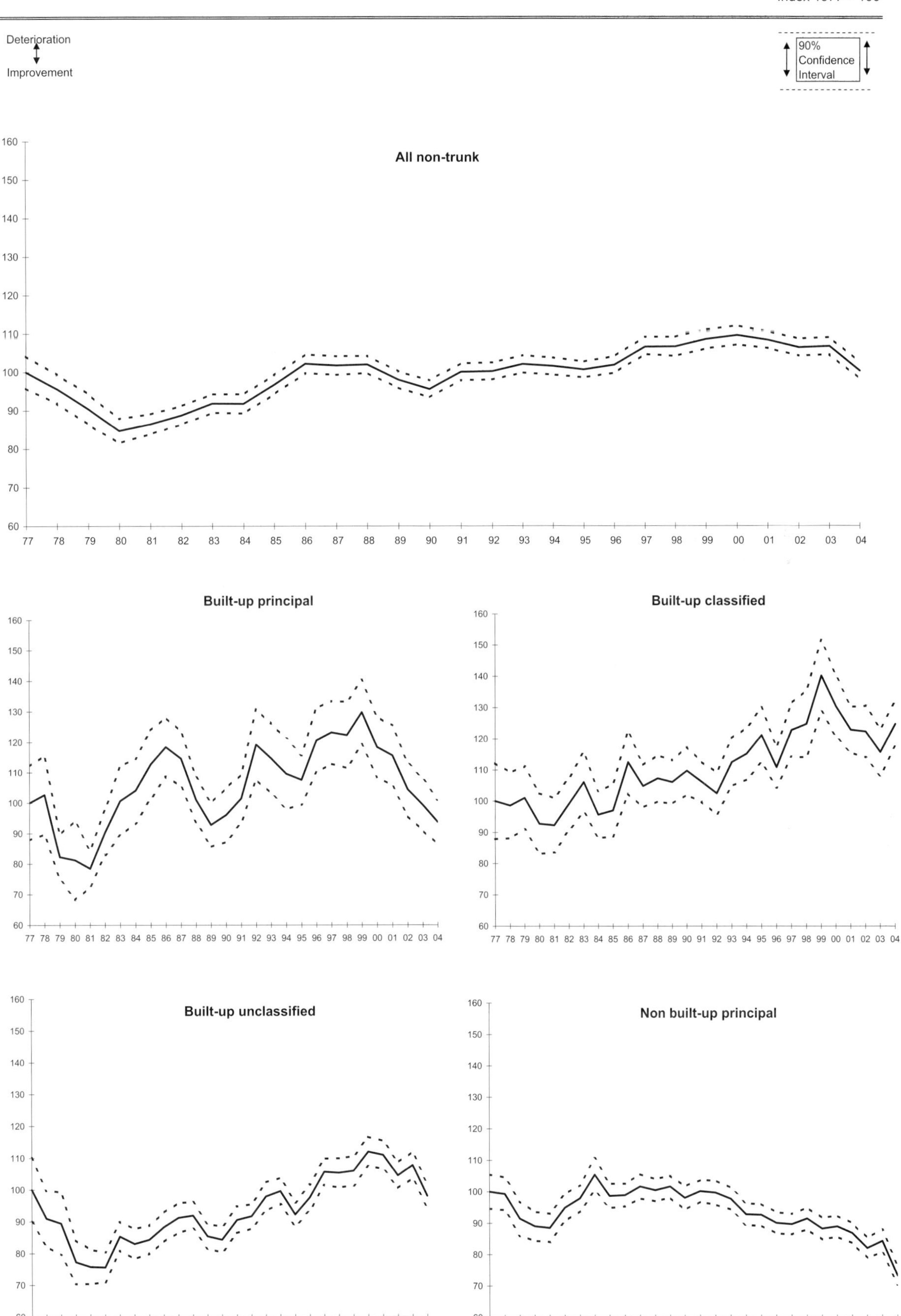

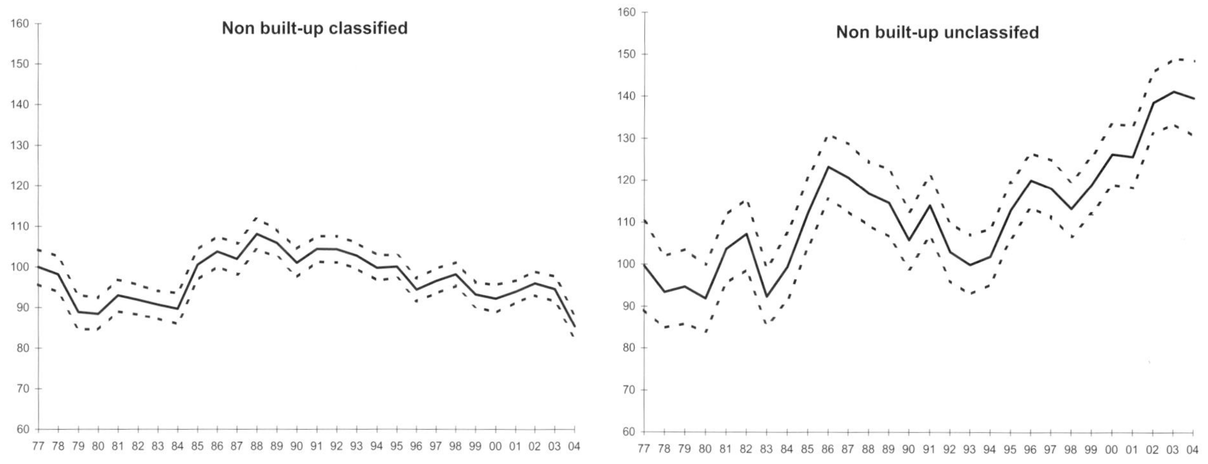

1. Built-up and non built-up were previously referred to as urban and rural. Results for all purpose trunk roads, and hence all roads, are not available from 2003.

☎020-7944 3092

Further details on National Road Maintenance Condition Survey 2004 are available at www.dft.gov.uk/transtat

7.18 Percentage contribution of defects to defects index: England and Wales: 2004 [1]

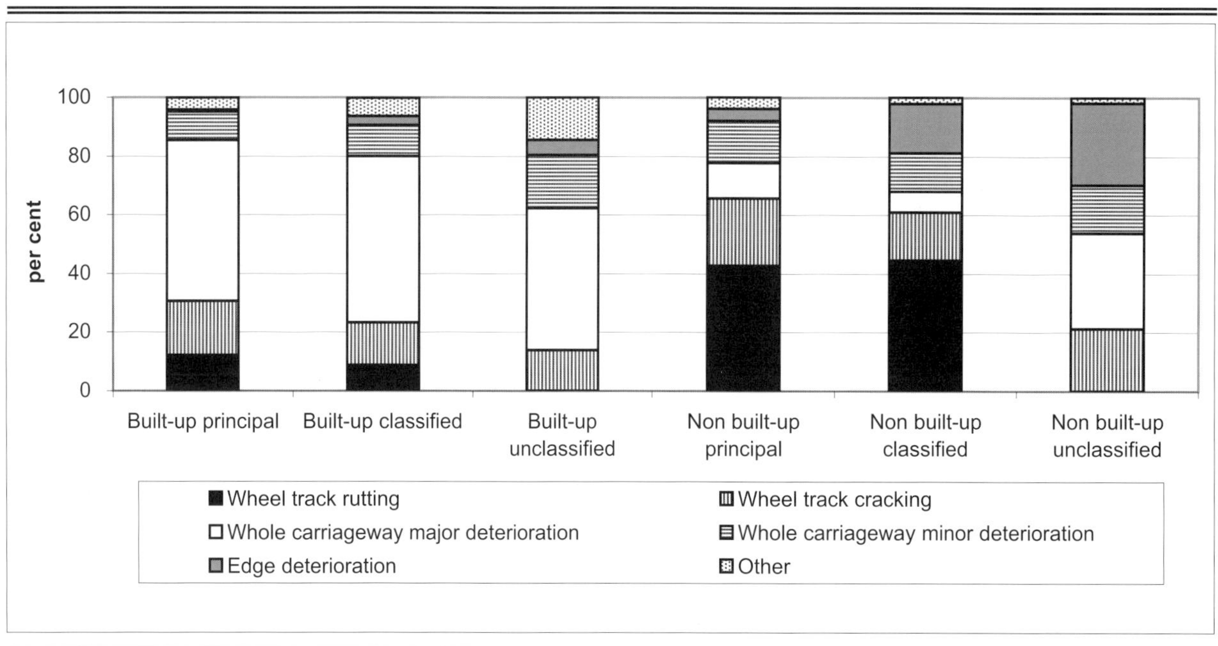

1 In practice, wheel track rutting alone would not generally be treated on unclassified roads and so the contribution is zero. Reliable results for all purpose trunk roads are not available. Built-up and non built-up were previously referred to as urban and rural.

☎020-7944 3092

Further details on National Road Maintenance Condition Survey 2004 are available at www.dft.gov.uk/transtat

7.19 Footways condition[1]: England and Wales: 1984 to 2004

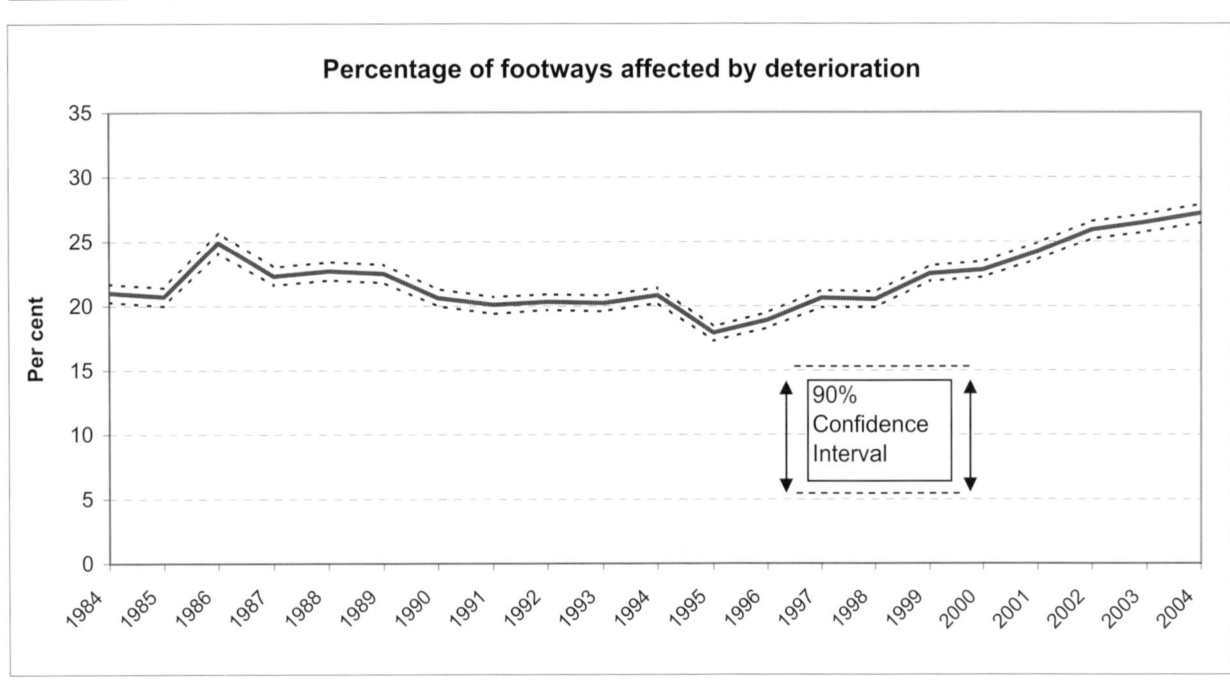

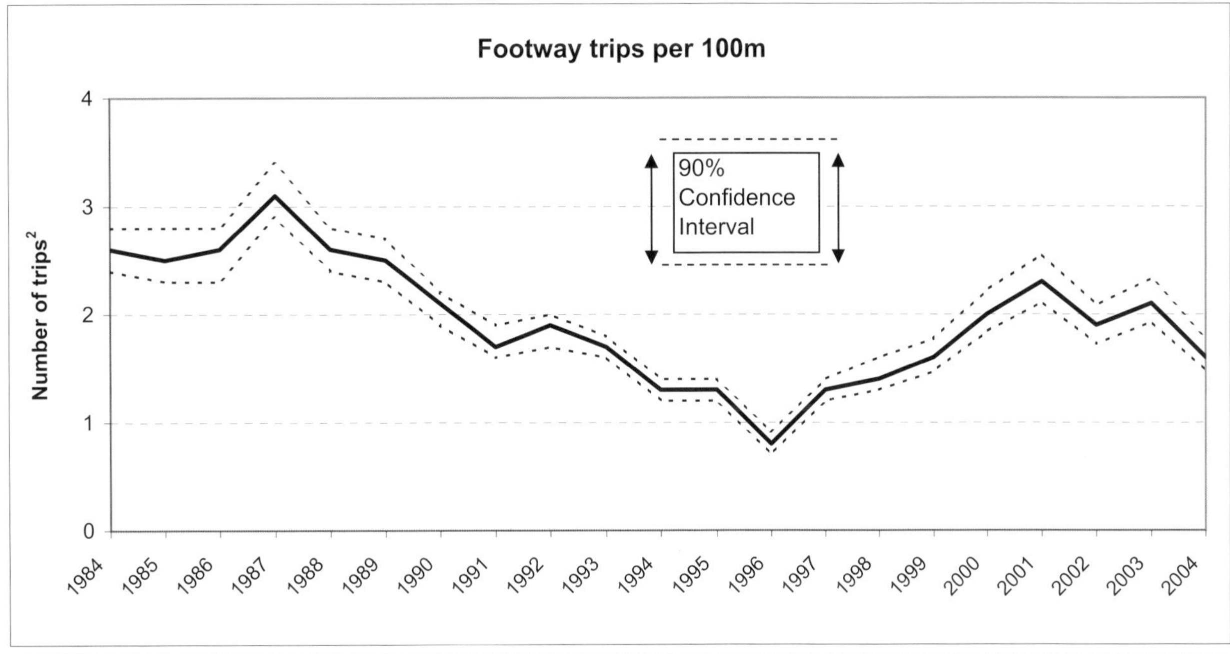

1 Figures are for local roads from 1999. Prior to that they include all purpose trunk roads although this will have little effect on the overall total.

2 The average number of spot conditions in every 100 metres which constitute a specific danger to pedestrians.

☎020-7944 3092

Further details on National Road Maintenance Condition Survey 2004 are available at www.dft.gov.uk/transtat

7.20 Percentage of verge area and kerb lengths[1] affected by deterioration: England and Wales: 1984 to 2004

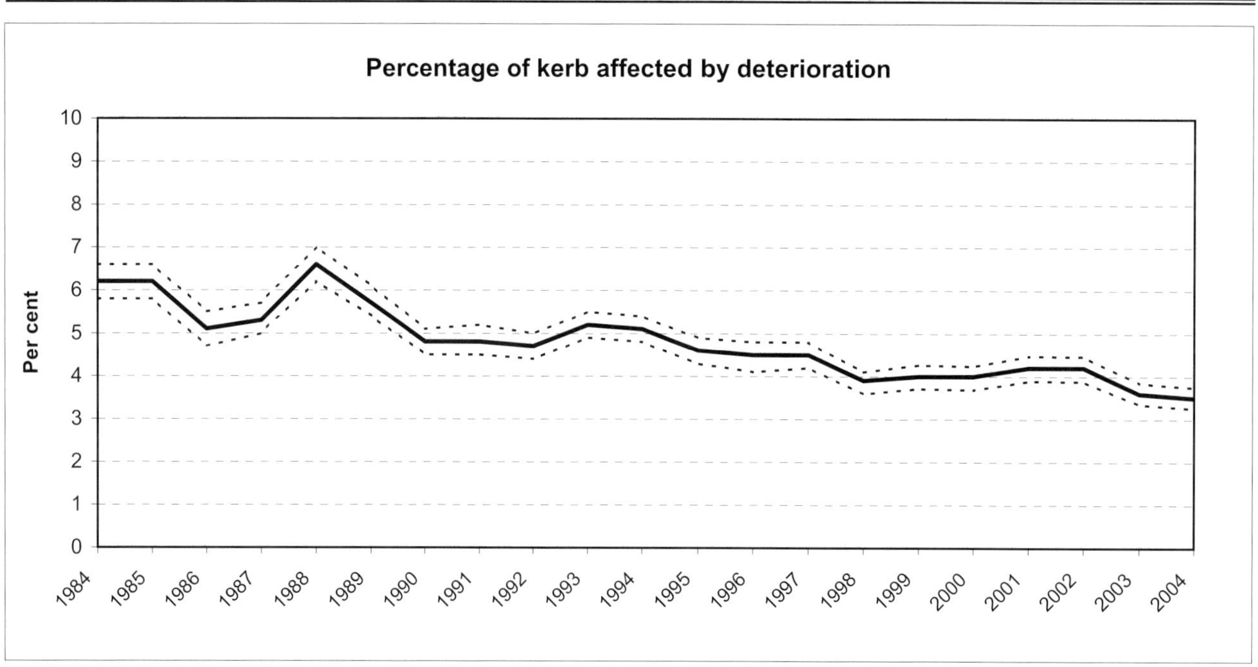

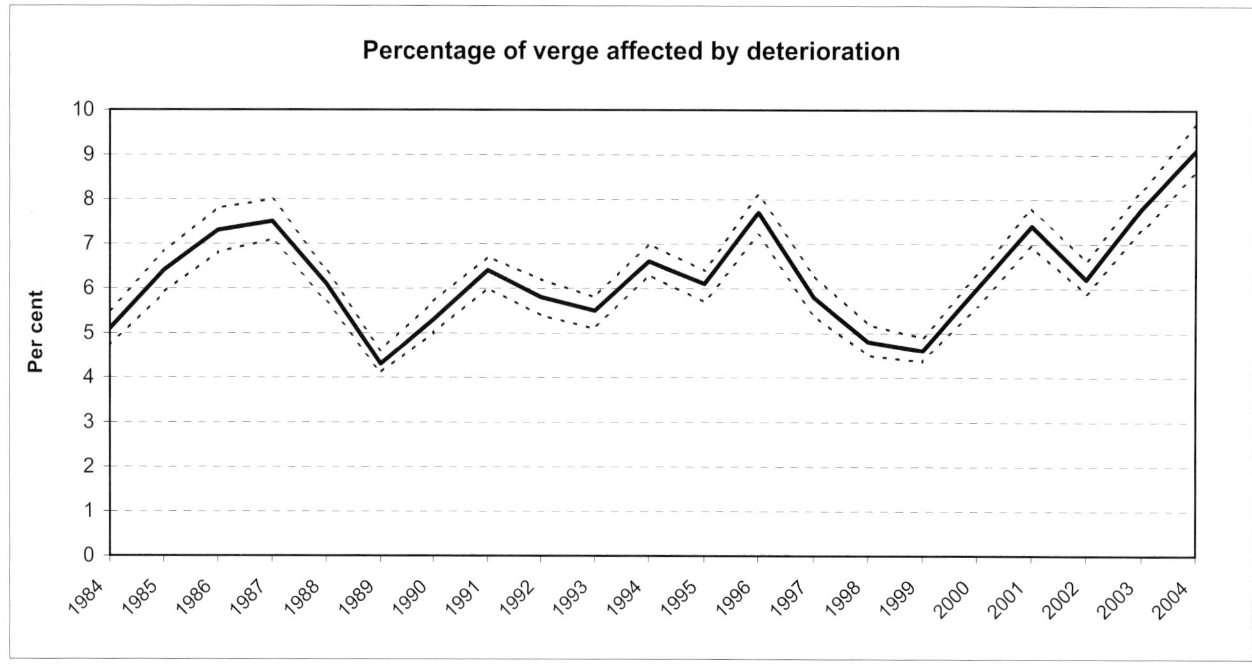

1 Figures are for local roads from 1999. Prior to that they include all purpose trunk roads although this will have little effect on the overall total.

☎020-7944 3092

Further details on National Road Maintenance Condition Survey 2004 are available at www.dft.gov.uk/transtat

8 Transport Accidents and Casualties:

Notes and Definitions

Road accidents and casualties: 8.1

Accident: Involves personal injury occurring on the public highway (including footways) in which at least one road vehicle or a vehicle in collision with a pedestrian is involved and which becomes known to the police within 30 days of its occurrence. The vehicle need not be moving and accidents involving stationary vehicles and pedestrians or users are included. One accident may give rise to several casualties. "Damage-only" accidents are not included in this publication.

Fatality: Since 1954 fatality is defined as 'death within 30 days', conforming to the Vienna Convention. Prior to 1954 the definition was two months. The effect of the change was an approximate 5 per cent reduction in fatalities.

Road Accidents: 8.2-8.5

In these tables the underlying definitions of personal injury road accidents involving road using vehicles and pedestrians in addition to those described for Table 1.7 are:

Adults: Persons aged 16 years and over (except where otherwise stated).

Children: Persons under 16 years of age (except where otherwise stated).

Failed breath test: Drivers or riders tested with a positive result, or who failed or refused to provide a specimen of breath.

Goods vehicles: These are divided into two groups according to vehicle weight (see below). They include tankers, tractor units travelling without their semi-trailers, trailers, articulated vehicles and pick-up trucks.

Heavy goods vehicles (HGV): Goods vehicles over 3.5 tonnes maximum permissible gross vehicle weight (gvw).

Light goods vehicles (LGV): Goods vehicles, mainly vans (including car derived vans), not over 3.5 tonnes maximum permissible gross vehicle weight (gvw).

Cars: . Includes taxis, estate cars, three and four wheel cars and minibuses except where otherwise stated. Also includes motor caravans prior to 1999.

Mopeds: Two-wheel motor vehicles with an engine capacity not over 50 cc, a maximum design speed of 30 mph, a kerbside weight not exceeding 250 kg and an index plate identifying them as mopeds (i.e. as defined in the Road Vehicles (Construction and Use) Regulations 1986).

Motor cycles: Mopeds, motor scooters and motor cycles (including motor cycle combinations).

Motorways: "M" roads and "A"(M) roads.

For traffic purposes *Urban roads* are major and minor roads within an urban area defined on the basis of population density. The exact definition is based on the 1991 ODPM (DTLR) definition of urban settlements. *Rural roads* are major and minor roads outside those urban areas.

Other roads: All "B", "C" class and unclassified roads.

Other vehicles: Other motor vehicles include ambulances, fire engines, trams, refuse vehicles, road rollers, agricultural vehicles, excavators, mobile cranes, electric scooters and motorised wheelchairs etc. Other non motor vehicles include those drawn by an animal, ridden horses, invalid carriages without a motor, street barrows etc.

Severity: Of an accident: the severity of the most severely injured casualty (fatal, serious or slight). Of a casualty: killed, seriously injured or slightly injured.

Slight accident: One in which at least one person is slightly injured but no person is killed or seriously injured.

Speed limits: Permanent speed limits applicable to the roadway.

Motoring offences: 8.6-8.7

Breath tests: Section 25 and Schedule 8 of the Transport Act 1981 amended the drinking and driving provisions of the Road Traffic Act 1972. These sections of the Act were renumbered (but otherwise unchanged) in the Road Traffic Act 1988. The police can require a person to take a screening breath test if they have reasonable cause to suspect that the person has been driving or attempting to drive or had been in charge of a vehicle with alcohol in his or her body, or that he or she has committed a moving traffic offence, or that he or she has been involved in an accident. A person failing to provide a breath test without reasonable excuse is guilty of an offence.

For the purposes of evidence in court, breath analysis was introduced in May 1983. The prescribed alcohol limit is 80 milligrams (mg) of alcohol in 100 millilitres (ml) of blood or 107mg per 100ml urine. The equivalent breath alcohol limit is expressed as 35 micrograms of alcohol per 100ml breath. In April 1996 the Association of Chief Police Officers recommended that drivers in all injury accidents should be breath tested.

An evidential breath test is required to be taken at a police station after a positive screening test, or where a screening test was refused or could not be provided. It may also be required after arrest for impairment or in certain other cases, e.g. where a person arrested for theft of a motor vehicle is suspected of having consumed alcohol.

A suspect will normally be asked to provide two specimens of breath to establish the amount of alcohol in his or her body. The lower result is taken as evidence of the person's breath alcohol concentration. Where the lower result is between 36 and 50 micrograms the suspect may request a blood or urine test. In certain limited circumstances a suspect can be required to provide a specimen of blood or urine instead of breath.

The introduction of a simplified statistical return on 1 January 1987 was associated with increased reporting of breath tests.

Findings of guilt at all courts: Includes all motoring offences which have resulted in a finding of guilt either after a summary trial at Magistrates' Court or else at the Crown Court. A person appearing in court can be dealt with for more than one offence at that appearance, and in this table the number of offences is counted, not the number of persons appearing at court.

Fixed penalty notices: A large number of motoring offences are dealt with by fixed penalty notices. In 1999, for example, an estimated 67 per cent of offences were dealt with in this way. However there is a wide variation by type of offence, with 99 per cent of obstruction, waiting and parking offences being dealt with by fixed penalty compared to only 47 per cent of other offences. Under the extended fixed penalty system introduced by the Transport Act 1982, now incorporated in Part III of the Road Traffic Offenders act 1988, the police can issue fixed penalty notices for a wide range of offences. The court can automatically register an unpaid notice as a fine without any court appearance. Offences for which a fixed penalty notice cannot be given include causing death or bodily harm, dangerous driving, driving after consuming alcohol or taking drugs, careless driving, accident offences, unauthorised taking or theft of a motor vehicle, certain driving licence, insurance, and record keeping offences and vehicle test offences. When court proceed-ins are instituted following non-payment of a fixed penalty, the offence may be included twice in the table.

Written warnings: These include cautions given in lieu of prosecutions for offences where there would have been enough evidence to support a prosecution. Informal warnings and advice, whether oral or written, are not included.

Motor insurance: 8.8

The data given in Table 8.8 are the latest available figures from insurance companies' DTI returns, the statutory returns which insurers are required to file with the Department of Trade and Industry. Only insurance companies are obliged to complete the returns and so the data does not include business written by Lloyd's underwriters. The data has been provided by the Association of British Insurers from the SynThesys Non-Life database of returns.

Table 8.8 gives claim data for the period 1997 to 2003. The figures are for all insurance claims and will include those arising from fire or theft as well as from road accidents. Exposure (expressed in million vehicle years) is the exposure to risk and is the product of the number of vehicles insured and the proportion of the year for which each vehicle was covered. The claim frequency shows the proportion of policyholders who made a claim.

For further information, see the Association of British Insurers web site at: www.abi.org.uk

Railway accidents: 8.9-8.11

These tables give the number of train accidents and casualties on all railway undertakings in Great Britain. Railway undertakings are required to report accidents, failures and dangerous occurrences to the Secretary of State for Transport under the regulatory safety legislation. As well as Network Rail and London Transport railways, the tables also cover accidents on Eurotunnel, tram systems and minor railways.

Casualty figures in Table 8.9 are shown in the categories below. Casualty figures are subdivided into casualties resulting from:

- train accidents
- accidents through movement of railway vehicles (but excluding train accidents) e.g. boarding or alighting from trains, opening or closing carriage doors at stations,
- accidents on railway premises not connected with movement of railway vehicles e.g. falling on steps at stations, slipping on platforms,
- injuries and fatalities of trespassers and suicides on railway land.

Table 8.10 is based on passenger casualties owing to train accidents and movement accidents. This is the basis for comparisons with other modes of transport.

Table 8.11 shows the total number of train accidents (collisions, derailments etc) reported irrespective of whether personal injury was involved. The figures include accidents on non-passenger lines and lines closed to normal traffic while engineering work took place.

8.1 Road accidents and casualties: 1950-2004

For greater detail of the years 1994-2004 see Table 8.2 or 8.3

		Casualties											
		Killed (number)					Injured (thousands)						
Year	Accidents (thousands)	Pedest-rians	Pedal cyclists	Motor cyclists	All other road users	All	Serious	Slight	All	All casualties (thousands)	Casualty rate per 100 million vehicle kilometres	All traffic (billion vehicle Km)
1950	167	2,251	805	1,129	827	5,012	49	148	196	201	276	73
1951	178	2,398	800	1,175	877	5,250	52	159	211	216	272	80
1952	172	2,063	743	1,142	758	4,706	50	153	203	208	248	84
1953	186	2,233	720	1,237	900	5,090	57	165	222	227	265	86
1954	196	2,226	696	1,148	940	5,010	57	176	233	238	269	89
1955	217	2,287	708	1,362	1,169	5,526	62	200	262	268	281	95
1956	216	2,270	650	1,250	1,197	5,367	61	201	263	268	276	97
1957	219	2,225	663	1,425	1,237	5,550	64	205	268	274	284	96
1958	237	2,408	668	1,421	1,473	5,970	69	225	294	300	280	107
1959	261	2,520	738	1,680	1,582	6,520	81	246	327	333	283	118
1960	272	2,708	679	1,743	1,840	6,970	84	256	341	348	279	124
1961	270	2,717	645	1,544	2,002	6,908	85	258	343	350	262	133
1962	264	2,681	583	1,323	2,122	6,709	84	251	335	342	248	138
1963	272	2,740	589	1,279	2,314	6,922	88	261	349	356	246	145
1964	292	2,986	583	1,445	2,806	7,820	95	282	378	385	240	160
1965	299	3,105	543	1,244	3,060	7,952	98	292	390	398	234	170
1966	292	3,153	514	1,134	3,184	7,985	100	285	384	392	219	179
1967	277	2,964	463	920	2,972	7,319	94	269	363	370	199	186
1968	264	2,762	391	877	2,780	6,810	89	254	342	349	181	193
1969	262	2,955	402	791	3,217	7,365	91	255	346	353	179	197
1970	267	2,925	373	761	3,440	7,499	93	262	356	363	177	205
1971	259	2,939	411	800	3,549	7,699	91	253	344	352	163	216
1972	265	3,083	367	729	3,584	7,763	91	261	352	360	159	226
1973	262	2,806	336	750	3,514	7,406	89	257	346	354	149	238
1974	244	2,642	282	797	3,162	6,883	82	236	318	325	139	234
1975	246	2,344	278	838	2,906	6,366	77	241	319	325	138	236
1976	259	2,335	300	990	2,945	6,570	80	254	333	340	137	248
1977	266	2,313	301	1,182	2,818	6,614	82	260	341	348	138	253
1978	265	2,427	316	1,163	2,925	6,831	83	260	343	350	134	262
1979	255	2,118	320	1,160	2,754	6,352	80	248	328	335	128	260
1980	252	1,941	302	1,163	2,604	6,010	79	243	323	329	119	277
1981	248	1,874	310	1,131	2,531	5,846	78	241	319	325	115	282
1982	256	1,869	294	1,090	2,681	5,934	80	249	328	334	115	291
1983	243	1,914	323	963	2,245	5,445	71	233	303	309	105	294
1984	253	1,868	345	967	2,419	5,599	73	246	319	324	105	309
1985	246	1,789	286	796	2,294	5,165	71	241	312	318	101	316
1986	248	1,841	271	762	2,508	5,382	69	247	316	321	97	331
1987	239	1,703	280	723	2,419	5,125	64	242	306	311	87	356
1988	247	1,753	227	670	2,402	5,052	63	254	317	322	85	381
1989	261	1,706	294	683	2,690	5,373	63	273	336	342	83	412
1990	258	1,694	256	659	2,608	5,217	60	275	336	341	82	416
1991	236	1,496	242	548	2,282	4,568	52	255	307	311	75	417
1992	233	1,347	204	469	2,209	4,229	49	257	306	311	75	417
1993 [1]	229	1,241	186	427	1,960	3,814	45	257	302	306	74	416
1994	234	1,124	172	444	1,910	3,650	47	265	312	315	74	426
1995	231	1,038	213	445	1,925	3,621	46	261	307	311	71	434
1996	236	997	203	440	1,958	3,598	44	272	317	321	72	445
1997	240	973	183	509	1,934	3,599	43	281	324	328	72	454
1998	239	906	158	498	1,859	3,421	41	281	322	325	70	462
1999	235	870	172	547	1,834	3,423	39	278	317	320	68	471
2000	234	857	127	605	1,820	3,409	38	279	317	320	68	471
2001	229	826	138	583	1,903	3,450	37	273	310	313	65	479
2002	222	775	130	609	1,917	3,431	36	263	299	303	62	491
2003	214	774	114	693	1,927	3,508	34	253	287	291	59	495
2004	207	671	134	585	1,831	3,221	31	246	278	281	56	502

☎020-7944 3078

1 See Notes and Definitions in Section 7 for details of discontinuity in road traffic figures from 1993 onwards.
From 1993 the data has been estimated using the expansion factors and the new methodology for measuring road lengths, they are not directly comparable with the figures for 1992 and earlier.

8.2 Road accident casualties by road user type and severity: 1994-2004

Number

	1994	1995	1996	1997	1998	1999	2000	2001	2002	2003	2004
Child pedestrians: [1]											
Killed	160	132	131	138	103	107	107	107	79	74	77
KSI	4,610	4,400	4,132	3,954	3,737	3,457	3,226	3,144	2,828	2,381	2,339
All severities	19,263	18,590	18,510	18,407	17,971	16,876	16,184	15,819	14,231	12,544	12,234
Adult pedestrians: [2]											
Killed	953	897	858	835	803	760	750	712	688	695	589
KSI	8,114	7,716	7,300	6,925	6,592	6,221	6,112	5,745	5,644	5,422	5,005
All severities	28,129	27,178	26,827	26,223	25,827	24,806	24,481	23,463	23,258	22,531	21,404
Child pedal cyclists: [1]											
Killed	42	48	54	33	32	36	27	25	22	18	25
KSI	1,234	1,249	1,231	1,016	915	950	758	674	594	595	577
All severities	8,075	8,133	8,217	7,899	6,930	7,290	6,260	5,451	4,809	4,769	4,682
Adult pedal cyclists: [2]											
Killed	129	164	148	150	126	135	98	111	107	95	109
KSI	2,710	2,673	2,517	2,542	2,345	2,172	1,954	1,951	1,801	1,776	1,697
All severities	16,097	16,140	15,778	16,181	15,326	14,834	13,630	12,974	11,712	11,643	11,366
Motorcyclists [3] and passengers:											
Killed	444	445	440	509	498	547	605	583	609	693	585
KSI	6,666	6,615	6,208	6,446	6,442	6,908	7,374	7,305	7,500	7,652	6,648
All severities	24,354	23,524	23,133	24,492	24,610	26,192	28,212	28,810	28,353	28,411	25,641
Car drivers and passengers:											
Killed	1,764	1,749	1,806	1,795	1,696	1,687	1,665	1,749	1,747	1,769	1,671
KSI	23,892	23,461	24,048	23,191	21,676	20,368	19,719	19,424	18,728	17,291	16,144
All severities	195,154	194,027	205,336	211,448	210,474	205,735	206,799	202,802	197,425	188,342	183,858
Bus/coach drivers and passengers:											
Killed	21	35	11	14	18	11	15	14	19	11	20
KSI	815	836	695	601	631	611	578	562	551	500	488
All severities	10,090	9,278	9,345	9,439	9,839	10,252	10,088	9,884	9,005	9,068	8,820
LGV drivers and passengers:											
Killed	64	69	61	64	67	65	66	64	70	72	62
KSI	1,101	1,106	989	928	949	867	813	811	780	765	631
All severities	7,558	7,200	7,215	7,476	7,672	7,124	7,007	7,304	7,007	6,897	6,166
HGV drivers and passengers:											
Killed	41	57	63	45	60	52	55	54	63	44	47
KSI	571	635	555	573	560	540	571	500	524	429	406
All severities	3,370	3,331	3,245	3,302	3,444	3,484	3,597	3,388	3,178	3,061	2,883
All road users: [4]											
Killed	3,650	3,621	3,598	3,599	3,421	3,423	3,409	3,450	3,431	3,508	3,221
KSI	50,190	49,154	48,097	46,583	44,255	42,545	41,564	40,560	39,407	37,215	34,351
All severities	315,359	310,687	320,578	327,803	325,212	320,310	320,283	313,309	302,605	290,607	280,840

1 Casualties aged 0-15.

2 Casualties aged 16 and over.

3 Includes mopeds and scooters.

4 Includes other motor or non-motor vehicle users, and unknown road user type and casualty age.

Note: KSI = Killed and seriously injured.

☎020-7944 3078

8.3 Road accidents and accident rates: by road class and severity: 1994-2004

Number/rate per 100 million vehicle kilometres

	1994	1995	1996	1997	1998	1999	2000	2001	2002	2003	2004
Motorway/A(M) roads											
Fatal	135	154	153	159	157	176	161	180	175	184	149
Fatal and serious	1,118	1,153	1,100	1,204	1,148	1,218	1,190	1,235	1,162	1,166	1,047
All severities	7,225	7,392	7,787	8,678	8,861	9,118	9,394	9,128	8,942	8,746	9,072
Rate [1]	*10*	*10*	*10*	*11*	*10*	*10*	*11*	*10*	*10*	*9*	*9*
Urban roads [2]											
A roads:											
Fatal	758	663	693	716	601	587	611	628	636	639	533
Fatal and serious	11,083	11,012	10,612	10,439	9,827	9,123	9,255	8,879	8,543	7,941	7,237
All severities	72,401	70,124	70,513	71,752	70,779	69,062	70,094	68,163	65,098	62,432	58,665
Rate [1]	*92*	*87*	*87*	*88*	*86*	*84*	*86*	*83*	*79*	*76*	*70*
Other roads:											
Fatal	628	615	614	563	562	588	554	573	491	532	518
Fatal and serious	13,831	13,427	12,926	12,345	11,828	11,222	10,809	10,594	10,307	9,686	8,991
All severities	85,148	84,216	86,405	86,735	86,388	85,129	84,353	82,127	79,361	75,907	73,327
Rate [1]	*85*	*83*	*85*	*84*	*82*	*79*	*78*	*75*	*70*	*66*	*64*
Rural roads [2]											
A roads:											
Fatal	1,230	1,223	1,165	1,219	1,184	1,169	1,157	1,177	1,182	1,207	1,134
Fatal and serious	9,146	8,905	8,745	8,649	8,332	8,128	7,837	7,799	7,593	7,370	6,811
All severities	37,364	37,109	38,114	39,211	38,802	37,706	36,922	36,880	37,041	35,890	35,699
Rate [1]	*32*	*31*	*31*	*31*	*30*	*29*	*28*	*28*	*27*	*26*	*25*
Other roads:											
Fatal	567	628	646	635	626	578	602	585	636	683	642
Fatal and serious	7,360	7,209	7,143	6,919	6,548	6,444	6,303	6,070	5,982	5,961	5,625
All severities	31,717	31,293	32,988	33,460	33,569	32,504	31,709	31,511	30,767	30,795	30,487
Rate [1]	*54*	*53*	*55*	*55*	*55*	*52*	*51*	*51*	*47*	*47*	*46*
All roads [3]											
Fatal	3,326	3,286	3,274	3,298	3,137	3,138	3,108	3,176	3,124	3,247	2,978
Fatal and serious	42,621	41,787	40,601	39,628	37,770	36,405	35,607	34,764	33,645	32,160	29,726
All severities	234,254	230,544	236,193	240,287	238,923	235,048	233,729	229,014	221,751	214,030	207,410
Rate [1]	*55*	*53*	*53*	*53*	*52*	*50*	*50*	*48*	*45*	*43*	*41*
All A roads:											
Fatal	1,990	1,887	1,860	1,939	1,788	1,782	1,782	1,826	1,821	1,847	1,669
Fatal and serious	20,276	19,959	19,402	19,128	18,201	17,388	17,204	16,761	16,168	15,328	14,055
All severities	109,974	107,428	108,803	111,165	109,807	107,474	107,544	105,548	102,378	98,436	94,429
Rate [1]	*56*	*54*	*53*	*53*	*52*	*50*	*51*	*49*	*47*	*44*	*42*
Other non-motorway roads:											
Fatal	1,201	1,245	1,261	1,200	1,192	1,180	1,165	1,170	1,128	1,216	1,160
Fatal and serious	21,227	20,675	20,099	19,296	18,421	17,799	17,213	16,768	16,315	15,666	14,624
All severities	117,055	115,724	119,603	120,444	120,255	118,456	116,791	114,338	110,431	106,848	103,909
Rate [1]	*74*	*73*	*74*	*73*	*72*	*70*	*69*	*66*	*62*	*59*	*57*

1 Figures have been revised from those published in previous years, see Notes and Definitions for more details. ☎020-7944 3078
2 The definition of urban and rural roads is different to that of built-up and non built-up shown in editions prior to 2003.
3 Includes unallocated roads.

8.4 Casualties by hour of day: 2004

(a) Weekdays

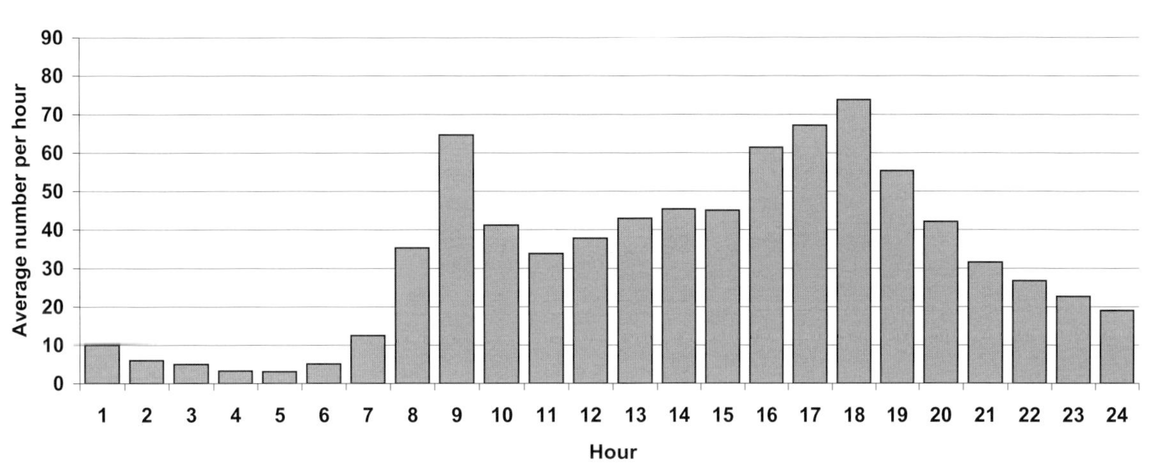

(b) Weekends

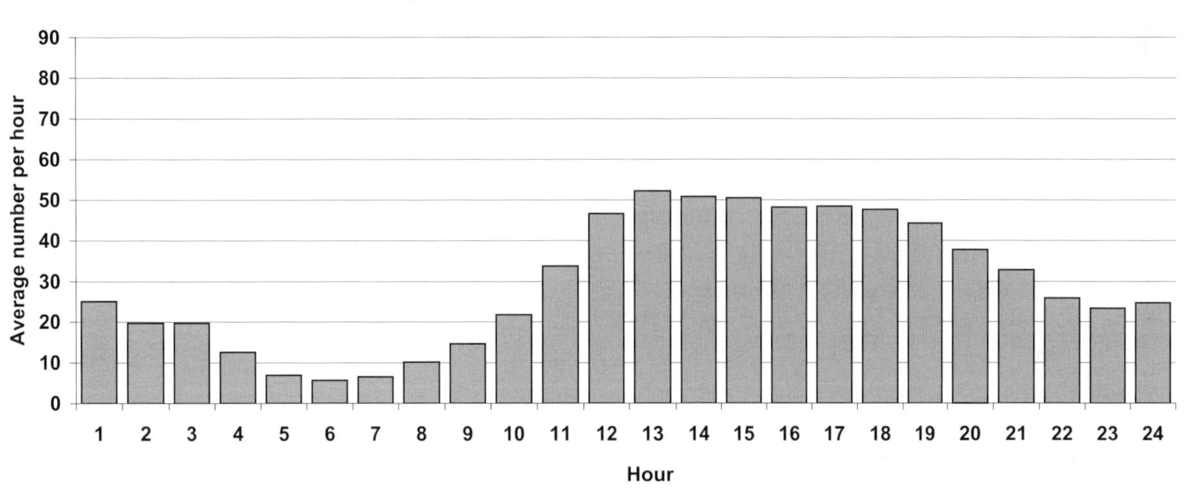

Note: The hours are defined as 1 being between midnight and 1 am, and 12 being between 11 am and midday, etc.

☎020-7944 3078

8.5 Road accidents: breath tests performed on car drivers and motorcycle riders involved in injury accidents: Great Britain: 1994-2004

Number/percentage

	1994	1995	1996	1997	1998	1999	2000	2001	2002	2003	2004
Car drivers involved	322,946	318,083	331,091	338,924	337,794	329,866	329,846	321,900	314,568	299,333	291,842
Breath tested [1]											
Number	91,927	99,631	133,347	157,373	173,610	175,916	172,840	163,540	159,782	151,442	149,430
Percentage of drivers involved	*28*	*31*	*40*	*46*	*51*	*53*	*52*	*51*	*51*	*51*	*51*
Failed breath test [1]											
Number	6,366	6,639	7,303	7,087	6,690	6,669	7,124	7,264	7,285	7,289	6,655
Percentage of drivers tested	*7*	*7*	*5*	*5*	*4*	*4*	*4*	*4*	*5*	*5*	*4*
Motorcycle riders involved	25,127	24,219	23,798	25,211	25,514	27,122	29,236	30,084	29,503	29,523	26,857
Breath tested [1]											
Number	5,159	5,720	7,906	9,926	11,416	12,970	13,945	13,725	12,992	13,178	12,422
Percentage of riders involved	*21*	*24*	*33*	*39*	*45*	*48*	*48*	*46*	*44*	*45*	*46*
Failed breath test [1]											
Number	450	438	408	428	426	443	442	446	441	510	423
Percentage of riders tested	*9*	*8*	*5*	*4*	*4*	*3*	*3*	*3*	*3*	*4*	*3*

1 Includes refusals.

☎020-7944 3078

8.6 Motor vehicle offences: drinking and driving: summary of breath tests and blood or urine tests: England and Wales: 1993-2003

Number/percentage

	1993	1994	1995	1996	1997	1998	1999	2000	2001	2002 [2]	2003
Screening breath test: number required (inc. refused/not able)	600,000	679,000	703,000	781,000	800,000	815,000	764,000	714,800	623,900	570,200	534,300
Of which: positive/refused [1]	89,000	93,000	94,000	101,000	104,000	102,000	94,000	95,000	100,000	103,500	106,300
Result (per cent)											
Positive/Refused	*15*	*14*	*13*	*13*	*13*	*13*	*12*	*13*	*16*	*18*	*20*
Negative	*85*	*86*	*87*	*87*	*87*	*87*	*88*	*87*	*84*	*82*	*80*
Total	*100*	*100*	*100*	*100*	*100*	*100*	*100*	*100*	*100*	*100*	*100*

1 Includes persons unable to provide a breath test specimen.

2 The figures for 2002 have been revised.

☎020-8760 1546

Source - Home Office

For further details on vehicle offences see Home Office Statistical Bulletin, Issue 06/05 Motoring Offences - - England & Wales 2003 and associated Supplementary Tables - England & Wales 2003. Copies of this report and other RDS publications can be downloaded free from the Home Office web site at: http://www.homeoffice.gov.uk/rds/index.htm

For details on motor vehicle offences in Scotland see Scottish Executive Criminal Justice Series Statistical Bulletin, Criminal Procedings in Scottish Courts 2003. The Scottish Executive ☎0131-244 2227

8.7 Motor vehicle offences: findings of guilt at all courts, fixed penalty notices and written warnings: by type of offence: England and Wales: 1993-2003

Thousands of offences

	1993	1994	1995	1996	1997	1998	1999	2000	2001	2002	2003
Offence type:											
Dangerous, careless or drunken driving etc	192	190	189	191	199	190	183	144	137	171	177
Accident offences	27	24	23	22	22	21	19	18	18	18	19
Speed limit offences	519	602	680	752	881	962	1,001	1,188	1,391	1,538 [1]	2,223
Unauthorised taking or theft of motor vehicle	49	46	41	40	37	37	36	32	31	32	30
Licence, insurance and record keeping offences	858	872	874	846	829	817	807	785	769	819	953
Vehicle test and condition offences	310	314	313	293	286	277	261	243	226	228	241
Neglect of traffic signs and directions and pedestrian rights	251	260	272	276	282	271	245	232	218	213	264
Other offences relating to motor vehicles (except obstruction, waiting and parking)	280	276	278	311	349	353	488	315	290	239 [1]	280
All offences (except obstruction, waiting and parking)	2,489	2,584	2,670	2,730	2,885	2,927	2,401	2,958	3,080	3,259	4,186
Obstruction, waiting and parking offences	3,418	2,723	2,290	2,302	2,219	2,139	1,828	1,611	1,341	1,180	1,058
All offences	5,907	5,307	4,960	5,031	5,104	5,066	4,700	4,569	4,421	4,439	5,244

1 These figures for 2002 have been revised

☎020-8760 1680

Source - Home Office

For further details on vehicle offences see Home Office Statistical Bulletin, Issue 06/05 Motoring Offences - England & Wales 2003 and associated Supplementary Tables - England & Wales 2003. Copies of this report and other RDS publications can be downloaded free from the Home Office web site at: http://www.homeoffice.gov.uk/rds/index.htm

For details on motor vehicle offences in Scotland see Scottish Executive Criminal Justice series Statistical Bulletin Criminal Procedings in Scottish Courts, 2003. Contact the Scottish Executive ☎0131-244 2227

8.8 Collation of motor insurance figures: United Kingdom: 1997-2003

							Million vehicle years
(a) Exposure	1997	1998	1999	2000	2001	2002 [1]	2003 [1]
Private car (comprehensive):	14.0	15.1	15.4	16.7	16.9	17.9	18.0
Private car (non-comprehensive):	3.9	3.2	3.0	2.9	3.3	3.3	3.3
Motor cycle	0.4	0.4	0.5	0.5	0.5	0.5	0.5
Commercial vehicle (including fleet)	4.7	4.9	4.9	4.8	4.2	4.5	4.5
All vehicles	23.1	23.6	23.8	24.9	25.0	26.2	26.4
(b) Number of claims							Millions
Private car (comprehensive):	2.49	2.71	2.78	2.93	2.99	3.05	3.10
Private car (non-comprehensive):	0.36	0.31	0.27	0.24	0.29	0.29	0.25
Motor cycle	0.02	0.03	0.03	0.03	0.04	0.03	0.04
Commercial vehicle (including fleet)	0.98	1.03	1.08	1.03	0.95	0.88	0.85
All vehicles	3.86	4.09	4.16	4.23	4.26	4.25	4.24
(c) Estimated cost of claims							£ million
Private car (comprehensive):	3,199	3,684	3,969	4,479	4,644	4,841	5,174
Private car (non-comprehensive):	753	654	630	643	756	846	889
Motor cycle	69	72	87	72	77	84	94
Commercial vehicle (including fleet)	1,662	1,827	1,882	1,885	1,835	1,904	2,052
All vehicles	5,683	6,236	6,568	7,078	7,311	7,675	8,210
(d) Claim frequency							Percentage
Private car (comprehensive):	*17.9*	*18.0*	*18.0*	*17.6*	*17.6*	*17.0*	*17.2*
Private car (non-comprehensive):	*9.3*	*9.7*	*8.9*	*8.2*	*8.9*	*8.7*	*7.7*
Motor cycle	*5.4*	*7.1*	*6.9*	*5.9*	*7.1*	*6.4*	*6.9*
Commercial vehicle (including fleet)	*20.7*	*21.2*	*22.0*	*21.3*	*22.3*	*19.8*	*18.8*
All vehicles	*16.8*	*17.3*	*17.5*	*17.0*	*17.1*	*16.2*	*16.1*
(e) Average claim							£'s
Private car (comprehensive):	1,283	1,359	1,429	1,527	1,553	1,590	1,671
Private car (non-comprehensive):	2,072	2,080	2,345	2,649	2,614	2,906	3,492
Motor cycle	2,885	2,290	2,722	2,623	1,985	2,437	2,632
Commercial vehicle (including fleet)	1,696	1,775	1,748	1,833	1,939	2,157	2,407
All vehicles	1,472	1,526	1,580	1,673	1,714	1,804	1,936
(f) Annual percentage change in claim frequency							Percentage
Private car (comprehensive):	*-6.3*	*0.8*	-	*-2.2*	*0.3*	*-3.6*	*1.1*
Private car (non-comprehensive):	*-7.2*	*4.0*	*-8.2*	*-7.9*	*8.2*	*-2.0*	*-11.4*
Motor cycle	*4.0*	*31.8*	*-2.8*	*-14.5*	*19.5*	*-9.6*	*7.6*
Commercial vehicle (including fleet)	*-1.7*	*2.4*	*3.8*	*-3.2*	*4.9*	*-11.3*	*-5.1*
All vehicles	*-2.9*	*3.0*	*1.2*	*-2.9*	*0.4*	*-5.0*	*-0.8*
(g) Annual percentage change in average claim							Percentage
Private car (comprehensive):	*8.7*	*5.9*	*5.2*	*6.9*	*1.7*	*2.4*	*5.1*
Private car (non-comprehensive):	*12.7*	*0.4*	*12.7*	*13.0*	*-1.3*	*11.2*	*20.1*
Motor cycle	*44.6*	*-20.6*	*18.9*	*-3.6*	*-24.3*	*22.8*	*8.0*
Commercial vehicle (including fleet)	*0.2*	*4.7*	*-1.5*	*4.9*	*5.8*	*11.2*	*11.6*
All vehicles	*6.3*	*3.7*	*3.5*	*5.9*	*2.5*	*5.3*	*7.3*

1. Subject to minor revisions.

☎020-7944 3078
The figures in this table are outside the scope of National Statistics
Source - ABI

8.9 Railway accidents: casualties: by type of accident: 1993/1994-2003/04

Number

		1993/94	1994/95	1995/96	1996/97 [1]	1997/98	1998/99	1999/00	2000/01	2001/02	2002/03	2003/04
Train accidents:												
Killed:	Passengers	0	3	1	1	7	0	29	10	0	6	0
	Railway staff	0	5	1	0	0	0	2	4	0	1	2
	Others	6	4	5	0	3	3	2	3	5	3	8
	Total	6	12	7	1	10	3	33	17	5	10	10
Major injuries:	Passengers	5	11	1	.	.	.	.	.	.	.	.
	Railway staff	4	8	15	9	2	2	3	6	6	0	0
	Others	2	5	7	.	.	.	.	.	.	.	.
	Total	11	24	23	9	2	2	3	6	6	0	0
Minor injuries:	Passengers	129	179	61	.	.	.	.	.	.	.	.
	Railway staff	91	75	60	52	37	29	20	36	17	23	11
	Others	15	18	22	.	.	.	.	.	.	.	.
	Total	235	272	143	52	37	29	20	36	17	23	11
Public injuries:	Passengers	.	.	.	180	190	40	290	178	21	128	25
	Railway staff	.	.	.	.	.	.	.	.	.	.	.
	Others	.	.	.	14	15	13	19	15	8	15	18
	Total	.	.	.	194	205	53	309	193	29	143	43
Accidents through movement of railway vehicles:												
Killed:	Passengers	14	12	7	13	15	17	14	7	7	14	6
	Railway staff	3	3	2	2	3	1	2	3	4	2	4
	Others	9	12	8	5	14	11	11	7	10	16	9
	Total	26	27	17	20	32	29	27	17	21	32	19
Major injuries:	Passengers	41	58	52	.	.	.	.	.	.	.	.
	Railway staff	23	14	18	31	34	35	37	25	26	26	42
	Others	2	1	5	.	.	.	.	.	.	.	.
	Total	66	73	75	31	34	35	37	25	26	26	42
Minor injuries:	Passengers	2,168	2,157	2,808	.	.	.	.	.	.	.	.
	Railway staff	134	187	188	222	215	246	289	296	293	313	313
	Others	5	0	7	.	.	.	.	.	.	.	.
	Total	2,307	2,344	3,003	222	215	246	289	296	293	313	313
Public injuries:	Passengers	.	.	.	559	617	668	569	610	573	556	541
	Railway staff	.	.	.	.	.	.	.	.	.	.	.
	Others	.	.	.	16	17	13	13	18	17	13	15
	Total	.	.	.	575	634	681	582	628	590	569	556
Accidents on railway premises:												
Killed:	Passengers	2	2	2	3	4	3	4	3	3	3	6
	Railway staff	5	1	2	0	0	3	1	1	1	4	3
	Others	1	0	0	1	2	1	0	1	2	1	1
	Total	8	3	4	4	6	7	5	5	6	8	10
Major injuries:	Passengers	159	135	161	.	.	.	.	.	.	.	.
	Railway staff	235	230	192	270	315	339	300	269	319	323	305
	Others	13	23	20	.	.	.	.	.	.	.	.
	Total	407	388	373	270	315	339	300	269	319	323	305
Minor injuries:	Passengers	4,309	4,250	4,601	.	.	.	.	.	.	.	.
	Railway staff	3,365	3,149	3,896	1,568	1,836	1,795	1,756	1,803	1,713	1,744	1,622
	Others	163	146	176	.	.	.	.	.	.	.	.
	Total	7,837	7,545	8,673	1,568	1,836	1,795	1,756	1,803	1,713	1,744	1,622
Public injuries:	Passengers	.	.	.	1,710	1,940	1,963	1,883	2,007	1,807	1,861	1,925
	Railway staff	.	.	.	.	.	.	.	.	.	.	.
	Others	.	.	.	120	95	75	53	51	67	55	59
	Total	.	.	.	1,830	2,035	2,038	1,936	2,058	1,874	1,916	1,984

8.9 Railway accidents: casualties: by type of accident: 1993/1994-2003/04 (continued)

Number

	1993/94	1994/95	1995/96	1996/97 [1]	1997/98	1998/99	1999/00	2000/01	2001/02	2002/03	2003/04
Overall totals:											
Killed: Passengers	16	17	10	17	26	20	47	20	10	23	12
Railway staff	8	9	5	2	3	4	5	8	5	7	9
Others	16	16	13	6	19	15	13	11	17	20	18
Total	40	42	28	25	48	39	65	39	32	50	39
Major											
injuries: Passengers	205	204	214	.	.	.	.	.	.	.	.
Railway staff	262	252	225	310	351	376	340	300	351	349	347
Others	17	29	32	.	.	.	.	.	.	.	.
Total	484	485	471	310	351	376	340	300	351	349	347
Minor											
injuries: Passengers	6,606	6,586	7,470	.	.	.	.	.	.	.	.
Railway staff	3,590	3,411	4,144	1,842	2,088	2,070	2,065	2,135	2,023	2,080	1,946
Others	183	164	205	.	.	.	.	.	.	.	.
Total	10,379	10,161	11,819	1,842	2,088	2,070	2,065	2,135	2,023	2,080	1,946
Public											
injuries: Passengers	.	.	.	2,449	2,747	2,671	2,742	2,795	2,401	2,545	2,491
Railway staff	.	.	.	.	.	.	.	.	.	.	.
Others	.	.	.	150	127	101	85	84	92	83	92
Total	.	.	.	2,599	2,874	2,772	2,827	2,879	2,493	2,628	2,583
Trespassers and suicides:											
Deaths	262	254	246	252	265	247	274	300	275	256	246
Injured	97	85	82	106	136	149	144	177	179	137	142

1 Under the RIDDOR 95 accident reporting system, brought into force on 1 April 1996, there is no distinction between a major or minor injury for a member of the public. The reporting trigger for a public injury is that they are taken from the site of the incident to hospital for treatment. The criteria for major and minor injury remains for railway staff and contractors (see notes and definitions section at start of Chapter 8).

☎020 7944 3094
The figures in this table are outside the scope of National Statistics
Source - HSE

8.10 Railway movement accidents: passenger casualties and casualty rates: 1993/94-2003/04

Number/rate per billion passenger kilometres

	1993/94	1994/95	1995/96	1996/97 [2]	1997/98	1998/99	1999/00	2000/01	2001/02	2002/03	2003/04
Casualties: [1]											
Deaths	15	15	9	14	22	17	43	18	10	20	6
Major injuries	46	69	53	.	.	.	.	.	.	.	.
Minor injuries	2,297	2,336	2,869	739	807	708	859	788	594	684	566
All casualties	2,358	2,420	2,931	753	829	725	902	806	604	704	572
Casualty rates:											
Deaths	*0.4*	*0.4*	*0.2*	*0.4*	*0.5*	*0.4*	*0.9*	*0.4*	*0.2*	*0.4*	*0.1*
Major injuries	*1.3*	*2.0*	*1.4*	.	.	.	.	.	.	.	.
Minor injuries	*62.7*	*66.4*	*77.9*	*19.1*	*19.4*	*16.2*	*18.6*	*16.9*	*12.5*	*13.9*	*13.8*
All casualties	*64.4*	*68.8*	*79.6*	*19.4*	*19.9*	*16.6*	*19.5*	*17.3*	*12.7*	*14.3*	*13.9*

1 Passenger casualties involved in train accidents and accidents occurring through movement of railway vehicles.
2 Under the new Accidents Reporting Regulations (RIDDOR 95) brought into force on 1 April 1996, there is no distinction between major and minor injury to members of the public. All injuries to members of the public are now shown as either minor injuries or killed. The reporting trigger for minor injuries is that the person is taken to hospital for treatment.

☎020-7944 3094
The figures in this table are outside the scope of National Statistics
Source - HSE

8.11 Railway accidents: train accidents: 1993/94-2003/04

Number

	1993/94	1994/95	1995/96	1996/97 [1]	1997/98	1998/99	1999/00	2000/01	2001/02	2002/03	2003/04
Collisions	135	125	123	120	127	121	94	106	101	69	59
Derailments	113	149	104	119	93	117	89	93	88	67	62
Running into level crossing gates and other obstructions	445	397	488	741	680	690	753	693	557	495	448
Fires	247	217	256	302	344	343	340	301	291	292	297
Damage to drivers' cab windscreens [2]	.	.	.	468	619	564	617	607	665	498	393
Miscellaneous	37	19	18	3	0	0	2	1	2	0	0
All accidents	977	907	989	1,753	1,863	1,835	1,895	1,801	1,704	1,421	1,259

1 New Accidents reporting regulations (RIDDOR 95) came into force on 1 April 1996.
2 Category now reportable under RIDDOR 95.

☎020 7944 3094
The figures in this table are outside the scope of National Statistics
Source - HSE

9 Vehicles:

Notes and Definitions

Vehicles registered for the first time and vehicles currently licensed: 9.1-9.8

Changes in the vehicle taxation system: There have been three major sets of changes to the vehicle taxation system in recent years:

From 1 October 1982, all general goods vehicles less than 1,525 kgs unladen weight were assessed for vehicle excise duty at the same rate as private vehicles and the old 'private car and van' taxation class was replaced by the new 'Private and Light Goods' (PLG) taxation class. Also goods vehicles greater than 1,525 kgs unladen weight were to be taxed with reference to their gross vehicle weight and axle configuration, as opposed to unladen weight as in previous years (farmers' light goods vehicles and showmen's light goods vehicles, ie. vehicles of less than 1,525 kgs unladen weight, were allocated to their own distinct taxation classes and were not included in the PLG taxation class).

From 1 October 1990, goods vehicles less than 3,500 kgs gross vehicle weight was transferred from the 'Goods Vehicle' taxation class to the 'Private and Light Goods' class. (Farmers' and showmen's goods vehicles of less than 3,500 kgs gross vehicle weight, but more than 1,525 kgs unladen weight, were transferred to the 'Light Goods Farmers' and 'Light Goods Showmen's taxation classes.)

Important changes to the vehicle taxation system were introduced from 1 July 1995, with the intention of removing many of the complications in the existing structure. The strategy was to link VED rates for as many vehicles as possible either to the rate for the private and light goods group (PLG), or the basic minimum rate for heavy goods vehicles (HGVs).

To achieve this, three 'umbrella' taxation groups were created: an emergency vehicles group exempt from VED; a special concessionary group including agricultural machines, snow ploughs, gritting vehicles, electric vehicles and, later, steam powered vehicles; and a special vehicles group, limited to vehicles over 3,500 kgs, including mobile cranes, works trucks, digging machines, showmen's vehicles, etc.

In addition, the goods vehicle taxation system was itself considerably simplified by the abolition of separate goods vehicle classes for farmers and showmen. All remaining light goods vehicle taxation classes were also abolished and vehicles in those groups transferred to the PLG class. At the same time, the basis for calculation of excise duty for goods vehicles was amended to 'revenue weight'. Revenue weight means either 'confirmed maximum gross weight' as determined by plating and testing regulations, or 'design weight' for vehicles not subject to plating and testing (formerly known as Restricted HGVs).

The process also included further simplifications and 'tidying' arrangements. These included cases in which vehicles of less than 3,500 kgs gross weight were moved into the private and light goods taxation class rather than remaining in specialised taxation classes and groups, and the reallocation of some tax classes into more appropriate groups. The changes were completed by the introduction of a new exempt class in the November 1995 budget for vehicles previously in the private and light goods or motor cycle groups over 25 of years of age, and the reallocation of a small number of minor tax classes.

In general, the process of implementing these changes was gradual, and vehicles were allowed to remain in their current class until a new tax disk was required, whereupon they were transferred into other groups and classes as appropriate. Since tax disks may run for up to a year, some vehicles remained legitimately taxed in abolished groups at end 1995.

Current taxation system: Following the reforms introduced in 1995, the vehicle taxation system consists of the following main groups.

Exempt vehicles: The exempt vehicles includes a number of distinct sub-groups and classes, of which the most important are:-

- Emergency vehicles.
- Crown vehicles.
- Disabled driver and disabled passenger carrying vehicles.
- Vehicles previously in PLG, motor cycle or tricycle tax groups manufactured before 1993.

The emergency vehicles group was created from 1 July 1995. These vehicles are required to obtain and display an annual tax disk but pay a nil rate of duty. Similarly, vehicles exempt because of age are still required to obtain and display an annual tax disk but pay a nil rate of duty.

Vehicles owned by Government Departments and operated under Certificates of Crown ownership (apart from those belonging to the Armed Forces) are registered but exempt from vehicle excise duty. The exempt vehicle statistics exclude cars and motor cycles used temporarily in Great Britain before being privately exported under the personal export and direct export schemes by non-United Kingdom citizens. Electric vehicles, which were previously an exempt class, fall into the special concession group from 1st July 1995.

General haulage: General haulage vehicles may not be used for carrying loads or transporting goods except on the trailer which it is towing, where, unlike articulated heavy goods vehicles, the trailer does not form an integral part of vehicles. Many vehicles taxed for general haulage are agricultural tractors.

Goods vehicles: Goods vehicles over 3,500 kgs gross vehicle weight. Now limited to two main groups, class 01 for heavy goods vehicles, and class 02 for goods vehicles paying additional trailer duty. Goods vehicles on certain off-shore islands may qualify to tax in class 16-small island goods. Reductions are available for goods vehicles meeting certain emission standards and generally the VED rates are based on the maximum gross vehicle weight and the number of axles used by the vehicles. Rates are lower for vehicles that have a lower average weight per axle, since these will cause less damage to the roads. The VED system for HGV's has been simplified to reduce the number of different rates in operation.

Motorcycles, scooters and mopeds: No distinction between these different types of machine is made for taxation purposes. The vehicle excise duty payable depends upon the engine capacity of the bike. The numbers licensed are influenced by seasonal factors and peaks in the summer months.

Private and light goods: Includes all vehicles used privately. The bulk of this group consists of private cars (whether owned by individuals or companies) and vans and light goods vehicles. The group also contains a number of important minority groups including private buses and coaches, private heavy goods vehicles, and some vehicles not exceeding 3,500 kgs which before 1st July 1995 were taxed in specialised taxation classes. A substantial number of motorcars are now taxed in the exempt disabled driver class. Taxation for private and light goods vehicles has changed in recent years. From June 1999, a reduced rate has been available for vehicles with smaller engine sizes. For existing vehicles, a reduced rate is currently in operation for those vehicles with an engine size of 1549cc or less. For new vehicles, from March 2001, taxation rates will be based upon the CO_2 emissions from the vehicle with five graduated bands, dependent upon the vehicle's fuel type. Twelve month VED rates in these four bands range from £70 to £155 for a petrol car.

Public transport vehicles: All vehicles classified for taxation purposes as class 34 - Bus (introduced 1 July 1995). These are vehicles used for public conveyance, with more than 8 seats. Prior to 1st July 1995 public transport vehicles were taxed in class 35 Hackney, used, similarly for public transportation but with no lower limit on seating capacity. Tables in part 9 concerned with public transport vehicles show time series for class 35 (Hackney vehicles) up to the end of 1994 and class 34 (Bus) thereafter, with retrospective estimates for class 34 wherever possible. Buses and coaches not licensed for public conveyance, and operated and used privately, are excluded and are classified for excise licensing with private and light goods. Taxis and private hire cars are now included in the private and light goods group and are not separately identified within the VED taxation system. Regulation and control of taxis and private hire cars is through local authorities who issue appropriate hackney and hire car plates. As with goods vehicles, reduced rates are available for reduced pollution public transport vehicles.

Special concessionary group: This class includes agricultural vehicles which are now exempt from duty. Also included are electric vehicles, gritting vehicles and snow ploughs, and steam powered vehicles. However, works trucks, mobile cranes and digging machines previously in the 'agricultural and special machines' group are no longer included and are in the special vehicles group.

Special vehicles group: This group consists of vehicles over 3,500 kgs, which do not pay VED as heavy goods vehicles nor qualify for taxation in the special concessionary group. Vehicles in this group pay VED at the basic minimum rate for HGVs. Types include road rollers, works trucks, digging machines, mobile cranes and showman's vehicles.

Other vehicles: This group includes three-wheeled cars and vans not exceeding 450 kgs unladen weight, recovery vehicles and general haulage vehicles, as described above. Motorised tricycles are included but motor cycle combinations are included with motor cycles.

Trade licences: These are issued to manufacturers and repairers of, and dealers in, motor vehicles but as they do not relate to particular vehicles they are not included in any of the tables relating to current licences or new registrations.

Vehicles owned by the Armed Forces: Vehicles officially belonging to the Armed Forces, except for a small number which for particular reasons, are licensed in the ordinary way, operate under a special registration and licensing system operated by them. Such vehicles are excluded from vehicle registration figures.

New registrations: 9.2

Census method: The statistics in this section are based on a complete analysis of new registrations and not on a sample count. Monthly analyses are compiled from the records of the Driver and Vehicle Licensing Agency (DVLA).

Statistics in this table are based on a complete analysis of new registrations and not on a sample count. In addition to the information already provided for Table 9.2, there are other historical licensing changes that affect the data.

In the past these were obtained from monthly returns of licensing authorities' records of new registrations. On 1 October 1974, the Driver and Vehicle Licensing Centre (DVLC) at Swansea took over responsibility for the licensing of vehicles from Local Taxation Offices (LTO). Initially, DVLC dealt only with new registrations, but from 1 April 1975 they began to take on the registration of older vehicles from the Local Vehicle Licensing Offices, which replaced the LTOs. On 1 April 1990, DVLC became the Driver and Vehicle Licensing Agency (DVLA). From July 1995 new tax arrangements applied to many minor taxation groups.

Vehicles currently licensed: 9.1, 9.3-9.8

Census Method: The census methods employed to estimate vehicles currently licensed fall into three distinct periods. Prior to 1978, information on vehicle stock had been obtained mainly from a sample of vehicles, and, for purely administrative reasons, counts of licensed vehicles at Local Taxation Offices included any vehicle licensed for at least one month during the third quarter of the year.

Estimates of vehicles currently licensed were based on the record of licensed vehicles at DVLA. The first such census was taken on 31 December 1978, and subsequent counts were also been taken on the last day of the year. Censuses derived from DVLA records were based on a single point (one day) in time, and were a complete count of all vehicles determined to be licensed on that specific day.

The 1995 changes did not produce any major change in total number of vehicles taxed within the PLG group, and the PLG series has not been subject to any retrospective adjustment or recalculation. Retrospective series have been estimated for the new 'bus' taxation class and are included in the tables.

Regional analysis: The only regional information easily obtainable from vehicle records held on computer by DVLA is the post code of the registered keeper of the vehicle (which may be a company car or a private individual). This can be used to determine the county in which the keeper lives. The regional analysis of body type cars in Table 9.5 has been compiled in this way. In this table, the figures for Great Britain include vehicles whose county is unknown. The number of cars licensed per 1,000 population is based on 2003 mid-year population estimates. This table is based upon cars in all taxation classes, whereas figures in Table 9.3 are different since they are for cars in the PLG tax class only. For an analysis by county and for more detailed information on vehicle stock and new registrations see *Vehicle Licensing Statistics 2004*, available from DfT, as a free statistical bulletin, or from the DfT website at: www.dft.gov.uk/transtat

In addition to the information provided for Tables 9.1, 9.3-9.8, the following is also relevant. Up to 1974, the figures for motor vehicles currently licensed were compiled from information received by the Department for Transport from all registration/licensing authorities or Local Taxation Offices (County, County Borough and Borough Councils) in Great Britain, which administered the Vehicles (Excise) Act 1971. Since October 1974, all new vehicles have been registered at the Driver and Vehicle Licensing Agency (DVLA), and records for older vehicles have also been transferred there, the process being completed in March 1978. For 1975 and 1976, the census was based on a combination of records held at Local Taxation Offices and at DVLA. Because of the closure of Local Taxation Offices, it was not possible to produce census results in 1977.

The first census based entirely on the record of licensed vehicles at DVLA was taken on 31 December 1978.

Figures for the period 1950-1976 are at 30th September; the 1977 census results are estimates; those for 1978-1993 are at 31st December. For years up to 1992, estimates are taken from the annual vehicle census analyses, based on the Driver and Vehicle Licensing Agency main vehicle file. From 1992, estimates of licensed stock are taken from DfT's Vehicle Information Database. From July 1995 new tax arrangements applied to many minor taxation groups.

Goods vehicles: 9.6-9.8

Vehicles included fall mainly into the goods vehicles taxation classes which include HGV, trailer HGV, and restricted HGV, for general goods, showman's goods and farmer's goods. Also included are vehicles in the Small Island goods, crown, electric vehicles and exempt taxation classes, which exceed 3.5 tonnes gross weight and have goods vehicle body type. Legislative changes have had an effect on the distribution of lorry weights. From the beginning of 1999, vehicles with 5 or more axles have been permitted to operate at a gross weight of 40 tonnes and since the start of 2001, 6 axle vehicles are allowed to run at 44 tonnes.

Trailer tests: 9.9

Although there is no registration system for trailers which carry goods, there is still a requirement to have them tested each year under the DfT's plating and testing scheme. These tests carried out by the Vehicle and Operator Services Agency provide the best current estimate of the number of trailers in use and includes a breakdown according to number of axles.

Vehicle testing scheme (MOT): 9.10-9.13

The following information gives some background on the testing process:

- 1 January 1977: stop lamps, indicators, windscreen wipers & washers, horn and the condition of the wheels, seat belts, exhaust systems, bodywork and suspension became testable;
- 1 January 1980: introduction of new testing station approval standards;
- 1 November 1991: introduction of exhaust emissions testing;
- 1 January 1992: minimum tyre tread depth raised from 1mm to 1.6mm;
- 1 January 1993: inspections of field of vision/ condition of glass, mirrors, fuel tanks and pipes, bodywork and body security, seat security, security of doors and other openings, registration plates, vehicle identification numbers, rear registration plate lamps, rear fog lamps, hazard warning signal devices, and diesel (smoke emission) were added to the test. The diesel smoke emission test was withdrawn in February 1993, but reintroduced in February 1994;
- 1 September 1995: the emissions limit for petrol and diesel engine vehicles in classes IV, V and VII were lowered.
- 1 January 1996: new limits for certain catalyst equipped petrol engine class IV vehicles, registered on or after 1 August 1992 were introduced. The tests were extended to include large petrol fuelled cars and petrol fuelled light goods vehicles from 1 August 1997.
- 1 August 1998 changes were made to the seat belt installation checks.

In 1999/00, there were 18,899 authorised examiners for the private MOT scheme. In addition there were 92 other MOT test stations operated by Post Offices, designated local authorities, the Crown or police authorities.

From 1 July 1970 to date a 2 per cent sample of all tests has been the basis on which vehicle testing statistics have been compiled. Computerisation of the MOT system has begun and will, once data are available, ensure a greater level of detail and accuracy. The 2 per cent sample gives:

- an estimate of the total number of vehicles presented for testing each year, with the actual total lying within 2.5 per cent of the estimate;
- a percentage breakdown of the total into 4 separate classes, normally within 0.1 per cent of the true percentage figure;
- for each class of vehicle an estimated failure rate within 0.2 per cent of the true figure for light goods vehicle, cars and other passenger vehicles and within 0.8 per cent for motor cycles;

Prohibition notice (PG9): Is a ban on the use of a vehicle on the public road. A Prohibition will normally be issued where a vehicle is found by an examiner to be, or likely to become, unfit for use or where driving the vehicle would involve a risk of injury to any person. For further details on Prohibition Notices, see publication *Categorisation of Defects on Road Vehicles*, available from the Vehicle and Operator Services Agency Publications Unit (☎01792 454267).

Road passenger service vehicle testing scheme: 9.11

EEC Directive 77/143 stipulated that all class VI (Public Service Vehicles) in use for more than one year must by 1 January 1983 have undergone a road-worthiness examination and be subject to an annual inspection thereafter. To meet this deadline, statutory testing of class VI vehicles commenced on 1 January 1982.

Goods vehicles over 3.5 tonnes testing scheme: 9.12

Table 9.12 shows from 1993 and up to including 2003 the number of tests carried out on heavy goods vehicles under the DfT's plating and testing scheme. Vehicles subject to plating and testing have to undergo a test when they are 1 year old and are tested annually thereafter; the term 'first test' refers to the first test of a vehicle in a particular year. The figures quoted cover the 52 week period ending on the Friday which precedes the first Monday in April.

For the purposes of this section, the vehicles are goods vehicles with a gross weight (gross train weight for articulated vehicles) exceeding 3,500 kgs. Further information on all vehicle testing schemes may be purchased from:

> Vehicle and Operator Services Agency, Welcombe House
> 91-92 The Strand, Swansea, SA1 2DH
> (☎ 01792 454233).

Households with regular use of cars: 9.14

Data from 1961 onwards are derived from household surveys. Figures for earlier years are estimates. Also, see notes to Table 9.15.

Private motoring: 9.15 and 9.16

The mid-year estimates of the percentage of households with regular use of a car or van in Tables 9.15 (a) and (b) are based on combined data from the National Travel Survey (NTS), the Expenditure and Food Survey (previously the Family Expenditure Survey) and the General Household Survey, where available. Comparisons with Census data are also shown. Table 9.15 (c) by area type is based on data from the NTS only. The percentage of driving licence holders in Table 9.16 is based on data from the NTS, and the estimated number of licence holders based on the mid-year resident population estimates from ONS.

Annual mileage of 4-wheeled cars: 9.17

These figures are based upon annual estimates for each purpose (commuting, business and other private) per vehicle as reported by participants in the National Travel Survey (NTS). The data are for 4-wheeled cars only. Company cars provided by an employer for the use of a particular employee (or director) are included, but cars borrowed temporarily from a company pool are not.

Private motoring: 9.18

Driving tests data are supplied by the Driving Standards Agency: contact: (☎ 0115 901 2873).

9.1 Motor vehicles currently licensed: 1950-2004

Thousands

Year	Private and light goods: Private cars	Private and light goods: Other vehicles	Goods vehicles	Motor cycles etc	Public transport vehicles	Special machines/ Special concessionary[1]	Other vehicles	Special Vehicles group	Crown and exempt vehicles[1]	All vehicles
1950	1,979	439	439	643	123	262	24	.	61	3,970
1951	2,095	457	451	725	123	250	26	.	63	4,190
1952	2,221	477	450	812	119	270	29	.	86	4,464
1953	2,446	516	446	889	105	289	30	.	88	4,809
1954	2,733	566	450	977	97	307	32	.	88	5,250
1955	3,109	633	462	1,076	92	326	35	.	89	5,822
1956	3,437	685	471	1,137	89	336	37	.	95	6,287
1957	3,707	723	473	1,261	87	355	41	.	96	6,743
1958	4,047	772	461	1,300	86	367	46	.	96	7,175
1959	4,416	824	473	1,479	83	383	55	.	96	7,809
1960	4,900	894	493	1,583	84	392	65	.	101	8,512
1961	5,296	944	508	1,577	82	400	76	.	106	8,989
1962	5,776	1,002	512	1,567	84	401	83	.	107	9,532
1963	6,462	1,092	535	1,546	86	412	88	.	115	10,336
1964	7,190	1,184	551	1,534	86	421	90	.	120	11,176
1965	7,732	1,240	584	1,420	86	417	91	.	127	11,697
1966	8,210	1,283	577	1,239	85	399	87	.	142	12,022
1967	8,882	1,358	593	1,190	85	416	89	.	147	12,760
1968	9,285	1,388	580	1,082	89	409	92	.	157	13,082
1969	9,672	1,408	547	993	92	398	90	.	162	13,362
1970	9,971	1,421	545	923	93	385	89	.	121	13,548
1971	10,443	1,452	542	899	96	380	92	.	126	14,030
1972	11,006	1,498	525	866	95	371	95	.	128	14,584
1973	11,738	1,559	540	887	96	373	97	.	137	15,427
1974	11,917	1,547	539	918	96	380	96	.	149	15,642
1975	12,526	1,592	553	1,077	105	384	108	.	166	16,511
1976	13,184	1,626	563	1,175	110	387	117	.	156	17,318
1977	13,220	1,591	559	1,190	110	393	115	.	167	17,345
1978	13,626	1,597	549	1,194	110	394	111	.	177	17,758
1979	14,162	1,623	561	1,292	111	402	106	.	359	18,616
1980	14,660	1,641	507	1,372	110	397	100	.	412	19,199
1981	14,867	1,623	489	1,371	110	365	95	.	427	19,347
1982	15,264	1,624	477	1,370	111	371	91	.	454	19,762
1983	15,543	1,692	488	1,290	113	376	86	.	621	20,209
1984	16,055	1,752	490	1,225	116	375	82	.	670	20,765
1985	16,454	1,805	485	1,148	120	374	78	.	695	21,159
1986	16,981	1,880	484	1,065	125	371	73	.	720	21,699
1987	17,421	1,952	485	978	129	374	68	.	744	22,152
1988	18,432	2,096	502	912	132	383	83	.	761	23,302
1989	19,248	2,199	505	875	122	384	77	.	785	24,196
1990	19,742	2,247	482	833	115	375	71	.	807	24,673
1991	19,737	2,215	449	750	109	346	65	.	840	24,511
1992	20,116	2,230	437	688	108	324	59	.	891	24,853
1992[2]	19,870	2,198	432	684	107	324	59	.	903	24,577
1993	20,102	2,187	428	650	107	318	55	.	979	24,826
1994	20,479	2,192	434	630	107	309	50	.	1,030	25,231
1995[2]	20,505	2,217	421	594	74	274	44	28	1,169	25,369
1996	21,172	2,267	413	609	77	254	40	48	1,424	26,302
1997	21,681	2,317	414	626	79	249	38	48	1,522	26,974
1998	22,115	2,362	412	684	80	243	37	47	1,558	27,538
1999	22,785	2,427	415	760	84	241	36	47	1,573	28,368
2000	23,196	2,469	418	825	86	233	34	46	1,590	28,898
2001	23,899	2,544	422	882	89	233	33	45	1,602	29,747
2002	24,543	2,622	425	941	92	.	32	46	1,855	30,557
2003	24,985	2,730	426	1,005	96	.	32	47	1,887	31,207
2004	25,754	2,900	434	1,060	100	.	32	50	1,929	32,259

1 The "Special Concession" vehicles form part of the "Crown and exempt taxation class from 2002.

2 Changes to the taxation system have meant that there are some discontinuities in the series.

☎020-7944 3077

Further details on Vehicle Licensing Statistics are available at www.dft.gov.uk/transtat

9.2 Motor vehicles registered for the first time: 1951-2004

Thousands

Year	Private and light goods	Goods vehicles	Motor cycles etc	Public transport vehicles	Special machines and special concessionary[1]	Exempt and Other vehicles[1]	All vehicles
1951	136.2	84.5	133.4	7.8	34.4	17.6	413.9
1952	187.6	81.8	132.5	5.4	35.3	16.0	458.6
1953	295.1	97.2	138.6	5.0	33.5	14.1	583.5
1954	386.4	109.6	164.6	5.5	35.2	17.1	718.4
1955	500.9	153.5	185.2	5.6	39.2	22.1	906.5
1956	399.7	148.0	142.8	5.1	31.9	23.3	750.8
1957	425.4	140.5	206.1	5.0	39.8	19.9	836.7
1958	555.3	172.6	182.7	4.9	47.2	18.9	981.6
1959	645.6	191.7	331.8	5.1	49.0	29.7	1,252.9
1960	805.0	225.9	256.7	6.4	42.5	32.9	1,369.4
1961	742.8	220.2	212.4	6.1	46.4	31.4	1,259.3
1962	784.7	192.3	140.2	5.5	42.8	26.7	1,192.2
1963	1,008.6	206.4	165.5	6.4	47.9	31.2	1,466.0
1964	1,190.6	229.3	205.1	6.5	46.1	33.6	1,711.2
1965	1,122.5	229.4	150.9	6.8	45.4	45.7	1,600.7
1966	1,065.4	227.2	109.4	6.8	48.4	36.4	1,493.6
1967	1,116.7	221.5	137.7	6.5	53.9	38.9	1,575.2
1968	1,116.9	231.7	112.0	7.1	57.0	37.2	1,561.9
1969	987.4	239.6	85.4	7.1	49.3	33.0	1,401.8
1969 [2]	1,133.2	93.8	85.4	7.1	49.3	33.0	1,401.8
1970	1,248.1	85.2	104.9	7.7	48.8	30.2	1,524.9
1971	1,462.1	74.2	127.9	9.5	37.9	30.0	1,741.6
1972	1,854.8	74.9	152.5	9.8	47.6	44.1	2,183.7
1973	1,851.3	82.7	193.6	10.0	49.7	43.0	2,230.3
1974	1,399.6	68.0	189.8	7.8	45.6	39.6	1,750.4
1975	1,317.2	67.0	264.8	7.8	48.5	44.6	1,749.9
1976	1,401.8	63.9	270.6	8.7	51.8	41.2	1,838.0
1977	1,445.0	68.8	251.3	8.8	48.3	39.8	1,862.0
1978	1,745.8	79.8	225.3	9.1	50.0	41.4	2,151.4
1979	1,891.5	91.3	285.9	9.1	47.7	44.4	2,370.0
1980	1,679.2	74.7	312.7	8.8	36.7	43.5	2,155.6
1980 [2]	1,699.2	54.9	312.7	8.8	36.7	43.5	2,155.8
1981	1,643.6	39.9	271.9	7.5	32.6	34.8	2,030.3
1982	1,745.5	41.2	231.6	7.1	38.9	39.6	2,103.9
1983	1,989.1	46.6	174.5	7.3	42.1	47.9	2,307.5
1984	1,932.6	49.6	145.2	7.2	40.1	64.2	2,238.9
1985	2,029.5	51.7	125.8	6.8	40.1	55.4	2,309.3
1986	2,070.7	51.4	106.4	8.9	34.8	61.5	2,333.7
1987	2,212.6	54.0	90.8	8.7	37.7	70.1	2,473.9
1988	2,437.0	63.4	90.1	9.2	45.2	78.6	2,723.5
1989	2,535.2	64.5	97.3	8.0	42.5	81.4	2,828.9
1990	2,179.9	44.4	94.4	7.4	34.2	78.4	2,438.7
1991	1,708.5	28.6	76.5	5.2	26.1	76.6	1,921.5
1992	1,694.4	28.7	65.6	5.1	24.1	83.9	1,901.8
1993	1,853.4	32.8	58.4	5.4	30.0	93.8	2,073.8
1994	1,991.6	41.1	64.6	6.7	35.3	109.7	2,249.0
1995 [2]	2,024.0	48.0	68.9	5.2	33.3	127.1	2,306.5
1996	2,093.3	45.5	89.6	6.5	25.7	149.5	2,410.1
1997	2,244.3	41.8	121.7	6.6	21.7	161.7	2,597.7
1998	2,367.9	49.1	143.7	7.4	15.2	157.0	2,740.3
1999	2,342.0	48.3	168.4	8.0	24.9	174.3	2,765.8
2000	2,429.8	50.4	182.9	7.5	24.0	176.3	2,870.9
2001	2,709.7	48.6	177.1	6.8	26.7	168.8	3,137.7
2002	2,815.6	44.9	162.2	7.8	-	199.0	3,229.4
2003	2,820.7	48.4	157.3	8.4	-	197.1	3,231.9
2004	2,784.7	48.0	133.7	8.3	-	210.7	3,185.4

1 The "Special Concessionary" vehicles form part of "Exempt and other vehicles" as they are exempt from tax from 2002.

2 Changes to the taxation system have meant that there are some discontinuities in the series.

☎020-7944 3077

Further details on Vehicle Licensing Statistics are available at www.dft.gov.uk/transtat

9.3 Motor vehicles currently licensed at end of year: by type of vehicle: 1994-2004

(a) Private and light goods — Thousands

Year		1994	1995 [1]	1996	1997	1998	1999	2000	2001	2002	2003	2004
Body type cars classified by cylinder capacity												
Over	Not over											
	700cc	54	46	42	37	29	18	19	23	29	37	47
700cc	1,000cc	1,905	1,757	1,678	1,564	1,459	1,435	1,415	1,368	1,314	1,237	1,199
1,000cc	1,200cc	2,261	2,258	2,327	2,336	2,293	2,275	2,228	2,244	2,252	2,221	2,210
1,200cc	1,500cc	5,337	5,225	5,321	5,418	5,497	5,600	5,677	5,819	5,894	5,939	6,089
1,500cc	1,800cc	6,276	6,345	6,540	6,655	6,766	6,922	6,992	7,124	7,241	7,284	7,405
1,800cc	2,000cc	3,088	3,274	3,550	3,828	4,090	4,389	4,604	4,869	5,166	5,398	5,686
2,000cc	2,500cc	759	791	851	925	1,003	1,094	1,159	1,275	1,400	1,520	1,639
2,500cc	3,000cc	486	494	524	548	574	608	630	666	704	762	841
3,000cc		313	315	340	371	403	443	473	510	543	587	638
All capacities		20,479	20,505	21,172	21,681	22,115	22,785	23,196	23,899	24,543	24,985	25,754
Other vehicles		2,192	2,217	2,267	2,317	2,362	2,427	2,469	2,544	2,622	2,730	2,900
All private and light goods		22,672	22,722	23,439	23,998	24,477	25,212	25,666	26,443	27,165	27,715	28,654

(b) Motor cycles, scooters and mopeds: by engine size

Over	Not over	1994	1995 [1]	1996	1997	1998	1999	2000	2001	2002	2003	2004
	50cc	129	112	105	96	102	117	141	154	155	159	161
50cc	125cc	187	170	162	143	143	148	160	172	177	182	189
125cc	150cc	2	1	1	1	1	1	1	1	1	1	1
150cc	200cc	18	14	13	12	12	12	13	13	14	16	16
200cc	250cc	50	46	46	44	42	41	38	35	33	33	33
250cc	350cc	15	12	11	10	10	9	9	8	8	9	9
350cc	500cc	45	43	48	54	57	61	62	62	70	74	75
500cc		186	196	223	265	317	371	403	437	482	531	576
All over 50cc		502	482	504	530	582	642	685	727	786	845	899
All engine sizes		630	594	609	626	684	760	825	882	941	1,005	1,060

1 The vehicle taxation system was subject to substantial revisions from 1 July 1995.

☎020-7944 3077

9.4 Motor vehicles currently licensed in 2004: by method of propulsion

Thousands

Taxation class	Petrol	Diesel	Petrol/Gas	Gas/GasBi Fuel/Gas-Diesel	Electric & Hybrid-Electric	Steam	All
Private and light goods	21,167.5	7,437.9	26.2	19.8	2.9	0.0	28,654.2
ow: Private cars	20,880.6	4,834.2	24.4	11.8	2.8	0.0	25,753.8
Motor cycles, scooters and mopeds	1,058.4	1.0	0.1	0.1	0.3	0.0	1,059.9
Bus	1.0	98.7	0.1	0.1	0.0	0.0	99.9
Goods	2.1	431.7	-	0.2	0.0	0.0	434.1
Special vehicles group	0.4	47.6	0.6	1.1	0.1	-	49.9
Other vehicles	14.7	16.9	-	-	0.0	0.0	31.7
Exempt vehicles of which:	1,317.5	595.6	1.1	1.6	11.7	1.9	1,929.3
former Special concessionary group	11.8	254.6	0.1	0.1	8.3	0.4	275.4
Total All Vehicles	23,561.6	8,629.4	28.1	22.9	14.9	1.9	32,258.9

☎020-7944 3077

9.5 Body type cars currently licensed: by government office region: 2004

			2004			
			Body type cars in all taxation classes			
	1994 (thousand)	2003 (thousand)	(thousand)	Per 1000 population	Average vehicle age	Percentage first registered in 2004
North East	756	948	982	387	5.7	*9.8*
North West	2,407	2,942	3,056	449	5.9	*10.8*
Yorkshire and the Humber	1,656	2,039	2,110	421	6.0	*9.5*
East Midlands	1,451	1,965	2,001	471	6.5	*10.7*
West Midlands	2,116	2,612	2,675	503	6.1	*12.8*
East of England	2,218	2,711	2,757	505	6.8	*9.3*
London	2,343	2,480	2,523	341	7.1	*8.6*
South East	3,263	4,162	4,248	526	6.6	*10.1*
South West	1,980	2,523	2,571	514	7.2	*7.4*
Total England	18,191	22,382	22,921	460	6.5	*9.9*
Wales	982	1,305	1,357	462	6.7	*7.5*
Scotland	1,603	2,031	2,076	411	5.7	*10.5*
Great Britain [1]	21,199	26,240	27,028	467	6.5	*9.6*

1 Totals for Great Britain include vehicles for which the region is unknown

☎020-7944 3077

Further details on Vehicle Licensing Statistics are available at www.dft.gov.uk/transtat

9.6 Goods vehicles over 3.5 tonnes currently licensed: 2004

Thousands

Body type	Over / Not over	3.5 t / 7.5 t	7.5 t / 12 t	12 t / 16 t	16 t / 20 t	20 t / 24 t	24 t / 28 t	28 t / 32 t	32 t / 33 t	33 t / 37 t	37 t / 38 t	38 t	All weights
Rigid vehicles													
Box Van		66.7	4.5	6.8	21.5	1.4	3.0	0.1	-	-	-	0.1	104.1
Tipper		21.3	0.8	1.0	5.5	0.2	6.3	15.0	-	-	-	-	50.3
Flat Lorry		8.1	1.0	1.2	4.4	0.8	3.7	0.9	-	-	-	0.1	20.2
Dropside Lorry		12.2	0.9	1.2	5.2	0.3	1.8	0.2	-	0.0	-	-	21.6
Goods		7.0	0.7	1.3	3.4	0.6	2.1	1.2	-	-	0.2	0.6	17.2
Insulated Van		6.9	0.8	1.7	3.8	0.4	1.2	-	0.0	0.0	-	-	14.7
Refuse Disposal		0.7	0.3	0.3	1.7	2.0	6.3	1.7	0.0	0.0	-	0.0	12.8
Skip Loader		1.2	0.2	0.3	5.6	0.2	0.8	2.1	-	-	-	-	10.4
Panel Van		7.3	0.1	-	0.2	-	-	-	-	0.0	0.0	1.0	7.7
Tanker		0.4	0.3	0.3	2.3	0.1	2.7	0.8	-	0.0	-	-	7.0
Concrete Mixer		-	-	0.2	0.5	-	2.9	0.7	-	-	-	1.0	4.3
Van		2.5	0.1	0.1	0.2	-	-	-	0.0	0.0	-	1.0	2.9
Livestock Carrier		2.6	0.2	0.1	0.2	-	0.2	-	0.0	0.0	0.0	-	3.4
Street Cleansing		1.6	0.1	1.9	0.3	-	0.1	-	0.0	0.0	0.0	1.0	4.0
Car Transporter		1.0	0.2	0.1	1.3	0.8	-	-	0.0	-	-	-	3.5
Luton Van		1.9	0.1	0.2	0.2	-	-	-	0.0	-	0.0	0.0	2.4
Float		1.7	-	-	0.0	0.0	0.0	0.0	0.0	0.0	0.0	0.0	1.7
Tractor		0.4	-	0.1	0.6	0.2	1.0	0.3	-	-	0.3	0.8	2.9
Truck		0.9	0.1	0.1	0.2	-	0.1	-	0.0	-	-	-	1.6
Specially Fitted Van		0.7	0.1	0.1	0.2	-	0.1	-	-	0.0	0.0	0.0	1.3
Pantechnicon		0.2	-	0.1	0.3	0.1	-	-	0.0	0.0	0.0	0.0	0.7
Tower Wagon		1.1	0.1	-	-	0.0	-	-	0.0	0.0	0.0	0.0	1.2
Skeletal Vehicle		0.6	0.1	0.2	0.3	-	0.1	0.2	-	0.0	0.0	-	1.4
Curtain Sided		5.9	0.4	0.4	4.5	0.2	1.7	-	0.0	-	-	-	13.3
Glass Carrier		0.2	-	-	0.2	-	-	-	0.0	0.0	0.0	0.0	0.5
Mobile Plant		0.2	-	-	0.1	-	0.1	-	0.0	0.0	-	0.0	0.5
Special Mobile Unit		0.3	0.1	-	0.1	-	-	-	0.0	0.0	0.0	0.0	0.5
Airport Support Unit		0.1	-	-	0.2	0.0	-	0.0	0.0	0.0	0.0	0.0	0.3
Others or not known		4.4	0.6	1.0	2.0	0.3	0.8	0.7	2.4	-	-	0.8	10.7
Total		158.2	11.9	18.8	64.6	7.9	35.1	24.2	2.4	0.1	0.6	1.7	323.1
Articulated vehicles [1]													
Total		0.2	0.1	-	0.4	1.5	9.0	4.3	2.0	3.1	22.8	75.3	118.7
Rigid and articulated vehicles													
Total		158.5	11.9	18.9	65.0	9.5	44.0	28.5	4.4	3.2	23.4	77.1	441.8

1 Body type refers to that of the trailer, or most frequently used trailer. The majority of these are recorded as "Goods" or are not known. Consequently there is insufficient reliable data for articulated vehicles by body type.

☎020-7944 3077

Further details on Vehicle Licensing Statistics are available at www.dft.gov.uk/transtat

9.7 Goods vehicles over 3.5 tonnes currently licensed at end of year: 1994-2004

Thousands

Year	Rigid vehicles	Articulated vehicles: Not over 28 tonnes	Articulated vehicles: Over 28 tonnes	Articulated vehicles: All	All vehicles
1994	312	13	91	103	416
1995	311	13	94	107	418
1996	311	13	96	110	421
1997	310	13	99	112	422
1998	310	13	98	111	421
1999	311	14	98	112	423
2000	311	14	100	114	425
2001	314	13	102	115	430
2002	316	12	104	117	433
2003	317	12	105	117	433
2004	323	11	107	119	442

☎020-7944 3077

9.8 Goods vehicles over 3.5 tonnes gross weight by axle configuration: 2004

Thousands

(tonnes) Over	Not over	Rigid: 2 axles	Rigid: 3 axles	Rigid: 4 axles	Rigid: All rigid vehicles	Articulated: 2 axle tractive unit	Articulated: 3 axle tractive unit	Articulated: All articulated vehicles
3.5	16	188.4	0.4	0.1	188.9	0.3	0.1	0.3
16	24	64.2	8.2	0.1	72.5	1.9	0.1	1.9
24	28	0.4	34.3	0.4	35.1	8.5	0.4	9.0
28	32	0.2	0.1	23.9	24.2	4.0	0.3	4.3
32	33	-	-	-	-	1.7	0.3	2.0
33	37	-	-	-	0.1	2.7	0.4	3.1
37	38	0.1	0.1	0.4	0.6	15.1	7.7	22.8
38		0.1	0.2	1.4	1.7	9.3	66.0	75.3
All weights		253.5	43.4	26.3	323.1	43.4	75.3	118.7

☎020-7944 3077

9.9 Trailer tests by axle type: 1996/97-2004/05

National totals									Thousands
First / Annual tests in:	1996/97	1997/98	1998/99	1999/00	2000/01	2001/02	2002/03	2003/04	2004/05
1 axle	9.4	8.6	8.1	7.5	7.1	6.7	6.4	6.0	5.6
2 axle	111.3	104.9	98.1	89.8	82.2	74.1	68.9	63.9	58.4
3 axle	111.9	121.7	131.8	143.2	151.2	156.7	166.5	171.5	177.9
4 axle	0.1	0.1	0.1	0.1	0.1	0.1	0.1	0.1	0.2
5 axle	-	-	-	-	-	-	-	-	-
Total	232.8	235.3	238.1	240.6	240.6	237.6	241.9	241.5	242.1

☎01792 454296
The figures in this table are outside the scope of National Statistics
Source - VOSA

9.10 Road vehicle testing scheme (MOT): test results: 1994/95-2004/05

											Thousand/percentage
(a) Motor cycles	1994/95	1995/96	1996/97	1997/98	1998/99	1999/00	2000/01	2001/02	2002/03	2003/04	2004/05
Tested	508.6	580.4	582.1	541.1	564.4	513.8	567.8	568.4	584.9	745.0 [1]	801.0
Failed	119.9	139.7	151.4	116.0	124.4	114.4	112.9	113.1	108.4	126.5	166.4
Percentage failed	*24*	*24*	*26*	*21*	*22*	*22*	*20*	*20*	*19*	*17*	*21*
(b) Cars, light goods vehicles, private passenger vehicles and other passenger vehicles											Million/percentage
Cars and other passenger vehicles:											
Tested	22.6	22.5	21.7	21.5	22.2	22.0	22.8	22.8	22.8	22.5	20.7
Failed	8.4	8.4	7.8	7.8	7.9	7.4	7.2	7.3	7.1	6.6	6.0
Percentage failed	*37*	*37*	*36*	*36*	*36*	*34*	*32*	*32*	*31*	*29*	*29*
Light goods vehicles:											
Tested	0.2	0.2	0.2	0.3	0.2	0.3	0.3	0.3	0.4	0.5	0.6
Failed	0.1	0.1	0.1	0.1	0.1	0.1	0.1	0.1	0.1	0.2	0.2
Percentage failed	*33*	*36*	*36*	*37*	*37*	*33*	*36*	*34*	*35*	*34*	*33*
Private passenger vehicles: [2]											
Tested	0.03	0.03	0.03	0.03	0.03	0.03	0.03	0.03	0.03	0.04	0.03
Failed	0.01	0.01	0.01	0.01	0.01	0.01	0.01	0.01	0.01	0.01	0.01
Percentage failed	*39*	*33*	*29*	*28*	*30*	*21*	*25*	*21*	*20*	*25*	*17*
(c) All vehicles											Million/percentage
Tested	23.3	23.3	22.5	22.3	23.0	22.9	23.7	23.7	23.8	23.8	22.2
Failed	8.6	8.6	8.1	8.0	8.1	7.6	7.4	7.5	7.3	6.9	6.3
Percentage failed	*37*	*37*	*36*	*36*	*35*	*33*	*31*	*32*	*31*	*29*	*29*

1 This reflects an increase in small cc scooters, bikes and mopeds being tested
2 Vehicles with more than 12 passenger seats.

☎0117 9543471
The figures in this table are outside the scope of National Statistics
Source - VOSA

9.11 Road passenger service vehicle testing scheme (PSV tests): 1994/95-2004/05

Number of tests and failure rates

Year	1994/95	1995/96	1996/97	1997/98	1998/99	1999/00	2000/01	2001/02 [1]	2002/03 [1]	2003/04 [1]	2004/05
First tests:											
Passed	62,422	62,663	64,198	64,769	62,950	67,219	67,016	65,899	65,458	67,528	67,425
Failed	11,758	11,766	11,071	11,001	12,332	11,216	11,583	14,290	14,515	13,832	13,045
Total tested	74,180	74,429	75,269	75,770	75,282	78,435	78,599	80,189	79,973	81,360	80,470
Re-tests:											
Passed	10,544	10,497	10,054	9,894	11,443	10,417	10,533	13,207	13,731	13,067	11,608
Failed	1,079	1,017	989	998	1,141	980	1,053	1,265	1,318	1,197	1,076
Total tested	11,623	11,514	11,043	10,892	12,584	11,397	11,586	14,472	15,049	14,264	12,684
Percentage failed:											
First test	*15.9*	*15.8*	*14.7*	*14.5*	*16.4*	*14.3*	*14.7*	*17.8*	*18.1*	*17.0*	16.2
Re-tests	*9.3*	*8.8*	*9.0*	*9.2*	*9.1*	*8.6*	*9.1*	*8.7*	*8.8*	*8.4*	8.5
All tests	*15.0*	*14.9*	*14.0*	*13.8*	*15.3*	*13.6*	*14.0*	*16.4*	*16.7*	*15.7*	15.2

1 Due to revisions of testing policy fewer defects are now allowed to be rectified at the testing station, resulting in a decrease in passes, an increase in failures and an increase in retests.

☎01792 454296
The figures in this table are outside the scope of National Statistics
Source - VOSA

9.12 Goods vehicles over 3.5 tonnes testing scheme (HGV Motor vehicles & Trailers): 1994/95-2004/05

Thousands of tests and failure rates

Year	1994/95	1995/96	1996/97	1997/98	1998/99	1999/00	2000/01	2001/02 [1]	2002/03 [1]	2003/04 [1]	2004/05
First tests:											
Passed	521.6	521.6	530.0	531.7	535.5	536.1	530.0	510.5	511.5	526.9	538.9
Failed	151.6	152.8	155.4	157.2	158.2	163.1	166.4	192.1	196.6	182.3	168.6
All	673.2	674.4	685.4	688.9	693.6	699.2	696.4	702.6	708.0	709.1	707.4
Re-tests:											
Passed	144.2	145.8	148.9	149.9	150.3	150.7	153.9	179.1	182.7	169.5	148.0
Failed	23.0	22.5	21.6	21.5	22.0	23.7	24.4	31.5	29.9	25.8	23.9
All	167.2	168.3	170.5	171.4	172.3	174.4	178.3	210.6	212.6	195.3	171.9
Percentage failed:											
First test	*22.5*	*22.7*	*22.7*	*22.8*	*22.8*	*23.3*	*23.9*	*27.3*	*27.8*	*25.7*	*23.8*
Re-tests	*13.8*	*13.4*	*12.7*	*12.5*	*12.8*	*13.6*	*13.7*	*15.0*	*14.1*	*13.2*	*13.9*
All tests	*20.8*	*20.8*	*20.7*	*20.8*	*20.8*	*21.4*	*21.7*	*24.5*	*24.6*	*23.0*	*21.9*

1 Due to revisions of testing policy fewer defects are now allowed to be rectified at the testing station, resulting in a decrease in passes, an increase in failures and an increase in retests.

☎01792 454296
Figures in this table are outside the scope of National Statistics
Source - VOSA

9.13 Road vehicle testing scheme (MOT): percentage of vehicles failing: by type of defect: 1994/95-2004/05

Percentage

	1994/95	1995/96	1996/97	1997/98	1998/99	1999/00	2000/01	2001/02	2002/03	2003/04	2004/05
Motor cycles: [1]											
Brakes	8.7	8.9	9.3	7.9	7.4	8.6	6.5	6.1	5.7	5.7	7.1
Steering	9.5	10.4	10.1	8.3	8.9	9.2	7.9	6.6	6.7	6.7	7.4
Lights	12.3	12.3	12.6	10.7	11.4	11.6	10.1	9.8	9.5	9.1	9.5
Tyres	6.6	6.4	6.7	5.2	5.5	6.2	4.9	4.4	4.4	4.0	4.3
Other	8.9	10.0	10.3	7.5	7.2	5.9	6.4	6.2	5.8	5.4	6.2
Cars and other passenger vehicles: [2]											
Brakes	15.5	15.4	14.7	15.1	14.3	13.4	12.4	12.4	12.0	11.1	10.6
Steering	17.3	17.4	16.7	16.8	16.8	15.8	14.4	13.9	13.5	12.3	11.4
Lights	20.3	20.0	18.6	18.4	18.0	17.6	15.9	16.1	15.8	15.7	14.9
Tyres	9.6	9.6	10.0	9.2	9.3	8.9	8.1	8.0	8.2	8.0	7.7
Petrol emission	6.0	7.4	7.9	7.1	6.4	5.6	4.3	3.1	2.4	1.8	1.4
Diesel emission	8.5	10.6	9.6	8.5	7.3	5.9	6.1	5.5	5.0	4.4	3.8
Other [3]	18.0	18.0	16.4	16.4	15.6	14.0	12.8	12.1	11.2	9.9	9.0
Light goods vehicles: [4]											
Brakes	15.4	16.7	18.4	18.7	18.1	14.2	16.8	15.9	16.4	14.9	14.1
Steering	17.5	20.5	22.1	21.2	20.3	17.3	19.3	17.0	19.1	16.3	16.0
Lights	19.6	22.7	22.9	22.5	22.4	18.7	21.2	19.9	20.5	20.4	19.0
Tyres	7.5	8.5	9.6	9.2	8.1	7.0	7.2	7.7	7.9	6.7	7.0
Petrol emission	5.9	7.7	9.4	8.4	6.9	5.6	5.0	4.4	4.8	2.8	2.2
Diesel emission	4.0	8.3	7.4	6.4	5.6	4.6	4.6	4.0	4.3	4.0	3.1
Reg. plates and VIN	1.9	2.2	2.4	2.0	1.8	2.1	1.9	1.7	1.7	2.0	1.6
Other [3]	16.9	20.4	18.5	19.8	18.6	13.9	16.7	15.8	15.3	13.8	12.7
Private passenger vehicles: [5]											
Brakes	15.5	12.6	8.5	13.0	9.7	7.8	7.8	7.1	6.4	10.6	6.2
Steering	15.7	15.8	8.6	10.6	10.8	8.1	7.6	7.5	6.7	9.3	6.2
Lights	20.8	17.2	10.1	12.7	12.3	10.0	9.8	8.2	8.4	14.0	8.9
Tyres	8.2	6.9	3.3	5.9	4.3	3.0	4.0	3.0	2.5	5.2	2.5
Petrol emission	8.6	6.9	9.8	4.5	4.1	2.5	2.6	1.4	1.7	1.6	2.0
Diesel emission	4.2	5.6	6.2	3.8	5.1	3.7	3.2	3.4	3.0	5.7	2.0
Other [3]	22.9	18.4	10.2	14.1	19.2	12.6	10.7	8.9	10.2	11.6	8.3

1 Emissions testing is not carried out on motorcycles.
2 Cars, 3 wheeled vehicles, motor caravans, vehicles with up to 12 passenger seats, taxis, goods vehicles not exceeding 3000kg gross weight
3 Figures include seat belts.
4 Gross weight over 3000kg upto 3500kg
5 Private passenger vehicles and ambulances with 13 or more passenger seats (including community buses) etc

☎ 0117 9543471
The figures in this table are outside the scope of National Statistics
Source - VOSA

9.14 Households with regular use of car(s): 1951-2003

For details of household car ownership by region and area type, see Table 9.15

Percentage

Year	No car	One car	Two cars	Three or more cars	All Households
1951	*86*	*13*	*1*	-	*100*
1952	*84*	*14*	*1*	-	*100*
1953	*83*	*16*	*1*	-	*100*
1954	*81*	*17*	*2*	-	*100*
1955	*80*	*19*	*2*	-	*100*
1956	*78*	*20*	*2*	-	*100*
1957	*76*	*22*	*2*	-	*100*
1958	*74*	*24*	*2*	-	*100*
1959	*73*	*25*	*2*	-	*100*
1960	*71*	*27*	*2*	-	*100*
1961	*69*	*29*	*2*	-	*100*
1962	*67*	*30*	*3*	-	*100*
1963	*64*	*33*	*3*	-	*100*
1964	*62*	*34*	*4*	-	*100*
1965	*59*	*36*	*5*	-	*100*
1966	*55*	*39*	*6*	-	*100*
1967	*53*	*41*	*6*	-	*100*
1968	*51*	*43*	*6*	-	*100*
1969	*49*	*45*	*6*	-	*100*
1970	*48*	*45*	*6*	*1*	*100*
1971	*48*	*44*	*7*	*1*	*100*
1972	*48*	*44*	*8*	*1*	*100*
1973	*46*	*43*	*9*	*1*	*100*
1974	*45*	*44*	*10*	*1*	*100*
1975	*44*	*45*	*10*	*1*	*100*
1976	*45*	*44*	*10*	*1*	*100*
1977	*43*	*45*	*10*	*1*	*100*
1978	*44*	*45*	*10*	*1*	*100*
1979	*43*	*44*	*11*	*2*	*100*
1980	*41*	*44*	*13*	*2*	*100*
1981	*40*	*45*	*13*	*2*	*100*
1982	*40*	*44*	*13*	*2*	*100*
1983	*39*	*44*	*14*	*2*	*100*
1984	*39*	*44*	*14*	*3*	*100*
1985	*38*	*45*	*15*	*3*	*100*
1986	*38*	*45*	*15*	*3*	*100*
1987	*36*	*45*	*16*	*3*	*100*
1988	*35*	*44*	*17*	*3*	*100*
1989	*34*	*44*	*18*	*4*	*100*
1990	*33*	*44*	*19*	*4*	*100*
1991	*32*	*45*	*19*	*4*	*100*
1992	*32*	*45*	*20*	*4*	*100*
1993	*31*	*45*	*20*	*4*	*100*
1994	*32*	*45*	*20*	*4*	*100*
1995	*30*	*45*	*21*	*4*	*100*
1996	*30*	*45*	*21*	*4*	*100*
1997	*30*	*45*	*21*	*5*	*100*
1998	*28*	*44*	*23*	*5*	*100*
1999	*28*	*44*	*22*	*5*	*100*
2000	*27*	*45*	*23*	*5*	*100*
2001	*26*	*45*	*23*	*5*	*100*
2002	*26*	*44*	*24*	*5*	*100*
2003	*26*	*44*	*25*	*5*	*100*

Note: Data from 1961 onward are derived from household surveys.
Figures for earlier years are estimates.

☎020-7944 3097

Sources - Family Expenditure Survey, ONS;
General Household Survey, ONS;
National Travel Survey

9.15 Private motoring: households with regular use of cars

Historic details from 1951 are available in Table 9.14

(a) 1993-2003 — Percentage

	No car	One car	Two cars	Three or more cars	All Households
Combined survey data[1]					
1993	31	45	20	4	100
1994	32	45	20	4	100
1995	30	45	21	4	100
1996	30	45	21	4	100
1997	30	45	21	5	100
1998	28	44	23	5	100
1999	28	44	22	5	100
2000	27	45	23	5	100
2001	26	45	23	5	100
2002	26	44	24	5	100
2003	26	44	25	5	100
Census data					
1991	33	44	19	4	100
2001	27	44	23	6	100

(b) By Government Office Region: 2003 [1] — Percentage

	No car	One car	Two or more cars	All Households
North East	37	44	19	100
North West	28	45	27	100
Yorkshire and the Humber	30	44	26	100
East Midlands	22	46	32	100
West Midlands	25	42	33	100
East of England	18	44	38	100
London	36	43	20	100
South East	17	42	41	100
South West	19	47	34	100
England	25	44	31	100
Wales	25	46	29	100
Scotland	31	43	25	100
Great Britain	26	44	30	100

(c) By area type : 2004[2] — Percentage/number

	Cars per Household	No car	One car	Two or more cars	All Households
London Boroughs	0.81	41	41	18	100
Metropolitan areas	0.91	34	44	22	100
Other urban areas with population:					
Over 250 thousand	1.11	24	46	29	100
25 to 250 thousand	1.03	26	48	26	100
10 to 25 thousand	1.10	25	46	29	100
3 to 10 thousand	1.15	23	44	33	100
Rural areas	1.47	11	41	48	100
Great Britain	1.08	26	45	29	100

1 Based on combined survey data sources - Family Expenditure Survey, ONS; General Household Survey, ONS; National Travel Survey, DfT

2 Based on National Travel Survey data.

☎020 7944 3097

9.16 Private motoring: full car driving licence holders by age and gender: 1975/1976 - 2004

Percentage/number (millions)

	Age								
(a) All adults	17-20	21-29	30-39	40-49	50-59	60-69	70 or over	All adults	Estimated number of licence holders
1975/1976	*28*	*59*	*67*	*60*	*50*	*35*	*15*	*48*	19.4
1985/1986	*33*	*63*	*74*	*71*	*60*	*47*	*27*	*57*	24.3
1989/1991	*43*	*72*	*77*	*78*	*67*	*54*	*32*	*64*	27.8
1992/1994	*48*	*75*	*82*	*79*	*72*	*57*	*33*	*67*	29.3
1995/1997	*42*	*73*	*81*	*82*	*74*	*64*	*39*	*68*	30.2
1998/2000	*41*	*74*	*84*	*84*	*78*	*68*	*41*	*71*	31.5
2002	*32*	*67*	*82*	*84*	*81*	*70*	*45*	*71*	32.1
2003	*28*	*68*	*82*	*84*	*79*	*73*	*45*	*70*	32.3
2004	*26*	*65*	*83*	*83*	*81*	*72*	*47*	*70*	32.2 P
(b) Male									
1975/1976	*36*	*78*	*85*	*83*	*75*	*58*	*32*	*69*	13.4
1985/1986	*37*	*73*	*86*	*87*	*81*	*72*	*51*	*74*	15.1
1989/1991	*52*	*82*	*88*	*89*	*85*	*78*	*58*	*80*	16.7
1992/1994	*54*	*83*	*91*	*88*	*88*	*81*	*59*	*81*	17.0
1995/1997	*48*	*79*	*89*	*89*	*88*	*83*	*65*	*81*	17.2
1998/2000	*45*	*81*	*90*	*92*	*89*	*84*	*65*	*82*	17.5
2002	*34*	*74*	*88*	*91*	*89*	*85*	*68*	*81*	17.7
2003	*31*	*74*	*88*	*91*	*90*	*87*	*69*	*81*	17.9
2004	*29*	*69*	*89*	*89*	*91*	*87*	*72*	*81*	17.9 P
(c) Female									
1975/1976	*20*	*43*	*48*	*37*	*24*	*15*	*4*	*29*	6.0
1985/1986	*29*	*54*	*62*	*56*	*41*	*24*	*11*	*41*	9.2
1989/1991	*35*	*64*	*67*	*66*	*49*	*33*	*15*	*49*	11.1
1992/1994	*42*	*68*	*73*	*70*	*57*	*37*	*16*	*54*	12.2
1995/1997	*36*	*67*	*74*	*74*	*61*	*46*	*22*	*57*	13.0
1998/2000	*37*	*69*	*78*	*77*	*68*	*54*	*22*	*60*	14.0
2002	*31*	*60*	*77*	*79*	*74*	*56*	*28*	*61*	14.4
2003	*24*	*62*	*77*	*78*	*69*	*59*	*27*	*61*	14.4
2004	*24*	*61*	*78*	*77*	*71*	*58*	*27*	*61*	14.4 P

☎020-7944 3097

9.17 Annual mileage of cars by type of car and trip purpose: 2004

Miles/percentage

	Business Mileage	Commuting mileage	Other private mileage	Total mileage	Proportion of cars in sample
All company cars	7,760	7,410	5,530	20,700	*5*
Self-employed business car	4,500	3,350	5,160	13,000	*3*
Household car used for work	3,820	4,040	4,650	12,500	*12*
Other household car	40	2,220	5,300	7,560	*80*
All private cars	660	2,480	5,220	8,360	*95*
All cars	1,040	2,740	5,230	9,020	*100*
All cars:					
1992/1994	1,770	2,720	5,200	9,690	*9*
1995/1997	1,620	2,720	5,090	9,430	*7*
1998/2000	1,510	2,860	5,040	9,410	*8*
2002	1,200	2,680	5,120	9,000	*6*
2003	1,170	2,770	5,160	9,100	*5*
2004	1,040	2,740	5,230	9,020	*5*

☎020 7944 3097

9.18 Private motoring: driving tests: 1994-2004/05

Thousands/rate

	1994	1995	1996	1997	1998/99	1999/00	2000/01	2001/02	2002/03	2003/04	2004/05
Applications											
received [1]	1,608	1,631	1,741	1,206	1,286	1,205	1,263	1,315	1,468	1,526	1,675
Tests conducted	1,483	1,489	1,685	1,122	1,166	1,130	1,015	1,216	1,344	1,399	1,668
Passed:											
Male	346	342	366	257	267	256	229	273	300	304	365
Female	351	342	382	269	268	240	214	254	283	295	340
Total	697	684	748	526	535	496	443	527	583	598	706
Pass rate, by sex:											
Male	*53*	*51*	*50*	*52*	*51*	*48*	*48*	*47*	*47*	*46*	*46*
Female	*43*	*42*	*40*	*43*	*42*	*40*	*40*	*40*	*40*	*40*	*39*
Total	*47*	*46*	*44*	*47*	*46*	*44*	*44*	*43*	*43*	*43*	*42*

1 These are gross figures and take no account of applications which do not mature into a test due to cancellations etc.

☎020-7944 3077
The figures in this table are outside the scope of National Statistics
Source - DSA

10 International Comparisons:

Notes and Definitions

This section gives some broad comparisons between transport in the United Kingdom and transport in other major industrialised countries, based on statistics obtained from international publications. Although efforts have been made to achieve comparability, there are still hazards in international comparisons because of differences in the statistical methods and definitions, so the figures should be used with caution.

In most tables the figures relate to 1995 and 2002. For some countries recent data are not available and figures for earlier years are shown as best estimates with appropriate footnotes.

To ease comparisons, much of the data in the tables have been rounded, typically to three significant figures or fewer, but it should not be assumed that figures are always accurate to the precision shown.

Some United Kingdom (or Great Britain) figures differ from comparable tables in other sections of *Transport Statistics Great Britain*, as they conform to slightly different definitions for consistency with figures for other countries.

Data sources

The data are from a wide variety of sources. Population and Gross Domestic Product estimates are from *National Accounts (OECD).* Other data come from; the EU publication *Transport in Figures, Rail Statistics (IRU), World Road Statistics (IRF),* and *Annual Bulletin of Transport Statistics (UN/ECE & UNESCAP)*, or from national statistics.

Road vehicles by type: 10.3

Stock of road vehicles: The number of road vehicles registered at a given date in a country and licensed to use roads open to public traffic. This includes road vehicles exempted from annual taxes or license fees; it also includes imported second-hand vehicles and other road vehicles according to national practices. The statistics should exclude military vehicles.

Passenger car: Road motor vehicle, other than a motor cycle, intended for the carriage of passengers and designed to seat no more than nine persons (including the driver). This, therefore, includes taxis and hired passenger cars provided that they have fewer than ten seats. This category may also include pick-ups.

Goods vehicle: Any single road motor vehicle designed to carry goods. This excludes articulated tractors and semi-trailers.

Motorcycles etc: Includes motorcycles and mopeds.

Motorcycle: Two-wheeled road motor vehicle with or without side-car, including motor scooter, or three-wheeled road motor vehicle not exceeding 400kg unladen weight. All such vehicles with a cylinder capacity of 50cc or over are included, as are those under 50cc which do not meet the definition of moped.

Moped: Two- or three-wheeled road vehicle fitted with an engine with a cylinder capacity of less than 50cc and a maximum authorised design speed in accordance with national regulations.

Buses and coaches: Passenger road motor vehicle (including mini-buses) designed to seat more than nine persons (including the driver).

Road traffic: 10.4

The Great Britain figures are gathered from traffic counts as described in Section 7 of this volume: for Great Britain, the traffic measured includes that by Great Britain registered (national) vehicles together with a small amount by foreign vehicles on British roads. Other countries' figures are generally for national vehicles, but comparable statistics are not always available since not all countries have a regular monitoring programme. Some countries rely on roadside interviews, fuel consumption and vehicle ownership data to derive the road traffic statistics.

For Great Britain, vehicle kilometres for buses and coaches relate to vehicles with bus and coach body types as opposed to just those taxed as hackneys with nine or more seats. This differs from Table 10.3 and may differ from other countries.

Freight Transport: 10.5

Road traffic: In general estimates are for freight carried by all vehicles on national territory. 1991 and 2001 estimates are not comparable with earlier years, as previous estimates show only national vehicles for some countries

Inland waterway traffic: Includes all transport loaded and moved on a country's inland waterways on inland waterway craft. It excludes traffic on vessels passing from the sea to an inland waterway.

Rail traffic: Includes all traffic on the country's network.

Passenger transport: 10.6

There are substantial differences in methods used to estimate passenger kilometres, so that results give only a broad indication of variation between countries.

Road deaths: 10.7

The data shown in this table are reproduced from the OECD International Road Traffic and Accident Database, with the permission of the German Federal Highway Research Institute.
International definition (Vienna Convention 1968) of road death: Any person who was killed outright or who died within 30 days as a result of the accident. Some countries use different definitions but adjustments are made for international comparability to a common 30 day basis.

Fuel prices: 10.8

The figures comparing the price of petrol and diesel are supplied by the Department of Trade and Industry, and are extracted from the weekly *EC Oil bulletin*.

The use of the term Tax in part (b) of this table is necessary because some other European countries impose other taxes and fees on fuel. For the United Kingdom this includes just fuel duty and VAT.

The figures in Table 10.8 differ from those in Table 3.3 because of the differences in availability and timing of data collection. The international comparisons in Table 10.8 are based on averages over the year. Table 3.3 attempts to be as up to date as reasonably possible.

Principal fleets: 10.9

Fleets: Includes all trading ships of 100 gross tons and over, so that totals given here for the United Kingdom are not comparable with those given in Table 5.14 which includes trading ships in excess of 500 gross tons.

Airlines: 10.10

The data have been extracted from Table 2.3 of the publication *Civil Aviation Statistics of the World*, published by ICAO. Airlines have been allocated to the country in which they are registered, apart from Cathay Pacific, which is based in Hong Kong, and which has been excluded from the United Kingdom figures. Traffic of the Scandinavian Airline System (SAS) has been divided 2:2:3 between Denmark, Norway and Sweden, respectively. The freight tonne-kilometres shown are those carried on freight-only flights.

Because they are not necessarily based on the same airlines each year, for some states figures will not strictly be comparable over time.

Carbon dioxide emissions from transport: 10.11

This table is based on data compiled by the European Environment Agency (EEA). From these submissions by member states, the EEA compiles its annual report on greenhouse gas emissions for the United Nations Framework Convention on Climate Change (UNFCCC). The full report and data can be found under "Content" at:

http://reports.eea.eu.int/technical_report_2005_4/en

The data follow the International Panel on Climate Change (IPCC) definitions of emissions, and are on the source basis. Land use change and forestry emissions (LUCF) have been excluded from the totals, so the country totals are broadly comparable with the data in Table 3.8 (a). The remaining difference (0.3 million tonnes of carbon in 2003) is due to direct soil emissions and emissions from forest and grassland conversion also being excluded from Table 10.11.

Transport emissions of carbon dioxide are based on fuel purchases in the country in question. International aviation and shipping are not included.

10.1 General Statistics: 2003

Country	Population (millions)	Area (1000 sq kms)	Population per square kilometre	Gross Domestic Product at current prices: At market exchange rates: $ (billion)	At market exchange rates: $ per head of Population	At purchasing power parity: $ (billion)	At purchasing power parity: $ per head of Population
Great Britain	57.9	230	252	..	..	..	..
Northern Ireland	1.7	14	120	..	..	..	..
United Kingdom	59.6	244	244	1,798	30,189	1,775	29,800
Austria	8.1	84	96	255	31,635	248	30,700
Belgium	10.4	31	340	304	29,329	307	29,600
Denmark	5.4	43	125	211	39,187	165	30,700
Finland	5.2	330	15	162	31,038	149	28,600
France	59.8	544	110	1,789	29,934	1,691	28,300
Germany	82.5	357	231	2,443	29,615	2,285	27,700
Greece	11.0	132	84	173	15,694	225	20,400
Irish Republic	4.0	70	56	152	38,477	132	33,300
Italy	57.5	301	191	1,468	25,545	1,535	26,700
Luxembourg	0.5	3	175	27	59,735	24	54,000
Netherlands	16.2	42	391	513	31,601	493	30,400
Portugal	10.4	92	114	147	14,097	196	18,800
Spain	41.9	506	83	881	21,039	1,051	25,100
Sweden	9.0	450	20	302	33,668	260	29,000
Cyprus	0.7	9	77	..	..	..	..
Czech Republic	10.2	79	129	90	8,861	176	17,300
Estonia	1.4	45	30	..	..	..	..
Hungary	10.1	93	109	82	8,109	153	15,100
Latvia	2.3	65	36	..	..	..	..
Lithuania	3.5	65	53	..	..	..	..
Malta	0.4	-	1,257	..	..	..	..
Poland	38.2	313	122	210	5,485	443	11,600
Slovak Republic	5.4	49	110	33	6,078	71	13,200
Slovenia	2.0	20	99	..	..	..	..
Norway	4.6	324	14	221	48,335	169	37,100
Switzerland	7.3	41	178	322	43,824	239	32,600
Japan	127.6	378	338	4,291	33,624	3,573	28,000
USA	291.0	9,363	31	10,951	37,627	10,943	37,600

☎020-7944 3088

The figures in this table are outside the scope of UK National Statistics

Sources - National Accounts (OECD)

10.2 Road and rail infrastructure: 1995 and 2002

Thousand kilometres

	Road network						Rail network					
	All roads		*ow:* motorways		All roads per 1,000 square kilometres (kilometres)		In operation		*ow:* electrified		Rail network per 1,000 square kilometres (kilometres)	
	1995	2002	1995	2002	1995	2002	1995	2002	1995	2002	1995	2002
Great Britain	386	392	3.3	3.5	1,681	1,704	16.7	16.7	5.2	5.2	72	72
Northern Ireland	24	25	0.1	0.1	1,690	1,731	0.3	0.3	..	..	21	21
United Kingdom	410	417	3.4	3.6	1,680	1,708	17.0	17.0	5.2	5.2	70	70
Austria	130	134	1.6	1.6	1,551	1,594	5.7	5.6	3.3	3.3	68	67
Belgium	143	149	1.7	1.7	4,687	4,884	3.4	3.5	2.4	2.9	110	115
Denmark	71	72	0.8	1.0	1,649	1,668	2.3	2.8	0.4	0.8	55	65
Finland	78	79	0.4	0.7	230	233	5.9	5.9	2.0	2.4	17	17
France	893	893	8.3	10.2	1,641	1,642	31.9	31.3	13.7	15.7	59	58
Germany	..	..	11.2	12.0	..	..	41.7	35.8	17.7	19.7	117	100
Greece	117	..	0.4	0.7 [1]	887	..	2.5	2.4	..	0.1	19	18
Irish Republic	93	96	0.1	0.1 [1]	1,316	1,362	1.9	1.9	-	0.1	28	27
Italy	..	..	6.4	6.5	..	..	16.0	16.0	9.9	11.3	53	53
Luxembourg	5	..	0.1	0.1	1,933	..	0.3	0.3	0.3	0.3	106	106
Netherlands	121	..	2.2	2.5	2,911	..	2.8	2.8	2.0	2.0	68	68
Portugal	..	..	0.7	1.8	..	..	3.1	2.8	0.5	1.1	33	30
Spain	..	..	7.0	9.9	..	..	16.3	16.5	6.9	9.4	32	33
Sweden	..	213	1.1	1.5	..	474	10.9	11.1	7.2	7.7	24	25
Cyprus	10	12	0.2	0.3	1,097	1,253	-	-	-	-	-	-
Czech Republic	..	127	0.4	0.5	..	1,613	9.4	9.6	2.6	3.0	120	122
Estonia	..	56	0.1	0.1	..	1,237	1.0	1.0	..	0.1	23	21
Hungary	159	160	0.3	0.5	1,705	1,715	7.6	7.7	2.3	2.8	82	83
Latvia	60	60	-	-	930	936	2.4	2.3	..	0.2	37	35
Lithuania	61	77	0.4	0.4	942	1,183	2.0	1.8	-	0.1	31	27
Malta	..	2	-	-	-	-	-	-	..	..	-	-
Poland	372	365 [1]	0.2	0.4	1,191	1,166 [1]	24.0	21.1	..	12.6	77	67
Slovak Republic	..	43	0.2	0.3	..	880	3.7	3.7	1.4	1.6	75	75
Slovenia	15	20	0.3	0.5	729	1,000	1.2	1.2	..	0.5	59	61
Norway	90	92	0.1	0.2	278	283	4.0	4.1	2.4	2.4	12	13
Switzerland	71	71	1.2	1.3	1,721	1,725	5.0	5.1	5.0	5.1	122	122
Japan	1,144	1,172 [1]	6.1	6.9 [1]	3,028	3,101	20.3	23.7 [1]	11.9	16.5 [1]	54	63 [1]
USA	6,238	6,378 [1]	89.2	89.9 [1]	666	681	..	315.3 [1]	1.7	..	-	34 [1]

1 2001 data.

☎020-7944 3088

The figures in this table are outside the scope of UK National Statistics

Sources: All roads - IRF; others - EU Transport in Figures (EUROSTAT)

10.3 Road vehicles by type, at end of year: 1995 and 2002[1]

Thousands

	Cars and taxis		Goods vehicles [2]		Motor cycles etc [3]		Buses and coaches	
	1995	2002	1995	2002	1995	2002	1995	2002
Great Britain	21,394	25,782	2,505	2,968	594	941	74	92
Northern Ireland	523	677	63	85	..	..	5	5
United Kingdom	21,917	26,460	2,568	3,053	..	..	80	97
Austria	3,594	3,987	290	320	546	595	10	9
Belgium	4,273	4,787	402	541	..	..	15	15
Denmark	1,679	1,888	324	389	..	..	14	14
Finland	1,901	2,195	252	320	159	222	8	10
France	25,100	29,160	3,597	5,354	2,289	2,441	82	87
Germany	40,404	44,660	2,215	2,619	3,920	5,135 [4]	86	86
Greece	2,205	3,730	876	1,099	..	2,340 [4]	25	31
Irish Republic	990	1,460	142	239	..	33 [4]	5	8
Italy	30,301	33,706	2,709	3,752	7,906	10,156	75	92
Luxembourg	232	287	16	23	29	30 [4]	1	1
Netherlands	5,664	6,855	583	917	848	1,002	12	11
Portugal	3,751	5,788	1,175	1,829	839	604	15	21
Spain	14,212	18,733	2,937	4,092	3,402	3,525	47	57
Sweden	3,631	4,044	308	409	259	330 [4]	15	14
Cyprus	220	288	100	117	50	40	3	3
Czech Republic	3,043	3,647	203	323	1,125	760	20	21
Estonia	383	401	66	80	..	7	7	5
Hungary	2,245	2,630	292	369	157	..	21	18
Latvia	332	619	61	92	16	22	17	16
Lithuania	718	1,180	101	94	..	21	18	1
Malta	181	201	41	45	8	13	1	1
Poland	7,517	11,028	1,299	2,052	..	..	85	83
Slovak Republic	1,016	1,327	148	164	..	..	12	11
Slovenia	710	915	39	55	8	..	3	2
Norway	1,685	1,897	145	158 [4]	198	277	33	36 [4]
Switzerland	3,229	3,701	256	281	722	745	37	42
Japan	44,680	54,541	21,934	19,219	15,587	13,540	243	233
USA	128,387	137,633 [4]	71,122	92,045 [4]	3,767	4,903 [4]	686	750 [4]

1 Some revisions have been made to the figures since last year.
2 There are differences in definitions between countries which limit comparisons.
3 Includes mopeds and three-wheeled vehicles but excludes pedal cycles.
4 2001 data.

☎020-7944 3088
The figures in this table are outside the scope of UK National Statistics
Source: EU Transport in Figures (EUROSTAT)

10.4 Road traffic on national territory: 1995 and 2002

Billion vehicle kilometres

	Cars and taxis		Goods vehicles [1]		Motor cycles etc [2]		Buses and coaches	
	1995	2002	1995	2002	1995	2002	1995	2002
Great Britain	351.1	392.9	69.9	83.3	3.7	5.1	4.9	5.2
Austria	..	..	..	..	..	..	..	..
Belgium	80.2	..	..	..	..	..	..	..
Denmark	33.2	38.9	6.8	7.4	..	0.6	0.5	0.6
Finland	35.8	41.7	5.8	6.5	..	..	0.6	0.6
France	351.0	422.0	102.0	120.0	..	4.0	2.5	2.4
Germany	507.0	..	58.4	..	11.5	..	3.6	..
Greece	..	..	..	..	..	..	0.5	..
Irish Republic	22.5	27.5 [3]	4.8	6.0 [3]	0.2	0.3 [3]	0.3	0.4 [3]
Italy	..	..	..	..	..	..	..	..
Luxembourg	3.0	..	0.5	..	..	..	-	..
Netherlands	89.1	..	14.2	..	1.7	..	0.6	..
Portugal	38.4	..	39.0	..	1.2	..	0.7	..
Spain	108.0	189.2 [3]	18.9	31.6 [3]	0.7	1.4 [3]	2.1	3.6 [3]
Sweden	57.4	57.9	6.7	13.1	0.6	1.2	0.8	1.0
Cyprus	..	..	..	..	..	..	..	..
Czech Republic	24.5	..	2.4	..	0.6	..	..	..
Estonia	..	5.4	..	1.2	..	..	..	0.2
Hungary	..	15.8	..	7.1	..	..	..	..
Latvia	..	..	..	..	..	..	..	..
Lithuania	..	..	2.2	1.1	..	..	0.2	0.2
Malta	..	..	..	..	..	..	..	..
Poland	75.2	94.6 [3]	32.7	37.9 [3]	3.2	4.8 [3]	5.1	5.6 [3]
Slovak Republic	8.3	..	2.5	0.2	0.1	..	-	0.3
Slovenia	6.5	8.6	0.8	1.1	-	-	0.1	0.1
Norway	22.6	28.7	2.5	4.8	..	1.0	..	..
Switzerland	43.8	52.2	5.0	6.7	1.7	2.1	0.1	0.1
Japan	446.4	526.4 [3]	267.1	257.6 [3]	..	..	6.8	6.8 [3]
USA	3,586.0	4,223.5	286.7	345.4	15.8	15.4	10.3	11.0

1 Including light vans.
2 Including mopeds and three wheeled vehicles but excluding pedal cycles.
3 2001 data.

☎020-7944 3088
The figures in this table are outside the scope of UK National Statistics
Source - IRF

10.5 Freight moved by mode on national territory: 1995 and 2002[1]

Billion tonne-kilometres

	Road		Rail		Inland waterway excluding coastal and one port traffic		Inland pipeline 50km long and over	
	1995	2002	1995	2002	1995	2002	1995	2002
Great Britain	149.6 [2]	157.3 [2]	13.3	18.7	0.2	0.2	11.1	10.9
Northern Ireland	3.0 [2]	4.2 [2]	-	-	..	..	0.0	0.0
United Kingdom	152.6 [2]	161.5 [2]	13.3	18.7	0.2	0.2	11.1	10.9
Austria	20.9	29.5	13.2	17.1	2.0	2.8	6.8	8.0
Belgium	34.6	39.6	7.6	7.3	5.7	8.1	1.4	1.6
Denmark	14.7	17.9	2.0	1.9	..	..	3.1	5.1
Finland	23.2	29.0	9.3	9.7	0.1	0.1	..	..
France	227.1	277.2	48.1	50.0	6.6	8.3	22.3	21.0
Germany	279.7	349.3	70.5	76.3	64.0	64.2	16.6	15.2
Greece	14.8	20.4	0.3	0.3	..	..	..	..
Irish Republic	5.5 [2]	10.7 [2]	0.6	0.4	..	..	..	..
Italy	174.4	192.7	21.7	20.4	0.1	0.1	9.7	10.8
Luxembourg	1.9	2.9	0.6	0.6	0.3	0.3	..	..
Netherlands	42.2	41.4	3.0	4.0	35.5	40.8	5.3	6.0
Portugal	11.6	14.7	2.0	2.2	..	..	..	..
Spain	94.6	161.3	11.0	11.6	..	..	5.9	7.8
Sweden	29.3 [2]	31.8 [2]	19.4	18.7	..	..	..	..
Cyprus	..	..	..	..	..	..	..	..
Czech Republic	..	..	22.6	15.8	0.4	0.1	2.3	1.7
Estonia	..	..	3.8	9.7	0.0	..	..	..
Hungary	..	..	8.4	7.8	1.5	1.7	1.6	2.0
Latvia	..	..	9.8	15.0	..	..	5.3	5.1
Lithuania	..	..	7.2	9.8	-	0.0	2.0	4.9
Malta	..	..	..	..	..	..	..	..
Poland	..	..	68.2	47.7	0.9	1.1	13.5	20.9
Slovak Republic	..	..	13.7	10.4	1.5	0.6	..	..
Slovenia	..	..	3.1	3.1	..	..	..	..
Norway	9.7	15.4	2.7	2.7	..	..	5.3	3.6
Switzerland	14.0	..	8.8	10.0 [3]	0.2	0.1 [3]	1.2	0.2
Japan	..	313.0 [3]	..	22.0 [3]	..	..	..	..
USA	1,345.0	1,534.0 [3]	1,906.0	2,183.0 [3]	534.0	505.0 [3]	878.0	841.0 [3]

1 Some revisions have been made to the figures since last year.
2 Only includes freight moved by vehicles registered in the country.
Other countries include all freight moved, regardless of the nationality of the vehicle.
3 2001 data.

☎020-7944 3088
The figures in this table are outside the scope of UK National Statistics
Source: EU Transport in Figures (EUROSTAT)

10.6 Passenger transport by national vehicles on national territory: 1995 and 2002

Billion passenger kilometres

	Cars		Buses and coaches		Rail excluding metro systems		Total of these modes	
	1995	2002	1995	2002	1995	2002	1995	2002
Great Britain	592.0	634.0	44.3	46.0	30.0	39.7	666.3	719.7
Austria	68.1	69.8	10.5	13.4	9.6	8.3	88.2	91.5
Belgium	97.5	109.4	13.1	13.6	6.8	8.3	117.3	131.3
Denmark	54.3	59.9	8.7	9.0	4.9	5.7	67.9	74.6
Finland	50.0	58.3	8.0	7.7	3.2	3.3	61.2	69.3
France	640.1	740.6	41.6	40.3	55.6	73.2	737.3	854.1
Germany	730.0	700.8	77.0	75.7	71.0	71.4	877.9	847.8
Greece	58.8	86.6	20.2	22.4	1.6	1.8	80.6	110.8
Irish Republic	23.2	37.2	5.2	6.4	1.3	1.6	29.6	45.2
Italy	614.7	711.7	87.1	97.5	43.9	46.0	745.7	855.2
Luxembourg	4.7	5.3	0.9	0.9	0.3	0.4	5.9	6.5
Netherlands	131.4	144.2	8.0	7.2	13.0	15.5	152.4	166.9
Portugal	61.4	94.7	11.3	9.9	4.8	3.7	77.5	108.3
Spain	250.4	335.9	39.6	50.1	15.3	19.5	305.3	405.4
Sweden	86.8	93.8	8.5	10.1	6.8	9.1	102.1	113.0
Cyprus	..	..	..	0.6	-	-	..	..
Czech Republic	54.5	65.2	11.8	9.7	8.0	6.6	74.3	81.5
Estonia	..	..	2.0	2.3	0.4	0.2	..	..
Hungary	45.8	47.1	16.6	18.7	8.4	10.5	70.8	76.3
Latvia	..	6.2	1.8	2.4	1.4	0.7	..	9.3
Lithuania	..	..	4.2	2.0	1.1	0.5	..	..
Malta	..	..	..	0.1	-	-	-	..
Poland	110.7	167.4	34.0	29.3	26.6	20.7	171.4	217.4
Slovak Republic	18.0	25.0	11.2	8.2	4.2	2.7	33.4	35.9
Slovenia	10.4	9.7	3.3	1.7	0.6	0.7	14.3	12.1
Norway	43.7	49.3	3.8	4.1	2.3	2.5	49.7	55.9
Switzerland	75.5	84.3 [1]	3.2	3.1 [1]	11.7	12.1	90.4	99.4
Japan	..	753.0 [1]	..	86.0 [1]	..	385.0 [1]	..	1,224.0 [1]
USA	5,702.0	6,544.0 [1]	219.0	238.0 [1]	22.0	24.0 [1]	5,943.0	6,806.0 [1]

1 2001 data.

☎020-7944 3088

The figures in this table are outside the scope of UK National Statistics

Source: EU Transport in Figures (EUROSTAT)

10.7 International comparisons of road deaths for selected OECD countries: 1993 - 2003[1]

	1993	1994	1995	1996	1997	1998	1999	2000	2001	2002	2003	Rate of road deaths in 2003 per 100,000 population [2]	Rate of road deaths in 2003 per billion motor-vehicle kilo-metres [2]
Great Britain	3,814	3,650	3,621	3,598	3,599	3,421	3,423	3,409	3,450	3,431	3,508	*6.0*	*7.2*
Northern Ireland	143	157	144	142	144	160	141	171	148	150	150	*8.8*	*6.5*
United Kingdom	3,957	3,807	3,765	3,740	3,743	3,581	3,564	3,580	3,598	3,581	3,658	*6.1*	*7.1*
Austria	1,283	1,338	1,210	1,027	1,105	963	1,079	976	958	956	931	*11.5*	*11.7*
Belgium	1,660	1,692	1,449	1,356	1,364	1,500	1,397	1,470	1,486	..	..	..	..
Denmark [3]	559	546	581	514	489	499	514	498	431	463	432	*8.0*	..
Finland	484	480	441	404	438	400	431	396	433	415	379	*7.3*	*7.6*
France	9,568	9,019	8,891	8,541	8,444	8,918	8,487	8,079	8,160	7,655	6,058	*10.2*	*10.9*
Germany	9,949	9,814	9,454	8,758	8,549	7,792	7,772	7,503	6,977	6,842	6,613	*8.0*	*9.7*
Greece	2,159	2,253	2,411	2,157	2,105	2,182	2,116	2,037	..	..	..	..	..
Irish Republic	431	404	437	453	472	458	413	415	411	376	335	*8.4*	..
Italy [3]	7,177	7,104	7,033	6,688	6,724	6,849	6,633	6,649	6,682	6,739	6,015	*10.5*	..
Luxembourg	76	66	70	71	60	57	58	76	70	62	53	*11.8*	..
Netherlands	1,252	1,298	1,334	1,180	1,163	1,066	1,090	1,082	993	987	1,028	*6.4*	*7.7*
Portugal	2,368	2,196	2,377	2,394	2,210	2,126	1,995	1,860	1,671	1,675	1,546	*14.8*	..
Spain	6,378	5,615	5,751	5,483	5,604	5,957	5,738	5,776	5,517	5,347	5,399	*12.8*	..
Sweden	632	589	572	537	541	531	580	591	554	532	529	*5.9*	..
Czech Republic	1,524	1,637	1,588	1,568	1,597	1,360	1,455	1,486	1,334	1,431	1,447	*14.2*	*31.7*
Hungary	1,678	1,562	1,589	1,370	1,391	1,371	1,306	1,200	1,239	1,429	1,326	*13.1*	..
Iceland	17	12	24	10	15	27	21	32	24	29	23	*7.9*	..
Norway	281	283	305	255	303	352	304	341	275	312	282	*6.2*	..
Poland	6,341	6,744	6,900	6,359	7,310	7,080	6,730	6,294	5,534	5,827	5,640	*14.8*	..
Switzerland	723	679	692	616	587	597	583	592	554	513	546	*7.1*	*9.0*
Australia [3]	1,954	1,938	2,013	1,970	1,768	1,755	1,758	1,817	1,737	1,715	1,621	*8.2*	*8.0*
Canada [3]	3,615	3,263	3,351	3,091	3,064	2,934	2,972	2,927	2,779	2,931	2,766	*8.7*	*8.9*
Japan	13,269	12,768	12,670	11,674	11,254	10,805	10,372	10,403	10,060	9,575	8,877	*7.0*	*11.2*
New Zealand	600	580	581	514	540	502	509	462	455	404	461	*11.5*	..
USA	40,150	40,716	41,817	42,065	42,013	41,501	41,717	41,945	42,116	42,815	42,643	*14.7*	..

☎020-7944 6595

The figures in this table are outside the scope of UK National Statistics

Source - OECD International Road and Traffic Accident database

1 In accordance with the commonly agreed international definition, most countries define a fatality as one being due to a road accident where death occurs within 30 days of the accident. The official road accident statistics of some countries however, limit the fatalities to those occurring within shorter periods after the accident. Numbers of deaths and death rates in the above table have been adjusted according to the factors used by the Economic Commission for Europe and the European Conference of Ministers of Transport, to represent standardised 30-day deaths: Italy (7 days) +8%; France (6 days) +5.7%; Portugal (1 day) +14%

2 Population and car kilometres taken from the OECD's International Road and Traffic Accidents Database and may differ from the figures in tables 10.1 and 10.4.

3 Figures have been revised from those published in previous years.

10.8 (a) Petrol and diesel in the European Union: current retail prices: 1994 - 2004

Premium unleaded petrol (95 RON): per 100 litres											US Dollars
	1994	1995	1996	1997	1998	1999	2000	2001	2002	2003	2004
United Kingdom	79	85	88	101	108	113	121	110	110	125	147
Austria	89	112	108	97	90	87	87	81	82	99	118
Belgium	92	104	111	104	96	96	97	90	92	115	142
Denmark [1]	85	104	111	101	96	102	103	99	104	125	140
Germany	96	108	108	96	91	93	94	91	99	123	141
Finland	88	111	119	106	104	106	105	99	101	124	146
France	95	113	117	106	102	101	101	93	96	115	132
Greece	77	82	85	78	70	69	72	67	69	84	101
Irish Republic	83	90	95	89	84	80	82	80	81	98	118
Italy	98	106	116	107	101	102	100	94	99	120	140
Luxembourg	71	84	84	76	71	74	76	72	73	88	112
Netherlands	104	118	118	109	107	107	107	103	113	131	161
Portugal	91	103	103	93	90	86	80	81	83	109	128
Spain	79	86	88	79	74	75	76	73	77	92	108
Sweden	97	105	117	108	101	101	104	91	96	116	136
Lead replacement petrol [2]: per 100 litres											
United Kingdom	87	94	96	110	118	125	130	115	115	131	155
Austria	..	..	..	..	..	..	..	..	..	..	..
Belgium	102	115	120	112	105	103	101	97	99	..	..
Denmark	89	107	..	..	..	..	..	..	..	..	..
Germany	104	118	117	..	..	..	..	..	..	..	..
Finland	..	..	..	..	..	..	..	..	..	..	..
France	101	118	121	110	107	106	108	100	103	124	142
Greece	83	88	91	84	75	75	76	71	74	89	108
Irish Republic	89	97	102	98	98	95	96	..	..	..	..
Italy	105	112	122	113	107	107	104	98	..	..	..
Luxembourg	81	95	94	85	80	..	..	..	..	..	..
Netherlands	113	128	127	..	..	..	..	..	..	..	..
Portugal	93	104	105	96	93	89	..	..	..	..	..
Spain	81	91	93	82	78	79	81	77	82	100	117
Sweden	102	111	122	121	106	105	107	..	..	..	..
Diesel: per 100 litres											
United Kingdom	79	86	90	102	109	117	123	112	113	128	150
Austria	69	85	87	77	70	68	72	67	68	82	101
Belgium	75	83	85	75	69	68	75	70	68	84	109
Denmark	66	77	83	79	77	80	88	84	86	103	114
Germany	70	78	81	72	65	68	94	73	79	100	116
Finland	64	81	82	73	69	73	78	73	74	91	103
France	70	77	84	76	72	73	78	72	73	90	110
Greece	53	60	65	59	51	56	62	56	59	72	92
Irish Republic	82	85	93	85	79	75	78	73	73	91	110
Italy	77	82	93	85	79	81	82	78	81	99	117
Luxembourg	60	68	70	62	57	58	64	59	60	72	86
Netherlands	86	96	100	77	72	74	78	73	74	90	110
Portugal	61	66	71	64	59	58	60	60	61	80	98
Spain	81	89	98	87	79	60	64	62	65	78	94
Sweden	89	101	100	89	84	81	92	84	86	100	116

10.8 (b) Petrol and diesel in the European Union: Tax as a percentage of retail prices: 1994 - 2004

Premium unleaded petrol (95 RON)											Percentage
	1994	1995	1996	1997	1998	1999	2000	2001	2002	2003	2004
United Kingdom	70	74	76	77	81	81	75	76	77	76	74
Austria	64	67	67	65	68	68	61	63	64	64	62
Belgium	72	72	73	73	76	74	66	67	69	67	66
Denmark [1]	67	71	71	70	72	73	67	68	70	70	68
Germany	76	76	74	72	75	74	69	72	73	74	71
Finland	71	74	75	75	78	74	67	68	70	72	68
France	79	80	80	78	81	79	70	71	74	74	72
Greece	71	70	68	65	67	63	53	55	56	55	52
Irish Republic	66	66	66	67	68	68	59	56	64	64	64
Italy	74	73	73	72	75	73	65	66	68	68	66
Luxembourg	66	67	65	62	66	64	56	58	59	59	60
Netherlands	74	74	72	72	75	73	66	69	68	71	67
Portugal	70	71	71	70	73	68	49	46	69	68	67
Spain	66	68	67	65	69	67	59	59	62	62	59
Sweden	72	74	74	73	76	73	67	68	70	70	68
Lead replacement petrol [2]											
United Kingdom	75	76	79	80	83	81	74	76	78	76	72
Austria	..	..	..	..	..	..	..	..	..	..	..
Belgium	75	75	75	74	77	76	64	64	67	..	..
Denmark	69	74	..	..	..	..	..	..	..	..	..
Germany	78	77	74	..	..	..	..	..	..	..	..
Finland	..	..	..	..	..	..	..	..	..	..	..
France	81	82	81	80	83	81	70	72	74	75	72
Greece	76	75	72	69	70	67	56	58	58	58	54
Irish Republic	68	68	66	67	70	69	61	..	..	..	..
Italy	77	76	75	74	76	74	66	68	..	..	..
Luxembourg	68	71	68	66	69	..	..	..	..	..	..
Netherlands	77	77	75	..	..	..	..	..	..	..	..
Portugal	74	75	74	73	74	67	..	..	..	..	..
Spain	69	70	69	68	71	69	60	60	63	62	59
Sweden	77	78	79	78	81	78	72	..	..	..	..
Diesel											
United Kingdom	68	73	75	77	82	81	74	74	76	74	72
Austria	58	59	60	58	63	62	54	55	57	57	55
Belgium	64	65	62	61	64	63	53	54	59	58	55
Denmark	63	66	66	64	64	61	56	59	60	61	60
Germany	67	68	64	63	68	67	61	63	66	67	64
Finland	57	54	62	62	67	63	54	55	57	58	56
France	70	72	71	70	75	73	62	64	66	66	64
Greece	67	67	64	62	65	64	52	54	55	54	48
Irish Republic	60	63	60	63	64	64	55	48	57	58	59
Italy	70	70	68	68	71	70	60	61	64	63	60
Luxembourg	61	63	60	59	63	60	50	52	53	53	50
Netherlands	65	67	56	63	67	65	56	57	59	59	57
Portugal	60	64	62	61	64	63	52	51	57	57	55
Spain	61	64	62	60	64	62	53	54	56	56	53
Sweden	54	54	59	60	62	60	55	55	57	59	59

1 Regular unleaded (92 RON) prices have been used from 2000 to date.
2 Refers to Four star petrol in earlier years.

☎020-7215 2722
The figures in this table are outside the scope of UK National Statistics
Source - DTI

10.9 Principal trading fleets by type of vessel and flag at mid year: 1994 and 2004

Gross tonnage (million)

	All trading ships of 100 gross tons and over		of which: Tankers		Bulk carriers		Container ships		General cargo	
	1994	2004	1994	2004	1994	2004	1994	2004	1994	2004
United Kingdom and Crown Dependencies	5.0	17.3	2.2	6.2	0.4	2.1	1.0	5.3	0.5	1.6
Denmark	5.1	7.6	1.6	2.3	0.4	0.0	1.8	4.4	0.8	0.4
France	4.2	4.7	2.3	2.8	0.5	0.3	0.6	0.6	0.3	0.2
Germany	4.8	6.0	0.3	0.2	0.4	0.0	2.5	5.2	1.3	0.2
Greece	29.5	32.2	14.1	17.6	12.7	10.8	0.6	1.9	1.3	0.4
Italy	6.7	10.1	2.6	3.5	1.8	1.4	0.4	0.6	0.8	2.1
Netherlands	3.7	6.4	0.7	0.6	0.2	0.2	0.9	1.8	1.3	2.9
Bahamas	22.1	33.5	11.0	14.9	4.7	5.8	0.8	1.9	4.1	5.9
Bermuda	3.0	5.0	2.6	1.4	0.2	1.9	0.1	0.5	0.1	0.2
China	14.3	18.4	2.2	3.3	5.8	7.5	1.2	2.3	5.0	4.9
Cyprus	22.8	21.6	5.3	4.2	12.1	11.8	1.0	2.8	4.2	2.5
Hong Kong	7.7	23.5	0.9	5.6	5.5	13.3	0.6	2.9	0.6	1.6
India	6.1	6.7	2.4	4.2	2.9	2.0	0.1	0.1	0.8	0.3
Japan	21.9	12.1	8.9	5.7	6.4	2.6	1.4	0.5	3.8	2.0
Liberia	54.4	53.1	31.2	27.3	14.7	10.6	3.0	11.7	4.6	3.5
Malaysia	2.2	5.7	0.9	3.0	0.6	1.4	0.3	0.7	0.4	0.6
Malta	14.2	24.0	5.5	8.5	5.7	11.0	0.4	1.1	2.3	3.2
Marshall Islands	2.2	19.9	1.6	14.0	0.5	3.1	0.0	1.4	0.0	1.2
Norway	20.8	18.7	12.3	9.7	4.9	3.9	0.2	0.1	2.7	3.9
Panama	58.0	125.8	20.9	34.4	17.5	52.6	5.0	18.8	13.9	17.5
Philippines	8.4	5.0	0.4	0.4	6.0	2.8	0.1	0.0	1.7	1.2
Russia	10.5	6.1	2.4	1.6	1.8	0.8	0.4	0.3	5.7	3.3
St Vincent and the Grenadines	5.2	6.0	1.1	0.5	1.9	2.6	0.2	0.2	1.9	2.5
Singapore	11.0	23.8	5.0	11.8	2.8	5.4	1.5	3.9	1.6	2.7
South Korea	6.3	6.4	0.7	1.2	3.5	3.3	1.1	0.8	0.9	1.0
Taiwan	5.7	3.6	0.8	0.9	2.5	1.5	2.1	1.0	0.2	0.1
Turkey	5.2	4.8	1.1	0.6	3.2	2.5	0.0	0.3	0.9	1.2
USA	14.2	10.5	6.5	2.9	1.5	1.3	2.8	3.1	3.0	2.9
World total [1]	437.4	589.7	168.2	211.8	137.0	176.9	32.6	81.4	84.7	92.2

1 Including other trading fleets not listed.

☎020-7944 4443
The figures in this table are outside the scope of UK National Statistics
Source - Lloyds Register - Fairplay

Further details on Maritime Statistics are available at: www.dft.gov.uk/transtat/maritime

10.10 Selected outputs of airlines: 1994 and 2004

State of airline registration	Scheduled services: International and domestic traffic: Aircraft kilometres flown (million) 1994	2004	Freight[1] tonne-kilometres flown (billion) 1994	2004	Passenger kilometres flown (billion) 1994	2004	International passenger kilometres flown (billion) 1994	2004	Non-scheduled services: International and domestic passenger kilometres flown (billion) 1994	2004
United Kingdom[2]	636	1,198	3.5	5.7	104.0	183.0	99.0	173.0	67.0	90.0
Austria	79	149	0.1	0.5	5.9	17.5	5.9	17.4	2.9	3.7
Belgium	107	125	0.5	0.7	7.5	4.7	7.5	4.7	0.0	0.0
Denmark	65	85	0.1	0.2	5.1	8.1	4.3	7.8	1.3	1.9
Finland	67	109	0.2	0.3	6.7	11.2	5.9	10.0	2.7	5.0
France	511	911	4.4	5.6	68.2	124.0	44.8	93.2	12.5	6.3
Germany	528	1,193	5.4	8.1	58.3	170.0	53.0	161.8	83.5	24.6
Greece	64	96	0.1	0.1	8.4	9.2	7.5	7.4	0.2	0.6
Irish Republic	42	236	0.1	0.1	4.9	34.6	4.9	34.6	0.7	0.2
Italy	249	407	1.4	1.4	31.8	43.2	24.8	32.1	5.3	1.1
Luxembourg	9	78	0.5	4.7	0.4	0.6	0.4	0.6	0.0	0.6
Netherlands	263	467	3.2	4.8	42.4	76.1	42.4	76.1	3.7	5.0
Portugal	74	149	0.2	0.2	7.9	16.1	6.6	13.6	0.4	2.6
Spain	237	520	0.6	1.0	26.9	64.1	18.2	43.5	20.8	15.0
Sweden	125	135	0.2	0.3	9.4	11.9	6.4	9.3	2.4	4.9
Cyprus	21	32	-	-	2.8	4.2	2.8	4.2	0.3	0.2
Czech Republic	24	67	-	-	2.0	6.0	2.0	6.0	0.2	2.8
Estonia	4	8	-	-	0.1	0.5	0.1	0.5	0.1	0.1
Hungary	26	52	-	-	1.7	3.5	1.7	3.5	0.5	0.8
Latvia	7	13	-	-	0.2	0.6	0.1	0.6	0.2	0.2
Lithuania	7	13	-	-	0.2	0.6	0.2	0.6	0.1	0.1
Malta	18	23	-	-	1.6	2.3	1.6	2.3	0.7	0.4
Poland	38	73	0.1	0.1	3.7	5.9	3.6	5.6	0.1	1.0
Slovak Republic	1	13	0.0	-	-	0.9	-	0.9	0.1	0.6
Slovenia	6	14	-	-	0.3	0.7	0.3	0.7	0.2	0.2
Norway	106	133	0.1	0.2	7.7	11.3	4.3	7.4	0.9	1.0
Switzerland	174	172	1.4	1.1	18.9	20.6	18.7	20.5	0.3	4.2
Japan	628	852	6.0	8.9	118.0	154.4	62.8	84.2	0.2	1.2
USA	7,901	11,665	19.1	37.5	823.7	1,164.4	228.9	306.2	18.5	20.8
Russian Federation	859	694	0.8	1.4	64.2	62.0	14.2	25.2	8.1	20.9

1 Excludes mail.
2 Source: CAA.

☎020-7944 3088
The figures in this table are outside the scope of UK National Statistics
Source: ICAO

10.11 Carbon dioxide emissions from transport: by source: 1993 and 2003

Million tonnes of carbon

	Road transport		Railways		Civil aviation		Shipping		All domestic transport[1]		All sources	
	1993	2003	1993	2003	1993	2003	1993	2003	1993	2003	1993	2003
United Kingdom	30.7	32.6	0.5	0.3	0.4	0.6	1.0	0.9	32.5	34.4	154	152
Austria	3.7	6.0	-	-	-	-	-	-	3.9	6.2	16	21
Belgium	5.6	6.8	0.1	-	-	-	0.3	0.1	6.0	6.9	32	34
Denmark	2.7	3.2	0.1	0.1	0.1	-	0.2	0.2	3.1	3.5	16	16
Finland	2.7	3.1	0.1	-	0.1	0.1	0.1	0.1	3.1	3.6	15	20
France	32.4	36.1	0.2	0.2	1.2	1.4	0.5	0.7	34.4	38.6	107	111
Germany	44.9	43.6	0.7	0.4	0.9	1.2	0.6	0.2	48.1	46.4	251	236
Greece	3.6	4.9	-	-	0.4	0.3	0.5	0.5	4.6	5.8	23	30
Irish Republic	1.4	3.0	-	-	-	-	-	-	1.5	3.1	9	12
Italy	27.9	31.7	0.1	0.1	0.5	0.8	1.5	1.7	30.1	34.4	116	133
Luxembourg	0.9	1.6	-	-	0.0	0.0	-	-	0.9	1.6	3	3
Netherlands	7.5	9.1	-	-	-	-	0.1	0.2	7.7	9.3	45	48
Portugal	3.1	5.1	-	-	0.1	0.1	0.1	0.1	3.3	5.3	13	18
Spain	15.4	23.8	0.1	0.1	0.9	1.5	0.5	0.6	16.9	26.0	64	90
Sweden	4.6	5.0	-	-	0.2	0.2	0.1	0.2	4.9	5.5	15	15
Cyprus	..	..	..	..	..	..	..	..	0.3	0.5	2	2
Czech Republic	..	..	..	..	..	..	..	..	2.1	3.7	37	35
Estonia	..	..	..	..	..	..	..	..	0.5	0.6	6	5
Hungary	..	..	..	..	..	..	..	..	1.8	2.6	17	16
Latvia	..	..	..	..	..	..	..	..	0.5	0.7	3	2
Lithuania	..	..	..	..	..	..	..	..	1.4	1.0	8	3
Malta	..	..	..	..	..	..	..	..	0.1	0.1	1	1
Poland	..	..	..	..	..	..	..	..	7.5	9.2	99	88
Slovak Republic	..	..	..	..	..	..	..	..	1.1	1.4	4	4
Slovenia	..	..	..	..	..	..	..	..	0.8	1.1	12	12

1 Includes a small amount of emissions from other transport sources.

☎020-7944 4276

The figures in this table are outside the scope of UK National Statistics

Sources - European Environment Agency (EEA)

Abbreviations used in Transport Statistics Great Britain: 2005 Edition

AAIB: Air Accident Investigation Branch
ABI: Association of British Insurers
ABP: Associated British Ports
AES: Annual Earning Survey
APEG: Airborne Particles Expert Group
BAA: British Airports Authority
BEA: (French) Bureau Enquetes Accidents
BR: British Rail
BRB: British Railways Board
BRF: British Road Federation
BW: British Waterways
CAA: Civil Aviation Authority
CfIT: Commission for Integrated Transport
CTRL: Channel Tunnel Rail Link
CVTF: Cleaner Vehicles Task Force
DBFO: Design, Build, Finance and Operate (contracts)
DDA: Disability Discrimination Act
DfT: Department for Transport
DLR: Docklands Light Railway
DPM: Deputy Prime Minister
DiPTAC: Disabled Persons Transport Advisory Committee
DSA: Driving Standards Agency
DTI: Dept. of Trade and Industry
DTLR: Department for Transport, Local Government and the Regions.
DVLA: Driver and Vehicle Licensing Agency
EC: European Community
EPS: European Passenger Services Ltd (ex-BR subsidiary)
EST: Energy Saving Trust
ETC: European Transport Council
EuroNCAP: EU New Car Assessment Programme
EUTC: European Union Transport Council
FDR: Fuel Duty Rebate
FFG: Freight Facilities Grant
FTA: Freight Transport Assn.
GLA: Greater London Authority
GMDSS: Global Maritime Distress and Safety System
GMPTE: Greater Manchester Passenger Transport Exec.
GOL: Gov. Office for London
Grt: Gross registered tonnage
GT: Gross Tonnage
HA: Highways Agency
HERL: Heathrow Express Rail Link
HGV: Heavy Goods Vehicle
HSC: Health and Safety Commission
HSE: Health and Safety Exec.
ICAO: Int. Civil Aviation Org.
ICC: International Climate Change
Int: International
IPS: International Passenger Survey
IRF: International Road Federation
IRFT: International Rail Freight Terminal
KSI: Killed or seriously injured
LA(s): Local Authority(s)
LCA: London City Airport
LCR: London and Continental Railways
LDDC: London Docklands Development Corporation
LFS: Labour Force Survey
LGV: Light Goods Vehicle
LoLo: Lift-on Lift-off
LRT: London Regional Transport
LT: London Transport
LTP: Local Transport Plan
LU: London Underground
MAIB: Marine Accident Investigation Branch
MCA: Marine and Coastguard Agency
MMC: Monopolies & Mergers Commission.
MML: Midland Mainline (rail)
MPV: Multi-purpose vehicle
NATS: National Air Traffic Services
NBC: National Bus Company
NDLS: National Dock Labour Scheme.
NEG: National Express Group
NET: Nottingham Express Transit
NEXUS: Tyne and Wear Passenger Transport Exec.
NTO: National Training Organisation
NTS: National Travel Survey
OECD: Organisation for Economic Co-operation and Development
ONS: Office for National Statistics

OPEC:	Organisation of Petroleum Exporting Countries
ORR:	Office of Rail Regulation
OTIF:	International Railway Transport Organisation
PCO:	Public Carriage Office
PFI:	Public Finance Initiative
PHV:	Private Hire Vehicle
PLG:	Private Light Goods (vehicle)
PPM:	Public Performance Measure
PPP:	Public-Private Partnership
PSV:	Public Service Vehicle
PTA:	Passenger Transport Area
PTE:	Passenger Transport Exec.
RBSG:	Rural Bus Subsidy Grant
RDS-TMC:	Radio Data System - Traffic Message Channel
RID:	Regulations concerning the International Carriage of Dangerous Goods by Rail
RITC:	Rail Industry Training Council
Ro-Ro:	Roll-on Roll-off (passenger) ferries
RPI:	Retail Price Index
RTRA:	Road Traffic Reduction Act
RVAR:	Rail Vehicle Accessibility Regulations
SACTRA:	Standing Advisory Committee on Trunk Road Assessment
SBG:	Scottish Bus Group
SMMT:	Society of Motor Manufacturers and Traders
SPAD:	Signal Passed at Danger
SPTE:	Strathclyde Passenger Transport Exec.
SRA:	Strategic Rail Authority
STAG:	School Travel Advisory Group
SYPTE:	South Yorkshire Passenger Transport Executive
TAG:	Track Access Grant
TCF:	Transport Card Forum
TfL:	Transport for London
TEN:	Trans European Network
TfL:	Transport for London
TGWU:	Transport and General Workers Union
TMC:	Traffic Message Channel
TRL:	Transport Research Laboratory
TSO:	The Stationery Office
TWA:	Transport and Works Act
TWPTE:	Tyne and Wear Passenger Transport Executive
UA:	Unitary Authority
VED:	Vehicle Excise Duty
VI:	Vehicle Inspectorate
VOSA:	Vehicle and Operator Services Agency
WHR:	Welsh Highland Railway
WYPTE:	West Yorkshire Passenger Transport Executive

Index

Figures indicate table numbers.

accidents and casualties
  air 1.7, 2.9
  bicycles 1.7, 8.2
  buses 1.7, 8.2
  car 1.7, 8.2
  coastguard 5.18
  goods vehicles 8.2
  marine 5.17
  motorcycles 1.7, 8.2
  motorways 8.3
  pedestrians 1.7, 8.2
  rail 1.7, 8.9, 8.10
  road
    breath tests 8.5
    deaths 10.7
    historical comparison 8.1
    by hour of day 8.4
    by road class 8.3
    by user type & severity 8.2
  vans 1.7
  water 1.7, 5.17, 5.18
aerodromes, civil 2.1
air transport
  accidents and casualties 1.7
  aircraft
    kilometres flown 2.4, 10.10
    noise 3.10
    pollutant emissions 3.8, 3.9
    proximity 2.10
    in service at end of year 2.6
  airports
    activity at 2.7
    air transport movements 2.2, 2.7
    government expenditure 1.15
    investment in infrastructure 1.14
    punctuality at 2.3
    terminal passengers 2.2, 2.7
    traffic at 2.2
  employment 1.16, 1.17, 1.18, 2.11
  forecasts 2.5
  freight 2.2, 2.4, 2.7, 10.10
  historical comparison 1.1
  international comparison 10.10
  international passenger movements 2.8
  overseas travel 1.10, 1.11
  passenger kilometres 1.1, 2.4, 2.12, 10.10,
  passenger seat occupancy 2.4
  passenger traffic via international airlines 2.12
  passengers uplifted 2.4
  petrol consumption 3.1, 3.2
bicycles
  accidents and casualties 1.7, 8.2
  average distance travelled 1.3
  commuter traffic to central London 1.6
  historical comparisons 1.1
  journeys
    distance 1.5
    purpose 1.4
  passenger kilometres 1.1
  road traffic 7.2, 7.4
  transport to work by region 1.8
  vehicle kilometres 7.2, 7.4
breath tests 8.5, 8.6
buses (and coaches)
  accidents and casualties 1.7, 8.2
  accompanied vehicles by sea 5.6, 5.7
  average distance travelled 1.3
  commuter traffic to central London 1.6
  employment 1.16, 6.12
  fares 1.19, 6.15
  government revenue support 1.15
  historical comparisons 1.1
  international comparisons 10.3, 10.4, 10.6
  journeys
    distance 1.5
    purpose 1.4
  licensed 9.1, 9.4
  local authority support 6.14
  operating costs 6.16
  overseas travel 1.10, 1.12
  passenger journeys by area 6.13
  passenger kilometres 1.1, 10.6
  pollutant emissions 3.6
  receipts 6.11
  registration 9.2
  road taxation revenue 7.15
  road traffic 7.2, 7.4, 7.5, 10.4
  speeds 7.10, 7.11
  transport to work by region 1.8
  vehicle kilometres 7.2, 7.4, 7.5, 6.9, 10.4
  vehicle stock 6.10
car drivers
  breath tests performed on 8.5
  driving tests 9.18
  emissions 3.6, 3.8, 3.9
  license holders 9.16
car ownership 9.15
  forecast 7.5
  historical comparison 9.15
car parks
  government expenditure on 1.15
carbon dioxide emissions
  projection 3.7
  from road vehicles in urban conditions 3.6
  from transport and other end users 3.9
carbon monoxide emissions 3.6, 3.9
cars

accidents and casualties 1.7, 8.2
accompanied vehicles by sea 5.6, 5.7
average distance travelled 1.3, 9.17
commuter traffic to central London 1.6
fuel consumption 3.4, 3.5
historical comparisons 1.1, 7.1
international comparisons 10.3, 10.4, 10.6, 10.7
investment in 1.14
journeys
distance 1.5
purpose 1.4
licensed 9.1
by engine size 9.3
historical comparison 7.1
by method of propulsion 9.4
by region 9.5
MOT results 9.10, 9.13
overseas travel 1.10, 1.12
passenger kilometres 1.1, 10.6
pollutant emissions 3.6, 3.8, 3.9
registration 9.1, 9.2
road deaths 10.7
road taxation revenue 7.15
road traffic 7.2, 7.4, 7.5, 10.4
speeds 7.10, 7.11
transport to work by region 1.8
vehicle kilometres 7.2, 7.4, 7.5, 10.4
casualties see accidents and casualties
central London see London
Channel Tunnel
freight 6.8
traffic to and from Europe 6.8
civil aerodromes 2.1
civil aircraft
pollutant emissions 3.8, 3.9
coaches see buses (and coaches)
coastguard incident statistics 5.18
commuter traffic (central London) 1.6
construction tender price index for roads 7.14
consumption of unleaded petrol 3.1
CO_2 emissions see carbon dioxide emissions
Crown and exempt vehicles 9.1, 9.4
cycles see bicycles
deaths
aviation accidents 2.9
coastguard incidents 5.18
marine 5.17
by mode of transport 1.7
railway accidents 8.9, 8.10
road accidents 8.2, 8.3, 10.7
defects
road conditions 7.17
vehicle in MOT tests 9.13

diesel
car consumption 3.4
duties 3.3
as percentage of price 10.8(b)
prices 3.3
international comparison 10.8
vehicles currently licensed by 9.4
distance
average travelled 1.3, 9.17
journeys 1.5
drinking and driving 8.5, 8.6, 8.7
driving licenses 9.16
driving tests 9.18
duties
petrol and diesel 3.3, 10.8(b)
vehicle excise 7.15
emissions see pollutant emissions
employment
airlines 1.16, 1.17, 1.18, 2.11
buses 1.16, 6.12
London Underground 6.1
by occupation group and industry 1.16
railways 1.16, 1.17, 1.18
in transport related occupations 1.17
seafarers 1.16
by sex and employment status 1.18
energy consumption
by transport mode 3.2
see also fuel consumption
expenditure, government
airports 1.15
car parks 1.15
ports 1.15
railways 1.15
roads 1.14, 1.15
regional 7.13
shipping 5.16
transport 1.15
exports
shipping 5.16
fares
buses 1.19, 6.15
rail 1.19, 6.3
taxi 6.17
ferry traffic
goods vehicles outward to Europe 4.11, 4.1
fixed penalty notices 8.7
fleets see trading vessels
forecasts
air traffic 2.5
car ownership 7.5
carbon dioxide emissions 3.7
buses 7.5
HGVS & LGVs 7.5
road traffic 7.5
freight transport
air 2.2, 2.4, 2.6, 2.7, 10.10

bilateral traffic between EC and UK 4.9
Channel Tunnel 6.8
by commodity 4.2, 4.3, 4.4, 4.5
goods vehicles 4.4, 4.5, 4.6
grants 1.15
historical comparison 4.1
inland waterways 5.8, 5.10, 10.5
international comparison 10.5
map of ports, rivers and inland waterways used for 5.9
by mode of transport 4.1, 4.3
by pipeline 4.1, 4.2, 4.3, 10.5
rail 4.1, 4.2, 4.3, 10.5
road 4.3
by commodity 4.2
forecast 7.5
goods lifted by goods vehicles 4.5
goods moved by goods vehicles 4.4
historical comparison 4.1
international comparison 10.5
international haulage 4.7, 4.8, 4.9
length of haul by goods vehicles 4.6
on major rivers 5.10
shipping industry's revenue from 5.16
waterborne 4.1, 4.2, 4.3, 5.8, 5.10, 10.5
fuel consumption
average car 3.4
average new car 3.5
railways 3.1, 3.2
road 3.1, 3.2
see also diesel; petrol
fuel tax 7.15
goods vehicles
accidents and casualties 8.2
employment 1.16
ferry traffic outward to Europe 4.11, 4.12
freight transport 4.4, 4.5, 4.6
historical comparisons 4.1, 7.1, 9.1
international comparisons 10.3, 10.4,10.5
international road haulage 4.7. 4.8, 4.9
licensed 9.1, 9.5, 9.7
by axle configuration 9.8
by engine size 9.3
historical comparison 7.1
by method of propulsion 9.4
overseas travel by sea 1.12
pollutant emissions 3.6
registered 9.1, 9.2
road taxation revenue 7.15
road traffic 4.1, 7.2, 7.4, 7.5, 10.4
testing scheme 9.10, 9.12, 9.13
trailer tests by axle type 9.9
vehicle kilometres 4.1, 7.2, 7.4, 7.5, 10.4

government expenditure see expenditure government
grants and subsidies
freight transport 1.15
greenhouse gases see pollutant emissions
Gross Domestic Product
international comparison 10.1
Retail Prices Index inflators 1.20
haulage, international see international road haulage
heavy goods vehicles
accidents and casualties 8.2
speeds 7.10, 7.11
historical comparisons
bicycles 1.1
car ownership 9.14
civil aerodromes 2.1
freight transport 4.1
goods vehicles 4.1, 7.1, 9.1
licensing of motor vehicles 9.1, 9.2
motorcycles 1.1, 7.1, 9.1, 9.2
passenger transport by mode 1.1
ports 5.1
rail length and passenger travel 6.1
registration
motor vehicles 9.1
trading vessels 5.14
road accidents and casualties 8.1
road lengths 7.6
road traffic 7.1
HM Coastguard Incident statistics 5.18
household
car ownership 9.14, 9.15
hydrocarbon emissions 3.6
imports
ports 5.1
shipping 5.16
inland waterways
freight 5.8, 5.10, 10.5
map of principal 5.9
international
passenger movements
by air 2.8
by sea 5.11, 5.12
road haulage 4.7, 4.8, 4.9
international comparisons
airline output 10.10
cars 10.3, 10.4, 10.6, 10.7
freight transport 10.5
general statistics 10.1
goods vehicles 10.3, 10.4, 10.5
motorcycles 10.3, 10.4
passenger transport 10.6
petrol and diesel prices 10.8
road deaths 10.7
road and rail infrastructure 10.2
road vehicles by type 10.3
trading fleets 10.9

international road haulage
goods vehicles 4.7, 4.8, 4.9
investment
expenditure in London Underground 6.7
in transport 1.13, 1.14
journeys, passenger
British Rail 6.1
bus 6.13
distance 1.5
London Underground 6.7
purpose 1.4
length of route
National Rail 6.1
licensing 9.1
car driver license holders 9.16
goods vehicles 9.1, 9.4, 9.6, 9.7, 9.8, 7.1
historical comparison 9.1
light goods vehicles 9.3, 9.4
by method of propulsion 9.4
by region 9.5
taxis 6.27
by type of vehicle and engine size 9.3
light goods vehicles
accidents and casualties 8.2
licensed 9.3, 9.4
MOT results 9.10, 9.13
road traffic forecast 7.5
speeds 7.10, 7.11
lighting
regional expenditure on 7.13
local authorities
support for local bus services 6.9
London
average traffic speeds 7.12
commuter traffic 1.6
main mode of transport to work 1.8
time taken to travel to work 1.9
London Underground
average distance travelled 1.3
historical comparison 6.1
investment expenditure 6.7
journeys
distance 1.5
purpose 1.4
by type of ticket 6.7
operating account 6.7
operational facilities 6.1
operations 6.7
passenger kilometres 6.1, 6.7
peak periods 1.6
performance indicators 6.7
receipts 6.7
stations 6.2
transport to work by 1.8
lorries see goods vehicles
maps
principal ports, rivers and inland waterways 5.9
motorway network 7.7
marine accident casualties 5.17
minicabs see taxis
MOT
failures by type of defect 9.13
test results 9.10
motor cars see cars
motorcycles
accidents and casualties 1.7, 8.2
average distance travelled 1.3
breath tests performed in accidents 8.5
commuter traffic to central London 1.6
historical comparisons 1.1, 7.1, 9.1, 9.2
international comparisons 10.3, 10.4
journeys
distance 1.5
purpose 1.4
licensed 9.1
by engine size 9.3
historical comparison 7.1
by method of propulsion 9.4
MOT results 9.10, 9.13
passenger kilometres 1.1
pollutant emissions 3.6
registered 9.1, 9.2
road taxation revenue 7.15
road traffic 7.1, 7.2, 7.4, 10.4
speeds 7.11
transport to work by region 1.8
vehicle kilometres 7.1, 7.2, 7.4, 10.4
motoring offences see offences, motoring
motorways
accidents and casualties 8.3
international comparison 10.2
network map 7.7
new construction 7.16
regional expenditure 7.13
road length 7.8, 7.9. 10.2
road traffic 7.3, 7.4
vehicle speeds 7.10
nitrogen oxide emissions 3.6
noise
aircraft 3.10
offences, motoring 8.5, 8.6, 8.7
operating costs
buses and coaches 6.16
overseas travel
accompanied passenger vehicles 5.6, 5.7
by air 1.10, 1.11
by sea 1.10, 1.12
visits to and from UK 1.10
see also international passenger movemen
particulate emissions 3.8
passenger journeys see journeys, passenger

passenger kilometres
air transport 1.1, 2.12, 10.10
historical comparison 1.1
international comparison 10.6
London Underground 6.1, 6.8
by mode 1.1
see also individual types of transport
passenger receipts see receipts, passenger
passenger aircraft seat occupancy 2.4
passenger transport
historical comparison 1.1
international comparison 10.6
by mode 1.1
peak periods London Underground 1.6
pedal cycles see bicycles
pedestrians
accidents and casualties 1.7, 8.2
average distance travelled 1.3
journeys
distance 1.5
purpose 1.4
transport to work by region 1.8
performance indicators London Underground 6.8
petrol
car consumption 3.4, 3.5
consumption by transport mode 3.1, 3.2
duties 3.3
as percentage of price 10.8
motor vehicles currently licensed by 9.4
prices 3.3, 10.8
use of unleaded
pipeline
freight 4.2, 4.3, 10.5
pollutant emissions
carbon dioxide emissions
projection 3.7
from road vehicles in urban conditions 3.6
from transport and other end users 3.8
carbon monoxide emissions 3.6, 3.8
civil aircraft 3.8, 3.9
hydrocarbon emissions 3.6
lead emissions 3.8
nitrogen oxide emissions 3.6
percentage of road vehicles failing MOT 9.13
road vehicles in urban conditions 3.6
population 10.1
ports
accompanied passenger vehicles 5.6, 5.7
exports 5.1
ferry traffic 4.11, 4.12
foreign, coastwise and one-port traffic 5.2
foreign and domestic traffic by port 5.3
foreign and domestic unitised traffic 5.4
government expenditure 1.15
imports 5.1
international sea passenger movements 5.12
investment in infrastructure 1.14
map of principal 5.9
prices
petrol and diesel 3.3
international comparison 10.8
private motoring
car ownership 7.5, 9.14, 9.15
driving licence holders 9.16
driving tests 9.18
proximity
aircraft 2.10
public expenditure see expenditure, governme
public transport
commuter traffic to central London 1.6
government expenditure 1.15
registered vehicles 9.1
see also buses (and coaches); railways;
punctuality
airports 2.3
rail 6.6
rail - (national rail network)
average distance travelled 1.3
historical comparison 1.1, 1.2, 6.1
journeys
distance 1.5
purpose 1.4
length of route 6.1
passenger journeys 6.2
passenger kilometres 6.2
railways
accidents and casualties 1.7, 8.9, 8.10
commuter traffic to central London 1.6
employment 1.16, 1.17, 1.18
fares 1.19, 6.3
freight 4.1, 4.2, 4.3, 9.14, 10.5
fuel consumption 3.1, 3.2
government expenditure 1.15
historical comparisons 1.1, 1.2, 6.1
infrastructure 10.2
international comparisons 10.2, 10.5, 10.6
investment in 1.14
passenger kilometres 1.1, 6.4, 10.6
pollutant emissions 3.8, 3.9
punctuality and reliability 6.6
receipts 6.3
route open for traffic 6.5
stations 6.2
transport to work by region 1.8
receipts, passenger
buses 6.11
London Underground 6.7
rail 6.3
regional comparisons
car ownership 9.15
expenditure on roads 7.13
licensing of cars 9.5

mode of transport to work 1.8
time taken to travel to work 1.9
registration
aircraft in service at year end 2.6
buses & coaches 9.2
cars 9.2
goods vehicles 9.2
motorcycles 9.2
historical comparison 9.1
trading vessels 5.14
historical comparison 5.13
Retail Prices Index
bus fares 6.15
Gross Domestic Product 1.20
transport components 1.19
rivers
freight traffic on major 5.10
map of principal 5.9
road accidents and casualties
breath tests 8.5
deaths 10.7
historical comparison 8.1
by hour of day 8.4
by road class 8.3
by user type and severity 8.2
road class
accidents 8.3
motor vehicle traffic 7.3
road conditions 7.17
road length 7.8, 7.9
road traffic 7.4
vehicle speeds 7.10
road freight 4.3
by commodity 4.2
goods lifted by goods vehicles 4.5
goods moved by goods vehicles 4.4
historical comparison 4.1
international comparison 10.5
international haulage 4.7, 4.8, 4.9
length of haul by goods vehicles 4.6
road PSV testing scheme 9.11
road traffic 7.2
forecast 7.5
historical comparison 7.1
international comparison 10.4
by road class 7.3
by type of vehicle and class of road 7.4
road transport
fuel consumption 3.1, 3.2
international comparison of vehicle type 10.3
investment in 1.14
pollutant emissions 3.6, 3.8, 3.9
taxation revenue 7.15
roads
conditions 7.17
construction tender price index 7.14
expenditure
government 1.15
investment in infrastructure 1.14
regional 7.13
infrastructure 10.2
length
by class of road and country 7.9
historical comparison 7.6
international comparison 10.2
by road type 7.8
motorway network 7.7
new construction 7.16
passenger kilometres 1.1
vehicle speeds on 7.10, 7.11
roll-on roll-off ferry
traffic 4.11, 4.12
sea transport
accidents and casualties 1.7, 5.17, 5.18
accompanied passenger vehicles 5.6, 5.7
coastguard statistics 5.18
employment of seafarers 1.16
freight 5.8
international passenger movements 5.11, 5
overseas travel 1.10, 1.12
shipping
exports 5.16
imports 5.16
international revenue & expenditure 1.
pollutant emissions 3.8, 3.9
trading vessels
international comparison 10.9
registered 5.14, 5.15
historical comparison 5.13
speed limit offences 8.7
speeds, vehicle
heavy goods vehicles 7.10, 7.11
London traffic 7.12
on non-urban roads 7.10
on urban roads 7.11
staff see employment
taxes and duties 7.15
on petrol and diesel 3.3, 10.8
taxis
average distance travelled 1.3
employment 1.16
fares 6.17
licensed 6.17
testing
goods vehicles 9.12
road passenger service vehicles 9.11
road vehicles (MOT) 9.10
failure of by defect type 9.13
trailer by axle type 9.9

trading vessels 5.15
international comparison 10.9
registered 5.14
historical comparison 5.13
traffic also see road traffic
at airports 2.2
to and from Europe by Channel Tunnel 6.8
trailer tests 9.9
trains see railways
transport
components, Retail Prices Index 1.19
expenditure, government 1.15
Underground see London Underground
unleaded petrol
consumption 3.1
prices and duties 3.3, 10.8
vans
average distance travelled 1.3
casualty rates 1.7
pollutant emissions 3.6
road traffic 7.2, 7.4
vehicle excise duty 7.15
vehicle kilometres
bicycles 7.2, 7.4
buses (and coaches) 7.2, 7.4, 7.5, 6.7, 10.4
cars 7.2, 7.4, 7.5, 10.4
goods vehicles 7.2, 7.4, 7.5, 10.4
motorcycles 7.2, 7.4, 10.4
vehicle stock
buses (and coaches) 6.10
vehicle testing scheme see testing
vessels see trading vessels
volatile organic compounds (VOCs) 3.9
walking see pedestrians
water transport
accidents and casualties 1.7, 5.17, 5.18
employment 1.17, 1.18
freight 4.2, 4.3, 5.8, 5.10, 10.5
petrol consumption 3.1, 3.2
see also ports; shipping
work
main mode of transport to by region 1.8
time taken to travel to by region 1.9

CLIP TRANSPORT STATISTICS

CLIP Transport Statistics (CLIP-TS) is a sub-group of the Central and Local (Government) Information Partnership (CLIP), the main forum for discussion between central and local government on statistical matters.

Its formal terms of reference are:

- To act as a forum for consultation between DfT and local authorities on any transport statistics of interest to either side that are not dealt with by other groups; and on any gaps in the Department's coverage.

- To act as a point of contact between local authorities and DfT on statistical matters of common concern, including the statistics needed for the monitoring of Local Transport Plans, Best Value Indicators, Regional Statistics and other relevant matters.

CLIP-TS is comprised of a Local Authority side and a DfT side. The LA side represents the Local Government Association, Association of London Government, Passenger Transport Authorities, Shire Counties, Unitary Authorities and London Boroughs. London Transport also attends in observer status.

Recent work of the group has centred on the information requirements of Local Transport Plans. This and other useful information will be shown on the group's website which can be found at:
http://www.clip.gov.uk/subgroups.asp?lsection=6&ccat=15

Who sits on the group?

Barbara Noble - Chief Statistician, Statistics Travel Division, Department for Transport (Chair)
Ray Heywood - Leeds City Council (LA Lead)
Position Vacant - Department for Transport (Secretary)
Alan Oliver - Chief Statistician, Transport Statistics Roads Division, Department for Transport
Stephen Reynolds - Statistician, Local and Regional Statistics, Department for Transport
Keith Oates - South Yorkshire Passenger Transport Executive
Piers Cockroft - Solihull MBC
Mike Collop - Transport for London
Position Vacant - Association of London Government
Sam Horstead - Government Office for Yorkshire and the Humber
John Lameris - Staffordshire County Council
John Marriott - Leicestershire County Council
John Pitt - Surrey County Council
Frank Cashmore - Bristol City Council
Vince Christie - Local Government Association
Juliet Whitworth - Local Government Association

For further information contact;

Mr Ray Heywood
Policy Monitoring Manager
Leeds City Council
Development Department
The Leonardo Building
2 Rossington St
Leeds, LS2 8HB

Tel: 0113 247 6342
Fax: 0113 247 8015
Email: ray.heywood@leeds.gov.uk